# Key Works in Critical Pedagogy

Bold Visions in Educational Research
Volume 32

*Series Editor*
**Kenneth Tobin**, *The Graduate Center, City University of New York, USA*

*Tribute*
**Joe L. Kincheloe** was the founding co-editor of the series. Long before we had the series Joe had the idea to have a Key Works feature and invited me to write such a book. It is fitting that Joe's Key Works is a part of the series that was primarily his idea. It is indeed an honor to publish Joe L. Kincheloe's Key Works because this collection of scholarly works and the associated commentaries will be essential reading for serious educational scholar researchers.

*Scope*
*Bold Visions in Educational Research* is international in scope and includes books from two areas: *teaching and learning to teach* and *research methods in education*. Each area contains multi-authored handbooks of approximately 200,000 words and monographs (authored and edited collections) of approximately 130,000 words. All books are scholarly, written to engage specified readers and catalyze changes in policies and practices. Defining characteristics of books in the series are their explicit uses of theory and associated methodologies to address important problems. We invite books from across a theoretical and methodological spectrum from scholars employing quantitative, statistical, experimental, ethnographic, semiotic, hermeneutic, historical, ethnomethodological, phenomenological, case studies, action, cultural studies, content analysis, rhetorical, deconstructive, critical, literary, aesthetic and other research methods.

Books on *teaching and learning to teach* focus on any of the curriculum areas (e.g., literacy, science, mathematics, social science), in and out of school settings, and points along the age continuum (pre K to adult). The purpose of books on *research methods in education* is **not** to present generalized and abstract procedures but to show how research is undertaken, highlighting the particulars that pertain to a study. Each book brings to the foreground those details that must be considered at every step on the way to doing a good study. The goal is **not** to show how generalizable methods are but to present rich descriptions to show how research is enacted. The books focus on methodology, within a context of substantive results so that methods, theory, and the processes leading to empirical analyses and outcomes are juxtaposed. In this way method is not reified, but is explored within well-described contexts and the emergent research outcomes. Three illustrative examples of books are those that allow proponents of particular perspectives to interact and debate, comprehensive handbooks where leading scholars explore particular genres of inquiry in detail, and introductory texts to particular educational research methods/issues of interest to novice researchers.

# Key Works in Critical Pedagogy

*Joe L. Kincheloe*

**Edited by**

kecia hayes
*Montclair State University*

Shirley R. Steinberg
*University of Calgary; University of Barcelona*

Kenneth Tobin
*City University of New York*

Giuliana Cucinelli, cover artist is a professor of media and youth culture, and an independent artist and filmmaker. Giuliana was as close to Joe Kincheloe as a daughter and was with Joe and Shirley when he died. She was a source of love and strength. She can be reached at gcucinelli@gmail.com.

The royalties generated by sales of this volume will be paid to: The Friends of Joe L. Kincheloe Foundation for The Paulo and Nita Freire International Project for Critical Pedagogy (*http://freireproject.org*).

SENSE PUBLISHERS
ROTTERDAM/BOSTON/TAIPEI

A C.I.P. record for this book is available from the Library of Congress.

ISBN: 978-94-6091-395-2 (paperback)
ISBN: 978-94-6091-396-9 (hardback)
ISBN: 978-94-6091-397-6 (e-book)

Published by: Sense Publishers,
P.O. Box 21858,
3001 AW Rotterdam,
The Netherlands
www.sensepublishers.com

*Printed on acid-free paper*

All Rights Reserved © 2011 Sense Publishers

No part of this work may be reproduced, stored in a retrieval system, or transmitted in any form or by any means, electronic, mechanical, photocopying, microfilming, recording or otherwise, without written permission from the Publisher, with the exception of any material supplied specifically for the purpose of being entered and executed on a computer system, for exclusive use by the purchaser of the work.

# TABLE OF CONTENTS

Foreword: For My Next Trick, I'll Need a Volunteer ............................................. ix
Shirley R. Steinberg

Learning from a Good Mate: An Introduction ....................................................... xv
Kenneth Tobin

1. Exposing the Technocratic Perversion of Education: The Death
   of the Democratic Philosophy of Schooling ....................................................... 1
   Joe L. Kincheloe

   Teachers Reversing the Cycle: Checking the Dangers of NCLB ..................... 21
   Connie Titone and Robert A. Duggan, Jr.

2. Willie Morris and the Southern Curriculum: Emancipating the
   Southern Ghosts ................................................................................................ 27
   Joe L. Kincheloe

   Goin' South ....................................................................................................... 49
   Shirley R. Steinberg and Chaim M. Steinberg

3. A Tentative Description of Post-formal Thinking: The Critical
   Confrontation with Cognitive Thinking ........................................................... 53
   Joe L. Kincheloe and Shirley R. Steinberg

   Reconceptualizing Educational Psychology: The Promotion of a Critical
   Consciousness ................................................................................................... 77
   Raymond A. Horn, Jr.

4. Meet Me Behind the Curtain: The Struggle for a Critical Postmodern
   Action Research ................................................................................................ 85
   Joe L. Kincheloe

   A Dialogic Encounter with Joe Kincheloe's "Meet Me Behind the
   Curtain": Catalyst for an Evolving Contemporary Critical Theory of
   Teachers' Work ............................................................................................... 101
   John Smyth

5. Schools Where Ronnie and Brandon Would Have Excelled: A
   Curriculum Theory of Academic and Vocational Education ......................... 107
   Joe L. Kincheloe

TABLE OF CONTENTS

    Reflections on Joe Kincheloe's Schools Where Ronnie and Brandon Would Have Excelled: A Curriculum Theory of Academic and Vocational Education ................................................................................. 123
    *Gene Fellner*

6. The New Childhood: Home Alone as a Way of Life ..................................... 129
    *Joe L. Kincheloe*

    Welcome to Shermerville .............................................................................. 149
    *Lee Gabay*

7. McDonald's, Power, and Children: Ronald McDonald (Aka Ray Kroc) Does it All for You ....................................................................................... 155
    *Joe L. Kincheloe*

    The Corporate Paradise of a Subverted Urban Kinderculture ...................... 171
    *kecia hayes*

8. Describing the Bricolage: Conceptualizing a New Rigor in Qualitative Research ..................................................................................... 177
    *Joe L. Kincheloe*

    Kincheloe's Bricolage .................................................................................. 191
    *Bal Chandra Luitel and Peter Charles Taylor*

9. Critical Ontology: Visions of Selfhood and Curriculum .............................. 201
    *Joe L. Kincheloe*

    Critical Ontology and Teacher Agency ........................................................ 219
    *Elizabeth J. Meyer*

10. The Knowledges of Teacher Education: Developing a Critical Complex Epistemology ................................................................................................ 227
    *Joe L. Kincheloe*

    The Knowledges of Teacher Education in Action ........................................ 245
    *Elizabeth P. Quintero*

11. On to the Next Level: Continuing the Conceptualization of the Bricolage ................................................................................................ 253
    *Joe L. Kincheloe*

    Embracing Radical Research: A Commentary on to the Next Level: Continuing the Conceptualization of the Bricolage ..................................... 279
    *Kathleen S. Berry*

TABLE OF CONTENTS

12. Rethinking Critical Theory and Qualitative Research .................................. 285
    *Joe L. Kincheloe and Peter McLaren*

    Reflecting on Critical Theory and Qualitative Research ............................. 327
    *kecia hayes*

13. Critical Ontology and Indigenous Ways of Being: Forging
    a Postcolonial Curriculum ............................................................................ 333
    *Joe L. Kincheloe*

    On Critical Ontology and Indigenous Ways of Being: Framing
    a Kincheloean Agenda for Education ........................................................... 351
    *Christopher Emdin*

14. The Southern Place and Racial Politics: Southernification,
    Romanticization, and the Recovery of White Supremacy ............................ 357
    *Joe L. Kincheloe*

    Kincheloe and Interracial Recovery: A Child of the South on Dialogic
    Engagement .................................................................................................. 379
    *Aaron David Gresson III*

15. Critical Pedagogy and the Knowledge Wars of the
    Twenty-First Century ................................................................................... 385
    *Joe L. Kincheloe*

    The Anti-Imperialist Pedagogy of Joe L. Kincheloe ..................................... 407
    *Curry Stephenson Malott*

16. Selling a New and Improved Jesus – Christotainment and the Power
    of Political Fundamentalism ......................................................................... 413
    *Joe L. Kincheloe*

    Joe Kincheloe: A Proponent of Democracy and Christianity? ..................... 429
    *Douglas J. Simpson*

Afterword: The Music ........................................................................................ 437
    *John Willinsky*

About the Contributors ...................................................................................... 443

SHIRLEY R. STEINBERG

# FOR MY NEXT TRICK, I'LL NEED A VOLUNTEER

*Foreword*

Joe Lyons Kincheloe, Jr. was born on December 14, 1950, in Kingsport, Tennessee. He was the son of a rural school principal, Joe Sr., and a third grade teacher, Libby Bird. Since he was a junior, he was called Jodie until his thirties. An only child of older parents, he found himself alone a lot, and found ways to amuse himself. Jodie learned to do what he called "routines" in the mirror, mimicking the characters he observed as a kid, and teaching himself the piano.

For the first twelve years of his life, he was apprenticed to his uncle, Marvin Kincheloe, a rural circuit preacher in the Methodist Church. Every Sunday, dressed in his Sunday best, Joe visited the elderly and sick parishioners, and attended Marvin's church. At 12, Joe realized he would never be saved, and refused to continue along the soul saving path. However, he did learn how to preach.

Joe's parents were staunch democrats, unusual in the mountains of Tennessee. He describes his youth: "Growing up among grotesque forms of classism and racism in the South of the 1950s and 1960s, I soon found a means, while still in high school, to bring people together and move them as a blues musician and songwriter." By 16, he was the leader of the VIPs, a 4 piece band of white kids in Kingsport who played weekly at school dances. Joe began writing songs at a very young age, and wrote well over 600. He also started a satirical newspaper in 8th grade with his friends, called *DRUT*, TURD spelled backward.

Obsessively and consciously political, Joe's grades were never great, and he tended to piss teachers off with his disagreements, his dislike of segregation, and his defense of underdogs. His high school counselor told him that his aptitude tests showed that he could never be more than a piano tuner, and he should seriously consider vocational school. Joe went to Emory and Henry College, a small Methodist College in Virginia, where he was promptly put on probation for his participation in anti-war rallies and his long hair. He did eventually graduate with a C average, and went to the University of Tennessee for a Master's in history, a Master's in education (where he read Paulo Freire's *Pedagogy of the Oppressed)*, and a Doctorate in educational history—he completed his dissertation on the evangelical camp meetings of fundamentalist Christians in the 1800s in 1980.

I titled this preface after a song by Warren Zevon. Joe was a volunteer, both metaphorically and literally. Joe followed in his parents' footsteps as a crazed, insane follower of the Tennessee Volunteers Football team. All things Tennessee orange were his, and he made sure everyone who knew him, knew the Volunteers. *Who ever heard of a team called the Volunteers?* His orange passion was legendary, and

## FOREWORD

there is not a friend, neighbor, or student alive that wasn't aware of Joe's team. Every September heralded in the next great hope for his beloved Vols, and he relished the start of NCAA football like the arrival of a most welcomed guest. One winter holiday, we all schlepped to Arizona to watch the Vols play in the National Championship. Partnered by an orange-painted Chaim, Joe was a bouncing little kid watching his team clench the championship. Along with the Vols, he was a fervent Braves fan, and as the Vols began their season, he often would stress at the Braves' inability to consummate a world series...they did it once. Joe never lost hope, and followed his teams from the beginning of each season...He never abandoned them, and had no respect for fair-weather fans. Joe was always aware of the contradictions in male sports. He celebrated the crashing of some barriers and raged against others. He understood the complexity of gender relations yet didn't essentialize them...and he was an unabashed lover of the game. I smile when I recall his absolute disdain for the Boston Red Sox—they were the last team to integrate, he would never, ever cheer for them.

Joe's first job was probably his most significant, serving as the department chair of the education department at Sinte Gleska College on the Rosebud Sioux Reservation in South Dakota. It was there he began to publish and research on the disenfranchisement of Native Americans. In 1982, Joe was given the Lakota Sioux ceremonial name of *TiWa Ska*, meaning clear, loving, or brilliant mind. His time on the Rosebud informed his work, his life, and his context. Those two years allowed him the time to establish himself as a scholar, and to do work which really, really made a difference.

After two years on the reservation, Joe became an assistant professor at Louisiana State University, in Shreveport, where he started a doctoral program in curriculum studies. In 1988 he moved to Clemson University as a full professor having published his first two books. In 1989, he attended the Bergamo Conference–a radical Marxist, feminist, reconceptualist curriculum conference in Dayton, Ohio. Joe and I met when he overheard me talking about working on the Blackfoot Reserve. He politely interrupted my conversation and said that he had worked on the Rosebud Sioux Res. He was very proud that he knew I was living in Canada, as he heard me refer to the *Reserve* not the res, or the reservation. He wanted to continue our conversation, and after he assured me that he was neither gay nor married, we engaged in the one-night stand that never ended.

Although I lived with my four kids in Alberta, within six months we were all in Clemson, South Carolina; and Joe was the father of four: Ian, Meghann, Chaim, and Bronwyn. How he loved those kids: they were spiritually his. We raised them in several states at different universities. We lived through Hurricane Andrew two weeks after moving to Florida International University, and Joe often said it was the most relaxing time of his life, he couldn't write—he just had to find food, ice, and water.

While at FIU, and after several new books, we began editing a book series. We were committed to publishing voices that had been marginalized by mainstream educational discourse. We moved to Penn State in 1994 and Joe and Henry Giroux became colleagues. Henry had been a huge inspiration and support to Joe, publishing

FOREWORD

his work and giving advice, and advocating his hire at Penn State—how cool was that, to work with Henry? I finished my doctorate, and in 1997, Joe was offered an endowed chair at Brooklyn College. After two years in this position, he was invited to join the CUNY Graduate Center faculty and to create the urban education doctorate. Joe marveled at the fact that he had become (in his words) a calloused, urbane sophisticate. This kid from East Tennessee was an *endowed chair*, and a man who co-created the doctoral program at the Grad Center, wow...and he never stopped the wonder. The doctoral program flourished, joined by Phil Anderson and Ken Tobin (Joe relished that he could have two colleagues with the intellect and humor as did Phil and Ken), the program drew from urban teachers who were committed to teach urban kids. And as far as groups of students go, the students Joe worked with at the Grad Center were magnificent; Joe celebrated their successes til the day he died. By the end of the century, Joe had written about 40 books, hundreds of articles, and edited well over 400 volumes in our combined series. He was an international speaker, traveling over the world discussing critical pedagogy, cultural studies, and education...all tied to the notion of social justice and equity. He did love to preach.

In 1998, we hosted a luncheon in San Diego and invited several friends/scholars to dine with us and discuss the possibility of their contributing a volume to our Westview series. I sat between Joe and John Willinsky, and we quickly determined that discussing rock n' roll was far more important than pontificating social theory. John said he had been working feverishly to learn the electric guitar, and I told him that Joe played keyboards and was an old rock n' roll band member. I think it was my idea (Joe always said it was his), but around the same time, the three of us decided to start a band. The band would play every year at the American Educational Research Association. John knew a drummer and a bass player. In those days we called the band the SIG GIG...and a couple of years later, it morphed into Tony and the Hegemones. Next to our family, friends, students, and his teams, this incarnation of rock n' roll became the center of Joe's life. John and Joe were soul brothers, and quickly our annual band became twice a year, three times a year, four times a year...practices occurred from New York to British Columbia, and gigs were planned from coast to coast, North to South, between Canada and the US. John was our long lost sibling, and the three of us bonded through music, loud laughter, silly routines, sarcasm, and the reality that the academy was just a tad better than bullshit. Those years were precious, those gigs the absolute best. I know that Joe and John spent more than a few hours and a few dollars cooking up their next gig, next recording scheme. By the new millennium, conferences became places to have a gig, speeches and presentations the vehicle to get to the gig—and sometimes there were back-to-back gigs, lasting much longer than any scholarly presentation. In the last few years, the band started to highlight Joe's music. I think that was the ultimate compliment to him—that John would urge him to sing and play his songs. At that point, I was happy to be *with the band.*

We stayed in New York City until 2005, when Joe was hired to come to McGill University as a Canada Research Chair (the chair award was given by the Prime Minister of Canada). Once again, the kid from the Blue Ridge Mountains had

FOREWORD

attained a rank previously held for Ivy Leaguers and the politically mediocre. He was full of wonder. Joe founded The Paulo and Nita Freire International Project for Critical Pedagogy. The only one of its kind in the world, the Project is a virtual and literal archives of global initiatives in critical pedagogy; deeply committed to the study of oppression in education... how issues of race, class, gender, sexuality, and colonialism shape the nature and purpose of education. In the spirit of Freire's work, Joe understood the project as a means to "support an evolving critical pedagogy that encounters new discourses, new peoples, with new ideas, and continues to move forward in the 21$^{st}$ Century. The project is understood as continued evolution of the work of Paulo Freire." He chose to name it after Paulo and his wife, Nita, as a celebration of their partnership and radical love. *After Joe died, I was told the Project didn't fit the mandate of the Faculty of Education, and it was scheduled to close. I took the virtual Project off campus, where it remains strong and global.*

Joe was simultaneously writing his 56$^{th}$, 57$^{th}$, 58$^{th}$, 59$^{th}$, and 60$^{th}$ book when he died, and editing eight different book series. He was the senior and founding editor of *The International Journal of Critical Pedagogy* and the blogmaster to the several thousand registered readers and bloggers of the Freire Project blog. In addition to his scholarship, Joe remained committed to teaching classes and supervising students. 2008 was a long year: Joe realized that the greener grass in Montreal was parched, and felt that he didn't want to spend any more years there. The lack of collegial support was strong, and a passive aggressive environment drove him to search for another job. We were poised to leave in 2009, and that notion gave him peace of mind. When we left for Jamaica, Joe was ready to relax and chill. He was burnt out, and mentioned that the only good to come out of 2008 was the election of Obama. After losing our dear friend, Marisa Terrenzio, on the day of the American election, Joe remarked that death was not his greatest fear. Indeed, he said that other than leaving the kids and me, he was looking forward to the next chapter, the next level, and elevated cognitive and spiritual states. He also said he had so many more books to write.

On his 58$^{th}$ birthday, December 14, 2008, Joe attended the Whitehouse, Jamaica Church of God of Prophecy with our dear friends Sadie and Mackie Gordon and our beloved Giuliana Cucinelli. The pastor asked him to speak, and he took the microphone and preached a mini sermon on the importance of faith, humility, and the human body as the vessel for great minds. Giuliana caught this on her camera. As a cynical Jew, I stayed back at the house, waiting for their return. That was the last time Joe spoke in public, and what an audience. One can barely hear his words on the tape, over the Amens, Hallelujahs, and Praises shouted by all. The next few days were spent floating in the warm waters of Jamaica, laughing with friends and our students, Myunghee, Suhun, Maria, and Giuliana. He died in Kingston, Jamaica on December 19, 2008, after spending the day before with Giuliana and me in *9 mile*, Bob Marley's home. I have a vivid image of Joe joining in with the Rasta men singing Marley's *Three Little Birds*. This is exactly how Joe would have chosen to spend his last week. His last Facebook post was: *Joe is regenerating.*

Joe was passionate, he had many radical loves: his family, rock n' roll, his students, and writing. Joe's passion fueled his struggles against inequality, oppression in all

# FOREWORD

of its varied forms, and the stupidification of education. He is recognized for his scholarly contributions to a range of topics that include postformal thinking, critical constructivism, critical multiculturalism, critical indigenous knowledge, and the work we did on critical cultural studies topics such as the notion of *kinderculture* and *christotainment*. In addition to his scholarship, Joe taught countless classes and supervised scores of doctoral students, most of whom are now well-established scholars and professors all over the world.

Joe Lyons Kincheloe, Jr.–Jodie, lived a full and loving life. He was humble as he was confident, gentle as he was strong, a father to Ian, Christine, Meghann and Ryan, Chaim and Marissa, and Bronwyn, a *zaide* to his precious Maci, Luna, Hava, Cohen, Tobias, and Seth. Joe was loud when he yelled at the TV, watching a bad play in the second quarter of the Florida/Tennessee game; he was quiet when he looked out on our snowy birch trees and smelled the fresh, cold night air. Joe was a passionate lover of people, and a radical hater of those who oppressed. Joe was patient with others, impatient with himself…he told me that he just didn't know if he had time to write all the songs, all the books he wanted to write. He never sought out approval, just hoped for respect; you didn't have to like him, he just wanted to do his thing and love his peeps.

On October 27, 2009, Milo Joe was born to Chaim and Marissa, the sweet punctuation of the bitter sentence of 2009. Milo Joe has ushered in our gentle memories and strong commitment to continue Joe's work. I hope that we will commit ourselves to a better world, a better way to articulate, a better path to educate, and a hell of a lot more rock n' roll.


This book is a collection of some of Joe's seminal chapters and articles. Each chapter is followed by a commentary from a dear friend and colleague, who wanted to punctuate Joe's work and impact in pedagogy and in life. An italicized commentary prefaces each chapter. As Joe was the ultimate contextualizer, I wrote each mini-preface in order to give a polysemic body to the text, and to place Joe within each piece.

KENNETH TOBIN

# LEARNING FROM A GOOD MATE

*An Introduction*

A big part of growing up in Australia involved being with my mates, peers with whom I developed strong social bonds in the process of my day-to-day life. Mates were close friends I looked out for, enjoying their successes, helping them when they were in trouble, confiding in them knowing they would protect my interests, and when necessary giving them advice, even when it was not invited. When I came to the United States I missed my mates and even more so the institution of mateship. However, Joe Kincheloe, who was from Tennessee, was an exception—he was my mate.

It was Joe Kincheloe's idea to have a Key Works series of books. I was visiting him at Penn State and he excitedly told me about an idea he and Shirley Steinberg had to publish a collection of papers that represented a scholar's career trajectory. He invited me to contribute to the series and the idea was immediately appealing—although I have yet to submit my own collection of articles as a contribution to the series. Neither Joe nor I would have imagined at the time of our meeting at Penn State that his Key Works would precede mine, a selection of articles that reflect Joe's stellar career as a leading scholar.

As the articles in this collection of key works clearly attest, Joe Kincheloe made a huge contribution to education through his prolific writing over a career that came to a premature ending with his death in Jamaica. As a science educator I became aware of Joe's scholarship through Deborah Tippins, who was co-author with Joe and Shirley on the book entitled *The Stigma of Genius* (Kincheloe, Steinberg, & Tippins, 1999). Having been alerted to Joe's work I was anxious to meet him because it was evident that he was not only a distinguished contributor to education research but also was a person who reached out to junior faculty to get them involved in publishing their work. Subsequently I met Joe at an annual meeting of the American Educational Research Association where, even though it was almost impossible to get uninterrupted time with him, he was friendly, articulate, jovial, witty, and deeply substantive. Based on my very positive impression of him, I invited Joe to present a keynote address at a large science education conference I was organizing in Miami, Florida. The meeting involved several hundred elementary and middle school science educators who were immediately in sync with Joe's presentation on critical pedagogy.

As my career aligned more closely with urban education Joe and I communicated frequently and eventually became colleagues at the Graduate Center and neighbors in a small city in South Amboy, New Jersey. For several years we collaborated over our ongoing research projects, including work of doctoral students. I had mixed feelings when Joe was appointed to the prestigious Canada Research Chair at McGill University–delighted with the opportunities this position afforded him and his line of research, and disappointed to no longer have the proximity of a close friend and colleague. The loss of his intellectual prowess at the Graduate Center was enormous. Joe was a tower of strength in terms of designing and enacting the doctoral program in urban education. Whereas he was open to improving the program in myriad ways, Joe steadfastly resisted efforts from outsiders to hijack the program and enact changes in ways that would better align with their interests rather than those of students.

## TEACHERS AS RESEARCHERS

Joe and I shared a strong interest in teachers and students doing research on their own practices. Also, we had strong interests in the ways in which sociocultural theory could provide a methodology for urban education and a framework for substantive issues to focus research and inquiry in urban education. I had the privilege of sitting in core and elective courses Joe taught in the urban education doctoral program. I read books and articles he assigned and participated in rich dialogues that unfolded in those classes. Almost without exception, students were enthusiastic and active participants. Many of the urban education students worked with Joe as advisor, but many did not, including those who opted to work with me. As an advisor I soon found that I could rely on the fact that students who had been taught by Joe were extremely well prepared to understand the methodologies we employed in our research and to raise important questions concerning the teaching and learning of science, mathematics and literacy in urban schools–especially those in New York City. Joe's teaching was highly influential and in many ways inspirational for students who worked with him. They brought a critical edge to their scholarship and willingness to continue to learn throughout their careers. As is often the case, I soon took this for granted and it was only after Joe left the Graduate Center that the magnitude of his contributions became apparent. The constantly positive impact of his teaching was sorely missed, even though his products accrued at an amazing rate and were accessible not only to scholars at the Graduate Center but to scholars around the world. I rationalized his departure with the thought that at McGill University Joe was well placed to have an even greater impact on the world at large, especially because he received a national grant to establish the Paulo and Nita Freire International Project for Critical Pedagogy.

There are many purposes for teachers and other school participants to design and enact research on their practices. Chief among these is the identification of oppression and the resources to overcome disadvantage. However, Joe made it clear that doing research involved much more than interpreting the status quo. It would not be sufficient to look at test scores and figure out ways to reduce the gaps associated with social categories such as social class, gender, sexual orientation, ethnicity, and proficiency in the use of English. Effectively enacting practitioner research necessarily involved new ways of thinking about education and places in which it is conducted. Understanding teaching and learning in schools necessitates deep understandings of the communities in which schools are embedded, including their histories, not only as they are portrayed through the voices of the mainstream, but also those histories as they are expressed in the voices and lives of those who are oppressed and represent minorities. Just as Lawrence Stenhouse advocated teachers as researchers as a hedge against the domineering effects of positivism (Stenhouse, 1975), Joe regarded teachers as researchers as a hedge against the perpetuation of oppression through the well-intentioned efforts of educators (Kincheloe, 1991). Whereas Joe identified positivism as pervasive and dangerous, he also recognized many other dangerous ideologies and associated practices that reproduced disadvantage and oppression (Kincheloe & Tobin, 2009). Accordingly, Joe regarded practitioner research as a priority.

## THEORY AND RESEARCH

Joe embraced the necessity for researchers to inform their intellectual work with rich theoretical frameworks. Doing research was necessarily more than an empirical activity and may not involve empiricism at all. Accordingly, another standpoint we shared was opposition to the tradition of describing research in terms of the qualitative/quantitative binary. Many of Joe's students described their approach to research as theoretical–as if to emphasize a non-empiricist stance. After Joe's death I worked with a number of his former students and was forced to address just exactly what was meant by theoretical research. A side remark from a colleague at the Graduate Center reminded me that this was an important issue when he asked in a whisper (during a doctoral examination of one of Joe's former students)–"do you think this is research?" At the time I was astonished and answered emphatically "absolutely!" What I did not realize was this perspective was the tip of an iceberg. Many of my colleagues embraced an axiology of preferring/requiring empirical studies for doctoral education in urban education. The whispered remark was a sign of a widespread problem acceptance of an empirical ideology that included continued use of a qualitative/quantitative binary.

It is surprising to me that scholars accept a qualitative/quantitative binary as a viable way of thinking about preparing researchers. Due largely to Joe's careful planning we have a core course in the urban education doctoral degree called the *Logics of Inquiry*. The course examines different ways of undertaking scholarly inquiry in education through the lenses of a variety of theoretical frameworks–in other words, the course allows doctoral students to examine the viability of a range of methodologies, including positivism and behaviorism, constructivism (e.g., social, radical, critical), cultural historical activity theory, hermeneutics, phenomenology, historicity, cultural sociology, and the sociology of emotions. Also, the theoretical underpinnings are examined for research that employs (for example) quasi-experimental designs, inferential statistics, ethnography, conversation analysis, and discourse analysis. Unfortunately, the course is a direct challenge to the qualitative/quantitative binary and many of my colleagues do not value the course or support its presuppositions.

They adopt the view that what students need are research methods and prefer a structure that stipulates that all students should study at least one quantitative and one qualitative methods course. They like to use the term mixed methods and what they mean is to use a combination of qualitative and quantitative data. Hidden beneath their preference for this binary system is a reality that most research is profoundly theoretical and that the theories permeate the methods employed and the research issues that focus the research. Unwillingness to probe the theoretical standpoints associated with research methods can lead to unwitting acceptance of ideologies such as positivism and empiricism, just to name two.

The preoccupation with methods is associated with good intentions–to ensure that doctoral graduates are well educated to produce and consume research. A common argument is that doctoral students should do a minimum of three methods courses, having at least one qualitative and one quantitative course. Often the purpose underlying this standpoint is to prevent students from dodging quantitative courses (assumed to be hard), focusing instead on qualitative courses (assumed to be easy). The well-intentioned goal is to ensure that all students can be literate consumers of published research, with an often-unstated intention that they should be able to understand data tables and associated statistical analyses. This deficit-laden position has many shortcomings, including several that I briefly touch on. First, the binary classification system of qualitative and quantitative methods is an empiricist standpoint that masks more complex systems that reveal the impossibility of studying all useful methods in a doctoral degree. Second, studying just one quantitative course fails to acknowledge that any one course would be a palpably inadequate preparation for making sense of publications with a statistical orientation. Advocates of lifelong learning might argue in favor of allowing doctoral students to specialize in learning methods that are germane to their scholarly interests and to learn other methods when and as necessary.

## PURPOSES OF EDUCATIONAL RESEARCH

There are many purposes for doing research in education. Some of my collaborators, such as Wolff-Michael Roth, embrace an axiology that research should emphasize the development of theory. In contrast, since I first began to work with graduate students in science and mathematics education in the 1980s my research program has been oriented toward the teaching and learning of science and mathematics in classrooms. Accordingly, there has been a strong focus on improving the quality of teaching and learning while learning more about learning and learners, teaching and teachers, and learning environments. As I moved from doing statistically oriented research prior to the mid-1980s toward genres of research grounded in hermeneutics, phenomenology, and ethnomethodology, I adopted an ethical stance that all participants in a study should benefit directly from their participation in the study. This standpoint is grounded in ethical concerns I had with researchers who argued that benefits could accrue when the results of research were applied in practice at some time after the research had been completed. Also, the hermeneutic approach we adopted in our research emphasized learning from different perspectives, bringing into question the assumed ascendancy of coherence and parsimony over difference and complexity. Initially we ensured that we understood what was happening in our research from the perspectives of the participants—using approaches that embraced polyphonia. Since we were also cognizant of people who are placed differently in social space having different stories to tell, we gradually incorporated polysemia into our research. In the late 1980s we adopted Guba and Lincoln's authenticity criteria as a basis for planning and judging our research (Guba & Lincoln, 1989). Accordingly, all studies in which I was involved were planned to have ontological, educative, catalytic, and tactical authenticity. The first two criteria (i.e., ontological and educative) oriented toward theoretical products and the second two (i.e., catalytic and tactical) toward transformation of the institutions and people involved in the research.

Because we were involved in participative observation types of studies in which we rejected the researcher/researched binary, all participants were considered to be researchers and all were considered to be learners and teachers. For this reason it made sense when Joe suggested that all participants should change their ontologies as a result of being involved in research. Previously, we had aimed for the university researchers to show evidence of progressive subjectivity–i.e., gradual changes in both the stories they used to represent what they had learned and evidence provided to support assertions pertaining to the research. Joe pointed out that all participants should change their stories as a result of them changing their positions in social space as they participated in research on their own education and that of their peers. Because of the symmetry we sought in the roles of all participants, it made sense to consider the ethics of research as a priority and to regard the four authenticity criteria as dialectical constituents of a whole; equally applicable to all participants in a study.

## LEARNING COLLABORATIVELY

One of Joe's ever-present virtues was his willingness to listen attentively to what was being said and to comment on it, as often as necessary, and with hermeneutic intent. His oral contributions oriented toward making sense of what was being proposed, testing possibilities, and responding in an emotionally positive way to others' contributions. Joe wrote about this process in a revision of a book he and I co-edited, referring to it as radical listening (Tobin & Kincheloe, 2010). Making an effort to understand others' standpoints without seeking to change them is referred to as radical listening. When persons enact radical listening they listen attentively to a speaker, ensure that they understand what has been said, and identify the key components of the speaker's standpoint. Then, rather than arguing a case against what is being proposed; radical listeners endeavor to adopt that standpoint, thereby exploring the possibilities. Only when the possibilities have been reviewed in terms of their viability for the collective are alternatives considered based on different standpoints. Radical listening, therefore, is a respectful way to deal with others' ideas, thereby increasing the possibility of adopting good ideas associated with others' culture.

Attentive listening is at the heart of effective dialoguing. Radical listening is a process that has the clear purpose of making sense of others' oral contributions with the express purpose of ascertaining what they can contribute. Each person listens carefully and when questions are asked and comments are made their purposes are hermeneutic, to push on the idea and figure out the affordances the idea provides. Any talk is oriented toward expanding the conversation around a particular contribution, not to suggest alternatives but to identify possibilities and boundaries, strengths and weaknesses. The goal is an expansion of the dialogue not contraction and certainly not to provide alternatives that pursue different directions. Accordingly, a dialogue that involves radical listening will thoroughly explore the contributions of all participants, regarding them as resources for the group, structures to expand possibilities and accomplishments. Only when consensus has been reached and the group has taken a given idea as far as it can go can alternatives be introduced as part of the ongoing dialogue. When radical listening is a constituent of dialogue all contributions are offered for the purposes of expanding collective agency, structures that can afford the process of attaining a group's motives. At the same time oral contributions, as structures, are associated with passivity. As such all participants create culture as they listened attentively to the ongoing verbal interactions within the context of an ethical commitment to speaking only for the purpose of testing ideas that are already on the table and expanding them in ways that align with the group's motives.

## RESEARCH ON AND WITH COGENERATIVE DIALOGUE

Cogenerative dialogue (i.e., cogen) has been a path for ongoing research for more than a decade (Tobin, 2010). We designed cogen as a field in which teachers, students, and others with a stake in the quality of teaching and learning could come together to discuss ways in which enacted curricula could be improved. At the time we did not have radical listening as a construct. However, the rules for cogen addressed the necessity to share the number of turns at talk and the duration of talk among all participants. Furthermore, it was the responsibility of all participants to ensure that everybody was involved. If a person was silent others had the responsibility to bring that person into the conversation in productive ways. We embraced the idea that talking should be not only for the self but also for the other. We also had a rule that the topic of conversation should not be changed until the group had reached consensus on what was to be done regarding that topic in future lessons. Taken together these rules are consistent with radical listening, which we adopted as part of the rule structure for cogen as soon as we knew about it. At the present time we regard it as central to effective cogen.

As is the case with all social constructs, radical listening is theorized to expand the possibilities of the construct. For example, polyphonia necessitates all participants contributing to the dialogue, saying what is on their mind in regards to a given topic. It is important that all individuals' rights to participate by speaking their mind is respected by all participants and no matter what is said, all contributions are considered thoughtfully in relation to the ongoing dialogue. An important axiological component of radical listening and cogen is the respect shown for all contributions and the value given to difference as a resource for a group. Difference is accepted as a resource in the sense that each structure is considered as an expansion of the capital produced and created within the field. Similarly, acceptance of polysemia allows a group to focus on the hermeneutics of making sense of each oral contribution, examining its potential to contribute, rather than questioning its viability. If all oral contributions are regarded as potentially viable then the group's motives can orientate toward working collectively to expand possibilities.

An important outcome of the research we undertook in Philadelphia, before I came to New York City, was that cogen was a seedbed for the production and creation of culture. When we first envisioned the field of cogen we selected participants to be different from one another in as many ways as possible. The rationale for so doing included polyphonia and polysemia. We expected the participants in cogen to learn from difference, and we expected each participant to learn different things in different ways while contributing to the group's motives. After a number of years of research it became apparent that the participants in cogen learned to produce success through the creation and production of new culture. At this time the outcomes of cogen began to focus more on what happened during the cogen rather than what happened subsequently in the whole class. It was not as if the class suddenly became unimportant, but that success was occurring without the necessity for all participants to become the same. The valuing of difference afforded participants interacting successfully with one another, while focusing on reaching consensus on shared goals/ motives and how to succeed.

Our project on cogen incorporates a standpoint that includes myriad dialectical relationships between social constructs that are often regarded as binaries. For example, we recognize the salience of the individual | collective dialectic and acknowledge the importance of individuals accomplishing their goals while contributing to the group's motives. Both are important. Accordingly, it does not make sense for individuals to be held accountable solely for their personal success or for a group's success. On the contrary, all participants in cogen, for example, are responsible for one another's successes and failures. The failure of any one individual to be successful is a matter of concern not only for the individual but also for the group. Not surprisingly, in a field that is structured as cogen is structured, a strong sense of solidarity emerges that is conducive to forging new identities associated with the group's accomplishments in cogen.

## THEORETICAL RESEARCH

I had to struggle with the idea of theoretical research and its nuances. Initially, I understood theoretical research to involve narratives that presented personal experiences of various sorts, explicating salient issues through the aegis of theory. It was not that human subjects were not involved in this research, but that the experiences on which the research focused had already happened at the time the study was designed. A researcher reflected on experiences and designed a study to highlight issues that were of salience. Research of this sort readily emerged from critical pedagogy, where issues of power, oppression, equity and social justice are studied in everyday life. In this genre of research a scholar's day-to-day experiences become the focus of deconstruction. Many of the chapters in this book are of this genre. For example, Joe's experiences with McDonald's afforded *The Sign of the Burger: McDonald's and the Culture of Power* (Kincheloe, 2002), a social analysis that examined the globalization of the problems within the framework of American ideology–including capitalism, democracy, and neoliberalism (Kincheloe, 2002). Hence, some of the ingredients of theoretical research, as it was often described, were history, existing data of various sorts, and narratives. For the most part the research consisted of narratives into which theory was woven. Points were made usually through storytelling rather than analysis of qualitative and quantitative data resources. In this genre of research, which I regard as hermeneutic/phenomenological, the approach is essentially non-empirical.

In my own research I had used narrative as a part of ethnography ever since I began to do interpretive research in 1984 (Tobin, 2000). Initially, my approach to analysis was highly reductionist and I viewed stories/narratives as resources for identifying themes and associated contradictions. That is, my approach was empiricist. Recently, I am very much more aware of the importance of stories being holistic representations of systems of knowing. Much can be missed when reductionist approaches are used in a process of learning from stories. Once stories have been told and included as part of the research it can be left for the reader to make from the stories whatever meanings are possible. For this reason, stories can be included as wholes in research reports, including dissertations. This approach acknowledges the holistic aspects of narrative and recognizes that reductionist attempts at analysis will not produce the best meaning, the only meaning, or complete meaning. Whereas I would once proclaim that stories cannot speak for themselves, I now acknowledge that stories can be included as artifacts in research reports; resources for the hermeneutic endeavors of readers. Basically the stories can be objects on which to focus dialogues from which meanings can unfold.

Other artifacts can be regarded in an analogous way. For example, we have used text boxes to allow for "voice over" techniques to be used in research reports. The texts provided in text boxes are not part of the ongoing flow of the manuscript but are related to it in a variety of possible ways. The idea is to present texts as multiple voices; an approach grounded in an axiological preference for polyphonia. Of course, the text inserted into a text box might be from many different genres including songs and poems. The text box may contain graffiti or a combination of text and picture. The possibilities are endless. The idea is to display many texts and allow the "reader as hermeneut" to build meaning through single and multiple readings.

Photographs, pictures, video files, and other artifacts can contribute to the communication of meaning in research. Obviously, it is not possible to include all artifacts in textboxes and the ways in which research is packaged will expand in the next several years. If this is the case it seems important that educators move beyond oversimplified binaries such as qualitative/quantitative when it comes to describing research genres. It is important that researchers have the theoretical tools to undertake thoughtful research that makes a difference in the variety of ways that creative individuals seek to improve the quality of social life.

## BRICOLAGE

As a bricoleur a researcher can appropriate multiple methodologies (i.e., theories of method) to employ in a study and also utilize multiple theories to frame substantive research. The foci for the research unfold as the research is enacted and there is no need to settle on a focus at the stage a study is designed. Also it is desirable neither to lock in on a genre of research that must begin with questions nor to rule out entirely the possibility that at some stage questions will focus a study or part of it. Why limit the repertoire of possibilities when it comes to doing research? Joe laid out the possibilities in his work on bricolage, using a pastiche of methodologies and theoretical frameworks in research that is ongoing. Initially, I thought of bricoleur and bricolage in relation to a particular study, but more recently I perceive bricolage in relation to grain size. Like most social constructs bricolage can be used to zoom in and zoom out—to focus at micro, meso, macro and global levels of social life. Accordingly, I find it useful to examine my methodologies and frameworks over a research career and stand amazed at the rich breadth of theory that has informed my research. Similarly, at a given point in time I can see my methodologies and frameworks in terms of bricolage and seek to unsettle equilibria so that what we do is always under scrutiny in terms of its viability. When we come to the table to do research it is always appropriate to subject what we are doing and what we are not doing to detailed scrutiny from within. Since, whenever culture is enacted, it is both reproduced and transformed, it is as well to incorporate searching for possibilities for change as part of the methodology for research, both in the immediate and long term futures.

## ... AND IN THE FUTURE ...

Joe was a prolific writer who loved to write every single day. His many books and articles represent a vast reservoir from which we can continue to learn through Joe's accessible written texts. Like a good mate, Joe told it as he saw it, looking at social life through a plethora of rich social frames. The collection we have assembled in this volume and the associated companion texts honor a trajectory that shows brilliance, willingness to learn from others, and emerging maturity. Through these works and many others like it Joe L. Kincheloe continues his scholarly tradition of being an exemplary teacher | learner. Mate, we appreciate all you have done and commit to learning from your endeavors.

## REFERENCES

Guba, E., & Lincoln, Y. S. (1989). *Fourth generation evaluation*. Newbury Park, CA: Sage Publications.
Kincheloe, J. L. (1991). *Teachers as researchers: Qualitative paths to empowerment*. New York: Falmer.
Kincheloe, J. L. (2002). *The sign of the burger: McDonald's and the culture of control*. Philadelphia: Temple University Press.
Kincheloe, J. L., Steinberg S. R., & Tippins, D. J. (1999). *The stigma of genius: Einstein, consciousness, and education*. New York: Peter Lang Publishing.

Kincheloe, J. L., & Tobin, K. (2009). The much exaggerated death of positivism. *Cultural Studies of Science Education, 4*, 513–528.
Stenhouse, L. (1975). *An introduction to curriculum research and development*. London: Heinemann.
Tobin, K. (2000). Interpretive research in science education. In A. E. Kelly & R. Lesh (Eds.), *Handbook of research design in mathematics and science education* (pp. 487–512). Mahwah, NJ: Lawrence Erlbaum Associates.
Tobin, K. (2010). Collaborating to transform and reproduce science education. *Enseñanza de las Ciencias*.
Tobin, K. & Kincheloe, J. L. (Eds.), (2010). *Doing educational research: A handbook* (2nd ed.). Rotterdam, NL: Sense Publishing.

*Joe was a younger brother to the Giroux generation, which ushered in a welcomed cynicism to federal educational interventions; he was disgusted and angry at the Republicans' attempts to change schooling by launching empty initiatives and slogans. This article highlights the technocratic, deskilling nature of schooling, and is an early discussion of the intervention of technology into the modern era. Never a Luddite, and never a technological genius, Joe was aware of the challenges we were to face with the advent of a media society. One of the first to buy a fax machine, he would sit cross-legged on the floor to fax work back and forth to colleagues, and started an early theoretical read of the need of immediate gratification and the new nature of cognition due to technology. This piece highlighted his awareness and fear of positivism, a theme which would follow him throughout his writing, alas, one of his final pieces was with Ken Tobin, attempting to shed light on the continued academic obsession with what Joe called, the God of Objectivity. SS*

JOE L. KINCHELOE

# 1. EXPOSING THE TECHNOCRATIC PERVERSION OF EDUCATION

*The Death of the Democratic Philosophy of Schooling*

INTRODUCTION: TECHNIQUE AT THE EXPENSE OF UNDERSTANDING

In *Anna Karenina*, Leo Tolstoy writes an interesting passage concerning the meaning of the word "technique." Some art patrons are discussing an artist's work in which Christ is a main figure.

> "Yes—there's a wonderful mastery!" said Vronsky... "There you have technique." ...The sentence about technique has sent a pang through Mihailov's [the artist's] heart, and looking angrily at Vronsky he suddenly scowled. He had often heard this word technique, and was utterly unable to understand...a mechanical facility for painting or drawing, entirely apart from its subject.[1]

Tolstoy's passage provides insight into the themes we attempt to develop in the following pages. In modern American society and modern American education technique often takes precedence over meaning. Colleges of education in their teacher-education curricula have often moved away from the exploration of educational meaning. In the process, they have devoted more and more time to teaching technique—techniques examined outside of a social, political, and philosophical context.

Like Tolstoy's painter, Mihailov, we are disturbed by the use of the word "technique" in the contemporary discussion of education. The over-emphasis on technique at the expense of contextual understanding is in part a product, we think, of twentieth-century technological development. In the following pages we attempt to delineate the impact of technology on school and society. In our discussion we refer to the concept of technocracy—a situation in which society is guided by the demands of the current technology and not by democratic concerns about the welfare of people. In other words, in a technocracy the technology becomes the master of the people not their servant. We also refer to technicalization. This term is used to describe the process by which technique comes to take precedence over purpose. In the technologically-driven society we argue that technique is viewed as an end in itself—in Tolstoy's words, "entirely apart from its subject."

To avoid the dehumanization that such over-emphasis on technique brings about, educators must first recognize that there is a problem. Once recognizing the problem, they must attend to the subtle and insidious ways that technicalization invades our workplaces, our schools, and our assumptions about human nature and education. This chapter is not in tune with the *Zeitgeist* of the 1990s—a time whose spirit is marked by too much complacency and unquestioned acceptance of the technocratic spirit. We hope that our essay serves to, at least momentarily, disrupt that spirit.

## THE NATURE OF TECHNOCRACY

Americans have traditionally placed great faith in the power of technology to solve the myriad of social, economic, and political problems which have faced us. Often in our enthusiasm for technological benefits, however, we failed to anticipate the social and environmental side effects of technological innovation. As Issac Asimov had maintained, anyone could have predicted the automobile, but few could have forecast the traffic jam; anyone could have predicted the television, but few could have forecast the soap opera. We would extend Asimov's paradigm to technological change in general. Anyone could have predicted the assembly line but few could have forecast the ____ (fill in the blank). Anyone could have predicted behavioral objectives but few could have forecast the ____ (fill in the blank). Anyone could have predicted the computer, but few could have forecast the ____ (fill in the blank). It must be the concern of educators to complete the statement. Our modern obligation is to devote attention not merely to the sophistication of educational technique, but to the educational and social side effects of the new technology.

Despite our historical faith in technology, a tradition of technological suspicion has emerged in the last two centuries. This fear of unchecked technology can be traced in the literature of science fiction from Samuel Butler's *Erewhon* written in 1872 to Ray Bradbury's *Fahrenheit 451*, Arthur C. Clarke's *2001: A Space Odyssey* and countless other works of the modern era. For example, consider just a few of the authors who have pointed to the possibility of dangerous side effects of computers. Butler, writing in 1872, warned of machines with artificial intelligence that might turn on their makers. These machines of great calculating ability, he wrote, may enslave man and supersede him. "Have we not engines which can do all manner of sums more quickly and correctly than we can?" The wise man of Erewhon fears that humans will someday relate to the intelligence machines as cattle now relate to man. Moved by his argument the inhabitants of Erewhon destroy these proto-computers. Thus begins the science fiction tradition of the computer as villain.[2]

The Industrial Revolution alerted many individuals to the underside of technological progress. The fear of the sociopolitical side effects of technological change is well-documented by Karl Marx. Social revolutions, he wrote, occur when a new mode of production breaks the constraints of established laws and relationships. Those who control the new "technology," Marx argued, emerge as a new class destined to become the ruling elite. Technology has created "new modes of production" as the information and service sectors of the economy have surpassed the agricultural and industrial sectors. Indeed, the gap between the information economy and other modes or production continues to grow. The implications of Marx's analysis for the future of the American economy are interesting. If his interpretation is applicable to the modern era, then modern technology and the information society it brings with it may widen the gap between management and labor and rich and poor. Thus, it becomes more important than ever to study education in the context of technological change. To view educational goals and teaching outside of this larger context is to misunderstand the forces which direct educational policy.

Albert Einstein argued that the results of technology have posed a threat to mankind since they have fallen into the hands of morally blind exponents of political power. Echoing Marx, Einstein maintained that technological innovation has "led to a concentration of economic and also of political power in the hands of small minorities which have come to dominate completely the lives of the masses of people who appear more and more amorphous."[3] But what is even worse is that this concentration of power made possible by technological innovation has served to prevent the development of truly independent human personalities. Again, the theme emerges—unchecked technological change limits human freedom. Like the warnings of the science fiction writers, technology comes to enslave human beings.

How exactly does technology come to limit human freedom? When most of us think about technology we often concentrate on its labor saving aspects which grant us greater control over our time. In this context technological innovation does *not* constrain human activity but allows greater choice over how we live our lives. The automobile and the interstate highway, for example, grant us more expendable time than our ancestors could have ever envisioned.

There is another side to technological innovation, however. Other than labor-saving devices, technology has rarely served to make for a humane workplace in modern America. In fact, technological innovations such as the assembly line and accompanying efficiency procedures have often served to limit worker options. New technologies of worker control, often called scientific management, may have extended the tendency of industrial supervisors to view workers as objects to be manipulated. Too infrequently have techniques of scientific management served to encourage a view of workers as human beings with emotions to be considered and individual talents to be cultivated.

Industrial managers have often sought specific worker personality types to meet the needs of the technicalized workplace. According to many industrial analysts, workers who possess the following personality traits are more valuable to the enterprise than employees who do not: 1) an acceptance of a subordinate role in the hierarchy; 2) submission to the rigid discipline required by the bureaucracy of the workplace; 3) comfort with the lack of concern for human emotions and the subtle dynamics of human interaction that are characteristic of the technicalized, bureaucratized workplace; 4) and acceptance of innovation based not on the value of the work itself but on external reward structures such as monetary incentives.

The role of education often revolves around the production of these personality traits in students. Men and women are students before they are workers. Workers who give up their control of the planning and direction of the activities which comprise their jobs, first surrender their autonomy to a teacher. This teacher plays the role of the boss, granting rewards and assessing penalties. As far as discipline is concerned, the schools succeed in preparing the future worker for the requirements of the dehumanized, bureaucratic workplace. Some of us have experienced that workplace directly through our own work histories. Others have experienced it vicariously through the stories of our friends or by reading about the line workers in Studs Terkle's *Working*. It is a structured world marked by highly standardized routines and degrading requirements of conformity to time schedules, regulations, and stifling technocratic procedures. Schools prepare our psyches for such a place with their, paraphrasing Charles Silberman, oppressive and petty rules which govern student behavior.

The schools often condition students to remove their emotions from their schoolwork—a characteristic highly valued in the workplace. The more "dehumanized" a bureaucracy becomes the more "success" it attains. When love, hatred, irrationality, and other emotional elements are removed from the official business, then rules and regulation can work more predictably. Thus, as educational studies have indicated, teachers tend to value student personality traits related to the cognitive mode of expression. Students with highly developed affective personality traits are often not rewarded for their compassion and emphatic insight. Also, students like workers frequently are not intrinsically interested in their work. In both cases the organization has to rely on external rewards such as grades, pay incentives, class ranks, or titles to motivate the individual.

What are the implications here? Simply put, this view of schooling turns our conventional notions upside down. To see one of the roles of school as the production of personality types which better suit the needs of those who run the technical workplace challenges the assumptions on which many modern discussions of education rest. We often look at schooling as a force which frees us from ignorance, helps us envision alternatives, gives us choice in the direction of our lives, and opens the doors of opportunity. Viewed in the context of "personality adjustment" school serves not as a force for freedom but as a vehicle of constraint. Instead of granting us power to shape our lives, it often manipulates us so that we better serve the needs of the workplace. This is not the way many Americans interpret the role of schools in a democratic society.

If schools serve this sometimes manipulative role, why don't more Americans understand that this is the case? Why do we rarely hear this view expressed in the public discussion of education? The answers to such questions are very complex and ambiguous and this is not the forum for a full discussion of them. Suffice it to say that many Americans intuitively understand that something was wrong with their education—they have just not articulated precisely what it is. Many Americans, especially those who have worked in low-status factory jobs, know that school was similar to work. And in neither school nor the workplace do these Americans feel that their talents were appreciated or that they have much input into what went on. It is important that these voiceless workers, these victims of technocracy, understand that school does not have to be an institution which limits choice. It is important that the concerns of these Americans be considered in the national conversation over educational policy. The concepts of technocracy and technicalization are valuable in the attempt to understand the role of schooling, for they provide us with a means of articulating our vague feelings that modern society and modern education are somehow hostile to individuality.

What is the nature of the process by which technocracy squashes the individuality of the worker? Because of its complexity and subtlety it is often unrecognized. The process merits examination in some detail.

Employers to exist must extract labor from their workers. In this society the employer must make an effort to avoid the appearance of treating labor harshly. The ideal situation, employers have reasoned, would involve a labor force which "voluntarily" cooperated with management to increase profit margins and to boost productivity.

Through the use of scientific management employers have found several ways to avoid harsh treatment of labor and to contribute to the creation of a cooperative workplace. The procedure which has worked best, however, has been to design technologies which simplify and specify the activities of workers. If the technology is sufficiently sophisticated, workers will not have to think for themselves as they merely follow a redesigned routine. The employer does not have to worry as much about supervision, as the workers relinquish their control of the process of production. The technology not the employer forces the employee to follow orders.

One of the most important outcomes of this technicalization of the workplace is the creation of a strict hierarchy. The hierarchy accentuates the division of labor and de-emphasizes thinking and decision making by the workers. Such a workplace conditions workers to take orders. Since workers do not control decision-making about the execution of their jobs the hierarchical structure necessitates the hiring of many foremen and supervisors, quality-control specialists, administrators to co-ordinate production, efficiency engineers, and researchers and consultants to provide the information necessary for the few at the top to make intelligent decisions. Unfortunately, this description of the technicalization of the workplace and the solidification of the workplace hierarchy sounds hauntingly familiar to the organization of our school systems.

The hierarchy in the workplace keeps those workers at the lowest rung of the ladder ignorant of the way the production process works as a whole. The low level workers see only a minute part of the process and they see it in isolation from the logic of the process. This ignorance requires that these workers accept the fact that decisions regarding their work be made by higher-ups. Some workers sometimes think that they could perform jobs at a higher level of the hierarchy just as well as the people who now hold them. They are discouraged by the higher formal education requirements necessary for such high level jobs. Seeing access to higher education as limited, the low level worker gives up his or her aspirations to higher positions. Thus, in many cases workers come to accept the view that their "ignorance" justifies management's relegation of them to non-thinking jobs.

Workers in this situation come to separate their "spirit" from their work. Work is not a time of fulfillment of creative impulses nor is it a time of unification of themselves with other workers. As a result, the workers seek gratification in other spheres of his or her life. Some analysts have argued that workers turn toward consumption of goods as an activity for happiness and fulfillment. A new boat, car, motorcycle, computer, or swimming pool substitutes for meaningful work activity. As a recent pop song puts it, employees start "working for the weekend." Older workers work for retirement.

As workers find that the possibility of promotion to higher level jobs is minimal and learn to devote their energies to concerns outside of work, management devises new ways to minimize their indifference to their work. One such way is the use of mini-hierarchies or job ladders for low level employees. Such ladders give workers hope of at least some advancement and encourage stable work behavior. The ethic of "not rocking the boat" or "not making waves" comes to dominate the workplace. Workers who offer too many creative suggestions or appear to be too enthusiastic about doing a job are not viewed as ideal employees but as potential troublemakers. Left unrestrained, these workers may disrupt the orderly flow of daily events and initiate discontent among fellow workers. Employers come to want employees with a moderate interest in their work—enough interest to do what they have to do but not enough to want to devise ways to do it better. Thus, technocracy in a bizarre way celebrates mediocrity.

Another result of the hierarchical structure produced by the technocratic workplace is the disruption of common interests between the workers. As low-status employees gain seniority and conform to the ethic of the workplace, they move up the rungs of the mini-ladder. As a result they acquire an interest in the preservation of the system and lose concern for the welfare of their workmates on the lower rungs. Worker camaraderie is further damaged by the fact that management arranged a situation where the lower-level workers rarely come into contact with persons near the top of hierarchy. The agent who supervises them is another worker—a foreman, an efficiency supervisor, or a quality control administrator. Their frustrations and resentments are directed toward one another. This serves to hide the exploitative role of both the technology and individuals at the top of the hierarchy who use it to control worker behavior.

Our schools tend to prepare students for the place in hierarchy which best fits their social class origins. Thus, the poorer kids are trained to adopt the personality traits necessary for low-status jobs. The more affluent children are socialized for managerial and professional roles. Most of the time such differential training takes place within individual schools, rationalized by so-called ability grouping and level testing. Any observer can notice the difference between the management of a "low group" and an "advanced group." The low group is subjected to a high degree of external discipline. There are copious rules accompanied by rigid disciplinary procedures. In these situations students learn to take orders and respect authority. Low-level students have few choices, as they are prepared for their low-status role in the workplace.

Advanced students are subjected to fewer rules with less consistent enforcement of rules which exist. For such students conflicts are often settled through negotiation and discussion rather than through the arbitrary action of authority. Such experiences serve to prepare the more affluent students for decision-making managerial or professional positions. The relative freedom of school will correspond to the relative freedom such students will find in their adult roles in the workplace as bosses.[4]

As technology changes in modern society the type of education provided slowly changes. Schools in America typically are designed to meet the needs of industry. It logically follows, therefore, that when technology mandates new types of industry, schools slowly adjust their curricula to produce new types of workers. It is true that the job market of the next quarter-century will see a need for more scientifically-trained students. Indeed, the "high-tech" economy will be an important part of American life in the first decade of the twenty-first century, but it will require relatively few workers. The fastest growing employment category will be service jobs, e.g., secretaries, office workers, etc. with the decline of jobs in hard industries, such as steel and automobiles, the nature of the American workplace is changing. It probably was not necessary that an automobile assembly-line worker educated in 1955 be able to read and write to perform his job. To perform competently the new service worker in addition to the "desirable" personality traits of the workplace must possess basic literacy skills. Thus, it is not surprising that 1983 was the year when the National Commission on Excellence in Education (NCEE) called for a dramatic reform of education to rescue "a nation at risk."[5]

## NATIONAL COMMISSION ON EXCELLENCE IN EDUCATION AND TECHNOCRACY

What is the relationship between the reform movement initiated by the NCEE and the technocracy with which we are concerned? The NCEE assumed that the role of school was fundamentally an economic one. When all is said and done, present "excellence" reformers agree, schools serve economic ends and curricula can be justified only to the degree those ends are accomplished. In the present economic situation technological improvement is paramount. Thus, education is viewed as a means of furthering technological improvement and providing workers to serve the new technology.

American business in the 1980s found itself in a technological crisis. Let us briefly examine the genesis of that technological crisis and its effect on education. Such an examination may help illustrate the role education plays in a technocracy.

The 1970s were years marked by declining productivity, reduced capital investment by American industry, and high employment, especially among young, entry-level workers. High unemployment resulted from the baby boomers coming of age and entering the workforce. Because of this circumstance, governmental education policy focused on youth unemployment. Career education and vocational education were pushed by all levels of government.

American business responded to the labor surplus by becoming more labor intensive and by reducing expenditures on new machinery. Many companies decided to add second and third shifts in lieu of replacing equipment which had grown old and obsolete. As a result, productivity declined—American workers were producing less than their Japanese and Western European counterparts. Between 1960 and 1977, American productivity remained virtually the same, while Japanese productivity increased by 255%.

In the 1980s the situation changed dramatically. The baby boom ran its course and fewer and fewer youths were entering the job market. In the 1970s, 2.5 million workers were entering the labor force annually—in the late 1980s that number decreased to around 1.5 million new workers per year. Simply stated, there were fewer young people in the 1980s than there were in the 1970s—in the 14 to 24 age group, about 20% less.

What is important to our discussion of technocracy in this brief economic history involves the response of American business. There were two main business responses in the educational sphere: 1) business sought to improve the basic education of youth who would have been marginally employable in the 1970s; and 2) business sought to improve the technological training (math and science) of those who would work in high-prestige industrial jobs (engineers, scientists, and technicians).

Let's examine the first response. As the baby boom subsided fewer qualified employees were available for entry-level jobs. Knowing that too great a decrease in labor will drive up wages, business responded in its own best interest and sought to maximize the number of potential laborers. Thus, business concerned itself with improving the academic competence of the marginally employable student of the 1970s. It called for a renewed concern for "the basics" and strict accountability to insure that such basic teaching and learning took place.

The second business response also merits further analysis. Because of the reluctance of manufacturers in the 1970s to improve equipment, American business had to face the consequences of a technological crisis in more recent years. One result, of course, was reduced productivity. When productivity declined, American industry found itself less able to compete equally with foreign competition. Thus, like with the challenge presented by Sputnik in the late 1950s, American business in the late 1980s and early 1990s called on the schools to supply them with technically competent professionals.[6] Business leaders have consistently called for increased math and science requirements for high school graduation. Reading the NCEE report, one is reminded of a call to arms against a more technologically competent enemy.

> Our nation is at risk. Our once unchallenged preeminence in commerce industry, science, and technological innovation is being overtaken by competitors throughout the world...If an unfriendly foreign power had attempted to impose on America the mediocre educational performance that exists today, we might well have viewed it as an act of war...The risk is not only that the Japanese make automobiles more efficiently than Americans and have

government subsidies for development and export. It is not just that the South Koreans recently built the world's most efficient steel mill, or that American machine tools, once the pride of the world, are being displaced by German products. It is also that these developments signify a redistribution of trained capability throughout the globe. Knowledge, learning, information, and skilled intelligence are the new raw materials of international commerce and are today spreading throughout the world as vigorously as miracle drugs, synthetic fertilizers, and blue jeans did earlier.[7]

The NCEE report reflects the concerns of the business community and its desire to solve its technological problems. Many of the members of the NCEE were directly associated with the Shell Oil Company, Bell Labs, the California Farm Bureau, and the Foundation for Teaching Economics. The economic concerns of these organizations were translated into the educational concerns of "A Nation at Risk." When the NCEE report is compared with other studies of American education (such as John Goodlad's or Ernest Boyer's) the economically motivated technological focus of the NCEE becomes apparent.

The strategy business has taken involves marshalling public support of the business-directed educational goals of expanding the numbers of potential employees—a move which will reduce wages. If business is successful, the job market by the late 1990s will be flooded with: 1) high school graduates with the "proper" personality traits and minimum literacy skills for entry-level jobs and; 2) college trained, highly qualified scientists and engineers. If such events take place, schools (from the perspective of the business-oriented reformers) will have performed their jobs well. The needs of business will have been met.

Many educators are uncomfortable with the business-oriented call for reform and its assumptions about the role of education. These detractors argue that: 1) schools do not exist to meet the short-term needs of business and industry; 2) the short-term demands of business and industry do not necessarily result in benefits for the economy in general or the individual in particular; 3) the technological and labor problems of business and industry were not caused by the failure of the public schools. Indeed, it was not school leaders who chose not to invest in new plants and equipment in the 1970s; 4) it is difficult to predict manpower needs for business and industry and there is little agreement that an educational curriculum specifically designed to address those needs even accomplishes its goal. Many agree that a general education steeped in the sciences as well as the humanities may in the long run best serve not only the nation's economic but even its spiritual needs.[8]

Thus, the business-oriented educational reforms of the 1980s served as a celebration to technocracy. If technocracy implies that the demands of the prevailing technology come to outweigh our democratic concerns about the welfare of people, then American education is in part a servant of the technocracy. The curriculum, if the business-oriented reformers prevail, will not be dictated by the desire to learn those skills and that knowledge which are of most worth; students will be presented material that best prepares them to adjust to the technology of the workplace. In the process, humane concerns in educational planning disappear; democratic participation is ignored as a goal for schooling; and the celebration of the individual as the free agent who plots his or her destiny is viewed as an inefficient impediment to economic growth. What matters is determined by the technological demands of the moment. Humans surrender to the needs of the machine in the name of international competition.

## THE TECHNICALIZATION OF EDUCATION: CHANGING OUR VIEW OF THE NATURE OF LEARNING

The technocratic culture implicitly asserts that any subject which fails to lend itself to quantification is, by definition, not worthy of the label, basic. This technocratic mentality invests more faith in the IQ than in human judgment and in the multiple choice test than observable behavior. In this technocratic context the jargon of education is transformed into a perverse lexicon. Technocratic educational language originated in the industrial revolution—not in any revolution of learning. To the terms "input," "output," and "quality control," the technicalized culture has added its latest and most pervasive component of technocratic language, "behavioral objective." If subject matter cannot be arranged in behavioral objectives, then it is not worthy of inclusion in the curriculum. What the technology measures not only takes on exaggerated importance but in a sense becomes "reality."

There is religious dimension to this process of technicalization. Only through technicalization can we discover what is true and valuable. Modern TV promotes this technical religious creed in many of its programs and especially in its commercials. Analyze a random sample of current TV commercials. What is the solution each one promotes to the problem it poses? The omniscient, quasi-divine voice dubbed over the babblings of the mere mortals lamenting their ring around the collar, tells us that we shall find happiness and fulfillment through the application of a specific technology. The voice tells us that there is a vegetable cutter that will end kitchen drudgery, a mouthwash that will grant us social acceptance, an analgesic which will kill our pain, a cake mix that will insure the love of our family, or a car that will open new vistas on our sex life. The technology, not God or human reason, provides salvation and by implication we mere mortals must kneel humbly in the presence of its power.

Overawed by the superiority of technology (an idea so aggressively promoted by the modern information environment), we begin to lose confidence in the human ability to think, analyze, and assign value. As a result we willingly transfer these functions to the technology and let the technical instrument place a numerical designation on human intelligence. The technicalization process in all phases of human life insists on the measurement of everything for everyone. All of our information will be objective; all human subjectivity will be defeated. Those irritating elements of the education process that are complex and ambiguous will be substituted with the precision of technocratic salvation. In the millennium of complete technicalization we will always know, to the nearest hundredth of a point, how well we are achieving our goals.

Technology is always an idea disguised as a piece of machinery. For example, the IQ is an idea or an assumption about the nature of intelligence, the ways it is expressed, and its relationship to time. In many Native American cultures the mark of a wise person is that he or she pauses to think about an answer to a question for a few moments before offering a response. The silent period following the question is used to survey a wide range of experiences and to formulate a well-conceived answer based on the information available. Often a questioner with a European heritage will misinterpret the silence as inability to answer and will interrupt what he or she perceives as an uncomfortable interlude with forced conversation. Euro-questioners may attempt to clarify the question or answer it themselves. Thus, they may leave the conversation with the impression that the Native is intellectually shallow or "slow." Given the biases of Western culture, the word, slow, commonly means unintelligent.

Operating within the confines of Western culture, the IQ test accepts the proposition that intelligence and time of response are directly related. Placed into the context of the IQ testing situation, the wise Native who values a thoughtful, measured response would "test" low on the scale. Because of the culturally-biased "ideas" behind the IQ test, the native's behavior is not perceived as intelligent. Thus, technicalization has occurred when the educator in doubt deems the technique as right and life as wrong. The story of the Native American gives us a good example of the technocratic approach. Though reality may tell us that the Native American is wise and holds great insight into the nature of life, his or her IQ is 85 and *that* is below normal.

This distortion of reality emerging from the need to quantify reflects the way we often choose to study education. In an attempt to emulate the empirical research methods of physical science, modern education research emphasizes the measuring or quantification of experience. Often this need for quantification takes precedence over the need to understand the *significance* of educational experience. Why don't we better understand the social and political results of education? Stated another way, why don't we know more about the impact education makes on the lives of individuals from various social backgrounds? These are complex questions, but one reason for our limited success in this area concerns our method of studying educational phenomena. Many argue that we are bound by what is called a "culture of positivism." This culture of positivism serves in the long run to further the technicalization of education.

## THE CULTURE OF POSITIVISM AND THE GOD OF OBJECTIVITY

Positivism is a way of "knowing" which assumes that knowledge worthy of being known can be derived from sense experience. Thus, positivism revolves around the quest for certainty and the need to reduce experience to a set of measurable facts. Researchers and educators caught in the culture of positivism focus on explaining the components of experience, predicting future situations, and controlling future experience by manipulation of technical means. Critics have charged that research methods which lean toward positivism often ignore questions concerning *what should be*. The attempt to produce "facts" which are empirically verifiable takes precedence over the search for purpose, meaning, and ethical outcomes.[9]

When analysts offer this critique of positivism and its uses in an educational context, they do not mean to imply that quantification never has a role in educational research. Quantification is a necessary component of research in any field. Some questions are best answered by the use of quantitative inquiry. The point is that there are many questions—especially questions in the people-centered field of education—which do not lend themselves to quantification. The attempt to quantify these experiences results in a violation of their nature. Thus, a new type of research methodology must be utilized to understand these types of experiences. The new research must ask qualitative questions. Such questions examine the quality of the experience, analyzing those aspects of experience which transcend its measurable factual nature. The qualitative researcher attempts to understand the unspoken assumptions behind an experience and the context in which an experience takes place. They examine the unity of the experience, meaning they attempt to take into account all features of an experience which ultimately give the experience meaning.[10]

The means of researching questions in education are very important to our discussion of tecnicalization. Without a research methodology which examines questions of implicit assumption, context, and larger meaning of experience, the process of technicalization remains unrecognized and unchallenged. The connection between academic research and the concern for improvement in the human condition has been torn apart in the twentieth century. The classical Greeks were concerned with the connection between the search for truth (research) and ethical outcomes. Many researchers in the field of education in the present era have forgotten the ends that research once served. In the name of *objectivity* researchers justify the separation between improvement of the human condition and research.

This notion of objectivity in research rests on some questionable assumptions. Knowledge itself is assumed to be objective and value free. Questions concerning how we deem certain knowledge worth knowing, how we organize and use knowledge, and how we evaluate it are not considered subjective features. Indeed, many times they are not even considered at all. Knowledge taken from the subjective world of intuition, insight, human-based learning, and lived experience is not viewed as real knowledge—it is "unverified." Values are viewed as emotional responses and are viewed as the opposite of that which is "factual." The proceeding points constitute a specific, value-laden position. Yet, it is this position which is defined as objective. All positions which disagree with it are subjective and thus inferior. In this way the culture of positivism has established the rules for inquiry in modern society.

When knowledge and research are separated from values many argue that the interests of learning are served. The fact is that when such a separation takes place, more is hidden than uncovered. The notion of objectivity in any field reflects the values and assumptions of the scholars working in that field. In the name of objectivity these values and assumptions are hidden. It is impossible to separate values from facts and inquiry from ethics. Think about a map maker's attempt to draw a map that represents every physical and human-made detail on a specific territory. Space on the map limits what can be represented. The map maker must decide what to leave out and what to include. He or she must make a value judgment concerning the importance of each feature. Even an object like a map represents a subjective set of decisions by its maker.

When in educational research we study the effect of certain teaching strategies on student performance we are like the map maker. While claiming to be objective, we constantly make assumptions and value judgments in the research process. One of the most important assumptions in such studies involves our acceptance of the validity of our evaluative instruments. In order for a quantitative evaluation to proceed, we must assume that the standardized, "objective" tests administered to our subjects of study are accurate measures of performance. Such tests are usually factually-based. A factually-based test assumes that the salient feature of the learning experience is the acquisition of facts. What about conceptual learning? If significant conceptual learning took place would it be measured by the tests? What about the interest students possessed before they came into the study? We assume that differences in student interests do not affect the outcomes of learning. It is a variable we cannot control. What about hard to define, subtle differences in teacher personality? Might such personality differences bring about important changes in student responses regardless of what method is used? We assume that the effect of teacher personality is unimportant, for in this situation we are focusing on a question concerning which teaching strategy is better. In complex human situations such variables are infinite and uncontrollable.

The effects of such a research methodology are numerous. The most obvious effect is the inaccurate picture we get of social phenomena. Cursed with a distorted picture of reality, we find it difficult to recognize problems which exist in our political and educational life. Another effect involves the removal of larger questions of ethics and political context from educational decision making. Devoid of this ethical and political dimension, educational questions become merely technical problems with technical solutions. Our quest becomes not to figure out what ethically and politically is desirable but what is technically possible—a key characteristic of technicalized education. In social studies education, for example, we sometimes fail to ask what types of historical and political knowledge are of most worth; instead, we ask what information delivery system most effectively serves to raise standardized tests scores. The question of technique takes precedence over the question of purpose. For all of the assumptions the culture of positivism makes, it fails to base its view of the world on the pretext that humans should be free to direct their own lives. Filling the vacuum left by this failure to embrace human emancipation is an insidious form of social engineering. It is insidious in the sense that it does not admit its true nature. It is social engineering in the sense that it views humans as entities to be manipulated. The positivistic culture consistently denies the possibility that it begins with specific presuppositions. Examined thoughtfully, the failure to assume that the furtherance of human freedom is basic to any truly humane view of the world or any research question is a frightening assumption. The nonpositivistic advocates of human freedom may begin their research with an assumption; but at least it is an openly-stated assumption.

Worshipping the god of objectivity, the culture of positivism succumbs to what has been called the "fallacy of objectivism." This fallacy occurs when a research methodology is self-limiting to the point that *it cannot reflect on its own presuppositions*. It cannot reflect on presuppositions because it claims they do not exist.

Trapped by its adulation of empirically-grounded fact, the culture of positivism fails to acknowledge the historical and social context which gave birth to it. Devoid of such context it fails to see itself clearly—it cannot perform self-analysis. Thus, it renews with a vengeance its focus on "what is." Typically, the result of the analysis of "what is" is that the status quo is basically sound. Teaching that is based on this culture uncritically passes "facts" along to students outside of any social or historical context.

## POSITIVISM, TECHNOCRACY, AND THE FRAGMENTATION OF HUMAN EXPERIENCE

To meet the requirements of positivistic investigation all human activity must be fragmented. Schools steeped in the culture of positivism teach the outcomes of such fragmentation—isolated facts. The attempt to comprehend the world as a network of interconnections is lost. North American students are taught to attack problems as if they emerged in isolation, detached from the dynamic social and political forces which bestow meaning.

Let us examine more closely the educational implications of this fragmentation of human experience. Teaching only the outcomes of this empirical fragmentation, school curricula fall prey to what we might call, ready-made subject matter that composes our standardized tests. It is the successful rote memorization of this ready-made subject matter that separates the successful from the unsuccessful student. It is the possession of this information that defines the educated person. Unfortunately, it is often the case that the manner in which this subject matter is learned as well as the subject matter itself contributed only minimally to the creation of thoughtful, analytical scholars.

The subject matter is ready-made in the sense that it is presented as an end in itself. It does not have to be connected to any other experience; it has only to be committed to memory. Not only does the knowledge come ready made, but it is second hand as well. It is second hand in the sense that it is the result of other people's exploration and discovery. Where the knowledge came from or how it was arrived upon is not important. Devoid of context, like other reflections of the culture of positivism, the second-hand knowledge is learned in isolation from lived experience.

Analysis of the process by which the knowledge was discovered, provides the learner insight into the logic behind the knowledge. It is this study of the process of discovery which allows for the understanding of context and significance. It is the critical analysis of the process which helps the student understand the nature of knowledge production or in other words, research. Thus, by studying the process by which knowledge is produced the student learns about the nature of learning. It is in this way that students accomplish that all important goal of education—learning to teach oneself. One who learns to teach himself or herself has engaged in one of the most basic acts of human emancipation. Because it is unconcerned with the attempt of humans to control their own destiny, the culture of positivism is indifferent to learning which pushes beyond the acquisition of second-hand, ready-made facts.

When the culture of positivism fails to embrace the norms based on a belief in people's right to control their own destiny, it extends its passive model of humans. As it extends this passivity, the culture leaves humans vulnerable to the manipulation of the modern era. Passive individuals cannot protect themselves from the manipulations of the workplace, the mass media, advertisers, and religious zealots. The soullessness of this objective quest for certainty suppresses the free will of the individual and the collective, shared interest of human beings. The culture of positivism contributes to the despair of existential loneliness. The community of men and women is fragmented and individuals see themselves alone in an impersonal world. Emphasis on those hard to quantify qualities which constitute our humanness is de-emphasized. As the culture of positivism studies the world, facts continue to be empirically registered but the basic questions about humanity remain unasked.[11]

One of the larger goals of school, many argue, is to produce critical thinking. (By the 1980s and 1990s critical thinking has become a popular buzzword in educational circles—universally accepted but rarely examined.) Too often the critical thinking promoted by the schools is a diluted form of analytical thought, presented without social or historical context emphasizing only technical academic skills. The critical thinking exercises are presented with only minimal information and are calculated to elicit a pre-determined outcome. The form of sequential logic required is also pre-determined, and the narrow range of outcomes acceptable does not challenge prevailing wisdom. Admittedly, the level of thought necessary for these so-called critical thinking exercises is more demanding than mere memorization, but the process is still controlled and pre-determined. Political and socio-economic power relationships are undisturbed, and the larger assumptions of the technocracy are unchallenged. The critical thinking lessons we have observed in the schools rarely give consideration to the social consequences of the knowledge acquired or the method used to acquire it. Examination of the application of the knowledge in the historical past or an exploration of its use in the future is irrelevant.

## THE ESCAPE FROM TECHNOCRACY: THE POLITICS OF CRITICAL THINKING

Critical thinking is by nature an active process which encourages individuals to examine contextually the meaning of the information encountered so as to better understand the world and to contribute to the control of their own lives. If these assertions are valid, then the culture of positivism takes a specific political position, as it serves as an impediment to this process. It is a political position because the act of controlling one's own life (emancipation) is always a political act. Such a desire dictates the political position one must take in particular circumstances.

Critical thinking itself is a political act in that it is a mode of reasoning which supports the realization that "I am able." One might ask at this juncture, "what about objectivity?" If critical thinking with its emphasis on the origin, development, and purpose of knowledge constitutes a specific political act, then isn't it unethical for schools to promote that value? Advocates of human emancipation reply, "what is the choice?" The alternative is to deny the importance of human emancipation, and such denial is undoubtedly an act with specific political consequences.

Think of some specific examples which illustrate the implicit political consequences of educational acts. Ask any fundamentalist conservative about the political implications of educational policy in modern American schooling. He or she will argue that curricular design not only has political but theological implications as well.

While by no means endorsing a New Right critique of American education, we would argue that on one level the fundamentalist is correct. There are tacit aspects of the modern curriculum which do challenge fundamentalist precepts. The efforts of curriculum planners to move the classroom toward more critical thinking has raised a red flag in the faces of the soldiers of the New Right. Though it is heard more at the theoretical level than witnessed in the classroom, this emphasis on critical thinking, with its analysis and questioning, rubs against some basic fundamentalist assumptions concerning learning.

We have previously referred to critical thinking as a political act—political in the sense that it empowers the learner to understand a cultural norm in such depth that the assumptions which undergird it may be analyzed. When assumptions behind these ideas are laid bare then the learner is more capable of rejecting or accepting such norms. This allows the learner more confidence in questioning conventional wisdom—a frightening possibility to the fundamentalist conservative. Instead of serving to buttress traditional theological, political and economic "truths" through catechistic training, critical thinking serves to undermine them by exposing the vulnerability of their assumptions. The result, the fundamentalists know all too well, is that the status quo is challenged. In fundamentalist words, traditional values are destroyed by their political enemies—the forces of evil.

Though the process of critical thinking may be threatened by the advocates of absolutist political or religious dogmas and may be stymied by the culture of positivism, education which does not promote it is an impediment to human self-determination. Critical thinking as a political act means that men and women can take an active part in the affairs of the world. Instead of being controlled by history, individuals can help shape history. In other words, critical thinking enables humans to "transcend" their own histories or backgrounds so that they can escape the helplessness which comes from an unexamined heritage. Before one can achieve personal emancipation or liberation, a person must understand the social, political, religious, ethnic, economic, and educational forces which molded him or her. Only through contextual analysis (an act basic to critical thinking) can one accomplish that liberation which comes from an understanding of personal formation.[12]

## WHAT IS TO BE DONE?

What might the average teacher or administrator learn from the preceding discussion of the process of technicalization in education? Hopefully the analysis of technicalization forces us to think more clearly about the purpose of education, the powers that determine the purposes, and what the purposes should be. Before American educators can arrest the continuing drift toward technicalization they must understand how technicalized education conflicts with the various goals of education in a democratic society. It is difficult to think about the purposes of democratic education without a few references to John Dewey.

Dewey's writings on education were founded on the assumption that we should be working toward the most democratic society possible. An education which allows the self-interest of business to dictate its purpose cannot reach its democratic potential. An education which hallows the self-perpetuating momentum of an educational bureaucracy to mandate goals cannot be responsive to democratic impulses. Democratic education seeks purposes which serve the best interests of as many groups and individuals as possible. Purpose should be determined by asking: what knowledge is of most worth? It should not be determined by asking: what knowledge is of most worth to powerful interests?

In modern discussion of educational purpose many commentators connect educational purpose to vocational preparation. Dewey warned against such a connection early in the twentieth century. Students, he argued, should be encouraged to develop their abilities to the point they are capable of choosing their own careers. The spirit of democratic opportunity is lost when schools attempt to fit students in advance to specific work roles. There is a direct relationship, he argued, between the social and economic conditions of one's birth and the vocational role typically chosen. The purpose of democratic education is not vocational preparation. Educational purpose in a democracy certainly is not a form of vocational preparation designed by industrialists for the needs of industry. Teachers and administrators need to understand this.[13]

Dewey argued that school should not train students for specific jobs. Education should be an end in itself with no specific outcomes outside of an increased intellectual ability and a heightened capacity to understand the ethical dimensions of human situations. When students are trained for specific jobs other areas not ostensibly related to the job are neglected. The pursuit of intellectual and ethical goals is thus stifled and the student is left with merely the technical aspects of a vocational skill. Unable to understand the larger social, political, and economic picture, the student has difficulty gaining control of his own life. He or she is left in a permanently subordinate position. Seventy years ago Dewey recognized the tendency in a technicalized, industrialized society for the conception of work to be separated from its execution: specifically trained workers find themselves in the position of "executing the intelligence of others who have a calling which permits more flexible play and readjustment."[14]

Schools, Dewey contended, must not become merely the extension of manufacturing, industry, and commerce. He warned that education will be pressured to transform itself into an undemocratic trade education. If this were to occur, schooling would become an instrument of perpetuating the existing industrial order of society. Many would argue that Dewey's fears have moved closer to becoming reality as the forces of business have played an increasingly larger role in determining educational goals.

What is the proper relationship between work and school? Education should begin with the assumption that every person desires to be occupied in work which will make the lives of others better worth living. Such a view of work accentuates the ties which bind human beings together; it tears down the antidemocratic walls which separate us from one another. Guided by such ideas, one role of educators involves the development of ideas which lead to the expansion of socially beneficial jobs. Educators need to ponder what constitutes "good work." Part of the educator's role as a democratic citizen is to support the policies of business, government, and education which help create dignified, worker-involved employment and to oppose those policies which fail to do so.

One of the great evils of technicalization is that it increases the numbers of people who work in jobs which do not appeal to their intelligence, creativity, and democratic social concern. There is a great difference, Dewey recognized decades ago, between jobs where the employee merely carries out the plans of others and those jobs where he or she forms original plans. Teachers and administrators must seek to disrupt an educational system which determines who will go into one of these job categories or another on the basis of socio-economic background.

How do teachers and administrators disrupt such an unfortunate form of educational predetermination? They must recognize and resist technicalization in every form—from pre-designed curriculum materials to business-designed curricula. They must make the school "vocational" in a new way. The vocational education we refer to here does not involve the training of certain students to master certain technical skills of the workplace. It is vocational only in the sense that it uses the world of vocations as a curricular starting place—a point to begin our study of the world.

The vocational education we promote engages students to understand the relationship between academic skills and the world of work. In other words it uses work as a real context in which the academic disciplines gain significance. It uses work as a laboratory where academic knowledge is applied. This new type of vocational education examines the intellectual and social meaning of work in a democratic society. This requires historical examination of how present conditions in an occupation came to be. Sociology, economics, political science, and geography are studied by the future worker to acquaint him or her with the problems of work and the society at large. The meaning of work and what constitutes good work in a democratic society are considered. Such studies would include not only an examination of problems but explorations of the various strategies offered to solve them. Science would be studied in order to understand the agencies of production in a modern industrial state. It would be viewed in a context which allows future workers to make sense of the technology which will confront them. In other words, this new vocational education grants students more control of their work lives; it provides them with the power to escape being victimized by the technical obsolescence which comes from narrow technical training combined with a constantly changing workplace.

Please do not misinterpret our vision of what schooling can be. Vocational considerations alone do not determine our curriculum! Schools exist to teach the fundamental skills of reading, writing, math, and analytical thinking. Aesthetic education is a basic component of any well-rounded program. We enthusiastically support the inclusion of health and physical education.

In a society increasingly beset by a dehumanization of the workplace, however, it is essential that education avoid anti-democratic policies which contribute to deskilling and technicalization. The use of a reconceptualized vocational education as a means of gaining insight into the context in which modern work developed, the scientific principles on which the means of production rests, the nature of the problems of the workplace and the possible solutions offered is a realistic way of improving America's workforce. It is an excellent means of tying the school to the lived world. Such educational policies would be designed by community members and educators for the benefit of students. They would not be designed by business people for the benefit of profit margins.

This vision is not offered as a panacea. It is naïve to think that school alone can solve such a pervasive and complex problem as the technicalization of our work and society. It is offered simply as a question-raising device which seeks to move the school away from the anti-democratic domination of business. If successful, such a reevaluation of the social role of school would produce more thoughtful workers and citizens. The outcome we envision is very modest. It would involve the creation of a corps of thinking American workers whose thoughtfulness would allow them to avoid manipulation by those members of society who want to use others for their own self-interests. Indeed, it would involve the creation of a corps of American citizens capable of using their minds to identify, understand, and even offer solutions to problems created by the developing and ever-changing cultures of this planet.

## NOTES

[1] Leo Tolstoy, Anna Karenina quoted by Carol Bly, *Letters from the Country* (New York: Penquin Books, 1981), p. 62.
[2] Marcia Ascher, "The Computer as Seen Through Fiction." In Irene Taviss, *The Computer Impact* (Englewood Cliffs, NJ: Prentice Hall, 1970), pp. 289–91.
[3] Albert Einstein, "Message to the Italian Society for the Advancement of Science" (delivered in 1950), *Ideas and Opinions* (New York: Dell Publishing, 1954), p. 348.
[4] William H. Behn, Martin Carnoy, Michael A. Carter, Joyce C. Crain, & Henry M. Levin, "School is Bad: Work is Worse." In Martin Carnoy and Henry M. Levin, *The Limits of Educational Reform* (New York: David McKay Company, 1976), pp. 219–244.
[5] Ray M. Winegar, "The National Commission of Excellence in Education and the Limits of Educational Reform." Paper presented to the Southeast Philosophy of Education Society; Mobile, Alabama, February 10, 1984, pp. 2, 11, 18, 22–23.
[6] Joel Spring, "Education and the Sony War," *Phi Delta Kappan*, LXV (April, 1984), pp. 534–537.
[7] See National Commission of Excellence in Education, *A Nation at Risk: The Imperative for Educational Reform* (Washington, D. C.: U.S. Government Printing Office, 1983).
[8] Winegar, "The National Commission of Excellence in Education," pp. 15–23; Spring, "Education and the Sony War," pp. 534–537.
[9] Henry A. Giroux, *Ideology, Culture, and the Process of Schooling* (Philadelphia: Temple University Press, 1981), pp. 37–62.
[10] James M. Giarelli and J. J. Chambliss, "Philosophy of Education and Qualitative Inquiry," *Journal of Thought*, XIX (Summer, 1984), pp. 34–36; Robert R. Sherman, Rodman B. Webb, and Samuel D. Andrews, "Qualitative Inquiry: An Introduction," *Journal of Thought*, XIX (Summer, 1984), pp. 24–33.
[11] Giroux, *Ideology, Culture, and the Process of Schooling*, pp. 37–62.
[12] Henry A. Giroux, *Ideology, Culture, and the Process of Schooling*, pp. 37–62. For an expansion of these ideas of critical (or what I call post-formal) thinking see Joe L. Kincheloe, *Teachers as Researchers: Qualitative Paths to Empowerment* (London: Falmer Press, 1991).
[13] John Dewey, *Democracy and Education* (New York: Macmillan Company, 1916), p. 119.
[14] Ibid, p. 311. (Selected articles as modified used with permission of Editor of *Review Journal of Philosophy and Social Sciences*.)

**Reprinted with permission: Kincheloe, J. L. (1991). Exposing the technocratic perversion of education: The death of the democratic philosophy of schooling. In J. J. Van Patten (Ed.), *The socio-cultural foundations in education and the evolution of education policies in the U.S.* (pp. 193–226). Lewiston, NY: Edwin Mellen Press.**

CONNIE TITONE AND ROBERT A. DUGGAN, JR.

# TEACHERS REVERSING THE CYCLE

*Checking the Dangers of NCLB*

Joe Kincheloe was always ahead of the curve; he seems to have seen and thought beyond what we experience in the present. Joe saw so far ahead of the curve that the curve became a circle, or rather a cycle that he saw strengthening as it spiraled out of control. In his 1991 chapter "Exposing the Technocratic Perversion of Education: The Death of the Democratic Philosophy of Schooling" in James J. van Patten's *[T]he socio-cultural foundations of education and the evolution of education policies in the United States*, Kincheloe recognized the same cycle of technicalization in education and society that envelops us today. Technocratic society imposes technique-centered policies upon education, which then feed technocratic-minded citizens back into the society to perpetuate the cycle. Kincheloe engages dialectically with recent historical and current educational and cultural dynamics in anticipation of the No Child Left Behind (NCLB) Act, which threatens to be the centerpiece of the societal technocratic overtaking of teaching. Although NCLB was not enacted until 2002, 11 years after the publication of Joe's piece, in it he demonstrates his ability to foresee "the subtle and insidious ways that technicalization invades our workplaces, our schools, and our assumptions about human nature and education" (1991, p. 194), which he believed would be created by a laser-pointed, unconsidered focus on one-size-fits-all standardized testing.[1]

Kincheloe's philosophy is grounded in a participatory, critical theory of democratic education—one that promotes the interests of the people and practices social equality. At the conclusion of the van Patten chapter, in a section called "what is to be done," Kincheloe lays out what are some of the guiding principles of his argument. On page 220, he insists that the "continuing drift toward technicalization" in education "conflicts with the various goals of education in a democratic society." Referencing John Dewey, the father of American progressivism, Kincheloe maintains that we should be in a constant state of creating "the most democratic society possible." He asserts that the truly democratic society "would serve the best interests of as many individuals and groups as possible." Furthermore, democratic schools would be committed to passing along learning and knowledge to prepare and empower individuals and groups who would serve the ideals of democracy. His model school would not assign students social roles or career goals, but rather would teach learners to think deeply, critically, and freely; and to attempt to understand all dimensions of the human experience, so that they would be capable of choosing their own best-suited career paths. These schools would be liberatory for students, "free[ing] [them] from ignorance" (1991, p. 199). He says, "Education should begin with the assumption that every person desires to be occupied in work which will make the lives of others better worth living" (1991, p. 222). What Kincheloe exposes is the technicalization in education which he predicts will tempt teachers to teach to tests at the cost of context and meaning and thus manipulate students to perpetuate the status quo. Students (and teachers) shaped in this way cannot possibly serve as citizens who would further the aims of a free, constantly improving, lively, democratic society. "To avoid the dehumanization that such over-emphasis of technique brings about," Kincheloe believes, "educators must first recognize that there is a problem" (1991, p. 194). Recognizing the problem, however, requires a breaking of the technique-focused mindset and, thus, the technocratic cycle.

Joe's prediction has been borne out, perhaps beyond even his expectations. In 2005, after witnessing the effects of the first few years of NCLB, Kincheloe decries that "[i]n the twenty-first century, the idea that teachers understand the complexity of the educational world is a radical proposition in and of itself," with "many educational reformers see[ing] no need for teachers to be rigorous scholars" (2005, p. 5). "Indeed," Kincheloe continues, "the No Child Left Behind reforms require disempowered teachers who do what they're told and often read pre-designed scripts to their students" (2005, p. 5). The disempowerment of the citizenry thus begins with the disempowerment of the public school teacher—the focal point of education for the majority of our young people and the leaders in the classroom. "[S]uch actions" as the NCLB reforms "are insulting to the teaching profession and are designed ultimately to destroy the concept of public education itself," Kincheloe concludes (2005, p. 5). In his 1991 article Kincheloe outlines the subversive, perverting effects of technicalization that find their logical conclusion in NCLB. In the 14 years between his first article and Kincheloe's 2005 critique, he watched NCLB insult the teaching profession, as well as individual teachers themselves, and begin the process of destroying the credibility and functionality of public schooling if not the notion of public education itself.

One of the most devastating consequences of high-stakes testing is the phenomenon of cheating by teachers. A series of *Dallas Morning News* stories in 2004 reports finding extensive test cheating on the elementary school level in Texas (Benton and Hacker, 2004). A state investigation identifies 22 teachers and other educators in poor, urban schools in Dallas and Houston as improperly assisting students on the TAKS test, including distributing answer keys in some cases. The false "Texas miracle" stands as the most infamous but just one of many cases of principals and teachers knowingly participating in academic fraud. (See also Grow [2004] for an overview of nationwide NCLB cheating by teachers.) In this extreme case, teachers were pressured by the educational and political systems, as well as their principals, to demonstrate that students could achieve passing (or improved) test scores—even if they did not, or could not. The stakes in the standardized test score game range in severity depending on many different factors, perhaps most importantly the amount of local funding of the school. If a loss of federal funding represents a significant piece of the school's financial pie, the test results weigh that much heavier on a teacher's mind. Disempowered, dehumanized as Joe predicted, and perhaps unconscious of the long-term consequences, these lost and desperate educators discredit their profession and insult their students and themselves by buying into the power of the test rather than questioning its validity as a measure of the worth of their professional efforts. Moreover, teachers infected with such thought-destroying fear and confusion could never provide rich, challenging, and intellectual curriculum to their students. They would not have the mental freedom to focus on such a project.

Headline-grabbing stories of dishonesty such as those described in the "Texas miracle" rise as peaks in the new landscape of education under NCLB, but the general terrain is also destructive in a much quieter, "subtle and insidious" as Kincheloe put it (1991, p. 194), yet equally devastating way. Knowing that the standardized test waits, and dreading the consequences of failing scores, some teachers are resigned to aligning too strictly to the course set out for them. To teach for broad and deep understanding, to follow either their own interests or the interests of the students, seems a dangerous and ill-advised path when the allocation of time and resources can result in loss of funding for programs or schools. As Kincheloe argued in 2005, here is where "many educational reformers see no need for teachers to be rigorous scholars" (p. 5), because the "rigorous scholarship" has already been done for the teachers by those who set the curriculum. Teachers become mere technocrats, facilitators of the material and neutral conduits of an agenda-driven educational program. In these schools, we begin the process of removing students' emotions from the learning environment. We dehumanize them. "The more 'dehumanized' a bureaucracy becomes," Joe Kincheloe warned, "the more 'success' it attains," with "success" defined as the creation of a place where "rules and regulations can work more predictably" (1991, p. 198). The "successful" teacher thus becomes one who simply reads the assigned script designed to shape a new generation of passive citizens and workers. Certainly subject content needs to be conveyed to the student, but that content is too often fragmented by the technocratic method rather than integrated meaningfully, as Kincheloe desires. Instead of opening up new worlds to students by way of expansive lesson plans that teach students to link complex ideas together, teachers narrow their teaching and deny their students the possibility of meaningful learning. When young people are deprived of learning to think, what is the significance of passing scores on a standardized test? When young people cannot take a position on a complex issue, and compose an argument supporting that position, what is the value of achieving the targeted score on a standardized test? If we are not asking (and attempting to answer) in public schools the most difficult questions that life and society pose, what becomes of the abilities of the more than 2, 649, 594 students who graduate from our public schools each year (Stillwell and Hoffman, 2009)? What can we expect from them as citizens and parents?

It should be no surprise that the consequences of a steady diet of prescribed learning can have a serious impact on prospective teachers. Since the implementation of NCLB in January 2002, a large cohort of students who experienced only that mode of education through secondary school and higher education now stand poised to become the next generation of educators. Ironically, another component of the NCLB Act is focused on providing a "highly qualified teacher" for every classroom. What can that mean in practice? In a recent graduate-level course at the very beginning of the program cycle, an exercise focused on the uses of active listening in facilitating group discussion became a snapshot of the effect of NCLB on what students think about learning and teaching. (See Gordon and Burch, 1974, pp. 90–94, for the original script.) A scripted role-playing scenario was acted out in which a high-school level teacher asks an open-ended question about a reading on the Spanish-American War. The teacher's objectives for the lesson are not stated, but the students inquire as to the role of girls and the perspectives of the Spanish people at the time of the war. Eventually the discussion focuses on whether or not history books can be (should be) accepted as accounts of truth—actual, partial, or biased—and what standards one should use when reading history books. The teacher allows the students to engage in the discussion for some time and at the end of the script, she incorporates the students' interests in assigning tasks to be accomplished in a future class.

After the role-play ended, the professor initiated a debriefing session on students' assessments of the teacher's handling of the discussion. The majority of the graduate students disagreed with the teacher's approach—in fact, they called it a digression—because the students did not spend enough time on discussing the war. They said that you must "teach to the test" or else NCLB will "cost you your job" and cost the students their school. The pre-service teachers labeled such rich discussions risky and irrelevant because they could lead students off the task of memorizing information that would be regurgitated on a standardized test. These graduate students initially resisted the counterargument that such digressions, such discussions, although requiring an investment of time away from the narrow conception of the mandated curriculum, could serve as a significant and valuable perspective-taking activity, enlarging students' perceptions of a complex social reality as it existed during the Spanish-American War period. Even before facing any real possibility of lost jobs or funding, something they may never actually confront, these pre-service teachers allowed propagandized fear and dread to limit their thinking.[2] We would argue, as Kincheloe did decades ago, that indoctrination into the NCLB mode, in which the teacher relinquishes her responsibility to create complex and meaningful curriculum compels new and old teachers alike to steer a straight path along a fixed curriculum and to avoid any "detours" no matter what benefits (i.e. interest, inspiration, and motivation) might accrue to students because of them.

After eight years of NCLB, many former students now looking to become teachers themselves know no other model of education than that infected by NCLB. The "perversion of education" Kincheloe speaks of in his title comes to fruition as the fact-peddling educational system itself creates its own future fact-peddlers. NCLB has successfully socialized students to value isolated facts over narratives that string those facts together into meaningful wholes. "North American students are taught to attack problems as if they emerged in isolation," Joe writes, "detached from the dynamic social and political forces which bestow meaning" (1991, p. 215). Sadly, the idea that the Spanish-American War might have been an imperialist war of choice (or any of the other implications or repercussions of the conflict) loses the battle with names, dates, and other trivia that are truly "trivial" in the sense of lacking relevance for today. "The subject matter is ready-made in the sense that it is presented as an end in itself," Kincheloe warns (1991, p. 216). Rather than students learning to question, critique, and understand, a prescribed body of knowledge becomes the ultimate educational end as embodied by items on standardized tests. Instructors, including instructors-to-be, pass on the passivity of this approach to their students by thwarting active thinking, labeling it as wasteful digression rather than mind-opening and horizon-widening cognition.

The values of education thus become perverted to the point of being turned around almost 180 degrees, pointing the system, the students, and new generations of teachers in a counter-productive direction.

How then can education, as he saw it, in the age of NCLB, be pointed back in the right direction? While he warns of "the implicit consequences of educational acts" (1991, p. 218) that serve the agenda of positivism and the creation of a passive, unquestioning citizen, he believes that the answer lies in the hands of the teacher and his/her ability to take a critical and creative approach in the classroom. "Critical thinking enables humans to 'transcend' their own histories or backgrounds so that they can escape the helplessness which comes from an unexamined heritage," Kincheloe asserts (1991, p. 219). To enable students to experience this transcendence, teachers must transcend prescriptive thinking through critical re-evaluations of their own. They must reflect and manifest a critical mindset in their dealings with young people and once that cognitive shift happens, critical and creative sparks begin to fly. "This emphasis on critical thinking with its analysis and questioning rubs against some basic fundamentalist assumptions [of NCLB and positivists] concerning learning," Kincheloe argues (1991, p. 219). From this friction, generated when the positivist definition of learning rubs up against the critical theory definition of learning, emerge the human warmth and intellectual emancipation and enlightenment which are needed to cast off the chill and the emptiness of education as mere, disconnected facts. "Too often the critical thinking promoted by the schools is a diluted form of analytical thought," Kincheloe posits, "presented without social or historical context emphasizing only technical academic skills" (1991, p. 217). Students are taught just enough critical-type thinking to be of service but not enough to pose a danger to the status quo either at work or of the government. "[E]ducation which does not promote [critical thinking] is an impediment to human self-determination," Kincheloe believes (1991, p. 219).

Through critical mindedness, students themselves can ask for a better system of education and exercise their democratic right of self-determination. Teachers can inspire and guide students to question the educational system and participate in their own learning, thus becoming active agents, "responsible subjects… in the search for self-affirmation" (Freire, [1970] 1993, p. 18) instead of passive receptacles. In many schools, education conducted in the NCLB mode becomes the Freirian model of banking education (Freire, p. 53) which he, too, names dehumanizing. No one has a bigger stake in education than students, although they may not be awake to that fact. Teaching students the importance of assuming their rightful role in the educational process and authorizing them to take up the power of agency prepares them for a lifetime of participating in the workplace and government. With empowered students, Joe's envisioned "modest" result of "a corps of American citizens capable of using their minds to identify, understand, and even offer solutions to problems created by the developing and ever-changing cultures of this planet" (1991, p. 224) could be realized. Society's hope and the true education's bonus will be the ever-questioning, critically-minded graduate. The downward spiral of the technocratic cycle could thus be reversed into an upward spiral, beginning with the foundation of education and then cycling out of technocracy's control to the workplace, the voting booth, and the global community.

## NOTES

[1] Joe L. Kincheloe wrote his 1991 article soon after Goals 2000, which some argue began the modern American fascination with accountability in schools. Standardized testing programs subsequently grew substantially after Goals 2000 to determine if U.S. students were meeting the goals.
[2] This limited thinking of these pre-service teachers recalls Freire's idea of "limit-situations," i.e. obstacles that are more mental states than actual impediments ([1970] 1993, p. 80). "[I]t is not the limit-situations in and of themselves which create a climate of hopelessness," Freire wrote, "but rather how they are perceived by women and men at a given historical moment: whether they appear as fetters or as insurmountable barriers" ([1970] 1993, p. 80). These pre-service teachers exhibit "a dominated consciousness which has not yet perceived a limit-situation in its totality [and] apprehends only its epiphenomena and transfers to the latter the inhibiting force which is the property of the limit-situation" (Freire, [1970] 1993, p. 85). In this case, the student teachers hand over power to such "epiphenomena" as "teaching to the test" at the expense of disempowering themselves and their students. This transference of power reinforces the resistance to a liberated mindset, as displayed by the pre-service teachers after the exercise, and is predicted by Freire ([1970] 1993, p. 85). By casting off the "fetters" of technocracy that compel them to "teach to the test," however, these future educators can liberate themselves and their students to greater opportunities for learning.

## REFERENCES

Benton, J., & Hacker, H. K. (2004, December 19). Poor schools' TAKS surges raise cheating questions. *Dallas Morning News*. Retrieved August 25, 2009, from http://www.dallasnews.com/sharedcontent/dws/news/longterm/stories/121904dnmetcheating.64fa3.html
Freire, P. (1993). *Pedagogy of the oppressed* (M. B. Ramos, Trans.). New York: Continuum. (Original work published 1970)
Gordon, T., & Burch, N. (1974). *T. E. T.: Teacher effectiveness training*. New York: Peter H. Wyden.
Grow, B. (2004, July 5). A spate of cheating—by teachers. *Business Week*. Retrieved August 25, 2009, from http://www.businessweek.com/magazine/content/04_27/b3890129_mz021.htm
Kincheloe, J. L. (2005). *Critical constructivism*. New York: Peter Lang.
Kincheloe, J. L. (1991). Exposing the technocratic perversion of education: the death of the democratic philosophy of schooling. In J. J. van Patten(Ed.), *The socio-cultural foundations of education and the evolution of education policies in the United States* (pp. 193–226). Lewiston, NY: Edwin Mellen Press.
Stillwell, R., & Hoffman, L. (2009). *Public school graduates and dropouts from the common core of data: school year 2005–06* (NCES 2008-353rev). Washington, DC: National Center for Education Statistics, Institute of Education Sciences, U.S. Department of Education. Retrieved August 25, 2009, from http://nces.ed.gov/pubsearch/pubsinfo.asp?pubid=2008353re

*Not long after we moved in together, Joe received an enormous parcel in the mail from SUNY Press. It was the galleys of the book that he was co-editing. He explained to me that we had to "proof" the galleys. Other than my own writing, I knew nothing about publishing, and that fall day in Clemson, South Carolina was my first day in thousands...writing with Joe, proofing, editing, and reading. I was given the task of proofing Joe's Morris piece. Well-tutored, I had been reading Southern novels, specifically Willie Morris, Pat Conroy, and Bobbie Ann Mason; and as a drama director I certainly had my share of Tennessee Williams. My Southern cultural capital had grown considerably while with Joe, and I read and proofed his piece with gusto. This is probably one of the best pieces Joe Kincheloe ever wrote. The chapter is an example of Joe's lyrical, literary, informed style. His love of the South had always been a contradiction. The ghosts, the horrendous actions of Southerners were a counterpoint to the New Orleans ladies, the gentle breeze in the Blue Mountains, the raspy, rasty riffs of country musicians, and the accented voices distinguishable from town to town. Joe loved the South with every fiber of his being, and he hated much of its past. This article speaks to those issues, and celebrates both the brilliance of Willie Morris, certainly one of Joe's favorite authors, and the genius of Joe's own words. SS*

JOE L. KINCHELOE*

## 2. WILLIE MORRIS AND THE SOUTHERN CURRICULUM

*Emancipating the Southern Ghosts*

In his speculations on the nature of a curriculum theory of southern studies, William Pinar draws upon the various strands of research that have informed reconceptualized curriculum theorizing. Grounded in critical theory and psychoanalysis, the southern curriculum is dedicated to a *social* psychoanalysis aided by the methodologies of historiography, ethnography, phenomenology, gender studies, autobiography, and literary criticism. In many ways Willie Morris brings together these approaches to southern studies in his corpus of work on his South.

Morris's nonfiction draws upon historiographical and ethnographic traditions. His autobiographical sensitivity is innocently phenomenological, as he responds poetically to the southern ghosts that haunted his mind and body. His work is permeated with references to the process by which gender role is fashioned in the South. These references are sometimes presented consciously, other times they are uncovered only by gender sensitive readers who discover manifestations of gender role formation by interrogating that psychic realm that is evidently not conscious to the author himself and is determined by subtle social conditioning. For a plethora of reasons, the work of Willie Morris is valuable in the reconceptualized southern curriculum.

Morris's work is primarily autobiographical, constantly relating his personal story to the story of his place. He carries on a grand southern literary convention: The writer's exploration of the southern traditions and his or her attempt to document the personal struggle to come to terms with those traditions in his or her own life. Morris is a student of the southern traditions, and the southern mythologies—he understands their variations, their nuances, and their death throes. He moves easily among the structures and codes of southern literature, invoking the vocabularies that were used by his literary ancestors without self-consciousness. As the twentieth century with its interstate highways and McDonald's mute the old voices, Morris seems determined to pour through the family album one more time before consigning it to the attic. His work is a eulogy—the interment will follow.

By the time Morris published his first book *North Toward Home* in 1967, the journalistic motif of Southerner-in-struggle had fossilized. The ghosts had done their job well. The liberal sons and daughters of the South found themselves without a home, their small towns and cities haunted by the specters of racism, violence, and poverty. Critics sometimes blasted Morris's work for its stylized quality—Faulkner without the urgency. While such criticisms hold some truth, they miss some important aspects of Morris's work and place in southern literary history. Morris writes of structures of feelings that are no longer his; he utilizes literary conventions whose rules have been determined not by his but previous generations. The homage he pays to the southern memories is self-consciously temporary—tomorrow, we feel, Morris must move on to the business of the present. Today, however, he is showing his kids "how it was" when he grew up. Indeed, Willie Morris is the weigh station between Faulkner and postmodernist southern writer, Barry Hannah, the movement from Southern League baseball to Lynyrd Skynyrd, from moonshine to cocaine.

Faulkner was truly a regional writer. No doubt, he challenged the myths, but the myths still held the imagination. The modernist tendencies that Faulkner expressed were couched in southern terms. Where Faulkner's work is of the South in a particular place and time, Morris finds his influences outside the temporal and spatial boundaries of Yoknapatawpha. Morris's South is lost to him: he is no longer a small town Southerner (though he eventually moves back to Oxford, Mississippi); and his land is lost to itself as the myths fade away from memory.

This analysis of Morris concerns itself with emancipation or liberation, the diversity of its expression, and the peculiar textures of southern life as they relate to the concept of liberation. We are all familiar by now with the discourse of emancipation, its poetic tone, and its dangerous implications for the preservers of the status quo. We understand its attempt to render problematic that which had previously been accepted as given, and its exhortation to reflect upon the essence of that which before had only been considered in terms of its use, its instrumental value. More and more educators have come to realize that liberation embodies a form of rationality that involves the capacity to think about thinking (Gouldner, 1976).

Emancipation has come to be seen as praxis, that is, an understanding of the ways in which human beings are dominated as well as forms of actions that serve to counter dominating forces (Giroux, 1981). Emancipation involves a form of critical thinking that moves us beyond common sense assumptions into a new territory marked by an understanding of genesis and purpose (McLaren, 1989). In our new dialectical mode, we see past isolated events, as we begin to think in terms of processes. Thus, emancipator thinking allows individuals to participate in the socio-historical transformation of their society, as they begin to bring their work under their own control (Freire, 1985).

In our attempt to understand the conventions of our place and how they have shaped us, we engage in what William Pinar and I, in our introduction label "social psychoanalysis." This social psychoanalysis may be referred to as "critical historiography." Emerging from a critical theoretical tradition this social psychoanalysis/critical historiography is an essential feature of southern curriculum theorizing. Jurgen Habermas considers Freudian psychoanalysis a model for a critical science, for it is only psychoanalysis that serves as an example of a science incorporating a methodical process of self-reflection (Habermas, 1970).

As the psychoanalyst attempts to remedy the mystified self-perceptions of the analysand, the social psychoanalyst sees myth invalidation as an important step toward social progress (Held, 1980). Such an attempt, just like the effort of the psychoanalyst to confront patients with actual forces that helped shape their psyches, is thwarted by many factors: for example, the success of the logic of capital in late industrial societies in reifying existing social, political, and economic relationships; and the psychological distortions of past racial, gender, and social class role definitions in say southern culture. In the modern industrialized South, both of these pre-mentioned factors may work in concert creating a symphony of unique distortions (Marcuse, 1964; Marcuse, 1978).

The power of such distortions on the individual and social level is undeniable—history is frozen and viewed as rational, as if it could be no other way (Jacoby, 1975). Until free people invalidate the myths and conceive of the possibilities offered by emancipation, slim is the possibility of authentic self-direction on the individual and social levels. The less social and individual self-direction which exists, the more it appears that society is governed by rational and intractable natural laws (Marcuse, 1960). This is the concern of the reconceptualized southern curriculum—to demystify southern experience in such a manner that distortions are confronted. In this way southern consciousness can be renegotiated with all participants—especially those previously excluded at the bargaining table. Such an undertaking allows for a language of possibility (Giroux and McLaren, 1989). The southern ghosts, who siphon their energy from the frozen history of race, class, and gender, find themselves exposed—they can no longer haunt with anonymity.

## MYTH

Our discussion of social distortion—especially in the context of literature—cannot proceed without an examination of a Barthesian notion of myth. Roland Barthes reflects Marcuse's concern with the existence of natural and rational law as he focuses his notion of semiology on myth. Myth, Barthes argues, provides a *natural* image of reality, as it ignores the existence of the dialectical relationship between activities and human actions. Myth renders such activities "a harmonious display of essences." Barthes contends that myth in talking about things, purifies them, makes them innocent, gives them a natural and eternal justification. Myth, he continues:

> abolishes the complexity of human acts, it gives them the simplicity of essences, it does away with all dialectics, with any going back beyond what is immediately visible, it organizes a world which is without contradictions because it is without depth, a world wide open and wallowing in the evident, it establishes a blissful clarity: things appear to mean something by themselves.[1]

Thus, the historical quality of things is lost. When myth conquers, individuals lose the memory that things were once made. As a complicated network of arguments, beliefs, and metaphors, myths become the vehicles through which societies deny historical origin and in the process support and authenticate their identities. Richard Gray writes that it is the recovery of the memory that Barthes is talking about here— "that things were once made"—that separates good southern literature from the mediocre (Gray, 1986, p. 272). For example, Faulkner demanded that we examine the codes and the hidden structures that grant insight into myth etiology. As Gray puts it, Faulkner "offers an examination of the way the world has been placed into words" (Gray, p. 272).

The myths of the South are great deceivers. The Patriarchal Myth of a cultural gentry with a superior notion of civilization, the Lost Cause Myth with its implicit justification of the Civil War aims, the Myth of Southern Womanhood with its glorification of feminine passivity, the Myth of the Happy Darkie on the benevolent plantation, the Gentlemanly Code of Honor Myth with its frozen notion of masculinity all claim to be drawing upon history, centering human action historically. The myths are charlatans, reifying the status quo, presenting themselves as an accurate account of essence of things. In providing answers to our southern identity search, the myths simplify and "explain" our origins. The only way to maintain our identity is via myth invocation and imitation—a process that Southerners have mastered over the decades, especially through their literature.

Myths may be used in a variety of ways. Political demagogues may employ the myth manipulatively to create allegiance to practices and symbols that serve the interest of the demagogue. Myths may be used innocently, as they are every day, to make sense of the world around us, to provide certainty in the chaotic lived world. In a critical sense myths may be employed by the demystifier. Like Claude Levi-Strauss, the demystifier may accomplish the task of deciphering the myth for all to see; or the demystifier may seek to locate the myth historically and understand the social forces that contributed to its sanctification. Whatever the process or combination of processes, the act of demystification is an act of social psychoanalysis as it uncovers the existence of social distortion, its genesis, its nature, and its effects. Curriculum theory grounded in social psychoanalysis and place is informed by Barthesian myth analysis and the subsequent process of demystification and myth explication.

The demystification process necessitates a well-developed sense of the past—a sense that must distinguish between history and myth. Traditionally preoccupied with the past, Southerners must draw upon their non-mythical historical sense to overcome the malformations of the present. Southern writer William Humphrey describes the historical sense of the region, arguing that: "If the Civil War is more alive to the Southerner than the Northerner it is because all the past is." Colonel Sartaris in Faulkner's *Flags in the Dust* (and many of his other characters as well) is so overpowered by things past that he seems pale in their reflection. In some ways, Willie Morris appears as a Faulknerian character in his own autobiographical writing—so powerful are his ghosts. Certainly this historical sense has begun to fade in the fast food, TV age. Contrary to more sanguine interpretations, the social amnesia that attends this fading does not destroy the myths. The mythological foundations of southern society remain intact—indeed, they are rendered more impervious to challenge—as the fading memory is accompanied by the fading possibility. The southern curriculum must draw sustenance from this traditional southern sense of the past.

Faulkner recognized the possibility of memory. The past was never seen as inert or buried but as a living presence always capable of growth (Gray, 1986, p. 181). Along with Robert Penn Warren and Allen Tate, Faulkner recognized the dialectical interaction between past and present—a recognition carried on by Willie Morris in *North Toward Home* and maybe most profoundly in *The Courting of Marcus Dupree*. This dialectical relationship involves alteration on both sides of the coin. Tate's "Ode to the Confederate Dead" examines a man in crisis standing in a Confederate graveyard. As he imagines what the lives of those buried there were like, he measures his failure against them. The ghosts are there, but they are the ghosts of the man's own invention—he constructs them with the bits of evidence available. The existence of *Tradition*, an ossified mythology, is not assumed in the poem. Tate's concern is that tradition doesn't merely exist, it is made. His character is making tradition, reinventing the past. Not only, the reader is reminded, does the past shape the present, but the present also shapes the past. The dialectic is celebrated, possibility is restored (Tate, 1970, p. 18). R. G. Collingwood reflected this idea of the human construction of the past when he wrote that all history is the reenactment of the past through the mind of the historian. We are not passive beings who surrender to the spell of others' interpretations of the past, to the spell of *Tradition*. History, he concluded, is an active process, a reenactment of past thought. The reenactment takes place in the context of the historian's own knowledge (Collingwood, 1962, pp. 215, 242–43).

We must become our own storytellers, Eudora Welty states. Nothing ever happens once and is finished, the past lives on. As Southerners tell their stories, enhance their reputations as raconteurs, they construct their individual versions of the past. Welty, too, views history as a dialectical process—an interchange between the "out there" (the objective) and the "in here" (the subjective). Each time a story is told there is a reweaving of facts—some details are omitted, some reemphasized. Tradition is challenged, the presentation of past as myth is overcome.

The southern victimization by Tradition takes many forms. Morris documents the power of the southern myths to evoke unquestioned allegiance from his fellow delta dwellers. Was it the power of the myths that elicited such zealous support from the poor and non-slaveholding South that individuals were willing to give their lives to protect a "peculiar Institution" that certainly did not serve their economic interests? Erich Fromm examines this southern phenomenon psychoanalytically. Using Freud's notion of narcissism, Fromm develops a theory of social narcissism to explain the tendency of some suppressed classes to be loyal to their social superiors and their rulers.

For an organized group to survive, it is important that the members of the group possess narcissistic energy. The members must consider the group as important or even more important than their own lives. Fromm labels the social narcissism benign if it is based on pride in a great achievement. It is malignant, he contends, if it is based not on something the group has produced but on something it has, for example, its splendor, its past achievements, its skin color, its code of gentlemanly behavior, and so forth... For those who are economically poor and socially excluded, narcissistic pride in belonging is an important source of satisfaction. Since their confined existence evokes little outlet for interest and little possibility for various forms of mobility, they may develop an exaggerated form of narcissism. The most extreme form of southern racism has traditionally come from the lower middle classes as its members view themselves as superior to the "inferior" Blacks; for example, the Bourbon protection of Blacks from lower middle-class Whites in post-Reconstruction era, the lower middle class following of George Wallace in the late 1960s and early 1970s.

> Even though I am poor and uncultured, I am somebody important because I belong to the most admirable group in the world—I am White.[2]

Thus, Southerners must escape the ravages of Tradition and the psychic mutilations it carries with it. Critical theoretical analysis with its discomfort with surface explanations offers hope.

Paulo Freire extends our thinking about the relationship between these psychic mutilations, historical location, anthropological context, and liberation. Arguing for a liberatory education, which frees humans from the oppression that traps them in the web of their historical reality, Freire ponders the *risk* of their emancipation. "Existence is not despair, but risk," he tells us. Those who seek liberation must risk themselves, though the "form of the risk" will vary from individual to individual and from place to place. The liberatory risk of a Brazilian is quite different from that of a Swiss; indeed, the liberatory risk of a New Yorker is quite different from that of a Mississippian. Our sociohistorical context shapes the form of our risk. The attempt to universalize the form and content of the liberating risk is ill-advised and unacceptable, Freire posits, to anyone who thinks dialectically.

## CHILDREN OF THE SOUTHERN PLACE

I am a child of the South, one who had sought to understand the rhythms of southern life and their effects on me. For many reasons, my first exposure to Willie Morris about twenty years ago provided much insight into my own *southern* consciousness.

So profound was the effect that I adopted Morris's *North Toward Home* for my introduction to education classes when I came to Louisiana to teach. An excellent educational autobiography, I hoped that the work would touch the consciousness of my students. I hoped that it would promote an introspective analysis of personal educational experience that might lead to a better understanding of the social forces that shaped southern students.

Emerging from the Yazoo City, Mississippi of the 1940s and early 1950s, Willie Morris chronicles his journey from a small town provincial to New York editor of *Harper's* to writer in residence at the University of Mississippi. Haunted by the power of Yazoo (even the sound of the word conjures ghosts), Morris struggles to comprehend the sway of the South in his life. Never far away from the consciousness of the southern sense of place, Morris presents a corpus of work that sheds light on the nature of liberation, its ambiguity, and its contextual contingency.

"Where are you from?" the Mississippian asked.

"What do you mean?"

"Well, where are you from? Where did you go to high school?"

The other man mentioned an Eastern prep school.

"But where did you grow up? Where are your parents?"

"Well, my father is in Switzerland, I think, and my mother is asleep in the next room."[3]

Morris reports this conversation between a young Mississippian and a Harvard man. Awakened by the traumatic interchange the Mississippian confides: "For the first time in my life, I understood that not all Americans are *from* somewhere." I think of myself as a teacher on the first day of class calling the roll and asking each student where they are from—somehow it is important as I match names with faces and attempt to learn something about them. To those from the small rural towns and parishes around Shreveport it is a natural question, and they talk with ease about life in Vivian, Greenwood, Plain Dealing, or Cotton Valley; to others, it is a strange, irrelevant question and they dismiss it—sometimes not even attempting an answer.

So strong is the southern awareness of place that when people from different towns meet they talk at length not only about where they are from but also where their parents are from. More often than not, the stranger will know exactly the location of the little hometowns. I know intimately the terrain and the now long dead personalities of my parents' original homes in Bland, Virginia, and Hawkins County Tennessee. For Southerners, Thorton Wilder wrote, "place, environment, relation, repetitions are the breath of their being." It is the charge of each Southerner to work out the power of *place* in his or her own existence (Morris, 1983b).

While Southerners have traditionally found themselves divided by lines of race, class, and gender, a sense of ambivalence (a sense that frustrates attempts to generalize about the South) renders such divisions problematic. This elusive southern consciousness of place seems to cut across racial and class lines, forming a tacit alliance between the South's professors, journalists, Black preachers, and hot rodders with Confederate flags on their rear bumpers. Indeed, both Black preachers and Klansmen agree that "the South is a good place to raise children" (Yoder, 1967). Morris recollects that during his exile in New York, he shared far more understanding with Black Mississippians than with the Yankee Wasps he met daily (Morris, 1967). *North Toward Home*[4] is filled with references to his friendship with Black authors and fellow southern expatriates, Al Murray and Ralph Ellison. On New Year's Day 1967, Morris describes their feast at Al Murray's apartment in Harlem of bourbon, collard greens, black-eyed peas, ham hocks, and cornbread—the traditional southern New Year's Day good luck dinner (p. 387). These southern connections are complex and often incomprehensible to outsiders. Consider C. vann Woodward's recollecttions of his thought while marching with Martin Luther King on the road to Montgomery: "I looked to the side of the road, and I saw the red-necks lined up, hate all over their faces, distrust and misunderstanding in their eyes. And I'll have to admit something. A little part of me was there with them" (Woodward, p. 399).

## THE GHOSTS

The struggle for emancipation for the Southerner is thus a complex enterprise inhabited by a potpourri of regional ghosts. *Morris ponders the mindless racism, the origins of the acts of violence he and his boyhood friends committed against isolated Black children.*

Hiding in the shrubbery, twelve-year-old Willie watched a young Black girl and her little brother walk down a deserted Yazoo sidewalk.

The older girl walked by first, and the child came along a few yards behind. Just as he got in front of me, lurking there in the bushes, I jumped out and pounced on him. I slapped him across the face, kicked him with my knee, and with a shove, sent him sprawling on the concrete.

Morris saw this violent display as more than a mere gratuitous act of childhood cruelty: "It was something else, infinitely more subtle and contorted." Blacks were always viewed ambivalently by the Yazoo Whites. "They were always ours to do with as we wished" with their degenerate lifestyles and distasteful habits. Dirty Whites "kept house like a nigger"; a "nigger car" was dilapidated and didn't run well; staying out all night and being seen with a variety of male companions made a woman guilty of "nigger behavior"; and conversation filled with lies and superstition was "nigger talk." Yet, despite all of this, Whites harbored a vague feeling for a mutual past with Blacks—a bond of shared place.[5]

*He relives the religious tyranny, the public school teachers and the Sunday School "church ladies" who imposed a Christianity by fear and rote.*

As a fourth grader, Willie found himself entrusted to public school teacher Miss Abbott and her white-bearded, king of clubs, American sympathizing anthropomorphic God. Miss Abbott passed along God's pronouncements on the niggers and the Japs while the children of Yazoo spent a good portion of their morning memorizing and reciting Bible verses. The lessons, buoyed by the omnipresent threat of hell, were not lost on the Yazoo youth. "Our fundamentalism was so much a part of us that its very sources, even its most outrageous gyrations and circumlocutions, went unquestioned." So unchallenged was the Yazoo fundamentalism that Willie and his friends would go near the local Catholic Church only when they were taunted and dared. Knowledge of the exact nature of God's will was rarely deemed problematic and was used to arrest the impulses of Willie and his adolescent peers.[6]

*He describes the important struggle for the honor of being a "good old boy," marked by self-conscious anti-intellectualism and male bonding rituals.*

Nothing was more important than good old boyism. In the presence of one's male peers, it was incumbent that the good old boy exhibit a well-cultivated cynicism about academic concerns. A boy's real friends, those among whom he felt comfortable being himself, were to be found in the male peer group, for association with popular and attractive girls was not pursued merely for its intrinsic worth—such associations brought with them increased status in the male group.[7]

*He writes of an elementary and high school education divorced from reality, a ritual so obsessed with form that knowledge of the outside world or knowledge of self was consciously repressed.*

I read the books, Morris writes, to stay on the good side of the teachers and to get A's, but they meant nothing to me and made no impact on the way I lived or saw experience. "I didn't understand my own intelligence...I was extraordinarily dependent on the judgment of my elders...All the things I wrote and read in high school I relegated to the farther crevices of my mind." High school was a preparation for entry into educated land gentry of Mississippi; it was designed to conform sensibilities to the needs of such a life not to understand its origins and contradictions. The Yazoo schools had left Morris ignorant of himself and the "world of moving objects" he was about to enter. Had he understood that great books "were for one's own private soul rather than mere instrumentalities for achieving those useless trinkets on which all American high schools...base their existence" maybe he would have better understood the delta ghosts:

> ...perhaps I would have found in Faulkner some dark chord, some suggestion of how this land had shaped me, how its isolation and its guilt-ridden past had already settled so deeply into my bones.[8]

*He reconstructs a southern middle-class enculturation, a process that explicitly delineated what exactly constituted the dominant cultural capital and the specific ways it was to be acquired.*

All the middle-class kids in Yazoo tacitly understood that they would make it through school all right, someday becoming the leaders of the community—the planters, store owners, druggists, and lawyers. We were the ones, Morris writes, who "read faster and better than the slower children of the families from 'out in the country'...we knew we were the teachers' favorites; we knew that the stirring challenges they laid down were secretly meant only for us" (Morris, pp. 20–21). Morris' first months as a student at the University of Texas were merely an extension of the quest for cultural capital. Surrounded by fraternity men in search of fun and status, Morris received sartorial advice and harsh criticism about his table manners (Morris, p. 151). Joining a number of organizations, Morris was comforted by the assurance of his social success.

> Versatility, gregariousness, the social graces, these were the important things, just as they had been in Yazoo; these were what the University of Texas could provide only bigger and better.[9]

*He reflects on his familiarity with an intense sense of belonging to Yazoo, a comfort that was sufficiently powerful to crush the latent, shadowy desire of his friends and acquaintances to go beyond it.*

It was a land that elicited love, Morris tells us (Morris, 1981). The sense of community that persists ties everything to everything else, everybody to everybody else. "Everything makes waves," Neshoba County scholar-in-residence Seena Kohl observed (Morris, 1983b). Morris saw his place in Yazoo; he imagined marrying his majorette, buying his land, and settling into the warm southern comfort. What more could there possibly be, he only occasionally wondered. After a Saturday night of high school partying at the house of some Yazoo parents who had traveled to Oxford for the Old Miss football game, Morris was satisfied.

> I was with the little plantation girl I loved, and old friends who had been friends for as long as I could remember in a town as familiar and settled to me as anything I would ever know, I would never wander very far away.[10]

Along with these regional ghosts exists an omnipresent sense of trauma in the southern upbringing, a blood and darkness which, on the one hand, obviously crushes the emancipatory impulse, but, on the other hand, provides a fertile ground for its cultivation. Morris refers to this thought as "the grace of character gained through suffering and loss." Could it be the "dialectic of place?" Does liberation require trauma? The tyrannies of southern life are all too real: its shattered dreams, the failures of its history, the insights gained from living with a great human wrong, and an "un-American" poverty (Morris, 1981). Liberation, I believe, *does* require myth confrontation. Morris the high school senior was comfortable with the Patriarchal Myth with its notions of gentility and a superior civilization. The existence of the tyrannies of southern life simply did not fit the myth; thus, consciousness of the tyrannies was repressed and the party continued.

Such realities provide Southerners the possibility of a unique vantage point (I see it in my students) from which they may come to understand their own history, American history in general, and the irony of modern affluent America (Morris, 1967). The ghosts won't let us forget. With its historical sense ever close to the surface, the south holds the possibility of memory with all of the subversive power memory provides. A sense of history allows us to understand the traditions that have formed our autobiographies and the textures of our intersubjective relationships (Giroux, 1981). Recognizing the sources of suffering in our past, we are empowered to initiate a discourse that refuses to assume that the present has been naturally or rationally constructed (Freire and Macedo, 1987).

The southern historical consciousness has been profoundly touched by the omnipresence of Black culture. Marked by an interesting dialectic of political, economic, and social marginality on one hand and cultural power on the other, Blacks represent the South's blood and darkness. The Black man and woman are compelling emblems of Original Sin. In Faulkner's *Go Down Moses*, young Roth Edmonds realizes that he can no longer sleep beside Henry Beauchamp, the Black boy who had been his closest friend. There was no specific event that motivated Roth's decision, Faulkner writes. Just one day the old curse of his fathers came down on him; he inherited the racial prejudice and guilt of his ancestors. Hence, he re-enacts their Original Sin in his own life (Faulkner, 1960, p. 91). William Styron's Stingo in *Sophie's Choice* is another inheritor of southern Original Sin as he fights with the guilt derived from his awareness that he is the progeny of the slaveholders and has profited at whatever distance from the buying and selling of human flesh (Styron, 1980, p. 249).

Morris is aware of the power of this historical consciousness—an impulse that by its nature creates that sense of critical distance necessary for emancipation. There is a painful quality to the distance necessary for liberation, and Morris with his southern sense of the tragic is drawn to it. To really understand a place in one's heart, he laments, "his heart must remain subtly apart from it." The liberated Southerner must "always be a stranger to the place he loves, and its people." While he may be shaped by the historical sense of the southern place and recognize the beauties within it, he knows that there are too many ghosts to embrace it completely. "He must absorb without being absorbed" (Morris, 1981). Faulkner understood this axiom on a variety of levels. Oxford, Mississippi was Faulkner's expertise but it could not ever completely become his home. Richard Gray argues that Faulkner could only half enter it. Alternately in love with it and offended by it (again the dialectic place?), Faulkner had to pull back. His stories are authored by a double agent, "an insider and outsider" (Gray, 1986, p. 171). Standing on the football field at Philadelphia (Mississippi) High School with legendary running back Marcus Dupree, Willie Morris listened to this untraveled, Black high school football star talk about how much he wanted to stay in Mississippi. Reflecting back on the ghosts, Morris told Dupree: "Sometimes we have to leave home, Marcus, before we can really come back" (Morris, 1983b).

But what moved Willie himself to leave Mississippi is not exactly clear to him. There were fleeting awarenesses of worlds other than Yazoo. Reading Booth Tarkington's Seventeen in high school study hall set the stage of an "out of mind" experience:

> I gazed out the window and lazily soaked in the soft spring afternoon, and all of a sudden I felt overcome for no reason at all by the likelihood of a great other world somewhere out there—of streamlined express trains and big cities, and boats sailing to other countries; the teacher snapped, "Willie, get back to that book!"[11]

Morris is haunted by the attempt to uncover the genesis of his desire to leave Mississippi. What constituted the abrasive grain of sand in his perception of things that scratched hidden ambitions and stirrings of independence? Though never exactly sure, Morris attributes his desire to remove himself from his deepest loyalties to his imagination. It was his imagination that held his will hostage when he was commissioned to write the prophecy of the Class of 1952 of Yazoo High School. His presentation of an irreverent, harshly satirical projection of the fate of his classmates elicited an angry response from his previously adoring teachers. You might as well leave here, one teacher told him, "because it's pretty clear that you don't appreciate the people around you" (Morris, p. 144). His imagination was beginning to formulate a vision of life beyond the honor roll, popularity, and the comforts of delta life. The limitations of a life that focused on delta courtesies and delta manners were slowly becoming apparent; indeed, a deeper level of human understanding was possible. The word may have been unfamiliar to the graduating senior, but Morris was in the first stages of the search of his *Lebenswelt*.

Though he possessed a latent potential for liberation, Morris did little to expand the envelope of his consciousness in his first months at the University of Texas. As a fraternity boy, he endured lost night, the fatuous initiation ceremonies, and the sundry humiliations of pledging. His association with the student newspaper, *The Daily Texan*, opened a window of escape. His first assignment was a weekly column surveying what was being reported by college publications around the country. Here he encountered strange ideas like racial integration, academic freedom, and the possibility that Ike might be something of a bore. Such topics were the exceptions, as most student papers were more concerned with turning over a new leaf at the beginning of each semester, giving blood to the blood drive, collecting wood for the pep rally bonfire, or the virtue of using leisure time more wisely. "Something was out of order here," Willie observed, but the exact nature of his discomfort eluded him (Morris, p. 162–63).

During the early period at Austin, Morris was invited to the apartment of a young graduate student and his wife. Morris was in awe of the books that lined their walls. Were they some special exhibit? Reflecting on the experience, Morris writes that it is disconcerting for many southern young people to see great quantities of books in a private home and to listen to ideas seriously discussed away from school. They were talking about ideas for pleasure! When the wife of the graduate student asked him what he wanted to do after graduation, Morris answered that he hoped to become a writer. Surprised by his response, Willie wondered why he had chosen that answer rather than sports announcer—his first vocational choice. That night, fascinated by the discussion and all the books, Morris went to the library determined to read every important book ever written (Morris, pp. 163–64).

Something had happened. Such exposures were beginning to provide Morris "an interest and a curiosity in something outside his own parochial ego." He was beginning to attend not only to the power of language, but also the exotic world of experience and evocation made accessible by language. Books and literature did not exist for simple casual pleasure but were as "subversive as Socrates and expressions of man's soul." One "dangerous idea" led to another, as Willie's provincial Yazoo mindset succumbed to the subversion of ideas (Morris, p. 165). Willie's journalism began to focus on such precarious issues as the oil industry's control of academic life of the University of Texas, the racism of the student body, and the spiritual vacuum of the university community (Morris, pp. 169–171).

Just as he was immersing himself in the controversial issues of the early 1950s, Morris traveled back to Yazoo for a few days with family and friends. The locals were buzzing with conversations about a meeting to form a local chapter of the White Citizen's Council. The chapter was a response to an NAACP targeting of Yazoo as a location where the Supreme Court desegregation decision would be put in effect. When Morris arrived at the meeting, it was apparent that most of the White citizens of the town were in attendance. He knew them all. Amid cries of "let's get them niggers," the council delegated a list of steps that would be taken. Local Blacks who had signed an NAACP desegregation petition would be immediately evicted by their landlords, barred from buying supplies from White grocers, and fired from their jobs. Morris watched the proceedings with visceral revulsions (Morris, pp. 176–179). He was confronted with the realization that he was not the same person who had lived all his previous life here.

> I looked back and saw my father, sitting still and gazing straight ahead; on the stage my friends' fathers nodded their heads and talked among themselves. I felt an urge to get out of there. Who are these people? I asked myself. What was I doing there? Was this the place I had grown up in and never wanted to leave? I knew in that instant, in the middle of a mob in our school auditorium, that a mere three years in Texas had taken me irrevocably, even without me realizing it, from home.[12]

The existential separation of Morris and Yazoo was thus effected. Liberated from unexamined delta consciousness, Morris, like a child taking his first steps, entered gingerly the ranks of that strange group known as southern intellectuals. Southern intellectuals, Morris writes, always had the sense that they were the lucky ones, miraculously freed from all the disastrous alternatives of their isolated lower or middle class rearings. So different was the experience of the eastern Jewish intellectuals who struggled to determine which set of ideas they would accept. For southern intellectuals ideas were not a part of childhood or adolescence, and their discovery in early adulthood as entities worth living by was not taken lightly. We discovered not *certain* books, Morris reflects, "but the simple *presence* of books, not the nuances of idea and feeling, but idea and feeling on their own terms." Because of such a late blooming, southern intellectuals are always cursed and blessed with a hungry, naïve quality that eclipses some insights but unveils others.

The southern intellectual is always a man or woman in danger. The exiled Southerner in search of liberation is ever vulnerable to the temptation to turn one's back on his or her own past in the pursuit of some convenient or trendy sophistication. He or she must be aware of the seductions that move one to be dishonest with the most distinctive things about one's self (Morris, pp. 381–19). The attempts of outsiders to dictate what a Southerner *ought* to feel about the South must be resisted. Morris was always impressed with Ellison and Murray's refusal to view their own southern pasts as unmitigated disasters despite the prevailing consensus that they should do so (Morris, pp. 385–86). Since his awakening at the University of Texas, Morris had been ashamed of his Mississippi origins. While in New York, he came to realize that he must transcend such a sentiment, for shame was a simplistic and debilitating emotion, "too easy and predictable—like bitterness." The challenge was to *understand* the southern experience, to comprehend its distinctiveness and meaning in relation to the experiences of humans who came from other places (Morris, p. 386).

Another threat to Southerners in search of liberation (and to all Southerners for that matter) comes from the rationality of the twentieth century with its industrialization and alienation—the advent of the New South movement. The city of my birth, Jackson, Mississippi, Morris writes, has endured two distinct destructions. The first was engineered with surgeon-like precision by General Sherman in 1863; the second, by ostensibly friendlier hands, came at the urging of the New South developers and entrepreneurs of recent years. These deceivers wrapped themselves in the magical banner of progress while they laid waste the old neighborhoods and city blocks. Rising in the dust were the soulless shopping malls and suburbias—tombstones to much of that sense of continuity, that awareness of human history (Morris, 1981).

Of course, the South by any human measure had to reform, but the reform was effected via homogenization. Like in other regions of twentieth century, industrialized America, community in the South began to fade, the ties that bound us together began to disintegrate. There is a painful, twisted ambiguity to the New South of the malls and suburbs. To conquer its racism, sexism, and blood, does the South have to trade in its sense of community for the rampant commercialism that the Europeans call "Americanization?" (Morris, 1981, p. 239). The question is omnipresent as Morris stares at a picture of William Faulkner next to a portrait of Ronald McDonald in the new McDonalds near the Ole Miss campus. We cannot avoid the question when we listen to a member of the Greenwood, Mississippi Chamber of Commerce asks Willie, "What can we do to improve Mississippi's image?" Let the people of the Bronx or Boston worry about Mississippi's image, Morris replied, let Mississippians "concern themselves with their image among one another" (Morris, p. 243). "When the material can coerce the human spirit," he laments, "we are doomed" (Morris, 1967).

The question inevitably arises: Has the South died and been reincarnated as the Sunbelt? Have the changes for emancipation bred in pain and suffering already been lost in a media-soaked postmodern nihilism? Walker Percy sardonically teases radical hopes with his portrayal of Blacks in his novels. Black Southerners are, as always, estranged in Percy's South, but this time their estrangement is not the result of the traditional prejudice and oppression; it finds its genesis in alienation, the anomie of late capitalism. Like their enslavers, they are spiritually alienated, separated from the world and themselves. Thus, Black progress toward economic equality, from Percy's perspective, is similar to the South's quest for mobility—achieved only at a high psychic cost. The southern Blacks who "make it" economically contract through their exposure to the alienated marketplace and its accompanying values the displacement disease. What a strange form of racial equality Percy proposes—Blacks and Whites united in their disconnection from history, a postmodern racial rapprochement (Percy, 1971; Percy, 1977).

The Southerner who seeks authenticity must be aware of modern industrial alienation, the nature of its southern manifestation, and its effect on the soul of the individual. The instrumental rationality that accompanies this alienation precipitates a dishonesty with the most distinctive things about one's self; indeed, this destruction of self-knowledge may be its most insidious aspect. We are so physically mutilated by this alienation that we hold in disdain those who force introspection by inducing us to look beyond our prevailing common sense view of ourselves so that we might glimpse our essences. While I was in high school, Willie reflects, "I joined easily and thoughtlessly in the Mississippi middle-class consensus that Faulkner, the chronicler and moralist, was out for the Yankee dollar" (Morris, 1967, p. 142). Without an understanding of self, Morris could not possibly understand how he would hold on to and reinterpret that "Mississippi" that would be forever in his soul. Without self-understanding, however, he could not see the connections between himself and Mississippi; he had to transcend it to find it. He had to transcend it to find himself. The southern curriculum must confront the sources of the modern alienation by using its social psychoanalytical methodology. The etiology of the industrial and self-alienation of the sons and daughters of the "good ole boys" and their wives, "the little ladies" must be exposed. The literature on the subject is extensive.

## THE TREASURES

The "southern treasures" that all of us native sons and daughters to some degree hold within us are powerful virtues—virtues not to be romanticized but to be interrogated in their dialectical relationship with the ghosts.

*The South is a place where people maintain a closeness to the land and a feel for the rhythms of nature.*

The powerful delta land, Willie writes, with all of its mysteries and strengths was always tugging at his soul. During one of his drives through the Mississippi countryside, Willie came upon a Black family in the September fields, burlap sacks of yesteryear draped over their shoulders, picking cotton. As he watched their silhouettes against a darkening sky, he was reminded in that instant of who he was, and where his people came from (Morris, 1983). We were never far away from the land, the growing plants, and nature's wilder moods, he tells us. Like the southern past, there was nothing gentle about nature: "It came at you violently, or in a rush, by turns disordered and oppressively somnolent." The overflowing Yazoo River and the tornadoes were especially hard on the poor Blacks, destroying their shacks on stilts built in the river bottoms (Morris, 1967). One's closeness to the textures of the land with its sensual if not erotic rhythms staved off at least one form of alienation, as it constantly confronted one with births and deaths, the long forgotten victories and tragedies, and the sadnesses and joys of human existence in this unique place (Morris, 1981).

*The South is a place where people cherish the importance of friendships that exist in reality, not in the effort—as in a Dale Carnegie "relationship".*

Morris is dismayed by the appearance of books in the 1980s on how to cultivate friendships. Such books could only appear in an alienated society where community is crumbling. Friends, in the southern sense of the term, were people one saw frequently and informally, and the word, friendship, carried with it a reverence: "I rank the betrayal of a friend—even a friend from an earlier part of one's life—as dastardly almost as child-abuse or manslaughter" (Morris, p. 188). In the South, you could organize a party on the spur of the moment and have trouble getting everyone to leave.

You shared certain things: a reverence for informality, an interest in what other friends were doing, a regard for geographic places, an awareness of a certain set of beloved landmarks in themselves important to one's everyday existence, a mutual but usually unexpressed sense of community (Morris, 1967, p. 408). When in New York, Morris, with his southern sensibilities was particularly attentive to the concept of friendship. One could designate a person a "friend," he observed, if "you saw him once every four or five months, talked for a while, and got along." It was absolutely not appropriate to drop in on one's "friends" without warning. "We lunch twice a year," a New Yorker told Willie of a good friend of his. He reported this to me, Willie confides, "without a trace of irony" (Morris, 1967, p. 409).

*The South is a place where people appreciate the aesthetic of sport while lamenting the questionable values and aggrandizements that threaten its integrity in modern America.*

Only with the knowledge that sports was a nexus for what was meaningful to Southerners (Morris, 1983a), can we possibly understand that when Willie last spoke with his father as he lay dying of cancer, the subject was baseball. The conversation was by no means trivial; it was very loving and intensely personal (Morris, 1967). So were his late night conversations with his grandmother, as they sat together on the front porch of her home discussing the subtleties of the Jackson Senators baseball game and eating her fried chicken that had been soaked overnight in buttermilk (Morris, 1981).

The significance of the rituals of sport for Southerners never ceases to impress Willie, who has devoted two of his books about the southern experience to sport. In *The Courting of Marcus Dupree*, Morris uses a Black running back, his high school football career, and the drama of his recruitment to the college ranks as the setting for the story of desegregation in Mississippi. Football illustrates to the Southerner the spectacle of the human adventure and as an observer of the South, Morris contends, he is obliged to watch football not only for its intrinsic aesthetic but also "for the ironic and picturesque detail and for the shadow behind the act" (Morris, 1983b). Nothing that mattered so much could fail to reveal something about who we really are. There is a magic to baseball, he writes, a quality that moves the children of the South to a new level of reality ("a dreamy and suspended state") where nothing can penetrate their consciousness while they chase outfield flies (Morris, p. 103). Sport in the rural South shapes us. Willie recollects the coach of American legion baseball team, a poor farmer known as Gentleman Joe. Before Yazoo's championship game with Greenwood, Gentleman Joe delivered his inspirational sermon to the team.

*Gentlemen*, he said, using that staple designation which earned him his nickname, "I'm just a simple farmer. Fifteen acres is all I got, and two mules, a cow, and a lot of mouths to feed." He paused between his words and his eyes watered over. "I've neglected my little crop because of this team, and the weevils gave me trouble last year, and they're doing it again now. I ain't had enough rain, and I don't plan to get much more. The corn looks so brown, if it got another shade browner it'd flake right off. But almost every afternoon you'd find me in my pickup on the way to town to teach you gentlemen the game of baseball..." Then with his pale blue eyes flashing fire, half whispering and half shouting, he said: "Gentlemen, I want us to pray, and then...I want you to go out there on that field and win this Miss'ippi championship. You'll be proud of it for the rest of your lives... You'll think about it when you're dyin' and your teeth are all gone."[13]

*The South is a place where people gain a special sensitivity to the struggle of our national experience through the medium of strained racial relations.*

In the South, Black and White people actually know each other, and in that knowledge and the knowledge of how they "knew one another" in the past they gain insight into the truth and struggle of America's national experience. A young Midwestern journalism professor told Willie that Black people in Chicago are often strangers to one another, not to mention to White people (Morris, 1983b). In the South, there is a shared community between White and Black that hopefully will be strengthened by remembering the past and by confronting its scars. "I like the way White and Black people banter with each other," Willie writes, referring to the racially-conscious kidding that is becoming more and more common in the South as the wounds start to heal (Morris, 1981). Only those who genuinely understand the backgrounds of one another can turn the word, "nigger" inside out in order to parody its traditional red-neck usage. Thus, the word is demystified and the tension engendered by it diffused. Such a taboo-smashing demystification promotes interracial understanding and unity, not hatred and divisiveness. During his years in Texas, Willie often debated where the South ends. At first he thought the boundary was somewhere a little west of Shreveport but later he came to realize that it ended where this ambiguous but evolving relationship between Black and White died and one's feel for the guilt of the land faded away (Morris, p. 77).

*The South is a place where people hold the belief that time is a precious entity that an individual controls by not letting it be filled with other-directed and organized activity.*

Though the instrumental ethos of the industrialized New South is subverting the effort, Southerners control time better than many. Those long and heavy southern afternoons with nothing doing (Morris, 1967), the mystical twilights when one is comforted by the appearance of old friend Venus in the western sky as it oversees the fading of the oranges, violets, mauves, roses, and lavenders below it, the humid evening when the crickets and frogs provide a musical concert for the patient porch sitter all contribute to an appreciation of the preciousness of time. These are times when one feels best equipped to resist the time thieves with their insidious ability to engender anxiety about the demands of the marketplace. We must never abandon the southern fight to make time stand still without concurrently developing our ability to transcend the blinders of the temporal.

*The South is a place where people love storytelling and believe that this tradition builds community by linking us to our past.*

In the South, Willie writes, a story worth telling is worth telling again. The storyteller assigns his or her listeners the responsibility to pass the tale along to a different audience, hopefully in a distant future. In this way family and cultural continuity is assured. The stories are the proper province of one's oldest living relative. They are most effective, Morris maintains, when they are told:

> in the dark of a summer evening, the whole family gathered on a screened porch, quiet in their listening so that the thumping of the night-flying beetles against the screens and the whine of locusts and cicadas merge with the storyteller's voice to become part of the tale. Such a setting, reaching past into the fiber of childhood, endures as vividly in the memory as the tale itself.[14]

The stories, Willie recalls, detailed the eccentric lives of old ladies of previous generations, recalled the impact of funerals of war heroes and other townspeople, traced tragic love affairs that were never consummated, and painted verbal portraits of old gentlemen with "tobacco stains on their whiskers" (Morris, pp. 239–40). My own southern heritage is exposed by the importance of storytelling in my childhood. The realization that the subjects of my father and mother's stories—their cousins, uncles and aunts (most of whom I never knew)—are more familiar to me in my mind's eye than some of the people I have called close friends in my life in the America of the late twentieth century is disconcerting. Eudora Welty extends Morris's reverence for southern storytelling. In the South, status is gained via one's proficiency as a raconteur. One of her characters expresses her desire to marry a particular man for his storytelling ability. Each tale belongs to a larger oral tradition—as Richard Gray puts it:

> a continuum of storytelling: stories knit into one another, one anecdote recalls another in the series, and tales which we learn have been told many times before…[15]

Indeed, the stories help create place and, for that matter, the past.

*The South is a place where people revere the impulses of the imagination that shape our speech, our music, our literature, our love of place, and our potential.*

The atmosphere of small southern towns, Willie argues, did amazing things to the imagination of its children. When clocks moved slowly the southern sense of fancy had time to develop: "One had to work his imagination out on something" (Morris, 1967). Our imagination is our greatest asset; it saved Willie from the philistine concerns of the small town bourgeoisie of Yazoo and it can save the South from the ravages of modern alienation. A student asked Morris if in the face of all the "progress" and "development" Mississippi can retain its spirit:

> I told him I did not know. I went on to suggest to the young student, however, that the preservation of those qualities must derive, in the future of Mississippi, from those old impulses of the imagination which have made the literature of Mississippi so impressive. It is no accident, I said, that Mississippi produced

Faulkner, and Eudora Welty and Tennessee Williams, and Walker Percy…and the distinguished others.[16]

The southern treasures are real and they still breathe despite the standardization of the region. They are found in unlikely places among Black and White, rich and poor, male and female. The obvious caution that must be taken when a writer celebrates such treasures involves the tendency toward romanticization. The innocent country boy (who lives inside me) who played happily and carelessly in the mountains of East Tennessee must not impose his happy images of his South upon my present attempt to garner a mature understanding of the region. The treasures may exist, but they live within a complex dialectic of pain and malformations. Without a critical grounding, the treasures lapse into an apologia for the status quo and the myths that sustain it. Without the treasures, the critical analysis of the South lacks fullness and possibility.

## THE POSSIBILITY OF PLACE

The genre of southern apologia has a long history. At the same time that Willie Morris published *North Toward Home*, Richard Weaver's posthumous defense of the "southern tradition" found its way into print as *The Southern Tradition at Bay*. Weaver's exemplar of the apologia genre highlights the difference between the southern curriculum's guarded celebration of the treasures and a right-wing defense of *Tradition*. To Weaver and his followers the Patriarchal Myth represented the foundation of a southern greatness marked by Christian values, chivalry, men who lived by a gentlemanly code, and the last bastion of honor in the world. There was little room for gender or racial equality, the deconstruction of social role, socioeconomic mobility, the values of peace, or social evolution in Weaver's *Tradition*. Weaver is a self-proclaimed member of the Old Order who understands that the intrusions of the twentieth century are destroying the place he loves. It is his identification with the myths, which grants him the insight needed to understand the changes: "It is not the …progressives…who discern what is at issue…. It is the men of the old order who see…the implications of the new" (Weaver, 1968, pp. 43–44). The South can continue on its present course to an amorphous standardized culture, Weaver concludes, or it can embrace the "fulfillment represented by the Old South" (Weaver, p. 391). This is *not* the message conveyed by our exploration of the southern treasures.

Willie Morris senses that buried in the experience of the South there exists something of great value for America. The project of the critical analyst of the southern curriculum is to unearth the buried treasures, to chip away the sediments of racism, sexism, and poverty, and to pursue a new level of consciousness. The South of the late twentieth century is a story of people trying—trying to forge a new life amid the impediments. As usual as the words may sound in a southern context, I feel that embedded in the southern treasures is a piece of the *utopian vision* of community—a vision that may serve as an antidote to the alienation of modern America. The southern treasures may give us direction in America's coming fight to gain a sense of community and to repair the ravages of the twentieth century.

What happens in small town Mississippi, Morris contends, will be of enduring importance to America's quest for its soul (Morris, p. 123).

Intelligence alone is not enough to fight this twentieth century alienation. Many of the intellectuals Morris encountered in the Northeast had an empty space where human understanding and toleration should have been. The partisans of intellectual thrills, Morris observes, seem "to desperately lack in experiences… They seemed devoid of any serious concern with real human beings in real human situations" (Morris, 1967). Thus, the southern curriculum based on social psychoanalysis seeks to explore the experiential in relationship to larger social forces. Cora Kaplan writing of the subordination of women captures the idea when she calls for an analysis of structures of feelings. Where Kaplan asks what feelings induce particular women to rebel or submit, the southern curriculum asks what feelings move a southern woman to reject the myth of Southern Womanhood (Kaplan, 1986). When confronted with modern southern alienation such analysis of feeling asks what allows some individuals to sense, expose, and overcome the deleterious effects of alienation in their lives and what blinds others to its existence.

Henry Giroux writes that one way technical/instrumental rationality contributes to the alienation of twentieth century life involves the fact that scholarship, theory, and intellectual pursuit are seen to possess no ethical dimension (Giroux, 1988). Scholarship serves the end of collecting "objective facts" that can be empirically verified. Thus, modern scholarship of this like has turned its back on the classical Greek notion that academic activity was designed as a method to free humans from dogma so that they could pursue ethical action (Giroux, 1981). Reflecting on his teacher, Texas newspaper editor Ronnie Dugger, Morris tells us that Dugger didn't simply teach him the techniques of reporting and writing, but how to view public life as an ethical process (Morris, 1967).

I revere the southern treasures; their humanity, authenticity, and ethical orientation make me confront who I really am and the relationship between that person and who I would really like to be. The southern personality treasures offer a stark contrast to the so-called objective view of the world often taught in our elementary schools, high schools, and colleges, promoted in our businesses, and ground into our consciousness by television. The southern sense of history, its collective memory, may yield an American sense of possibility. Joan Didion writes that a "place belongs forever to whoever remembers it most obsessively, wrenches it from itself, shapes it, renders it, loves it so radically that he remakes it in his image" (Morris, 1981). Our memory, our understanding of the historical forces that pull our puppet strings, can liberate us, and hopefully save us. It is this vision that inspires the southern curriculum.

*To "Manny" Pridgen, a southern scholar, who first introduced me to the South as "place."

## NOTES

[1] Roland Barthes, *Mythologies* (New York: Hill and Wang, 1972), pp. 142–43.
[2] Eric Fromm, *The Heart of Man* (New York: Harper and Row, 1980), p. 79.
[3] Willie Morris, *Terrains of the Heart* (Oxford Miss: Yoknapatawpha Press, 1981), pp. 30–31.

[4] Willie Morris, *North Toward Home* (Oxford Miss: Yoknapatawpha Press, 1967), p. 77.
[5] Ibid., pp. 77–78.
[6] Ibid., pp. 40–43, 52–54.
[7] Ibid., pp. 135, 140–41.
[8] Ibid., pp. 141–42.
[9] Ibid., p. 153.
[10] Ibid., pp. 139–140.
[11] Ibid., p. 123.
[12] Ibid., pp. 179–80.
[13] Ibid., p. 121.
[14] Morris, *Terrains of the Heart*, p. 230.
[15] Richard Gray, *Writing the South* (New York: Cambridge University Press, 1986).
[16] Morris, *Terrains of the Heart*, p. 242.

Reprinted with permission: Kincheloe, J. L. (1991). Willie Morris and the southern curriculum: emancipating the southern ghosts. In J. L. Kincheloe and W. Pinar (Eds.), *Curriculum as social psychoanalysis: Essays on the significance of place* (pp. 123–154). Albany, NY: SUNY Press.

SHIRLEY R. STEINBERG AND CHAIM M. STEINBERG

# GOIN' SOUTH

**Shirley:** October 19, 1989, Dayton Ohio…The Bergamo Conference Center

A long-haired dirty-blonde man interrupted me during a conversation with someone at the reception. After we exchanged information and flirtations, I asked him: "Where's your accent from?" Not one for short explanations, Joe launched into an elongated description of being from the mountains of East Tennessee. He painted a landscape of his Appalachians and punctuated it by inviting me to see the "10,000 shades of green." Five weeks later, he met me at the Atlanta airport, handed me strawberry incense, a bottle of beer, kissed me and said: "Welcome to the South."

If you haven't been there, you won't understand that *the South* is a distinct geographic, metaphysical, cosmic place…that there may be a North, a West, or an East, but *the South* embodies so much more than the directional title it implies. This is what I learned in November of 1989.

**Chaim:** I remember the exact date I left Canada. It was July 12, 1990. My older sister and I were leaving by way of the airport in Great Falls, Montana. The trip took a little over three hours and I imagine we spent most of it in silence, our biological father driving down wide highways in an old blue and white van that had a middle row of captain's seats. What I remember most about the trip was the left over ice cream cake that we ate out of a purple-brown Tupperware container. Compared to the small town in Southern Alberta that I had grown up in, Great Falls was a metropolis, and its airport seemed to be the greatest hub in the history of aviation.

As we stumbled wearily and warily through the Minneapolis and Atlanta airports, marked by little plastic pilot's wings, it quickly became apparent how small our horizons had been. By the time we reached Atlanta and met Shirley and Joe, it was about 10:00 at night and the cool breezy prairie summer of western Canada had been replaced by the gloriously humid summer of the American southeast. We piled into a red Toyota van, and made the two hour trip east to Clemson, South Carolina; finally pulling into a little development of houses a little after midnight. It was my tenth birthday.

**Shirley:** Who would have imagined that less than 9 months later, Joe and I would be importing all four Albertan kids to live with us in South Carolina? I remember finding each day a marvel of cultural collisions. My first time at a supermarket, walking down two full aisles of pork products. Standing in line to check out, waiting for what seemed like hours while the cashier and customer exchanged lengthy "hey, howya doin'?" In fact, I waited all the time, the slow pace of the South dragged me like I was fixed in sludge. I learned quickly to take deep breaths and try to indulge in listening to the conversations and dialects, which never hurried along.

*k. hayes et al., (eds.), Key Work in Critical Pedagogy: Joe L. Kincheloe, 49–52.*
*© 2011 Sense Publishers. All rights reserved.*

**Chaim:** It is not often the case that we can assign an exact date and time to life's major changes, but for me the journey south always begins on the day I turned ten. Growing up in Canada I experienced Chinooks (warm winds off the prairies that could raise the temperature 50 degrees and melt mountains of ice), amazement at the 22 channels available on my grandmother's cable, at least one Halloween dressed as a vampire stamping through 2–3 feet of snow, and an intensity of demographic homogeneity. But the South was entirely different. School would be cancelled for the threat of an inch or so of snow. Summers were hot, sticky, cut your way through the humid air, but at least there were fireflies.

If there were fireflies in Alberta, I don't remember them. I do remember the idea of fireflies, popular in children's books and TV shows, magic creatures that could be put in jars and used in place of a desk lamp or overhead light, but I can't recall having ever seen them. A few nights after arriving in South Carolina, Joe took us for a walk around the neighbourhood introducing us to kudzu and cooling asphalt. I'm sure most of the woods that surrounded that little development have since been ploughed over and turned into student housing, but in 1990 they were full of fireflies. Luminous spots appeared by the thousands, a mini-Milky Way dumped like two scoops of raisins onto an unsuspecting landscape.

**Shirley:** The South has a smell, its very own scent. It is a scent of heat, of fried food, of sweat, work, poverty and privilege. It has themes: of narrative, of storytelling, of old couches on the front porch, of beer, of beat up cars, and people raising their hand slowly to greet every passing car. Becoming a Southernphile demanded work, I wanted to learn everything there was to know about the South. Why was it so different? So closed off from the other three directions of the US? Why was it so brutal? So soft? One of the first questions I asked Joe in Ohio that October day was "who was right? Neil Young or Lynyrd Skynyrd?" Without a beat, he replied: "Neil Young." As much as he loved the South, he was painfully aware of her ghosts, and felt Neil had seen their aura. He did, however, feel Neil was uninformed as to the nuances of the South, and had Young spent time in the South, his Canadian dismissal of "Southern Man," as simply barbaric and racist would have been more informed. That was one of the mysteries of the South: racism and hatred could be spewed by a working stiff, a redneck, yet that same man could be a daddy to his babies and twirl his own mama around a dance floor on Mother's Day. The complexity of loving the words and music of Gregg Allman and the Brothers from Macon, Georgia, but knowing we would never cast the same votes for social change.

**Chaim:** While there was an undeniable magic to southern nights, the days had their own special qualities.... reruns. Not to offend the good people at the Canadian Broadcasting Corporation, but child cannot live by *Mr. Dressup* and *The Raccoons* alone. I'm grateful to Canada for its universal health care, its generous social net, the appreciation it has for all things frozen, but why did I grow up watching *The Beachcombers*, when I could have been watching reruns of *MASH* and *Batman*? There was nothing more glorious to ten year old sensibilities than Adam West and Burt Ward BAM, SPIFF, and SPLORTING their ways through the ranks of King Tut, the Joker, and Catwoman. ... Catwoman. I was not the first, nor am I the last young boy to have special place in my heart for Eartha Kitt and Julie Newmar.

**Shirley:** Joe introduced us to music. I mean *really* introduced us. I thought I was a pretty seasoned rock n' roller, loving the blues and more savvy than most females of my generation. Joe *was* music. He saw music in his South, in the gentle waves of the trees, the deep drawls of voices, and he was an expert at imitating every different Southern accent. When Joe would hear someone speak and note that it wasn't the local accent, he would approach them and ask if they were from Bull's Gap, or Greenville, or Memphis ... wherever. He usually hit it within 20 miles. I fancy Joe saw himself as the Southern Henry Higgins, parsing out linguistic differences. He had the kids learning his routines, and tutored them in the fine art of Southernification. They are still able to fall into a slow drawl when prompted.

**Chaim:** My biggest case of culture shock centred on one particular aspect of life.... Black people.... Travelling to Alberta, one would notice, at least in the early '90s, that there was not a lot of ethnic diversity. I recall one Black family from my first ten years; they were so notable that I even remember where they lived: in a small house under a big tree next to the Bank of Montreal branch office. South Carolina was of a different color, many different colors. It was my first introduction to the vagaries of race and racial politics. Being so inexperienced in the issue, I had no idea it was even a big deal, one person seemed as normal as another. Gradually, I noticed that there was only one Black student in the advanced track of classes, and then I started seeing *David Duke for President* stickers on cars, leading up to the 1992 Presidential Primary season. A friend invited me to come along with him and his family to a Klan meeting, informing me, "we're not racist, we just think everybody has a certain place in society." Our house became, and continues to be, a highway of students: Black, Hispanic, White, Asian, etc... an environment grossly at odds to what existed within the halls of the local schools and university. Clemson was a university with buildings named after administrators (Tillman Hall) who had bestrode the doorway armed with a pitchfork, like a colossus of segregation, trying to keep the Black students out.

**Shirley:** I worked as a teacher development leader at a local pre-school. We decided to invite all the teachers to our house for a party, along with friends and students. I'll never forget Cheryl and Bede, the infants teachers, taking me aside: "Miss Shirley, you don't have to invite us." I told them we wanted them to come over, and they told me they had never been invited to a white person's house before. A few weeks later, I saw Cheryl at the store, and called out to her, she put her head down, I thought she didn't hear me. So I went over to her, she greeted me quietly and whispered: "don't feel like you have to speak to me in public."

As our friendship grew, Cheryl and Bede mentored me in the curriculum of being Black in the South. Joe enhanced my education by introducing me to Pat Conroy, Bobbie Ann Mason, Willie Morris, and the Southern treasures. My romance with the South became full of love and hate. Southerness had multiple facets, and each South was filled with both love and hate, each bump was filled with contradictions. One day I went to visit Bede at her place. She gave me specific directions to get there: Go up the highway, turn at the old night club on Vista, drive about a half mile, and turn at the Black church. I drove back and forth from that night club, and I couldn't find the black church. Finally, I went home and called Bede and told her I couldn't find her house. She asked where I had been, and I told her I followed her directions exactly, but when I passed the club, I only saw a red brick church, it was the only one there. Bede belted out a scream, started laughing, and told me that *was* the Black church…the Black church. I never ceased to be surprised at the ghosts.

**Chaim:** The move to Clemson was not only my first exposure to Southern life, but also to Americana. As is often the case with life's first experiences, my sense of America is nonetheless deeply colored by the south. I hate boiled peanuts, but I appreciate their soggy place in the world. Southern baseball and college football are the important contributions to sports. You can't live without pork and bottle rockets. Pepsi is Coke's bastard cousin, and I may not like iced tea, but I'll drink sweet tea any day. There was also shotgun shacks, redlining, implicit and explicit discrimination, family values for some families, but not others, and school field trips across the street so a local church could give us faux-leather bound, green copies of the *New Testament* without violating the establishment clause. America is a dichotomy, and nowhere is that more obvious than the American South. And to no one is that less obvious, except in hindsight, than to a ten-year-old from the western prairies of Canada.

**Shirley:** Joe's article on Willie Morris helped me understand the South. It taught me that literature could speak as a multi-layered, polysemic cultural study of place. It taught me that place was more than *a place*…that place was integral to one's being and one's story. I never had a sense of place as a child. I used to blame it on my mother's constant moves, but after internalizing place, I understand that it isn't an *it*. Place defines us as we define place. From Blanche's naïve refusal to eat an "unwashed grape," to Willie Morris's passion for pigskin, *the South* can be read in many ways, and sung to limitless riffs. And of course, for Chaim, for me, and for Ian, Meghann, and Bronwyn, Joe, with all his contradictions, was our Southern treasure.

*In 1990, Joe was finishing his second book,* Teachers as Researchers: Qualitative Inquiry as a Path to Empowerment. *As we had just bought a new Mac, the first word processing computer with a hard drive, I offered to type the book for him. In those days, word processing was still quite cumbersome, and the nuances of cutting, pasting, and saving, didn't always work well. Long story short, after the book came out, Joe noticed that I had missed an entire chapter. I was embarrassed; he was depressed, so I said I would do anything to make it up to him. He quickly suggested that I co-author and re-work the missing chapter and create a piece for a journal, preferably, the Harvard Educational Review. We worked on the piece for a year, and it was submitted in 1992, it was during that time that my work on Piaget merged with Joe's reconceptualization of cognition, and we developed Post Formalism. Joe mentored me with patience (and impatience) in the specific way to produce for an academic journal...he also allowed me the privilege of dealing the editors of the HER, a decidedly anal and serious group. I learned the primary lesson of higher education: that sometimes, writing for a "top tiered" journal was a pain in the ass. SS*

JOE L. KINCHELOE AND SHIRLEY R. STEINBERG

# 3. A TENTATIVE DESCRIPTION OF POST-FORMAL THINKING

*The Critical Confrontation with Cognitive Thinking*

*In this article, Joe Kincheloe and Shirley Steinberg critique and challenge the reductionist conceptions of intelligence that underlie cognitive developmental theory. The authors formulate a post-Piagetian cognitive theory that is informed by and extends critical, feminist, and postmodern thought. By delineating the features of what they refer to as a "post-formal" way of thinking, the authors provide practitioners with a framework for reconsidering both curricular and pedagogical practices.*

Postmodern analysis, though diverse in the ways it is conceptualized, has consistently laid bare the assumptions of Cartesian logic by exposing the ways that the structure of traditional science constructs imaginary worlds. Science, like a novel, is "written"; both the novel and science operate according to the arbitrary rules of a language game. Such postmodern understandings confront us with a dramatic socio-educational dilemma: how do we function in the midst of such uncertainty?

The contemporary debate over postmodernism is often framed in all-or-nothing terms—we can either completely accept or completely reject Western modernism. In our work, we have sought a middle ground that attempts to hold onto the progressive and democratic features of modernism while drawing upon the insights postmodernism provides concerning the failure of reason, the tyranny of grand narratives, the limitations of science, and the repositioning of relationships between dominant and subordinate cultural groups. In such complex and changing times, we, as critical educators, turn to our emancipatory system of meaning, grounded as it is in feminist notions of passionate knowing, African-American epistemologies, subjugated knowledges (ways of knowing that have been traditionally excluded from the conversation of mainstream educators), liberation-theological ethics, and the progressive modernist concerns with justice, liberty, and equality. As we temper our system of meaning with a dose of postmodern self-analysis and epistemological (or maybe post-epistemological) humility, we move to a new zone of cognition—a *post-formal* way of thinking.

Formal thinking a la Piaget implies an acceptance of a Cartesian-Newtonian mechanistic worldview that is caught in a cause-effect, hypothetico-deductive system of reasoning. Unconcerned with questions of power relations and the way they structure our consciousness, formal operational thinkers accept an objectified, unpoliticized way of knowing that breaks a social or educational system down into its basic parts in order to understand how it works. Emphasizing certainty and prediction, formal thinking organizes verified facts into a theory. The facts that do not fit into the theory are eliminated, and the theory developed is the one best suited to limit contradictions in knowledge. Thus, formal thought operates on the assumption that resolution must be found for all contradictions. Schools and standardized test-makers, assuming that formal operational thought represents the highest level of human cognition, focus their efforts on its cultivation and measurement. Students and teachers who move beyond formality are often unrewarded and sometimes even punished in educational contexts.

This article attempts to define the type of thinking that might occur when individuals, and teachers in particular, move beyond the boundaries of Piagetian formality. Many theorists (Lave, 1988; Walkerdine, 1984, 1988) over the last two decades have sought to formulate a post-Piagetian cognitive theory. Too often, however, they have not used a social theoretical analysis to construct a critique and a new vision of cognitive theory. In some ways, Piaget anticipated our theoretical project as he and Rolando Garcia (Piaget, & Garcia, 1989) discussed the impact of social and epistemic paradigms in shaping cognitive systems. Unfamiliar, however, with critical postmodern analysis of subjectivity and power, Piaget was limited as to how far his intuitions could take him. Even with such limitations, Piaget often understood far more than many of his students about the situated nature of cognition (Walkerdine, 1984, 1992). Nevertheless, he did not connect this situatedness with any effort to break the confines imposed by the abstract rationality of the formal stage. Grounded in an understanding of critical and postmodern advances in social theory, we attempt to develop a *socio-cognitive* theory that draws upon these evolving discourses and moves beyond the monolithic essentialism of the past.

Moving to post-formality, critical educators politicize cognition; they attempt to disengage themselves from socio-interpersonal norms and ideological expectations. The post-formal concern with questions of meaning, emancipation via ideological

## A TENTATIVE DESCRIPTION OF POST-FORMAL THINKING

disembedding, and attention to the process of self-production rises above the formal operational level of thought and its devotion to proper procedure. Post-formalism grapples with purpose, devoting attention to issues of human dignity, freedom, authority, and social responsibility. Many will argue that a post-formal mode of thinking with its emphasis on multiple perspectives will necessitate an ethical relativism that paralyzes social action. A more critical post-formality grounded in our emancipatory system of meaning does not cave in to relativistic social paralysis. Instead, it initiates reflective dialogue between critical theory and postmodernism—a dialogue that is always concerned with the expansion of self-awareness and consciousness, never certain of emancipation's definition, and perpetually reconceptualizing the system of meaning. Critical theory, in brief, refers to the tradition developed by "the Frankfurt School" in Germany in the 1920s. Max Horkheimer, Theodor Adorno, and others attempted to rethink the meaning of human self-direction or emancipation, to develop a theory of non-dogmatic social transformation, to expose the hidden social relationships of the everyday world, and to analyze the problems of social theories that celebrated social harmony without questioning the assumptions of the larger society. In a sense, the dialogue between critical theory and postmodernism produces a theoretical hesitation, a theoretical stutter.

One of the main features of post-formal thinking is that it expands the boundaries of what can be labeled sophisticated thinking. When we begin to expand these boundaries, we find that those who were excluded from the community of the intelligent seem to cluster around exclusions based on race (the non-White), class (the poor), and gender (the feminine). The modernist conception of intelligence is an exclusionary system based on the premise that some people are intelligent and others aren't (Case, 1985; Klahr, & Wallace, 1976). Intelligence and creativity are thought of as fixed and innate, while at the same time mysterious qualities found only in the privileged few. The modernist grand narrative of intelligence has stressed biological fixities that can be altered only by surgical means. Such an essentialism is a psychology of nihilism that locks people into rigid categories that follow them throughout life (Bozik, 1987; Lawler, 1975; Maher, & Rathbone, 1986). Howard Gardner's work, though not situated in the postmodernist tradition, has criticized this type of rigid modernism. This article positively draws from Gardner's critiques and theories. At the same time, it attempts to move beyond some of Gardner's ideas by connecting the political realm to the cognitive (Gardner, 1983, 1989, 1991).

The developmentalism of Piaget, while claiming a dialectical interaction between mind and environment, still falls captive to the grand narrative of intelligence. The theory walks into its own captivity because it views intelligence as a process that culminates in an individual's mastery of formal *logical* categories. The development of thinking seems to come from thinking itself, separate from the external environment. This reflects the innate fixity of earlier Cartesian-Newtonian views of intelligence as a specter emerging from innate inner structures. The early Piaget, in particular, maintained that the desired pedagogical course was to move students' development away from the emotions so that rationality could dominate the progress of the mind. Stages were thus constructed around this logocentrism—stages that would become key supports in the commonsense, unquestioned knowledge about intelligence (Piaget, 1970, 1977; Piaget, & Inhelder, 1968).

Feminist theory challenges this meta-narrative, arguing that cognizance of social construction of individuals and the inseparability of rationality and emotion cause us to question essential categories of human development. Feminists ask us to examine the difference between masculine and feminine ways of knowing (Belenky, Clinchy, Goldberger, & Tarule, 1986). The masculine, of course, represents the "proper" path for human cognitive development. Proposing that intelligence be reconceptualized in a manner that makes use of various ways of thinking, feminist theorists teach us that intelligence is not an innate quality of a particular individual, but, rather something related to the interrelationship among ideas, behaviors, contexts, and outcomes (Bozik, 1987; Lawler, 1975; Walkerdine, 1984).

Developmental psychological principles have become so much a part of teacher education programs that it is hard to see where questions about them might arise. Not understanding the etymology of cognitive developmentalism, educators are unable to see it as a system of scientific classification. Developmentalism hides behind its claim of "freeing the child" from traditional methods of instruction, protecting its identity as an order of regulation on which child-centered pedagogy has been established. Critical constructivism (a constructivism grounded on an understanding of critical theory and postmodernism) along with post-formal thinking seeks to expose developmentalism as a specific sociohistorical construction grounded in a specific set of assumptions about the mind. Developmentalism is not the only way to view intelligence. As we have come to see individualized instruction and child-centered pedagogy as a set of regulated and normalized progressive stages, we have missed the rather obvious point that individuals operate simultaneously at divergent cognitive stages. For example, an eight-year-old may employ particular skills with a computer that certainly reflect a formal-like thinking, while his or her understanding of U.S. politics reflects a more concrete-like cognitive stage. Indeed, is what Piaget described as formal thinking a "universal" stage in cognitive development? When we examine the percentage of adults who "fail" when assessed by this formal standard, its universality is brought into question. The irony in the twentieth century's history of developmental psychology is that in its concern with individual freedom and the production of a rationality that could save human beings in their struggle for survival, it produced a system of cognitive and pedagogical apparatuses that delimited and rigidly defined the normalized individual. The biological capacities developmentalism has designated have insured that even *progressive* teachers often view the child as an object of scientific pronouncement and, in the process, have undermined the liberation promised (Maher, & Rathbone, 1986; Riegal, 1973; Walkerdine, 1984).

Indeed, the child in the developmentalist discourse is often viewed, within an ethic of Lockean individualism, as an isolated entity. Critical studies (Bourdieu, & Passeron, 1977; McLaren, 1986; McLeod, 1987) have long maintained that children come to school with disparate amounts of cultural capital or awareness that can be traded in for advantage in the school microcosm. Knowledge of White middle-class language, concern for academic success, and the ability to deport oneself

## A TENTATIVE DESCRIPTION OF POST-FORMAL THINKING

in a "courteous" manner all contribute to one's advantage at school. Metaphorical constructs and meaning-making frameworks brought to school by Mexican-American, Latino, or other children who do not come from White middle-class backgrounds are often dismissed as developmentally inappropriate. Because developmentalism fails to ground itself within a critical understanding of the power relationships of dominant and subordinate cultures, it has often privileged White middle-class notions of meaning and success (O'Loughlin, 1992).

Liberatory outcomes are far from the consciousness of many curriculum makers who ground their work in the discourse of child development. Liberatory intent is also betrayed when we fail to address the critical constructivist concern with the social construction of mind. In the same way that Cartesian-Newtonian science strips away the layers of the social from our analysis, cognitive development is essentialized. The social features (race, class, gender, place) that influence patterns and definitions of development are ignored, allowing what are actually social constructions to be seen as natural processes. Here rests the practical value of the postmodern critique with its decentering of the subject. Not allowing for a pre-existent essence of self, postmodernism denies the existence of men and women outside of the socio-historical process. The grand narrative of liberal individualism is thus subverted, for objects of any type (especially knower and known, self and world) cannot be defined in isolation to one another. Cognitive development, then, is not a static, innate dimension of human beings; it is always interactive with the environment, always in the process of being reshaped and reformed. We are not simply victims of genetically determined, cognitive predispositions (Lawler, 1975; Walkerdine, 1984).

The postmodern critique not only undermines cognitive essentialism, it also subverts socio-cognitive reductionism. The normalization of social control along the lines of scientifically validated norms of development and conduct implicit within developmentalism is not the outcome of some repressive power broker determined to keep individuals in their place. Power manifests itself not through some explicit form of oppression, but via the implicit reproduction of the self. Thus, advocates of critical thinking will operate within the boundaries of developmentalism with its predetermined definitions of normality; these advocates teach and learn within its gravitational field. The task of those who understand both the social contextualization of thinking and the postmodern critique of its discursive practices is to overthrow these reductionistic views of the way power works. When we view the effect of power on the way we define intelligence, or when we construct consciousness as some simple cause-effect process, we forfeit our grasp on reality and lose our connection to the rhythms of social life (deLauretis, 1986; Walkerdine, 1984). Post-formal thinking attempts to conceive cognition in a manner that transcends the essentialist and reductionist tendencies within developmentalism, coupling an appreciation of the complexity of self-production and the role of power with some ideas about what it means to cross the borders of modernist thinking.

Since one of the most important features of post-formal thinking involves the production of one's own knowledge, it becomes important to note in any discussion of the characteristics of post-formality that few boundaries exist to limit what may be considered post-formal thinking. Post-formal thinking and post-formal teaching become whatever an individual, a student, or a teacher can produce in the realm of new understandings and knowledge within the confines of a critical system of meaning. Much of what cognitive science, and in turn the schools, have measured as intelligence consists of an external body of information. The frontier where the information of the disciplines intersects with the understandings and experience that individuals carry with them to school is the point where knowledge is created (constructed). The post-formal teacher facilitates this interaction, helping students to reinterpret their own lives and uncover new talents as a result of their encounter with school knowledge.

Viewing cognition as a process of knowledge production presages profound pedagogical changes. Teachers who frame cognition in this way see their role as creators of situations where student experiences could intersect with information gleaned from the academic disciplines. In contrast, if knowledge is viewed as simply an external body of information independent of human beings, then the role of the teacher is to take this knowledge and insert it into the minds of students. Evaluation procedures that emphasize retention of isolated bits and pieces of data are intimately tied to this view of knowledge. Conceptual thinking is discouraged, as schooling trivializes learning. Students are evaluated on the lowest level of human thinking—the ability to memorize without contextualization. Thus, unless students are moved to incorporate school information into their own lives, schooling will remain merely an unengaging rite of passage into adulthood.

The point is clear; the way we define thinking exerts a profound impact on the nature of our schools, the role that teachers play in the world, and the shape that society will ultimately take. As we delineate the following characteristics of post-formal thinking, each feature contains profound implications for the future of teaching. Indeed, the post-formal thinking described in the following section can change both the tenor of schools and the future of teaching. Self-reflection would become a priority with teachers and students, as post-formal educators attend to the impact of school and society on the shaping of the self. In such a context, teaching and learning would be considered acts of meaning-making that subvert the technicist view of teaching as the mastering of a set of techniques. Teacher education could no longer separate technique from purpose, reducing teaching to a deskilled act of rule-following and concern with methodological format. A school guided by empowered post-formal thinkers would no longer privilege White male experience as the standard by which all other experiences are measured. Such realizations would point out a guiding concern with social justice and the way unequal power relations in school and society destroy the promise of democratic life. Post-formal teachers would no longer passively accept the pronouncements of standardized-test and curriculum makers without examining the social contexts in which their students live and the ways those contexts help shape student performance. Lessons would be reconceptualized in light of a critical notion of student understanding. Post-formal teachers would ask if their classroom experiences promote, as Howard Gardner puts it, the highest level of understanding that is possible (Gardner, 1991).

Our search for such understanding is enhanced by a delineation of the following four features of post-formal thinking: *etymology*—the exploration of the forces that

## A TENTATIVE DESCRIPTION OF POST-FORMAL THINKING

produce what the culture validates as knowledge; *pattern*—the understanding of the connecting patterns and relationships that undergird the lived world; *process*—the cultivation of new ways of reading the world that attempt to make sense of both ourselves and contemporary society; and *contextualization*—the appreciation that knowledge can never stand alone or be complete in and of itself.

### ETYMOLOGY

*The origins of knowledge.* Many descriptions of higher order thinking induce us to ask questions that analyze what we know, how we come to know it, why we believe it or reject it, and how we evaluate the credibility of the evidence. Post-formal thinking shares this characteristic of other descriptions of higher order thinking, but adds a critical hermeneutic and historical epistemological dimension to the idea. In order to transcend formality, we must become critically exposed to our own tradition (and other traditions as well) so that we may understand the etymology of the cultural forms embedded within us. Antonio Gramsci (1988) noted that philosophy cannot be understood apart from the history of philosophy, nor can culture be grasped outside the history of culture. Our conception of self and world, therefore, can only become critical when we appreciate the historicity of its formation. We are never independent of the social and historical forces that surround us—we are all caught at a particular point in the web of reality. The post-formal project is to understand what that point in the web is, how it constructs our vantage point, and the ways it insidiously restricts our vision. Post-formal teachers struggle to become aware of their own ideological inheritance and its relationship to their own beliefs and value structures, interests, and questions about their professional lives (Cherryholmes, 1988; Codd, 1984; Daines, 1987; Greene, 1988).

As historical epistemologists, post-formal thinkers understand the etymology of knowledge, the way that knowledge is produced and the specific forces that contribute to its production. The *Zeitgeist* influences knowledge production as it directs our attention to certain problems and potentialities—for example, the questions of equity emerging from the civil rights movement, or the nature of religious fundamentalism coming from the rise of the New Right, or of gender bias growing out of the women's movement. As the *Zeitgeist* changes or as multiple *Zeitgeists* compete in the same era, some bodies of information go out of fashion and are forgotten for the time being. Other bodies of knowledge are shelved because they seem to be tied to one particular research methodology and are not amenable to extension into different contexts. Thus, social and educational knowledge is vulnerable to the ebb and flow of time and the changing concerns and emotional swings of different eras. This vulnerability to the temporal will probably continue, for social science shows no sign of developing consistent universal strategies for evaluating the validity of these various forms of knowledge. Indeed, such a strategy would be positivistic and suggest regression to a more formalistic mode of thinking (Fiske, 1986).

Post-formal thinkers concerned with epistemological etymology and their own subjective etymology have identified with Michel Foucault's (1984) notion of genealogy. By epistemological and subjective etymology, we are referring to: 1) the process by which social forces shape our understanding of what constitutes knowledge (is it a scientific process or are there other legitimate ways of knowing?); and 2) the process by which social forces shape our subjectivities or, less subtly, our identities. Foucault uses the term genealogy to describe the process of tracing the formation of our own subjectivities. By recognizing the ambiguities and contradictions in the construction of their own subjectivities, post-formal teachers can better understand the complexities of their students' consciousnesses. As they engage in self-critical genealogy, draw on our critical system of meaning, and employ action-research techniques, post-formal teachers become "ungrounded" and "unrigorous" from the perspective of the technicists who wag their fingers at their lack of technical procedure and formal systemization. Indeed, the self-critical genealogy and the critical action research that grows out of it constitute an emancipatory "rite of post-formal passage," as teachers leave behind their cognitive past (Kincheloe, 1991). Exercising new insights, they come to formulate more penetrating questions about their professional practice, see new levels of activity and meaning in their classrooms, decipher connections between sociocultural meanings and the everyday life of school, and reconceptualize what they already "know." As post-formal teachers grow to understand the etymology of the race, class, and gender locations of the students and others they study, they come to appreciate their own etymology, their location, and the social relationships such locations produce (Aronowitz, 1992; Miller, 1990; Reinharz, 1982).

*Thinking about thinking—exploring the uncertain play of the imagination.* Like William Pinar's notion of *currere* (the Latin root of the word "curriculum," meaning the investigation of the nature of the individual experience of the public), post-formal thinking about thinking allows us to move to our own inner world of psychological experience. The effort involves our ability to bring to conscious view our culturally created, and therefore limited, concept of both self and reality, thus revealing portions of ourselves previously hidden (Pinar, 1975). Indeed, we are again involved in an etymological exploration, the explanation of the origins of our consciousness. To think about one's own thinking in a post-formal manner involves understanding the way our consciousness is constructed and appreciating the forces that facilitate or impede our accommodations. Post-formal thinking about thinking involves our ability to engage in ideological disembedding, the ability to remove ourselves from socio-interpersonal norms and expectations. This post-formal concern with questions of meaning and attention to the process of self-production rises above the formal level of thought and its concern with proper procedure. Our conception of post-formal thinking about thinking never allows us to be content with what we have cognitively constructed. Never certain of the appropriateness of our ways of seeing and always concerned with the expansion of self-awareness and consciousness, post-formal thinkers engage in a running meta-dialogue, a constant conversation with self (Codd, 1984; Kegan, 1982).

Ancient Greeks mythologically portrayed this dialogue with self. They were fascinated by the lulls of profound silence that periodically spread across a room filled with conversation. The Greeks postulated that at such moments Hermes had entered the room. By silencing the everyday babble, Hermes allowed the Greeks to tap their imaginations, fears, hopes, and passions. Through this awareness they were freed from acting out socially constructed expectations they really didn't understand. Hermes came to symbolize the penetration of boundaries—boundaries that separated one culture from another, work from play, fantasy from reality, and consciousness from unconsciousness. As he connects us with the unconscious, Hermes becomes another in a long line of trickster gods whom ancients associated with the power of the imagination.

Post-formal thinking about thinking draws upon the boundary trespasses of Hermes and the playful parody of postmodernism to transgress the official constraints of our consciousness construction, to transcend modern convention by exposing its etymology and its ironic contradictions (Bohm, & Peat, 1987; Combs, & Holland, 1990; Hutcheon, 1988; Kramer, 1983; van Hesteran, 1986). As Peter McLaren explains the postmodern double reading of the social world, he writes of a teaching disposition that encourages students to think about their thinking in a post-formal manner. Students learn to construct their identities in a way that parodies the rigid conventions of modernism, thus assuming the role of postmodern stand-up comics, social satirists (McLaren, forthcoming). Hermes, the playful trickster, mysteriously pops up everywhere with his fantasies, surprise inspirations, and other gifts of the imagination; they are ours for the taking if we can hold onto the silence long enough to listen to him, if we have not let social expectations crush our propensity for play (Kristeva, 1980).

*Asking unique questions—problem detection.* The technical rationality of modernism has long ignored the ability to ask unique questions and to detect problems as important aspects of higher order intelligence. This modernist tradition has often reduced intelligence, and in turn the work of teachers, to problem-solving. Such cognitive reductionism restricts teaching to the level of formal thinking and captures practitioners in a culture of bureaucratic technicalization where they simply seek solutions to problems defined by their superiors (Munby, & Russell, 1989; Schon, 1983). When the work of teachers is reduced to mere problem-solving, a practitioner's ability to identify the problems of the classroom and to ask unique questions about them is neglected. Indeed, pedagogies of problem-solving and tests of intelligence that focus upon problem-solving ignore the initial steps of questioning and problem detecting, which are prerequisites to creative acts of learning and post-formal thinking (Courtney, 1988). Problem detecting is a far more holistic act than problem-solving, in that problem detecting demands understanding of the goals of social justice and the etymology of those forces that undermine them. Such etymological appreciations shape our post-formal ability to detect contradictions, conflicts in the social order.

Problem detecting is undoubtedly a necessary precondition for technical problem-solving, although problem detecting is not itself a technical problem—it cannot be approached in a formalist procedural (technical) way. As a problem is detected, questions are formulated about a situation. In the process, a coherence is imposed on the situation that exposes asymmetries and helps cultivate an intuition for what might need to be changed about the situation. The context is framed from which an observation will be made. A body of past experiences and understandings are applied in this framing process to the situation in question. Problem detecting and the questioning that accompanies it become a form of world making in that the way these operations are conducted is contingent on the system of meaning employed. For example, a teacher in a multicultural education classroom may find that the texts recommended and the conception of the classroom conveyed by the course description encourage students to ask questions about the cultural identity of a variety of minority groups. Though it is not framed as a problem in the traditional conversation about multicultural education, the post-formal teacher might detect a problem in the discourse's erasure of "Whiteness" as an ethnicity—indeed, an ethnicity with a cultural identity. Raising this issue as a problem might open a new window of insight into the ways that White ethnocentrism is constructed and how the power of dominant culture reveals itself. Such problem detecting exposes the ways White people are sometimes shielded from forms of self-reflection that might reveal the origins of condescending views of "the other." With their focus on meta-awareness, post-formal thinkers are cognizant of the relationship between the way they themselves and others frame problems and ask questions about the nature of the system of meaning they employ. They possess an understanding of the etymology of frames, even when the individual involved fails to recognize the origin of a question or a problem.

Without this meta-awareness of a system of meaning, we, as teachers and administrators, may learn how to construct schools but not how to determine what types of schools to construct. We will not grasp the connection between political disposition and the types of education that are developed. Grounded on an understanding of such connections, post-formal teachers, administrators, and teacher educators realize that school problems are not generic or innate. They are constructed by social conditions, cognitive assumptions, and power relations, and are uncovered by insightful educators who possess the ability to ask questions never before asked, questions that may lead to innovations that promote student insight, sophisticated thinking, and social justice (Munby, & Russell, 1989; Ponzio, 1985; Schon, 1987).

## PATTERN

*Exploring deep patterns and structures—uncovering the tacit forces, the hidden assumptions that shape perceptions of the world.* Physicist David Bohm helps us conceptualize this aspect of post-formal thinking with his notion of the "explicate" and "implicate" orders of reality (Bohm, & Edwards, 1991; Bohm, & Peat, 1987). The explicate order involves simple patterns and invariants in time—that is, characteristics of the world that repeat themselves in similar ways and have recognizable locations in space. Being associated with comparatively humble orders of similarities and differences, explicate orders are often what is identified by the categorization and generalization function of formal thought. The implicate order is a much deeper structure of reality. It is the level at which ostensible separateness vanishes and all things seem to become a part of a larger unified structure. The implicate order is a process, an enfolded sequence of events like the process of becoming an oak embedded in an acorn. The totality of these levels of enfolding cannot be made explicit as a whole. They can be exposed only in the emergence of a series of enfoldings. In contrast to the explicate order (which is an unfolded order) where similar differences are all present together and can be described in Cartesian-Newtonian terms, the implicate order has to be studied as a hidden pattern, sometimes impenetrable to empirical methods of inquiry (Bohm, & Peat, 1987).

Post-formal thinking's concern with deep structures is, of course, informed by an understanding of the implicate order. Many have speculated that at higher levels of human consciousness, we often peek at the implicate pattern. Profound insight in any field of study may involve the apprehension of structures not attainable at the explicate order of reality. At these points we transcend common sense—we cut patterns out of the cosmic fabric (Combs, & Holland, 1990). "Artists don't reproduce the visible," Paul Klee wrote; instead they "make things visible" (Leshan, & Margenau, 1982). Similarly, Albert Einstein often referred to his physics as based on a process of questioning unconscious assumptions so as to reveal the deep structures of the universe. The theory of relativity itself emerged from his probing of the tacit assumptions underlying classical physics, in particular, absolute conceptions of time and space (Reynolds, 1987). As Einstein exposed deep physical structures of the shape of space, he was at least approaching an implicate order of the physical universe.

Post-formal thinking works to get behind the curtain of ostensible normality. Post-formal teachers work to create situations that bring hidden assumptions to our attention and make the tacit visible. For example, an American history teacher can create a hermeneutic atmosphere, a safe learning situation where students are encouraged to seek meaning, to interpret, even to be wrong at times. In this context, the teacher could point out the implicate patriarchal order of the required U.S. history text. Predominantly a story of male triumph in the political and military spheres, the book is arranged as a story of exploration, conquest, consolidation of power, and the problems of ruling the expanding empire. Questions of women's history, the history of poverty, racial justice, moral self-reflection, the history of ideas and culture, if addressed at all, are secondary. What may be the most important dimension of such a classroom may involve the post-formal uncovering of hidden assumptions of U.S. textbook publishers. Post-formal students may come to recognize patterns of exclusion, identifying historical themes or events that are typically erased from the "American Pageant." Virginia Woolf argued that artists possess many of these same abilities: they uncover hidden realities and communicate them to their readers. These hidden realities are inseparable from implicate orders that ultimately are to be found at the base of all experience. Formal thinking has not been attuned to such a reality, possibly because the expansionist, conquest-oriented goals of the Cartesian-Newtonian paradigm emphasized the explicate order of things. The social world is in many ways like an onion—as we peel off one layer, we find another beneath. An outside layer of socio-educational reality is the standardized test performance of a school. A second layer is the assumptions behind the language that is used in discussing the curriculum. A third layer is the unspoken epistemological assumptions of the curricular reforms. A fourth layer is the body of assumptions about learning that students bring to school, ad infinitum (Bohm, & Peat, 1987; Briggs, 1990; Greene, 1988).

Unfortunately, the formalist analysis of school is grounded in the explicate order in which deep structures remain enfolded and out of sight. The dominant culture's conversation, not only about education but also about the political process, racism, sexism, and social-class bias, is formalist and focuses on the explicate order. Educators come to understand, for example, that the most damaging form of racism is not an explicate "George Wallace in 1963" variety, but an institutional racism built into the enfolded structure of schools, corporations, professional sports, and other institutions. Critical postmodern theory has taught us that little is as it appears on the surface (Giroux, 1992; Kanpol, 1992; McLaren, 1989; Pagano, 1990). When post-formal observers search for the deep structures that are there to be uncovered in any classroom, they discover a universe of hidden meanings constructed by a variety of socio-political forces. These meanings often have little to do with the intended (explicate) meanings of the official curriculum. A post-formal analysis of curriculum is grounded on the recognition that there are implicate orders of forces that shape what happens in schools—some complimentary, others contradictory, some emancipatory, others repressive. When this post-formal analysis of deep structures is applied to education, the implications for change are infinite. Imagine the way we might post-formally reconceptualize evaluation, supervision, administration, and so on. The reductionism of the explicate approach to these areas would be overthrown.

*Seeing relationships between ostensibly different things—metaphoric cognition.* Post-formal thinking draws heavily on the concept of the metaphor. Metaphoric cognition is basic to all scientific and creative thinking and involves the fusion of previously disparate concepts in unanticipated ways. The mutual interrelationships of the components of a metaphor, not the components themselves, are the most important aspects of a metaphor. Indeed, many have argued that patterns of relationships, not objects, should be the basis of scientific thinking (Gordon, Miller, & Rollock, 1990; Grumet, 1992; Rifkin, 1989). When thinking of the concept of mind, the same thoughts are relevant. We might be better served to think of mind not in terms of parts, but in terms of the connecting patterns, the dance of the interacting parts. The initial consciousness of the "poetic" recognition of this dance involves a non-verbal mental vibration, an increased energy state. From this creative tension emerges a perception of the meaning of the metaphor and the heightened consciousness that accompanies it. Post-formal teachers can model such metaphoric perception for their students. Such perception is not simply innate, it can be learned (Bohm, & Peat, 1987; Fosnot, 1988; Talbot, 1986).

Pondering the question of what is basic in education, Madeleine Grumet (1992) argues that the concept of relation, of connecting pattern, is fundamental. Ironically, she argues, it is relation that we ignore when asked to enumerate the basics. Education involves introducing a student to modes of being and acting in the world that are new to his or her experience. Grumet concludes that it is the relation, the dance between the student's experience and knowledge that separates education from training or indoctrination (Grumet, 1992). Post-formal thinkers recognize that relationships, not discrete objects, should be the basis for definitions in the sciences and humanities. From this perspective, the physical and social worlds are seen as dynamic webs of interconnected components. None of the parts of the webs are fundamental, for they follow the dance of their relationship with the other parts. The nature of their interconnections shapes the form the larger web takes. The educational implications of such a realization are revolutionary. The uncovering and interpretation of the dance becomes a central concern of teachers and students. Curricular organization, evaluation techniques, teacher education, and definitions of student and teacher success cannot remain the same if this post-formal characteristic is taken seriously (Capra, 1982; Fosnot, 1988; Talbot, 1986).

In the attempt to understand more than the explicate order of school, post-formal thinkers might draw upon the perspectives of oppressed peoples (Welch, 1991). Taking a cue from liberation theologians in Latin America, post-formal analysts begin the cognitive process of understanding the way an institution works by listening to those who have suffered most as the result of its existence. These subjugated knowledges allow post-formal thinkers to gain the cognitive power of empathy—a power that enables them to take a picture of reality from different angles, to analyze the deep patterns and structures of oppression. The intersection of these angles and the connections of these deep patterns allow for a form of analysis that moves beyond the isolated, fragmented analysis of modernity. With these ideas in mind, post-formal thinkers seek a multicultural dialogue between eastern cultures and western cultures, as well as a conversation between the relatively wealthy northern cultures and the impoverished southern cultures (Bohm, & Peat, 1987). In this way, forms of knowing that have traditionally been excluded by the modernist West move post-formal teachers to new vantage points and unexplored planetary perspectives. Understanding derived from the perspective of the excluded or the culturally different allows for an appreciation of the nature of justice, the invisibility of the process of oppression, and a recognition of difference that highlights our own social construction as individuals.

In this spirit, post-formal teachers begin to look at their lessons from the perspectives of their Asian students, their Black students, their Latino students, their White students, their poor students, their middle- and upper-middle-class students, their traditionally successful students, their unsuccessful students. They examine their teaching from the vantage points of their colleagues or outside lay observers, which helps them reveal the hidden patterns and assumptions that shape their approaches. Thus, they step out of their teacher bodies and look down on themselves and their students as outsiders. As they hover above themselves, they examine their technicist teacher education with its emphasis on bulletin board construction, behavioral objective writing, discussion skill development, and classroom management. They begin to understand that such technicist training reflects a limited formality, as it assumes that professional actions can be taught as a set of procedures (Nixon, 1981).

*Uncovering various levels of connection between mind and ecosystem—revealing larger patterns of life forces.* As a result of a dinner conversation with Albert Einstein, Carl Jung theorized his notion of synchronicity, the meaningful connection between causally unconnected events (Combs, & Holland, 1990). Jung maintained that at the center of the mind a level of consciousness existed that connected the inner world of the psyche with the outer world of physical reality. The inner world of the psyche, Jung argued, is a mirror of the outer world—thus, the origin of his notion of the collective consciousness or deep unconsciousness as a collective mirror of the universe. Such a theory implies a level of connection between mind and reality or ecosystem that opens a realm of cognition untouched by cognitive science. Peter McLaren (forthcoming) taps this post-formal level of cognition when he writes of the realm of "impossible possibility" where teaching begins to search for connections between causally unconnected phenomena. As we move beyond the Cartesian-Newtonian borders in the explosion of our postmodern cognitive revolution, we begin to transcend our current disposition of being-in-the-world, our acceptance of boredom, alienation, and injustice. In a way, we become the science fiction writers of education, imagining what is admittedly not yet possible; but because of the fact that we can conceive of it, like sci-fi writers who imagined trips to the Moon, it becomes possible (Combs, & Holland, 1990).

Post-formality is life-affirming as it transcends modernism's disdain and devaluation of the spiritual. Post-formalism, in its postmodern deconstructive manner, contests the "meaning of life"—that is, the actual definition of life. In the process of the deconstruction, it begins the task of reshaping on multiple, possibly contradictory levels, the definition of living. Transcending Cartesian-Newtonian fragmentation, post-formal thinkers understand that life may have less to do with the parts of a living thing than with patterns of information, the "nothing" of the *relations* between parts, the "dance" of a living process—that is, life as synchronicity. Postmodernism is the consummate boundary crosser, ignoring the no-trespassing signs posted at modernism's property line of certainty. It is possible that postmodernism and its socio-cognitive expression, post-formality, will lead us across the boundary dividing living and non-living. Those characteristics that modernism defined as basic to life are present in many phenomena in the universe—from sub-atomic particles to weather to seahorses. Because all life on the planet is so multi-dimensionally entwined, it is extremely hard to separate life from non-life. Indeed, some scientists have already begun to argue that the best definition of life is the entire Earth. Seen from this perspective, modernism's lack of concern with ecological balance is suicidal on many levels (Talbot, 1986). Post-formal teachers can design lessons that illustrate the physical and spiritual connections between self and ecosystem. For example, a post-formal biology teacher might design a research project that seeks to define where animate objects end and inanimate objects begin. Students would be encouraged to define "life-force" and to develop an alternative taxonomy of living entities.

The world around us (maybe more precisely, the world, an extension of us) is more like an idea than a machine. Post-formality's concern with etymology, pattern, process, and contextualization expresses a similar thought on the social level. Human beings cannot be simply separated from the contexts that have produced them. Post-formality assumes the role of the outlaw, as it points out modernism's tendency to fragment the world. Indeed, post-formality recognizes none of the official boundaries that define our separateness. This post-formal transgression of boundaries is the feminist concept of connectedness writ large (Belenky, Clinchy, Goldberger, & Tarule, 1986), a holistic connectedness that opens cognitive possibilities previously imaginable only by the dreamers. As a hologram, the brain may interpret a holographic universe on a frequency beyond Newtonian time and space (Ferguson, 1980). The only definition left for life in the postmodern world is not some secret substance or life-force, but an information pattern. This definition of life as an information pattern elevates the recognition of relationship from the cognitive to the spiritual realm, for it is the relationship that is us. The same is true for consciousness; that is, sensitive intelligence is present wherever an entity can tune into the woven mesh of cosmic information, the enchanting pattern, the implicate order of the universe. From this definition, then, the ecosystem is conscious—the "nothing" of perceived pattern is the very basis of life and mind. Post-formal thinkers thus become ambassadors to the domain of the *pattern*. The cognitive revolution initiated by post-formality reshapes the school in a way in which life and its multi-dimensional connectedness resides at the center of the curriculum. Thinking is thus conceived as a life-sustaining process undertaken in connection with other parts of the life force.

## PROCESS

*Deconstruction—seeing the world as a text to be read.* The post-formal thinker reads between the lines of a text, whether the text be, as with a physical scientist, physical reality or, for a teacher, the classroom and students. Thus, a text is more than printed material, as it involves any aspect of reality that contains encoded meaning to be deconstructed (Scholes, 1982; Whitson, 1991). Deconstruction can be defined in many ways—as a method of reading, as an interpretive process, and as a philosophical strategy. For post-formality, it involves all three of these definitions since it views the world as full of texts to be decoded, to be explored for unintended meanings. Jacques Derrida (1976) has employed deconstruction to question the integrity of texts, meaning that he refuses to accept the authority of traditional, established interpretations of the world. He has characteristically focused on elements that others find insignificant. His purpose is not to reveal what the text really means or what the author intended, but to expose an unintended current, an unnoticed contradiction within it (Culler, 1981, 1982).

When post-formal teachers view the world as a text, deconstruction can revolutionize education. No longer can the reader be passive, a pawn of text producers. Whether the text is produced by an author or by tradition, "areas of blindness" are embedded within it. When these areas are exposed, they reveal insight into the nature of how our consciousness is constructed. All texts are silent on certain points, and the task of deconstruction is to reveal the meanings of such silences (Scholes, 1982). Operating in the spirit of deconstructionism, post-formal thinkers come to realize that what is absent is often as important, or maybe more important, than what is present in a text. Employing the deconstructive process, post-formal teachers and students gain a creative role that transcends the attempt to answer correctly questions about what the author meant. After deconstruction, we can never again be so certain and comfortable with the stability of the world's meanings. Here rests a key element of post-formal thinking. Aware of the instability of meaning, post-formal thinkers abandon the quest for certainty, for closed texts. Unlike more formal thinkers in search of solutions to logical problems, post-formal thinkers are not uncomfortable with ill-structured problems with ambiguous answers.

Deconstruction represents the contemporary postmodern extension of a century of attempts in art, literature, psychology, and physics to penetrate surface appearances, to transcend the tyranny of common sense, to expose the unconsciousness of a culture. Within a deconstructive framework, consider what has happened to the Cartesian-Newtonian concept of reality in the twentieth century. The work of Albert Einstein, Werner Heisenberg, Sigmund Freud, and Carl Jung planted mines in the sea of modernity. Laying dormant until armed by the postmodernists, the mines were detonated by the ships of absolute truth. In the explosions, certainty was destroyed. In the wake of the destruction, the postmodern critique has taught us that, like fiction, science is a text. It produces "truth" no more absolute than the truth of Mozart or Dickens—it is an inventive act, a creative cognitive process.

*Connecting logic and emotion—stretching the boundaries of consciousness.* Feminist theory, Afrocentrism, and Native-American ways of knowing have raised our consciousness concerning the role of emotion in learning and knowing (Uensen, 1984; Myers, 1987; Nyang, & Vandi, 1980). In Afrocentrism and Native-American epistemologies, reality has never been divided into spiritual and material segments. Self-knowledge lays the foundation for all knowledge in these traditions, and a unified process of thinking has moved these traditions to appreciate the continuum of logic and emotion, mind and body, individual and nature, and self and other. Such appreciations have often caused great historical problems. It is only in the last thirty years that some European peoples have begun to recognize the epistemological sophistication of the African and Native-American paradigms, with their recognition of unity in all things. Thus, from the post-formal perspective, that which is deemed primitive by Western observers becomes a valuable source of insight in the attempt to attain higher levels of understanding (Kincheloe, 1991).

Feminist constructivists have maintained that emotional intensity precedes cognitive transformation to a new way of seeing. Knowing, they argue, involves emotional as well as cognitive states of mind. As such, emotions are seen as powerful knowing processes that ground cognition (Mahoney, & Lyddon, 1988). Formal thinkers in the Cartesian-Newtonian lineage are procedural knowers who unemotionally pay allegiance to a system of inquiry—indeed, they often see emotion as a pollutant in reason. Post-formal thinkers grounded in feminist theory unite logic and emotion, making use of what the emotions can understand that logic cannot. Emotionally committed to their thoughts, post-formal thinkers tap into a passion for knowing that motivates, extends, and leads them to a union with all that is to be known. Feminist scholar Barbara DuBois describes passionate scholarship as "science making, [which is] rooted in, animated by and expressive of our values" (cited in Belenky, Clinchy, Goldberger, & Tarule, 1986, p. 141).

Using a cognitive process created by the union of reason and emotion, feminist thinkers have revealed unanticipated insights gleaned from the mundane, the everyday lived world. They have exposed the existence of silences and erasures where formal thinkers had seen only "what was there." Such absences were revealed by the application of women's lived experience to the process of analysis, thus forging new connections between knower and known. Cartesian-Newtonian formalists had weeded out the self, denied their emotions and inner voices, and in the process produced restricted and object-like interpretations of social and educational situations. Using empirical definitions, these formalist object like interpretations were certain and scientific; feminist self-grounded interpretations were inferior, merely impressionistic, and journalistic. Feminist theorists came to realize that the objective cognitive process described by Piagetian formality was released from any social embeddedness or ethical responsibility. Objectivity in this sense became a signifier for ideological passivity and an acceptance of a privileged socioeconomic position. Thus, formalist objectivity came to demand a separation of logic and emotion, the devaluation of any perspective maintained with emotional conviction. Feeling is designated as an inferior form of human consciousness—those who rely on logical forms of thinking and operate within this framework can justify their repression of those associated with emotion or feeling. Feminist theorists have pointed out that the thought feeling hierarchy is one of the structures historically used by men to oppress women. In heterosexual relationships, these theorists assert, if a man is able to represent the woman's position as an emotional perspective, then he has won the argument—his is the voice worth hearing (Belenky, Clinchy, Goldberger, & Tarule, 1986; Reinharz, 1979).

The way of knowing ascribed to "rational man" defines logical abstraction as the highest level of thought—symbolic logic, mathematics, signifiers far removed from their organic function. Piaget's delineation of formality fails to appreciate these androcentric forces of decontextualization. Unlike Piaget's objective cognition, women's ways of knowing are grounded on an identification with organic life and its preservation. Rational man contends that emotions are dangerous because they exert a disorganizing effect on the progress of science. Informed by feminist perspectives and critical constructivist epistemology, post-formal teachers admit that, indeed, emotions do exert a disorganizing effect on traditional logocentric ways of knowing and rationalistic cognitive theory. But, they argue, such disorganization is a positive step in the attempt to critically accommodate our perceptions of ourselves and the world around us. Emotions thus become powerful thinking mechanisms that, when combined with logic, create a cognitive process that extends our ability to make sense of the universe (Fee, 1982; Mahoney, & Lyddon, 1988; Reinharz, 1979).

*Non-linear holism—transcending simplistic notions of the cause-effect process.* Post-formality challenges the hegemony of Cartesian-Newtonian logocentric formality, as it reverses the hierarchy of cause-effect, the temporality of modernist cause-effect rationality. In formalist thinking, cause has always been considered the origin, logically and temporally prior to effect. Post-formality upsets the certainty of this easy process by asserting that effect is what causes the cause to become a cause. Such a displacement requires a significant re-evaluation of common sense in the mundane, in everyday language. In this context, we begin to understand that while the formal operational orientation functions on the basis of the Cartesian assumption of linear causality, the post-formal perspective assumes reciprocity and holism (Kramer, 1983; van Hesteran, 1986). Holism implies that a phenomenon can't be understood by reducing it to smaller units; it can be appreciated only by viewing it as a non-linear process, an integrated whole. It is the opposite of reductionism. For example, in a film the value and significance of a particular image is lost when considered in isolation. When perceived in relationship to the rest of the film's images, it is understood as part of an organic whole. The film is the process, the totality—not a succession of discrete images (Bohm, & Peat, 1987; Talbot, 1986).

This returns us again to David Bohm's conception of the implicate order. The implicate order of a film, or a piece of music, or a painting is constantly unfolding from an original perception in the mind of the artist. More traditional conceptions of the creative process use a machine model, implying that the whole emerges out of an accumulation of detail—the whole is built out of a set of pieces. Thus, we see an important distinction between formal and post-formal thinking: creative unfolding representing a post-formal act and the sequential accumulation of detail representing a formal act. In any creative act there is an implicate order that emerges as an expression of the creator's whole life. The formal attempt to separate this holism into parts misses the essence of the creative process. Indeed, the attempt to teach based on this formalist, linear assumption will contribute little to the cultivation of creativity (Bohm, & Peat, 1987).

Thus, creative thinking originates in the holistic depths of an implicate order. Such an order does not operate in a Newtonian universe of absolute, linear time. Events happen simultaneously rather than in a particular order of succession. When Einstein or Mozart or Da Vinci saw whole structures of physics, music, or art in a single flash of insight, they grasped the implicate order, the overall structure of a set of relationships all at once. Cognitive theorists have spoken of simultaneity for years, but they have rarely dealt with how to accomplish it. Post-formality can be more specific as it reconceptualizes the process of analysis. The flash of insight where all things are considered at once involves connecting to the current of the implicate order. It is not easy to teach products of Cartesian-Newtonian consciousness construction, to think in terms of this simultaneous cognitive process and the holism it implies. Modernist thinkers have become accustomed to thinking that formal cognition with its scientific method is the zenith of human consciousness. We learn in the formal milieu to direct our attention to partial aspects of reality and to focus on a linearity consistent with our metaphors for time. In this formalist partiality we leave the whole stream of continuity, as we separate the humanities from the sciences, work from play, love from philosophy, reading from painting, the private from the public, and the political from the cognitive. The cognitive process as conceptualized by post-formalism invokes deconstruction to undermine the simple literalism of intended meanings. At the same time, this process embraces a holism that subverts formal thinking's notion of cause-effect linearity. Teachers who employ this post-formal cognitive process will be far better equipped to "read" their classrooms and the requirements of educational bureaucracies. Such teachers will be prepared to articulate the contradictions between society's educational and social goals and the realities of school practice.

## CONTEXTUALIZATION

*Attending to the setting.* The development of a context in which an observation can assume its full meaning is a key element in the construction of a post-formal mode of thinking. The literal meaning of context is "that which is braided together." Awareness of this braiding induces post-formal thinkers to examine the ecology of everything, as they realize that facts derive meaning only in the context created by other facts. For instance, only in recent years has the medical profession begun to examine the context of disease—some physicians even argue that we should study the milieu and not simply the symptoms (Ferguson, 1980). In the same way, post-formal educators have begun to acknowledge that the contextualization of what we know is more important than content. In response to technicist educators who argue the importance of content, the need to "master" the basics as an initial step of learning, post-formal teachers maintain that once a fabric of relevance has been constructed, content learning naturally follows (Ferguson, 1980).

An example of the way meaning is dependent on context might involve a listener who lacks adequate context to understand the "order" of a musical form. In many cases, such a listener will judge an avant-garde composition as meaningless. Europeans, upon hearing African music, for instance, attempted to assess it in the terms of another musical form. Unable to appreciate the context that gave meaning to the African music, the Europeans did not hear the intentions of the composers and performers with their subtle rhythms and haunting melodies. They heard primitive noise (Bohm, & Peat, 1987).

Cartesian-Newtonian thinking fails to convey a valuable perspective on cognition and teaching, as it fails in its reductionism to account for context. In modern empirical research, so-called scientific controls contribute to a more perfect isolation of the context being investigated. Attention to circumstances surrounding the object of inquiry must be temporarily suspended. This suspension of attention is based on the assumption that these extraneous circumstances will remain static long enough to allow the study to be validated. Of course, these extraneous circumstances never remain static. They are constantly interacting and shaping. To exclude them is to distort reality (Longstreet, 1982). In settings such as schools, student and teacher behavior cannot be understood without careful attention to the setting and the individuals' relationships to the traditions, norms, roles, and values that are inseparable from the lived world of the institutions. The inability of Cartesian-Newtonian researchers to say very much that is meaningful about school life is due in part to their lack of regard for the context—the often invisible, but foundational aspects of organizational life (Eisner, 1984; Wilson, 1977). John Dewey (1916) reflected this idea long ago when he argued that many thinkers regard knowledge as self-contained, as complete in itself. Knowledge, Dewey contended, could never be viewed outside the context of its relationship to other information. We only have to call to mind, Dewey wrote, what passes in our schools as acquisition of knowledge to understand how it is decontextualized and lacks any meaningful connection to the experience of students. Anticipating our notion of post-formality, Dewey concluded that an individual is a sophisticated thinker in the degree to which he or she sees an event not as something isolated, "but in its connection with the common experience of mankind" (Dewey, 1916).

*Understanding the subtle interaction of particularity and generalization.* Grounded in the Cartesian-Newtonian universe, formal thinking often emphasizes the production of generalizations. The post-formal teacher's concern with the particular, the unique experience of each learner, seems rather unscientific to the modernist educational scientist. To the post-formal teacher, the scientism, the obsession with generalization of the formal thinker is not especially helpful in the everyday world of the classroom. Formal generalization is out of sync with the rhythm of everyday life with its constant encounters with the novel and the unexpected—the particular.

When thinking is captured by Cartesian-Newtonian generalization, the nature of the particular is missed when it is treated as a sample of a species or a type—it is not itself, it is a representative. Viewed in this way, the particularistic, the individualistic has no proper name; it is alienated and anonymous. Children are interesting to the empirical researcher only as they represent something other than themselves. Joe Kincheloe and William Pinar's (1991) theory of place, which grounds post-formality's transcendence of mere generalization or mere particularity, fights formality's reductionist tendency. Place, as social theory, brings the particular into focus, but in a way that grounds it contextually in a larger understanding of the social forces that shape it. Place is the entity that brings the particularistic into focus; a sense of place sharpens our understanding of the individual and the psychological and social forces that direct her or him. Place, in other words, grounds our ways of seeing by providing the contextualization of the particular—a perspective often erased in formal forms of abstract thinking. Such contextualization connects post-formal thinkers with the insight of the visceral—its lust, fear, joy, love, and hate.

Post-formal thinking returns the particular to the educational conversation. Existing educational research focuses, for example, on public activities. Questions of social justice are public questions, often uninterested in the particularity of individual or family experience. As we are acculturated by the school, such tendencies induce us to repudiate the intimacy of our own autobiographies. Concepts as personal as epistemology are transformed into the height of abstraction, as our way of knowing becomes a public word connected with abstract theory. Indeed, the mere implication that epistemology is personal raises collegial eyebrows. In such a context, concern with the general and the abstract turns us away from place. The particularity, for example, of our home lives marked by thrilling, frightening, shameful, and proud moments is out-of-bounds in the public discourse of generalization. Such notions are translated into the everyday practice of schooling. As our children progress to the upper grades, too often they are taught to leave their particular autobiographies behind; these narratives have no place in the "real work" of school. Teachers who let themselves be known too well by students are immediately under suspicion. The curriculum is a public domain, as education leads us out of our intimate place to a world of public anonymity. Post-formal teachers fight such tendencies by drawing on student autobiography, theater, and literature to connect public knowledge to our private lives, to the formation of our subjectivities (Grumet, 1988).

*Uncovering the role of power in shaping the way the world is represented.* The way we make sense of the world around us is not as much a product of our own ability to assimilate information as it is the result of dominant ideologies or forces of power in the larger society. This dominant power insidiously blocks our ability to critically accommodate. As it blocks our recognition of exceptions, it undermines our attempt to modify our assimilated understandings of ourselves and the world. When educational leaders use particular words, metaphors, and models to design programs and policies, they reflect the effects of the influence of power. When teachers unquestioningly accept these models and metaphors and employ them to ground their instructional practices, they unwittingly allow power to shape their professional lives. Power, as Foucault (1980, 1984) argued, has served to censor and repress like a great superego; but, he continues, it also serves to produce knowledge, creating effects at the level of the formation of consciousness. As a censor in our thinking as practitioners, power serves to reward particular ways of seeing and acting. For example, teachers who desire to be recognized as successful learn to follow particular norms and conventions that may have little to do with teaching and learning per se. When teachers internalize these norms and conventions, they allow power to create a context that dictates their views of appropriate "ways of being" (Cherryholmes, 1988; Giroux, 1992; McLaren, 1989).

Post-formal thinkers, operating at a meta-cognitive level, are able to understand the way power shapes their own lives. Post-formal teachers realize that in school, power often silences the very people that education purports to empower. This is the great paradox of contemporary schooling and teacher education: educators speak of empowerment as a central goal, but often ignore the way power operates to subvert the empowerment of teachers and students. Failing to ask how curricular knowledge is produced, educational analysts infrequently address which social voices are represented in the curriculum and which voices are excluded. When such questions are not asked, the attempt to move to a higher order of cognition is undermined as both teachers and students fail to explore the ways that social forces have contributed to the production of their identities, their ability to function in the world (Giroux, & McLaren, 1988). Does it matter that we come from rich or poor homes, White or non-White families? These questions are not recognized as cognitive questions or questions of power—indeed, they are often not recognized at all. In the post-formal attempt to contextualize cognition, such questions of power must be seriously considered.

## CONCLUSION

If knowledge and consciousness are social constructions, then so is post-formal thinking—for it also emerges from a particular historical and social location. Recognizing post-formal thinking as historically situated, we in no way intend for it to be portrayed as an essential list of what constitutes higher order thinking. We offer it simply as a heuristic, an aid to further one's thinking about cognition. Post-formal thinking always includes an elastic clause—a rider that denies any claim of the objective existence of a post-formal way of thinking. It is one perspective from a particular point in the web of reality; a mere starting point in our search for what constitutes a higher level of understanding.

## REFERENCES

Aronowitz, S. (1992). *The politics of identity: Class, culture, and social movements.* New York: Routledge.
Belenky, M., Clinchy, B., Goldberger, N., & Tarule, J. (1986). *Women's ways of knowing: The development of self, voice, and mind.* New York: Basic Books.
Bohm, D., & Edwards, M. (1991). *Changing consciousness.* San Francisco: Harper.
Bohm, D., & Peat, F. (1987). *Science, order, and creativity.* New York: Bantam Books.
Bourdieu, P., & Passeron, J. (1977). *Reproduction: In education, society, and culture.* Beverly Hills, CA: Sage.
Bozik, M. (1987, November). *Critical thinking through creative thinking.* Paper presented to the Speech Communication Association, Boston.
Briggs, J. (1990). *Fire in the crucible.* Los Angeles: Jeremy Tarcher.
Capra, F. (1982). *The turning point: Science, society, and the rising culture.* New York: Simon, & Schuster.
Case, R. (1985). *Intellectual development: Birth to adulthood.* New York: Academic Press.
Cherryholmes, C. (1988). *Power and criticism: Post-structural investigations in education.* New York: Teachers College Press.
Codd, J. (1984). Introduction. In J. Codd (Ed.), *Philosophy, common sense, and action in educational administration* (pp. 8–28). Victoria, Australia: Deakin University Press.
Combs, A., & Holland, M. (1990). *Synchronicity: Science, myth, and the trickster.* New York: Paragon House.
Courtney, R. (1988). *No one way of being: A study of the practical knowledge of elementary arts teachers.* Toronto: MGS.
Culler, J. (1981). *The pursuit of signs: Semiotics, literature, deconstruction.* Ithaca, NY: Cornell University Press.
Culler, J. (1982). *On deconstruction: Theory and criticism after structuralism.* Ithaca, NY: Cornell University Press.
Daines, J. (1987). Can higher order thinking skills be taught? By what strategies? In R. Thomas (Ed.), *Higher order thinking: Definition, meaning and instructional approaches* (pp. 3–6). Washington, DC: Home Economics Education Association.
de Lauretis, T. (1986). Feminist studies/critical studies: Issues, terms, and contexts. In T. de Lauretis (Ed.), *Feminist studies/Critical studies* (pp. 1–19). Bloomington, IN: Indiana University Press.
Derrida, J. (1976). *Of grammatology.* Baltimore: Johns Hopkins University Press.
Dewey, J. (1916). *Democracy and education.* New York: Free Press.
Eisner, E. (1984). Can educational research inform educational practice? *Phi Delta Kappan, 65,* 447–452.
Fee, E. (1982). Is feminism a threat to scientific objectivity? *International Journal of Women's Studies, 4,* 378–392.
Ferguson, M. (1980). *The Aquarian conspiracy: Personal and social transformation in our time.* Los Angeles: J. P. Tarcher.
Fiske, D. (1986). Specificity of method and knowledge in social science. In D. Fiske & R. Shweder (Ed.), *Metatheory in social science: Pluralisms and subjectivities* (pp. 61–82). Chicago: University of Chicago Press.
Fosnot, C. (1988, January). *The dance of education.* Paper presented to the annual conference of the Association for Educational Communication and Technology, New Orleans.
Foucault, M. (1980). *Power/knowledge: Selected interviews and other writings, 1972–1977* (C. Gordon, Ed.). New York: Pantheon.

Foucault, M. (1984). *The Foucault reader* (P. Rabinow, Ed.). New York: Pantheon.
Gardner, H. (1983). *Frames of mind: The theory of multiple intelligences.* New York: Basic Books.
Gardner, H. (1989). *To open minds.* New York: Basic Books.
Gardner, H. (1991). *The unschooled mind: How children think and how schools should teach.* New York: Basic Books.
Giroux, H. (1992). *Border crossings: Cultural workers and the politics of education.* New York: Routledge.
Giroux, H., & McLaren, P. (1988). Teacher education and the politics of democratic reform. In H. Giroux (Ed.), *Teachers as intellectuals: Toward a critical pedagogy of learning.* Granby, MA: Bergin, & Garvey.
Gordon, E., Miller, F., & Rollock, D. (1990). Coping with communicentric bias in knowledge production in the social sciences. *Educational Researcher, 19*(3), 14–19.
Gramsci, A. (1988). *An Antonio Gramsci reader* (D. Forgacs, Ed.). New York: Schocken Books.
Greene, M. (1988). *The dialectic of freedom.* New York: Teachers College Press.
Grumet, M. (1988). *Bitter milk: Women and teaching.* Amherst, MA: University of Massachusetts Press.
Grumet, M. (1992). The curriculum: What are the basics and are we teaching them? In J. L. Kincheloe & S. R. Steinberg (Eds.), *Thirteen questions: Reframing education's conversation.* New York: Peter Lang.
Hutcheon, L. (1988). *A poetics of post modernism.* New York: Routledge.
Jensen, K. (1984). Civilization and assimilation in the colonized schooling of Native Americans. In P. Altbach & G. Kelly (Eds.), *Education and the colonial experience* (pp. 155–179). New Brunswick, NJ: Transaction Books.
Kanpol, B. (1992). *Towards a theory and practice of teacher cultural politics: Continuing the postmodern debate.* Norwood, NJ: Ablex.
Kegan, R. (1982). *The evolving self: Problem and process in human development.* Cambridge, MA: Harvard University Press.
Kincheloe, J. (1991). *Teachers as researchers: Qualitative paths to empowerment.* New York: Falmer Press.
Kincheloe, J., & Pinar, W. (1991). Introduction. In J. Kincheloe & W. Pinar (Eds.), *Curriculum as social psychoanalysis: Essays on the significance of place* (pp. 1–23). Albany, NY: State University of New York Press.
Klahr, D., & Wallace, J. (1976). *Cognitive development: An information processing view.* Hillsdale, NJ: Erlbaum.
Kramer, D. (1983). Post-formal operations? A need for further conceptualization. *Human Development, 26*, 91–105.
Kristeva, J. (1980). *Desire in language: A semiotic approach to literature and art* (L. S. Roudiez, Ed.). New York: Columbia University Press.
Lave, J. (1988). *Cognition in practice.* Cambridge, England: Cambridge University Press.
Lawler, J (1975). Dialectical philosophy and developmental psychology: Hegel and Piaget on contradiction. *Human Development, 18*, 1–17.
Leshan, L., & Margenau, H. (1982). *Einstein's space and van Gogh's sky: Physical reality and beyond.* New York: Macmillian.
Longstreet, W. (1982). Action research: A paradigm. *The Educational Forum, 46*(2), 136–149.
Maher, F., & Rathbone, C. (1986). Teacher education and feminist theory: Some implications for practice. *American Journal of Education, 94*(2), 214–235.
Mahoney, M., & Lyddon, W. (1988). Recent developments in cognitive approaches to counseling and psychotherapy. *The Counseling Psychologist, 16*(2), 190–234.
McLaren, P. (1986). *Schooling as ritual performance: Towards a political economy of educational symbols and gestures.* London: Routledge.
McLaren, P. (1989). *Life in schools.* New York: Longman.
McLaren, P. (forthcoming). Postmodernism/post-colonialism/pedagogy. *Education and Society.*
McLeod, J. (1987). *Ain't no makin' it.* Boulder, CO: Westview Press.
Miller, J. (1990). *Creating spaces and finding voices: Teachers collaborating for empowerment.* Albany, NY: State University of New York Press.
Munby, H., & Russell, T. (1989). Educating the reflective teacher: An essay review of two books by Donald Schon. *Journal of Curriculum Studies, 21*, 71–80.

Myers, L. (1987). The deep structures of culture: Relevance of traditional African culture in contemporary life. *Journal of Black Studies, 18*(1), 72–85.
Nixon, J. (1981). Postscript. In Nixon (Ed.), *A teachers' guide to action research*. London: Grant McIntyre.
Nyang, S., & Vandi, A. (1980). Pan Africanism in world history. In M. Asante & A. Vandi (Eds.), *Contemporary black thought: Alternative analyses in social and behavioral science*. Beverly Hills, CA: Sage.
O'Loughlin, M. (1992, September). *Appropriate for whom? A critique of the culture and class bias underlying developmentally appropriate practice in early childhood education*. Paper presented to conference on Reconceptualizing Early Childhood Education: Research, Theory, and Practice, Chicago.
Pagano, J. (1990). *Exiles and communities: Teaching in the patriarchal wilderness*. Albany, NY: State University of New York Press.
Piaget, J. (1970). Piaget's theory. In P. Mussen (Ed.), *Manual of child psychology* (Vol. 1, pp. 703–732). New York: Wiley.
Piaget, J. (1977). *The essential Piaget* (H. Gruber & J Voneche, Eds.). New York: Basic Books.
Piaget, J., & Garcia, R. (1989). *Psychogenesis and the history of science* (H. Feider, Trans.). New York: Columbia University Press.
Piaget, J., & Inhelder, B. (1968). *The psychology of the child*. New York: Basic Books.
Pinar, W. (1975). The analysis of educational experience. In W. Pinar (Ed.), *Curriculum theorizing: The reconceptualists*. Berkeley, CA: McCutchan.
Ponzio, R. (1985). Can we change content without changing context? *Teacher Education Quarterly, 12*(3), 39–43.
Reinharz, S. (1979). *On becoming a social scientist*. San Francisco: Jossey-Bass.
Reinharz, S. (1982). Experiential analysis: A contribution to feminist research. In G. Bowles & R. Klein (Eds.), *Theories of woman's studies* (pp. 162–191). Boston: Routledge, & Kegan Paul.
Reynolds, R. (1987). Einstein and psychology: The genetic epistemology of relativistic physics. In D. Ryan (Ed.), *Einstein and the humanities* (pp. 169–176). New York: Greenwood Press.
Riegel, K. (1973). Dialectic operations: The final period of cognitive development. *Human Development, 16*, 346–370.
Rifkin, J. (1989). *Entropy: Into the greenhouse world*. New York: Bantam Books.
Scholes, R. (1982). *Semiotics and interpretation*. New Haven, CT: Yale University Press.
Schon, D. (1983). *The reflective practitioner: How professionals think in action*. New York: Basic Books.
Schon, D. (1987). *Educating the reflective practitioner*. San Francisco: Jossey-Bass.
Talbot, M. (1986). *Beyond the quantum*. New York: Bantam Books.
Walkerdine, V. (1984). Developmental psychology and the child-centered pedagogy: The insertion of Piaget into early education. In J. Henriques, W. Hollway, C. Urwin, C. Venn, & V. Walkerdine (Eds.), *Changing the subject* (pp. 153–202). New York: Methuen.
Walkerdine, V. (1988). *The mastery of reason: Cognitive development and the production of rationality*. London: Routledge.
Walkerdine, V. (1992, April). *Redefining the subject in situated cognition theory*. Paper presented to the American Educational Research Association, San Francisco.
Welch, S. (1991). An ethic of solidarity and difference. In H. Giroux (Ed.), *Postmodernism, feminism, and cultural politics: Redrawing educational boundaries* (pp. 83–99). Albany, NY: State University of New York Press.
Whitson, J. (1991). *Constitution and curriculum*. New York: Falmer.
Wilson, S. (1977). The use of ethnographic techniques in educational research. *Review of Educational Research, 47*, 245–265.
van Hesteran, F. (1986). Counselling research in a different key: The promise of human science perspective. *Canadian Journal of Counselling, 20*(4), 200–234.

Reprinted with permission: Kincheloe, J. L., & Steinberg, S. R. (1993). A tentative description of post-formal thinking: the critical confrontation with cognitive thinking. *Harvard Educational Review, 63*, 296–320.

RAYMOND A. HORN, JR.

# RECONCEPTUALIZING EDUCATIONAL PSYCHOLOGY

*The Promotion of a Critical Consciousness*

Joe L. Kincheloe and Shirley R. Steinberg's (1996) concept of postformal thinking is essentially about the critical interpretation of reality—the dynamically ever changing process through which we socially construct the knowledge that mediates and informs our actions. Their critical confrontation with modernistic cognitive theory provides a critical cognitive alternative that is not only germane to but also essential in our confrontation with the global, local, and personal challenges of the 21st century. These challenges range from environmental crises on a planetary level, a state or region's budgetary struggle to balance income/expenditures and the provision of basic human needs, to an individual's struggle for self-identity. To critically engage these exigent challenges, Kincheloe (1999) states, "Moving beyond the certainty and authority of modernist formality is a central goal of a postformal approach" (p. 19). In opposition to the modernist/formal "focus on hidden assumptions, false notions of objectivity, and contextualization of scholarly disciplines historically and socially" (p. 19), postformalism adopts a self-critical stance that "leads to a search for new literacies that address the unique interpretive demands of hyperreality's visual imagery" (p. 19).

An additional challenge that can be significantly informed by postformal thinking deals with the nature of democracy. As a social construct, the meaning of democracy is constantly renegotiated and contested by various ideologically driven interest groups. The social justice implications of this democratic process are significant for the arrangement of power and personal identity within a society. Questions that are indicative of this challenge include: What kind of democracy should be representative of society? What kind of democracy should schools promote? What would be the nature of a democracy whose project is social justice for all? How can oppressive ideologies and regimes of practice be resisted? Postformal thinking provides a meta-cognitive process that can engage the complexity of the meaning and practice of democracy through a critical interrogation of the socio-historical context in which the meaning of democracy is embedded.

THE NATURE OF POSTFORMAL THINKING

As conceived by Kincheloe and Steinberg (1996), postformal thinking provides a multi-faceted sociocognitive process through which complex problems can be effectively detected, critically interrogated, and potentially resolved while maintaining a critical concern for social justice, democratic participation, and an ethic of care. This multilogical process draws insight from a diversity of perspectives such as "critical theory, feminist theory, critical multiculturalism, cultural studies, ecological theory, postmodernist epistemologies, indigenous knowledges, situated cognition, and post-structuralist psychoanalysis" (Kincheloe, 1999, p. 5). Kincheloe (1999) expresses the purpose behind this process:

> Using ideas taken from this variety of discourses, my purpose here involves the tentative formulation of a democratic educational psychology that is ethically and culturally grounded and that supports a critical pedagogy. Such a psychology I will refer to as postformal thinking in its cognitive manifestation and as postformal educational psychology in a more holistic sciences-of-the-psyche expression. Such an holistic discipline would include the domains typically addressed by cognitive studies, psychoanalysis, and social psychology (pp. 5–6).

Postformal thinking promotes a body of pluralistic knowledge and a bricolage of methodology that acknowledge the inherent complexity of human activity. One way that postformal thinking departs from other modernistic processes in understanding reality is in its attempt to politicize and humanize—or as Kincheloe (2004a) characterizes, "contextualize humanness" (p. 14)—the process of problem detection, critical interrogation of the situational context, and the generation of potential egalitarian solutions. Another significant difference is that, as a sociocognitive theory, postformalism "blurs boundaries separating cognition, culture, society, epistemology, history, psychoanalysis, philosophy, economics, and politics" (Kincheloe, 2004b, p. 863).

The complex nature of the challenges of our age, in relation to a desire for social justice, creates an added relevance and urgency for the promotion of postformal thinking. The processes used to detect and solve these challenges are fundamental to the successful and equitable resolution of these challenges. To a large degree, those who engage in serious attempts of problem detection and solution are now somewhat aware of the ecological nature of these problems, and of the inherent and dynamic interconnectedness and interrelationship of multiple problems and the components that comprise one specific situation. Also, some attention is given to the highly contextual nature of problems, including how the personal mediates and informs our deliberations, conclusions, and actions in relation to engaging a problem.

However, the "amoral technicism" (Kincheloe, 2004a, p. 30), systematic, procedure-based, and empirical decontextualized nature of these reductionist processes alone cannot result in a socially just resolution of a problem. Postformal thinking, as the foundation for a postformal educational psychology, provides the potential to critically interrogate the systemic and local context, the social and personal context, and the processes employed to address the issue. As this foundation, "Postformalism understands that intelligence, justice, emotion, activity, disposition, context, access, power, justice, tools, process, and ethics ad infinitum cannot be separated in the study of educational psychology" (Kincheloe, 2004a, p. 34).

Additionally, what is required is a meta-awareness that begins when "postformal thinkers are cognizant of the relationship between the way they themselves and others frame problems and ask questions about the nature of the system of meaning they employ" (Kincheloe, & Steinberg, 1996, pp. 178–179). Kincheloe and Steinberg (1996) propose that postformal thinkers operate at a meta-cognitive level, and are able to understand the way power shapes their lives (p. 191); or, as Kincheloe (2004a) proposes, "to bring individuals to a literacy of power" (p. 33). In essence, the resolution of current and future global, local, and personal problems is grounded in how we think—more accurately, in how we are able to think critically. "Postformalism grapples with purpose, devoting attention to issues of human dignity, freedom, power, authority, domination, and social responsibility" (Kincheloe, 1999, pp. 21–22). Through this meta-awareness, postformalism challenges the fact that, "Modernist psychology not only failed to study power relations and the interaction of the social and the individual but was complicit in power's shaping of subjectivity and individual perception" (Kincheloe, 1999, p. 36).

Postformal thinking provides a critical alternative to the mechanistic and rationalistic processes of cognition that are limited in scope due to their failure to include the additional contexts of human activity (e.g., the social, political, economic, cultural, etc.) and their singular emphasis on quantitative method and data. In postformal thinking Kincheloe (2004a) reports, "…no individual activity exists in simple isolation" (p. 13). Kincheloe (2004a) states, "The mechanistic tradition of educational psychology from behaviorism to cognitivism has emphasized the quantifiable behavior of groups of individuals—focusing in particular on producing generalizable empirical data about these aggregates of people" (p. 3). Kincheloe succinctly summarizes the critical consequences of this narrow modernist view of human activity. "Indeed, we have often found the social, political, pedagogical, economic, and philosophical influences of this dominant impulse to be profoundly harmful to those—especially those marginalized because of race, class, gender, national origin, ethnicity, geographic place, etc.—who are vulnerable to its power" (p. 3).

Kincheloe and Steinberg (1996) theorized that postformal thinking involved a meta-awareness of etymology, pattern, process, and contextualization in the discernment of a situation. Fundamental to this meta-awareness is the realization that knowledge and consciousness, as well as the postformal thinking process, are social constructions and emerge from a particular historical and social location (Kincheloe, & Steinberg, 1996, p. 192). "The critical hermeneutic that postformality incorporates is a socio-historical analysis that seeks to understand the circumstances under which knowledge and meaning are produced (by scholars and the powerful) and received (by students and other consumers)" (Kincheloe, 1999, p. 22). After all, "We are never independent of the social and historical forces that surround us—we are all caught at a particular point in the web of reality" (Kincheloe, & Steinberg, 1996, p. 175).

In relation to the humanizing potential of postformal thinking, Kincheloe (1999) describes the meta-analytic range of postformal thinking. "In this context the new psychology emphasizes the impact of power on the 1) intrapersonal—the domain of consciousness; 2) interpersonal—the domain of relationships, social interactions; and 3) corporeality—the domain of the body and behavior, people's physical presence in the social world" (p. 36).

Another central aspect of the range of postformal thinking is its attention to knowledge production, especially in relation to how an individual interrogates self-knowledge. Kincheloe and Steinberg (1996) state, "Since one of the most important features of postformal thinking involves the production of one's own knowledge, it becomes important to note in any discussion of the characteristics of postformality that boundaries exist to limit what may be considered postformal thinking. Postformal thinking and postformal teaching become whatever an individual, a student, or a teacher can produce in the realm of new understandings and knowledge within the confines of a critical system of meaning" (p. 173).

## CHALLENGING COMPLEXITY: A CRITICAL PRAXIS

Postformal thinking acknowledges and critically engages the inherent complexity of reality. Unlike modernist psychology's claim of objectivity that ignores the theoretical presuppositions present in any act of knowledge production (Kincheloe, 1999, p. 42), postformal thinking represents "a multidisciplinary psychology with social, economic, cultural, political, and philosophical dimensions" (Kincheloe, 2004a, p. 8) that, through an epistemological pluralism and a diversity of paradigmatic perspectives, engages the complexity of reality and its oppressive dimensions.

Kincheloe postformally addresses social complexity through the employment of a multilogic perspective of a research bricolage. "Bricolage involves taking research strategies from a variety of disciplines and traditions as they are needed in the unfolding context of the research situation. Such a position is pragmatic and strategic, demanding a self-consciousness and an awareness of context from the researcher" (Kincheloe, 1998, p. 120). Integral to this bricolage are all the definitions of deconstruction, "as a method of reading, as an interpretive process, and as a philosophical strategy" (Kincheloe, & Steinberg, 1996, p. 184).

Building upon the multidisciplinary terrain of interpretivism (2004a, p. 13), Kincheloe's reconceptualization of a postformal bricolage synergetically connects with his understanding of critical theory, critical pedagogy, and critical multiculturalism. Kincheloe's perspective on bricolage foundationally resonates with the precepts of postformal thinking—etymology, pattern recognition, process, and contextualization. Within this perspective, the postformal bricoleur engages multiple epistemologies, intertextuality, underlying cultural assumptions, the role of power, interconnectedness and difference, and the interdisciplinarity of knowledge (Kincheloe, 2004a). Through this postformal inquiry, the bricoleur "moves into a new zone of emergent complexity" (Kincheloe, 2004a, p. 38) in which "knowledge must be enacted—understood at the level of human beings' affect and intellect" (p. 38).

This more complex understanding of social reality "promotes a meta-understanding of power that is aware of the ways all frames of reference and all approaches to research are shaped by dominant ideologies, discourses, and values" (Kincheloe, 2004c, p. 99). In turn, this meta-awareness facilitates a critical praxis informed by a critical consciousness. Indeed as Kincheloe (2004d) proposes, the multilogicality of bricolage rests at the heart of postformalism (pp. 879–880). It is through this postformal praxis that individuals can engage in a cycle of critical reflection and action to transform themselves and their world.

## A CRISIS OF CONSCIOUSNESS

Bela Banathy (1996) has written about a crisis of consciousness in our society because "we have yet to create a unity of consciousness" (pp. 315–316). Others have linked considerations of consciousness to human social evolution because "during the past 30 years, our basic social and economic systems have attempted to maintain the status quo despite the many warnings that the old ways, particularly in the developed world, were no longer sustainable. In many instances our existing systems are not humane; homelessness, hunger, disease, and poverty consume the lives of hundreds of millions of people and the environment continues to degrade" (Hubbard, 1998, p. 11). Related to this line of thought are the contributions from fields other than education that refer to the intricate and interwoven pattern, structure, and organization of human activity systems (Goerner, 1999), as well as the multi-dimensional aspect of the order of reality (Bohm, 1980; Bohm, & Edwards, 1992; Capra, 1991). All of this is germane to the process of postformal thinking and its central project.

Postformal thinking provides a theoretical foundation and a critically pragmatic praxis to deal with the crisis of consciousness and advance social evolution. Postformalism has the potential to be an integral mediating and synergizing process in the conscious evolution of our thinking, feeling, knowledge production, and socially responsible actions. This can be accomplished through the development of a critical consciousness and the promotion of critical, pragmatic and emancipatory praxis.

Within individual and collective contexts, postformalism connects the processes that we can use to the state of consciousness that we want to attain. Kincheloe (1999) addresses this connection. "The concept of negation, central to critical theory and to accommodation [in the Piagetian process of cognitive development], involves the continuous criticism and reconstruction of what one thinks she knows. For example, critical theorist Max Horkheimer argued that through negation we develop a critical consciousness that allows us to transcend old codified world views and incorporate our new understandings into a new reflective attitude" (p. 14).

Because of the "interrelationship between consciousness and culture" (Kincheloe, 2004a, p. 30), a time in which there is a crisis of consciousness demands the promotion of a critical consciousness and the subsequent employment of a critical praxis. In his critique of Piaget's concept of accommodation, Kincheloe (1999) proposes a critical accommodation, or "new ways of seeing" (p. 15) that allows us "to think in terms of anticipatory accommodation, that is we anticipate what we might encounter in similar situations, what strategies might work in our attempt to bring about emancipatory outcomes" (p. 18).

Central to a postformal confrontation with the crisis of consciousness is the development of a "new mode of selfhood" (Kincheloe, 2004e, p. 894). Kincheloe (2004a) proposes, "To describe cognitive processes without an understanding of the construction of identity and selfhood or devoid of insight into the nature of consciousness provides little help in the larger effort to make sense of human beings and their relationship to the processes of teaching and learning" (p. 13). From a critical ontological perspective, "in a postformalist critical ontology we are concerned with understanding the sociopolitical construction of the self in order to conceptualize and enact new ways of being human. These new ways of being human always have to do with the critical interpretivist psychological insight that selfhood is more a relational than an individual dynamic" (Kincheloe, 2004a, p. 36).

The development of a postformal critical consciousness is predicated on the idea that "identity itself must be contextualized. Identity thus is decentered by its social, power-related, and linguistic situatedness" (Kincheloe, 1999, p. 23). This decentering of one's identify allows the self to engage alternate rationalities, which "employ forms of analysis sensitive to signs and symbols, the power of context in relation to thinking, the role of emotion and feeling in cognitive activity, and the value of the psychoanalytic process as it taps into the recesses of (un)consciousness" (Kincheloe, 2004b, p. 863). Postformally, engaging alternate rationalities allows a critical interrogation of one's self and socially constructed identify. "Such a critique interrogates the deep structures that help shape our consciousness as well as the historical context that gave birth to the deep structures" (p. 862). Kincheloe (2004b) maintains, "In this sociohistorically contextualized postformal effort to uncover the sources of consciousness construction, we attempt to use such insights to change the world and promote human possibility" (p. 862).

As a holistic paradigm, postformalism further engages a crisis of consciousness through a reconceptualization of the relationship between emotion, intuition, and reason. Unlike the modernistic bifurcation of emotion and reason, a critical consciousness that is grounded in postformalism recognizes that "emotion can connect us to the world in ways that reason cannot—and vice versa" (Kincheloe, 1999, p. 7). Kincheloe and Steinberg (1996) note that "emotions do exert a disorganizing effect on traditional logocentric ways of knowing and rationalistic cognitive theory," however, "such disorganization is a positive step in the attempt to critically accommodate our perceptions of ourselves and the world around us" (p. 187). In addition, "instead of being conflictual, the relationship between intuition and reason is synergistic" (Kincheloe, 1999, p. 26). In valuing and utilizing these three manifestations of humanness individually and as interrelated, the critically conscious postformal thinker is empowered within a critical praxis.

## CONCLUSION

Those who are mired in a modernistic view of reality may ask questions such as, what is the value of postformalism, or why should we challenge our traditional understanding of reality? These questions could be answered in a theoretical context by explaining how the development of a postformal literacy helps us develop a critical awareness that can result in the implementation of a critically informed praxis. Or, we could discuss how postformal inquiry results in the construction of a postformal container in which personal and collective consciousness is both interrogated and nurtured. In addition, postformal inquiry promotes the construction of metacognitive leverage points that make personal and social constructions accessible to further critique through the employment of postformal analytical lenses.

Also, a more critical pragmatic stance could be offered as an answer. This stance could identify the necessity of building epistemological and research capacity for postformalist public intellectuals to provide a way out, an escape from the ideological blinders of the mechanistic worldview (Kincheloe, 2004a, p. 32) Through the use of postformal theory and practice, these public intellectuals could protect idealistic visions from developing uncritical essentializing metanarratives that merely replace the outdated modernistic metanarratives.

Through postformal conversation, postformalism acts as a safeguard in the interrogation of the coexistence of societal elements of modernism and postmodernism. Kincheloe and Steinberg allude to this coexistence in the intent of their postformal proposition. "We have sought a middle ground that attempts to hold onto the progressive and democratic features of modernism while drawing upon the insights postmodernism provides concerning the failure of reason, the tyranny of grand narratives, the limitations of science, and the repositioning of relationships between dominant and subordinate cultural groups" (1996, p. 168). In this context, postformalism can protect and enhance idealistic visions, "expanding our understanding of complexity and challenging critical theory itself" (Kincheloe, 2004a, p. 29). Postformalism allows individuals to enact reflective, contextualized, and critical forms of thinking that connect our ability to think critically with issues of ethical sensibility and social reform (Kincheloe, 2004a, p. 33).

Finally, Joe Kincheloe (1999) talked about the "wounded spirit," and "cognitive illness" that permeates contemporary human activity. To counter these deleterious conditions of spirit and cognition, Kincheloe (2004a) proposes, "As it integrates the powerful insights emerging from the interpretivist tradition in educational psychology, constructivism, situated cognition, enactivism, and multiple forms of criticality, postformal pushes the cognitive envelope" (p. 38). Or simply, as Joe Kincheloe said, "I want 'smartin' up' in all the complexity that our study of these multiple and interrelated domains informs us" (p. 34).

## REFERENCES

Banathy, B. H. (1996). *Designing social systems in a changing world*. New York: Plenum Press.
Bohm, D. (1980). *Wholeness and the implicate order*. New York: Routledge.
Bohm, D., & Edwards, M. (1991). *Changing consciousness*. San Francisco: Harper.
Capra, F. (1991). *The Tao of physics*. Boston: Shambhala.
Goerner, S. J. (1999). *After the clockwork universe: The emerging science and culture of integral society*. Edinburgh, UK: Floris Books.
Hubbard, B. M. (1998). *Conscious evolution: Awakening the power of our social potential*. Novato, CA: New World Library.
Kincheloe, J. L. (1998). Critical research in science education. In B. Fraser & K. Tobin (Eds.), *International handbook of science education* (pp. 1191–1205). Boston: Kluwer Academic Publishers.
Kincheloe, J. L. (1999). Trouble ahead, trouble behind: Grounding the postformal critique of educational psychology. In J. L. Kincheloe & S. R. Steinberg (Eds.), *The postformal reader: Cognition and education* (pp. 4–54). New York: Falmer Press.
Kincheloe, J. L. (2004a). Introduction: Educational psychology—Limitations and possibilities. In J. L. Kincheloe & R. A. Horn (Eds.), *The Praeger handbook of educational psychology* (pp. 3–40). Westport, CT: Praeger.
Kincheloe, J. L. (2004b). Critical constructivism and postformalism: New ways of thinking and being. In J. L. Kincheloe & R. A. Horn (Eds.), *The Praeger handbook of educational psychology* (pp. 855–863). Westport, CT: Praeger.

Kincheloe, J. L. (2004c). Redefining and interpreting the object of study. In J. L. Kincheloe & K. S. Berry (Eds.), *Rigour and complexity in educational research: Conceptualizing the bricolage* (pp. 82–102). London: Open University Press.

Kincheloe, J. L. (2004d). Postformalism and critical multiculturalism: Educational psychology and the power of multilogicality. In J. L. Kincheloe & R. A. Horn (Eds.), *The Praeger handbook of educational psychology* (pp. 876–883). Westport, CT: Praeger.

Kincheloe, J. L. (2004e). Postformalism and critical ontology—Part 2: The relational self and enacted cognition. In J. L. Kincheloe & R. A. Horn (Eds.), *The Praeger handbook of educational psychology* (pp. 892–898). Westport, CT: Praeger.

Kincheloe, J. L., & Steinberg, S. R. (1996). A tentative description of postformal thinking: The critical confrontation with cognitive theory. In P. Leistyna, A. Woodrum, & S. A. Sherblom (Eds.), *Breaking free: The transformative power of critical pedagogy* (pp. 167–198). Cambridge, MA: Harvard Educational Review.

*Etymologically speaking, this article was a single parent to Joe's articulation of bricolage a decade later. As he began to chair dissertation committees, he became aware of the lack of heart within even the qualitative research methods. He saw most qualitative research as removed from the personal, and removed from alternative methods. The work needed to be moved from the modernist notion of staying within a "methodology," and to a way in which to create a researcher/writer/scholar, one intricately and personally connected to the work. Naturally, this construct was not heralded in with trumpets, and indeed, to this day, there is still the need to convince committee members that it is not unscholarly to insert and intertwine oneself within the research...to blend the knower and the known. When Joe wrote this piece, I remember him contacting many of the scholars he cited, and starting to create lifelong friendships and scholarship with them. Joe was quick to humbly contact someone whose work he read and admired, mention the influence of their work on his own, and engage them in new projects or concepts. SS*

JOE L. KINCHELOE

## 4. MEET ME BEHIND THE CURTAIN

*The Struggle for a Critical Postmodern Action Research*

Teacher education's historical encounters with the domain of research have produced very few benefits. Assuming this failure, this chapter analyzes the action-research movement in a critical postmodern context, attempting in the process to theorize new ways of conceiving of teachers as researchers engaged in reflective and democratic practice. The research component of teacher education programs has typically involved a watered-down statistics course in master's curricula and nothing at all in pre-service programs. Action-research concepts such as the promotion of greater teacher self-understanding of his or her practices, conceptual change, and an appreciation of the social forces that shape the school are ignored in the traditional teacher research classes. Such classes with their circumscribed notions of research miss the specificity of the teaching act, the uniqueness of the teaching workplace, the ambiguity of practitioner ways of knowing. If we are serious about the production of critical, reflective practitioners, then *democratic* action research cannot be separated from a single component of teacher education. The postmodern form of this democratic action research demands interrogation.

I will begin that questioning with an examination of the roots of this contemporary action-research movement in education. As early as the 1940s Kurt Lewin called for action research in social psychology. Taking their cue from Lewin, leaders in spheres as disparate as industry and American Indian affairs advocated action research. During the post-world War II era Stephen Corey at Teacher's College led the action-research movement in education. Corey argued that action research could help reform curriculum practice, as teachers applied the results of their own inquiry. There was considerable enthusiasm for the movement in the post-war period, but by the late 1950s action research became the target of serious criticism and started to decline. Analysts have posited that the decline was precipitated by the bifurcation of science and practice which resulted from the growth of the cult of the expert. As policymakers came to rely more and more on expert educational research and developmental laboratories, the development of curriculum and pedagogical practices was dictated from the top down. Thus, the production of research was separated from the ambiguous and complex world of the practitioner.

When action research was rediscovered in the United Kingdom in the 1970s, motivation for its resuscitation involved the growing acceptance of the positivistic view of knowledge with its emphasis on specified, measurable learning outcomes and its degradation of the role of teacher as self-directed professional. Educators were beginning to question the usefulness of positivism's abstract generalizations in the concrete and usefulness of positivism's abstract situations in which they operated on a daily basis (McKernan, 1988, pp. 174–79; Elliott, 1989a, p. 5). Still, however, teacher education continues to assume a research dimension of professional studies that involved the training of teachers in the use of quantitative methods. Research was defined as a positivistic form of data gathering and generalization production. So ingrained and unchallenged were such definitions of research that when action research advocates involved teachers in on-site teacher inquiry projects, the teachers reported that they did not consider themselves, to have taken part in "real" research. Even those who felt that they had taken part in research maintained that it was a very low quality activity. Their college of education-generated definition of research as a controlled experimental design, replete with systematic statistical analysis, seemed to undermine their ability to reconceptualize what form research might take or how it might be connected to their lives as practitioners (van Hesteran, 1986, pp. 217–18; Ross, 1984, p. 114).

Fighting the image of research in the conventional wisdom, advocates of action research began to evoke new interest in the late 1970s. Aligning themselves with the attempt to redefine teacher professionalism, action researchers gained unprecedented respectability in the 1980s. In the midst of its success, action research found itself being molded and defined by many of the same people who had promoted the traditional forms of research in colleges of education. More critical teacher educators began to express concerns over the foundations of what often passed for teacher action research. Fearing a technocratic co-optation of such inquiry, Patti Lather argued in 1986 that much of the action research conducted in schools was not critically grounded. Lather was correct then and now, as, unfortunately, much of the teacher research in the 1990s remains ahistorical and apolitical. As such, it lends itself to subversion by educational leaders who are tempted to employ a technical form of action research as a means of engineering practitioner "improvements" (Lather, 1986, p. 263).

For example, many school projects have viewed teachers as researchers as implementers of theoretical strategies devised by researcher experts or administrators. In such situations teacher research involves testing how well particular strategies work through the analysis of particular techniques in their own classrooms. Promoted as teacher-friendly, these projects in the name of creating democratic workplaces actually promote a very restricted view of the role of teachers. Teachers are supporting actors incapable of playing leading roles, that is, in developing critical perspectives at the level of ideas (Connelly and BenPeretz, 1980, pp. 90–100)—teachers in this context are still seen as mere executors. Advocates of teacher research who support this implementation orientation are quite naive when it comes to the realm of ideology. They do not realize that the act of administrators selecting problems for teachers to research is an ideological act, an act that trivializes the role of teachers. When administrators select problems for teacher researchers to explore, they negate the critical dimension of action research.

When the critical dimension of teacher research is negated, the teacher-as-researcher movement can become quite a trivial enterprise. Uncritical educational action research seeks direct applications of information gleaned to specific situations—a cookbook style of technical thinking is encouraged, characterized by recipe-following teachers. Such thinking does not allow for complex reconceptualizations of knowledge and as a result fails to understand the ambiguities and the ideological structures of the classroom. Teachers, in this context, retreat to cause-effect analysis, failing to grasp the interactive intricacy of a classroom. The point that educational problems are better understood when considered in a relational way that transcends simple linearity is missed. Thus, teacher research becomes a reifying institutional function, as teachers, like their administrators and supervisors, fail to reveal the ways that the educational bureaucracy and the assumptions that support it constrain one's ability to devise new and more emancipatory understandings of how schools work (Orteza y Miranda, 1988, p. 31).

Teacher research is co-opted, and its democratic edge is blunted. It becomes a popular grassroots movement that can be supported by the power hierarchy—it does not threaten, nor is it threatened. Asking trivial questions, the movement presents no radical challenges or offers no transformative vision of educational purpose, as it acts in ignorance of deep structures of schooling such as the positivistic view of educational knowledge. Teachers are assumed to be couriers, that is, information deliverers and are accorded a corresponding lack of status in the workplace (Ruddick, 1989, p. 9; Ponzio, 1985, pp. 39–43). Uncritical educational action research fails to recognize that inquiry must always subject its findings to assessment and some form of critical analysis—and critical analysis is always dangerous in its unpredictability and transformative character.

What exactly is the difference between a co-opted form of teacher research and a critical form of teacher research? In both *Teachers as Researchers: Qualitative Inquiry as a Path to Empowerment* (1991) and *Toward a Critical Politics of Teacher Thinking: Mapping the Postmodern* (1993), I have attempted to delineate the requirements of critical action research. First, it rejects Cartesian-Newtonian notions of rationality, objectivity, and truth. Critical action research assumes the methods and issues of research are always political in character. Second, critical action researchers are aware of their own value commitments, the value commitments of others and the values promoted by the dominant culture. In other words, one of the main concerns of critical action research involves the exposure of the relationship between personal values and practice. Third, critical action researchers are aware of the social construction of professional consciousness. Fourth critical action researchers attempt to uncover those aspects of the dominant social order which undermine our effort to pursue emancipatory goals. And fifth, critical action research is always conceived in relation to practice—it exists to improve practice.

When conducted with these criteria in mind, critical action research is the consummate democratic act, as it allows teachers to help determine the conditions of their own work. Critical action research facilitates the attempt of teachers to organize themselves into communities of researchers dedicated to emancipatory experience for themselves and their students. When teachers unite with students and community members in the attempt to ask serious questions about what is taught, how it is taught, and what should constitute the goals of a school, not only is critical self-reflection promoted but group decision making becomes a reality (Carr and Kemmis, 1986, pp. 221–23; Aronowitz and Giroux, 1985, p. 81).

Action research as defined here becomes the (logical) educational extension of a postmodern critical social theory. Since critical theory is grounded in a recognition of the existence of oppression, it stands to reason that the forces of this oppression have to be identified. Action research serves as a perfect vehicle for such a search. Without this critical recognition of domination and oppression, action researchers will simply consider the school site as value neutral and their role as disinterested, dispassionate observers. Change in this context is irrelevant—and according to Cartesian-Newtonian perspectives on research, this is the way it should be. Researchers are to maintain an uncommitted view toward the actions they encounter. In a world of oppression, critical theorists argue, ethical behavior demands that such dispassion must be confronted (Giroux and McLaren, 1991, p. 70; Codd, 1984, pp. 10–11).

Whenever we dispense with values, political considerations, or historical context, our attempt to understand the situation we are researching is weakened. Our appreciation of an educational situation is contingent on the context within which we encountered it and the theoretical frames we brought with us to the observation. Cartesian-Newtonian modernism has told us that our research must serve no specific cause but critical postmodernism has caused us to realize that every historical period produces rules that dictate what non-partisanship entails. In other words, different rules privilege different causes. Thus what we "see" as researchers is shaped by particular world views, values, political perspectives, conceptions of race, class, and gender relations, definitions of intelligence, and so on. Research, thus, can never be nonpartisan for we must choose the rules that guide us as researchers; critical theory's exposé of the hidden ideological assumptions within educational research marked the end of our innocence (Aronowitz, 1983, p. 60; Elliott, 1989b, p. 214).

To be critical is to assume that humans are active agents whose reflective self-analysis, whose knowledge of the world, leads to action. Action research is the logical extension of critical theory in that it provides the apparatus for the human species to look at itself. Critical action research that is aware of the postmodern perspectives on the production of subjectivity and the context of hyperreality can contribute to the sociocognitive emancipation of men and women. Such a sociocognitive emancipation is the first step in our cognitive revolution; our postformal effort to see the world and ourselves from new angles. Based on a democratic dialogue, an awareness of historical moment, and a passionate commitment to the voice of the oppressed, the postmodern insurrection redefines research, in the process producing a knowledge between the cracks, information previously swept under the rug.

In schools the firsthand, up-close perspectives of teachers previously relegated to a lesser significance are valued by action research as kinetic knowledge—that is, knowledge with potential to wreak havoc. This information gained through action research's emphasis on observation and reflection promotes democratic change grounded on the understanding of participants. In the modernist discourse of science such an emphasis constitutes a radical change of approach (Codd, 1984, pp. 27–28; Young, 1990, pp. 149, 158). Action that reflective individuals take to correct the social and individual pathologies uncovered by teachers can be negotiated after the action-research process is completed. The critical core of critical action research involves its participatory and communally discursive structure and the cycle of action and reflection it initiates. Such a cycle does not produce a set of rules and precise regulations for the action it promotes. Critical postmodern action research provides a provisional framework of principles around which action can be discussed rather than a set of procedures. Teachers who engage in critical action research are never certain of the exact path of action they will take as a result of their inquiry (Young, 1990, p. 158; Popkewitz, 1981).

A central art of this action involves the redefinition of knowledge. There are many dimensions to this redefining process, but one of the most important involves democratizing access to knowledge in schools and society. If knowledge is a form of cultural capital, then lack of access to it spells major problems for those on the margins of the culture of knowledge. Foucault has convinced us that knowledge is power, and though it is a hard pill for advocates of teacher empowerment to swallow, part of the reason that the teaching corps is delegated to the margins is that too many of them are ill-educated in colleges and teacher education programs. Teachers with weak academic, theoretical, and pedagogical backgrounds must defer to the judgments of educational leaders, the certified experts. The culture of technicist teacher education has tacitly instructed teachers across the generations to undervalue the domain of theory while avoiding questions of the ideological, psychological, and pedagogical assumptions underlying their practice. The power that comes from such understanding is a prerequisite for the critical attempt to redefine knowledge. Teachers must understand the social and political factors that contribute to knowledge production—indeed, the gaining of such an awareness should be a central concern of critical action research (May and Zimpher, 1986, pp. 94–95; Porter, 1988, p. 508; Maeroff, 1988, p. 508; Tripp, 1988, p. 19; Giroux, 1992, pp. 98–99, 238).

Critical knowledge production begins when action researchers illuminate the taken-for-granted. Dewey focused our attention on such a process when he argued that teachers should operate on the basis of a reflective action that disembodies moral, ethical, and political issues from mundane thinking and practice. As action researchers maintain such a perspective in their everyday experience, they are able to explore the tacit forces that have encoded their own lives and their students' lives. In a sense, critical action researchers relearn the way they have come to view the world around them—indeed, they awaken from the modernist dream with its unexamined landscape of knowledge and unimaginative consciousness construction. Once awake, critical teachers as researchers begin to see schools as human creations with meanings and possibilities lurking beneath the surface appearances. Their task becomes the interpretation of schools, not just the chronicling of surface characteristics devoid of context (Hultgren, 1987, p. 28; May and Zimpher, 1986, p. 94; Lesko, 1988, p. 147).

What do particular forms of teacher evaluation tell us about the purposes and values of my school, teacher researchers ask. Looking below the surface of standardized-test driven, behavioral assessment models of teacher evaluation, action researchers begin to uncover patterns of technicalization that erase teacher input into the determination of their own professional lives. Empowered with such knowledge, teachers gain the language to argue a case for their involvement in school policy. When principals and supervisors, for example, argue that teacher evaluation instruments necessitate particular forms of assessment, teachers will be able to point out that embedded within such instruments is an entire set of political, epistemological, cognitive, and pedagogical assumptions. Thus teachers will enter into a sophisticated, theoretically grounded negotiation with administrators about the terms of their evaluations, the terms of their professional lives.

Obviously, critical theory-based action research attempts not simply to understand or describe the world of practice but to change it. Proponents of such inquiry hope teacher education students will learn to use action research in a way that will empower them to shape schools in accordance with well-analyzed moral, ethical, and political principles. Teachers who enter schools with such an ability are ready to make a cognitive leap—indeed, the stage has been set for movement to the realm of a postmodern practitioner thinking. As critical action researchers endowed with a vision of what could be and a mechanism for uncovering what is, these teachers are able to see the sociopolitical contradictions of schools in a concrete and obvious manner. Such recognitions force teachers to think about their own thinking, as they begin to understand how these sociopolitical distortions had tacitly worked to shape their worldviews and their self-images. With a deeper appreciation of such processes, practitioners recognize the insidious ways power operates to create oppressive conditions for some groups and privilege for others. Thus critical teacher research opens new ways of knowing that transcend formal analysis (May and Zimpher, 1986, pp. 94–95; Hultgren, 1987, pp. 27–30).

Such teachers as researchers cannot help but turn to biographical and autobiographical analysis in their inquiry. Aware of past descriptions of higher-order thinking, such teachers in this situation become researchers of themselves, researchers of the formation of their own cognitive structures. Such inquiry produces a meta-awareness of an omnipresent feature of the role of critical postmodern teachers. They are always in the process of being changed and changing, of being analyzed and analyzing, of being constructed and constructing, of learning and teaching, of disembedding and connecting. The purpose of critical action research, thus, is not to produce data and better theories about education—it is to produce a metatheoretical understanding supported by reflection and grounded in sociohistorical context (Carr and Kemmis, 1986, pp. 39, 56, 123; May and Zimpher, 1986, p. 94).

The metatheoretical and the self-reflective qualities of teacher research are forever intertwined with the process of sharing this practitioner research with others. One practitioner sharing his or her research with another is the best way known to foster a healthy questioning and a meaningful dialogue between practitioners. Successful dialogues will produce "felt responses" and further introspection, further revelations of ideological domination. Such interactions will move teachers to expose the sociopolitical values in their research and teaching, uncover the ideological assumptions that have directed their practices, and reveal the impact of their own race, class, gender, and religious affiliations on their everyday lives (Reinharz, 1982, pp. 182–83). This self-reflective quality of the teacher as researcher brings to center stage an extremely important dimension that the uncritical teacher research misses. As the critical action researcher begins to reflect on his or her own consciousness, the realization begins to emerge that it has been shaped by a panoply of ideological forces—forces that often blind the teacher to an understanding of a multitude of important dimensions of classroom life.

If this is true of the practitioners themselves, then the same ideological forces must work to shape the everyday understanding, the self-perceptions of research subjects, namely, people in general. The very essence of critical teacher research involves the return to this realization—that subjects participating in social practices understand what is happening in their own lives, their own microcosms.

Of course, the way we teach or conduct research are products of these influences (Cherryholmes, 1988, pp. 111). If we are to ever operate as emancipated self-directed adults, we must confront the power of these forces. Indeed, in this confrontation we are obliged to deconstruct the power relations and the assumptions embedded in the term, emancipation. When post-structuralism confronts emancipation, some interesting things begin to happen. Action researchers should carefully watch the encounter. First, emancipation can no longer claim to be the "blessed redeemer" of educational and sociopolitical life once exposed to the provisionality of post-structuralism. Second, after a poststructuralist interrogation, emancipation's patriarchal foundations are revealed—as Gayatri Spivak (1987, pp. 88–89) points out, no concept is free of the Nietzschean will to power. Third, informed by poststructuralist concerns, advocates of emancipation never again allow emancipation to escape questioning, to assume the position of a grand narrative. Fourth, humbled by poststructuralist deconstruction, emancipation is promoted as *one* way that an educational or a political situation could be improved, not as *the* way.

Despite this poststructuralist humility the problem remains—the goals of critical postmodern action research violate the neutrality, the nonpolitical claim of the dominant school culture's view of inquiry. Attempts of critical teacher researchers to examine and expose the forces that shape our consciousness and the assumptions of our research are viewed as efforts to politicize the research process. Again, poststructuralism forces us to question more deeply social and discursive assumptions. Rejecting a binary opposition between subjectivity and objectivity, we begin to uncover a modernist cult of objectivism. Devotees of the cult attempt to make invisible their own social beliefs and practices (the political domain) while concurrently pointing to the subjectivities and "bizarre" customs of the individuals they are studying (Roman and Apple, 1990, p. 40). They don't seem to realize that reality is tattooed by power, that the world's imprint on knowledge cannot be removed (McLaren, 1992a, p. 83).

What mainstream empirical researchers cannot seem to understand is that meaning is a contested entity. What an event, an action, or a text means may depend on what question is asked about it or what is hidden from an observer. When operating from this perspective, analysts of research divert their attention from questions concerning the bias of the data to questions concerning the interests served by the bias—questions of whose meanings prevail. Such questions forsake the positivist search for a privileged reference point from which the truth of educational practice may be discerned. Thus what mainstream researchers once termed *human* predispositions, researchers informed by critical theory and postmodernism refer to as discursive imprints on subjectivity namely, the consciousness construction that results from immersion in particular language games (McLaren, 1992b, pp. 321–322; Lather, 1992, p. 14).

Opponents of critical postmodern attempts to problematize the constancy of meaning have trouble understanding that the definition of objectivity always involves a power struggle. In the late-twentieth-century struggle the guardians of orthodoxy (the progeny of Umberto Eco's blind monk in *The Name of the Rose*) guard the objective canon as the postmodern barbarians at the gate pose critical challenges to their sequestered elitism (Scott, 1989, pp. 688–90). Patti Lather describes this struggle for objectivity as a dinosaur culture fighting to maintain its dominance against the forces of chaos (Lather, 1991, p. xvi). If the dinosaurs lose, the last pillars of Western civilization and the cult of objectivity will have been sabotaged. In no way should this critical postmodern challenge be interpreted to imply a lack of concern with empirical validity. Critical action research understands that even though objectivity is a social construction, data credibility can still be achieved by systematic approaches to reflective methods. Such methods involve interaction between researcher and researched. Such systematic interaction lessens the possibility that action researchers will simply impose meanings on situations instead of construct meanings via a give and take with those they have studied (McLaren, 1992a, p. 78; Lather, 1991, p. 110).

Based on their negotiations with those they have researched, critical action researchers assess information on the basis of its ability to move its consumers and producers in an emancipatory and humanistic direction, namely, to help them achieve empowerment and self-direction through an understanding of the ideological forces that shape humans. For example, if action researchers are unaware of the unequal power relations in the school in which they are conducting their inquiry how can they possibly grasp the importance and meaning of what they might perceive? When studying the school performances of a select group of students, action researchers would be handicapped if they failed to account for the interaction between socio-economic class and a student's language usage. A student's usage of language, of course, seriously affects how well he or she does on a standardized test. Embodied in particular discursive fields students from specific backgrounds as well as the action researchers who analyze them will tend to perceive in the context of these fields (McLaren, 1992a, p. 79). If action research is to be praxiological, then such understandings are central and must be shared with those being researched. As students from cultures shaped by repressive forces of race, class, and gender begin to understand the power discourses that have molded them, appreciate the causes of powerlessness, and take such insights to form the basis of collective and individual actions to change repressive conditions, they are empowering themselves in the critical sense of the term (Shapiro, 1989, pp. 80–82; Lather, 1991, pp. 3–4).

Such considerations, however, are conceptual light-years away from the forms of action research approved for use in the school. Arguing from a different set of assumptions, noncritical advocates of action research maintain that the everyday knowledge of teachers is the most important form of educational knowledge we possess. While the everyday knowledge of teachers is more insightful than the positive knowledge of propositional language, it is not enough. It is not all that teachers need to know. Action research in education critically defined is not content to confine teachers as researchers to the task of collating what they and their colleagues already know. Even though the packaging of noncritical action research appears new and fresh, its flavor is the same. The theoretical assumptions are tailored to the cult of objectivity, which blinds participants to the complex forces that move events in educational settings. The critical teacher researcher asks questions of deep structure of his or her school or classroom settings. The critical teacher researcher, in other words, he or she takes Habermas's notion of the emancipatory interest of knowledge seriously. Thus, critical teacher research will always aim to aid individuals in the attempt to take control of their lives, assuming that such autonomy is a moral right of human beings. This moral principle extends into the process of action research, as it demands that individuals who are studied have the right to participate in decisions that tend to produce knowledge about them. The concept of the dignity of those being researched is revered when power is shared in both the application and the production of knowledge about them. Such power sharing allows the researchers to gain new insights into the deep social structures that shape them, thus, enhancing the possibility of self-determination.

Bringing everyday practical knowledge to the forefront of our consciousness may be the first step in such a process but it is not the last—it must be supplemented by an awareness of the ideological construction of our consciousness and the educational and political results of such construction. Given such a purpose for critical postmodern action research, Patti Lather has proposed the notion of catalytic validity. Catalytic validity points to the degree to which research moves those it studies to understand the world and the way it is shaped in order for them to transform it. Noncritical action researchers who operate within an empiricist discursive community will find catalytic validity to be a strange concept. Action research that possesses catalytic validity will display not only the reality-altering impact of the inquiry process but it will also direct this impact so that those under study will gain self-understanding and self-direction (Altrichter and Posch, 1989, p. 28; van den Berg and Nicholson, 1989, pp. 16–18; Lather, 1991; Kincheloe and Steinberg, 1993, pp. 303–304).

Teacher research that ignores the emancipatory interest ends up only ankle-deep in the school ocean, missing a kaleidoscope of undersea activity. Educational action research needs to move beyond exclusive concern with the individual and institutional levels of inquiry toward an understanding of the social and cultural structures that help shape the educational lives of individuals and help determine the consequences of schooling. When all three levels of inquiry are pursued by teacher researchers, a view of education far more sophisticated than the one produced by an uncritical attention to teacher practical knowledge emerges. It is more sophisticated in that it is multidimensional, genuinely practical, reflective, politically savvy, and emancipatory. This uncritical-action-research orientation is quite dangerous as it fosters severely limited views of teaching and the educational process in the name of innovation and democratic pedagogy. It covertly upholds the status quo, as it is unable to analyze the dominant forces that constrict teacher insight and school policy. As it ignores the wider social and political framework, it unwittingly reproduces extant ideology and denies teachers the privilege of questioning the authority of past educational practices (Ruddick, 1989, pp. 6–8).

As it denies teachers the right to self-direction, it also shuts its eyes to the values which appear throughout any effort to do research. It pretends that what counts as an educational improvement is obvious to all. If such a view is accepted, then research becomes simply a value free, neutral technique used to measure how well we have reached consensual goals. What we call "improvement" is always problematic, always embedded with tacit epistemology, politics, views of human psychology and ideology (Wallace, 1987, pp. 108–9). When researchers and educational leaders assert or even imply that there is consensus on educational goals, alarm bells should ring in the ideology-detection center staffed by critical teacher researchers.

Many of the pronouncements of advocates of uncritical action research illustrate an unawareness of our notion of social embeddedness, as they assume that everyday language is politically neutral and value free. John Elliott, for example, has argued that everyday teacher concepts, expressed in everyday teacher language, should substitute for outsider perspectives. While Elliott makes a valuable point when he argues that teachers should protect themselves from the domination of the expert, he comes across as xenophobic when he maintains a "conceptual isolationism" for teachers. Concepts from social theory, when presented with sensitivity for the unique role of the practitioner, are necessary in the development of deeper understandings of the everyday life of the classroom and alternative perspectives on the goals and purposes of teaching. When it is not viewed as verified truth and not presented as a justification for top-down imposed goals for teachers, social theory can of course be very valuable. Elliott himself suffers from the effects of this conceptual isolationism, as he fails to comprehend the social construction of consciousness. Teacher language and concepts seem to him somehow miraculously free of ideological interference. Elliott takes his analysis to another level.

Focusing his attention on critical educational action research, Elliott calls it a dangerous conception of the teacher-as-researcher movement. Action researchers, he tells us, influenced by Habermas have perpetuated the false notion that the self-understandings teachers hold of their everyday activities make up ideologically distorted misrepresentations of the world. The purpose of critical theory, according to Elliott, is to provide teachers with modes of analysis which explain how this ideology distorts teachers' views of themselves and their teaching and works to justify hegemony. Since he rejects the possibility that a teacher's perspective on the world could be ideologically shaped, Elliott sees the intent of critical action research as mere politicization. The most important effect of critical action research, Elliott contends, is that it requires a dialogue between the critical theorist and the teacher. The critical theorist thus becomes merely the latest in a long line of experts who impose their opinions on teachers.

Elliott seems to forget that most people, teachers included, identify with or embrace ways of seeing that do not serve their best interests. Thus when teacher perceptions of the world of school are left unquestioned, the effects of power are left invisible. No matter what the way of seeing in question is, critical deconstructive analysis points out the partiality of any perspective. As deconstruction alerts us to how our economic, gender and racial positions shape our comprehension of various phenomena, we begin to understand that the questions generated in our action research reflect where we are standing in the web of reality. In light of such postmodern understandings, Elliott's tendency to unprovisionally celebrate the perspectives of teachers conducting action research is misguided. Whether the perspective be that of the critical academic, the educational leader, the student, or the teacher as researcher, the historical and cultural placement of the subject must be exposed and analyzed. Without question, the voice of the teacher must be respected, but respect does not imply a disinclination to question positionality (Lather, 1991, pp. 68, 145; McLaren, 1992b, pp. 333).

Elliott neglects another important point in his critique of critical action research—as opposed to other "outsiders," critical advocates of action research are not a part of a bureaucratic power structure that mandates teacher behavior. Whenever critical theorists would, in the mode of positivism, force their perspectives top-down on teachers, I would join Elliott in his condemnation of them. At present this is not happening. No room for outside opinion exists in Elliott's view of teaching and action research; in a critical action research context, he laments, "Teachers' self-understandings cannot alone serve as the basis for their emancipation from ideological control." Elliott's view of hegemony is quite unusual; while it excludes the identification of many of the forces which reproduce power in our consciousness, for example, media, traditional teacher education, gender relations, and so on, it includes all outsiders who analyze educational situations (Elliott, 1989b, pp. 50–53).

Elliott's perspectives have influenced other supporters of action research who also condemn critical teacher research for its desire to end open-minded inquiry. Jim McKernan writes in the spirit of Elliott that action research cannot be "held hostage" to the political ideology of the critical theorists. While he supports the effort to link critique and education in education, McKernan contends that this educational action should involve education and *not* politics—it should be an action that concentrates on issues of curriculum and instruction, not on political matters like social justice. In the name of educational improvement and political neutrality positivism (in its modern postpositivist guise) pops up like a jack-in-the-box. McKernan's view is plausible only if we accept the positivist separation of facts and values and see the role of schools as politically neutral (McKernan, 1988, pp. 198–99). My reading of educational history tells a very different story—a tale of schools many times used for political purposes, schools undermined by unequal power distribution.

Such uncritical perspectives are not simply the province of traditional quantitative researchers or researchers who accept the tenets of positivism. The perspective is alive and well in, of course, the action-research movement and also within qualitative educational studies in general. The ability to make judgments is not viewed as a goal of qualitative research, many researchers argue. Of course, there is an element of truth in the pronouncement that we don't do qualitative research in order to judge how well a teacher is doing—but this is not the final word on judgment in a qualitative research content. We can refrain from making *personal* judgments while developing a set of criteria that allow us to judge the value of particular educational goals and outcomes—this is why it is so important for us to develop a provisional system of meaning. We need to ask and answer questions such as; Are these goals and outcomes just? are they respectful of human dignity? Whose interests do they serve? what are the epistemological assumptions embedded in these goals and outcomes? On what set of political beliefs are the grounded? This is judgment and, even in the name of neutrality, is also political—but to refrain from some form of judgment even in the name of neutrality is also political—critical awareness smokes us out of our pseudoneutral "high ground." We cannot avoid making political choices.

It seems obvious that any teacher's perspective unaided by different vantage points will guarantee that they remain unconscious of these tacit assumptions that direct their practice. They would be unaware, say, that they held sexist or racist viewpoints that affected their teaching or did not correspond to their authentically avowed principles. I do not doubt that those I refer to as the uncritical proponents of action research are genuinely concerned with granting teachers more insight into their professional practice, but such advocates fail to ask whether in the modern workplace teachers are free to initiate changes they consider necessary. Uncritical advocates of teacher research are uncomfortable with the so-called elitism of critical action researchers such as Wilfred Carr and Stephen Kemmis, who have focused on the theoretical and organizational structures that constrain the everyday practice of teachers. Can teachers make changes derived from their research and reflection, Carr and Kemmis ask. Often times the answer is no, given the self-perpetuating organization of schools and the ideological blindness of many school leaders. Uncritical action researchers, it seems, meet teachers only halfway—they throw one-half the length of the rope needed to pull them out of the water to safety. They speak the language of empowerment, and they concern themselves with the reflective power of teacher research, but they refuse to confront the structural conditions of schools and the larger society that preclude the translation of teacher reflection into emancipatory educational action (Wallace, 1987, pp. 108–9).

Uncritical advocates of teacher research are more and more using a critical vocabulary to describe their activities. Words such as "emancipation," "hegemony" and "domination" are heard and read quite often in the literature of action research. "Emancipation," for example is not employed in the same way by Elliott as it is by Giroux, McLaren, Carr and Kemmis, and myself. To Elliott (and many others) emancipation is a very specific situation—teachers freeing themselves from perspectives that emanate from outside the classroom. Giroux, McLaren, and Carr and Kemmis use the term to evoke the image of teachers freeing themselves from the hegemonizing influences of larger sociocultural forces. Elliott's concept of emancipation does not allow for a critical reconceptualization or decentering of dominant views of the purpose of teaching. Employing a language of critique in relation to particular teacher expectations, critical postmodern forms of questioning become, from Elliott's perspective, an unwelcomed political imposition from outside the school. Is it not possible to respect teachers and the sanctity of teacher knowledge and at the same time question particular interpretations and actions teachers derive from their reflection? (Elliott, 1989, pp. 2–3). Maybe an analogy outside an educational context would help. There is little doubt that a lawyer with thirty years of courtroom experience possesses a unique form of knowledge that could only be attained by this particular experience. This does not mean that we have no right to argue or disagree with his or her purposes for trying or not trying a case or for accepting one case and turning down another. Indeed, an outsider with a different set of experiences may provide valuable insight into particular aspects of the lawyer's work. Critical action researchers in education cannot allow their language to be co-opted and stripped of its emancipatory meaning by analysts who don't understand the reality of power relations, the socially constructed nature of knowledge, and the suffering that comes out of the existence of domination in the social and educational world.

Lest I be misunderstood, I will close with a few reminders. In our attempt to preserve a role for advocates of critical postmodern action research in the conversation about teacher research, we are not attempting—as Elliott and McKernan would suggest—to argue that teachers should not become authorities on the discourse of schooling. Educational poststructuralists demand respect of teachers and teacher knowledge and seek to expose the insidious ways that outside experts can come to dominate teachers. This is not, however, the position of Elliott and McKernan, as they fail to discuss the discursive and power restrictions on understandings derived from teacher-conducted action research. Neither are we attempting to pose as outside experts ready to come in and "correct" the false consciousness or distorted perceptions of teachers. As poststructuralist critic Teresa Ebert maintains, we are interested in uncovering the ways that all of us, teachers included, are shaped by the ways lives are connected to dominant relations of power (Ebert, 1988, p. 23). No one possesses a consciousness that situates him or her beyond history and political practices. None of us, as Peter McLaren contends, stands outside the policy structures of discourses. Our emotional investments shape our belief structures and our practices, what we "see" and what we look past (McLaren, 1992a, p. 77). Action researchers can always profit from encounters with those who encourage them to uncover how their own inquiry reflects ways that they have been taught to "see." Without such understandings, teacher researchers will never get beyond the curtain to see why the microcosm of education operates in the ways that it does.

## REFERENCES

Altrichter, H., & Posch, P. (1989). Does the 'Grounded Theory' approach offer a guiding paradigm for teacher research? *Canthridge Journal of Education, 19*(1), 21–31.
Aronowitz, S. (1983, December). The relativity of theory. *The Village Voice*, p. 60.
Aronowitz, S., & Giroux, H. (1985). *Education under seige.* South Hadley, MA: Bergin, & Garvey.
Carr, W., & Kemmis, S. (1986). *Becoming critical.* Phildelphia: Falmer Press.
Cherryholmes, C. (1988). *Power and criticism: Pcststructural investigations in education.* New York: Teachers College Press.
Codd, J. (1984). Introduction. In J. Codd (Ed.), *Philosophy, common sense, and action in educational administration.* Victoria, Australia: Deakin University Press.
Connelly, F., & Ben-Peretz, M. (1980). Teachers' roles in the using and doing of research and curriculum development? *Journal of Curriculum Studies, 12*(2), 95–107.
Ebert, T. (1988). The romance of patriarchy: Ideology, subjectivity, and postmodern feminist cultural theory. *Cultural Critique, 10*, 19–57.
Elliott, J. (1989a). *Studying the school curriculum through insider research.* Paper presented to the international conference on School-Based Innovations: Looking Forward to the 1990s, Hong Kong.
Elliott, J. (1989b). Action-Research and the emergence of teacher appraisal in the united kingdom. Paper presented to the American Educational Research Association, San Francisco.
Giroux, H. (1992). *Border crossings: Cultural workers and the politics of Education.* New York: Routledge.
Giroux, H., & McLaren, P. (1991). Language, schooling, and subjectivity: Beyond a pedagogy of reproduction and resistance? In K. Borman, P. Swami, & L. Wagstaff (Eds.), *Contemporary issues in U.S. education* (pp. 61–83). Norwood, NJ: Ablex Publishing.
Hultgren, F. (1987). Critical thinking: Phenomenological and critical foundations? In R. G. Thomas (Ed.), *Higher-order thinking: Definition, meaning and instructional approaches* (pp. 27–45). Washington, DC: Home Economics Education Association.
Kincheloe, J. L. (1991). *Teachers as researchers: Qualitative paths to empowerment.* London: Falmer Press.
Kincheloe, J. L. (1993). *Toward a critical politics of teacher thinking: Mapping the postmodern.* Granby, MA: Bergin & Garvey.
Kincheloe, J. L., & Steinberg S. R. (1993). A tentative description of postformal thinking: The critical confrontation with cognitive theory? *Harvard Education Review, 63*, 296–320.
Lather, P. (1991). *Getting smart: Feminist research and pedagogy with/in the classroom.* New York: Routledge.
Lather, P. (1986). Research as Praxis? *Harvard Educational Review, 56*, 257–277.
Lesko, N. (1988). *Symbolizing society: Stories, rites, and structure in a Catholic High School.* New York: Falmer Press.
Maeroff, G. (1988). A blueprint for empowering teachers? *Phi Delta Kappan, 69*(7), 472–477.
May, W., & Zimpher, N. (1986). An examination of three theoretical perspectives on supervision: Perceptions of preservice field supervision. *Journal of Curriculum and Supervision, 1*(2), 83–99.
McKernan, J. (1988). Teacher as researcher: Paradigm and Praxis. *Contemporary Education, 59*(3), 154–158.
McLaren, P. (1992a). Collisions with otherness: Traveling theory of post-colonial criticism, and the politics of ethnographic practice—The mission of the wounded ethnographer. *Qualitative Studies in Education, 5*(1):77–92.

McLaren, P. (1992b). Literacy research and the postmodern turn: Cautions from the margins? In R. Beach, et al. (Eds.), *Multi-Disciplinary perspectives on literacy research* (pp. 339–379). Urbana, IL: National Council of Teachers of English.

Orteza, Y., & Miranda, E. (1988). Broadening the focus of research in education. *Journal of Research and Development in Education, 22*(1), 23–28.

Ponzio, R. (1985). Can we change content without changing context? *Teacher Education Quarterly, 12*(3), 39–43.

Popkewitz, T. (1981). The study of schooling: Paradigms and field-based methodologies in education research and evaluation? In T. Popkewitz & B. Tabachrück (Eds.), *The study of schoolin*. New York: Praeger Publishers.

Porter, A. (1988). Indicators: Objective data or political tool? *Phi Delta Kappan, 69*(7), 503–508.

Ross, D. (1984). A practical model for conducting action research in public school settings? *Contemporary Education, 55*(2), 113–117.

Ruddick, J. (1989). *Critical thinking and practitioner research: Have they a place in initial teacher training?* Paper presented to the American Educational Research Association, San Francisco.

Scott, J. (1989). History in crisis: The others' side of the story. *The American Historical Review, 94*(3), 680–692.

Shapiro, S. (1989). Towards a language of educational politics: The struggles for a critical public discourse of education? *Educational Foundations, 3*(3), 79–100.

Spivak, G. (1987). *In other worlds: Essays in cultural politics.* New York: Methuen.

Tripp, D. (1988). *Teacher journals in collaborative classroom research.* Paper presented to the American Educational Research Association, New Orleans.

van den Berg, O., & Nicholson, S. (1989). *Teacher transformation in the South African context: An action research approach?* Paper presented to the international conference on School-based Innovations: Looking Forward to the 1990s, Hong Kong.

van Hesteran, F. (1986). Counselling research in a different key: The promise of human science perspective? *Canadian Journal of Counseling, 20*(4), 200–234.

Wallace, M. (1987). A historical review of action research: Some implications for the education of teachers in their managerial role. *Journal of Education for Teaching, 13*(2), 97–115.

Young, R. (1990). *A critical theory of education: Habermas and our children's future.* New York: Teachers College Press.

Reprinted with permission: Kincheloe, J. L. (1995). Meet me behind the curtain: the struggle for a critical postmodern action research. In P. McLaren and J. Giarelli (Eds.), *Critical theory and educational research* (pp. 71–89). Albany, NY: SUNY Press.

JOHN SMYTH

# A DIALOGIC ENCOUNTER WITH JOE KINCHELOE'S "MEET ME BEHIND THE CURTAIN"

*Catalyst for an Evolving Contemporary Critical Theory of Teachers' Work*

INTRODUCTION

Joe would have been absolutely delighted with the notion of a dialogic encounter with his work because dialogic engagement was the essence of his very being. He was an avid and gregarious conversationalist, always keen to use his formidable intellect to interrogate the most pressing issues of the time, to puncture and expose what they were up to, in order to construct a more democratic alternative. Nowhere was that more evident than in teacher education and what was happening (and is continuing to happen largely unabated) to teachers' work.

As I re-read Joe's "Meet Me behind the Curtain" (Kincheloe, 1995), this time with the sadness in my heart that I can no longer have an actual conversation with Joe, I am deeply struck by how little the issues have changed and how contemporary this paper is. The issues haven't really improved at all, and indeed if anything they have worsened in the decade and a half since the paper was published—only the names of the adversaries have moved around a bit. The neo-liberal project of co-opting, controlling, disparaging and denigrating the indigenous forms of knowledge of teachers is very much alive.

In this revisitation of one of Joe's most significant papers I want to engage in a dialogue with the key ideas Joe raised, explain how they have been a crucial catalyst in the evolution of a critical theroretical framework for teachers' work, and how in the process Joe's ideas are even more relevant today than when he first uttered them.

At the crux of Joe's paper is the distinction he makes between forms of teacher research that co-opts teachers, subjugates their knowledge, and humiliates them in order to domesticate them as annexes of capitalism, versus critical forms of teacher research which celebrate teaching as a form of crucial intellectual work committed to producing courageous young citizens, analytical of what is happening around them and prepared to speak back with an alternative.

The antidote to the dominant construction and presumption of teachers as "couriers" or complicit and compliant "deliverers" of information, and here I am reminded of Henry Giroux's (1988) colorful nomenclature of teachers as "clerks of the empire" (p. 91), is presented by Joe as residing in conceptualizations of teachers as active agents involved in the pursuit of critical action research around their own and one another's teaching. This is where Joe's capacity to present distinction becomes so crucial as he makes the point that even processes that have the inherent capacity to liberate, as action research does, are nevertheless still highly susceptible to being hijacked to technical and instrumental ends. As something of a biographic aside, I can clearly remember a couple of decades ago being approached by a senior educational administrator in Australia with a request to adopt across a state-wide system a version of critical action research which I was using with teachers. He wanted to know if I would give him permission to apply it teachers "without all that political stuff that comes with it!" My response was, of course, that I could not prevent him from using my work, but he would not receive any endorsement from me to gut it in the technicized way being suggested. I never did follow up to see what happened.

## TAKING ON THE BARBARIANS!

Joe provides five crucial framing distinctions that critical action researchers are committed to, and they are worth briefly alluding to.

First, unlike positivist research, which quite unashamedly and falsely purports to be neutral, objective and value free, critical action research is not at all shy about admitting to its avowedly political character—that seems to be a refreshingly honest approach. Second, a preparedness by critical action researchers to acknowledge their own value commitments, while at the same time naming the values promoted, maintained and perpetuated by the dominant culture. Third, there is a pervasive understanding by critical action researchers that "professional consciousness" is not simply the aggregate of individual personal biographies, but rather is socially and historically constructed. Fourth, critical action researchers regard it as a signature or the raison d'etre of what they do, to uncover how forms of hierarchy work, how they came to be, what holds them in place, and most importantly, what needs to be done to undermine, unhinge and supplant them with more emancipatory alternatives. Finally, the venue through which critical action is actually played out is not some distant vacuous policy vacuum, but rather teachers' actually existing classroom practices—it is always conceived of in terms of how to improve practice.

As Joe begins to unpeel the various layers of the claims to authenticity and legitimacy that are at the essence of critical action research, we begin to get a sense of the forensic nature of his intellect at work. He is unremitting in his castigation of forms of research that construct teachers as subjects, that treat them as demeaning targets of other people's exploitative agenda—are wrapped up and presented to appear as if it were innocent. To be clear, Joe does much more then merely name the source of oppression—like all good critical theorists he uses the scalpel of his critique to sculpt the basis of the features of a better and more socially just world. While the metaphor in the title of his chapter, "Meet me behind the curtain," is suggestive of something subversive or insurgent, what we take him to be saying is that those of us of a critical persuasion have to get behind the theatre played out when schools are treated like huge sausage machines. What Joe is alluding to is how through critical action research, teachers have the power to do profound things under the radar.

A few of his comments serve to highlight the quest Joe is on for a more socially just alternative—or as he repeatedly calls it "an evolving criticality":

...critical action research is the consummate democratic act, as it allows teachers to help determine the conditions of their own work" (p. 74)

...[S]ince critical theory is grounded in a recognition of the existence of oppression...[a]ction research serves as a perfect vehicle for such a search (p. 75)

Joe sutures these perceptive observations together to advance his argument that when action research does not have "domination and oppression" firmly in its sights, then it succeeds only in becoming part of the problem rather than a contestation of the status quo and its rejuvenation.

Permitting schools to be presented as if they were dispassionate "value neutral" sites, and allowing the role of those within them and those from outside who allegedly have the interests of students at heart to operate as if that were the case, is tantamount to being deceptive at best or grossly unethical at the worst. The way he puts it is that "in a world of oppression, critical theorists argue, ethical behavior demands that such dispassion must be confronted" (p. 75). When how power works is unveiled in this way, then we have genuinely begun to engage in the kind of unmasking and forms of exposé that Joe argues is crucial to advancing notions of criticality.

Joe was, of course, never averse to employing notions of subversion as a way of working between the cracks in order to pursue the kind of "postmodern insurrection" necessary to legitimate knowledge that would otherwise be "swept under the rug" (p. 75). What he is referring to here is the "up-close" and "firsthand" knowledge of teachers that is so unceremoniously dismissed as irrelevant by the mandarins of the so-called 'scientific' regime of randomized experimental field style of research. We should not be surprised, therefore to find Joe turning to the "biographical and autobiographical" as the basis upon which to craft teachers' counter-hegemonic forms of research. Reflecting on how their teaching came to be the way it is, what keeps it that way, and who it is working for (or against), is a way of bringing teachers to the realization of "the panoply of ideological forces" (p. 78) that often inhibit teachers from seeing how and why classroom life works the way it does.

## PAUSE TO THINK

In respect of these issues Joe was in many ways well ahead of his time. Recently, Appadurai (2006) has referred to what Joe was pitching at in his paper as the "need to de-parochialise...the idea of research" (p. 168). As it is generally understood, research is a systematic and disciplined process undertaken by those with formal training and who know how to enact the appropriate protocols, like the capacity to "review...literature, the strategic citation, the delineation of the appropriate universe" (Appadurai, 2000, p. 10) and the like. Working with groups who are oppressed or disposed produces a very different set of dynamics. Speaking from a background of working with the most marginalized and excluded slum dwellers in Mumbai, Appadurai (2006), argues for a view of "research which is not confined to the university or the professional elites, but which [is] part of the lives of ordinary people" (p. 173). What Appadurai (2006) is saying is that research ought to be regarded as a special kind of right which amounts to a "capacity to make disciplined inquiries into those things we need to know, but do not know yet" (p. 167), and that:

> All human beings are, in this sense, researchers since all human beings make decisions that require them to make systematic forays beyond their current knowledge horizons (p. 167).

Conceived of in terms of this quite different 'research imagination' being alluded to by Appaduarai, research actually inverts power relationships. In de-parochialising research and opening up the space in which the subaltern can speak, dramatically changes who owns knowledge, how it is shaped, and the forces making it that way. This was a matter Joe understood profoundly. He was as at pains to note how mainstream research was in denial through the way it purports to sustain the "cult of objectivism… [and the] attempt to make invisible their own social beliefs and practices" (Kincheloe, 1995, p. 79). What they don't seem to get "is that meaning is a contested entity" (p. 79) and that continuing to genuflect to what Joe dubbed a "dinosaur culture" of research, is to prop up an outdated "sequestered elitism" (p. 80). For Joe, it was not that critical action research was in any way dataless, or the case that anything goes, but rather that data derives its legitimacy through "interaction between researcher and researched" (p. 80). When action researchers negotiate meaning with their informants, then the veracity of meaning is significantly enhanced rather than being diluted or dissipated. The crucial point Joe is making is that:

> Such systematic interaction lessens the possibility that action researchers will simply impose meanings on situations instead of construct meanings via a give and take with those they have studied (p. 80).

For Joe, the underlying issue was the way in which critical action research enables teachers who are collaborating with outside action researchers, if that is indeed the case, to have a measure of genuine ownership, self-direction and control over what is happening in their lives. He uses the example of working with teachers to puncture hierarchies of class, gender and race, and revealing its genesis, in order to provide the individual and collective basis for speaking back.

It is easy to become confused here because even non-critical versions of action research can appear to be like a breath of fresh air compared to externally-driven positivist research, but they are actually mired in their own set of significant shortcomings. They appear to shift power from outsiders to teachers, and in a limited way that is true. It is also hard as Joe indicates to argue against the sensibility of the everyday knowledge of teachers, of the importance of teachers dialoguing about their teaching, and the efficacy of reflecting on their classroom practice. These are all smart things to do. It is not what happens in the foregrounding of teachers' knowledge that is the problem, but rather what is not going on, if that is all there is to it. What the critical teacher does is "ask…questions about the deep structure of his or her school or classroom setting" (p. 81).

I can perhaps best illustrate something of the journey of becoming critical through my own work, in seeking to develop teachers as critically reflective practitioners (Smyth, 1989; Smyth, 1992). My argument (Smyth, 1991; Smyth, 2001) going back over three decades is that moving teachers towards becoming critically reflective practitioners involves a carefully staged process. First, involving teachers in *describing* their practices—collecting data about the who, the what, the when, and where in their teaching and classrooms, usually with the assistance of a colleague. Second, using the descriptions thus obtained, to look for patterns, themes, similarities, relationships, surprises, or whatever—this is what I term *informing*—starting to dig into what might otherwise remain at the level of unreflective practice. For many teachers, this is as much as they feel comfortable with, and this is where they stop. Third, and this is where the critical aspect begins to emerge as teachers are urged to ask deeper questions about what lies behind the theorized instances they have described—Why do I teach this way? What assumptions lie behind this way of teaching? Indeed, what social practices are being expressed? Who says this is the way teaching ought to be? How come this has become part of my personal biography and professional repertoire? How is power working here? What constrains me? Who is being included/excluded? This is what I call *confronting*—and it involves a preparedness to ask questions about biography, history, and the political and ideological construction of consciousness. The fourth and more strategic moment which emerges from "unsettling beliefs" (Diem, & Helfenbein, 2008), the production of perplexity, or dissatisfaction, is how things might be changed—personally, institutionally, and culturally in the direction of making things more socially just. The overarching question here is: how can teaching be made more political in the sense of working for the most excluded and marginalized? I call this *re-constructing*.

Although Joe did not crystallize it out in quite the way I have just put it, he profoundly understood that to change teaching in the way I am suggesting, critical action research had to first understand the world in order to transform it. This is the crucial intersecting Freirean point for myself and Joe, or as he put it, "multidimensional, genuinely practical, reflective, politically savvy, and emancipatory" (Kincheloe, 1995, p. 82). It is not surprising that Joe had no truck with look-alike versions of action research that promulgated "severely limited views of teaching," that "covertly uphold the status quo," and that adamantly refuse to acknowledge the wider social and political domain. People like John Elliott who drew Joe's ire by dismissing critical action research as "mere politicization" (p. 83), were part of what Joe regarded as a politically naïve fraternity who were endorsing a view that was collapsing under the weight of evidence to the contrary, by refusing to see how schools were rampantly and blatantly being used for political purposes that are distorting, disfiguring and irreparably damaging the social institution of schooling through propping up gross inequalities of power.

CONCLUSION OR MORE LIKELY A STRONG RE-AFFIRMATION

It should be clear by now that I regard this as a seminal piece in the formidable legacy of work that Joe has left us. His perspicacity in noting trends, themes and ideological patterns was way ahead of its time and in many respects pointed the way to the antidote to No Child Left Behind, and its diminished offshoots in other countries.

In all of this Joe was far more than a critic of emaciated and domesticated one-dimensional views. In taking us behind the carefully contrived veils and masks of neo-liberalism, he has not only systematically decimated them with his blistering and compelling set of arguments, but he has also constructed an almost unassailable alternative. The challenge for those of us who seek to follow in his footsteps, is to have the unwavering courage Joe had to both 'speak the unpleasant' (Chavez, & O'Donnell, 1998), as well as to persist with the only democratic alternative.

## REFERENCES

Appadurai, A. (2000). Grassroots globalization and the research imagination. *Public Culture*, *12*(1), 1–19.

Appadurai, A. (2006). The right to research. *Globalisation, Societies and Education*, *4*(2), 167–177.

Chavez, R. & O'Donnell, J. (Eds.). (1998). *Speaking the unpleasant: The politics of (non) engagement in themulticultural education terrain*. Albany, NY: State University of New York Press.

Diem, J. & Helfenbein, R. (Eds.). (2008). *Unsettling beliefs: Teaching theory to teachers*. Charlotte, NC: Information Age Publishing.

Giroux, H. (1988). *Teachers as intellectuals: Toward a critical pedagogy of learning*. Granby, MA: Bergin, & Garvey.

Kincheloe, J. L. (1995). Meet me behind the curtain: the struggle for a critical postmodern action research. In P. McLaren & J. Giarelli (Eds.), *Critical theory and educational research*. Albany, NY: State University of New York University Press.

Smyth, J. (1989). A critical pedagogy of classroom practice. *Journal of Curriculum Studies*, *21*(6), 483–502.

Smyth, J. (1991). *Teachers as collaborative learners: Challenging dominant forms of supervision*. London: Open University Press.

Smyth, J. (1992). Teachers' work and the politics of reflection. *American Educational Research Journal*, *29*(2), 267–300.

Smyth, J. (2001). *Critical politics of teachers' work: An Australian perspective*. New York: Peter Lang Publishing.

*Soon after buying a home in Central, South Carolina, we decided we needed to finish the basement for the four kids, and add on an apartment for Joe's Mama and Daddy. We found two builders, Ronnie and Brandon. I learned very quickly, that Joe would pretty well prefer to hang out and laugh with our workers than just about anything else. This pattern was repeated for twenty years, and every home we moved into, naturally needed renovating. Joe vetted our builders, and by all means, became their friends. Not only was this piece significant in his articulation of admiration and enjoyment for those who worked with their hands, but in his own interest in vocational education. Following this chapter, Joe set to researching and wrote two books on vocational education, Toil and Trouble, and How Do We Tell the Workers? To this day, some of our oldest, faithful, and most beloved friends are those who drank a coke, a beer, or smoked a joint with Joe on a pile of 2 x 4's in our yard. This chapter is specifically a shoutout to Ronnie, Brandon, Mongo, Bob, Paul, Sandy, and G. SS*

JOE L. KINCHELOE

# 5. SCHOOLS WHERE RONNIE AND BRANDON WOULD HAVE EXCELLED

*A Curriculum Theory of Academic and Vocational Education*

Having recently completed a detailed study of Richard Herrnstein and Charles Murray's *The Bell Curve: Intelligence and Class Structure in American Life* (1994), I am acutely aware of elitist discourses in education and psychology. Few academic locales reveal a class-biased elitism more clearly than the conversation about intelligence in educational psychology. The dialogue becomes especially elitist and condescending when issues surrounding the intelligence of blue collar, low status workers are broached. My contention in this essay is that we must, as critical and democratic scholars, induce the academic community to rethink this elitism and restructure schools in light of that reconceptualization.

The elitism in *The Bell Curve* is omnipresent and oppressive, as the authors speak unabashedly about dysgenesis and the social havoc wrought by the poor (and non-white). Using what my co-authors (Shirley Steinberg and Aaron Gresson) label an "'us' verses 'them'" social theory, Herrnstein and Murray value abstract ways of knowing over hands-on, bodily modes of understanding. Schools, of course, reflect this tacit assumption in their privileging of the academic over the vocational curriculum. This elitist view of education inflicts immeasurable damage on economically and racially marginalized students. Every day, thousands of brilliant students are taught that they are stupid. My friends Ronnie and Brandon illustrate this point.

Ronnie and Brandon are carpenters who completed some renovation work on my house a couple of years ago. During that period they became good friends of mine who talked with me for hours about education–their own in particular. Like many individuals in the trades, they hated school. Convinced by their school experience that they were stupid, they sought vocations that ostensibly had little to do with the skills schools teach. In their everyday work, I watched them employ sophisticated geometric and algebraic abilities, solving unstructured problems with their improvisational math. When I pointed out the sophistication of their operations, they found my praise difficult to accept. "This is not really math it's not like the math you do in school," Ronnie told me. As I explained to them how their math was in many ways more sophisticated than what is typically taught in high school, they were fascinated. Focusing on their facility with unstructured problems as opposed to school's structured problems, I began to argue that they were not as dumb as they thought.

As I explained critical conceptions of class-bias in education and the exclusionary, elitist discourse of educational psychology's view of intelligence they began to understand the socially constructed nature of intelligence and how they had been victimized by the elitist viewpoint. The more we talked, the more excited they got. Initially reluctant to express their concerns about the elitism of schooling with a college professor who taught teachers, they began to share with me the anger and resentment they harbored toward formal education. In conversations with other men and women in the trades, I have encountered similar anger. Schooling has had little positive effect on their lives. It was a place of embarrassment and hurt feelings, a place where one's failures and inabilities took center stage. "I just kept my mouth shut and hoped the time would pass quickly," Ronnie told me. As long as we continue to demean manual forms of intelligence, a large percentage of students, like Ronnie, will suffer through an irrelevant and humiliating school experience.

What Ronnie and Brandon intuitively understood was their "place" in the elitism of the schools they attended and the lack of connection between schooling and everyday life. Even when they studied algebra and geometry, for example, they saw little relevance for their carpentry. "I had to learn it all over again when I started working," Brandon explained. The school Brandon and Ronnie attended operated under the logic that if students learn a body of general skills, these skills can be transferred to a variety of work situations when the need arises. The skills are taught as isolated subtasks and evaluated by a student's ability to successfully perform the task when called upon. The concept of employing skills in appropriate contexts appears irrelevant in most schools (Raizen, 1989). Brandon and Ronnie were put off by this decontextualized drill on fragmented little skills. Drawing upon their experiences, they quickly understood my explanation of the modernist cognitive illness with its privileging of mind over body and its fragmentation of knowledge in a way that separates schools from the world in which people live and work.

As I write this essay about a curriculum theory that addresses the elitism/class-bias that shapes the education of the poor and marginalized, I cannot help but personalize the ideas as they relate to Ronnie and Brandon. What kind of education would have spoken to them and addressed their needs? What curricular arrangements would have made schooling meaningful in their lives? As educators, how do we act upon our understandings of the elitism, class-bias, and fragmentation that undermine our democratic yearnings for meaningful change? These are the questions that form the conceptual infrastructure for this essay—a piece that offers some concrete notions about critically-grounded curricular reform. Critical scholars are often accused of not being sufficiently specific about their proposals for democratic school reform. While attempting to avoid an authoritarian blueprint for the reform of schools, the essay offers a tentative proposal for one way of acting on our critical and democratic imperative in a curricular context-the integration of academic and vocational education. I hope that Ronnie and Brandon and their colleagues in the trades would approve.

## THINKING ABOUT CURRICULAR INTEGRATION FOR ALL STUDENTS

In the integrated programs that now exist, possibilities for profound educational reform abound. Teachers loosened from the chains of top-down bureaucratic management discover surprising connections between academic and vocational content. Academic teachers often realize for the first time the teaching methods and the unique forms of motivation offered by vocational teachers. Vocational teachers in their collaborations with academic teachers discover windows through which they can contextualize vocational skills with academic knowledge. Long standing barriers between vocational and academic teachers are hurdled and in many situations the routine and boredom of the traditional school is shattered by integrative innovation. As students study vocational paths in an integrated manner, they take field trips, listen to talks from business and (too infrequently) labor leaders, and work in internships. New interest is generated in future occupations and the vocational consequences of curricular choices. Teachers come to realize the negative effects of their isolation from one another and of the isolation of their students from the outside world of business and politics. So far, these experiments in academic and vocational integration have provided a veritable seminar in the educational imagination for teachers and students alike (Beck, 1991; Grubb et al., 1991).

Discussions of academic and vocational integration have typically revolved around the reform of vocational education. The way integration will be viewed here, however, will concern the reform of education in general, both vocational and academic programs. Proponents point out that integration forces schools to reduce class size, improve student counseling, provide coherent programs of courses, offer greater contact between teachers and students, and create closer relationships with social institutions outside of school. Teachers in integrated programs are forced to confront and act to remedy the liabilities of the traditional organization of school including the fragmentations of curriculum from students' lives and of schooling from the world outside of school. With such understandings teachers in integrated settings are more prone to consider methodological innovations. Academic teachers, for example, find that the vocational connection provides the context in which engaging student projects that connect academic theory with vocational practice naturally emerge. Work education takes on new meaning in such situations as it positions teachers and students in closer contact with life than they have ever before experienced in school settings. As they gain an authentic connection to the lived world, teachers and students come to recognize far more clearly the academic, vocational, sociopolitical, and cognitive capacities that competent and morally courageous students and workers must possess. Such a recognition can serve to construct a revolutionary consciousness, a way of seeing that will not allow the world to remain the same (Grubb et al., 1991).

Integration will require special types of teachers with special insights and abilities. The fragility of such an innovation becomes apparent when one thinks of how easily the process can be destroyed by administrators and teachers without a vision of the larger purposes of integration. For example, vocational instructors who continue to teach narrow job skills without concern for student appreciation of the academic principles that contextualize them will undermine an integrated curriculum. Academic teachers who view vocational instruction condescendingly and refuse to grant credit for "applied academic classes" will destroy any chance for success. Teachers who enjoy their neat and tidy Madeline Hunter lesson plans and their coherent and orderly courses may pose a problem for integrated programs. In light of such threats, integration demands a reconceptualized form of teacher education. Academic teachers must become more familiar with work education issues such as production processes, the activity-based teaching methods of sophisticated vocational programs, and the vocational decisions that all students face. Vocational teachers will require greater involvement in the academic disciplines most relevant to their vocational fields, as well as more study of the social and political dimensions of work. All teachers will need more experience in cooperative curriculum development grounded in a multi-dimensional understanding of educational purpose (Copa, & Tebbenhoff, 1990; Beck, 1991).

With teachers who possess a sense of purpose and a democratic vision of integration, a major offensive can be launched against the class-based and race-based segregation of students within existing schools. The bifurcation of vocational and academic students has resulted in a division between college-bound and work-bound students. Of course, vocational courses are heavily populated by students of the lower socio-economic classes, highlighting the unconscionable class divisions within schools. Through the integration of academic and vocational education everyone, in a sense, would take vocational education. No longer would vocation based experiences carry a stigma of low status. Well-informed teachers could sophisticate vocation-based classes in such a way that students who thought of themselves as academic would be induced to take them. On the other hand, students who thought of themselves as vocational would be induced to take academic courses that were integrated with concrete vocational experiences in such a way that would make them attractive.

Thus, integration can offer a vision of what American education can become, a practical strategy to address the class-bias that cripples the opportunities of children not born into middle class homes. For example, savvy teachers in charge of an integrated program might be able to make positive use of business participation in school life. Previous participation of business in education has been trivial at best and repressive at worst, with corporations and industries attempting to open "untapped markets" in classrooms or to indoctrinate students into ideological positions uncritical of the social abuses of business. In thoughtful, well-designed programs business people (along with representatives of labor) can "put their resources where their mouths are" and provide summer jobs and future employment to worthy students. They can reinforce the need for students to learn both academic and vocational competencies and put in concrete terms the relationship between school learning and other aspects of life. In their collaboration with integrated programs, business people can make sure that vapid work placement programs characterized by repetitive job experiences and simple-minded academic experiences become mistakes of the past (Grubb et al., 1991).

## DUALISMS: *WHAT* AND *HOW*

Integration addresses a number of regressive modernist dualisms that serve to fragment reality. One of the most basic issues here involves addressing the distinction between knowing *what* and knowing *how*. Conventional wisdom positions this distinction as the separation of the learning of canonical knowledge through formalized teaching, that is grounded on textbooks, lectures, and other materials, from learning by doing through first-hand experience. Those who are deemed capable by school authorities of learning the *what* are placed in academic tracks; those deemed capable of learning the *how* are placed in vocational tracks. Caught within the gravitational pull of this distinction are several other false binarisms, including the separations of theory and practice, thinking and doing, and learning principles and devising applications. When Hume, in the seventeenth century, proclaimed that he was giving up philosophy so he could go play billiards, he was referring to yet another dualism within this orbit—separating the abstract from the concrete is ill-advised because we often learn more about an abstract notion by analyzing its concrete expression. Indeed, one of the categories of postformal thinking (see Kincheloe, 1995; Kincheloe, & Steinberg, 1993) involves the ability to connect generalization and particularity in a way that grants observers a far more textured view of reality (Raizen, 1989).

Focusing on the context of work education, this modernist tendency for dualism exposes itself in the distinction between education and training. "Low-ability" students, the argument goes, are trained for specific tasks, while *true* education is reserved for the academically talented. The student who is trained for his or her vocation is incapable of grasping theory or understanding the whole. The trained student employs rule-of-thumb procedures, while the educated student invokes theory as he or she solves problems and reflects upon the process (Feinberg, & Horowitz, 1990). Little reason exists to worry about the training of these "dullards"-the conventional wisdom has decided that they cannot be educated. On the basis of such beliefs the school curriculum is separated into different ability tracks, and the vocational school is even physically separated from the academic school. Such a physical separation makes integration quite difficult, as academic and vocational teachers find themselves isolated from one another. Often, in their isolation, "us-and-them" relations develop (Hillison, & Camp, 1985; Douglas, 1992).

When learning *what* is separated from learning *how*, the decontextualization of learning is justified. School knowledge is abstracted from the context in which it is learned and used, rendering the cultivation of postformal modes of thinking impossible. It requires little argument to justify the notions that vocational preparation should involve academics and academic preparation should involve the contextualizing influence of occupational processes. Even so, few educators have grasped the manner in which the dualisms serve to exacerbate learning pathologies in American schools. The Norwegian root word of "crazy" is *krasa*, which means fragmented, the separation of a whole that belongs together. Indeed, the panoply of dualisms to which we have made reference is nothing if not crazy. A critical pedagogy of work that integrates academic and vocational education seeks to end the crazy injustice that designates the poor and non-white as vocational students who are subsequently trained to fit into a repressive workplace.

John Dewey contended that the integration of academic and vocational education in American schools was directly related to the question of what type of life humans would produce in a technological civilization. Dewey understood that the act of academic and vocational integration signified a number of important understandings, including an appreciation of the subtle ways injustice is perpetuated at a tacit institutional level—a realization that present understandings of cognition do not adequately account for manual expressions of intelligence, and a cognizance of the fact that teaching methodology must be revolutionized. Dewey's symbiotic view of knowledge (as opposed to the dualist epistemological tradition) laid the foundation for a democratic society that valued both hand and brain, learning *how* and learning *what* and forms of knowing emerging from various subcultures including the subjugated knowledge of the poor and dispossessed (Wirth, 1983).

Now that the Perkins Act has mandated that academic and vocational education be integrated, the concept has new appeal and possibility (Hudelson, 1992). Even mainstream educators are arguing that vocational education can make academics more concrete and understandable, and that academic education can point out the vocational ramifications of all forms of learning (Beck, 1991). In this context, for example, vocational students in agriculture study environmental science gaining insights into the connections between farming and various forms of pollution. At the same time these students might study the politics of environmental damage, exploring the ways that powerful agriculture related businesses keep government from interfering with their ecologically insensitive practices. Home economics students uncover personal insights, studying the family from both psychological and sociological perspectives. In the course of such a study, students might examine the politics of the debate over family values, analyzing the assumptions that shape the various political positions. Auto mechanics students find physics and mathematics to be more meaningful and even easier to learn when considered in relation to cars (Rehm, 1989). In this situation, students might also explore the interesting history of automobile safety from both a technical and political perspective, analyzing the way the power wielded by U.S. auto manufacturers delayed the implementation of safety features.

This curriculum theory of academic and vocational education brings together five features in the attempt to address the rupture between learning *what* and learning *how*—academic learning, vocational learning, critical social concerns, worksite placement, and postformal thinking. Sensitive to the social and economic context in which it must operate, this critically grounded integration cultivates an awareness of the relationship between its goals and the existence of the postmodern hyperreality and the emerging post–Fordist economy. Dedicated to the critical goals of social and economic justice, good work, and the analysis of power relations, the integrated curriculum utilizes experiential knowledge gained from worksite placement of students to help produce workers and citizens of all varieties who are capable of sophisticated analysis. The model on page 79 may help us understand this curriculum theory.

## THE VALUE OF VOCATIONAL EDUCATION

As we explore the various dimensions of this theory of integration, the traditional question concerning what academic education can do for its step-child, vocational education, is turned on its head. The question of what vocational education can do for academic learning focuses our attention on the reform of high school for all students, whether they are college bound or work bound. Vocational education by its nature addresses the traditional criticisms of academic education—its aridity, boredom, teacher dominance, lecture-centeredness, and student passivity. At its best, vocational education requires more participatory instructional strategies, promotes activities that are intrinsically interesting, stimulates cooperative rather than competitive learning, and provides more possibility for student initiative.

Vocational education should not be seen as just another set of courses competing for a student's time. Such education should be carefully integrated with academic learning in a manner that facilitates young people's ability to understand and apply what they are learning in the academic core curriculum. Through this practical application of school knowledge, theoretical and conceptual ideas can gain new meaning for both students and teachers. Once integration takes place, teaching methods can never stay the same, as academic teachers begin to appropriate vocational strategies. Project-directed methods pursued in a specific context help academic teachers to transcend the decontextualized purposelessness that afflicts the high school. With this understanding, academic teachers begin to realize that the skills of general academic courses are not as transferable as educators have been comfortable thinking. Research seems to indicate that the degree to which academic or vocational experiences can be generalized depends on the resemblance between the conditions under which the learning takes place and the conditions under which it is to be applied. Of course, the point that once again emerges involves the context specificity of all learning (Copa, & Tebbenhoff, 1990; Grubb et al., 1991).

**CRITICAL POSTMODERN
INTEGRATION OF ACADEMIC AND
VOCATIONAL EDUCATION**

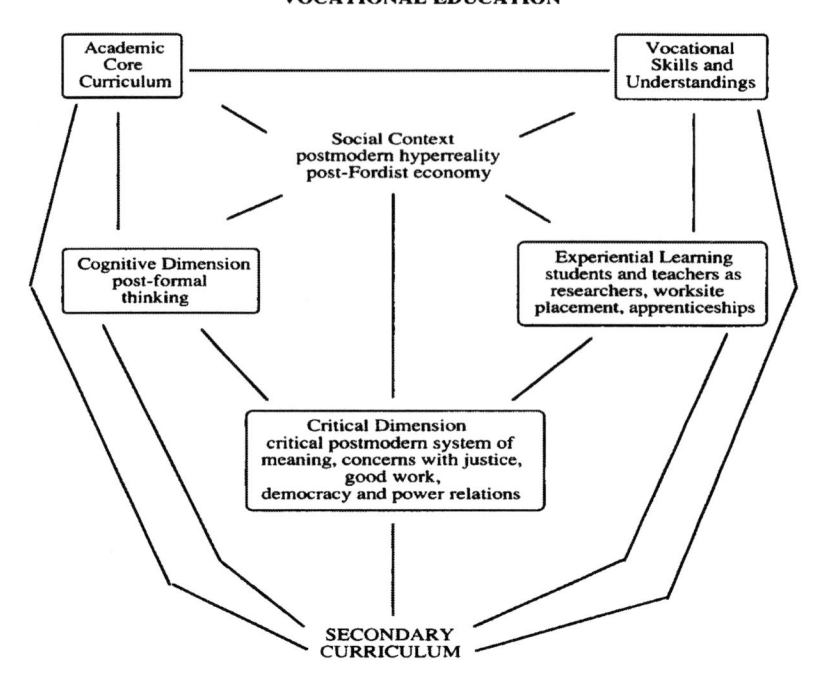

- Academic Core Curriculum
- Vocational Skills and Understandings
- Social Context: postmodern hyperreality, post-Fordist economy
- Cognitive Dimension: post-formal thinking
- Experiential Learning: students and teachers as researchers, worksite placement, apprenticeships
- Critical Dimension: critical postmodern system of meaning, concerns with justice, good work, democracy and power relations
- SECONDARY CURRICULUM

## LEARNING ACADEMIC SKILLS IN CONTEXT

Students of cognition who examine learning in context (situated cognition) have criticized traditional cognitive science for its individualistic focus—that is, its exclusive concern with individual mental activity. In this isolation, traditional cognitive science has marginalized the wider social and material context in which thinking is implanted. Such cognitive perspectives have led to schooling practices that involve the teacher as information deliverer, student as fact gatherer, and assessment as the testing of individual performance in a narrow setting. Utilizing anthropological and sociological ways of inquiring, students of situated cognition recognize the inadequacy of individualized and fragmented schooling. They realize that the world of the shop floor, hospital, or the family is a cosmos of constant change and ambiguity.

A critical postmodern pedagogy of work that integrates academic and vocational education understands that profound learning demands an education that takes place in a context that matters to the learner. Marginally literate adults enrolled in a workplace reading program experienced far greater improvement in job related reading than in general reading. Study after study indicates that learning which takes place in a meaningful context is more profound than decontextualized learning (Raizen, 1989). A critical curriculum of integration reorients schooling in a way that meaningfully contextualizes lessons in relation to work. Students learn academic skills in a vocational context where they can learn by doing with the freedom to profit from their mistakes (Harp, 1992; Schon, 1987). For example, a recent study analyzed a class attempting to teach students with weak math and reading skills to become electronics technicians. Traditional approaches provided remedial drills in math and reading before introducing students to the subject of electronics. In the program under analysis, Thomas Sticht, the instructor, began the course with what students already knew about flashlights, lamps, and radios. As students inspected the electrical devices, Sticht pointed out the systems-related and functional features of the equipment. Then, in the *context* of these familiar devices, reading, writing, diagramming, mathematics, critical thinking, problem detection and problem solving were integrated with the teaching of technical electronics (Raizen, & Colvin, 1991).

The way individuals learn in the context of their jobs is very different from the form learning takes in the traditional school. Not only, of course, is most workplace learning group based and cooperative, it relies on the use of simple and complex tools. In the work context, most workers, including even illiterate workers, acquire mathematical skills and formulate creative mechanisms to solve math problems. Studies of the computational skills of unschooled children who sell merchandise in the street markets of Recife, Brazil indicate that they constantly make complex mathematical calculations in their businesses. When confronted with the same problems in a paper and pencil school-type test, they were lost. Indeed, their attempts to follow school-based math teaching methods disrupted the children's ability to compute. Such findings don't mean that we should scrap traditional methods of teaching math, but they do tell us that we should seriously reconsider them. The formal algorithms taught in schools need to be learned in context in a way that expands an individual's thought processes so that problems can be identified and solved. Such an approach would revolutionize the teaching of math as it provided meaning to math lessons. Academic and vocational integration offers the context needed to initiate such changes.

## MAKING ACADEMIC SKILLS USABLE

The integration of academic and vocational education requires curriculum developers to consider how academic skills can be understood and used by students and teachers. Such consideration necessitates a brief reference to modernist and post-modernist epistemologies-objectivism and constructivism. In objectivism, facts are what they are, and truth can always be discerned by an appeal to the facts. A constructivist view of knowledge sees individuals constructing their meanings and interpretations of facts in light of their own experiences and contexts. The objectivist or modernist view of knowledge is a one-truth epistemology that has affected all aspects of Western life, education being no exception (Schon, 1987). Since objectivist knowledge (like a child's conception of pre-Columbian North America) is predefined and waiting to be discovered "out there," what use is it to teach speculative and interpretive strategies? Schools of the post-Enlightenment era emphasized not the production of knowledge but the learning of that which had already been defined as knowledge. Students of modernism's one-truth epistemology are treated like one-trick ponies, rewarded only for short-term retention of certified truths. Teachers learn in their "educational science" courses that knowledge is acquired in a linear skill or subskill process. Pre-identified in the context of adult logic, the linear process is imposed on children in a manner that focuses teacher/ parent attention away from the child's constructions of reality, away from the child's point of view. Thus, children's answers are often "wrong," when actually, given their point of view, the wrong answer may indicate ingenuity.

As a critical constructivist (see Kincheloe, 1993), I believe that learning is a form of "worldmaking." Engaging in thousands of acts of attention and inattention, naming, decoding, interpreting, and setting and transgressing borders, workers make their worlds and their know-how. Acting on this understanding, constructivist teachers avoid top-down curriculum designs where expert knowledge is transferred to students who memorize it. Instead, they teach for understanding and application, in the process researching students' original constructions of the subject at hand. A critical postmodern curriculum of integration takes student experience seriously, as its teachers attempt to discern the ways students give meaning to their lives and the role that schooling and work might play in that process.

The integration of academic and vocational education is connected to the core of this process, as it creates a context that allows schooling to connect with student interest. Operating in an integrated curriculum, a group of inner city high school students inquires into the forces that keep them out of the job market. In the process, they read literature on the relationships that connect work, racism, and class bias. Part of their inquiry involves conducting an ethnographic study of unemployed young people in their community, searching for patterns that grant insight into the origins, nature, and solutions to inner city unemployment. Not only are such students learning to read, write, communicate, and research, their interest in school is piqued, and they are learning to think in a critical, postformal manner. In addition, they begin to see that their lives are worthy of study, that they are intelligent, and that school learning could possibly play a role in improving the quality of their lives (MacLeod, 1987).

In harmony with advocates of situated learning, high school students scream for a real world context. Students studying physics in a critical integrated curriculum might seek apprentice-like experiences with a mechanical engineer at a local factory. A deal could be worked out between the firm and the school, designating particular times for engineer volunteers to work with a few students. During the apprenticeship, students would shadow the engineer at work, learning specific ways that the professional incorporated various forms of knowledge into his or her practice. Close cooperation between the firm and the school would inform the engineer of the specifics of the high school curriculum so that he or she could tailor the apprenticeship to directly connect with the students' experiences.

Such an apprenticeship would be part of a curriculum of experience that connects the needs and concerns of students to conceptual/theoretical understandings and to the insights gained from a practical context. Such an education becomes indistinguishable from everyday life with little discontinuity between daily activities and the learning of work-related skills and sophisticated forms of cognition. Many of the work-related activities in this integrated curriculum situate learning as something that is undertaken for its immediate use and value, rather than as something required for a degree or for next year's class. The learning that takes place does not proceed in a linear order that is determined by a curriculum guide—indeed, outside authority has little to do with the activities of students and teachers. Stories are very important in the integrated curriculum, as they share experiences, exemplify and personalize learning, and interpret the relationship between school knowledge and the life experiences students and teachers bring with them. When apprenticeship-like activities are connected with a critical integrated curriculum, possibilities for cognitive growth are unparalleled.

## ACTIVITY, CONCEPT, AND CULTURE

Senta Raizen argues that in a vocational learning situation, the work activity being studied, the conceptual device being employed to study the activity, the cultural context formed by the dynamics of the workplace, and the ways of seeing characteristic of the people involved in such work must all be understood by a successful student. Activity, concept, and culture are, thus, interdependent as students in a critical integrated program come to see the dynamic interaction of these components in all work situations. Learning conceived this way becomes, in a sense, a process of enculturation as students are introduced into a community with its own language, knowledge, ways of seeing, and conceptual tools (Raizen, 1989). A critical postmodern pedagogy of work disrupts the smooth functioning of such an enculturation, sensing that the term, enculturation, possesses a dangerous underside. Without a careful questioning, enculturation can come to mean *adjustment* to the world as it is. Such a vocational enculturation must always question the status quo in terms of a critical vision of a democratic, multicultural community.

Academic and vocational integration would allow for the construction of an educational situation that is aware of contextual factors in all learning. Students, for example, studying economic justice and democratic forms of work in an academically and vocationally integrated economics class would need to realize that, in the context of the existing American workplace, such an idea is viewed suspiciously. Understanding such a context, students would need to research the way workers deal with regressive management. In the process, students would develop strategies designed to address alienated workplaces in a way that is politically smart and contextually savvy. They could become agents of change who are aware of the fear their position engenders and of the conflict it could ignite.

At the same time, such students would come to understand the low regard this society holds for a curriculum that involves making a living. Detractors connect such studies with courses in underwater basket weaving, window cleaning, or mop jockeying. In their effort to ridicule the unfortunate tendency for "over-vocationalization," they over-generalize. To argue that concerns with making a living have no place in a liberal education is to contend that education has no connection to the larger social context. Traditional educational philosophy has often associated training for making a living with "dense" students (Beck, 1991). Education for the "less able" child included pottery, outdoor pursuits, weaving, woodworking, metalwork, domestic science and motherhood, and many other activities. Such activities have been thought to involve little or no reasoning and should be recommended for people with "limited intellect" (Carr, 1984). Students who study vocational topics will have to contend with these prejudices, not only in their education, but also in their work lives.

A critical integrated curriculum rejects these expressions of socio-economic class prejudice. Respecting the intellectual and creative potential of *all* learners, the advocates of critical integration recognize that crafts and trades involve higher orders of intellect at both the perceptual and bodily levels. Such advocates refuse to validate the common assumption within the culture of formal education that the theoretical ways of knowing of the academic disciplines are innately superior to the practical ways of knowing of the vocations (Rehm, 1989, p. 110). When one knows how to perform a certain task, he or she is able to deploy strategies that help accomplish a particular purpose. Traditionally, psychologists and philosophers have not regarded such activity as manifestations of intellect. Any curriculum theory that fails to acknowledge the educational importance of the practical knowledge of the trades and crafts is guilty not only of pedagogical ignorance but of class bias as well.

When teachers make the attempt to cultivate practical knowledge, changes begin to occur in the everyday life of schools. For example, when reading teachers work with high school students with low reading skills, connecting reading improvement with the attempt to gain practical knowledge, they begin to reverse the failure of traditional remediation. Reading-to-do and reading-to-learn strategies make reading more enjoyable, in the process better developing general reading skills. Low-skill students fascinated with riding and repairing motorcycles can improve their reading dramatically when a teacher assigns material on this topic. The teacher's role does not end with the assignment, as he or she monitors progress and assigns students activities that expand their ability to conceptualize, interpret, apply, contextualize, and understand. Using postformal thinking (Kincheloe, & Steinberg, 1993) as a benchmark, teachers connect reading improvement with cognitive development.

In this manner the curriculum of integration attempts to focus attention on the cognitive process—it attempts to induce teachers and students to think about their thinking, the connections between their academic knowledge and their practical knowledge. As students learn both *about* work and how to do it, they begin to concentrate on the transformative possibility of their experiences. Drawing upon critical democratic insights to analyze work and work education. Critical students and teachers make explicit the types of thinking that ground repressive and anti-democratic perspectives. In this context students and teachers involved in a critical integrated curriculum studying home construction could analyze the political assumptions embedded in questions concerning shelter. Guided by their political concerns, they could analyze the politics of zoning laws in the local community, questions of homelessness, and problems with building codes. No aspect of work education would be studied in isolation, apart from questions of human values, power, and democracy (Simon, Dippo, & Schenke, 1991).

## THE SPECIFICS OF INTEGRATION-THE NECESSITY OF TEACHER COLLABORATION

Integration, no matter what form it takes, should strengthen the teaching of all subjects. When adeptly executed, integration should make history, literature, and the social sciences come alive for previously unmotivated students. As long as such programs are grounded on a critical democratic understanding and are well-planned, locations such as an automobile garage can become places of unique and profound learning. Indeed, an integrated garage can become not merely a place to fix cars but a venue where physics, chemistry, and mathematics are studied in relation to cars. The physics of torque, the chemistry of gasoline as a fuel, and mathematics of horsepower could provide compelling experiences for all students, especially ones never engaged by the traditional methods of schooling (Freeman, 1992; Feinberg, & Horowitz, 1990).

One of the most important methodological features emerging in the integrated classroom involves the ability to move back and forth from concrete to the abstract in the quest for deeper levels of understanding. Research seems to consistently show that students understand more quickly and more profoundly when they begin with concrete examples and then move to abstract theoretical principles. In one research study, a vocational teacher taught his electronics class to draw a graphic illustration of integrated circuits and then to perform the task in actual practice. Many students were not able to accomplish the exercise. When the teacher asked his class to begin with the concrete (the actual practice) and then move to the abstract (the graphic representation of what they had done), almost all of the students were able to successfully complete the task (Wirth, 1983; Packer, 1992; Mjelde, 1987).

The integration of academic and vocational education requires teacher collaboration. Teachers working together is a relatively rare sight in contemporary schools, as teachers retreat to their private domains. The benefits of collaboration become quickly apparent, as teachers better appreciate the relationships between courses, the common purpose that unites them with other professionals, the meaning of deeper levels of understanding, postformal thinking and the relationship between good work and educational purpose. Collaboration does not mean that academic specialists would become interchangeable with vocational specialists, but it does mean that each would gain a far greater understanding of what the other does. With this understanding, and as they attend to the diverse aspects of a critical postmodern education and the synergisms created when one aspect is considered in relation to the others their ability to turn out good students and smart workers will dramatically increase.

## INTEGRATION SO FAR

With the passage of the Perkins Act, and with its mandate to integrate academic and vocational curricula, integration has gained momentum. Hopefully, the movement will avoid the fate of other progressive reforms that have lost their purposes and their critical edges in a sea of bureaucratic rules and regulations. Even in the early stages of the integration movement, we can identify unfortunate trends—schools rushing to meet the requirements of the Perkins Act by devising programs that are integrative in name only; the tendency for large industries and businesses to shift the emphasis of fledgling programs away from concerns with economic justice and democratic work toward more traditional attempts to adjust young workers to work as it presently exists; and the production of integrated curriculum materials that subvert the more critical and complex aspects of integration.

Nevertheless, promising examples of integration exist. In many schools vocational and academic instructors team teach applied academic courses. Observers note that in the best of these classes, it is very difficult to differentiate the academic from the vocational teacher. Both instructors are familiar with the academic content and the vocational application and easily move back and forth between the concrete and the theoretically abstract. In such classes students are engaged and highly motivated, as teachers offer compelling reasons for attending to what is going on. Students are constantly moving between seatwork in academic classrooms to vocational applications in adjacent laboratories. Teachers and students in field-based integration projects in construction have integrated their understandings of the world of work (including such domains as drafting, marketing, home economics, and horticulture) and their academic skills (for example, math, English, and science).

Critical dimensions of integrated programs seem to be more common in home economics than in other vocational areas. One program in Family and Technology, for example, examines the interrelationship between technological development and the work of the family. In such a context, students and teachers explore the ways that families construct meanings, develop values, and produce patterns of thinking. Another example of academic and vocational integration involves students learning the technology of filmmaking as they learn to research in various content areas. In one such program, high school students won several prizes in an international university-level film contest. In all of these examples of integration, there is one common thread—students and teachers were learning how to learn.

The possibilities for new curricula and methodological innovations are endless in programs that critically integrate academic and vocational education. Students and teachers have the possibility of opening new conversations about work and its role in their lives, its relation to various aspects of physical and social reality. Students, especially those from economically disadvantaged homes, have a chance to escape the oppressive tracking system that delegates them to second-class citizenship in America's schools. I envision a working class high school student deadened by eleven years of being labeled a failure entering an integrated auto mechanics/ physics class. Fascinated by engines, he has become adept at auto repair and is excited about the new class. Entering a classroom of untracked, heterogeneous students, he is intimidated until he realizes that, for the first time since he started to go to school, he holds the valued knowledge—he is the student who understands the workings of the engine and its component parts. The instructors ask him to help his more economically privileged peers with their attempt to identify the parts of the engine. In this situation he is the smart one for the first time he experiences school success. The effect is dramatic. His genius is recognized—Ronnie and Brandon's never was.

## REFERENCES

Beck, R. (1991). *General education: Vocational and academic collaboration.* Berkeley, CA: NCRVE.
Carr, H. (1984). We integrated the academics. *Vocational Education, 59*(2), 34–36.
Copa. G., & Tebbenhoff, E. (1990). *Subject matter of vocational education: In pursuit of Foundations.* Berkeley, CA: NCRVE.
Douglas, A. (1992). Mending the rift between academic and vocational education. *Educational Leadership, 49*(6), 42–43.
Feinberg, W., & Horowitz, B. (1990). Vocational education and the equality of opportunity. *Journal of Curriculum Studies, 22*(2), 188–192.
Freeman, M. (1992). Food for thought. *Vocational Educational Journal, 67*(8), 28–29, 72.
Grubb, N., Davis, G., Lum, J., Phihal, J., & Morgaine. C. (1991). *The cunning hand, the cultured mind: Models for integrating vocational and academic education.* Berkeley, CA: NCRVE.
Harp, L. (1992, September 23). Scuttled program's work. skill themes enjoying resurgence. *Education Week, 1,* 13.
Herrnstein, R., & Murray, C. (1994). The *bell curve: Intelligence and class structure in American life.* New York: The Free Press.
Hillison, J., & Camp, W. (1985). History and future of the dual school system for vocational education. *Journal of Vocational and Technical Education, 2*(1), 48–56.
Hudelson, D. (1992). Roots of reform: Tracing the path of workforce education. *Vocational Education Journal, 67*(7), 28–29.
Kincheloe, J. L. (1993). *Toward a critical politics of teacher thinking: Mapping the postmodern.* Westport, CT: Bergin and Garvey.
Kincheloe, J. L. (1995). *Toil and trouble: Good work, smart workers, and the integration of academic and vocational education.* New York: Peter Lang.
Kincheloe, J. L., & Steinberg S. R. (1993). A tentative description of postformal thinking: The critical confrontation with cognitive theory. *Harvard Educational Review, 63*(3), 296–320.
MacLeod, J. (1987). *Ain't no makin' it: Leveled aspirations in a low-income neighborhood.* Boulder, CO: Westview Press.
Mjelde, L. (1987). From hand to mind. In D. Livingstone & contributors(Eds.), *Critical pedagogy and cultural power.* South Hadley, MA: Bergin and Garvey.
Packer, A. (1992, May 27). School to work: Helping students learn a living. *Education Week* , p. 28.
Raizen, S. (1989). *Reforming education for work: A cognitive science perspective.* Berkeley, CA: NCRVE.
Raizen, S., & Colvin, R. (1991, December 11). Apprenticeships: A cognitive-science view. *Education Week,* p. 26.
Rehm, M. (1989). Emancipatory vocational education: Pedagogy for the work of individuals and society. *Journal of Education, 171*(3), 109–123.
Schon, D. (1987). *Educating the reflective practitioner.* San Francisco: Jossey-Bass Publishers.
Simon, R., Dippo, D., & Schenke, A. (1991). *Learning work: A critical pedagogy of work education.* New York: Bergin and Garvey.
Wirth, A. (1983). *Productive work in industry and schools.* Lanham, MD: University Press of American.

Reprinted with permission: Kincheloe, J. L. (1995). Schools where Ronnie and Brandon would have excelled: a curriculum theory of academic and vocational education. *Journal of Curriculum Theory, 11*(3), 61–83.

GENE FELLNER

# REFLECTIONS ON JOE KINCHELOE'S SCHOOLS WHERE RONNIE AND BRANDON WOULD HAVE EXCELLED

*A Curriculum Theory of Academic and Vocational Education*

In the Newark, New Jersey middle schools, where I mentor language arts teachers, the concept of integrating vocational and academic programs, that Joe so convincingly advocates for in his article, *Schools where Ronnie and Brandon would have excelled,* has no immediate possibility of becoming a reality. To begin with, there are no vocational courses as part of the curriculum on the middle school level. After eighth grade, students do have the option of applying to "vocational" schools that include academic learning, but the two are not integrated in the way Joe envisions they should be, indeed they are barely integrated at all. Vocational training exists alongside academic learning and they are seen as two distinct trajectories which have no bearing on each other. Meanwhile, in "academic" schools there is no "vocational" ingredient at all. This fragmented education then characterizes both schools labeled academic and vocational. Additionally, as Joe pointed out in his article, those schools labeled "vocational" are seen as "lesser" by the educational elite—in Newark they seem to be repositories for "low-performing" students in failing middle schools.

That eighth grade students in Newark's failing schools should be encouraged to apply to vocational high schools regardless of their aptitudes is seriously problematic. The eighth graders I have worked with are usually not in a position to declare what they want to do with the rest of their lives and most do not realize the import of choosing to attend a vocational vs. an academic high school. Just last week, I sat with eighth grade students who were writing entrance essays to get into high schools in Newark. One student with a keen mind and a passionate anti-racist and anti-homophobic streak who said he wanted to be a singer was applying to a school of technology but was not sure if they had a music program. I asked many of the other boys who were also applying to vocational schools what they wanted to study; one of them said "computers" but the others had no idea. They all agreed, though, that they wanted to play football. They didn't know, however, if the technology schools to which they were applying even had a football team.

That organically integrated academic-vocational curriculums do not exist constrains student possibilities in the future, denying them the range of educational experiences that could put them in touch with their talents, abilities, aspirations and dispositions and expose them to ideas and practices that could open up the world to them in a different way. It also rigidifies a false dichotomy between academic and vocational education and the elitism that privileges the former. This is to say that students, already stigmatized on so many levels for being poor, Black, and Latino, are further marginalized by educational structures that are informed by the very deficit epistemologies, ontologies and axiologies that Joe condemns in his article.

The imposition of these structures has served to constrain constructivist learning and participant agency without improving student scores on standardized tests. Fewer than 50% of Newark middle schoolers have passed these tests in every year since 2001 and indeed I work within schools that have been labeled failing schools by the state of New Jersey for over ten years. Joe's 1995 proposals for integrating vocational and academic education with the goal of assisting all students to fulfill their potential thus remains as pertinent and as critical as ever.

The administrators of Newark's middle schools and the policymakers who monitor and direct them would vociferously deny, as would many of the teachers, that the schools in which they work mediate against optimizing student learning. Indeed, they repeatedly announce to their students that "you will succeed," "you can be anything you want to be," and "failure is not an option," and many are sincere in believing that their unintegrated, teach-to-the-test curricula will serve their students well. But the structures that have been designed by educational decision makers and that determine how and what is being taught and the context within which "teaching" takes place, mediate against the realization of those very goals. Their imposition on students and teachers has rendered the schools ever more authoritarian while teaching has become increasingly formulaic. The design by which these schools are run, the "conceived space" of the educational planners and architects, overlays the daily lived lives of students, teachers and administrators and mediates the daily rhythm of their lives.

In one Newark middle school, for example, the language arts block is subdivided into five-to-fifteen minute units of scripted activities that are clocked to the minute by stop watches that some teachers use to assure their own adherence to the timed mandates—5 minutes warm up, 5 minutes read aloud, 10 minutes word study, 15 minutes mini-lesson, 10 minutes shared reading, 15 minutes group or independent reading. Any diversion from this schedule, for discussion, critical analysis, or arts infused work, is prohibited. Academic education in these schools follows the most oppressive features of the factory model, "training" students to comply with timed schedules without building any vocational skills or, arguably, any skills at all except that of obedience to routine. It is not surprising that so many students drop out. Teachers drop out as well. More than half of new teachers with advanced degrees leave full-time classroom teaching or migrate to schools in which they are not micromanaged as rigidly (Hunt, & Darling-Hammond, 2003). Foucault's analysis of schools as an extension of military and factory discipline and one more weapon in the service of hegemonic control is well illustrated here.

The elitism against blue collar jobs that Joe addresses and its correlation in the minds of educators with lesser intellectual abilities is given a perverse twist in the Newark schools in which I work. Skills categorized as strictly academic are taught as if they were assembly line products geared solely for functional use by low-ability "work bound" students in the same vein as the "vocational" subjects that Joe writes about. Academic subjects, even within a strictly "academic" framework, are torn away from any application they might have to the lives that the students are living, just as they were for Ronnie and Brandon. And so, in language arts classes, students who have never gone camping are asked to speculate on what they might have forgotten on a camping trip or are asked to write persuasive essays about things they care nothing about. This despite the fact that, in theory, the literacy strategies employed emphasize the importance of making connections between self and text and accessing student background knowledge. Their implementation, however, through routinized, inflexible, and imposed methods contradict their purpose. Constructivist epistemologies that Joe has done so much to further, illuminate and deepen have been tossed aside for rote learning that disparages and silences student knowledge and experience. Since No Child Left Behind, students in poor districts who are as brilliant, creative, talented, curious and funny as students anywhere else have been further marginalized and deprived of the educational options that they and their families seek and deserve. One of these options is education that embraces curriculum integration rather than the separation of vocational and academic learning.

The idea of curriculum integration, as Joe explained, is not new. John Dewey, in the years preceding the First World War, wrote that schooling should integrate work, study and play and advocated a borderless merging of schools and communities, academic and vocational skills, manual and intellectual talents, hearts and minds. He urged the education of the whole person with each individual progressing at her own pace along with teachers serving as guides. Students and teachers together would construct knowledge and reflect upon it. Dewey advocated apprenticeships, field trips, and the involvement of families and businesses in the educational development of the child. Education was to embrace vocational and educational learning and the arts. Dewey's world, like Joe's, was not an either-or world, a world of dichotomous thinking, and rigidified frontiers between disciplines. Rather it was an all embracing one in which everything flowed into everything else, sometimes seamlessly and sometimes uneasily but always interacting and evolving in a continuous dialectical cycle. And Dewey, like Joe, was ontologically and axiologically committed to a world in which students, teachers, citizens would work collaboratively for justice and peace without sacrificing their individuality and uniqueness. It is sobering that, a century later, Joe reasserted and focused Dewey's critique on the schools of today at a time when state governments and national educational policy, even under President Obama, are inventing evermore ways to categorize, quantify, fragmentize, and dichotomize an educational curriculum that excludes vocational education, hands-on knowledge, art and play from the curricula of schools in our most marginalized neighborhoods and seeks to transform teachers into mechanized cogs within an educational machine.

What can't be quantified, qualities like joy in learning, creativity, emotional fulfillment, curiosity, collaboration—knowledge of self and others has no official place in the curricula of the schools in which I teach. Teachers have been told that focusing on these unmeasurable criteria diverts energy from achieving academic excellence whereas Joe believed that they may serve as the very foundation for academic achievement. Teachers and administrators have been told that their jobs depend only on how well students perform on standardized tests (which are reserved for only language arts and math). The fact that in the middle schools where I work, the average score on the standardized literacy tests, is only 46% (School Digger. com, 2008) seven years after No Child Left Behind became law, which would, one might think, expose the contradictions involved in the deficit ontologies and epistemologies that are dominant today in the schools. Apparently, however, this is not the case. Instead of reassessing a failed policy that restricts educational options and ignores individual ways of learning, policymakers are narrowing the curriculum even more and stifling the talents of many of our students.

Recently, I was sitting in a Newark classroom with a number of literacy and math teachers who were eating lunch. I asked them how the school year was going. They were, unanimously, both furious and depressed. They told me that at the start of the year the principal told them that he had almost fired a number of teachers but decided, at the last minute, to continue with the teaching staff that he had. He wouldn't reveal which teachers he was dissatisfied with, but said he reserved the right to let go any teacher who was not working up to speed. The teachers said that, under the circumstances, they were frightened to voice any complaints they might have with the scripted curriculum or with the unprofessional way in which they were being treated. Meanwhile, they said, their workload had tripled. Under these conditions, the ideas that Joe puts forward—of teachers working together collaboratively, of loosening "top-down" management; of improving counseling and encouraging community involvement, of taking students' experiences seriously and connecting with them—is a dream still waiting to become reality. Principals, frightened that their schools will be closed because of poor test results create a climate of fear in the schools, a circle of symbolic violence that mediates against creating a community of knowledge construction that benefits all of its members.

I did not know Joe personally, but when I arrived at the CUNY Graduate Center to pursue doctoral studies in 2007, his presence was felt everywhere though he had already moved to McGill University where he had founded the Paulo and Nita Freire International Project for Critical Pedagogy. Among the faculty at CUNY, his presence had been clearly controversial, but every student I met who had worked with Joe adored him, credited him with opening their eyes and helping them to find and enrich their own passions in their own ways while sharpening the intellectual rigor that they brought to their studies. Ken Tobin always says that, more than any other person, Joe was able to put himself in the shoes of the students he was speaking to, see the world from their perspectives, help reveal their strengths, join in their enthusiasms for what they were engaged in and travel with them on the roads they chose to follow.

Joe demonstrates this ability in this article where he sees the world through the eyes of Ronnie and Brandon and helps them to realize their own talents and abilities and how, through practicing their vocation, they acquired math skills that they were not able to learn in schools where math appeared to be irrelevant to skills such as carpentry. It was the insight that Ronnie and Brandon learned "academic" skills through vocational work that was meaningful to them that helped Joe realize the importance of advocating for integrated curricula. Joe also realized that far from being oppositional, academic and vocational education enrich each other, they are constantly intertwining spurs that braid together to the benefit of mind, heart and soul in their differences and in their unity. Joe's work, and his article about integrated curricula reflect his belief that every child, every student, every person has the capacity to construct knowledge with others if only structures are in place that afford the possibility of doing so and that demonstrate the interconnection of vocational, educational and dare I say artistic ways of thinking.

In his article about Ronnie and Brandon and curriculum theory, Joe makes it clear how important these structures are, and how important to their construction are ontologies that see, value and seek to further the potential and the fulfillment of every member of the community. Because the structures of so many schools in Newark mediate against such liberatory ontologies and epistemologies and thus against the integrated curricula which is only one aspect of such a standpoint, it is not likely that the students I see will have the opportunities that Joe demands that they have. The fact that teachers are generally frightened to question authority and that collaborative resistance between them and their students is rare also mediates against the inclusion of the proposals that Joe made in his article. Nevertheless, as Foucault wrote, practicing liberty is always an option. Teachers and students can always, to some degree, resist and thus transform the structures that confine them. Joe, in this article and in his many other publications, provides us with theoretical foundations, creative proposals, and unwavering support to create structures that serve our goals.

## REFERENCES

Hunt, J. B., & Darling-Hammond, L. (2003, January). *No dream denied: A pledge to America's children.* National Commission on Teaching and America's Future.

School Digger. com. (2008). Schools in Newark, NJ. *Search for a school in New Jersey.* Retrieved November 28, 2008, from http://www.schooldigger.com/go/NJ/city/Newark/search.aspx

*1990, Winter holidays, Myrtle Beach, South Carolina. It was our goal to always get out of town during what is commonly known as Christmastime. Neither Joe nor I relished the annoying pleasantries, decorations, insane shopping, and Christianity of the holiday period. Each year we would come up with another way to entertain four children and ourselves, by avoiding the tripe that the holiday brought. In Myrtle Beach, we found long beaches for the kids to run and walk on, and, well, cold weather. So we decided to go to 3 movies a day and see everything the theaters had to offer. After boring our kids with grownup stuff, they convinced us we had to see Home Alone. We snuck in two cans of beer, and settled in with the progeny to watch a dreaded kid flick. The film was well produced, directed, and entertaining. But every few minutes, Joe and I would turn to one another and comment, or even just raise our eyebrows. We realized we had something. What was it with this mother hating, smartass filmmaker, who had the audacity to even sneak in an anti-Semitic scene? What was it with this over-stimulated blond brat, and the construct of the American family as kid-hating, kid fearing? On the drive home, we came up with Kinderculture. Americans did hate their kids, mothers were seen as failures, and corporate culture had redefined childhood. Joe would spend many hours watching the Home Alone and Parenthood films, and his work sophisticated the newly developed area of cultural studies and childhood. SS*

JOE L. KINCHELOE

# 6. THE NEW CHILDHOOD

*Home Alone as a Way of Life*

*Home Alone* (1990) and *Home Alone 2: Lost in New York* (1992) revolve around Kevin McAlister's (Macaulay Culkin) attempts to find his family after (1) being left behind on a family Christmas trip to Paris; and (2) being separated from his family on a Christmas trip to Miami. Wildly successful, the two movies portray the trials and tribulations of Kevin's attempts to take care of himself while his parents try to rejoin him. In the process of using these plots to set up a variety of comedic stunts and sight gags, the movies inadvertently allude to a sea of troubles relating to children and family life in the late twentieth century. As we watch the films, an entire set of conflicts and contradictions revolving around the lives of contemporary children begin to emerge. In this way *Home Alone 1* and *2* take on a social importance unimagined by producers, directors, and screenplay writers. In this essay I will use the family dynamics of the *Home Alone* movies as a means of exposing the social forces that have altered Western childhood over the last couple of decades. In both films a central but unspoken theme involves the hurt and pain that accompany children and their families in postmodern America.

## A GENERATION OF KIDS LEFT HOME ALONE

Childrearing is a victim of the late twentieth century. With divorces and two working parents, fathers and mothers are around children for less of the day. As parents are still at work in the afternoon when children get home from school, children are given 'latchkeys' and expected to take care of themselves. Thus, we have seen generations of "home aloners" – kids that in large part have had to raise themselves. The last thirty years have witnessed a change in family structure that must be taken seriously by parents, educators, and cultural workers of all stripes. Since the early 1960s the divorce rate as well as the percentage of children living with one parent has tripled. Only one-half of today's children have parents, who are married to each other. By the twenty-first century only one-third of U.S. children will have such parents. Among children under six-years old, one in four live in poverty. The stress that comes from the economic changes of the last twenty years has undermined the stability of the family. Family incomes have stagnated, as costs of middle class existence (home ownership, health care, and higher education) have skyrocketed. Since the late 1960s the amount of time parents spend with their children has dropped from an average of thirty hours per week to seventeen (Lipsky and Abrams, 1994; Galston, 1991). Increasingly left to fend for themselves, children have turned to TV and video games to help pass their time alone.

Any study of contemporary children must analyze the social conditions that shape family life. Rarely do mainstream social commentators make reference to the fact that the American standard of living peaked in 1973 creating a subsequent declining economic climate that demanded mothers work. While the effects of international competition, declining productivity, and the corporate reluctance to reinvent the workplace all contributed to a depressed economy, not all recent family problems can be ascribed to the declining post-Fordist economy. The decline of the public space and the growth of cynicism have undermined the nation's ability to formulate creative solutions to family dysfunction. The 1970s and 1980s, for example, while witnessing the birth and growth of a family value movement, also represented an era that consistently privileged individual gratification over the needs of the community (Paul, 1994; Coontz, 1992). Such an impulse justified the privatistic retreat from public social involvement that had been institutionalized in the 1980s as part of a larger right-wing celebration of self-reliance and efficient government. Unfortunately, it is often our children who must foot the cost of this perverse abrogation of democratic citizenship.

One scene in *Home Alone* particularly highlights the decline of the public space in postmodern America. While Kevin's parents attempt to arrange a flight from Paris to their home in Chicago, the rest of the family watches *It's a Wonderful Life* dubbed into French on TV. This positioning of movie within a movie confronts viewers with the distance between the America of Jimmy Stewart's George Bailey and Macaulay Culkin's Kevin McAlister. Kevin has no community, no neighbors to call for help—he is on his own in his "private space." George Bailey had a score of neighbors to help bail him out of his financial plight and to help him fight the capitalists' efforts to destroy the community. Kevin is not just home alone—he is socially alone as well. But such realizations are not present in the conscious mind of the movie-makers. On the surface the McAlisters live in a desirable community and are a perfect family. Like millions of other late twentieth century families, they are physically together but culturally and emotionally fragmented. Plugged into their various "market segments" of entertainment media they retreat into their "virtual isolation booths."

Like millions of other kids Kevin feels isolated in such an existence—isolation leads to powerlessness, hopelessness, and boredom. How could kids with everything handed to them, adults ask, become so alienated from their parents, schools, and communities? The answer to this question involves on some level the pervasive violation of childhood innocence. Popular culture via TV promised our children a *Brady Bunch* family circus, but they had to settle for alienated and isolated homes. The continuing popularity of *The Brady Bunch* is testimony to the mind-set of American children. *The Brady Bunch*, with its family values and two engaged parents, seemed to provide what our children found lacking in their own homes. This melancholy nostalgia for suburban family bliss indicates a yearning for a lost childhood. All those hours home alone have taken their toll (James, 1990; Rapping, 1994; Ferguson, 1994).

## THE UNWANTED

Although *Home Alone* 1 and 2 work hard to deny it, they are about a child unwanted by his family—as are many other films of the 1980s and early 1990s. The comedic forms of the movies supposedly render the unwanted theme harmless in the process revealing contemporary views of parenting and the abandonment of children. In one particular scene in the first *Home Alone* Kevin's mother (Catherine O'Hara) pays for abandoning her son by riding home to Chicago through Midwestern snow storms in a truck carrying a polka band leader (John Candy) and his band. In one dialogue mother and band leader engage in a confessional on bad parenting and child abandonment:

*Mother*: "I'm a bad parent"

*Band Leader*: "No, you're not. You're beating yourself up .... You want to see bad parents. We're [band] on the road *48* to 49 weeks out of the year. We hardly see our families. Joe over there, gosh, he forgets his kids' names half the time. Ziggy over there hasn't even met his kid. Eddie, let's just hope none of them [his children] write a book about him"

*Mother*: "Have you ever gone on vacation and left your child home?"

*Band Leader*: "No, but I did leave one at a funeral parlor once. Yeah, it was terrible. I was all distraught and everything. The wife and I, we left the little tyke there in the funeral parlor all day, ALL DAY. We went back at night when we came to our senses and there he was. Apparently, he was there alone all day with the corpse. He was O. K. You know after six or seven weeks he came around and started talking again. But he's O. K. They get over it. Kids are resilient like that."

*Mother*: "Maybe we shouldn't talk about it"

*Band Leader*: "You brought it up."

So comfortable are marketers with the theme of abandonment that promos on the home video of *Home Alone* 2: *Lost in New York* present a "*Home Alone* Christmas Album." Commodifying child abandonment, promoters urge viewers to "begin a tradition in your house." Something is happening in these movies and the promotions that surround them that is not generally understood by the larger society. 'By the early 1990s social neglect of children had become so commonplace that it could be presented as a comedic motif without raising too many eyebrows. There was a time when childhood accorded protected status-but that time is growing obsolete, as safety nets disintegrate and child supports crumble. Now, as children are left to fend for themselves, few public institutions exist to "address their needs."

In *Home Alone* 1 and 2 not only is Kevin left to take care of himself, but when his parents and family are on screen they treat him with disdain and cruelty, In one scene Kevin's uncle unjustifiably calls him a "little jerk." After understandably asking why he always gets "treated like scum" Kevin is banished to the attic upon which he proclaims for his generation: "families suck." These early experiences set up the comedic bread and butter of *Home Alone*: Kevin's transference of his anger toward his family to burglars Marv (Daniel Stern), and Harry (Joe Pesci) and his subsequent torture of them. *Home Alone* 1 and 2 are not the only movies of the era that address child abandonment and child revenge. In horror-thrillers *Halloween* and *Friday the 13th* the only individuals spared from violence are those who give time to and care for children. Those who neglect children must ultimately pay with their lives. As neglected social rejects, children are relegated to the margins of society. It is not surprising, therefore, that in *Home Alone 2* Kevin forges an alliance with a homeless pigeon lady who lives in Central Park—after all they are both social castoffs. Together they learn to deal with their cultural status.

## THE AMERICAN AMBIVALENCE TOWARD CHILDREN

After World War II, Americans began to realize that childhood was becoming a phase of life distinctly separate from adulthood. This distinction was most evident in the youth culture beginning to lake shape in the 1950s: it was this youth culture that convinced parents that they were losing the ability to shape the culture in which their children lived. As a result, they were losing control of their sons and daughters. This fear has informed the academic study of youth in the last half of the twentieth century, often focusing attention on children as "the problem." Too often refusing to question the dominant culture and values of the adult world and the tacit assumptions of the field of childhood studies itself, mainstream scholars have often viewed conflict between children and parents as dysfunctional. Childhood "experts" and the mainstream education establishment have often insisted in this academic context that children need to be instructed to follow directions. This functionalist orientation assumes that the order and stability of environments must be maintained (Paul, 1994; Lewis, 1992; Griffin, 1993; Polakow, 1992). This, of course, ensures that institutions such as schools become unable to accommodate change, as they regress into a state of "equilibrium" that is, rigidity.

The virtual ubiquity of parent-child alienation and conflict is rarely perceived at the individual level of human interaction as a social phenomenon. When such conflicting dynamics occur in almost all parent-child relations, it is not likely that fault rests solely with individual parents and individual children. As we said before, something larger is happening here. It seems as if individual children can't help but judge parents for their inconsistencies and shortcomings. On the other hand, parents can't help but resent their judgment and strike back with equal venom (Ventura, 1994). Adults must understand the social nature of this familial phenomenon and based on this recognition attempt to transcend the demand for order inscribed into their consciousness by the larger culture. Indeed, Americans don't understand their children or the dynamics of children's culture. Kids understand that adults just don't get it, as they listen and watch adults express and act on their misunderstandings of the differences between generational experiences and mindsets. Schools are perceived by children as virtually hopeless—indeed, they are institutionally grounded on a dismissal of these differences. Little has changed since the 1960s when Kenneth Keniston wrote that adult misunderstanding of youth contributed to the conclusion reached by many children: American mainstream culture offers us a little to live for (Lewis, 1992).

Understanding this adult-child alienation, children slowly begin to withdraw into their own culture. Culkin's Kevin has absolutely no need for adults, as he shops (with newspaper coupons even), takes care of the house, and defends himself against robbers all by himself. This is quite typical for the films of John Hughes, whose children and teenagers rule in a world where youth culture is the only one that matters. Parents in these films are notoriously absent either at work or on vacation; their advice is antiquated, consisting generally of pompous pronouncements about subjects they obviously know nothing about. Typical of the genre is *The Breakfast Club*, which revolves around the stupidity of parents and adult authority. While it is a flagrant attempt by Hughes to commodify and exploit youth culture, the film does point out the width and depth of the chasm that separates kids and adults (Rapping, 1994). Children's culture, of course, takes shape in shadows far away from the adult gaze—as well it should. The point here is that it behooves parents, teachers, social workers, and other cultural workers who are interested in the welfare of children to understand the social dynamics that shape children and their culture in the final years of the twentieth century. When parents intensify their anxiety about the threat of postmodern kinderculture (Kincheloe and Steinberg, 1996) and strike out against it, they simply widen the chasm between themselves and their children. In this situation, the assertion of parental control becomes simply an end in itself having little to do with the needs of children.

As adults in the 1950s and early 1960s began to understand the power of children's culture and the separations between childhood and adulthood it represented, parental and educator anxiety levels reached new highs. Adult fears that the kids were out of control expressed themselves in a variety of ways, none more interesting than in two British films of the early 1960s, *Village of the Damned* and its sequel, *Children of the Damned*. *Village of the Damned* is based on an invasion by an intergalactic sperm that impregnates earth women to produce a new race of mutant children who mature quickly and are capable of reading adult minds. Reflecting adult anxieties of the era concerning the growing partition between childhood and adulthood, the movie offers a "solution" to the youth problem. Though it is embraced with great difficulty, adults in *Children of the Damned* ultimately decide that they must kill their children. Understanding that child murder by necessity is suicidal in that it involves killing a part of oneself, parents sacrifice themselves in order to eradicate the iniquity their children embody. The youth rebellions of the mid-and late sixties that followed *Children of the Damned* would serve to raise the emotional ante expressed in the movie's fantasized infanticide.

The adult hostility toward children is omnipresent in *Home Alone* 1 and 2, but such issues are consistently hidden from overt recognition. Previous films—*The Other, The Exorcist, The Bad Seed, Firestarter, It's Alive*— recognized adult hostility but projected it onto evil children as a means of concealing it. The abundance of these evil children films points to a social tendency of parents to view their children as alien intruders. This child-based xenophobia positions children as foreigners whose presence marks the end of the family's configuration as a couple (Paul, 1994). Old routines are undermined and new demands must be met, as the child's power as a manipulator is experienced by harried adults. Such familial dynamics set the scene for the postmodern child custody case where lawyers, judges, and parents decide who *has* to take the kids.

Commercial children's culture understands what parents and educators don't— children and adolescents are wracked by desire that demands stimulation and often gets out of hand. We *see* its manifestation in children and children's culture with the constant struggle to escape boredom. Of course, most adults view this childhood desire as a monstrous quality to be squashed by any means necessary even if it requires the stupidification of young people in the process. In the *Home Alone* movies Kevin constantly feels as if he has done something terribly wrong, as if he were a bad kid. In *Home Alone* 2: *Lost* in *New York* Kevin prays to the Rockefeller Square Christmas tree: 'I need to see my mother, I need to tell her I'm sorry!' Exactly for what he should be sorry, no one is quite sure. One can only conclude that he is sorry for being a child, for intruding on the smooth operation of the family, of being goaded by his monstrous desire.

If we equate children with that which is monstrous, it is not a long jump to the position that the manipulative aliens are evil. In *The Bad Seed*, a successful novel, play, and movie of the mid 1950s Rhoda is an eight-year-old murderess endowed with a greed for material things—childhood desire run amuck. As the first work that explored this homicidal dimension of childhood, *The Bad Seed* equates youth with absolute malignancy-concealed at first in an innocent package. As Rhoda's landlady says of her: "she never gets anything dirty. She is a good child, a perfect child. She saves her money and keeps her room clean." The appearance of evil so close to goodness and innocence made the child monster that much more horrible.

Children who are so evil (or at least so capable of it) in a perverted sense justify child abuse. By 1990s this image of the bad child would be used for comic effect in *Problem Child* and *Problem Child 2* a year later. The way adults in the *Problem Child* movie reacted to the problem child is revealing:

*School principal*: "Being a principal's great 'cause I hate kids. I have to deal with the Weenies"

*Teacher to principal after he brings problem child to her class as new student*: "O God! Another one. How many kids are they going to make me teach?"

*Lawanda, the owner of the bank*: "What's this thing [referring to problem child] This Kid's a nightmare.... Kids are like bum legs. You don't shoot the patient, you cut off the leg."

*Problem child's, Grandfather*: "You little psycho—you're an evil boy. You got to learn to respect your elders."

*Lawanda*: "Listen you little monster. I'm going to marry your father and send you to boarding school in Baghdad."

*School principal*: "You rotten kids should be locked up in cages."

*Lawanda*: "I hate children. They ruin everything. If I had enough power I'd wipe them off the face of the earth."

Child murderer Susan Smith never stated it this clearly and unambiguously.

Whenever the problem child seeks to subvert the order of the status quo, viewers are alerted to what is coming by George Throughgood's blues guitar riff from "Bad to the Bone". Such innate "badness" cannot be indulged. As with the neo-folk wisdom in 1990s America that criminals could not be rehabilitated, there is no hope for the growth and development of the problem child. *Home Alone's* Kevin, who is certainly capable of "badness" and sadistic torture, is still struggling with parental forgiveness; the problem child is beyond all that. Parental and educational authority is concerned simply with control; the issue is naked power—there is no need for ameliorative 'window dressing' in this *realpolitik* for children. In this context kindness becomes the cause of juvenile delinquency, child advocacy the response of dupes and bleeding heart fools. Movie audiences want to see the problem child punished, if not physically attacked. Not too far from such sentiments looms child abuse.

In John Carpenter's *Halloween* the camera shows the audience an unidentified murderer's point of view of a middle-American suburban house occupied by two teenagers making love in an upstairs bedroom. As we watch from the murderer's eyes, he picks up a carving knife in the kitchen, observes the teenage boy leave the house, and walks back up the stairs to the bedroom where the teenage girl is now in bed alone. Looking directly into the gaze of the camera the girl expresses her annoyance with an obviously familial character wielding the knife. At this point the hand carrying the knife stabs the girl to death, principally focusing the attack on her bare breasts. It is only after the murder that we are granted a reverse angle shot of the killer, who is a six-year-old boy. By 1978 when *Halloween* was made, movie commentators made little of the age of the murderer (Paul, 1994). So accustomed was the American audience to the "innate" evil potential of children that movie makers perceived no need to explain the etymology of the child's violent behavior. By the end of the 1970s headlines such as "Killer Kids" and newspaper copy such as "Who are our children? One day they are innocent. The next they may try to blow your head off" (Vogel, 1994, p. 57) had made an impact. No more assumptions of innocence, no surprises. A new era had emerged.

## THE BLAME GAME

Clusters of issues come together as we consider the role of mothers and fathers in the family wars of the late twentieth century. The battle to ascribe blame for family dysfunction in general, and childhood pathology in particular, plays out on a variety of landscapes: politics, religion, and popular culture. On the political terrain, the 1990s have witnessed the Dan Quayle-Murphy Brown showdown over single mothers as parents, while on the religious battleground right-wing Christian fundamentalists have fingered feminism as the catalyst for mothers' neglect of their children. The analysis of this blame game expressed in popular culture offers some unique insights.

In *Home Alone* 1 and 2 Kevin's mother has internalized the right-wing blame of women for the neglect (abandonment) of Kevin in particular and family pathology in general. Though they are uncomfortable with a negative maternal figure, the screenplay writers of *Home Alone 1* and *2* leave no doubt as to who's to blame. Banished to the attic because he has been *perceived* as a nuisance, Kevin is (justifiably) hurt and angry.

*Kevin*: "Everyone in this family hates me."

*Mother*: "Then maybe you should ask Santa for a new family."

*Kevin*: "I don't want a new family. I don't want any family. Families suck."

*Mother*: "Just stay up there. I don't want to see you again for the rest of the night."

*Kevin*: "I don't want to see you again for the rest of my life. And I don't want to see anyone else, either."

*Mother*: "I hope you don't mean that. You'd be pretty sad if you woke up tomorrow morning and you didn't have a family."

*Kevin*: "No, I wouldn't"

*Mother*: "Then say it again. Maybe it'll happen"

*Kevin*: "I hope I never see any of you again."

The mother here is the provocateur, the one who plants the ideas that emerge as Kevin's wishes. Insensitive to his emotional hurt, she induces him to request a new family, she is the first to speak of not wanting to see him, she is the one who dares Kevin to tempt fate by wishing away his family (Paul, 1994). There is little doubt left by the *Home Alone* movies that child care is the mother's responsibility. John Heard's father character is virtually a non-entity. He is disinterested, condescending and hostile to Kevin. He knows (along with the audience) that he is not responsible for

Kevin's abandonment even though he was present during the entire episode. He has no reason to gnash his teeth or rend his garment in displays of penitence—this is the domain of the mother. And pay she does with her polka band trip in the first *Home Alone* and her frenzied running the nighttime streets of New York calling for her son in *Home Alone* 2, In an era when child abuse and child murder by mothers occupy national headlines, Kevin's mother's request for forgiveness may signify a much larger guilt. The right-wing male's blame of women for the ills of the family, however, is grotesquely perverse, implying as it does, that battalions of strong but tender men are struggling with their wives to let them take charge of child-rearing—not hardly (Rapping, 1994).

Feminist research and analysis of child abuse and domestic violence have subverted the happy depiction of family life as a safe haven far removed from pathologies emanating from internal power inequities. As such scholarship documented the ways that family life has oppressed women and children, pro-family conservative groups responded by calling for reassertion of patriarchal control in the home. Women, they argued, should return to child-rearing. Some conservatives have even maintained that women who don't adequately perform these "maternal" chores should have their children taken away and placed in orphanages. The most optimistic estimates place the number of children who would be institutionalized under this plan at over one million—the costs of such care would run over 36 billion dollars (Griffin, 1993; Morganthau et al., 1994). The male backlash to the assertive feminist critique has only begun with its depiction of women's political organization as the rise of a dangerous special interest group. Protectors of male power are waging an effective public relations battle: any campaign that is able to deflect blame for family failure from absent and often abusive fathers to mothers possesses a superior penchant for persuasion and little concern for truth.

*Home Alone* displays these gender dynamics in its complete refusal to implicate the father in the abandonment. Upon learning that Kevin is not in Paris with the family, his mother exclaims. "What kind of mother am I?" The lack of affect on the part of the adult males of the family, Kevin's Father and his uncle, is perplexing. The careful viewer can only conclude that they neither like nor care about the eight year-old. An explanation of the father's dismissiveness is never provided. All the viewer can discern is that the father and the uncle seem to be fighting for their manhood, expressing it perhaps in their resistance to the "breadwinner-loser" male character who forfeits his "male energy" in his domestication and subsequent acceptance of fidelity in marriage, dedication to job, and devotion to children (Lewis, 1992). Such a male figure was ridiculed by beatniks as square, by *Playboy* devotees as sexually timid, and by hippies as tediously straight. The search for a hip male identity along with a healthy dose of irresponsibility has undermined the family as a stable and loving environment. Indeed, to "do the right thing" in regard to one's family as a man is to lose status among one's fellow men.

An examination of adult male behavior in families indicates that many men are desperately concerned with peer group status. For example, men on average pay pitifully inadequate child support to their former spouses, if they pay it at all. Only half of women awarded child support ever receive what they are owed; another quarter receive partial payment, and the remaining quarter get nothing at all (Galston, 1991). This ambiguous role of the father in the family highlighted by the indifferent father of *Home Alone* is addressed in a more overtly oedipal manner in other movies of the last couple of decades (Paul, 1994). *The Shining*, for example, retrieves that which has always been repressed in Western culture, a father's hostility toward his own son, and builds an entire plot around it. Danny, the child protagonist in *The Shining*, develops the psychic power to see beyond the limits of time and space after his father (Jack Nicholson) in an alcoholic stupor broke Danny's arm. Danny's power, his shining, is expressed through his imaginary friend, Tony, who lives in Danny's mouth. Tony exists to help Danny cope with his violent and abusive father. Danny's presence and growth remind his father of his emasculation, his stultification by the family. The father's solution to his problem—the attempted ax murder of his wife and child—allows for none of the *Home Alone* ambiguity; the movie jumps headfirst into the maelstrom of the conflict between virile masculinity and the demands of domesticity.

As the screen image of the crazed ax-wielding Jack Nicholson fades into a blurred image of *Jurassic Park* (1993), the continuity of the child hating adult male remains intact even in this "child-friendly" Spielberg-produced dino-drama. The paleontologist (Sam Neill) holds such an extreme hatred of children that he won't ride in the same car with them. At one point in the film in response to a prepubescent boy's sarcastic question about the power of dinosaurs, Neill evokes the image of the violent Nicholson circling and threatening the child with the ominous claw of veliciraptor. The difference between *Jurassic Park* and *The Shining*, however, involves Neill's moment of epiphany; when the children are endangered by the dinosaurs, Neill sheds his hatred and like a good father risks mutilation and death to save their lives. As in the *Home Alone* movies, the issue of the father's hatred is buried in a happy McAlister family celebrating Christmas in a frenetic present-opening ritual. The demand for family values in the 1980s and 1990s had changed the cultural landscape: family values must triumph; adult men must be depicted as ultimately devoted to their children; the feminists' portrayal of the "bad father" must not be reinforced.

## AND AS IF THE AMBIGUITY WASN'T BAD ENOUGH, SOME KIDS MATTER MORE THAN OTHERS

It doesn't take long to discern that with the class dynamics of the 1990s, poor children in America don't matter as much as upper-middle-class children, that is, privileged children like the ones portrayed in the *Home Alone* movies. The frequent assertion that America is not a class society, uttered so confidently by mainstream politicians and educators, holds profound psychological and political consequences. This class silence undermines the well-to-do's understanding that they were granted a head start, while paralyzing the less successful with feelings of personal inferiority. On the political level as it sustains the fiction, the belief reifies the status quo: when the poor are convinced that their plight is self-produced, the larger society is released from any responsibility (Rubin, 1994).

An overt class silence pervades *Home Alone* 1 and 2. Even newspaper reviewers referred to the upper-middle class, white, and Protestant "bleached and sanitized" microcosm of the two movies (Koch, 1990). The McAlisters are very wealthy, living in their enormous brick colonial in a generic Chicago suburb filled with extravagant furnishings and conveniences. Indeed, they are an obnoxious, and loathsome crew, but being so privileged they believe they can act any way they want. The filmmakers go out of their way to make sure viewers know that the family deserves its money- as father McAlister (John Heard) drinks from crystal in first class on the plane to Paris, he alludes to his hard work and humble origins. The message is clear—the American dream is attainable for those willing to put in the effort. The McAlisters deserve their good fortune.

Into this restricted world of affluent WASPs, Harry and Marv (two small-time robbers with an attitude) make their appearance as the only poor people and the only non-WASPs in the two movies. Harry (Joe Pesci) and Marv (Daniel Stem) are quickly positioned as "the other" in both screenplays, they speak in specific lower socioeconomic class accents; obviously ethnic, Pesci exaggerates his working-class Italian accent, and just so we are not confused Stem signifies his Jewishness with a curiously gratuitous "Happy Hanukkah" reference as he steals money from a *toy* store; they are ignorant and uneducated—Pesci makes specific reference to the fact he never completed the sixth grade; they hold an irrational hatred of the affluent, their "crime signature" involves flooding affluent home after each robbery (they are known as the "wet bandits"). These class and ethnic specific traits set Marv and Harry apart to such a degree that the audience can unambiguously enjoy their torture at the hands of Kevin.

*Home Alone* 1 and 2 pull their weight in the larger social effort to erase class as a dynamic in late twentieth century American life; under interrogation the movies confess their class complicity as evidenced through the "otherization" of Marv and Harry. Compare Marv and Harry with Mr. Duncan, the toy store-owner who appears in *Home Alone* 2. Imbued with the sweetness and generosity of Joseph the angel in *It's a Wonderful Life*, Duncan is the most charming character in the *Home Alone* movies. After the McAlisters' reunification in *Home Alone* 2, he showers them with scores of presents. His only motivation for being in business is that he loves children and wants to see their happy faces when they open presents from his store. His loving smiles prove that capitalism cares and the status quo is just. He deserves every penny of his profits just as much as Marv and Harry deserve their torment. Such characterization gently dovetails with the dominant political impulses of the moment, marked by a callous acceptance of poverty, child poverty in particular, in the midst of plenty.

Over 12.6 million children live below the poverty line, making one out of every five American children poor. Too often unaware of even the existence of such class realities, Americans and their institutions are far removed from the insidious effects of such poverty. Poor children too infrequently escape the effects of living with parents scarred by their sense of shortcoming, of having to negotiate movie and TV images of ·the poor and working class as dangerous and oafish caricatures (as in *Home Alone* 1 and 2), and of confronting teachers and social workers who hold lower expectations for them than their middle and upper-middle class peers. A key feature "of the class dynamic in *Home Alone* 1 and 2 involves the public reaction to the McAlisters' child abandonment episodes as "good fun" as opposed to the real-life home alone cases that keep surfacing in the 1990s. While Kevin's parents report his having been left alone in New York to the police after they reach their vacation destination in Miami, it's no big deal. Even when they admit that abandoning the child has become "a family tradition," no one is excited—after all, the McAlisters are upper class, well-to-do people. Almost daily, parents (especially single mothers) who leave their young children home alone for sometimes just a few hours are arrested and forced to relinquish their child/children to foster care. With child-care often costing 200 to 400 dollars a month, poor mothers are placed into virtually impossible circumstances (Seligman, 1993). The society's refusal to address poor and single mothers' need for child care has contributed to the feminization of poverty (Polakow, 1992*). Home Alone* 1 and 2 indicate the double standard that dominates the American view of the rich and the poor and the mean-spirited class bias of some expressions of popular culture in this conservative age.

## THE POSTMODERN CHILDHOOD

Within *Home Alone* 1 and 2's bizarre mix of child abandonment and child-parent alienation, children caught in the crossfire of gender wars, crass class bias, and comedy resides something profound about the role of children in contemporary American culture. The movies could have been made only in a culture that had experienced a profound shift in the social role of children. For all individuals who have a stake in understanding children—parents, teachers, social workers, family counselors, and so forth—knowledge of these changing conditions becomes a necessity. A no-growth economy has mandated that all adults in the family must work outside the home; because of such needs, children find themselves saddled with daily duties ranging from house cleaning, baby-sitting, and grocery shopping to cooking, laundry, and organizing carpools. With the "family values" agenda of right-wing movements of the 1990s threatening to eviscerate the governmental support of poor and middle-class families, the economic problems of children look to get worse before they get better.

The new era of childhood, the postmodern childhood, cannot escape the influence of the postmodern condition with its electronic media saturation. Such media omnipresence produces a hyperreality that repositions the real as some thing no longer simply given but artificially reproduced as real. Thus, media-produced models replace the real-simulated TV kids on sitcoms replace real life children as models of childhood. In this true media-driven postmodern condition a cultural implosion takes place, ripping apart boundaries between information and entertainment as well as images and politics. As media push the infinite proliferation of meaning, boundaries between childhood and adulthood fade as children and adults negotiate the same mediascape and struggle with the same impediments to meaning making. Children become "adultified" and adults become "childified" (Aronowitz and Giroux, 1991; Best and Kellner, 1991). Boundaries between adulthood and childhood blur to the point that a clearly defined, "traditional," innocent childhood becomes an object of nostalgia—a sure sign that it no longer exists in any unproblematic form (Lipsky and Abrams, 1994; Postman, 1994).

There is nothing child-like about a daily routine of child care, cooking, and, shopping. In *Home Alone* 1 and 2 Kevin is almost completely adult-like in meeting the demands of survival on his own, He checks into hotels, uses credit cards, buys pizzas, and grocery shops (even with coupons), all as a part of a day's work. He needs no adult-figure; he can take complete care of himself. In the postmodern childhood being home alone is an everyday reality. Children now know what only adults used to know: postmodern children are sexually knowledgeable and often sexually experienced; they understand and many have experimented with drugs and alcohol; and new studies show they often experience the same pressures as single working mothers, as they strive to manage the stresses of school, work at home, and interpersonal family dynamics. When the cultural dynamics of hyperreality collide with post babyboom demographics and the economic decline of the early 1970s, 1980s, and 1990s, the world changes (Lipsky and Abrams, 1994). The daily life of media-produced family models such as the Cleavers from *Leave it to Beaver* is convulsed. June must get a job and Wally and Beaver must take *care* of the house. No longer can Beaver and his friends Larry and Whitey leisurely play on the streets of Mayfield after school. Anyway, it's dangerous—Mayfield is not as safe as it used to be.

Children under twelve of the mid-1990s belong to a generation only half the size of the baby boomers. As a result, children as a group garner less attention in 1996 than in 1966 and exert a correspondingly diminished voice in the society's social and political conversation. In such a context, youth issues are not as important as they once were. Add to this a declining economy complicated by rising expectations. As American manufacturing jobs have disappeared and dead-end service jobs have expanded, advertising continues to promote higher and higher consumer desire. Frustration levels among children and teenagers rise as a direct result of this socio-economic contradiction. Given the centrality of TV in the lives of this postmodern home alone, generation, the awareness of the desirability of children's consumer goods becomes a central aspect of their lives. Consumer desire, however, is only one aspect of the effect of TV and other electronic media on American children. TV is where children find out about American culture. Indeed, one doesn't have to be a movie critic to know how often Hollywood has drawn on the TV-taught-me-all-I-know theme. In *The Man Who Fell to Earth*, David Bowie as an alien learns all about earth culture from TV; in *Being There* Peter Sellers as idiot-savant Chauncey Gardner knows nothing about the world but what he has learned on TV. The movie ends with Chauncey on his way to a possible presidential candidacy—life imitates art? The robot in *Short Circuit*, the mermaid in *Splash*, the aliens in *Explorers*, and the Neanderthal in *Encino Man* all are completely socialized by TV (Lipsky and Abrams, 1994).

What does the repeated invocation of this theme say to observers of childhood? With the evolution of TV as a medium that attempts to more or less represent reality, children have gained an adult-like (not necessarily an informed) view of the world in only a few years of TV watching. Traditional notions of childhood as a time of sequential learning about the world don't work in a hyperreality saturated with sophisticated but power-driven views of reality. When a hotel porter asks Kevin McAlister in *Home Alone* 2 if he knows how the TV in his hotel room works, Kevin replies, "I'm ten years old, TV's my life." The point is well taken, and as a consciousness dominating, full disclosure medium TV provides everyone—sixty-year-old adults to eight-year-old children—with the same data. As postmodern children gain unrestricted knowledge about things once kept secret from non-adults, the mystique of adults as revered keepers of secrets about the world begins to disintegrate. No longer do the elders know more than children about the experience of youth -given the social/technological changes they often know less, for example, about video games, computers, TV programs, and so forth. Thus, the authority of adulthood is undermined, as kids' generational experience takes on character its own.

The social impact of such a phenomenon is profound on many levels. A subversive kinderculture is created where kids through their attention to child-targeted programming and commercials know something that mom and dad don't. This corporate-directed kinderculture provides kids with a body of knowledge adults don't possess, while their access to adult themes at least makes them conversant with marital, sexual, business-related, criminal, violent, and other traditionally restricted issues (Kincheloe and Steinberg, 1996). When combined with observations of families collapsing, the dynamics of the struggle of a single mother to support her family, parents involved in the "singles" scene, and post-divorce imposition of adult-like chores, children's TV experience provides a full-scale immersion into grown-up culture.

In the context of childhood education the postmodern experience of being a kid represents a cultural earthquake. The curriculum of the third grade is determined not only by what vocabulary and concepts are "developmentally appropriate" but by what content is judged to be commensurate with third grade experience in the lived world, (Lipsky and Abrams, 1994; Postman, 1994). Hyperreality explodes traditional notions of curriculum development—third graders can discuss the relationship between women's self-image amid the nature of their sexual behavior. While parental groups debate the value of sex education in the public schools, their children are at home watching a TV docudrama depicting a gang rape of a new inmate in the federal penitentiary. When teachers and the culture of school treat such children as if they know nothing of the adult world, the kids come to find school hopelessly archaic, out of touch with the times. This is why the postmodern subversive kinderculture always views school with a knowing wink and a smirk—how quaint school must look to our postmodern children.

There is nothing easy about the new childhood. Indeed, many teenagers and young adults speak of their stress and fatigue originating in childhood. If one has judged the responsibilities of adulthood since the age of seven, physical and psychological manifestations of stress and fatigue during one's adolescence should surprise no one. Adolescent suicide did not exist as a category during the "old childhood" – by 1980 it was second only to accidents as the leading cause of death of teenagers. By the 1990s, 400,000 young people were attempting suicide yearly and youth suicide was being described in the academic literature as an epidemic (Gaines, 1990).

THE NEW CHILDHOOD

The covenant between children and adults has been broken by parental and clerical child abuse and the pathological behavior of other caretakers. Too often children of the late twentieth century have callously been deposited in inadequate child care institutions administered on the basis of cost-efficiency concerns not on a larger commitment to the welfare of children. The tendency to segregate by age is well established in late twentieth century America, and unless steps are taken to reverse the trend more generational alienation and antagonism will result (Gaines, 1994; Polakow, 1992).

In the context of this child segregation, cultural pathologies manifest themselves. Excluded from active participation in the social order, children find themselves both segregated and overregulated by institutional forms of social control. The overegulators pose as experts on child raising, child development, child morality, and early childhood education with their psycho discourse on the rigid phases of child development and the strict parameters of normality, in the name of "proper child rearing techniques" experts tap into the larger ideology of personnel management that adjusts individuals to the demands of an orderly society. Like all strategies of personnel management mainstream child psychology masks its emphasis on control. Intimidated by the scientific language of the experts, parents lose faith in their own instincts and surrender control to the authority figure on *Sally*. Play gives way to skill development, as structure permeates all aspects of the child's life. While middle and upper-middle class children suffer from the hyper-structure of skill-development, poor children labeled "at risk" are medicated and drilled—led in the misguided effort to reduce chaos and disorder in their lives. In the name of order the experience of poor children is further bureaucratized (Seiter, 1993; Polakow, 1992).

## THE WORLDLINESS OF POSTMODERN CHILDHOOD: THE WISE ASS AS PROTOTYPE

The *Home Alone* movies can be understood only in the context of the postmodern childhood. Kevin McAlister is a worldly child. Light-years separate Kevin from Chip, Ernie, and Robbie Douglas on My *Three Sons* of the late 1950s and early 1960s. As a Black comedy for children, *Home Alone* struck an emotional chord with movie watchers that made it one of the most popular and profitable films, of all time. Kevin, as kiddie-nair hero, is a smart-kid with an attitude. Macauley Culkin's ability to portray that character turned him into an overnight celebrity, a role model for the pre-pubescent wise ass.

Kevin as postmodern wise ass could not tolerate children from the 1940s and 1950s with their simple-minded "the policeman is our friend" view of the world. Bizzare in their innocence, such children are viewed by postmodern kids as antimatter reflections of themselves without responsibilities or cynicism. "What would we talk about?" Kevin might ask of a meeting with such kids. Unless Kevin had watched old movies or lived near a separatist group such as the Amish, he would have never seen such unworldly children. Almost every child depicted on TV in the contemporary era—Alex Keaton on *Family Ties*, Michele in *Full House*, Lisa and Bart Simpson on *The Simpsons*, Rudi on *The Cosby Show*—are worldly and wise.

Bart Simpson may be an underachiever—but only in school, a place he finds boring, confining, and based on a childhood that no longer exists, Bart is not childish, the school is. The smart-ass child a la Culkin and Bart Simpson is the symbol for contemporary childhood. Imagine Bart's reaction to a "Yes, Virginia, there is a Santa Claus" adult monologue: "Right, daddy-o, now eat my shorts."

The wise-ass is the hero of the subversive kinderculture. The appeal of *Home Alone* 1 and 2 is connected to this insurgent response to middle-class propriety with its assumption of child helplessness and its worship of achievement. Child and adult are pitted against one another with the child as the sympathetic character. In the case of *Home Alone* 1 and 2 no one could feel much sympathy for Kevin's parents with their lack of empathy for Kevin's position in the family and their lack of attention to his needs. Kevin's behavior is an act of righteous resistance to this unjust status quo. Like his kindred spirits, Bart Simpson, and Beavis and Butthead, Kevin thrives on disorder—a chaos that undermines the social order constructed around bourgeois stability. As Beavis and Butthead might put it, order "sucks" disorder is "cool." The subversive kinderculture of the postmodern childhood thrives on this disorder.

Indeed, one of the subtexts running through both *Home Alone* movies involves the humorous juxtaposition of comments of family members concerning poor, helpless little Kevin with the visual depiction of Kevin happy and in control of the disorder of his solitude. The appeal of the film revolves around Kevin's ability to tell his parents: "Even in the middle of all this exciting chaos, I don't need you!" The self-sufficient, boy-hero of the postmodern era—what a movie marketing bonanza. He shows his remorse on learning that his parents have left him home alone: (with eyebrows raised Kevin speaks to the audience) "I made my family disappear." Compare this postmodern reaction to parent-child separation of Dorothy's in *The Wizard of Oz*—Judy Garland's *raison d'etre* is getting back home to Kansas. Kevin is self-actualized, living out the childhood fantasy of life without parental encumberment. Since he "can't trust anybody in his family" Kevin decides he would rather vacation alone than with "such a group of creeps." As a bellman scoops ice cream for him in his posh New York hotel room, it is obvious that Kevin's intuitions are correct. "*This* is a vacation," he sighs.

## CONFRONTING THE INTENSITY OF YOUTH IN A POSTMODERN CHILDHOOD

As parties interested in the status of contemporary childhood, we ask, what does the popularity of the *Home Alone* movies tells us about the inner-lives of children and their attempt to understand their relationship with the adult world? For a generation of home aloner's Culkin's Kevin is a character with whom they can identify, as he negotiates the cultural obstacles they also have had to confront. He offers them a sense of hope, a feeling that there is something heroic in their daily struggle. Once again, the corporate marketers are one step ahead of the rest of us, as they recognize the changing nature of childhood and colorize the psychological ramifications such changes produce. In retrospect it seems so easy: to canonize a child who is left home alone for Christmas is to flatter every postmodern child in the audience.

Kevin's predicament validates a generation's lived experience, transforming them from unwanted children into pre-teen Ninja warriors. If nothing else, *Home Alone* is a rite-of-passage story about a boy home alone, endangered, besieged who emerges victorious and transformed (Koch, 1990), "I'm no wimp," he proclaims as he marches off to battle, "I'm the man of the house."

In a postmodern era where children have already seen everything, have watched the media sell laundry detergent by exploiting a mother's love for her children, it is no surprise that kids of the 1990s experience difficulty with emotional investment. As a result the interpersonal affect of postmodern children tends to be—everything is kept at a distance and treated ironically (Grossberg, 1994). Kevin offers such children both something in which to invest, and a sense that their desire for real experience is not pathological. This childhood and adolescent desire for extremes, for intense sensation is typically viewed by the adult world as dangerous and misguided. Indeed, the very purpose of certain forms of traditional schooling and child rearing has been to tame such feelings. This visceral energy of the young—so central to Kevin in *Home Alone* and so enticing to young moviegoers—lays the foundation for a progressive postmodern childrearing and childhood education. Too often adults who are "in charge" of children forget the nature and power of this visceral energy filled force of young people. In their adult amnesia they fail to connect with the force and, as a result, relinquish the possibility of guiding it or being replenished by it. They often blame rock music, MTV videos, video games, communists, or Satanists for creating the energy, forgetting that historically-mediated forms of it have expressed themselves from ancient hunter-gatherer societies to modern and postmodern ones (Ventura, 1994; Rodriguez, 1994).

The suppression of childhood desire in the postmodern North American culture at the end of the twentieth century undermines our civic, psychological, and intellectual growth. The very qualities adults fear most in our children—their passion; visceral energy, and life force—can be used as the basis for a postmodern childhood education. In a sense the genie is out of the bottle and there is no way to get her or him back in. As the communication revolution has opened adult esoterica to children, we find there is no turning back. The endless debate over movie and record ratings are futile exercises; the question now revolves around: how do we provide children the type of emotional and intellectual supports that help them balance the interaction between their visceral energy and their newfound insights? Just as traditional forms of teaching and childhood curricular arrangements are passe given the "new times", forms of discipline and control strategies are obsolete. Can kids who hold Kevin's knowledge of the world in general and the anxieties and tribulations of adulthood in particular, be domesticated and controlled (not to mention the question of *should* they ...) in the same ways as children of a different era of childhood were? Custodial schooling is no longer adequate for children of the 1990s—indeed, it was never adequate for children no matter what the era.

Education for domestication assumes that the information a child encounters can be regulated and sequentially ordered (Polakow, 1992; Gaines, 1990). Much schooling and child rearing is still based on such an archaic assumption, resulting in strategies that negate children's exploration, invention, and play. Indeed, that purpose of many of these strategies is to prevent the interaction of acquired information from a variety of sources into the cognitive and emotional structure of an evolving personhood, that is, growth itself. Thus, childrearing insufficiently prepares children for adulthood or even postmodern childhood, as it ignores the world that surrounds children and shapes their lives. The lessons to be excavated from this quick analysis of the *Home Alone* movies are sobering in their urgency. The state of the family at the end of the twentieth century and the inability of the public conversation about it to transcend the most trivial forms of platitudes to the value of the family in our "national character" is distressing. An effort to examine the nature of kinderculture and the forces that shape it simply does not exist in the surreal image-based politics of the present era. The ambivalent adult relationship with children is a suppressed feature of the cultural landscape, rarely, if ever, addressed in even the professional schooling of child welfare professionals, child psychologists, or elementary educators. These silences must end.

## REFERENCES

Aronowitz, S., & Giroux, H. (1991). *Postmodern education: Politics, culture, and social criticism*. Minneapolis, MN: University of Minnesota Press.

Best, S., & Kellner, D. (1991). *Postmodern theory: Critical interrogations*. New York: The Guilford Press.

Coontz, S. (1992). *The way we never were: American, families and the nostalgia trap*. New York: Basic Books.

Ferguson, S. (1994). The comfort of being sad. *Utne Reader, 64*(July/August), 60–61.

Gaines, D. (1994). Border crossing in the USA. In A. Ross & T. Rose (Eds.), *Microphone fiends: Youth music, youth culture* (pp. 227–234). New York: Routledge.

Gaines, D. (1990). *Teenage wasteland: Suburbia's dead end kids*. New York: Harper Perennial.

Galston. W. (1991, December 2). *Home alone: What our policymakers should know about our children*. The New Republic, 40–44.

Griffin, C. (1993). *Representation of youth: TM study of youth and adolescence in Britain and America*. Cambridge, MA: Polity Press.

Grossberg, L. (1994). Is anybody listening? Does anybody care? On the state of rock. In A. Ross & T. Rose (Eds.), *Microphone fiends: Youth music, youth culture* (pp. 41–58). New York: Routledge.

James, C. (1990, December 23). Scrooge pens the screenplay. *New York Times*.

Kincheloe, J. L., & Steinberg S. R. (1996). *Kinderculture: The corporate construction of childhood*. Boulder, CO: Westview Press.

Koch, J. (1990, December 27). Home alone hits home with a powerful, disturbing pop-culture potion. *The Boston Globe*.

Lewis, J. (1992). *The road to romance and ruin; Teen films and youth culture*. New York: Routledge.

Lipsky, D., & Abrams, A. (1994). *Late bloomers, coming of age in Today's America: 'The right place at the wrong time*. New York: Times Books.

Morganthau, T., et al. (1994). The Orphanage. *Newsweek, 124*(24), 28–32.

Paul, W. (1994). *Laughing screaming: Modern Hollywood horror and comedy*. New York: Columbia University Press.

Polakow, V. (1992). *The erosion of childhood*. Chicago: University of Chicago Press.

Postman, N. (1994). *The disappearance of childhood*. New York: Vintage Books.

Rapping, E. (1994). *Media-tions: Forays into the culture and gender wars*. Boston: South End Press.

Rodriguez, L. (1994). Rekindling the warrior. *Utne Reader, 64*(July/August), 58–59.

Rubin, L. (1994). *Families on the faultline: America's working class speaks about the family, the economy, race, and ethnicity*. New York: HarperCollins.

Seiter, E. (1993). *Sold separately: Parents and children in consumer culture.* New Brunswick, NJ: Rutgers University Press.
Seligman, K. (1993, August 1). Poor kids often home alone. *San Francisco Examiner.*
Ventura, M. (1994). The age of endarkenment. *Utne Reader, 64*(July/August), 63–366.
Vogel, J. (1994). Throw away the key. *Utne Reader, 64*(July/August), 56–60.

Reprinted with permission from Elsevier (Oxford, England): Kincheloe, J. L. (1996). The new childhood: home alone as a way of life. In H. Jenkins (Ed.), *The children's culture reader* (pp. 159–177). New York: NYU Press.

LEE GABAY

# WELCOME TO SHERMERVILLE

Shermer, Illinois is the unspecified suburb on Chicago's North Shore where the film, *Home Alone*, takes place. In fact, this fictitious town is the backdrop for most of writer-director John Hughes' movies such as *Weird Science, the Breakfast Club, Ferris Bueller's Day Off, Sixteen Candles, Pretty in Pink* and *National Lampoon's Vacation*. In Kevin Smith's film *Dogma*, the characters Jay and Silent Bob mention a failed trip to Shermer. They were unaware that Shermer is fictional and wanted to visit because of its high ratio of beautiful girls to dorky guys (as seen in most of Hughes' Shermer–based films), and also because of its apparent lack of any competing drug dealers. Shermer is not a place; it is an idea, a social construct perhaps even a feeling.

Joe Kincheloe's essay, "The New Childhood: *Home Alone* as a Way of Life" brings the reader to the borders of Shermer by critically exploring our perceptions of the portrayal of children and parents within the oppressive social and political terrain of John Hughes' cinematic El Dorado. In the realm of popular cultural versus esoterica, the intensity of this fictional locale serves as a fertile landscape for Kincheloe to question the social agreements concerning the type of care parents provide for young children.

## DON'T YOU (FORGET ABOUT ME)

John Hughes directed eight films and wrote and produced dozens more mostly in the 1980s and 90s. His work embodied the pop culture of the age. Especially for those born between the Cuban missile crisis and Watergate, the phrase "a John Hughes movie" will instantly conjure a range of images and associations. As Shakespeare was to Elizabethan England, Hughes was the poet of American youth in the post-Vietnam War period. *Home Alone* was the inevitable and final step in John Hughes' evolution as a writer and filmmaker.

Hughes aimed to show children in a different light, with honesty and reverence, reversing the long-standing cinematic stereotype of caring parents with clueless offspring. He created an entirely new model of savvy teens juxtaposed to self-involved and hopelessly un-cool authority figures. In Hughes' films, parents are positioned as a kind of enemy; they are either irresponsible, or emotionally limited, or simply unaware. His movies are distinguished by their moving portrayals of ordinary adolescents engaged in mini-dramas involving class distinctions, family disconnect, peer pressure and crushes.

Hughes earned the devotion of an entire generation of young fans by doing what the adults in his films do not: paying attention to what kids have to say. The kids on screen and in the audience are united by their need to survive without any help from their elders. In order to establish this connection with his fans, his films adhere to a simple formula: mock traditional parental behaviors.

He tweaks normative gender roles in *Mr. Mom*; in *Pretty in Pink* the alcoholic father is taken care of by his daughter; in *Trains, Planes and Automobiles* the adults, due to many, often self-inflicted, mishaps, struggle to be home with their families for the holidays. The parents in *16 Candles* forget Samantha's birthday. In The *Breakfast Club*, Mr. Vernon the teacher, and primary authority figure, walks around with toilet paper dangling from his pants. In *Home Alone* Hughes presents us with the ultimate caricatures of the irresponsible authority figures: the parents who forgot their son at home while going on vacation.

In the essay, "The New Childhood: *Home Alone* as a Way of Life," Kincheloe posits a critique of the social forces that have altered Western childhood over the past couple of decades. Using the *Home Alone* franchise as its foci, his thesis seeks to identify the visible and powerful ways in which different styles of parenting can impact a child's life experience. One of the tasks of "The New Childhood: *Home Alone* as a Way of Life" is to establish the fundamental issues that operate at the center of familial relations in the 21$^{st}$ century. The ontological effort to peer into the conflicts and contradictions revolving around the lives of contemporary children taps into a frequent motif in Hughes' films: the narrative of rejection as a cultural metaphor for anxiety and loneliness. Kincheloe's take on youthful castaways considers, in addition to ontological, the epistemological. In his essay, Kincheloe cites the central and unspoken theme of the hurt and pain that accompanies familial interactions in postmodern America as the basis for this home life rupture.

*Home Alone*, which premiered on November 16, 1990, was a movie about a resourceful boy and careless parents. It was a unique pop culture phenomenon and the biggest moneymaking comedy in Hollywood history at the time. Kincheloe saw *Home Alone* as something larger than a cultural explosion and even deemed it a social movement.

## PRIVATE PROPERTY

The rise of John Hughes in the 1980s occurred during a reactionary period in American history when political, social, and cultural forces were responding to the political gains made by the progressive movements of the 1960s and 1970s. Devolution and small government were viewed as the solution to all of society's ills. Federal policy decisions to cut funding for public housing, to standardize education, and to crack down on crime reflected the growing cultural and political intolerance of causative factors such as early education failure, family disruption, drug abuse, and gang activity (Jacobson, 2007). During President Reagan's first term, the rates of divorce, single parent homes, youth suicide, and children on anti-depressant medication skyrocketed. Additionally the number of juveniles sent to adult prisons rose by almost 50 percent (Krisberg, 2005, Gaines, 1990). New policies that emphasized deterrence and punishment impacted the social context in which youth tried to survive on a day-to-day basis. The growing disparities tied to race, gender, and the distribution of wealth in the US during the Reagan era gave rise to three things: the prison industrial complex, hip hop and *Home Alone* as a way of life.

In the 1980s and 90s, many children lived in neighborhoods and attended schools where they were put down, shamed, humiliated, exploited and alienated by adults and institutions—or they were perpetuating the violence by doing this to each other. A John Hughes movie such as *Home Alone* provided fertile ground for resistance; the frustration and anger released by the movie emerged in response to systemic oppression and disempowerment. Young boys and girls, longing for salvation and agency and through television and movies, found an uncensored and often amplified platform from which to speak. John Hughes films screamed of young people's sense of exclusion from individual opportunity and diversity. The ideas of *Home Alone* were a prop used in meaning-making, propelling boys and girls toward deeply rooted escapist fantasies. They transformed familial abandonment into a scenario in which they are independent, heroic and ultimately beloved mini-versions of Dirty Harry or Rambo. Personal achievement is difficult in a world where most things seem contested, incoherent, and unrealized. *Home Alone* offered children something many were not receiving in school or from their parents: attention, affirmation, praise and a semblance of control within an ontologically insecure world.

Childhood alienation thus became vigilantism, or a way to achieve quick social mobility in the disjointed streets, communities and families. Protagonists such as *Home Alone*'s Kevin united disparate youth by empowering them with a new sense of worth. Within this framework, *Home Alone* can also be seen as a conservative, even reactionary, film, in which the celebration of rebellion draws more upon the middle class resentment that brought Reagan into office than the residual anti-establishment radicalism that preceded the era. The characters are in conflict with authority, but they are also stubborn in their individualism and often unapologetically materialistic. This assumed sense of uniformity and entitlement imparts a genuine expression of the American utopian ideal.

## HOMELAND INSECURITY

The *Home Alone* generation of American children is the most surveilled group of young people to date. Yet in his essay Kincheloe asserts that kids are being ignored at historic rates. Accepting both of these conflicting claims suggests that children are watched, but neither seen nor cared for. In the 1990s, government regulations were becoming substitute for local and individualized forms of care. The mechanical efficiency of modern forms of surveillance including mandatory car seat laws, baby on board bumper stickers, nanny cams, two way audio monitors, Meghan's law, AMBER alerts, and a host of other forms of legal and social micro-management were the zeitgeist. The anxieties created by these well-intentioned acts further established an emotional and intellectual disconnect from families. Somewhere along the way, however, the floodgates were opened and the coy innuendoes were replaced by gratuitous comic violence.

Many of the kids exposed to the *Home Alone* images, not to mention the accompanying dialogue, went on to create their own real-life alienation scenes, arguably before they had the maturity to do so. Children are constrained to view themselves without contextualizing the circumstance of the lives they lead. Thus, little priority is given to self-reflexiveness. *Home Alone*'s model formal thinking is too narrow. The movies' privileging of assimilation over accommodation therefore places people outside of their reality by removing them from their environment. This can be exemplified in Hughes' omission of politics, Black people, and harsh social and psychological realities within his cinematic context. In fact, it appears that keeping difficult social and political realities hidden was standard operating procedure during this era.

## HOME FORECLOSED

As Kincheloe points out, the first two *Home Alone* movies play on kids' fantasies of being left alone to do anything they want. Kevin got to play around the house and in New York, spend lots of money, watch violent movies, talk back to adults, and beat up bad guys. What little kid wouldn't want to be Kevin?

In the subsection of his essay entitled, "The American Ambivalence Toward Children," Kincheloe lists a host of horror films which reflect a pervasive adult hostility towards youth including, *The Exorcist, The Bad Seed,* and *Firestarter.* Although not classically representative of the genre, the few people who sat though *Home Alone 3* and *Home Alone 4* might equate the experience to seeing horror movies.

When the family foil failed to be fresh and exciting, and the franchise waned with the aging of Macauly Culkin, *Home Alone 3* found a different child and a different enemy—foreigners.

In *Home Alone 3,* four terrorists working for a North Korean group are sent by their boss to obtain a top-secret microchip that can act as a cloaking device for a missile. They succeed in retrieving the chip and hiding it in a remote controlled car, but due to a luggage mix-up at the airport with an old woman, the car lands in the hands of Alex (the young protagonist/hero) who lives down the street from the woman and receives the car as payment for snow-shoveling her driveway. Instead of being left truly "home alone" for an extended period of time, in the third movie Alex is just home sick with the chicken pox. Alex finds out about the chip in the car, and that it is sought by the terrorists. When they target his house, he sets traps in order to deter them.

The fourth and final installment of *Home Alone* came out as a made-for-TV movie on ABC's Wonderful World of Disney. Keeping in line with the theme of family dysfunction, Kevin, who in the previous three films has been left alone, lost in New York, and forced to carry out acts of espionage, finally experiences the pain and alienation of an enemy which threatens his family itself—divorce.

The remains of the franchise leave a trail of mortgaged relationships, abandoned souls and unoccupied feelings. The *Home Alone* experience both saturates and tries to deny one's openness; but the vulnerabilities simply end up expressing themselves in different ways for Culkin and many other young people—with violence, drugs and depression.

## IRRECONCILABLE DIFFERENCES

Childhood can be both a luxurious bubble and a gritty place, and it is difficult for youth to predict the dangers (and splendors) that lie ahead. The process of growing up can be overwhelming for many people, so they choose, as is the case of Culkin on and off screen, fear and materialism. The strongest survive, while others are destroyed.

While the character played by Macauly Culkin in *Home Alone* was abandoned by his parents in the fictional movie, off-screen, at the age of 14, Culkin was battling his real life parents in a courtroom, suing them for disputed custody. Essentially, Culkin was reenacting what his character Kevin did on screen—taking control of his own life. Subsequently, Culkin was legally emancipated, winning full custody of himself. According to reports, his emotionally abusive father, who had been his manager, forced the young and exhausted Culkin to make fourteen movies in six years.

His parents, who were also in the process of getting divorced, had legal guardianship of 20 percent of Culkin's money. The other 80 percent was in a trust that no one could touch, not even Culkin until he was 18-years-old. In a bold act not dissimilar to those devised by his alter ego Kevin, Culkin took his parents' names off the trust and signed it over to his accountant.

Kincheloe's essay, "The New Childhood: *Home Alone* as a Way of Life" is concerned with a certain form of acquired consciousness, a point of view that perceives the ills that befall families. Correcting these ills requires addressing the sources of dysfunction in the fundamental parent-child relationship, not simply addressing the symptoms of the disorder which seek to deny the experience of childhood, which in turn serves to further alienate kids from their parents.

Culkin, who has since retired from acting, has been married himself, divorced, and most recently made headlines for being arrested for the possession of marijuana and two controlled substances, namely Xanax and Clonazepam. Both are potent prescription anti-anxiety medications. Culkin was briefly jailed in Oklahoma and pleaded guilty to misdemeanor drug offenses. His lawyers reached a plea bargain with the state of Oklahoma; he received three one-year suspended prison terms, a probationary drug treatment program and a $540 fine.

The iconic movie image of Culkin holding his gasping face between his hands is more poignant, powerful and telling twenty years later. He is still the poster child of his generation: self medicated, isolated, and lost. This shift from adolescents self-medicating like adults looms large. Depression will be the second largest killer after heart disease by 2020 (McManamy, 2006). Since *Home Alone* was released, teenagers are still abandoned, alone, and even alienated from their surroundings. Pop culture in the 1990s offered the luxury of depression, promoting an often meaningless and existentially vapid American wasteland. This has affected all of us individually and institutionally as society has allowed for both. It is a social emergency when societal resources are insufficient for getting children through the day. Everyday dilemmas are created by the way the social structural system is organized.

## LEFT OF CENTER

Today, more than a decade after publication, as cutbacks loom in every sector of American economic life, the specter raised by "*Home Alone* as a Way of Life," with its intimations of deprivation and depredation, seems increasingly near as well. There seems to be even less time for the niceties of "traditional" family life. In this way, the *Home Alone* movies can evoke a fond nostalgia for life on a firmer and safer footing. The answers offered in *Home Alone* are emotionally generous but naïve. Many of the children emerging from *the Home Alone* era are lost, confused, scared and lacking a sense of self.

Both Joe Kincheloe and John Hughes were born in 1950. Both were just finishing high school in 1968. That summer, they both listened to The Doors singing the lyrics, "the old get older and the young get stronger" in the song *Five to One*, which was about the expanding ratio of youth to adults. They were exposed to images from the film *Wild in the Streets*, portraying a rebellious teen as president. The intergenerational fires of their generation were in full blaze during these impressionable years and likely informed their adult cognitive frameworks. The *Home Alone* generation is half the size of the baby boomer generation of which Kincheloe and Hughes are part. New media and mediated technologies increasingly direct young people to look to the media for guidance and life lessons. Yet these new media, which include Facebook, YouTube, and MySpace, are often driven by youth themselves. The enduring and unanswered question of "The New Childhood: *Home Alone* as a Way of Life" is: What lessons are being taught to young people and by whom?

A child's daily clash with adults is not new, but as a society, we must aid in resolving these conflicts. Whether that means guarding our youngest constituents by creating a safe space for exploring the issues dulled through psychotropic self-medication or by providing more than just lip-service when it comes to child exploitation, we must act. After all, it takes a village, a nation, or sometimes even just a home.

## REFERENCES

Gaines, D. (1990). *Teenage wasteland: Suburbia's dead end kids*. New York: Harper Perennial.
Jacobson, M. (2007) Testimony to a hearing of the joint economic committee. Mass Incarceration in the United States: at What Cost?
Kincheloe, J. L. (1996). The new childhood: Home alone as a way of life. *Cultural Studies, 1*, 219–238.
Krisberg, B. (2005). *Juvenile justice: Redeeming our children*. London: Sage.
Mcmanamy, J. (2006) *Living well with depression and bipolar disorder: What your Doctor doesn't tell you... That you need to know*. New York: Harper.

*When I met Joe, we were both vegetarians, and following a violent illness, both of us were so weak, we decided to reintroduce meat into our diets. It was at this time that he admitted to me that the ten years sans meat were some of his most difficult, and that indeed, he was addicted to McDonald's burgers and fries. I clearly remember going to McDonald's the day he went back to the burger, and watching him down two cheeseburgers and two bags of fries. I had always hated fast food in general, and McDonald's specifically, and was amazed that this man I loved could have hidden such an addiction. While we were at McDonald's he started to tell me an elongated story about his childhood, and the first McDonald's in Kingsport, Tennessee. As we sat and talked, he looked around, and started to make semiotic remarks about the restaurant. The conversation continued for weeks as Joe was determined to make up for lost hamburgers, and we paid very close attention to McDonald's TV ads. While in Atlanta (for my first time), I noticed that all the McDonald's TV ads contained only Black people, and that a decidedly African American text was used. I commented on the cholesterol issues plaguing Black men (recently on the news), and Joe started to franticly write. He said he would do an entire book on McDonald's as a cultural and political signifier. This was a piece in Kinderculture: The Corporate Construction of Childhood, and led to his book, The Sign of the Burger: McDonald's and the Culture of Power. After writing the book for Westview Press, the publishers refused to publish it due to their fear of litigation from McDonald's. Stanley Aronowitz made a call to Temple University Press and got Joe a new contract. SS*

JOE L. KINCHELOE

# 7. MCDONALD'S, POWER, AND CHILDREN

*Ronald McDonald (Aka Ray Kroc) Does it All for You*

IN HIS BOOK The Hawkline Monster: A Gothic Western (1974, p. 11), the late Richard Brautigan develops the character, Cameron, who is a counter:

> Cameron was a counter. He vomited nineteen times to San Francisco. He liked to count everything that he did. This had made Greer a little nervous when he first met up with Cameron years ago, but he'd gotten used to it by now.
>
> People would sometimes wonder what Cameron was doing and Greer would say, "He's counting something," and people would ask, "What's he counting?" and Greer would say, "What difference does it make?" and the people would say, "Oh."

People usually wouldn't go into it any further because Greer and Cameron were very self-assured in that big relaxed casual kind of way that makes people nervous.

I can relate to Cameron, for I, too am a counter. McDonald's also is a counter—and like the people who noticed Cameron's peculiar proclivity, most Americans don't go very far in analyzing the company's propensity for counting or, for that matter, anything else about the fast-food behemoth. Like Greer and Cameron, the company's self-assurance (that is, its power) must make people a little nervous.

I was destined to write about McDonald's, for my life has always intersected with the Golden Arches. As part of my undergraduate comedy shtick I told my listeners (truthfully) that I had consumed 6,000 McDonald's hamburgers before graduating from high school. In junior high and high school we were allowed to go off campus to eat. My friends and I (before we had our driver's licenses) would tromp through the Tennessee woods rain or shine to McDonaldland—by high school we drove. After six years of three-hamburger lunches, not to mention the Wednesday-night burgers with my parents and several more on weekend nights after cruising with friends, the count began to mount. A secondary bonus for my fifteen-cent burgermania involved the opportunity to count my cholesterol numbers as they crept higher and higher. Ray Kroc, the man who made McDonald's a household name, would have been proud.

Somewhere in my small-town Tennessee adolescent consciousness, I understood that McDonald's was the future. I couldn't name it, but the standardized hamburger was a symbol of some vague social phenomenon. Like Italian or Polish immigrants of another place and time, I was ethnic (hillbilly). And like all children of traditional ethnic parents I struggled for an American identity free from the taint of ethnicity. Though it hadn't yet assumed the mantle of all-American symbol around the world, I knew that the McDonald's of the early 1960s was mainstream American through and through. As such, my participation in the burger ritual was an act of shedding my ethnic identity. Understanding the company's regulation of customer behavior, I complied readily, knowing the menu in advance and placing my order quickly and accurately. My parents, in contrast, raised in the rural South during the early twentieth century, were lost at the ordering counter—never understanding the menu, always unsure of the expected behavior; the effort to shape their customer conduct was a bust.

On a very different level, however, my parents were seduced by McDonald's. Students of media have come to understand that readings of film, TV, and TV commercials are idiosyncratic, differing significantly from individual to individual. So it was in my home. As victims of the Great Depression in southern Appalachia (a double economic whammy), my mother and father came to see excessive spending as a moral weakness. Eating out, when it was possible to prepare food at home, was especially depraved. My father would darken the door of McDonald's only if he was convinced of its economic "good sense." Indeed, advertisers struck an emotional chord when they pitted fifteen-cent McDonald's hamburgers and twelve-cent French fries as an alternative to the extravagant cost of eating out. To my self-identified working-class father, eating McDonald's was an act of class resistance. He never really cared much for the food—he would have rather eaten my mother's country ham and cornbread. But as we McDined, he spoke with great enthusiasm about how McDonald's beat the price of other burgers around town by fifty or sixty cents. Such statistics made him very happy.

Like others in peculiar social spaces around the world, my father consumed a democratic, egalitarian ethos. French teenagers accustomed to the bourgeois stuffiness of French restaurants could have identified with my father's class-resistant consumption, as they are known to revel in the informality and freedom of the restaurants' "American atmosphere." The inexpensive fare, the informal dress, and the loud talk are class signifiers (Leidner, 1993). Such coding is quite ironic in light of the company's right-wing political history, its manipulations of labor, and its cutthroat competition with other fast-food enterprises. That McDonald's continues to maintain an egalitarian image is testimony to the power/expertise of its public-relations strategists. And here rest the major questions raised by this essay: What is the nature of these public-relations strategies? What do they tell us about McDonald's? And how do they affect American culture—its kinderculture in particular?

## SHAPING CULTURE, SHAPING CONSCIOUSNESS

Few Americans think in terms of how power interests in the larger society regulate populations to bring about desired behaviors. In America and other Western societies political domination shifted decades ago from police or military forces to the use of cultural messages. Such communications are designed to win the approval or consent of citizens for the actions taken by power elites (Giroux, 1988). The contributors to this book in their own particular ways are involved in efforts to expose the specifics of this process of cultural domination (it is often labeled hegemony). The process takes place in the everyday experience of our lives. The messages are not sent by a clandestine group of conspirators or devised by some secret ministry of propaganda; neither are they read by everyone in the same way—some people understand the manipulative intent and rebel against their authority (Goldman, 1992). The company's role in these power dynamics illustrates the larger process. If any organization has the power to shape the lives of children from Peoria to Moscow, it is McDonald's.

The construction of who we are and what we believe cannot be separated from the workings of power. Americans don't talk much about power; American politicians don't even talk about power. When the subject of power is broached in mainstream sociology, the conversation revolves around either the macro level—the political relations of governments—or the micro level—the personal relations between two people (Abercrombie, 1994). Power, as the term is used in this essay, is neither macro nor micro—nor does it rely on either legality or coercion. Power, as it has evolved at the end of the twentieth century, maintains its legitimacy in much more subtle and effective ways.

Consider the power generated by the company's use of the media to define itself not simply as an American institution but as America itself. As the "land we love" writ small. McDonald's attaches itself to American patriotism and the cultural dynamics it involves. Ray Kroc understood from the beginning that he was not simply selling hamburgers—he was selling America a vision of itself (Luxenberg, 1985). From the all-American marching band to the all-American basketball and football teams to the all-American meal served by all-American boys and girls, the all-American of the Year—Ray Kroc—labored to connect the American signifier to McDonald's. The American flag will fly twenty-four hours a day at McDonald's, he demanded. Using the flag as a backdrop for the hamburger count, Kroc watched the burger numbers supplant the Dow Jones closing average as the symbolic statistical index for America's economic health. In the late 1960s and early 1970s, Kroc saw the perpetually flying flag as a statement to the war protesters and civil rights "kooks" that McDonald's (America) would not stand for anyone criticizing or attempting to undermine "our" country (Kroc, 1977).

One of the reasons Americans don't talk much about power is that it works in such a subtle and hard-to-define manner. Ask Americans how McDonald's has shaped them or constructed their consciousness, and you'll draw blank stares. What does it mean to argue that power involves the ability to ascribe meanings to various features of our lives? Return to the McDonald's all-American ad campaign. Kroc and McDonald's management sanctioned the costliest and most ambitious ad campaign in American corporate history (Boas and Chain, 1976). All this money and effort were expended to imbue the hamburger—the McDonald's variety in particular—with a star-spangled signification. And it worked in the sense that Americans and individuals around the world began to make the desired connection. Described as the "ultimate icon of Americana," a "cathedral of consumption" where Americans practice their "consumer religion," McDonald's, like Disneyland, transcends status as mere business establishment (Ritzer, 1993). When McDonald's or Disney speaks, they speak for all of us. How could the Big Mac or Pirates of the Caribbean mislead us? They are us.

Just as Americans saw mystical implications in the deaths of Thomas Jefferson and John Adams on July 4, 1826, the fiftieth anniversary of the Declaration of Independence, contemporary Americans may see mystical ramifications in the fact that Ray Kroc and Walt Disney were in the same company in the U.S. army. Both having lied about their age, the two prophets of free enterprise-grounded utopian Americana fought the good fight for the American way. It takes nothing away from the mystery to know that Kroc described Disney as a "strange duck" (Donald? Uncle Scrooge? Daisy?) because he wouldn't chase girls (Kroc, 1977).

No expenses were spared, no signifiers were left free-floating in the grand effort to transfer reverence for America to McDonald's. The middle-class cathedral was decorated as a shrine with the obligatory plastic eagle replete with powerful wings and glazed, piercing eyes. A banner held in the bald eagle's beak read "McDonald's: The American Way" (Boas and Chain, 1976). These legitimation signifiers work best when they go unnoticed, as they effectively connect an organization's economic power to acquire property, lobby Congress, hire lawyers, and so on to its power to ascribed meaning and persuade. In the process the legitimated organization gains the power to create and transmit a view of reality that is consonant with its larger interests—American economic superiority as the direct result of an unbridled free-enterprise system.

A recent ad campaign paints a nostalgic, sentimentalized, conflict-free American family pictorial history. The purpose of the ad is to forge an even deeper connection between McDonald's and America by creating an American historical role for McDonald's where there was none before. You can almost hear the male voiceover: "Though we didn't yet exist, we were there to do it all for you—McDonald's then, McDonald's now." We're all one big, happy family with the same (European?) roots. "We" becomes McDonald's and America—"our" family (Goldman, 1992). The only thing left to buttress the all-American image would be some type of Santa Claus connection. Kroc's public-relations men quickly made their move, inducing Kroc himself to distribute hamburgers to Chicago's street-corner Santa's and Salvation Army workers. Newspapers noticed the event and, to Kroc's delight, linked Santa Claus to a chauffeur named McDonald's. The legend grew when the public-relations men circulated a story about a child who was asked where Santa had met Mrs. Santa. "At McDonald's," the child was reported to have said. Wire services picked up the anecdote, sending it to every town in the country (Boas and Chain, 1976). Whether with big ad campaigns or bogus anecdotes, McDonald's has used the media to create an American mythology.

Like other giant international corporations of the late twentieth century, McDonald's has used the media to invade the most private spheres of our everyday lives. Our national identifications, desires, and human needs have been commodified (that is, appropriated) for the purposes of commerce (Giroux, 1994; Kellner, 1992). Such media usage grants producers a level of access to human consciousness never before imagined by the most powerful dictator. One way such power is illustrated is in the resistance McDonald's elicits as signifier for America. Time and time again in the company's brief history, neighborhood organizers have reacted to its efforts to enter their communities. Seeing McDonald's as a form of cultural colonization that overwhelms locally owned businesses and devours local culture, individuals have fought to keep McDonald's out. In the 1970s opposition became so intense in New York City that Kroc ordered high walls built around construction sites to keep them hidden from local residents. At the same time in Sweden, radicals bombed two restaurants in hopes of thwarting "creeping American cultural imperialism" (Boas and Chain, 1976). For better and for worse, McDonald's had succeeded in positioning itself as America.

## MCDONALD'S IS A KIDS' KIND OF PLACE: E-I-E-I-O

Contrary to the prevailing middle-class wisdom, childhood is not and never has been an unchanging developmental stage of humanness. Rather, it is a social and economic construction tied to prevailing perceptions of what constitutes the "natural order" (Polakow, 1992). Forces such as urbanization and industrialization have exerted significant influences on the nature of childhood—as have the development of media and the techno-power it produces for those financially able to afford it. By the term *techno-power* I am attempting to illustrate the expansion of corporate influence via the use of recent technological innovation (Kellner, 1989; Harvey, 1989). Using techno-power, corporations like McDonald's have increased their ability to maximize capital accumulation, influence social and cultural life, and even help mold children's consciousness. Since childhood is a cultural construction shaped in the contemporary era by the forces of this media-catalyzed techno-power, the need for parents, teachers, and community members to study it is dramatic. Let us turn now to McDonald's and the late-twentieth-century construction of childhood.

Even the name—"McDonald's"—is kid-friendly, with its evocation of Old McDonald and his farm—E-I-E-I-O. The safety of McDonald's provides asylum, if not utopian refuge, from the kid-unfriendly contemporary world of child abuse, broken homes, and childnapping. Offering something better to escape into, the company's TV depiction of itself to children as a happy place where "what you want is what you get" is very appealing (Garfield, 1992). Thus, by the time children reach elementary school they are often zealous devotees of McDonald's who insist on McDonaldland birthday celebrations and surprise dinners. Obviously, McDonald's advertisers are doing something right, as they induce phenomenal numbers of kids to pester their parents for Big Macs and fries.

McDonald's and other fast-food advertisers have discovered an enormous and previously overlooked children's market. Children aged five to twelve annually spend $4.2 billion of their own money. They influence household spending of an additional $131 billion each year. Of this $131 billion, $82 billion goes to food and drinks (Fischer et al., 1991). Every month nineteen out of every twenty kids aged six to eleven visit a fast-food restaurant. In a typical McDonald's promotion where toys like Hot Wheels or Barbies accompany kids' meals, company officials can expect to sell 30 million to child customers. By the time a child reaches the age of three, more than four out of five know that McDonald's sells hamburgers. As if this level of child-consciousness colonization were not enough, McDonald's, along with scores of other companies, has targeted the public schools as a new venue for child marketing and consumption. In addition to hamburgers for A's programs and advertising-based learning packets for science, foreign language, and other subjects, McDonald's and other fast-food firms have attempted to operate school cafeterias (Hume, 1993; Ritzer, 1993; Giroux, 1994).

Make no mistake about it: McDonald's and its advertisers want to transform children into consumers—indeed, they see children as consumers in training (Fischer et al., 1991). Ellen Seiter (1993), however, warns against drawing simplistic conclusions about the relationship between advertisers and children, as have, she says, many well-intentioned liberal children's advocacy groups. ACT (Action for Children's Television), the leading voice against corporate advertising for children, fails to capture the subtle aspects of techno-power and its colonization of childhood. Seeing children as naïve innocents who should watch only "good" TV, meaning educational programs that portray middle-class values, ACT has little appreciation of the complexity of children's TV watching. Children at the end of the twentieth century are not passive and naïve TV viewers. As advertising professionals have learned, children are active, analytical viewers who often make their own meanings of both commercials and the products they sell. These social and psychological dynamics between advertiser and child deserve further analysis.

One of the most important of these dynamics involves the recognition by advertisers that children themselves feel oppressed by this middle-class view of children as naïve entities in need of constant protection. By drawing upon the child's discomfort with middle-class protectionism and the accompanying attempt to "adjust" children to a "developmentally appropriate" norm, advertisers hit upon a marketing bonanza. If we address kids as kids—a dash of anarchism and a pinch of hyperactivity—they will love our commercials even though parents (especially middle-class parents) will hate them. By the end of the 1960s, commercial children's TV and advertising were grounded on this premise. Such video throws off restraint, discipline, and old views that children should be seen but not heard. Everything, for example, that educational TV embraces—earnestness, child as an incomplete adult, child in need of correction—commercial TV rejects. In effect, commercial TV sets up an oppositional culture for kids.

One doesn't have to look far (try any middle-class home) to find that children's enthusiasm for certain TV shows, toys, and foods isolates them from their parents. Drawing on this isolation, children turn it into a form of power—they finally know something that dad doesn't. How many dads or moms understand the relationship between Mayor McCheese and the French Fry Guys? Battle lines begin to be drawn between children and parents, as kids want to purchase McDonald's hamburgers or action toys. Conflicts in lower-middle-class homes may revolve around family finances; strife in upper-middle-class homes may concern aesthetic or ideological concerns. Questions of taste, cultural capital, and self-improvement permeate child-adult interactions in such families. The child's ability to negotiate the restrictions of adult values is central to the development of an independent self. A very common aspect of this development of independence involves the experience of contradiction with the adult world. Children of upwardly mobile, ambitious parents may find it more difficult to negotiate this experience of contradiction because of the parents' strict views of the inappropriateness of TV-based children's culture. Thus, the potential for parent-child conflict and alienation may be greater in this familial context.

A covert children's culture has always existed on playgrounds and in schools. The children's culture of the past, however, was produced by children and propagated through child-to-child contact. Today's postmodern children's culture is created by adults and dispersed via television for the purpose of inducing children to consume. As they carefully subvert middle-class parenting's obsession with achievement, play as a serious enterprise, and self-improvement-oriented "quality time" (a subversion that in my opinion probably contributes to the public good), advertisers connect children's culture to their products. McDonald's commercials reflect these themes, although less blatantly than many advertisers.

Attempting to walk a tightrope between tapping the power of children's subversive culture and the possibility of offending the middle-class guardians of propriety, McDonald's has developed a core of so-called "slice-of-life" children's ads. Casting no adults in the commercials, advertisers depict a group of preteens engaged in "authentic" conversations around a McDonald's table covered with burgers, fries, and shakes. Using children's slang ("radical," "dude," "we're into Barbie") to describe toys in various McDonald's promotions, children discuss the travails of childhood with one another. In many commercials children make adults the butt of their jokes or share jokes that adults don't get (Seiter, 1993; Goldman, 1992).

Subtle though it may be, McDonald's attempts to draw some of the power of children's subversive culture to their products without anyone but the kids knowing. Such slice-of-life ads are opaque to the degree that adults watching them don't get it—they don't see the advertiser's effort to connect McDonald's with the subversive kinderculture.

## THE BLOODY FIGHT FOR CONFORMITY, COURTESY, AND ESTABLISHED VIRTUE: MCDONALDLAND, RONALD AND RAY

TV ads often serve as postmodern myths, as they resolve cultural contradictions, portray models of identity, and glorify the status quo. Although all McDonald's ads accomplish these mythic functions to some degree, none do it better than ads and promotions involving McDonaldland. To understand the mythic dynamics of McDonaldland, one must appreciate the psychological complexity of Ray Kroc. Born in 1902 in a working-class neighborhood on Chicago's West Side into what he called a "Bo-hunk" (Bohemian) family, Kroc was obsessed throughout his life with proving his worth as both a human being and a businessman. Having failed in several business ventures while in his twenties and thirties, Kroc had much to prove by the time the McDonald's opportunity confronted him at the age of 52 (Boas and Chain, 1976). Kroc defined McDonaldland the same way he defined himself—through consumption. Driven by an ambition to own nice things, Kroc's autobiography is peppered with references to consumption: "I used to comb through the advertisements in the local newspaper for notices of house sales in the wealthier suburbs...I haunted these sales and picked up pieces of elegant furniture" (Kroc, 1977, p. 27). Watched over by the messianic Ronald McDonald, McDonaldland is a place (your kind of place) where consumption was not only the sole occupation but the means through which its inhabitants gained their identities.

McDonaldland is a kid's text fused with Kroc's psyche that emerges as an effort to sell the system, to justify consumption as a way of life. As central figure in McDonaldland, Ronald McDonald emerges as a multidimensional clown deity, virgin-born son of Adam Smith, press secretary for free-enterprise capitalism. He is also Ray Kroc's projection of himself, his ego creation of the most loved prophet of utopian consumption in the McWorld. Ronald's life history begins in Washington, D. C., with Willard Scott, currently the *Today* weatherman. Struggling to make it as a junior announcer at WRC-TV during the early 1960s, Scott agreed to play Bozo the Clown on the station's show. When Scott donned the clown suit, he was transformed from Clark Kent to Superman, bumbling Willard to Superclown. The local McDonald's franchisees recognized Scott's talent and employed Bozo as a spokesperson for McDonald's. When the show was canceled by WRC, McDonald's lost a very effective advertiser. The local McDonald's owners worked with Scott to create Ronald McDonald (Scott's idea), debuting him in October 1963. Ronald was so successful, creating traffic jams every time he appeared in public, that the local operators suggested to the Chicago headquarters that Ronald go national (Love, 1986).

After a lengthy debate over whether they should employ Ronald McDonald as a clown, a cowboy, or a spaceman, corporate leaders and advertisers settled on the clown. Dumping Scott because he was deemed too fat for the image they wanted to promote, the company in 1965 hired Coco, an internationally known clown with the Ringling Brothers and Barnum, & Bailey Circus. Beginning with his first national appearance in Macy's Thanksgiving Day Parade on November 25, 1966, the deification of Ronald began. The press releases on Ronald issued by the McDonald's Customers Relations Center are sanctification documents cross-pollinated with frontier tall-tale boasting. "Since 1963, Ronald McDonald has become a household name, more famous than Lassie or the Easter Bunny, and second only to Santa Claus" (McDonald's Customers Relations Center, 1994).

All of the other characters in McDonaldland, the company's promotional literature reports, revere Ronald—aka Ray Kroc. He is "intelligent and sensitive...he can do nearly anything...Ronald McDonald is the *star*." If children are sick, the promos contend, Ronald is there. Even though he has become "an international hero and celebrity," Ronald is still the same friend of children he was in 1963. Ninety-six percent of all children, claimed a bogus "Ronald McDonald Awareness Study" fed to the press, can identify this *heroic* figure (Boas and Chain, 1976). Ronald was everything Kroc wanted to be: a beloved humanitarian, an international celebrity, a philanthropists, a musician (Kroc made his living for awhile as a piano player; Ronald has cut children's records). Even the sophisticates—a group whose affection Kroc sought throughout his life—loved Ronald, Kroc wrote in his autobiography. Unfortunately, he would have to settle for it vicariously through Ronald. Abe Lincoln, too, had been rejected by the sophisticates of his day; as twentieth-century Lincoln, Kroc prominently displayed the bust of Ronald adjacent to the bust of Lincoln on a table behind his desk at the Chicago headquarters (McCormick, 1993; Kroc, 1977).

According to the promotional literature designed for elementary schools, Ronald "became a citizen of [the McDonald's] International Division" in 1969 and soon began to appear on TV around the world. Kroc was propelled to a new level of celebrity as the corporation "penetrated" the global market. Now known everywhere on earth, Kroc/Ronald became the Grand Salesman, the successful postindustrial Willy Loman—they love me in Moscow, Belgrade, and New York. Stung by a plethora of critics, Kroc was obsessed with being perceived as a moral man with a moral company that exerted a wholesome influence on children around the world. Kroc wrote and spoke of his noble calling, establishing his "missions" with the Golden Arches as part of his neo-white man's burden. "I provide an humanitarian service," Kroc proclaimed: "I go out and check out a piece of property [that's] not producing a damned thing for anybody," he wrote in his epistles from California. The new franchise provides a better life for scores of people— "out of that bare ground comes a store that does, say, a million dollars a year in business. Let me tell you, it's great satisfaction to see that happen." Kroc/Ronald personified the great success story of twentieth-century capitalism. Kroc's and his franchisees' fortunes came to represent what happens when one works hard in the free-enterprise system. McDonaldland and the McWorld—signifiers for the McDonaldization of the planet.

The convergence of the growth of international megacorporations and the expanding technological sophistication of the media has prompted a new era of consumption. Some analysts argue that the central feature of the postmodern lifestyle revolves around the act of consuming. In McDonaldland, Ronald McDonald serves as CEO/archduke over his fiefdom of consumer junkies. The Hamburglar is "cute" in his addiction to hamburgers. According to the literature provided to schools about McDonaldland, the Hamburglar's main purpose in life is the acquisition of McDonald's hamburgers." Grimace is described as "generous and affectionate...[his] primary personality attribute is his love for McDonald's shakes." The most important passion of Captain Crook is his love of McDonald's Filet o' Fish sandwiches.

As free-enterprise utopia, McDonaldland erases all differences, all conflicts; social inequities are overcome through acts of consumption. As such messages justify the existence of extant power relations, conformity emerges as the logical path to self-production. The only hint of difference in McDonaldland involves Uncle O'Grimacey, the annual Irish visitor who speaks in brogue and is defined by his obsession with Shamrock shakes. The emphasis on standardization and "sameness" is so intense that all Ronald McDonald actors go to school to make sure they conform to a uniform image. The training system is so rationalized that students are tracked into one of two groups; throughout preservice and in-service experiences the clowns are either "greeting Ronalds" or "performing Ronalds." The most compelling manifestation of conformity in McDonaldland involves the portrayal of the French Fry Guys. As the only group of citizens depicted in the Hamburger Patch, these faceless commoners are numerous but seldom seen:

> They tend to look, act, and think pretty much alike. Parent French Fry Guys are indistinguishable from children, and vice versa. They are so much alike that, so far, no individual French Fry Guy has emerged as a personality identifiable from the others. They resemble little mops with legs and eyes and speak in squeaky, high-pitched voices, usually in unison. They always move quickly, scurrying around in fits and starts, much like the birds one sees on sandy beaches (McDonald's Customer Relations Center, 1994)

As inhabitants of a McDonaldized McWorld, the French Fry Guys are content to remove themselves from the public space, emerging only for brief and frenetic acts of standardized consumption—their only act of personal assertion.

Life in McDonaldland is conflict-free—the Hamburger Patch is a privatized utopia. It is late-twentieth-century America writ small, corporate-directed and consumer-oriented. Questions such as distribution of income among classes, regulation of corporate interests, free trade, minimum wage, and collective bargaining traditionally elicited passion and commitment—now they hardly raise an eyebrow. The political sphere where decisions are made concerning who gets what and who voted for what is managed by a small group. Their work and the issues they confront are followed by an ever-decreasing audience of new watchers tuned to CNN and C-SPAN. Politics, Americans have concluded, is not only useless but far worse in the mediascape—it is boring. It can't be too important; it gets such low Neilsens. The political structure of McDonaldland reflects this larger depoliticization with its depiction of the inept and superfluous Mayor McCheese. The school promotional literature describes him as a "silly" character not "to be taken seriously." As a "confused and bumbling" politician, Mayor McCheese would rather spend his time in the privatized space of McDonald's, eating cheeseburgers. The lesson is clear to children—politics don't matter, leave McDonald's alone, let these business*men* run their business the way they see fit.

The benign nature of capitalist production, with its freedom from serious conflict of any type, portrayed by McDonaldland and Kroc/Ronald is a cover for a far more savage reality. Business analysts, for example, liken McDonald's operations to the U.S. Marine Corps. When a recruit graduates from basic training (Hamburger University), he believes that he can *conquer* anybody (Love, 1986). Motivated by an econotribal allegiance to the McFamily, store operators speak of faith in McDonald's as if it were a religion. Kroc openly spoke of the Holy Trinity— McDonald's, family, and God in that order (Kroc, 1977). Released from boot camp on a jihad for a success theology, these faceless French Fry Guys have forced thousands of independent restaurant owners out of business (Luxenberg, 1985). Competing fast-food franchisees tell of their introductions to recent Hamburger University graduates and other McDonald's managers with amazement: "We will run you out of business and bury you," these Khrushchevs of fast food proclaim.

No matter how ruthless business might become, there is no room for criticism or dissent in McDonaldland. "I feel sorry for people who have such a small and wretched view of the system that made this country great," Kroc (1977) wrote in his autobiography. The "academic snobs" who have criticized McDonald's tapped a sensitivity in Kroc's psyche that motivated counterattacks until the day he died. This love-it-or-leave-it anti-intellectualism finds its McDonaldland expression in the Professor. Described as the proud possessor of various degrees, the Professor is a bumbling fool with a high-pitched, effeminate voice. As none of his theories or inventions ever work, he meets Kroc's definition of an overeducated man: someone who worries about inconsequential affairs to the degree that he is distracted from the normal problems of business. Kroc never liked books or school and saw little use for advanced degrees: "One thing I flatly refuse to give money to is the support of any college" (Kroc, 1977, p. 199). Intellectuals don't fit into the culture of the Hamburger Patch.

As much as the Professor is effeminate, Big Mac, McDonaldland's policeman, is manly. The promotional literature describes him as "the strong, silent type. His voice is deep and super-masculine; his manner is gruff but affectionate...his walk is a strut. His stance is chest out, stomach in." The gender curriculum of McDonaldland is quite explicit: Big Mac as the manly man; Birdie, the Early Bird, as the pert, nurturing female. As the only female in McDonaldland, Birdie is faced with a significant task. She is the cheerleader who encourages the male residents to jump into the activities of the new day. "Her enthusiasm and energy are infectious... her positive attitude is emphasized by her bright, perky, cheerful voice" (McDonald's Customer Relations Center, 1994). Once the McDonaldlanders have gobbled down their Egg McMuffins and are off to their respective occupations, Birdie retires to the sidelines as a passive observer.

The Kroc influence is alive and well in the gender dynamics of the corporation. Referring to himself in the third person as "Big Daddy," Kroc expressed a sometimes disturbing misogyny in his handling of company affairs. Ray's personality, one colleague observed, would never allow a woman to gain power (Love, 1986). To Kroc, women were to take care of frills, leaving the important work to men:

> Clark told me I should hire a secretary.
>
> "I suppose you're right," I [Kroc] said. "But I want a male secretary...I want a man. He might cost a little more at first, but if he's any good at all, I'll have him doing sales work in addition to administrative things. I have nothing against having a pretty girl around, but the job I have in mind would be much better handled by a man..." My decision to hire a male secretary paid off when I was hospitalized for a gall bladder operation and later for a goiter operation. [The male secretary] worked between our office and my hospital room, and we kept things humming as briskly as when I was in the office every morning (Kroc, 1977, pp. 48–49).

June Martino was a very talented woman who had been with Kroc from the earliest days of his involvement with McDonald's. Corporate insiders described her as a gifted businesswoman whose expertise often kept the company going during difficult times. Kroc's view of her reflected his view of women in general: "I thought it was good to have a lucky person around, maybe some of it would rub off on me. Maybe it did. After we got McDonald's going and built a larger staff, they called her 'Mother Martino.' She kept track of everyone's family fortunes, whose wife was having a baby, who was having marital difficulties, or whose birthday it was. She helped make the office a happy place" (Kroc, 1977, p. 84).

Such attitudes at the top permeated all levels of the organization and were expressed in a variety of pathological ways. Management's sensitivity to sexual harassment was virtually nonexistent well into the 1980s. Interviews with women managers reveal patterns of sexual misconduct involving eighteen- and nineteen-year-old women employees being pressured to date older male managers. Reports of sexual harassment were suppressed by the company bureaucracy; women who complained were sometimes punished or forced to resign. One successful manager confided that after she reported harassment, company higher-ups stalked her both on and off the job. She was eventually forced to leave the company. Not surprisingly, such an organization was not overly concerned with women's complaints about the exaggerated gender roles depicted in McDonald's commercials and promotions. From Birdie as cheerleader to Happy Meals with Barbies for girls and Hot Wheels for boys, McDonald's has never escaped Kroc's gender assumptions (Hume, 1993).

McDonald's perpetuates what Allen Shelton (1993) refers to as a hegemonic logic—a way of doing business that privileges conformity, zealously defends the middle-class norm, fights to the death for established virtue, and at all costs resists social change. As a passionate force for a Warren G. Harding "normalcy," McDonald's is the corporation that invites the children of prominent civic, military, and business leaders to the opening of its first McDonaldland Park—but leaves the daughters and sons of the not-so-rich-and-famous off the invitation list. This hegemonic logic holds little regard for concepts such as justice or morality—McDonald's morality is contingent on what sells. This concept is well illustrated in the company's emphasis on the primacy of home and family values in its advertising.

## WE'VE GOT OURSELVES A FAMILY UNIT: HOME IS WHEREVER RONALD MCDONALD GOES

Kroc and his corporate leaders unequivocally understood their most important marketing priority—to portray McDonald's as a "family kind of place." As they focused on connecting McDonald's to America and the family, they modified the red-and-white ceramic takeout restaurants to look more like the suburban homes that had sprung up throughout America in the late 1950s and 1960s. Ad campaigns proclaimed that McDonald's was home and that anywhere Ronald goes "he is at home." Like many other ads of the late twentieth century, these home and family ads privilege the private sphere, not the public sphere, as the important space where life is lived. As an intrinsically self-contained unit, the family is removed from the public realm of society, such a depiction, however, conceals the ways that politics and economics shape everyday family life. The greatest irony of these ads is that even as they isolate the family from any economic connections they promote the commodification of family life. A form of doublespeak is discernible in this situation: The family is an end in itself; the family is an instrumental consumption unit whose ultimate purpose is to benefit corporate profits and growth.

McDonald's ads deploy home and family as paleosymbols that position McDonald's as the defender of "the American way of life," Kroc (1977) never knew what paleosymbols were but he understood that McDonald's public image should be, in his words, a "combination YMCA, Girl Scouts, and Sunday School." Devised to tap into the right-wing depiction of the traditional family under attack from feminists, homosexuals, and other "screwballs," these so-called "legitimation ads" don't sell hamburgers—they sell social relations. In the midst of social upheaval and instability, McDonald's endures as a rock of ages, a refuge in a world gone mad. McDonald's bring us together, provides a safe haven for our children. The needs the legitimation ads tap are real; the consumption panacea they provide is false (Goldman, 1992). After its phenomenal growth in the 1960s, McDonald's realized that it was no longer the "cute little company" of the 1950s (Love, 1986). From Kroc's right-wing perspective, he saw the antiwar, civil rights, and other social movements of the 1960s as repugnant to all of his American values. Such views, when combined with the marketing need for McDonald's to legitimate itself now that it was an American "big business," made home and family the obvious battlefield in the legitimation campaign. As the public faith in corporations declined, McDonald's used the paleosymbols to create an environment of confidence. Going against the grain of a social context, perceived to be hostile to big business, the ads worked. The lyrics of accompanying music read:

You, you're the one.
So loving, strong, and patient.
Families like yours
made all the states a nation.
Our families are our past,
our future and our pride.
Whatever roots we come from,
we're growing sided by side (quoted in Goldman, 1992, p. 95).

The world of home and family portrayed by the McDonald's legitimation ads is a terrain without conflict or tension. In an ad produced during the early 1980s, as Reagan's family-values agenda was being established, a typical white middle-class family is returning to the small town of Dad's childhood. Excited to show his preteen son and daughter his childhood world, Dad tells the family that his old house is just up the street. As the "Greek chorus" sings "things have changed a bit since you've been around" as background music, Dad is shocked to discover new condominiums have replaced the old house. Dismayed but undaunted, Dad tells the family that his old friend Shorty's house is just around the corner. Shorty's house is also gone, replaced by a car wash. From the backseat the daughter tells her disappointed father that she hopes the place he used to eat at is still standing because she's hungry. Dad immediately begins to look for the unnamed eating place; the background chorus sings: "In the night, the welcome sight of an old friend." The camera focuses on Dad as his eyes brighten and a smile explodes across his face. The camera cuts to a car pulling into McDonald's, and the chorus sings: "Feels so right here tonight at McDonald's again."

Once again consumption at McDonald's serves to solve the problem of change. The consumptive act in this case serves to affirm family values in a world where the larger society threatens them. Nothing has changed at McDonald's, as Dad tells the perky, young counter girl that he had his first Big Mac at this McDonald's. The camera focuses across the dining room to a short man expressing surprise and disbelief. Of course, it is Shorty. As Shorty embraces Dad we find out that Dad's childhood name was Curly—ironic in the fact that he is now bald. The camera retreats to frame the old friends embracing in the light cast by the Golden Arches. Dad is at McDonald's, he is *home* with old friends and family. McDonald's made it all possible (Goldman, 1992). The turbulent 1960s are finally over. We (America) have "come home" to the traditional family values that made us great. The chorus has already reminded us that it "feels so right...at McDonald's *again.*" The key word here being "again." Reagan, whose candidacy Kroc and the McDonald's management fervently supported, has brought back traditional values—McDonald's wants viewers to know that McDonald's is an important aspect of the traditional family-values package.

In the final scene of this "Home Again" commercial, the camera shoots a close-up of the son and daughter. Having just watched the embrace between Dad and Shorty, the daughter turns to her brother and says with ironic inflection, "Curly?" Her brother shrugs and rolls his eyes in recognition of the generational rift between Dad's understanding of the scene as compared to their own. The camera tells us the reunion is irrelevant to the son and daughter as it focuses on the attention they pay to the hamburgers sitting in front of them—the only time, by the way, McDonald's food is displayed in the ad. McDonald's wants it both ways: the adult identification with Reagan, America, and the return to traditional family-values; and child identification with the subversive kinderculture described previously. The subversive kinderculture subtext of this ad involves the children's shared recognition of the father's fatuous pursuit of a long-dead past and his embarrassing public display of emotion. Dad blows his "cool pose." The "Curly irony" is the overt signifier for these deeper generational divisions—differentiations described by advertisers as market segments.

The grand irony of this and many other ads is that under the flag of traditional family values McDonald's actually undermines the very qualities it claims to promote. The McDonald's experience depicted does not involve a family sharing a common experience—each market segment experiences it in a different and even potentially conflicting way. The family depicted here, like so many American middle-class families, is an isolated unit divided against itself. In terms of everyday life McDonald's does not encourage long, leisurely, interactive family meals. The seats and tables are designed to be uncomfortable to the point that customers will eat quickly and leave. In the larger scheme of things, family values, America, and home are nothing more than cynical marketing tools designed to legitimate McDonald's to different market segments. Kroc himself made his feeling about family very clear—work comes first, he told his managers. "My total commitment to business had long since been established in my home" (Kroc, 1977, p. 89). The cynicism embedded in McDonald's ads and scores of other ads undermines the social fabric, making the culture our children inhabit a colder and more malicious place. Such cynicism leads corporations to develop new forms of techno-power that can be used to subvert democracy and justice in the quest for new markets. Such cynicism holds up Kroc/Ronald as heroes while ignoring authentic heroes—men and women who struggle daily to lead good lives, be good parents, and extend social justice.

## REFERENCES

Abercrombie, N. (1994). Authority and consumer society. In R. Keat, N. Whiteley, & N. Abercrombie (Eds.), *The authority of the consumer*. New York: Routledge.
Boas, M., & Chain, S. (1976). *Big Mac: The unauthorized story of McDonald's*. New York: E. P. Dutton.
Brautigan, R. (1974). *The Hawkline monster: A gothic western*. New York: Pocket Books.
Fischer, P., et al. (1991). Brand logo recognition by children aged 3 to 6 years. *Journal of the American Medical Association, 266*(22), 3145–3148.
Garfield, B. (1992). Nice ads, but that theme is not what you want. *Advertising Age, 63*(8):53.
Giroux, H. (1988). *Teachers as intellectuals: Toward a critical pedagogy of learning*. Granby, MA: Bergin and Garvey.
Giroux, H. (1994). *Disturbing pleasures: Learning popular culture*. New York: Routledge.
Goldman, R. (1992). *Reading ads socially*. New York: Routledge.
Harvey, D. (1989). *The condition of postmodernity*. Cambridge, MA: Basil Blackwell.
Hume, S. (1993). Fast-food caught in the middle. *Advertising Age, 64*(6), 12–15.
Keat, R., Whiteley, N., & Abercrombie, N. (1994). Introduction. In R. Keat, N. Whiteley, & N. Abercrombie (Eds.), *The Authority of the consumer*. New York: Routledge.
Kellner, D. (1989). *Critical theory, Marxism, and modernity*. Baltimore: Johns Hopkins University Press.
Kellner, D. (1992). Popular culture and the construction of postmodern identities. In S. Lash & J. Friedman (Eds.), *Modernity and identity*. Cambridge, MA: Basil Blackwell.
Kroc, R. (1977). *Grinding it out: The making of McDonald's*. New York: St. Martin's.
Leidner, R. (1993). *Fast food, fast talk: Service work and the routinization of everyday life*. Berkeley, CA: University of California Press.
Love, J. (1986). *McDonald's: Behind the arches*. New York: Bantam.
Luxenberg, S. (1985). *Roadside empires: How the chains franchised*. New York: Viking Penguin.
McCormick, M. (2003). Kid Rhino and McDonald's enter licensing agreement. *Billboard, 105*(8), 10–11.
McDonald's Customer Relations Center. (1994). *Handout to schools*.
Ritzer, G. (1993). *The McDonaldization of society*. Thousand Oaks, CA: Pine Forge Press.

Seiter, E. (1993). *Sold separately: Parents and children in consumer culture.* New Brunswick, NJ: Rutgers University Press.

Shelton, A. (1993). Writing McDonald's, eating the past: McDonald's as a postmodern space. *Studies in Symbolic Interaction, 15,* 103–118.

Reprinted with permission: Kincheloe, J. L. (1997). McDonald's, power, and children: Ronald McDonald (aka Ray Kroc) does it all for you. In S. R. Steinberg and J. L. Kincheloe (Eds.), *Kinderculture: The corporate construction of childhood* (pp. 249–266). Boulder, CO: Westview Press.

KECIA HAYES

# THE CORPORATE PARADISE OF A SUBVERTED URBAN KINDERCULTURE

Kinderculture, as a youth subcultural form, reflects young people's unique phenomenological perspectives of how they experience society. It represents the landscape wherein young people engage in a persistent discourse with the hegemonic dominant culture and with the subordinated cultures of their parents as they construct, disseminate, and perform their subcultural forms. They provide an essential counter-narrative that critically challenges the rhetoric of cultural normativity imbued in the generational culture of their parents that permeates our hegemonic society. In doing so, young people begin to cultivate a *crisis of democracy* but their efforts are subdued by the authoritarian parent culture. According to Chomsky, a *crisis of democracy* occurs when the masses attempt to reposition themselves as active, rather than passive, participants within the political, economic, and social arenas, and the ruling elite reacts to subdue the resistance to their authority.

In his essay, Joe Kincheloe demonstrates how McDonald's exploits social capital and power to shape culture and consciousness of civil society through its pernicious penetration of youth subculture. Unfortunately, McDonald's is not alone in this endeavor as other corporate capitalists are equally adept and unequivocal at leveraging the tools of co-optation and commodification to colonize kinderculture and thereby expand their socioeconomic power. The authenticity and revelatory potential of kinderculture is significantly threatened as young people are disempowered and their agency is silenced. This discussion considers the power dynamic within the co-optation and commodification of urban kinderculture, particularly in terms of how it falsely establishes urban youth as normatively problematic; and how it structures urban youth's complicit participation in their oppression.

## THE CO-OPTATION AND COMMODIFICATION OF URBAN KINDERCULTURE

Perhaps more than anything else, hip hop reflects a critical feature of urban youth's kinderculture. Consequently, it also has become the site of an extensive and strategic corporate effort to colonize the kinderculture of urban youth of color. The musical form emerged around the 1970s as a cultural apparatus constructed by urban youth of color to document and disseminate a discourse that worked to counter the publicly mediated dominant narrative of what it meant to be poor and Black or Latino. Some of its founding cultural agents operated as Gramscian counterhegemonic organic intellectuals who gave voice to a subjugated narrative that critically juxtaposed their lived experiences against the public discourse and imagery that characterized them and their communities as *welfare cheats, subculture of violence/poverty, crime-prone, gang-infested, crack-plagued, ghetto outcasts,* and *ghetto-poverty syndrome.*

It also challenged the prevailing idea that the era of the Civil Rights Movement had established a utopian social egalitarianism across race and class such that there were no valid reasons why they could overcome the debilitating social conditions that characterized our urban centers. Undeniably, these young people were deftly engaged in the production, dissemination, and interpretation of cultural identity politics, which "…starts from analyses of oppression to recommend, variously, the reclaiming, redescription, or transformation of previously stigmatized accounts of group membership. Rather than accepting the negative scripts offered by a dominant culture about one's own inferiority, one transforms one's own sense of self and community, often through consciousness-raising" (Heyes, p. 1). Through their phenomenological examination of their lived experiences, they challenged the rhetoric of the dominant culture as well as of the parent culture; and amplified the inherent social contradictions that victimized them.

The music is a way for urban youth of color to articulate disenchantment with and alienation from the dominant and parent cultures within civil society; and to issue calls for resistance against their continued oppression. "Hip hop is a reaction to institutionalized White racism, American classism, the material, spiritual, and psychological failures of the Civil Rights Movement, the United States government's abandonment of its war on poverty, the horrendous lack of vision and incompetence of "traditional" Black leadership…" (Powell, p. 8). Artists such as Afrika Bambaataa, dead prez, Common, Black Star, Nas, Public Enemy, KRS-One, Mos Def, The Coup, The Roots, Salt N' Pepa, Disposable Heroes of Hiphoprisy, and Queen Latifah incorporated discourses into their music that highlighted the racialized, classed, and gendered social inequities within civil society, particularly with respect to drugs, crime, and the prison industrial complex as well as the inadequacies of urban schooling. Through the messages embedded in their music, hip hop artists educated, politicized, mobilized, and stimulated the critical consciousness of urban youth.

Unfortunately, by the early 1990s, hip hop began to experience some fissures wherein the Black Nationalist and Afrocentric social critiques were overshadowed by messages of misogyny and hypermasculinity. This new focus, characteristic of the gangster rap genre, was thoroughly exploited by the music industry. In her interview with an executive of Rush Communications, Rose documents how record companies, through their A, & R departments, molded artists to fit the best selling genres so that as gangster rap gained market share, artists were steered to include that type of musical form in their overall repertoire. With commodification, elements of the young people's subcultural form were hijacked, decontextualized, compartmentalized, and repackaged into a marketable cultural product that was disseminated to the public via mass media outlets. The commodified cultural artifacts assumed new significations and meaning that were not necessarily understood by the public and consumers as inauthentic to the extent that they represent a public relations strategy rather than the phenomenological experiences and discursive intent of the artists.

The hypermasculinity that historically has been problematically characteristic of Black Nationalism was compartmentalized, distorted, intensified, and re-interpreted outside of the larger context of a nationalist agenda in preparation for mass dissemination through the mediated formats of recordings and music videos. The works of the genre that reinforced the hegemonically oppressive messagest were valorized while those that implicated hegemonic elites and social structures in acts of oppression were marginalized and erased. In her discussion of the commercialization of the hip hop/rap subcultural form, Blair cites the scholarship of Tony van Der Meer who believes that commercialization is the thing that threatens rap by "... preventing its genuine forms the freedom to fully develop. The expression of Black people is transformed when it is repackaged without any evidence remaining of the Black historical experience" (Blair, p. 574). Hip hop music, which began as the means by which the subculture sought to express its dissatisfaction with the social milieu in which they existed, was transformed into a commodity produced, disseminated, and controlled by the ruling class against which the subculture initially emerged to resist.

Blair utilizes a Gottdienerian three-stage model of mass culture, somewhat inspired by Marxian hegemony theory, to delineate the commercialization of the hip hop subculture. At the third stage, Blair explains that the "... transfunctionalized objects produced by the subculture become the raw material for cultural production by the mass culture industries. During this process, subcultural meanings are changed by mass producers (such as advertisers) into more marketable, less radical meanings" (Blair, p. 579). As a popular culture commodity, Black hypermasculinity is made devoid of any cultural context, which obfuscates the possibility of it being understood as a reactionary political discourse against the dominant culture's oppression and social injustice that historically has emasculated Black male identity. To be clear, this is not to ignore the deeply problematic role of hypermasculinity in the hip hop culture but only to suggest that it has been essentialized into a caricature through the process of corporate commodity production. As corporate elites create and market these mutations of urban kinderculture, they further entrench the dominant culture's problematic narrative of urban youth by portraying the commodified text's distorted image as real. All of us, including urban youth, accept the narrative as a normative *Truth* and it fundamentally shapes our beliefs of who they are and who they can become. Furthermore, corporate elites imbue the text with a contrived authenticity as they ensnare urban youth in its production and consumption.

## COMPLICITY IN A COLONIZED URBAN KINDERCULTURE

As hip hop culture became increasingly and aggressively commodified and commercialized by the corporate entertainment industry, urban young people were made complicatedly complicit in the production, dissemination, and consumption of a text that essentializes them as deficient and problematic youthful characterizations, across race, class, and gender. The young artists are alienated from their cultural artifacts and from the transmission of their cultural expressions, which diminishes their power to control the discursive elements of their subculture. They produce, market, and consume a cultural commodity that is no longer phenomenologically reflective of how they make sense of the range of their experiences within civil society.

In his discussion of didactics and self-production within hip hop, Maher leverages the experiences of dead prez to provide a particularly effective example of how hip hop artists are forced to confront their complicit participation in a colonized urban kinderculture. Dyson characterizes dead prez as "organic intellectual voices" and "hip hop Gramscians" who emerged within the hip hop underground as the era of the gangsta genre began to decline. According to Maher, dead prez eventually signed with an entertainment corporation that was not willing to release the group's more politicized musical discourses, which was viewed by the music industrialists as inflammatory material. This circumstance forced the group to invoke other strategies to disseminate their music. "When it came time to release their second studio album, *RBG: Revolutionary But Gangsta*, Columbia held back and, in an attempt to get their voices out while skirting contract restrictions, dead prez adopted the moniker "dpz" and began to release independent-label mixtapes: *Turn Off the Radio: The Mixtape Volume 1* in 2002 and *Get Free or Die Tryin': The Mixtape Volume 2*" (Maher, p. 143). In discussing the group's engagement with the entertainment industry, M-1 notes "[i]n a good way that experience of being bought and sold and feeling like a slave led us to think of ways to do-for-self on our own. That's when we produced the mixtape, *Turn off the Radio: Volume 1*.... that album helped us to make statements about Iraq and other issues, when there really were no avenues on the radio or anywhere else to do it" (Maher, p. 143). Interestingly, M-1 characterizes the experience of having the group's music or cultural form colonized by corporate elites as enslavement – an indicator of a more pernicious consequence of laboring in the colonized urban kinderculture. Hip hop artists must forego their creative freedoms as they become laborers within the industry that co-opted and commodified their cultural forms. Through this process, they can become complicit in their oppression as they labor to produce and market the distorted texts that essentialize urban young people as socially deficient and problematic.

Complicity also is evidenced in the ways in which young hip hop artists' politicized responses to problematic discursive elements with their subculture are silenced. In her examination of female hip hop artists' reaction to sexist comments by the 2 Live Crew, Rose notes that of five prominent female hip hop artists (Salt N' Pepa, MC Lyte, Queen Latifah, Sister Souljah, and Yo-Yo), only one member of Salt N' Pepa criticized 2 Live Crew for their comments and the critique reflected familiar Black nationalist calls for Black women to be respected. In contemplating why the other publicly progressive female artists did not criticize 2 Live Crew, Rose indicates that they were well aware of how their responses would be repackaged and reproduced within the dominant discourse of popular culture. "Cognizant that they were being constructed in the mainstream press as a progressive response to regressive male rappers, these female rappers felt that they were being used as a political baton to beat male rappers over the head, rather than being affirmed as women who could open up public dialogue to interrogate sexism and its effects on young Black women. Furthermore, they remain acutely aware of the uneven and sometimes racist way in which sexist offenses are prosecuted, stigmatized, and reported. And so, in several public contexts, women rappers defended male rappers' freedom of speech and focused their answers on the question of censorship rather than on sexism in rap lyrics" (Rose, p. 149). Within the colonized urban kinderculture, an artist's social positionality is made much more complex and precarious; and the artist's politicized voice can be silenced in an act of indirect complicity.

Another aspect of the complicity is urban youth's uncritical consumption of the commodified text. Unfortunately, there is little to no realization by the consumer that the commodity is performative rather than truly representative. According to Lipsitz, "culture comes to us as a commodity" and we often do not question its origins or the intentions of the artists behind the commodified cultural artifact. As we uncritically consume the commodities of a colonized urban kinderculture, it is nearly impossible to understand what is "keeping it real" or authentic (representative) vs. what is caricature (performative). Urban youth are made complicit in the entrenchment of the problematic dominant narrative of them as they consume the commodified texts of their colonized urban kinderculture. Through their repeated consumption, they begin to internalize the dominant narrative's false reality of who they are and what they can become – their beliefs about their potential in life become constrained by the images and the discourses that dominate the distorted text of their subculture.

## DECOLONIZATION OF URBAN KINDERCULTURE

The corporate co-optation and commodification of the artifacts of urban kinderculture substantively and substantially interrupts its original intent to destabilize the public transcript. Additionally, it problematically restructures the phenomenological expressions of the lived experiences of urban youth of color. To reclaim the power of potential inherent in the cultural artifacts that they create and imbue with meaning, urban youth need to reject the distortions of their commodified cultural forms and work to decolonize their kinderculture. "To acquiesce is to lose ourselves entirely and implicitly agree with all that has been said about us. To resist is to retrench in the margins, retrieve what we were and remake ourselves" (Tuhiwai, p. 4).

As Joe would admonish, any effective strategy to upend the brutal colonization of urban kinderculture and its members must be anchored within a framework of criticality. Urban youth must be engaged in learning experiences where they examine and deconstruct the dynamics of power that are embedded in the social intersections of pedagogy, the production and consumption of knowledge and culture, and evolving identity formations. He further would emphasize the need to situate urban kinderculture as an intellectual asset to leverage young people's development of a critical literacy that allows them to not only understand how power is deployed to enslave their hearts and minds within a colonized urban kinderculture, but to also understand how to strategically subvert that power so that they can reclaim their beliefs in their authentic and unfettered potential.

Our failure to substantively develop young people's critical perspectives and literacy will further cultivate fertile ground within urban kinderculture for the perpetuation of the hegemonic logic – "a way of doing business that privileges conformity, zealously defends the middle-class norms, fights to the death for established virtue, and at all costs resists social change" (Kinchele, p. 262). The reclamation of urban kinderculture is an urgent endeavor for our civil society because our young people, who are in the midst of transitioning into adulthood, need to develop the capacity to effectively leverage an emergent sociopolitical capital informed by an intentionality around social justice. In the end, it's not so much that we do this work for them but that we do it for ourselves and our democratic civil society.

## REFERENCES

Back, L. (1996). *New ethnicities and urban culture: Racisms and multiculture in young lives.* New York: St. Martin's Press.
Blair, M. E. (2004). Commercialization of the rap music youth subculture. In M. Forman & M. A. Neal (Eds.), *That's the joint!: The hip-hop studies reader.* New York: Routledge.
Chomsky, N. (2000). *Chomsky on miseducation.* New York: Rowman, & Littlefield Publisher, Inc.
Corrigan, P., & Frith, S. (1976). The politics of youth culture. In S. Hall & T. Jefferson (Eds.), *Resistance through rituals: Youth subcultures in post-war Britain.* London: Hutchinson, & Co. Ltd.
Gelder, K., & Thornton, S. (Eds.). (1997). *The subcultures reader.* New York: Routledge.
Heyes, C. (2009, Spring Edition). Identity politics. In E. N. Zalta (Ed.), *The Stanford Encyclopedia of Philosophy.* Retrieved from http://plato.stanford.edu/archives/fall2002/entries/identity-politics/
Kincheloe, J. L. (1997). McDonald's, power, and children: Ronald McDonald (aka Ray Kroc) Does it all for you. In S. R. Steinberg & J. Kincheloe (Eds.), *Kinderculture: The corporate construction of childhood.* Boulder, CO: Westview Press.
Maher, G. C. (2005). Brechtian Hip-Hop: Didactics and self-production in Post-Gangsta political mixtapes. *Journal of Black Studies, 36*(1), 129–160.
Martin, G. (2002). Conceptualizing cultural politics in subcultural and social movement studies. *Social Movement Studies, 1*(1), 73–85.
Nightingale, C. H. (1993). *On the edge.* New York: Basic Books.
Powell, K. (2004). The hip-hop generation. *Socialism and Democracy, 18*(2), 7–8.
Rose, T. (1994). *Black noise: Rap music and black culture in contemporary America.* Middletown, CT: Wesleyan University Press.
Smith, L. T. (2001). *Decolonizing methodologies: Research and indigenous peoples.* New York: Zed Books.
Thornton, S. (1996). *Club cultures: Music, media and subcultural capital.* New Hampshire: University Press of New England.

*Following Joe's demand to humanize, politicize, and transgress through qualitative research, it was natural for him to go to create a new strand of bricolage, a completely fresh approach to qualitative work. Looking at Levi Strauss's context of bricolage and the nods made to bricolage by Norm Denzin and Yvonna Lincoln, Joe was determined to continue to criticalize and rigorize the traditional ways in which to do multi-methodological research. Certainly humbled by the invitation to deliver the Egon Guba Lecture at the American Educational Research Association, he acknowledges the lineage he follows from those who came before. Certainly, one of the highlights of Joe's friendships was the one he shared with Egon Guba. We met Egon early in the 1990s, at his and Yvonna's home in Texas. Joe marveled at the pleasure and gifts he had been given to engage in a new friendship with one of his heroes. And Egon did not disappoint...a funny, passionately compelling and brilliant man, Egon exemplified the persona Joe admired. Egon's love for Yvonna added volumes to the beginning seeds of Joe's work in radical love. SS*

JOE L. KINCHELOE

# 8. DESCRIBING THE BRICOLAGE

*Conceptualizing a New Rigor in Qualitative Research*

*Picking up on Norman Denzin's and Yvonna Lincoln's articulation of the concept of bricolage, the essay describes a critical notion of this research orientation. As an interdisciplinary approach, bricolage avoids both the superficiality of methodological breadth and the parochialism of unidisciplinary approaches. The notion of the bricolage advocated here recognizes the dialectical nature of the disciplinary and interdisciplinary relationship and promotes a synergistic interaction between the two concepts. In this context, the bricolage is concerned not only with divergent methods of inquiry but with diverse theoretical and philosophical understandings of the various elements encountered in the act of research. The insights garnered here move researchers to a better conceptual grasp of the complexity of the research act— a cognizance often missed in mainstream versions of qualitative research. In particular, critical bricoleurs employ historiographical, philosophical, and social theoretical lenses to gain a more complex understanding of the intricacies of research design.*

As a preface to this essay, I want to express what an honor it is for me to deliver the Egon Guba Lecture. I consider Egon one of the most important figures in research in the 20th and 21st centuries and consider his career the best model I know for a

k. hayes et al., (eds.), *Key Work in Critical Pedagogy: Joe L. Kincheloe*, 177–189.
© 2011 Sense Publishers. All rights reserved.

life of rigorous, innovative scholarship in education. Every idea expressed in this essay is tied to concepts Egon developed over the past few decades. If they are insufficiently developed, it is an expression of my limitations, not his. In this spirit, I dedicate this lecture to Egon Guba and his innovative scholarship and pedagogy.

My desire to write this essay and ultimately a more comprehensive work on bricolage comes from two sources. The first involves my fascination with Denzin and Lincoln's (2000) use of the term in their work on research methods over the past decade. From my perspective, no concept better captures the possibility of the future of qualitative research. When I first encountered the term in their work, I knew that I would have to devote much effort to specifying the notion and pushing it to the next conceptual level. Secondly, coupled with this recognition of the power of bricolage was the experience several of my doctoral students brought back from their job interviews. Prepped and ready to answer in detail questions about their methods and research agendas, my students spoke of their theoretical embrace and methodological employment of the bricolage. Much too often for our comfort, search committee members responded quite negatively: "bricolage, oh I know what that is; that's when you really don't know anything about research but have a lot to say about it." Much to our dismay, the use of the concept persuaded such committee members not to employ the students. I had no choice, I had to respond.

Yvonna Lincoln and Norm Denzin (2000) used the term in the spirit of Claude Levi-Strauss (1966) and his lengthy discussion of it in *The Savage Mind*. The French word, *bricoleur*, describes a handyman or handywoman who makes use of the tools available to complete a task. Some connotations of the term involve trickery and cunning and remind me of the chicanery of Hermes, in particular his ambiguity concerning the messages of the gods. If hermeneutics came to connote the ambiguity and slipperiness of textual meaning, then bricolage can also imply the fictive and imaginative elements of the presentation of all formal research. Indeed, as cultural studies of science have indicated, all scientific inquiry is jerryrigged to a degree; science, as we all know by now, is not nearly as clean, simple, and procedural as scientists would have us believe. Maybe this is an admission many in our field would wish to keep in the closet. Maybe at a tacit level this is what many search committee members were reacting to when my doctoral students discussed it so openly, enthusiastically, and unabashedly.

## BRICOLAGE IN THE COSMOS OF DISCIPLINARITY AND INTERDISCIPLINARITY

My umbrage at the denigration of bricolage by my students' interlocutors should in no way be taken as disrespect for those who question the value of the concept. For those of us committed to theorizing and implementing such an approach to research, there are some profound questions that need to be answered as we plot our course. As we think in terms of using multiple methods and perspectives in our research and attempt to synthesize contemporary developments in social theory, epistemology, and interpretation, we must consider the critiques of many diverse scholars. At the core of the deployment of bricolage in the discourse of research rests the question of disciplinarity/interdisciplinarity. Bricolage, of course, signifies interdisciplinarity—a concept that serves as a magnet for controversy in the contemporary academy. Researching this article, I listened to several colleagues maintain that if one is focused on getting tenure he or she should eschew interdisciplinarity; if one is interested in only doing good research, she or he should embrace it.

Implicit in the critique of interdisciplinarity and thus of bricolage as its manifestation in research is the assumption that interdisciplinarity is by nature superficial. Superficiality results when scholars, researchers, and students fail to devote sufficient time to understanding the disciplinary fields and knowledge bases from which particular modes of research emanate. Many maintain that such an effort leads not only to superficiality but madness. Attempting to know so much, the bricoleur not only knows nothing well but also goes crazy in the misguided process (Friedman, 1998; McLeod, 2000; Palmer, 1996). My assertion in this article respects these questions and concerns but argues that given the social, cultural, epistemological, and paradigmatic upheavals and alterations of the past few decades, rigorous researchers may no longer enjoy the luxury of choosing whether to embrace the bricolage (Friedman, 1998; McLeod, 2000).

## THE GREAT IMPLOSION: DEALING WITH THE DEBRIS OF DISCIPLINARITY

Once understanding of the limits of objective science and its universal knowledge that escaped from the genie's bottle, there was no going back. Despite the best efforts to recover "what was lost" in the implosion of social science, too many researchers understand its socially constructed nature, its value-laden products that operate under the flag of objectivity, its avoidance of contextual specificities that subvert the stability of its structures, and its fragmenting impulse that moves it to fold its methodologies and the knowledge they produce neatly into disciplinary drawers. My argument here is that we must operate in the ruins of the temple, in a postapocalyptic social, cultural, psychological, and educational science where certainty and stability have long departed for parts unknown.

In the best sense of Levi-Straus's (1966) concept, the research bricoleurs pick up the pieces of what's left and paste them together as best they can. The critics are probably correct, such a daunting task cannot be accomplished in the time span of a doctoral program; but the process can be named and the dimensions of a lifetime scholarly pursuit can be in part delineated. Our transcendence of the old regime's reductionism and our understanding of the complexity of the research task demand the lifetime effort. It is this lifetime commitment to study, clarify, sophisticate, and add to the bricolage that this article advocates.

As bricoleurs recognize the limitations of a single method, the discursive strictures of one disciplinary approach, what is missed by traditional practices of validation, the historicity of certified modes of knowledge production, the inseparability of knower and known, and the complexity and heterogeneity of all human experience, they understand the necessity of new forms of rigor in the research process. To account for their cognizance of such complexity bricoleurs seek a rigor that alerts them to new ontological insights. In this ontological context, they can no longer accept the status of an object of inquiry as a thing-in-itself. Any social, cultural, psychological, or pedagogical object of inquiry is inseparable from its context, the language used to describe it, its historical situatedness in a larger ongoing process, and the socially and culturally constructed interpretations of its meaning(s) as an entity in the world (Morawski, 1997).

## RIGOR IN THE RUINS

Thus, bricolage is concerned not only with multiple methods of inquiry but with diverse theoretical and philosophical notions of the various elements encountered in the research act. Bricoleurs understand that the ways these dynamics are addressed—whether overtly or tacitly—exerts profound influence on the nature of the knowledge produced by researchers. Thus, these aspects of research possess important lived world political consequences, as they shape the ways we come to view the social cosmos and operate within it (Blommaert, 1997). In this context, Douglas Kellner's (1995) notion of a "multiperspectival cultural studies" is helpful, as it draws on numerous textual and critical strategies to "interpret, criticize, and deconstruct" the cultural artifacts under observation.

Employing Nietzsche's notion of perspectivism to ground his version of a multimethodological research strategy, Kellner (1995) maintains that any single research perspective is laden with assumptions, blindnesses, and limitations. To avoid one-sided reductionism, he contends that researchers must learn a variety of ways of seeing and interpreting in the pursuit of knowledge. The more perspectival variety a researcher employs, Kellner concludes, the more dimensions and consequences of a text will be illuminated. Kellner's multiperspectivism resonates with Denzin and Lincoln's (2000) bricolage and its concept of "blurred genres." To better "interpret, criticize, and deconstruct," Denzin and Lincoln call for bricoleurs to employ "hermeneutics, structuralism, semiotics, phenomenology, cultural studies, and feminism" (p. 3). Embedded in Kellner's (1995) and Denzin and Lincoln's (2000) calls is the proto-articulation of a new rigor—certainly in research but with implications for scholarship and pedagogy in general.

This rigor in the ruins of traditional disciplinarity connects a particular concept—in contemporary education, for example, the call for educational standards—to the epistemological, ontological, cultural, social, political, economic, psychological, and pedagogical domains for the purpose of multiperspectival analysis. In the second edition of their *Handbook of Qualitative Research*, Denzin and Lincoln (2000) maintain that this process has already taken place to some extent; they referred to it as a two-way methodological Diaspora where humanists migrated to the social sciences and social scientists to the humanities. Ethnographic methodologists snuggled up with textual analysts; in this context the miscegenation of the empirical and the interpretive produced the bricoleur love child.

Thus, in the late 20th and early 21st centuries, disciplinary demarcations no longer shape, in the manner they once did, the way scholars look at the world. Indeed, disciplinary boundaries have less and less to do with the way scholars group themselves and build intellectual communities. Furthermore, what we refer to as the *traditional disciplines* in the first decade of the 21st century are anything but fixed, uniform, and monolithic structures. It is not uncommon for contemporary scholars in a particular discipline to report that they find more commonalities with individuals in different fields of study than they do with colleagues in their own disciplines. We occupy a scholarly world with faded disciplinary boundary lines. Thus, the point need not be made that bricolage should take place—it already has and is continuing. The research work needed in this context involves opening an elastic conversation about the ways such a bricolage can be rigorously developed. Such cultivation should not take place in pursuit of some form of proceduralization but an effort to better understand the beast and to realize its profound possibilities (Friedman, 1998; Palmer, 1996; Young, & Yarbrough, 1993).

## BRICOLAGE AND THE DIALECTICAL VIEW OF DISCIPLINARITY

Questions of disciplinarity permeate efforts to theorize the research bricolage. Exploring such inquiries, one notes a consistent division between disciplinarians and interdisciplinarians: Disciplinarians maintain that interdisciplinary approaches to analysis and research result in superficiality; interdisciplinary proponents argue that disciplinarity produces naïve overspecialization. The vision of the bricolage promoted here recognizes the dialectical nature of this disciplinary and interdisciplinary relationship and calls for a synergistic interaction between the two concepts. Before one can engage successfully in the bricolage, it is important to develop a rigorous understanding of the ways traditional disciplines have operated. I maintain the best way to do this is to study the workings of a particular discipline. In the context of becoming a bricoleur, such a study would not take place in the traditional manner where scholars learned to accept the conventions of a particular discipline as a natural way of producing knowledge and viewing a particular aspect of the world.

Instead, such a disciplinary study would be conducted more like a Foucauldian genealogy where scholars would study the social construction of the discipline's knowledge bases, epistemologies, and knowledge production methodologies. As scholars analyzed the historical origins of the field, they would trace the emergence of various schools of thought, conflicts within the discipline, and the nature and effects of paradigmatic changes. In this genealogical context they would explore the discipline as a discursive system of regulatory power with its propensity to impound knowledge within arbitrary and exclusive boundaries. In this context, scholars would come to understand the ideological dimensions of the discipline and the ways knowledge is produced for the purposes of supporting various power blocs.

It is not contradictory, I assert, to argue in a dialectical spirit that at the same time this genealogical analysis is taking place, the bricoleur would also be studying positive features of the discipline. Even though the discipline operates in a power-saturated and regulatory manner, disciplinarians have often developed important models for engaging in a methodical, persistent, and well-coordinated process of knowledge production. Obviously, there are examples not only of genius within these domains but of great triumphs of scholarly breakthroughs leading to improvements in the human condition. The diverse understanding of these types of disciplinary practices empowers the bricoleur to ask compelling questions of other disciplines he or she will encounter. Such smart questions will facilitate the researcher's capacity to make use of positive contributions of disciplines while avoiding disciplinary parochialism and domination.

As bricoleurs pursue this dialectic of disciplinarity, gaining a deep knowledge of the literature and conversations within a field, they would concurrently examine both the etymology and the critique of what many refer to as the disciplines' arbitrary demarcations for arranging knowledge and structuring research. In a critical context, the bricoleur would develop a power literacy to facilitate his or her understanding of the nature and effects of the web of power relations underlying a discipline's official research methodologies.

Here bricoleurs would trace the ways these power dynamics shaped the knowledge produced within the disciplinary research tradition. Learning multiple lessons from their in-depth study of the discipline in particular and disciplinarity in general, the bricoleur becomes an expert on the relationships connecting cultural context, meaning making, power, and oppression within disciplinary boundaries. Their rigorous understanding of these dynamics possibly makes them more aware of the influence of such factors on the everyday practices of the discipline than those who have traditionally operated as scholars within the discipline (Freidman, 1998; Lutz, Jones, & Kendall, 1997; Morawski, 1997).

## QUESTIONING THE SOCIAL CONSTRUCTION OF INTERDISCIPLINARITY

Thus, bricoleurs operating within this dialectic of disciplinarity gain an indepth understanding of the "process of disciplinarity," adeptly avoiding any superficiality that might result from their interdisciplinary pursuits. At the same time, such researchers possess the insight to avoid complicity in colonized knowledge production designed to regulate and discipline. Such subtle expertise illustrates an appreciation of the complexity of knowledge work to which bricolage aspires. Understanding disciplinary processes and models of expertise while recognizing the elitist dimensions of dominant cultural knowledge technologies involves a nuanced discernment of the double edged sword of disciplinarity. Concurrently, bricoleurs subject interdisciplinarity to the same rigorous perusal. Accordingly, bricoleurs understand that interdisciplinarity is as much a social construction as disciplinarity. Just because bricolage is about interdisciplinarity, bricoleurs must not release the notion from the same form of power analysis used to explore disciplinarity.

In addition, bricoleurs must clarify what is meant by interdisciplinarity. A fuzzy concept at best, *interdisciplinarity* generally refers to a process where disciplinary boundaries are crossed and the analytical frames of more than one discipline are employed by the researcher. Surveying the use of the term, it quickly becomes apparent that little attention has been paid to what exactly interdisciplinarity implies for researchers. Some uses of the concept assume the deployment of numerous disciplinary methodologies in a study where disciplinary distinctions are maintained; other uses imply an integrated melding of disciplinary perspectives into a new methodological synthesis. Advocates of bricolage must consider the diverse approaches that take place in the name of interdisciplinarity and their implications for constructing the bricolage.

In light of the disciplinary implosion that has taken place over the past few decades and the "no going back" stance previously delineated, I feel no compulsion to preserve the disciplines in some pure, uncorrupted state of nature. Although there is much to learn from their histories, the stages of disciplinary emergence, growth and development, alteration, and devolution and decline, the complex view of bricolage I am presenting embraces a deep form of interdisciplinarity. A deep interdisciplinarity seeks to modify the disciplines and the view of research brought to the negotiating table constructed by the bricolage. Everyone leaves the table informed by the dialogue in a way that idiosyncratically influences the research methods they subsequently employ.

The point of the interaction is not standardized agreement as to some reductionistic notion of "the proper interdisciplinary research method" but awareness of the diverse tools in the researcher's toolbox. The form such deep interdisciplinarity may take is shaped by the object of inquiry in question. Thus, in the bricolage, the context in which research takes place always affects the nature of the deep interdisciplinarity employed. In the spirit of the dialectic of disciplinarity, the ways these context-driven articulations of interdisciplinarity are constructed must be examined in light of the power literacy previously mentioned (Freidman, 1998; Blommaert, 1997; Pryse, 1998; Young, & Yarbrough, 1993).

## BRICOLAGE AS DEEP INTERDISCIPLINARITY: THE SYNERGY OF MULTIPLE PERSPECTIVES

With these disciplinary concerns in the front of our mind, I will now focus attention on the intellectual power of the bricolage. It does not seem a conceptual stretch to argue that there is a synergy that emerges in the use of different methodological and interpretive perspectives in the analysis of an artifact. Historians, for example, who are conversant with the insights of hermeneutics, will produce richer interpretations of the historical processes they encounter in their research. In the deep interdisciplinarity of the bricolage the historian takes concepts from hermeneutics and combines them with historiographical methods. What is produced is something new, a new form of hermeneutical historiography or historical hermeneutics. Whatever its name, the methodology could not have been predicted by examining historiography and hermeneutics separately, outside of the context of the historical processes under examination (Varenne, 1996). The possibilities offered by such interdisciplinary synergies are limitless.

An ethnographer who is conversant with social theory and its recent history is better equipped to transcend certain forms of formulaic ethnography that are reduced by the so-called "observational constraint" on the methodology. Using the x-ray vision of contemporary social-theoretically informed strategies of discourse analysis, poststructural psychoanalysis, and ideology critique, the ethnographer gains the ability to see beyond the literalness of the observed. In this maneuver, the ethnographer-as-bricoleur moves to a deeper level of data analysis as he or she sees "what's not there" in physical presence, what is not discernible by the ethnographic eye. Synergized by the interaction of ethnography and the social theoretical discourses, the resulting bricolage provides a new angle of analysis, a multidimensional perspective on a cultural phenomenon (Dicks, & Mason, 1998; Foster, 1997).

Carefully exploring the relationships connecting the object of inquiry to the contexts in which it exists, the researcher constructs the most useful bricolage his or her wide knowledge of research strategies can provide. The strict disciplinarian operating in a reductionistic framework chained to the prearranged procedures of a monological way of seeing is less likely to produce frame-shattering research than the synergized bricoleur. The process at work in the bricolage involves learning from difference. Researchers employing multiple research methods are often not chained to the same assumptions as individuals operating within a particular discipline. As they study the methods of diverse disciplines, they are forced to compare not only methods but also differing epistemologies and social theoretical assumptions. Such diversity frames research orientations as particular socially constructed perspectives—not sacrosanct pathways to the truth. All methods are subject to questioning and analysis, especially in light of so many other strategies designed for similar purposes (Denzin, & Lincoln, 2000; Lester, 1997; Thomas, 1998).

This defamiliarization process highlights the power of the confrontation with difference to expand the researcher's interpretive horizons. Bricolage does not simply *tolerate* difference but *cultivates* it as a spark to researcher creativity. Here rests a central contribution of the deep interdisciplinarity of the bricolage: As researchers draw together divergent forms of research, they gain the unique insight of multiple perspectives. Thus, a complex understanding of research and knowledge production prepares bricoleurs to address the complexities of the social, cultural, psychological, and educational domains. Sensitive to complexity, bricoleurs use multiple methods to uncover new insights, expand and modify old principles, and reexamine accepted interpretations in unanticipated contexts. Using any methods necessary to gain new perspectives on objects of inquiry, bricoleurs employ the principle of difference not only in research methods but in cross-cultural analysis as well. In this domain, bricoleurs explore the different perspectives of the socially privileged and the marginalized in relation to formations of race, class, gender, and sexuality (McLeod, 2000; Pryse, 1998; Young, & Yarbrough, 1993).

The deep interdisciplinarity of bricolage is sensitive to multivocality and the consciousness of difference it produces in a variety of contexts. Described by Denzin and Lincoln (2000) as "multi-competent, skilled at using interviews, observation, personal documents," the bricoleur explores the use of ethnography, Pinarian currere, historiography, genre studies, psychoanalysis, rhetorical analysis, discourse analysis, content analysis, ad infinitum. The addition of historiography, for example, to the bricoleur's tool kit profoundly expands his or her interpretive facility. As bricoleurs historically contextualize their ethnographies, discourse analysis, and semiotic studies, they tap into the power of etymology. Etymological insight (Kincheloe, & Steinberg, 1993; Kincheloe, Steinberg, & Hinchey, 1999) involves an understanding of the origins of the construction of social, cultural, psychological, political, economic, and educational artifacts and the ways they shape our subjectivities. Indeed, our conception of self, world, and our positionalities as researchers can only become complex and critical when we appreciate the historical aspect of its formation. With this one addition, we dramatically sophisticate the quality and depth of our knowledge work (Zammito, 1996).

## EXPANDING THE BOUNDARIES: THE SEARCH FOR NEW FORMS OF KNOWLEDGE PRODUCTION

Operating as a form of deep interdisciplinarity, bricolage is unembarrassed in its effort to rupture particular ways of functioning in the established disciplines of research. One of the best ways to accomplish this goal is to include what might be termed *philosophical research* to the bricolage. In the same way that historiography ruptures the stability of particular disciplinary methods, philosophical research provides bricoleurs with the dangerous knowledge of the multivocal results of humans' desire to understand, to know themselves and the world. Differing philosophical/ cultural conventions have employed diverse epistemological, ontological, and cosmological assumptions as well as different methods of inquiry. Again, depending on the context of the object of inquiry, bricoleurs use their knowledge of these dynamics to shape their research design. It is not difficult to understand the epistemological contention that the types of logic, criteria for validity, and methods of inquiry used in clinical medicine as opposed to teacher effectiveness in teaching critical thinking will differ.

In making such an assertion the bricoleur is displaying philosophical/ epistemological/ontological sensitivity to the context of analysis. Such a sensitivity is a key element of the bricolage, as it brings an understanding of social theory together with an appreciation of the demands of particular contexts; this fused concept is subsequently used to examine the repertoire of methods the bricoleur can draw on and to help decide which ones are relevant to the project at hand. Practicing this mode of analysis in a variety of research situations, the bricoleur becomes increasingly adept at employing multiple methods in concrete venues. Such a historiographically and philosophically informed bricolage helps researchers move into a new, more complex domain of knowledge production where they are far more conscious of multiple layers of intersections between the knower and the known, perception and the lived world, and discourse and representation. Employing the benefits of philosophical inquiry, the bricoleur gains a new ability to account for and incorporate these dynamics into his or her research narratives (Bridges, 1997; Fischer, 1998; Madison, 1988; McCarthy, 1997).

This is what expanding the boundaries of knowledge production specifically references. In the particularities of the philosophical interactions with the empirical in a variety of contexts, bricoleurs devise new forms of rigor, new challenges to other researchers to push the methodological and interpretive envelopes. As bricoleurs study the subjective meanings that human beings make, for example, they use their philosophical modes of inquiry to understand that this phenomenological form of information has no analogue in the methods of particular formalist forms of empirical research. Thus, in an obvious example, a choice of methods is necessitated by particular epistemological and ontological conditions—epistemological and ontological conditions rarely recognized in monological forms of empirical research (Haggerson, 2000; Lee, 1997).

I want to be as specific as possible about the nature of these epistemological and ontological conditions. Although we have made progress, much of the research that is devoid of the benefits philosophical inquiry brings to the bricolage still tends to study the world as if ontologically it consists of a series of static images. Entities are often removed from the contexts that shape them, the processes of which they are a part, and the relationships and connections that structure their being-in-the-world. Such ontological orientations impose particular epistemologies, specific ways of producing knowledge about such inert entities. In this ontological context, the task of researchers is reduced, as they simply do not have to worry about contextual insights, etymological processes, and the multiple relationships that constitute the complexity of lived reality. In a reductionistic mode of research, these dynamics are irrelevant and the knowledge produced in such contexts reflects the reductionism. The bricolage struggles to find new ways of seeing and interpreting that avoid this curse and that produce thick, complex, and rigorous forms of knowledge (Karunaratne, 1997).

In this thick, complex, and rigorous context, bricoleurs in the social, cultural, psychological, and educational domains operate with a sophisticated understanding of the nature of knowledge. To be well prepared, bricoleurs must realize that knowledge is always in process, developing, culturally specific, and power-inscribed. They are attuned to dynamic relationships connecting individuals, their contexts, and their activities instead of focusing on these separate entities in isolation from one another. In this ontological framework, they concentrate on social activity systems and larger cultural processes and the ways individuals engage or are engaged by them (Blackler, 1995).

Bricoleurs follow such engagements, analyzing how the ever-changing dynamics of the systems and the processes alter the lived realities of participants; concurrently, they monitor the ways participants operate to change the systems and the processes. The complexity of such a mode of inquiry precludes the development of a step-by-step set of research procedures. Bricoleurs know that this inability to proceduralize undermines efforts to "test" the validity of their research. The researcher's fidelity to procedure cannot simply be checked off and certified. In the complex bricolage the products of research are "evaluated." The evaluation process draws on the same forms of inquiry and analysis initially delineated by the bricolage itself (Madison, 1988). In this context, the rigor of research intensifies at the same time the boundaries of knowledge production are stretched.

## LIFE ON THE BOUNDARIES: FACILITATING THE WORK OF THE BRICOLEUR

The bricolage understands that the frontiers of knowledge work rest in the liminal zones where disciplines collide. Thus, in the deep interdisciplinarity of the bricolage, researchers learn to engage in a form of boundary work. Such scholarly labor involves establishing diverse networks and conferences where synergistic interactions can take place as proponents of different methodologies, students of divergent subject matters, and individuals confronted with different problems interact. In this context, scholars learn across these domains and educate intermediaries who can build bridges between various territories. As disciplinary intermediaries operating as bricoleurs facilitate this boundary work, they create conceptual and electronic links that help researchers in different domains interact. If the cutting edge of research lives at the intersection of disciplinary borders, then developing the bricolage is a key strategy in the development of rigorous and innovative research. The facilitation and cultivation of boundary work is a central element of this process.

There is nothing simple about conducting research at the interdisciplinary frontier. Many scholars report that the effort to develop expertise in different disciplines and research methodologies demands more than a casual acquaintance with the literature of a domain. In this context, there is a need for personal interaction between representatives from diverse disciplinary domains and scholarly projects to facilitate these encounters. Many researchers find it extremely difficult to make sense of "outside" fields and the more disciplines a researcher scans the harder the process becomes. If the scholar does not have access to historical dimensions of the field, the contexts that envelop the research methods used and the knowledge produced in the area, or contemporary currents involving debates and controversies in the discipline, the boundary work of the bricolage becomes exceedingly frustrating and futile. Proponents of the bricolage must help develop specific strategies for facilitating this complicated form of scholarly labor.

In this context we come to understand that a key aspect of "doing bricolage" involves the development of conceptual tools for boundary work. Such tools might include the promotion and cultivation of detailed reviews of research in a particular domain written with the needs of bricoleurs in mind. Researchers from a variety of disciplinary domains should develop information for bricolage projects. Hypertextual projects that provide conceptual matrices for bringing together diverse literatures, examples of data produced by different research methods, connective insights, and bibliographic compilations can be undertaken by bricoleurs with the help of information professionals. Such projects would integrate a variety of conceptual understandings, including the previously mentioned historical, contextual, and contemporary currents of disciplines (Friedman, 1998; Palmer, 1996).

Kellner (1995) is helpful in this context with his argument that multiperspectival approaches to research may not be very helpful unless the object of inquiry and the various methods used to study it are situated historically. In this way, the forces operating to socially construct all elements of the research process are understood, an appreciation that leads to a grasp of new relationships and connections. Such an appreciation opens new interpretive windows that lead to more rigorous modes of analysis and interpretation. This historicization of the research and the researched is an intrinsic aspect of the bricolage and the education of the bricoleur. Because learning to become a bricoleur is a lifelong process, what we are discussing here relates to the lifelong curriculum for preparing bricoleurs.

Also necessary to this boundary work and the education of the bricoleur are social-theoretical and hermeneutical understandings. Social theory alerts bricoleurs to the implicit assumptions within particular approaches to research and the ways they shape their findings. With grounding in social theory, bricoleurs can make more informed decisions about the nature of the knowledge produced in the field and how researchers discern the worth of the knowledge they themselves produce. With the benefit of hermeneutics, bricoleurs are empowered to synthesize data collected via multiple methods. In the hermeneutic process, this ability to synthesize diverse information moves the bricoleur to a more sophisticated level of meaning making (Foster, 1997; Zammito, 1996). Life on the disciplinary boundaries is never easy, but the rewards to be derived from the hard work demanded are profound.

I'll mercifully stop here.... This is part of an expanding piece.

## REFERENCES

Blackler, F. (1995). Knowledge, knowledge work, and organizations: An overview and interpretation. *Organization Studies, 16,* 6.
Blommaert, J. (1997). *Workshopping: Notes on professional vision in discourse* [Online]. Retrieved from http://africana_rug.ac.be/texts/research-publications/publications_on-line/workshopping. htm
Bridges, D. (1997). Philosophy and educational research: A reconsideration of epistemological boundaries. *Cambridge Journal of Education, 27,* 2.
Denzin, N., & Lincoln, Y. (2000). *Handbook of qualitative research* (2nd ed.). Thousand Oaks, CA: Sage.
Dicks, B., & Mason, B. (1998). Hypermedia and ethnography: Reflections on the construction of a research approach. *Sociological Research Online, 3,* 3.
Fischer, F. (1998). Beyond empiricism: Policy inquiry in postpositivist perspective. *Policy Studies Journal, 26*(1), 129–146.
Foster, R. (1997). Addressing epistemologic and practical issues in multimethod research: Aprocedure for conceptual triangulation. *Advances in Nursing Education, 202,* 2.
Friedman, S. (1998). (Inter) disciplinarity and the question of the women's studies Ph. D. *Feminist Studies, 24,* 2.
Haggerson, N. (2000). *Expanding curriculum research and understanding: A mytho-poetic perspective.* New York: Peter Lang Publishing.
Karunaratne, V. (1997). *Buddhism, science, and dialectics* [Online]. Retrieved from http://humanism. org/opinions/articles.html
Kellner, D. (1995). *Media culture: Cultural studies, identity and politics between the modern and post-modern.* New York: Routledge.
Kincheloe, J. L., & Steinberg S. R. (1993). A tentative description of postformal thinking: The critical confrontation with cognitive theory. *Harvard Educational Review, 63*(3), 296–320.
Kincheloe, J. L., Steinberg S. R., & Hinchey, P. (1999). *The postformal reader: Cognition and education.* New York: Falmer.
Lee, A. (1997). What is MIS? In R. Galliers & W. Currie (Eds.), *Rethinking MIS.* London: Oxford University Press.
Lester, S. (1997). *Learning for the twenty-first century* [Online]. Retrieved from http://www.devmts. demon.co.uk/lrg21st.htm
Levi-Strauss, C. (1966). *The savage mind.* Chicago: University of Chicago Press.
Lutz, K., Jones, K., & Kendall, J. (1997). Expanding the praxis debate: Contributions to clinical inquiry. *Advances in Nursing Science, 20,* 2.
Madison, G. (1988). *The hermeneutics of postmodernity: Figures and themes.* Bloomington, IN: Indiana University Press.
McCarthy, M. (1997). Pluralism, invariance, and conflict. *The Review of Metaphysics, 51,* 1.
McLeod, J. (2000, June). *Qualitative research as bricolage.* Paper presented at the Society for Psychotherapy Research annual conference, Chicago.

Morawski, J. (1997). The science behind feminist research methods. *Journal of Social Issues, 53*(4), 667–682.
Palmer, C. (1996). Information work at the boundaries of science: Linking library services to research practices. *Library Trends, 44*(2), 165–192.
Pryse, M. (1998). Critical interdisciplinarity, women's studies, and cross-cultural insight. *NWSA Journal, 10*(1), 1–11.
Selfe, C., & Selfe, R. (1994). *The politics of the interface: Power and its exercise in electronic contact zones* [Online]. Retrieved from http://www. hu.mtu.edu/~cyselfe/texts/politics.html
Thomas, G. (1998). The myth of rational research. *British Educational Research Journal, 24*, 2.
Varenne, H. (1996). The social facting of education: Durkheim's legacy. *Journal of CurriculumStudies, 27*, 373–389.
Young, T., & Yarbrough, J. (1993). *Reinventing sociology: Mission and methods for postmodern sociologists* (Transforming Sociology Series, 154). Weidman, MI: Red Feather Institute.
Zammito, J. (1996). *Historicism, metahistory, and historical practice: The historicization of the historical subject* [Online]. Retrieved from http://home.cc.umanitoba.ca/~sprague/zammito.htm

Reprinted with permission: Kincheloe, J. L. (2001). Describing the bricolage: conceptualizing a new rigor in qualitative inquiry. *Qualitative Inquiry, 7*, 679–92.

BAL CHANDRA LUITEL AND PETER CHARLES TAYLOR

# KINCHELOE'S BRICOLAGE

A VIEW FROM WITHIN TRANSFORMATIVE EDUCATIONAL RESEARCH

*Introduction*

*Dear Joe*
Today, we are writing a different type of letter, one that celebrates the important *karmic* culmination of your recent lifetime and that presents our view on a number of issues you have discussed in "Describing the bricolage: Conceptualising a new rigor in qualitative research" (Kincheloe, 2001). It was this paper that introduced your textual self to me (Bal Chandra) for the first time in 2003 when, during my master's study at an Australian university, I was preparing to conduct an auto|ethnographic inquiry into the nature of culturally decontextualised mathematics education in Nepal. Whilst you were physically present on some other part of the Earth, I was busy making sense of many radical (and somewhat unclear) ideas of yours with the help of a thesaurus, dictionaries and encyclopaediae available in the English language, a language that still remains somewhat obscure to me. At that time, I wrote a letter asking you to clarify the concept of bricolage but I didn't send it because I felt that my curiosities, questions and concerns were not worthy enough for you to expend the precious academic time needed for generating more creative ideas instrumental to transforming educational research from the grip of positivistic mindsets.

When I started my doctoral research in mid-2006, I continued reviewing your paper wondering how your notion of 'new rigor' might be compatible with my emergent multi-paradigmatic research design. In the meantime, I read your subsequent paper (Kincheloe, 2005) in which you attempted to clarify some complex issues associated with the notion of bricolage. Fascinated by the notions of 'methodological diaspora', 'multi-methods' and 'transformative action', I spent some time thinking about the possibility of employing a bricolage of auto|ethnographic and philosophical inquiry in developing a transformative philosophy of mathematics education for Nepal, a country that hosts more than 90 different language groups and that is desperately waiting for mathematics education to be inclusive of multiple knowledge systems arising from students' multiple lifeworlds (Luitel, & Taylor, 2007). My notion of a transformative philosophy seems to resonate with yours, namely, that it is very important to make teachers and learners "more conscious of multiple layers of intersections between the knower and the known, perception and the lived world, and discourse and representation" (Kincheloe, 2001, p. 688). However, because you and I grew up in different cultural, linguistic and educational

*k. hayes et al., (eds.), Key Work in Critical Pedagogy: Joe L. Kincheloe, 191–200.*
*© 2011 Sense Publishers. All rights reserved.*

contexts, I may not be able to emulate your articulation of key methodological concepts, especially with reference to Western intellectual history.

With my autobiographical self as key author of this next letter, I am being partnered by my mentor, Peter Taylor. We do not intend to present a comprehensive review of your ideas, nor do we aim to present a critique of your notion of bricolage; rather, we shall focus on selected key methodological issues that are relevant to our own research program and that you have raised in/directly in two of your papers (Kincheloe, 2001, 2005). In this process of sharing our ideas with you we are speaking from a transformative perspective (Taylor, 2008), a standpoint from which we prepare educational researchers to (a) examine disempowering socio-cultural forces embedded in their practice, and (b) envision inclusive and socially just perspectives for continuously altering their practice towards an emancipatory praxis.

We start this letter by exploring interdisciplinarity in relation to the notion of a multi-paradigmatic research design space. We argue that such a design space provides bricoleurs with much needed explanatory heuristics for challenging the otherwise unchallenged hegemony of single paradigm research which is often employed in conjunction with a narrowly conceived view of disciplinarity. Next, we articulate multiple logics and genres that are essential for enabling the bricoleur to account for otherwise neglected alternative knowledge systems. Finally, we discuss how your 'new rigor' can be further articulated with the help of a set of recently developed quality standards. These standards are intended to facilitate the bricoleur's "complex understanding of research and knowledge production" (Kincheloe, 2001, p. 687), and to help us realize how knowledge generation and legitimation are intertwined in the broad spectrum of research possibilities. We have included boxed poems, where appropriate, to evoke readers' pedagogical thoughtfulness (Van Manen, 1991).

## MULTI-PARADIGMATIC RESEARCH DESIGN SPACE FOR THE BRICOLAGE

*Dear Joe*, we like your formulation of interdisciplinarity as making visible the invisible frames of historicity, epistemology and ontology of disciplines whilst also adopting best disciplinary methods and methodologies in constructing a bricolage. Indeed, individual disciplinary structures and strictures are not usually favourable to the examination of disempowering hidden agendas regulating disciplinary borders, especially those that serve the technical interest of promoting uncritical reproduction of *a priori* ideas and knowledge. We agree with your sentiment that hidden agendas tend to endorse exclusive and "elitist dimensions of dominant cultural knowledge technologies" (Kincheloe, 2001, p. 685) which often discourage researchers from contesting otherwise uncontested ontologies and epistemologies. We believe that raising critical awareness is a necessary first step in transforming educational research practice away from the 'crypto-positivistic' mindset. We would like also to share with you our belief in the importance of the next step in this process, namely, that researchers need to envision alternative socio-cultural landscapes, thereby better enabling themselves to embody and implement visionary changes in their professional contexts. For these two important stages of development to unfold successfully an enabling research design space is essential.

We argue that a multi-paradigmatic research design space is more helpful than a design space created by a single paradigm for enabling the researcher to "develop a rigorous understanding of the ways traditional disciplines have operated" (Kincheloe, 2001, p. 683) and to realize "the social, cultural, epistemological and paradigmatic upheavals and alternations" (Kincheloe, 2001, p. 681) taking place *within* and *without* disciplinary borders. A multi-paradigmatic research design space entails more than one research paradigm, thereby enabling researchers to include otherwise excluded realities, to employ multiple ways of knowing, and to embrace a set of value dimensions. For example, employing both interpretive and critical research paradigms a researcher can exercise multiple vantage points by embodying both nomothetic and ideographic ontologies, subjective and objective epistemologies, and value systems that are both contextualized (e.g., culturally contextualized pedagogies) and universalized (e.g., human rights). Through a bricolage of paradigmatic perspectives one can examine both disciplinarity and interdisciplinarity as processes co-existing side by side.

*Dear Joe*, a multiparadigmatic research design space is likely to capture your sentiment of employing a bricolage in a meaningful way, that is, by avoiding both interdisciplinary superficiality and disciplinary parochialism. In such a space a synergy of sometimes antagonistic worldviews (comprising distinctly different ontologies and epistemologies) can be created. The rigor of the bricoleur's task lies in conceiving explicitly the varying dimensions of the bricolage. For example, I created a bricolage of auto|ethnographic and philosophical inquiry for my doctoral research, a methodology that enabled me to conceive a transformative philosophy of mathematics education for Nepal (Luitel, 2009). Drawing mainly from the paradigms of interpretivism, criticism and postmodernism, I used numerous logics for constructing

---

Let Me Declare

Let me declare
From today and further
I change my direction
I challenge conventions
I walk in the fire
I dance on the water
I go totally wild
I fly opposite to the wind
Let me declare

Let me declare
This rage does not stop here
It travels on sand and water
It reaches to the ether
It creates a cyclone
It organises a hurricane
It sacrifices ignorance
It destroys borders

Let me declare
In this rage, singular becomes plural
Here turns out to be there
The rebellion alters many
Nothing is big and tiny
Rivers pass through desert
Vultures turn away from meat
Mice take charge of the cheese factory
Cats take care of rat zoos
Lions embrace compassion

Let me declare
From now and hereafter
I host a *tandav* dance
with lots of free entry tickets
You can access the inaccessible
You can think the unthinkable
Don't miss this opportunity
Look inside you and allow it entry
This is my final declaration
The rage has just begun

(Luitel, 2009, p. 93)

different forms of knowledge, I employed multiple genres for representing my (emergent) knowledge claims, and I conceived a range of quality standards for regulating explicitly different epistemic aspects of the inquiry.

We would like to explain our vision of the way in which multiple paradigms are treated in constructing the research design space. For us, paradigms constitute referential systems rather than frameworks. Much as an artist brings to the canvas a suite of concepts and techniques drawn creatively from a variety of sources, the bricoleur brings to the research design space a suite of epistemes, concepts and techniques drawn from multiple paradigms and combines them in a uniquely creative way. Rather than being constrained within the ontological framework of a particular paradigm, the bricoleur 'refers' to various paradigms as sources of epistemic inspiration; thereby making sense of, representing, and helping to restructure socio-cultural reality afresh. With multiple paradigms available as referents researchers "can no longer accept the status of an object of inquiry as a thing-in-itself" (Kincheloe, 2001, pp. 681–682), thereby giving primacy to hermeneutic and transactional use of paradigms over their monological use as frameworks. More so, we view the relationship between paradigms as holonic, meaning that every historically evolved paradigm subsumes and transcends pre-existing paradigms. Such a relationship gives a fractal-like image in which paradigmatic borders are no longer treated as permanent and impervious; instead, they are understood to be in-the-making (for a detailed explanation see Taylor, Settelmaier, & Luitel, in press).

---

My Voice

Where is my voice?
Concealed in dry statements
Trapped in ethereal ideas
Again it questions
Am I a slave of dry texts?

I say to my voice
Don't make a noise
Start minding the proposition
Conceal the humdrum opinion
Again it questions
Am I not worthy of consideration?
I say, these are big ideas
Caused by 'and causes of' other ideas

My voice questions
Cannot the chain of causation be in your mind?
Cannot that be simply your interpretive imposition?
My voice, gradually coming to the forefront, says
Exclusivity makes life defunct
Because it promotes a singular yardstick
for constructing a statement
for depicting the truth
If I am forever to be colonised by propositional logic
How can I ever see present fuzziness?
How can I account for blurred images?

Luitel (2009, p. 218)

---

The Reunion

Oh dear friend, wake up now
I will explain how—
You will come out of the confine
And, help me plan for a reunion

That reunion will be dramatised
For those who are tormented
By the wrath of muted symbols
By the command of motorized algorithms

That reunion will play a song
For our survival in the aggression
of a rigid structure over emergent kens
of a confined frame over open musings

*Dear Joe*, our argument for a multi-paradigmatic design space favours your "active view of research methodology" which questions "deterministic views of social reality that assume the effects of particular social, political and economic, and educational processes" (Kincheloe, 2005, p. 325). And so we advocate complex research methodologies for helping to challenge formerly colonised epistemic techniques and canons, thereby opening new ways of decolonising educational research enterprises. Whilst sympathising with your concerns about the reductionist and dualistic hegemony of positivistic passivity, we are equally vigilant about our own perspective being a source of unhelpful dualisms. Therefore, we are committed to working for increasing tolerance among competing research paradigms, thereby enabling bricoleurs "to transcend the objective certainty of positivism and the effort to avoid the nihilism of more radical modes of postmodernism" (Kincheloe, 2005, p. 331). This can be achieved, we believe, by employing a range of alternative logics and genres.

> That reunion will see dances
> challenging the unhelpful fences
> uniting the body and the mind
> saying no to their undue break
>
> That reunion will hear stories
> about Roll's theorem being adapted
> about new definitions of Nepali Calculus
> to be used by people of all walks
>
> That reunion will see a debate–
> inclusive versus elitist mathematics
> it helps construct some strategies
> ways of addressing many dualisms
> (Luitel, 2009, p. 96)

## MULTIPLE LOGICS AND GENRES FOR THE BRICOLAGE

*Dear Joe*, cannot we make a case for multiple logics to enable bricoleurs to transgress the narrowly conceived positivistic way of knowing? We envisage the necessity of multiple logics for viewing the socio-cultural world from multiple perspectives. The idea of multiple logics entails both new and old modes of reasoning arising from alternative and positivistic paradigms. Our list of new logics includes (but is not confined to) dialectical, poetic, narrative and metaphorical forms of reasoning. The aim of dialectical logic, as you have mentioned and we have discussed elsewhere (Luitel, & Taylor, 2008), is to develop synergy between (and sometimes a synthesis of) adversarial perspectives associated with contrasting ways of knowing, being and valuing; especially to transcend antithetical (and often Western imperialistic) dualisms such as rational or non-rational, masculine or feminine, legitimate or illegitimate. Dialectical logic is an empowering mode of reasoning that holds opposing ideas in productive and creative tension, thereby helping us to be more inclusive of and tolerant towards competing views and ideologies. Poetic logic enables us to explore ineffable meanings of elusive phenomena such as trust, identity and spirituality, whose roots lie largely beyond the non-empirical world of sense impressions. Likewise, with narrative logic at our disposal we can develop not just stories of our research contexts and co-participants, but also the love and compassion needed to articulate an holistic sense of knowing and being. With its key feature of elastic correspondence between different concepts, metaphorical reasoning helps us explore expanded meanings of ideas, problems or issues under consideration.

You may agree with us that metaphorical logic offers productive ways to conceive and employ multiple epistemologies via a host of epistemic metaphors such as *research as ideology critique, research as reconceptualising self, research as writing* and *research as envisioning.*

*Dear Joe*, don't you think that we also need new genres to represent multiple ways of knowing and knowledge production in the process of creating a bricolage? As transformative educational researchers, we have been employing a number of arts-based modes of representation, including narrative, poetic, performative and non-linguistic genres (Taylor, Settelmaier, & Luitel, in press). A narrative genre enables us to speak from a lived storied perspective that fuses place, moment and people, thereby bringing forth the complexity of human understandings. As culture studies researchers, bricoleurs can use their own cultural formats of story-telling as a basis for sharing both research process and outcomes. If we wish to go beyond clean (c. f., messy), linear (c. f., complex) and realist (c. f., impressionistic) texts for representing our knowledge claims, then poetic genres provide a sublime means for cultivating the aesthetic and imaginative dimensions of our knowing. According to Vedic sages and seers, poetry can help us to know the furthest locale of our inner landscapes through which to realise our true Self.

> The Moment I Speak To You
>
> The moment I speak to you
> I am not merely releasing words
> I am not merely uttering sounds
> I am not merely mimicking sentences
> I am not merely vibrating my lips
> The moment I speak to you
>
> The moment I speak to you
> I am sharing my vantage points
> I am drawing my picture of reality
> I am thinking of possible payoffs
> I am refreshing my beliefs
> The moment I speak to you
>
> The moment I speak to you
> I am calculating how much I owe you
> I am wondering how I can pay you
> I am undecidedly wandering
> I am asking: Why are thoughts meandering?
> The moment I speak to you
>
> The moment I speak to you
> I am telling a story of the day
> I am disrupting your way
> I am going far away and then
> I am coming to my inn
> The moment I speak to you
>
> The moment I speak to you
> I am longing for my presence
> I am making claims of my sense
> I am bespeaking complicities
> I am requesting a space
> The moment I speak to you
>
> (Luitel, 2009, p. 269)

Likewise, performative genres enable us to speak as advocates for transformative socio-cultural agendas, bringing to the textual foreground of knowledge creation the metaphor of *writing as performative praxis*. More so, performative genres can have an engaging dialogic quality with the help of plurivocal texts in the form of ethnodrama and ethnotheatre. Last but not least, via non-linguistic genres such as photographs, paintings, cartoons, collage, creative models, and digitised productions we can portray richly the visual dimension of our knowledge claims.

As with dialectical reasoning, we adhere to the notion of inclusivity in accounting for logics and genres arising from different research paradigms. Thus, we argue that there is also a place for the conventionial logics and genres (e.g., propositional, analytic, deductive, impersonal, descriptive, objective, voiceless) embedded in the positivistic research tradition, but only insofar as they do not continue to pose a totalitarian hegemony of knowledge production and legitimation. We acknowledge their immense value in enabling us to understand and represent the realist dimension of research inquiries. Indeed it is almost impossible to write an article or research report completely free from conventional logics and genres. You may agree with us that in the counter-hegemonic articles of yours that we are discussing here you have, to a very large extent, employed conventional logics and genres.

## QUALITY STANDARDS FOR THE BRICOLAGE

*Dear Joe*, we prefer to use the term 'quality standards' instead of your term 'rigor' because of the hegemony arising from its hidden historical meanings. Nevertheless, the sentiment reflected in your explanation of the term 'new rigor' seems to represent its post-apocalyptic sense, hinting at the need to enable bricoleurs to conceive and develop quality standards in accordance with the purpose and nature of their inquiry, which of course depends on the paradigms they are drawing on to generate their research epistemologies. How can this be made possible? Rather than attempting to present a prescription, we intend to outline several possibilities for constructing quality standards that we find meaningful in the context of our own transformative approaches to educational research.

First, we would like bricoleurs to articulate quality standards for their research texts. In drawing on the interpretive and postmodern paradigms, bricoleurs would need to be mindful of the concept of multi-textuality, a view that the meaning of a research text is not independent of person, time and space (Bloome, & Egan-Robertson, 1993). For example, if we value dialogical (c. f., monological) research texts we need to acknowledge a commitment to perspectivalism which helps us to "explore the realm of possibility, a kinetic epistemology of possible" (Kincheloe, 2005, p. 346). And so we need to make explicit the intended impact of our writing on our readers, especially if we wish to engage them in pedagogical thoughtfulness, as advocated by Max van Manen (1991), as a first step in considering the possibility of adopting transformative action in their professional contexts. The quality of our dialogic research text could be judged by the extent to which the text is evocative and interactive, has the potential to promote dialogue with our readers, and is likely to engage them in imagining themselves to be situated in one or many possibilities offered by the text.

Another important quality standard for bricoleurs pertains to the praxis dimension of their research. For us, the standard of critical reflexivity, drawn from the criticalist paradigm, reflects this dimension. The term reflexivity signifies the extent to which the researcher has made his/her background information available to readers. This basic notion of reflexivity needs further extension for examining critically the researcher's false (or unknowingly colonised) consciousness generated by subscribing ideologically to a particular epistemology, methodology or theoretical framework. The quality of critical reflexivity embedded in our research can be judged by the extent to which: (a) we have made the process of interpretation visible to readers; (b) we have reflected critically on our assumptions; (c) we have reflected consciously and critically on our evolving subjectivities throughout the process of the inquiry; and (d) our textual constructions have not arisen from isolated naval gazing, thereby constituting an authentic vision for our present and future praxis in our professional field.

Humility is an important quality that can help bricoleurs to be less presumptive about contentious issues and to demonstrate a commitment to self-evaluation, self critique and acceptance of self-weaknesses (Ho, 1995; Massoudi, 2002). We envisage that bricoleurs can uphold the quality standard of humility by demonstrating a heightened level of epistemic tolerance of adversarial traditions and perspectives associated with issues under study. To ascertain the extent to which a research text has met the standard of humility, readers may ask: Does the researcher appear to be less presumptive about contentious issues?' and 'Does the researcher appear to be aware of the limitations of the epistemologies being employed in this research?'

> One and Many
>
> *Don't show me this monochrome again*
> *I say to the photographer with passion*
> *Please bring images of different effects*
> *I say, the monochrome is not enough*
>
> *Why don't you like the realistic image?*
> *The photographer says,*
> *You have a surprising craze*
> *Rejecting what is real, true and exact*
> *What are you trying to achieve?*
>
> *How do you know your image is real?*
> *I question, why don't you think of multiple?*
> *Your exactness can be bounded*
> *Your truth can be misguided*
> *Come on, construct multicoloured image-icon*
> *Not just one from one, but many out of one*
>
> *Colourful images are inspirational*
> *Don't worry about real, unreal and nonreal*
> *I am happy with all of them*
> *But be aware I need a great deal of collection*
>
> The photographer begins to listen
> As if he is going to be educated soon
> I say, *strict boundaries have no charm*
> *Just like being restricted inside a locked room*
>
> I stress further, *images signify possibilities*
> *They embody normal, abnormal and otherwise*
> *My friend, use as many pixels as you can*
> I encourage, *use as many effects as you can*
> *Employ multiple lenses to capture dimensions*
> *Apply colour combinations for imaginations*
>
> Finally the photographer nods
> I continue with my proddings
> *The world is colourful and so are our beings*
> *Allow images to sprout freely from your lenses*
> *Remember many is the essence of one*
> *And one is a basis for and gives rise to many.*
>
> (Luitel, 2009, p. 288)

*Dear Joe*, we also recognise that bricoleurs need to address significant research issues and problems, thereby demonstrating strong connection with the field of their inquiry (e.g., mathematics education, science education, education policy). For this, we put forward two quality standards: incisiveness and illumination. The standard of incisiveness seeks to ensure that the research is focused clearly on significant issues relevant to the field of inquiry. For instance, in my recently completed doctoral research, I endeavoured to meet this quality standard with a clear focus on the macro level problem of decontextualised mathematics education that ignores the cultural capital students bring with them from their communities, a widespread problem in the education system of Nepal. Investigating this problem was highly significant for developing an overarching vision of culturally inclusive mathematics education for my country. I enhanced the incisiveness of the research also by focusing on micro level issues associated with widespread student underachievement, especially the unquestioned dominance of didactic classroom pedagogy, an entrenched hierarchical classroom culture, and an exclusively Western view of curriculum development.

Finally, the research standard of illumination concerns the extent to which the meanings of issues under investigation are enriched, deepened, made vivid and more complex, as advocated by leading advocates of arts-based educational research (e.g., Barone, 2006; Eisner, 2008). Bricoleurs can illuminate subtle but significant research issues by portraying their vividness and complexity via narrative, reflective, performative, poetic and non-linguistic genres. These genres help bricoleurs speak differently about issues being investigated. And when a bricoleur enhances his/her own visibility and the visibility of his or her research context through self-conscious and reflexive writing styles, such visibility is illuminative because it helps unpack the bricoleur's being and becoming as a complex textual collage of student, teacher, advocate of social justice and teacher educator, to name a few possible overlapping life roles.

## CODA

*Dear Joe*, in closing this letter of celebration of a small but significant part of your life's work we would like to express our gratitude for this opportunity to offer a dialogue with you about the powerful concept of the bricolage. Over the years we have learned much from you about the important counter-hegemonic work of bricoleurs in bringing a transformative dimension to educational research. We have taken this opportunity to demonstrate the value of your ideas many of which have enabled us to develop our own perspective on multi-paradigmatic transformative educational research. We hope that readers of this brief chapter might gain valuable insights from the intertextuality of our writings.

## REFERENCES

Barone, T. (2006). Arts-based educational research: Then, now, and later. *Studies in Art Education, 48*(1), 4–8.
Bloome, D., & Egan-Robertson, A. (1993). The social construction of intertextuality in classroom reading and writing lessons. *Reading Research Quarterly*, 305–333.
Eisner, E. W. (2008). Art and knowledge. In J. G. Knowles & A. L. Cole (Eds.), *Handbook of the arts in qualitative research: Perspectives, methodologies, examples, and issues* (pp. 3–12). Thousand Oaks, CA: Sage.
Ho, D. Y. F. (1995). Selfhood and identity in Confucianism, Taoism, Buddhism, and Hinduism: Contrasts with the west. *Journal for the Theory of Social Behaviour, 25*(2), 115–139.

Kincheloe, J. L. (2001). Describing the bricolage: Conceptualizing a new rigor in qualitative research. *Qualitative Inquiry, 7*(6), 679.

Kincheloe, J. L. (2005). On to the next level: Continuing the conceptualization of the bricolage. *Qualitative Inquiry, 11*(3), 323–350.

Luitel, B. C. (2009). *Culture, worldview and transformative philosophy of mathematics education in Nepal: A cultural-philosophical inquiry*. Unpublished PhD Thesis, Curtin University of Technology, Perth, Australia.

Luitel, B. C., & Taylor, P. C. (2007). The shanai, the pseudosphere and other imaginings: Envisioning culturally contextualised mathematics education. *Cultural Studies of Science Education, 2*(3), 621–638.

Luitel, B. C., & Taylor, P. C. (2008, Jan). *Globalization, ecological consciousness and curriculum as montage: A vision for culturally contextualized mathematics education*. Paper presented at the Southern African Association for Research in Mathematics Science and Technology Education. Maseru, Lesotho.

Massoudi, M. (2002). On the qualities of a teacher and a student: An Eastern perspective based on Buddhism, Vedanta and Sufism. *Intercultural Education, 13*(2), 137–155.

Taylor, P. C. (2008). Forum: Reflections on qualitative research writing: Warrants, perspectives, structure and theory? *Cultural Studies of Science Education, 3*(3), 684–693.

Taylor, P. C., Settelmaier, E., & Luitel, B. C. (in press). Multi-Paradigmatic transformative research as/for teacher education: An integral perspective. In K. Tobin, B. Fraser, & C. McRobbie (Eds.), *International handbook of science education*. Dordrecht, The Netherlands: Springer.

van Manen, M. (1991). *The tact of teaching: The meaning of pedagogical thoughtfulness*. New York: State University of New York Press.

*Joe always incorporated the idea of selfhood within his work. He was both a champion of autobiography and self study as legitimate qualitative research, and the greatest critic of its use. Joe saw self study and critical autobiography as necessary components for researchers/scholars to identify themselves within their own work. Most of his doctoral students were asked to complete self research and connect it to their own theoretical underpinnings, with a bit of phenomenological hermeneutic seasoning. Joe insisted that this work would contextualize exactly what it was they were doing and how they became to know what they know. Along with his work in self study, ontology, and autobiography, he was highly aware of the self-indulgent tripe written by many in the curriculum field. Students from this ilk tended to wallow in their own visions of previous victimization, in the case of middle class white women, many so-called "self study" mentors seemed to spawn a never-ending trail of whining privileged graduates, always in search of their own victimization. In the case of others, there was a bit more complexity, in that marginalized students would record their own autobiographical work, but then never pushed to the critical theoretical edge it so needed. Joe also critiqued the narcissistic rantings of some autobiographical writers, who so often reminded the reader of just how difficult it was to be a white, upper class, private school teacher to the other. As a critical writer, Joe was committed to never let pseudo scholarship get in the way of rigorous and contextualized work. As difficult as it is to walk the fine line of autobiographical theory, it is important for qualitative researchers to insist that the use of self be tightly rooted in the theoretical. SS*

JOE L. KINCHELOE

## 9. CRITICAL ONTOLOGY

*Visions of Selfhood and Curriculum*

There is nothing profound about asserting that the ways one teaches and the curricular purposes one pursues are tied to the ways teachers see themselves. Yet the ways teachers come to see themselves as professionals and learners–in particular the ways they conceptualize what they need to learn, where they need to learn it, and how the process should take place–shape their teacher persona (CPRE, 1995). Such a persona cannot be separated from the various forms of knowledge produced in the culture at large, in academic curricula and in the larger notion of "professional awareness." Too infrequently are teachers in university, student teaching, or in-service professional education encouraged to confront why they think as they do

k. hayes et al., (eds.), *Key Work in Critical Pedagogy: Joe L. Kincheloe, 201–217.*
© 2011 Sense Publishers. All rights reserved.

about themselves as teachers—especially in relationship to the social, cultural, political, economic, and historical world around them. Mainstream teacher education provides little insight into the forces that shape identity and consciousness. Becoming educated, becoming a critical teacher as researcher/teacher as scholar necessitates personal transformation based on an understanding and critique of these forces. This article explores these dynamics and in the process develops a notion of critical ontology for teachers. Such a concept explores self-production for the purpose of conceptualizing new, more just, and more complex ways of being human. Critical ontology as delineated here involves about 23 basic ideas. Such a concept understands the need:

- to move beyond mechanistic metaphors of selfhood.
- to transcend the alienation of disenchantment of abstract individualism and the notion of an essentialized, permanent, fixed self.
- to develop new forms of self-awareness and an understanding of consciousness construction.
- to appreciate the autopoietic (self-producing) aspect of the "self" in order to gain a more sophisticated capacity to reshape our lives.
- to understand the importance of socio-historical consciousness concerning the production of self.
- to discern the productive power of relationships in the (re)construction of self.
- to recognize dominant power's complicity in self-production vis-à-vis ideologies, discourses, and linguistics.
- to gain the ability to research oneself.
- to develop a critical ontological agency to act on self and world in a just and an intelligent manner.
- to conceptualize new ways of analyzing experience and apply it to the re-construction of selfhood.
- to construct a power literacy that alerts individuals to their placement in the web of reality–a web refashioned by the increasing influence of power wielders in electronic hyperreality.
- to avoid allowing the ontological quest for self knowledge and self reconstruction.
- to mutate into new forms of egocentrism and narcissism.
- to move schools to examine the ontological realm of self-production and the myriad of forces that affect it.
- to realize the complexity and rigor of studies designed to analyze the social construction and the critical reconstruction of the self.
- to become detectives of difference who search for new ways of being human.
- to gain awareness of the ontological implications of studying things-in-themselves as opposed to studying things-in-relationship to one another to their contexts.
- to become cognizant of the cognitive act as the basic activity of living systems–the process of establishing relationships and new modes of being.
- to grasp the notion that this ontological process of cognition constructs the world rather than reflecting an external world already in existence.

- to realize that the nature of this world, the meanings we make about it, and our relationships with it are never final–thus, humans are always in process.
- to see that the self is not pre-formed as it enters the world–that it *emerges* in its relationships to other selves and other things in the world.
- to conceptualize the emergent self as virtual; this means that depending on its relationships it is always capable of change and has no essential central controlling mechanism.
- to appreciate that political empowerment, community building, and the cultivation of both the individual and collective intellect require a constant monitoring of the relationships that shape us.
- to realize that the nature of the interactions in which the self engages actually changes the structure of the mind.

## HUMANS AS WELL-OILED MACHINES AND COMPUTERS: MOVIN' ON

In this context we engage in the excitement of attaining new levels of consciousness and "ways of being." In a critical context individuals who gain such an awareness understand how and why their political opinions, religious beliefs, gender role, racial positions, or sexual orientation have been shaped by dominant perspectives. A critical ontological vision helps us in the effort to gain new understandings and insights as to who we can become. Such a vision helps us move beyond our present state of being–our ontological selves–as we discern the forces that have made us that way. The line between knowledge production and being is blurred, as the epistemological and the ontological converge around questions of identity. As we employ the ontological vision we ask questions about ethics, morality, politics, emotion, and gut feelings, seeking not precise steps to reshape our subjectivity but a framework of principles with which we can negotiate. Thus, we join the quest for new, expanded, more just and interconnected ways of being human. A key dimension of a critical ontology involves freeing ourselves from the machine metaphors of Cartesianism. Such an ontological stance recognizes the reductionism of viewing the universe as a well-oiled machine and the human mind as a computer. Such ways of being subvert an appreciation of the amazing life force that inhabits both the universe and human beings. This machine cosmology has positioned human beings as living in a dead world, a lifeless universe. Ontologically, this Cartesianism has separated individuals from their inanimate surroundings, undermining any organic interconnection of the person to the cosmos. The life-giving complexity of the inseparability of human and world has been lost and social/cultural/pedagogical/psychological studies of people abstracted–removed from context. Such a removal has exerted disastrous ontological effects. Human beings, in a sense, lost their belongingness to both the world and to other people around them. The importance of indigenous (Semali and Kincheloe, 1999) and other subjugated knowledges emerges in this ontological context. With the birth of modernity and the scientific revolution, many pre-modern, indigenous ontologies were lost, ridiculed by Europeans as primitive.

While there is great diversity among pre-modern worldviews and ways of being, there do seem to be some discernible patterns that distinguish them form modernist perspectives. In addition to developing systems of meaning and being that were connected to cosmological perspectives on the nature of creation, most premodern viewpoints saw nature and the world at large as living systems. Western, often Christian, observers condescendingly labeled such perspectives as pantheism or nature worship and positioned them as an enemy of monotheism. Not understanding the subtlety and nuance of such indigenous views of the world, Europeans subverted the sense of belonging that accompanied these enchanted views of nature. European Christomodernism transformed the individual from a connected participant in the drama of nature to a detached, objective, depersonalized observer. The Western modernist individual emerged from the process alienated and disenchanted. As Edmund O'Sullivan (1999) puts it, Cartesianism tore apart "the relationship between the microcosmos and the macrocosmos" (p. 18). Such a fragmentation resulted in the loss of cosmological significance and the beginning of a snowballing pattern of ontological imbalance. A critical ontology involves the process of reconnecting human beings on a variety of levels and in numerous ways to a living social and physical web of reality, to a living cosmos. Teachers with a critical ontological vision help students connect to the civic web of the political domain, the biotic web of the natural world, the social web of human life, and the epistemological web of knowledge production. In this manner, we all move to the realm of critical ontology where new ways of being and new ways of being *connected* reshape all people. Philip Wexler (2000) picks up on these ontological issues, arguing that an intuitive disenchantment with this Cartesian fragmentation and its severing of the self-environment relationship is fueling a diffuse social revaluation. He employs the term, revitalization, for this mass, decentered movement taking place throughout Western societies. It constitutes an attempt, he contends, to resacralize our culture and ourselves. Such an effort exposes the impact of Eurocentrism and Cartesianism on what human beings have become, as, at the same time, it produces an ontological "change from within." Understanding the problems with Cartesianism's lack of self-awareness or concern with consciousness and interconnectedness, Wexler's resacralization picks up on wisdom traditions both premodern and postmodern, to lay the foundation for profound ontological change. In the emerging ontology the Cartesian bifurcation of the mind and body is repaired, and new relationships with the body, mind, and spirit are pursued. In the transcendence of modernist notions of bodily ego-greed, a new understanding of the body's role in meaning making and *human being* is attained. Picking up on these insights a critical ontology positions the body in relation to cognition and the process of life itself. The body is a corporeal reflection of the evolutionary concept of *autopoiesis*, self-organizing or self-making of life. Autopoiesis involves the production of a pattern of life organization. Cognition in this ontological context involves the process of self-production. Thus, life itself, the nature of being, is a cognitive activity that involves establishing patterns of living, patterns that become the life force through self-organization. If life is self-organized, then there are profound ontological, cognitive, and pedagogical implications. By recognizing new patterns and developing new processes, humans exercise much more input into their own evolution than previously imagined. In such a context human agency and possibility is enhanced. Indeed, evolution is not as random as previously thought. Life is self-produced in forms of escalating diversity and complexity. The interaction of different living forms can catalyze the self-production feature of living systems. In both its corporeal and cognitive expressions the autopoietic life process reaches out for difference, for novelty, to embrace its next ontological level (Wexler, 2000; Kincheloe and Steinberg, 1997; Steinberg, 2001; Capra, 1996). Teachers who understand this critical ontological process can use these notions to rethink their lives and their teacher persona. With these understandings, we can self-organize and reorganize the field to new levels of complexity where new patterns and processes allow us to rethink the nature of our being and the possibility of our becoming. Curriculum in this complex context takes on an unprecedented importance, as it pursues ways of knowing and being that shape the evolution of the human species.

## THE BEGINNING: HISTORICALLY SITUATING THE SELF

In this context I offer a notion of critical ontology with its complex, reflective engagement with the complications of self-production and the ways such factors shape teacher selfhood and professional awareness in the twenty-first century. With such dynamics in mind teachers are asked to confront their relationship to some long-term historical trends rarely discussed in the contemporary public conversation. Critical complex teacher educators maintain these trends hold profound implications for the development of both professional awareness and a teacher persona. In my own case the understanding of my personal historicization in light of five centuries of European colonialism from the fifteenth to the twentieth century—and new forms of economic, cultural, political and educational colonialism picking up steam in the contemporary era—is very important knowledge. Indeed, everyone in the contemporary U.S. is shaped by this knowledge in some way whether or not they are conscious of it. We cannot contemplate our professional awareness without reference to these last five hundred and some years and their effects. I was born in 1950, in the middle of the post-colonial rebellion against this half millennium of colonial violence emerging in Africa, Asia, Latin America, and throughout the indigenous world. While anti-colonial activity continues into the twenty-first century, such discontent reached its apex in the U.S. in the 1960s and early 1970s finding expression in the civil rights, women's, anti-Vietnam war, gay rights, and other liberation movements. By the mid-1970s a conservative counter-reaction was taking shape with the goals of "recovering" what was perceived to be lost in these movements. Thus, the politics, cultural wars, and educational debates, policies, and practices of the last three decades cannot be understood outside of these efforts to "recover" white supremacy, patriarchy, class privilege, heterosexual "normality," Christian dominance, and the European intellectual canon. I must decide where I stand in relation to such profound yet muffled historical processes. I cannot conceptualize my teacher persona outside of them. They are the defining macro-concerns of our time, as every topic is refracted through their lenses. Any view of education, any curriculum development, any professional education conceived outside of their framework ends up becoming a form of ideological mystification.

Once we turn our analysis to the examination of ontological knowledges vis-à-vis such historical processes, we set the teacher "self" in question. As self-images, inherited dogmas, and absolute beliefs are interrogated, teachers begin to see themselves in relation to the world around them. They perceive the school as a piece of a larger mosaic. With such a conceptual matrix teachers start to see an inseparable relationship between thinking and acting, as the boundary between feeling and logic begins to fade from the map of teacher thinking. In such an ontological context teachers derive the motivation to produce their own knowledge. If teachers hold power to produce their own knowledges, then they are empowered to reconstruct their own consciousness. The top-down tyranny of expert-produced interpretations of tradition and its oppressive power can be subverted and our futures can be reinvented along the lines of a critical and complex system of meaning making. If the right-wing ideological directives of the Bush Administration's Department of Education with their positivistic and *duplicitous* "No Child Left Behind" modes of conceptualizing teaching are unchallenged and allowed to prevail, then there is little hope for progressive reform. These issues of self-production will be removed from the consciousness of prospective teachers, as they memorize the generic theories and the fragments of the bogus "knowledge base." Relegated to a static state of being, teachers in this technicist paradigm are conceived as a unit of production of an assembly line—historically abstracted selves located outside of a wider social context. Standards reforms that decontextualize teachers and students in this manner are molded by the dynamics of history and social structure (Kincheloe and Weil, 2001). Identity is never complete and always subject to modification in relation to prevailing ideologies, discourses, and knowledges. A critical and complex teacher education encourages desocialization via ideological disembedding. Critical complex professional education coursework and practicum experiences focus on the ways in which the values of power-driven, information-saturated hyperreality of the twenty-first century shape the consciousness of both students and teachers (Britzman, 1991; Macedo, 1994; Carson, 1997; Soto, 2001; Apple, 1999; Gordon, 2001; Malewski, 2001a, 2001b). The rigorous study of cultural and historical context alerts prospective teachers to the ways dominant myths, behavior, and language shape their view of the teacher role and the curriculum without conscious filtering.

## ENGAGING A CRITICAL ONTOLOGY: TEACHERS AS RESEARCHERS OF SELF-PRODUCTION

The notion of critical ontology demands that teacher scholars who research the worlds of students, schools, and communities also research themselves. In this context teachers explore what it means to be human and to negotiate the social and ideological forces that shape their pedagogical consciousness. In light of a critical knowledge of power, we are pursuing a key dimension of critical ontology—a way of being that is aware of the ways power shapes us, the ways we see the world, and the ways we perceive our role as teachers. When teachers possess such understandings they are better prepared to support or critique what schools are doing, the goals they are promoting. In this context teachers become political agents who research their own practices and their own belief systems. In so doing they develop their own teacher persona, not one that has been insidiously constructed by tacit exposure to the machinations of oppressive power so dominant in the first decade of the twenty-first century. To gain this literacy of power (Macedo, 1994) teachers must transcend simplistic forms of reflection and move to specific questions about whose interests are being served by particular forms of pedagogy and curriculum development. How am I complicit in these political activities? Do I want to contribute to the political agenda being promoted by the existing school organization? Critical complex teachers learn that no teaching, curriculum development, knowledge production is value-free, no language is politically neutral, and no meaning making process is objective. In this context they understand that the teacher persona they create is committed to something, to the valuing of some politically inscribed educational purpose. Thus, human "being" itself is never a disinterested dynamic and must always be self-monitored for the ways it has been shaped by power. Thus, a critical ontology pursues human agency—the disposition and capacity to act on the world in ways that involve self-direction and the pursuit of democratic and egalitarian principles of community formation. A critical ontology insists that humans possess inalienable rights to knowledge and insight into knowledge production, to intellectual development, to empowerment, and to political agency in a democratic society. When teacher educators understand these ontological dynamics and work toward the political goals they portend, they have laid the foundation on which other aspects of professional education can be constructed. They have signaled to those around them that social justice must be integrated into every aspect of education—even the construction of teacher selfhood. With this sense of agency teachers are better prepared to sidestep the technical rationalism and the forces of race, class, gender, and sexual oppression that constantly work to shape education in the U.S. (Getzel, 1997; Grimmitt, 1999; Edwards, 2000; Horn, 2000, 2001; Segall, 2002). This is the goal-oriented dimension of critical ontology—the political agency of critical complex teacher educators and teachers. The goal orientation is never simplistic. It is much more of a hermeneutic dynamic that questions the notion of fixed goals even as it pursues them. Educators aware of this critical ontology always understand that different contexts demand different goals and that seen in light of different horizons goals will take on different forms. In this hermeneutic orientation toward goals teacher educators and teachers pay less attention to teaching and more attention to the intersection of empirical, normative, critical, experiential, ontological, and reflective-synthetic knowledges of education. In this context an informed agency develops that moves the individual teacher to new levels of understanding and action (Block, 1995; Morris, Doll, and Pinar, 1999; Edwards, 2000; Gordon, 2001). Ontological knowledge cannot be separated from experience. Indeed, some might define experience as knowledge translated into action (Ferreira and Alexandre, 2000). Thus, critical complex teacher educators always are comparing ontological knowledge to experiential knowledge, thinking about the relationship between who they are and what they do as educators. Critical ontology is obsessed with new and better ways of being human, being with others, and the creation of environments where mutual growth of individuals is promoted and symbiotic learning relationships are cultivated. Such actions are highly political, involving the knowledge and disposition to escape form technicist modes of social control and knowledge production. The aspect of education that moved me to become a teacher and teacher educator involves this *great escape* and the subsequent move to a new ontological domain. With this in mind we can engage in a form of ontologically-catalyzed knowledge production that results in a reconceptualiztion of our lives and, of course, our pedagogy.

### CRITICAL ONTOLOGY AND HUMAN POSSIBILITY: DEALING WITH THE MULTIDIMENSIONAL ALIENATION OF SELFHOOD

In a critical ontology context curriculum development and the learning process become profoundly exciting enterprises because they are always conceptualized in terms of what we can become–both in an individual and a collective context. In our socio-ontological imagination we can transcend the Enlightenment category of abstract individualism and move toward a more textured concept of the relational individual. While abstract individualism and a self-sufficient ontology seem almost *natural* in the Western modernist world, such is not the case in many non-Western cultures and has not been the case even in Western societies in previous historical eras. In ancient Greece, for example, it is hard to find language that identified "the self" or "I"–such descriptions were not commonly used because the individual was viewed as a part of a collective who could not function independently of the larger social group (Allen, 2000). In the "common sense" of contemporary Western society and its unexamined ontological assumptions this way of seeing self is hard to fathom. Enlightenment ontology discerns the natural state of the individual as solitary. The social order in this modernist Eurocentric context is grounded on a set of contractual transactions between isolated individual atoms. In other works I (Kincheloe, 1993) have referred to Clint Eastwood's "man with no name" cinematic character who didn't need a "damn thing from nobody" as the ideal Western male way of being–the ontological norm. Operating in this context, we clearly discern, for example, cognitive psychology's tradition of focusing on the autonomous development of the individual monad. In our critical complex ontology a human being simply can't exist outside the inscription of community with its processes of relationship, differentiation, interaction, and subjectivity. Indeed, in this critical complex ontology the relational embeddedness of self is so context dependent that psychologists, sociologists, and educators can never isolate a finalized completed "true self." Since the self is always in context and in process, no final delineation of a notion such as ability can be determined. Thus, we are released from the rugged cross of IQ and such hurtful and primitive conceptions of "intelligence." One can quickly discern the political consequences of such a Cartesian ontology. Human beings in Western liberal political thought become abstract bearers of particular civic rights. If individuals are relational, context-embedded beings, however, these abstract rights may be of little consequence. A critical complex ontology insists that individuals live in specific places with particular types of relationships. They operate or are placed in the web of reality at various points of race, class, gender, sexual, religious, physical ability, geographical place, and other continua. Where individuals find themselves in this complex web holds dramatic power consequences. Their location shapes their relationship to dominant culture and the psychological and curricular assumptions that accompany it. In other words the intelligence mainstream psychology and the curriculum and pedagogy it supports deem these individuals to possess, profoundly depends on this contextual, power-inscribed placement. A prime manifestation of ontological alienation involves a lack of recognition of the dramatic effect of these dynamics on everything that takes place in the psycho-educational cosmos. In the context of our critical ontology the autonomous self with a fixed intellectual ability becomes an anachronism. As an effort to appreciate the power of human beings to affect their own destinies, to exercise human agency, and to change social conditions, critical ontologists study selfhood in light of the sociological, cultural studies, cultural psychological, and critical analytical work of the last few decades. Much of what dominant psychology and education consider free will and expressions of innate intelligence are simply manifestations of the effects of particular social, cultural, political, and economic forces. While we can make decisions on how we operate as human beings, they are never completely independent of these structuring forces. This is true whether we are Diane Ravitch or Michel Foucault–neither person can operate outside of society or free from cultural, linguistic, ideological influences. It is important to note here that neo-positivist educational policy makers contend that their work takes place outside of the influence of these dynamics. They claim that their work avoids cultural values and morally inscribed issues and because of such diligence, they have presented us the truth about how students learn and how teachers should teach. In the critical ontological context developed here, such researchers must take a closer look at who they are and the structuring forces that have shaped their views of the world, mind, and self. Their inability to discern the effects of these forces reflects the ontological alienation referenced here. Such alienation undermines their ability to imagine new and better ways of being human both for themselves and for the teachers and students their knowledges and policies oppress.

## CRITICAL ONTOLOGY AND POWER: THE POLITICS OF SELF-PRODUCTION

A critical ontology understands that self-production cannot be understood outside the context of power. In this context, teachers pursuing a critical ontology employ a critical mode of hermeneutics and engage with texts for the purpose of gaining a new level of self-understanding. This question of gaining insight into personal identity is not a call to narcissism; indeed, it is quite the opposite. In this ontological context educators learn to understand the oppressive forces that shape them so–especially in contemporary Western culture–they can become less self-absorbed and individually oriented. In this context they learn to situate themselves historically and socially. With such knowledge they are far better equipped to make conscious decisions about who they want to be and how they will deal with the ideological socialization processes of twenty-first century electronic societies. In what might be described as the tacit ontology of Cartesianism students and teachers are not encouraged to confront why they tend to think as they do about themselves, the world around them, and their relationship to that world. In other words students and teachers gain little insight into the forces that shape them—that is, that construct their consciousness, and produce their subjectivity. In addition, this uncritical articulation of curriculum and pedagogy is virtually unconcerned with the consequences of thinking, as it viewed cognition as a process that takes place in a vacuum. Thinking in a new way always necessitates personal transformation; indeed if enough people think in new ways, social transformation is inevitable. One reason this situating of self often does not take place in contemporary schooling involves the fact that many of those who teach are denied the historical, philosophical, sociological, and cultural studies background to delineate what such an act might entail. Insights derived from these domains might have helped teachers discern the ways that dominant power has subverted democratic impulses in a variety of venues including the political, epistemological, psychological, and the curricular and pedagogical. Increasingly dominated by private interests, these domains operated to construct the identities of individuals in ways that were conducive to the needs of dominant power wielders. There were concerted attempts to make individuals more compliant to the needs of corporations, more accepting of government by the market, globalized capitalism, free market ideologies, the irrelevance of the political domain, etc.... The ideological deployment of schools as sorting mechanisms for the new corporate order has gone unchallenged by practitioners unaware of these forces. Where the self fits in these power-driven dynamics is, of course, irrelevant in too many pedagogical venues. Human efforts to make sense of self and the world are dominated by ideological forces that thwart our pursuit of individual goals. At the same time, particular forms of thinking and action reveal volition and a genuine motivation that transcends the confines of existing social forces. Social theorists have traditionally been guilty of not recognizing this ambiguity of consciousness construction, identity production, and social action. Not until the 1970s and 1980s with the influx of new theories of language analysis and cultural understanding did scholars appreciate the way power was embedded in language and knowledge and the implications of such inscriptions in the production of the self. Human beings are initiated into language communities where women and men share bodies of knowledge, epistemologies, and the cognitive styles that accompany them. These are powerful forces in the shaping of who we are. Thus, the manner in which we come to think about selfhood and pedagogy is inseparable from these language communities. Indeed, the nature of the curriculum we devise is inseparable from them. A critical ontology understands these dynamics; it understands that the sociohistorical dimensions of self-production are often manifested on the terrain of language. The schemas that guide a culture and its schooling and help produce subjectivity are too infrequently taught in the hyperrational schools of the twenty-first century. It was the recognition of this same absence in the Italy of the 1920s that social theorist Antonio Gramsci had in mind when he argued that philosophy should be viewed as a form of self-criticism. Gramsci asserted that the starting point for any higher understanding of self involves the consciousness of oneself as a product of sociohistorical forces. A critical philosophy, he wrote, involves the ability of its adherents to criticize the ideological frames that they use

CRITICAL ONTOLOGY

to make sense of the world. I watch my colleagues and myself struggle as teachers of a complex ontology, as we attempt to engage our students in Gramsci's pedagogical effort to understand themselves in sociohistorical context. The work is never easy as we complain and moan about our students' lack of preparation for engagement in such theoretical and introspective analysis. Teachers who engage a complex ontological curriculum must be patient and empathetic with their twenty-first century students. Our students have very few opportunities in the contemporary world of media and corporately influenced schooling to gain experiences that would equip them for such a task. In very specific terms a complex ontology is profoundly concerned with the production of self in the context of the influence of power blocs in contemporary society. Such concern reveals itself in a critical questioning of the social, cultural, political, economic, epistemological and linguistic structures that shape human consciousness as well as the historical contexts that gave birth to the structures. Such ontological analysis helps students and teachers explore the sociohistorical and political dimensions of schooling, the kind of meanings that are constructed in classrooms, and how these meaning are translated into student consciousness. Advocates of an ontologically impoverished curriculum often speak of student and teacher empowerment as if it were a simple process that can be accomplished by a couple of creative learning activities. One thing our ideological critique of self-production tells us is that the self is a complex, ambiguous, and contradictory entity pushed and pulled by a potpourri of forces. The idea that the self can be reconstructed and empowered without rigorous historical study, linguistic analysis, and an understanding of social construction is a trivialization of the goals of a critical ontology. A curriculum informed by a complex ontology asks the question: how do we move beyond simply uncovering the sources of consciousness construction in our larger attempt to reconstruct the self in a critical manner? Critical teachers must search in as many locations as possible for alternate discourses, ways of thinking and being that expand the envelopes of possibility. In this context teachers explore literature, history, popular culture, and ways of forging community in previously devalued, subjugated knowledges. In this context teachers develop their own and their students' social and aesthetic imaginations. Here we imagine what we might become by recovering and reinterpreting what we once were. The excitement of curriculum as an ontological quest is powerful.

## LAYING THE FOUNDATION FOR A CRITICAL ONTOLOGY

Employing an understanding of complexity theory, Maturana and Varela's Santiago enactivism as the process of life, critical theoretical foundations, the critique of Cartesianism, and poststructuralist feminist analysis, we can lay the conceptual foundations for a new mode of selfhood. Such a configuration cannot be comprehensively delineated here, but we can begin to build theoretical pathways to get around the Cartesian limitations on the ontological imagination. With Humberto Maturana and Francisco Valera's concept that living things constantly remake themselves in interaction with their environments, our notion of a new self or a critical ontology is grounded on the human ability to use new social contexts and experiences to reformulate subjectivity. In this context the concept of personal ability becomes a de-essentialized cognition of possibility. No essentialized bounded self can access the cognitive potential offered by epiphanies of difference or triggered by an "insignificant" insight. As we begin to identify previously unperceived patterns in which the self is implicated, the possibility of cognitive change and personal growth is enhanced. As the barriers between mind and multiple contexts are erased, the chance that more expanded forms of "cognitive autopoiesis"—self-constructed modes of higher-order thinking—will emerge is increased. A more textured, a thicker sense of self-production and the nature of self and other is constructed in this process. As we examine the self and its relationship to others in cosmological, epistemological, linguistic, social, cultural, and political contexts, we gain a clearer sense of our purpose in the world especially in relation to justice, interconnectedness, and even love. In these activities we move closer to the macro-processes of life and their micro-expressions in everyday life. A key aspect of the life processes is the understanding of difference that comes from recognition of patterns of interconnectedness. Knowing that an individual from an upper-middle class European background living in a Virginia suburb will be considered culturally bizarre by a group of tribespeople from the Amazon rainforest is a potentially profound learning experience in the domain of the personal. How is the suburbanite viewed as bizarre? What cultural practices are seen as so unusual? What mannerisms are humorous to the tribespeople? What worldviews are baffling to them? The answers to such questions may shock the suburbanite into reorienting her view of her own "normality." The interaction may induce her to ask questions of the way she is perceived by and the way she perceives others. Such a bracketing of the personal may be quite liberating. This interaction with difference could be another example of Maturana and Valera's structural coupling that creates a new relationship with other and with self. In Maturana and Varela's conceptualization a new inner world is created as a result of such coupling (Maturana and Varela, 1987; Varela, 1999; Sumara and Davis, 1997). Such explorations on the ontological frontier hold profound curricular implications. As students pursue rigorous study of diverse global knowledges, they come to understand that the identities of their peer groups and families constitute only a few of countless historical and cultural ways to be human. As they study their self-production in wider biological, sociological, cultural studies, historical, theological, psychological and counter-canonical contexts, they gain insights into their ways of being. As they engage the conflicts that induce diverse knowledge producers to operate in conflicting ways, students become more attuned to the ideological, discursive, and regulatory forces operating in all knowledges. This is not nihilism, as many defenders of the Eurocanon argue; this is the exciting process of exploring the world and the self and their relationship in all of the complexity such study requires. The processual and relational notions of self structurally couple with the socio-cultural context and can only be understood by studying them with these dynamics in mind. These characteristics of self hold profound implications politically, psychologically, and pedagogically. If our notion of the self emerges in its relationship with multiple dimensions of the world, it is by its nature a participatory entity. Such an interactive dynamic is always in process and thus demands a reconceptualization of the concept of individualism and self-interest (Pickering, 1999). The needs of self and others in this context begin to merge, as the concept of self-reliance takes on new meanings. Notions of educational purpose, evaluation, and curriculum development are transformed when these new conceptions of the personal domain come into the picture. In the first decade of the twenty-first century we stand merely on the threshold of the possibilities this notion of selfhood harbors.

## ENACTIVISM AS A WAY OUT: EXPLORING THE POSSIBILITIES

A critical ontology understands that the effort to explain complex cognitive, biological, social, or pedagogical events by the reductionistic study of their components outside of the larger processes of which they are a part will not work. It will not move us to new levels of understanding or set the stage for new, unexplored modes of being human. The social, biological, cognitive, or the curricular domain is not an assortment of discrete objects that can be understood in isolation from one another (Pickering, 1999). The fragmented pieces put forth in such studies do not constitute reality–even if commonsense tells Westerners they do. The deeper structures, the tacit forces, the processes that shape the physical world and the social world will be lost to such observers. As I argue in the introduction to *The Stigma of Genius: Einstein, Consciousness, and Education* (1999), Einstein's General Theory of Relativity could not have been produced without this understanding of connectedness, process, and the limitations of studying only things-in-themselves. For 250 years physicists had been searching for the basic building block of gravity–some contended it was a particle (a graviton), others argued it was a gravity wave. Einstein pointed out that it was neither, that it was not a thing at all. Gravity, he maintained, was a part of the structure of the universe that existed as a relationship connecting mass, space, and time. This insight, of course, changed the very nature of how we conceptualize the universe. It should have changed how we conceptualize epistemology, cognition, pedagogy, and ontology. Of course, it didn't–and that's what we are still working on. The emphasis on studying and teaching about the world as a compilation of fragmented things-in-themselves has returned with a vengeance, of course, in recent educational reforms. In this context the work of Humberto Maturana is instructive. Maturana and Varela's Santiago enactivism employs the same relational concept Einstein's used in the General Theory of Relativity to explain life as a process, a system of interconnections. Indeed, they argue, that the process of cognition is the process of life. In enactivism mind is not a thing-in-itself but a process–an activity where the interactions of a living organism with its environment constitute cognition. In this relationship life itself and cognition are indelibly connected and reveal this interrelationship at diverse levels of living and what are still considered non-living domains. Where mind ends and matter begins is difficult to discern, a situation that operates to overturn the long-standing and problematic Cartesian separation of the two entities. In Maturana's and Varela's conception mind and matter are merely parts of the same process–one cannot exist without the other. A critical ontology seeks to repair this rupture between mind and matter, self and world. In this re-connection we enter into a new phase of human history, new modes of cognition, and dramatic changes in pedagogy. According to the enactivists perception and cognition also operate in contradiction to Cartesianism, as they construct a reality as opposed to reflecting an external one already in existence. The interactive or circular organization of the nervous system described by Maturana is similar to the hermeneutic circle as it employs a conversation between diverse parts of a system to construct meaning. Autopoiesis as the process of self-production is the way living things operate. Self-construction emerges out of a set of relationships between simple parts. In the hermeneutic circle the relationships between parts "self-construct" previously unimagined meanings. Thus, in an ontological context meaning emerges not from the thing-in-itself but from its relationships to an infinite number of other things. In this complexity we understand from another angle that there is no final meaning of anything; meanings are always evolving in light of new relationships, new horizons. Thus, in a critical ontology our power as meaning makers is enhanced. Cognition is the process in which living systems organize the world around them into meaning. With this in mind critical ontology creates a new era of immanence– "what could be" has never implied so much. Specifically, Maturana and Varela argue that our identities do not come with us into the world in some neatly packaged unitary self. Since they "rise and subside" in a series of shifting relationships and patterns, the self can be described using the Buddhist notion that the "self is empty of self-nature." Understanding this, Francisco Varela (1999) maintains, self-understanding and self-change become more possible than ever before. The self, therefore, is not a material entity but takes on more a virtual quality. Human beings have the experience of self, but no self–no central controlling mechanism–is to be found. Much is to be gained by an understanding of the virtual nature of the self. As argued throughout this essay, such knowledge is an important dimension of a critical ontology. According to the enactivists this knowledge helps us develop intelligent awareness–a profound understanding of the construction and the functioning of selfhood. Intelligent awareness is filled with wisdom but devoid of the egocentrism that undermines various notions of critical knowing. In such a context intelligent awareness cannot be separated from ethical insight. Without this ontological understanding many of pedagogies designed to empower will fan the flames of the egocentrism they attempt to overcome. If nothing else a critical ontology cultivates humility without which wisdom is not possible.

## ENACTIVISM AND THE RELATIONAL SELF

From Maturana and Varela's perspective learning takes place when a self-maintaining system develops a more effective relationship with the external features of the system. In this context enactivism is highlighting the profound importance of *relationship* writ large as well as the centrality of the nature and quality of the relationships an organism makes with its environment. In a cognitive context this is an extension of Vygotsky's notion of the zone of proximal development to the ontological realm. In the development of a critical ontology we learn from these ideas that political empowerment vis-à-vis the cultivation of the intellect demand an understanding of the system of relationships that construct our selfhood. In the case of a critical form of curriculum development these relationships always involve students' connections to cultural systems, language, economic concerns, religious belief, social status, and the power dynamics that constitute them. With the benefit of understanding the self-in-relationship teachers gain a new insight into what is happening in any learning situation. Living on the borderline between self and external system and self and other, learning never takes place outside of these relationships (Pickering, 1999). Such knowledge changes our orientation to curriculum development and pedagogy. Thus, a critical ontology is intimately connected to a relational self (Noddings, 1990; Thayer-Bacon, 2000). Humans are ultimately the constructs of relationships, not fragmented monads or abstract individuals. From Varela's perspective this notion of humans as constructs of relationships corresponds precisely to what he is labeling the virtual self. A larger pattern–in the case of humans, consciousness–arises from the interaction of local elements. This larger pattern seems to be driven by a central controlling mechanism that can never be located. Thus, we discern the origin of traditional psychology's dismissal of consciousness as irrelevant. This not only constituted throwing out the baby with the bath water, but discarding the tub, the bathroom fixtures, and the plumbing as well. In this positivistic articulation the process of life and the basis of the cognitive act were deemed unimportant. A critical ontology is always interested in these processes because they open us to a previously occluded insight into the nature of selfhood, of human being. The autopoiesis, the self-making allows humans to perpetually reshape themselves in their new relationships and resulting new patterns of perception and behavior. There is no way to predict the relationships individuals will make and the nature of the self-(re)construction that will ensue. Such uncertainty adds yet another element of complexity to the study of sociology, psychology, and pedagogy, as it simultaneously catalyzes the possibilities of human agency. It causes those enamored with critical ontology yet another reason to study the inadequacies of Cartesian science to account for the intricacies of the human domain. Physical objects *don't necessarily* change their structures via their interaction with other objects. A critical ontology understands that human beings do change their structures as a result of their interactions. As a result the human mind moves light years beyond the lifeless cognitivist computer model of mind–a psychological way of seeing that reduced mental activity to information processing (Lapani, 1998).

The human self-organization process–while profoundly more complex than the World Wide Web–is analogous to the way the Web arranges itself by random and not-so-random connections. The Web is an autopoietic organism that constructs itself in a hypertextual mode of operation. Unanticipated links create new concepts, ways of perceiving, and even ways of being among those that enter into this domain of epistemological emergence. Such experience reminds one that a new cultural logic has developed that transcends the mechanical dimensions of the machine epistemologies and ontologies of the modernist industrial era. Consider the stunning implications that when numerous simple entities possessing simple characteristics are thrown together–whether it be websites on the Internet or individuals' relationships with aspects of their environments–amazing things occur. From such interactions emerge a larger whole that is not guided by a central controlling mechanism. Self-awareness of this process of creation may lead to unanticipated modes of learning and new concepts of human being. Curriculum theorists have no choice; they must deal with these ontological issues.

## REFERENCES

Allen, M. (2000). *Voice of reason*. Retrieved from http://www.curtin.edu.au/learn/unit10846/arrow/vorall.htm
Apple, M. (1999). *Power, meaning and identity: Essays in critical educational studies*. New York: Peter Lang.
Block, A. (1995). *Occupied reading: Critical foundations for an ecological theory*. New York: Garland.
Britzman, D. (1991). *Practice makes practice: A critical study of learning to teach*. Albany, NY: State University of New York Press.
Capra, F. (1996). The web of life: A new scientific understanding of living systems. New York: Anchor Books.
Carson, T. (1997). Reflection and its resistances: Teacher and education as living practice. In T. Carson & D. Sumara (Eds.), *Action research as a living practice*. New York: Peter Lang.
Center for Policy Research (CPRE). (1995). *Dimensions of capacity*. Retrieved from http://www.ed.gov/pubs/CPRE/rb18/rb18b.html
Ferreira, M., & Alexandre, F. (2000). *Education for citizenship: The challenge of teacher education in postmodernity*. Retrieved from http://www.ioe.ac.uk./ccs/conference2000/papers/epsd/ferreiraandalexandre.html
Getzel, G. (1997). *Humanizing the University: An analysis and recommendations*. Retrieved from http://humanism.org/opinions/articles.html
Gordon, M. (2001). Philosophical analysis and standards—philosophical and analytical standards. In J. L. Kincheloe & D. Weil (Eds.), *Standards and schooling in the United States: An Encyclopedia* (Vol. 3). Santa Barbara, CA: ABC-Clio.
Grimmett, P. (1999). Teacher educators as mettlesome mermaids. *International Electronic Journal for Leadership in Learning, 3*, 12. Retrieved from http://www. ucalgary. ca/~iejll
Horn, R. (2000). *Teacher talk: A postformal inquiry into education change*. New York: Peter Lang.
Horn, R. (2001). Texas—A postformal conversation about standardization and accountability in Texas. In J. L. Kincheloe & D. Weil (Eds.), *Standards and schooling in the United States: An encyclopedia* (3 Vols.). Santa Barbara, CA: ABC-Clio.
Kincheloe, J. L. (1993). *Toward a critical politics of teacher thinking: Mapping the postmodern*. Westport, CT: Bergin and Garvey.
Kincheloe, J. L., & Steinberg S. R. (1997). *Changing multiculturalism*. London: Open University Press.
Kincheloe, J. L., Steinberg, S. R., & Tippins, D. J. (1999). *The stigma of genius: Einstein, consciousness, and education*. New York: Peter Lang.
Kincheloe, J. L. & Weil, D. (Eds.). (2001). *Standards and schooling in the United States: An Encyclopedia* (3 Vols.). Santa Barbara, CA: ABC-Clio.
Lepani, B. (1998). *Information literacy: The challenge of the digital age*. Retrieved from http://www.acal.edu.au/lepani.htm
Macedo, D. (1994). *Literacies of power: What Americans are not allowed to know*. Boulder, CO: Westview Press.
Malewski, E. (2001a). Administration—Administrative leadership and public consciousness: discourse matters in the struggle for new standards. In J. L. Kincheloe & D. Weil (Eds.), *Standards and Schooling in the United States* (3 Vols.). Santa Barbara, CA: ABC-Clio.
Malewski, E. (2001b). Queer sexuality—The trouble with knowing: Standards of complexity and sexual orientations. In J. Kincheloe & D. Weil (Eds.), *Standards and schooling in the United States: An Encyclopedia*. Santa Barbara, CA: ABC-Clio.

Maturana, H., & Varela, F. (1987). *The tree of knowledge*. Boston: Shambhala.
Morris, M., Doll, M., & Pinar, W. (1999). *How we work*. New York: Peter Lang.
Noddings, N. (1990). Review symposium: A response. *Hypatia, 5*(1), 120–126.
O'Sullivan, E. (1999). *Transformative learning: Educational vision for the 21st century*. London: Zed.
Pickering, J. (1999). The self is a semiotic process. *Journal of Consciousness Studies, 6*(4), 31–47.
Segall, A. (2002). *Disturbing practice: Reading teacher education as text*. New York: Peter Lang.
Semali, L., & J. L. Kincheloe (1999). *What is indigenous knowledge? Voices from the academy*. New York: Falmer.
Soto, L. (2001). Bilingual Education—Silenced lives: The case of bilingual children. In J. L. Kincheloe & D. Weil (Eds.), *Standards and schooling in the united states* (3 Vols.). Santa Barbara, CA: ABC-Clio.
Steinberg, S. R. (2001). *Multi/intercultural conversations: A reader*. New York: Peter Lang.
Sumara, D., & Davis, B. (1997). Cognition, complexity, and teacher education. *Harvard Educational Review, 67*(1), 75–104.
Thayer-Bacon, B. (2000). *Transforming critical thinking: Thinking constructively*. New York: Teachers College Press.
Varela, F. (1999). *Ethical know-how: Action, wisdom, and cognition*. Stanford, CA: Stanford University Press.
Wexler, P. (2000). *The mystical society: Revitalization in culture, theory, and education*. Boulder, CO: Westview.

Reprinted with permission: Kincheloe, J. L. (2003). Critical ontology: visions of selfhood and curriculum. *Journal of Curriculum Theorizing, 19*(1), 47–64.

ELIZABETH J. MEYER

# CRITICAL ONTOLOGY AND TEACHER AGENCY

POSTFORMAL AUTOBIOGRAPHY AND ITS IMPACTS ON
RESEARCH AND PRACTICE

Know Thyself γνῶθι σεαυτόν *gnōthi seauton* (Temple of Apollo at Delphi)

The critical ontology of ourselves has to be considered not, certainly, as a theory, a doctrine, nor even a permanent body of knowledge that is accumulating; it has to be conceived as an attitude, an ethos, a philosophical life in which the critique of what we are is at one and the same time the historical analysis of the limits that are imposed on us and an experiment [*épreuve*] of their possible transcendence [*de leur franchissement possible*]. (Foucault, 1987, p. 174)

In light of a critical knowledge of power, we are pursuing a key dimension of critical ontology – a way of being that is aware of the ways power shapes us, the ways we see the world, and the ways we perceive our role as teachers (Kincheloe, 2003, p. 53).

Joe Kincheloe's 2003 article, "Critical Ontology: Visions of Selfhood and Curriculum," in the *Journal of Curriculum Theorizing*, argues for the importance of understanding identity construction in teacher education and, in so doing, advances a notion of critical ontology for teachers and teacher educators. He wrote, "Too infrequently are teachers in university, student teaching, or in-service professional education encouraged to confront why they think as they do about themselves as teachers – especially in relation to the social, cultural, political, economic, and historical world around them" (p. 47). This notion of critical ontology is more deeply philosophical and political than the more commonly used terms: self-study or autoethnography. As such, critical ontology demands a deeper engagement with philosophical questions about the self as well as a more focused attention on the socio-historical situatedness of the individual. Such ontological investigations require an examination of how power intersects with the ways educators make meaning of ourselves and the contexts in which our teaching and our identities are embedded. In this essay, I will discuss the key ideas advanced in Kincheloe's *JCT* article, how they relate to other similar schools of thought including self-study of teacher education and Pinar's *currere*. I will conclude with a discussion of how this article has shaped my own interpretations and applications of Joe's work in postformalism and critical pedagogy.

The concept of self-study, or deeply reflecting on one's experiences, ideas, and beliefs is not a new one. Socrates declared "the unexamined life is not worth living," and most proponents of forms of self-study can trace the roots of their philosophy to this ancient statement. More recently it has been popularized in the work of Parker Palmer in his book, *The Courage to Teach: Exploring the inner landscape of a teacher's life* (1998). In the first chapter of this book he writes, "teaching holds a mirror to the soul. If I am willing to look in that mirror and not run from what I see, I have a chance to gain self-knowledge – and knowing myself is as crucial to good teaching as knowing my students and my subject" (p. 2). However, much of the discourse around self-study and teachers doesn't challenge formal ways of understanding the self, nor does it address the key tenets of the critical ontology Kincheloe outlined in his article.

## KINCHELOE'S *CRITICAL ONTOLOGY*

As noted above, Kincheloe was not the first to argue for a greater emphasis on understanding oneself and one's ongoing evolution in the process of becoming a teacher; however his critical, historical, and philosophical approaches to making sense of the world distinguish his approach to self-study. He is best known for his work in postformalism (Kincheloe, & Steinberg, 1993) and contributions to the field of critical pedagogy (Kincheloe, 2005b) including the establishment of the Paulo and Nita Freire International Project for Critical Pedagogy (www.freireproject.org). Critical pedagogy is often critiqued for being dominated by white male scholars who often ignore or misrepresent issues related to race, gender, and sexuality in their work (Ellsworth, 1989; Tan, 2008). However, in Joe's writing and publications, he explicitly includes discussion of and works by scholars in the fields of: critical multiculturalism, critical race theory, post-structural feminism, indigenous knowledges, and queer theory. He explains the importance of exposing the impacts of colonial White male heterosexual hegemony on teacher education by asserting that, "the rigorous study of cultural and historical context alerts prospective teachers to the ways dominant myths, behaviour, and language shape their view of the teacher role and the curriculum without conscious filtering" (Kincheloe, 2003 #1864) (p. 52).

In his article, Joe identifies 23 basic ideas that clarify his proposed notion of critical ontology. I've made an attempt to distil this long and complex list of demands into the five categories of thought and action based on the five aspects of "Postformal Intrapersonal Intelligence" Kincheloe advanced in an earlier piece (1998, pp. 137–141) which include:

1. Meta-consciousness-expanding the capacity for self-reflection and the analysis of identity formation (#1–4, 17, 18, 20)
2. Transcendence of ego-centrism- the difficult journey outward (#6, 12, 22, 23)
3. The creation of integrated knowledge- understanding ourselves in relation to the way we make sense of the world, integrating personal knowledge into secular knowledge and vice versa (#8, 10, 14, 15, 16)
4. Recognition of non-hierarchical difference - connecting intrapersonal development with an understanding of other individuals (#5, 7, 9, 11, 13)
5. Developing self-reliance in the transcendence of authority dependence- confronting the culture of ethical and political passivity (#19, 21, 22)

Each of these five overarching categories is embedded in the theoretical approaches that Kincheloe identifies as providing the foundation for critical ontology: complexity theory, enactivism, critical theory, critique of Cartesianism, and poststructural feminist analysis. In his deeper excavation of the concept of critical ontology, he relies heavily on Maturana and Varela's concept of enactivism which he explains as the "concept that living things constantly remake themselves in interaction with their environments" (Kincheloe, 2003, p. 58), and this demonstrates the importance of recognizing our interconnectedness in constructing a "new inner world." Enactivism is related to critiques of Cartesianism by situating the self as the author of one's reality as opposed to "reflecting an external one already in existence" (Kincheloe, 2003, p. 61). Kincheloe explains that "Cartesianism has separated individuals from their inanimate surroundings, undermining any organic interconnection of the person to the cosmos...human beings lost their belongingness to both the world and to other people around them" (p. 49). Enactivism cultivates a sense of self that is deeply connected to others and thus requires a transcendence of ego-centrism that allows a deeper humility to develop, "without which wisdom is not possible" (p. 61). This complex, critical, and philosophical approach to self-study is different on many levels from other theorists who have also addressed the importance of self-study in teacher education.

## SELF-STUDY OF TEACHING PRACTICES (S-STEP)

In their book, *Self-study of teaching practices*, Samaras and Freese provide an introduction to and overview of the discipline from their perspectives. This primer explains that personal history self-study is "the study of the influence of one's culture, context, and history on one's teaching practices" (Samaras, & Freese, 2006, p. 7). The group of researchers that have built this self-study school of practice emerged in the early 1990s and is formally marked by the creation of the S-STEP Special Interest Group created at the 1993 Annual Meeting of the American Educational Research Association (p. 33).

Samaras and Freese identify three main purposes of teacher self-study: personal renewal, professional renewal, and program renewal (2006, p. 14). They also name three research paradigms which influence self-study: teacher inquiry, action research, and reflective practice (2006, p. 25). According to these authors, education-related life history is "a self-study activity that involves reflection on critical or nodal moments in one's learning past that may help to inform one's teaching" (Samaras, & Freese, 2006, p. 8). The work of the scholars in this SIG seems to focus primarily on examining one's behaviours in the classroom and less on the critical and philosophical questions that critical ontology makes central. Self-study is defined in their text as: "teachers' systematic and critical examination of their actions and their context as a path to develop a more consciously driven mode of professional activity" (Samaras, & Freese, 2006, p. 11).

This text provides a lengthy list of books and articles in its references, however it does not mention the *JCT* article, but briefly refers to one of Joe's earlier (1991) works: *Teachers as researchers: Qualitative inquiry as a path to empowerment.* They reference the epistemological concept he advances: that there is no knowledge without the knower, but do not explore this concept in-depth or interrogate their own conceptions of self-study through this deeper epistemological question (Samaras, & Freese, 2006, p. 44). Researchers who align themselves with the S-STEP approach to understanding the self and its impacts on the teaching act differ significantly from Kincheloe's notion of *critical ontology* in two important ways. First, although they acknowledge social and cultural influences and the impacts they have on the development of how an individual makes sense of their world, they don't explicitly examine the influence of hegemony: the roles that dominant discourses and systems of power play in shaping our understanding of and our relationships in this world. Second, since the methods described by S-STEP scholars don't include an analysis of power, there is little talk about agency and educators' roles in working to create an educational and social context that is more equitable and just. Examples of self-study projects presented in this primer focus more on micro-level changes to an individual's teaching practice such as classroom management and assessment strategies as opposed to macro-structural changes in how knowledge is constructed, or meta-conscious changes in how one understands teaching and learning and the way teachers and students make sense of themselves and their world (Samaras, & Freese, 2006). A second related approach to developing an understanding of the self that is more closely aligned with Kincheloe's critical ontology is William Pinar's *currere*.

## PINAR'S *CURRERE*

In an earlier piece discussing Pinar's notion of *currere*, Joe advanced some ideas that he builds on in greater detail in the *JCT* article and others (Kincheloe, 2005a, 2006, 2008). He wrote, "Pinar, through *currere* is asking us to become action researchers of ourselves. Teachers and students begin to systematically analyze how socio-political distortions have tacitly worked to shape their world views, perspectives on education, and self-images" (Kincheloe, 1998, p. 133). Kincheloe refers to *currere* as a form of postformal autobiography because it "involves individuals' attempts to disengage themselves from socio-interpersonal norms and ideological expectations" (2005a, p. 3; Kincheloe, & Steinberg, 1993). *Currere* is the latin root-word for curriculum which means "running the race course" and indicates ongoing activity and engagement. Pinar describes it as "a method focused on self-understanding" that is based in methodology borrowed from African-American autobiography (Pinar, 2004, pp. 4–5). Kincheloe builds on this definition by explaining that it "concerns the investigation of the nature of the individual experience of the public" and that this allows us to "loosen our identification with the contents of consciousness so that we can gain some distance from them. From our new vantage point we may be able to see those psychic realms that are formed by conditioning and unconscious adherence to social convention" (Kincheloe, 1998, p. 129). It is this psychic distancing from our constructed knowledge systems that allows for a more critical level of analysis and understanding as it takes the socio-historical context of our lives and experiences into consideration.

In a later essay, Kincheloe more explicitly acknowledges the influence of *currere* on his work by stating, "any notion of postformal autobiography is indebted to William Pinar's notion of *currere*" (Kincheloe, 2005a, p. 5). This action research method that has been introduced and refined through Pinar's work and writing explicitly asks educators to examine power relations and their impacts on our positionalities and perspectives on how we make meaning of ourselves and our world. Pinar acknowledged that this work is difficult yet pedagogically very important by explaining, "for heterosexually identified white men, finding the seams, discovering the traces of rejected fragments, and creating interior spaces may well prove pedagogically useful, potentially self-shattering" (Pinar, 2004, p. 51). The links between critical ontology and *currere* as a postformal autobiographical method are made clear in the following statement:

> Thinking about thinking in postformalism induces students to deconstruct their personal constructions of the purpose of their schooling...As a culture, we have little idea how our identities are shaped by power relations and the impact of such a process on how we define intelligence. Postformal thinking about thinking appropriates *currere's* ideological disembedding, pushing cognition into the complexity of self-production. Transcending Piagetian formalism with its disembodied abstraction and its concern for disinterested procedure, postformal thinking about thinking encourages a running meta-dialogue, a constant conversation with self. (Kincheloe, 1998, p. 132)

It is clear that the links between *currere* and critical ontology are strong and that these two important educational theorists were able to refine and deepen their explanations of their approaches to self-understanding through this ongoing dialogue with each other. My own work has been heavily influenced by both of these scholars as well, and I will now discuss the impacts of critical ontology in the context of my own research in teacher identity and activism.

## IMPACTS OF CRTICIAL ONTOLOGY

Engaging with this piece of Joe Kincheloe's work has encouraged me to revisit previous work I have done on self-study (Meyer, 2008b) and teacher identity (Meyer, 2008a, 2008c, 2009). It is appropriate that my first published autobiographical project was written for an edited collection of graduate student reflections on our individual journeys towards engaging with critical discourses. The book project was edited by one of Kincheloe's graduate students and emerged from one of their many philosophical conversations. The reflection I did in my chapter, "I am (not) a feminist: Unplugging from the heterosexual matrix" was an exercise in critical ontology. I was able to write creatively and with emotion about the deep learning that occurred from my first-hand experiences with privilege and oppression, discrimination and injustice, and how these experiences shaped my personal and professional identities. I used an ongoing metaphor from the film *The Matrix* to illustrate the deconstruction and reconstruction of how I made sense of the world around me. I concluded my piece with a call to action for social justice activism:

> It was my loss of heterosexual privilege that forced me to swallow the red pill and build a new understanding of the world. This is the language and the strength that critical theory has given me. I hope the story of my queer journey may help others to 'unplug' and work against oppression in all its forms. Follow the white rabbit (Meyer, 2008b, p. 42).

The explicit recognition of privilege and power relations linked with a call to action directly relates to several of Kincheloe's 23 basic tenets of critical ontology including: 5, 6, 7, 9, 18, and 22. The metaphor from *The Matrix* helps illustrate the concept of #18 that "the ontological process of cognition constructs the world rather than reflecting an external world already in existence" (p. 48). My closing challenge to "follow the white rabbit" encourages others to explore their agency as #22 states: "to appreciate that political empowerment, community-building, and the cultivation of both the individual and collective intellect require a constant monitoring of the relationships that shape us" (p. 48).

This exercise has also encouraged me to reconsider a theoretical model I developed to explain and illustrate the influences on teacher behaviours and agency that related to their own identities and school contexts (Meyer, 2007, 2008a). Upon rereading Kincheloe's article, I realized there was an essential element lacking from this model: the broader socio-historical context in which the teacher's life experiences and school culture were embedded. This revised diagram (Fig 1.1), gives an overview of the various factors that shape teacher agency. In the context of my research I was examining teachers' perceptions of and responses to forms of gendered harassment (sexual, sexual orientation, and gender non-conformity).

In my work with eight secondary teachers, I developed a model that shows how the external influences are filtered through each teacher's internal influences, like water poured through a coffee filter. The data indicated that both external and internal influences present *barriers* (in grey) and *motivators* (in white) to teachers' interventions. These influences vary based on teachers' identities and experiences

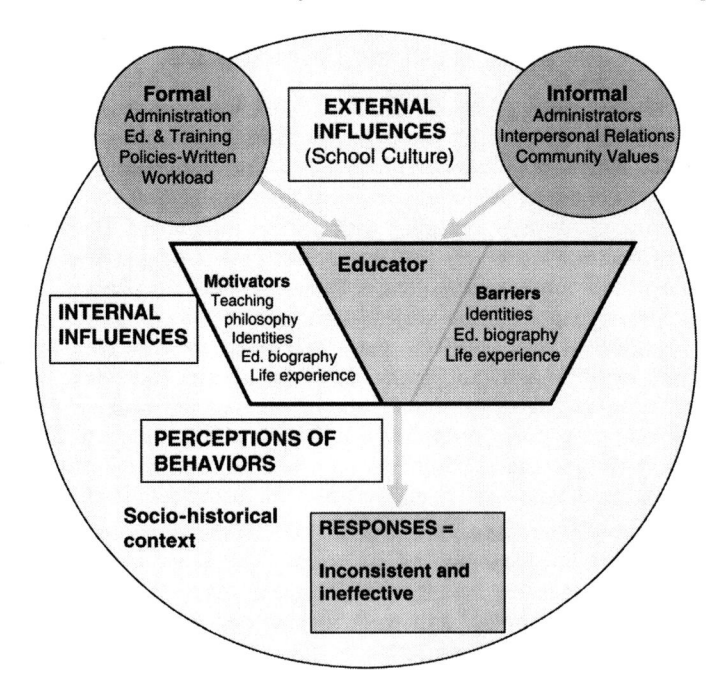

*Fig 1.1. Factors influencing teachers' critical ontological agency.*

in their school cultures, but in all cases in my study, the barriers outweigh the motivators for intervention. It was as if teachers' eyes are covered by institutional and social barriers that tell them not to see gendered harassment and not to intervene. However, their internal motivators often encourage them to see and to act in spite of these strong external barriers. This imbalance creates a constant struggle for the teachers who are trying to take action to challenge sexism, transphobia, and homophobia in their classrooms and schools. The spotted circle in the back of the diagram labelled "socio-historical influences" is what I added while working on this essay. I reflected on my findings and recognized that although I discussed the role of culture and life experience in shaping teachers' identities and school cultures, I hadn't effectively presented it in the visual representation of the theoretical model. I continue to be grateful to Joe Kincheloe for the insights his writings offer and the ways they allow me to continue reflecting on and improving my own work.

## CONCLUSION

Joe Kincheloe's critical ontology demands a deep level of engagement with one's self and community. This engagement goes beyond the self-reflection and "navel gazing" that some critics of self-study pronounce. The layer of empowerment, action, and human agency that Kincheloe writes about is an important distinguishing feature of this philosophy. He emphasizes that, "Critical ontology is obsessed with new and better ways of being human, being with others, and the creation of environments where mutual growth of individuals is promoted and symbiotic learning relationships are cultivated" (Kincheloe, 2003, p. 54). May we all be moved to new ways of conceptualizing ourselves and our relationships with others and be filled with the humility that made Kincheloe's work so authentic and powerful. If we are to take up the project of investing in educational research and teacher development activities that aim to make the world a more loving, humane and socially just place, then we must find new ways to understand and transform ourselves and our work. As Kincheloe so eloquently reminds us "thinking in new ways always necessitates personal transformation; indeed if enough people think in new ways, social transformation is inevitable" (Kincheloe, 2003, p. 56).

## REFERENCES

Ellsworth, E. (1989). Why doesn't this feel empowering?: Working through the repressive myths of critical pedagogy. *Harvard Educational Review*, Fall.
Foucault, M. (1987). What is enlightenment? In P. Rabinow & W. Sullivan (Eds.), *Interpretive social science: A second look* (pp. 157–174). Berkeley, CA: University of California Press.
Kincheloe, J. L. (1991). *Teachers as researchers: Qualitative inquiry as a path to empowerment*. London: Falmer Press.
Kincheloe, J. L. (1998). Pinar's Currere and identity in hyperreality: Grounding the postformal notion of intrapersonal intelligence. In W. F. Pinar (Ed.), *Curriculum: Towards new identities* (pp. 129–142). New York: Taylor and Francis.
Kincheloe, J. L. (2003). Critical ontology: Visions of selfhood and curriculum. *Journal of Curriculum Theorizing*, *19*(1), 47–64.

Kincheloe, J. L. (2005a). Autobiography and critical ontology: Being a teacher, developing a reflective persona. In W. M. Roth (Ed.), *Auto/Biography and Auto/Ethnography: Praxis of research method*. Rotterdam: Sense Publishers.

Kincheloe, J. L. (2005b). *Critical pedagogy*. New York: Peter Lang.

Kincheloe, J. L. (2006). Critical ontology and indigenous ways of being: Forging a postcolonial curriculum. In Y. Kanu (Ed.), *Curriculum as cultural practice: Postcolonial imaginations*. Toronto: Curriculum as Cultural Practice: Postcolonial Imaginations.

Kincheloe, J. L. (2008). An introduction to IJCP. *The International Journal of Critical Pedagogy, 1*(3), 3.

Kincheloe, J. L., & Steinberg S. R. (1993). A tentative description of postformal thinking: The critical confrontation with cognitive theory. *Harvard Educational Review, 63*(3), 296–320.

Meyer, E. J. (2007). *Gendered harassment in secondary schools: Understanding teachers' perceptions of and responses to the problem*. Unpublished doctoral dissertation, McGill University, Montreal, QC, Canada.

Meyer, E. J. (2008a). Gendered harassment in secondary schools: Understanding teachers' (non)interventions. *Gender, & Education, 20*(6), 555–572.

Meyer, E. J. (2008b). I am (not) a feminist: Unplugging from the heterosexual matrix. In A. H. Churchill (Ed.), *Rocking your world: The emotional journey into critical discourses* (pp. 35–44). Rotterdam, The Netherlands: Sense Publishers.

Meyer, E. J. (2008c). Who we are matters: Exploring teacher identities through found poetry. *LEARNing Landscapes, 1*(3), 195–210.

Meyer, E. J. (2009). *Gender, bullying, and harassment: Strategies to end sexism and homophobia in schools*. New York: Teachers College Press.

Palmer, P. (1998). *The courage to teach: Exploring the inner landscape of a teacher's life*. San Francisco: Jossey-Bass Publishers.

Pinar, W. F. (2004). *What is curriculum theory?* Mahwah, NJ: Lawrence Erlbaum and Associates.

Samaras, A. P., & Freese, A. R. (2006). *Self-study of teaching practices*. New York: Peter Lang.

Tan, E. (2008). Critical pedagogy and the great white hope dilemma. In A. H. Churchill (Ed.), *Rocking your world: The emotional journey into critical discourses* (pp. 147–156). Rotterdam, The Netherlands: Sense Publishers.

*Joe's ability to engage in a conversation with scholars, students, and teachers was unique. He understood the importance of creating an accessible teacher discourse without sacrificing the essential language of rigor. Indeed, in the past fifteen years, he chose to write in a style, which reinforced the need for rigor in critical studies. Bouncing against the faux arguments against critical pedagogy and critical theory, Joe's work recalled the essential elements within Freire's and Giroux's work: that teachers are political beings, that schooling is political, and that teachers as cultural workers must recognize and declare themselves as change agents. His own work in New York City informed him at an educational crossroads which began with Reagan-inspired Back to Basics schooling, fascist Giuliani anti-intellectualism, and Bush Daddy's 2000 vision. SS*

JOE L. KINCHELOE

# 10. THE KNOWLEDGES OF TEACHER EDUCATION

*Developing a Critical Complex Epistemology*

The first decade of the twenty-first century is an exciting and frightening time for supporters of a rigorous, practical, socially just, and democratic teacher education. It is a time of dangerous efforts to destroy teacher education and of brilliant attempts to reform it. A sense of urgency permeates discussions of the topic, as studies indicate that presently there is a need for more teachers in a shorter timeframe than ever before in U.S. history. About 1,025 teacher education programs graduate around 100,000 new teachers annually. The problem is that over the next few years 2 million teachers are needed in U.S. elementary and secondary schools. Many analysts argue that the problem will be solved by lowering standards for teacher certification or simply doing away with the certification process and admitting any one who breathes regularly into the teaching ranks (U.S. Department of Education, 1998). Such capitulation to short-term needs would be tragic.

I wish I had a dollar for every time someone in higher education or the professions reacted condescendingly upon learning that the individual with whom they were conversing was a professor of teacher education or pedagogy. Understanding the history of teacher education, one is provided with plenty of reasons to look at the domain askance—but not any more than other elements of higher/professional education. Too often the condescension toward teacher education and teacher educators is harbored for all the wrong reasons. Contempt for teacher education and pedagogy emanates not from knowledge of their historical failures but from a generic devaluing of the art and science of teaching as an unnecessary contrivance.

*k. hayes et al., (eds.), Key Work in Critical Pedagogy: Joe L. Kincheloe, 227–243.*
*© 2011 Sense Publishers. All rights reserved.*

"As long as one knows her subject matter," the clichéd argument goes, "she doesn't need anything else to teach." Anyone who makes such an assertion should be mandated to teach the fourth grade for six weeks. Such a crash immersion may induce a reconsideration of the platitude, as the complexity of doing such a job well becomes apparent.

Indeed, the complexity of the pedagogical process and the intricacies of a rigorous teacher education are central concerns of this article. What is a critical complex teacher education? What types of knowledges should professional educators possess? In a climate as hostile as the first decade of the twenty-first century the ability of teacher educators to articulate a case for particular knowledges is not merely important, it may just be a survival skill. In its devaluation, pedagogy has been rendered invisible in many higher educational settings. Teacher educators, teachers, and teacher education students must not only understand the complexity of good teaching, but stand ready to make this known to political leaders and the general population. If we are not successful in such a political effort, we will witness the death of the scholarly conception of teacher education to the degree it now exists. While such articulations of teacher education are not dominant, many scholarly, rigorous, and democratic teacher education programs exist and produce excellent teachers. At the same time in countless mediocre programs great teacher educators ply their trade in unfavorable conditions, turning out good teachers despite the circumstances.

## THE CRITICAL COMPLEX VISION: TEACHERS AS SCHOLARS AND POLICY MAKERS

The vision on which this essay is grounded involves the empowerment of teachers in an era where teacher professionalism is under assault. I want universities to produce rigorously educated teachers with an awareness of the complexities of educational practice and an understanding of and commitment to a socially just, democratic notion of schooling. Only with a solid foundation in various mainstream and alternative canons of knowledge can they begin to make wise judgments and informed choices abut curriculum development and classroom practice. In this context they can craft a teacher persona that enables them to diagnose individual and collective needs of their students and connect them to their pedagogical strategies and goals. It is naïve and dangerous to think that teachers can become the rigorous professionals envisioned here without a conceptual understanding of contemporary and past societies and the socio-cultural, political, and economic forces that have shaped them. Such knowledges are essential in the process of both understanding and connecting the cultural landscape of the twenty-first century to questions of educational purpose and practice (Bruner, 1997; Ferreira, & Alexandre, 2000; Horn, & Kincheloe, 2001; McGuire, 1996; McNeil, 2000).

Few seem to understand the demands of high-quality teaching of a critical democratic variety in the twenty-first century. After listening, for example, to former mayor of New York, Rudolph Guiliani and other high ranking city officials chastise and degrade New York City teachers over the last decade, I understand the anger

## THE KNOWLEDGES OF TEACHER EDUCATION

and cynicism these teachers harbor as they open their classroom doors to start the day. The emotional complexity of their lives haunts me as I engage them in rigorous graduate school analyses of the various knowledges demanded by the critical complex vision. "Why learn this," they sometimes ask me, "when the system won't let us apply it in our deskilled classrooms?" This is a tough question. I struggle for the right words, for inspirational words to let them know the value of the vision. Literally, there is little hope for educational reform if they do not gain detailed insight into:
– the context in which education takes place;
– the historical forces that have shaped the purposes of schooling;
– the ways dominant power uses schools for anti-democratic ideological self interest;
– how all of this relates to the effort to develop a democratic, transformative pedagogy;
– the specific ways all of these knowledges relate to transformative classroom teaching in general and to their particular curricular domain in particular.

Only with these and similar insights and skills can teachers build rigorous communities of practice (Edwards, 2000) that empower them to develop more compelling ways of teaching and conceptualizing pedagogy. And just as importantly, in these communities of practice they can mobilize the political power to educate the public about the nature of a rigorous, democratic education and the types of resources and citizen action that are necessary to making it a reality. Given the political context of the twenty-first century with its "reeducated" public and corporatized information environment, the friends of democracy and education have no other choice. Thus, critical complex teaching involves teachers as knowledge producers, knowledge workers who pursue their own intellectual development.

At the same time such teachers work together in their communities of practice to sophisticate both the profession and the public's appreciation of what it means to be an educated person. They ask how schools can work to ensure that students from all possible backgrounds achieve this goal (Bereiter, 2002; Horn, 2000; Smyth, 2001; Steinberg, 2001). In this context, such educators engage the public in developing more sophisticated responses to questions such as:
– What does it mean "to know" something?
– What is involved in the process of understanding?
– What are the moral responsibilities of understanding?
– What does it mean to act on one's knowledge and understanding in the world?
– How do we assess when individuals have engaged these processes in a rigorous way?

Teachers as scholars demand respect as they engage diverse groups in these and other questions about education in a democratic society. They alert individuals to the demands of democratic citizenship that require the lifelong pursuit of learning. In such a context no teacher, no concerned citizen is ever fully educated; they are always "in process," waiting for the next learning experience. As they claim and occupy such an important socio-political role, critical complex teachers dismantle the Berlin wall that separates educational policy form practice. Those who make educational policy almost never engage in classroom practice. These policy makers, especially in the recent standards reforms, have in many cases completely disregarded the expertise and concerns of classroom teachers and imposed the most specific modes of instructional practice on them (Elmore, 1997; Schubert, 1998). This type of imposition is unacceptable. Teachers in a democratic society have to play a role in the formulation of professional practice, educating the public, and educational policymaking.

## CATEGORIZING THE MULTIPLE FORMS OF PEDAGOGICAL KNOWLEDGE: DEVELOPING A META-EPISTEMOLOGICAL PERSPECTIVE

We are asking teachers and teacher education students to gain complex understandings not previously demanded of educational practitioners. What follows is a delineation of the types of knowledges required in a critical complex teacher education. This delineation is conceptually wrapped in what might be called a meta-epistemological package that grounds many of the categories of knowledges teachers need to know. A meta-epistemological perspective is a central understanding in a critical complex conception of teacher professionalism (Strom, 2000). Simply put, such an insight helps us approach the contested concept of a "knowledge base for education." In our meta-epistemological construction, the educational knowledge base involves the recognition of different types of knowledges of education including but not limited to empirical, experiential, normative, critical, ontological, and reflective-synthetic domains.

Such an assertion challenges more traditional and technical forms of teacher education that conceptualized teaching as a set of skills—not a body of knowledges. Thus, in the framework promoted here, teaching before it is anything else is epistemological—a concept that wreaks havoc in the pedagogical world. As an epistemological dynamic, teaching, as Hugh Munby and Tom Russell (1996) contend, "depends on, is grounded in, and constitutes knowledge" (p. 75). If the teaching profession doesn't grasp and embrace this understanding, as well as the different types of knowledge associated with teaching and the diverse ways they are taught and learned, teacher education will continue to be epistemologically bankrupt and viewed as an Philistine vocation. In the meta-epistemological domain critical complex teacher educators avoid this Philistinism by analyzing the epistemological and other types of tacit assumptions embedded in and shaping particular articulations of practice.

## EMPIRICAL KNOWLEDGE ABOUT EDUCATION

Empirical knowledge comes from research based on data derived from sense data/ observations of various aspects of education. Throughout my scholarship I have expressed reservations about the positivist version of empirical knowledge and its uses—but not about the concept of empirical knowledge itself. A critical complex teacher education demands more sophisticated forms of sense observational knowledges of education. A thicker, more complex, more textured, selfconscious form of empirical knowledge takes into account the situatedness of the researcher and the researched—where they are standing or are placed in the social, cultural, historical, philosophical, economic, political, and psychological web of reality. Such insight respects the complexity of the interpretive dimension of empirical knowledge production.

A critical complex, empiricism understands that there may be many interpretations of the observations made and the data collected, that different researchers depending on their relative situatedness may see very different phenomena in a study of the same classroom. Power dynamics such as ideological orientation, discursive embeddedness, disciplinary experience, ad infinitum may shape the research lenses of various researchers in diverse and even contradictory ways (Kincheloe, 2003). Once we understand these dynamics we can never be naïve researchers again. Empirical knowledge about education enters into an even more complex realm when educators ask what it tells them about practice. Since such knowledge has such a complex interaction with and multidimensional relationship to practice, there will always be diverse articulations of its practical implications. Too many teacher educators have not understood these dynamics.

A critical complex empiricism understands that knowledge about humans and their social practices is fragmented, diverse, and always constructed by human beings coming from different contexts. Such a form of knowledge does not lend itself to propositional statements—i.e., final truths. Indeed, a critical complex empirical knowledge does not seek validation by reference to universal truths. Rather it remains somewhat elusive, resistant to the trap of stable and consistent meaning. The way it is understood will always involve the interaction between our general conceptions of it and its relationship with ever-changing contexts. Thus, our conception of empirical knowledge is more dialectical than propositional. Simply put, there is not one single answer to any research question and no one question is superior to all others. Particular empirical descriptions will always conflict with others, tensions between accounts will persist, and alternative perspectives will continue to struggle for acceptance. As Elvis might have put it, "Man, you better believe this stuff is complicated." The technical rationality of positivism failed to heed Elvis's warning. In this articulation of the empirical project there was nothing too complex about educational knowledge production and its role in teacher education: researchers defined educational problems and solved them by rigorous fidelity to the scientific method.

These solutions were passed along to practitioners who put them into practice. A critical complex empiricism avoids this technical rationality and the certainty that accompanies it. It never prescribes precise content and validated instructional techniques for teachers' use. In the critical complex perspective there is no certain knowledge about:
− what subject matter to teach;
− the proper way to develop a curriculum;
− the correct understanding of students;
− the right way to teach. (Center for Policy Research in Education (CPRE), 1995; Pozzuto, Angell, & Pierpont, 2000; Report of Undergraduate Teacher Education Program, 1997). The relationship between such knowledge and practice in its complexity is always open to discussion and interpretation.

In this discussion a critical complex empiricism refuses to undermine other types of educational knowledges and exclude them from the process. For example, the experiential knowledge teachers derive from teaching is deemed very important in this context. Traditional positivist perspectives created a chasm between empirical knowledge and experience, as they excluded teachers from the knowledge production dimension of the profession. The concept of great teachers as virtuosos who produce brilliant pieces of pedagogical performance/knowledge was alien to the positivist conception of empirical knowledge about education. In a positivist context teachers were expected to follow empirical imperatives, not to produce masterpieces (Britzman, 1991; Horn, 2000; Segall, 2002). If teachers don't belong at the conference table of knowledge production in education, then the table deserves to be dismantled.

Critical, complex empirical knowledge about education avoids the positivist tendency to represent itself as a distinct, autonomous object—a thing-in-itself. Here critical, complex knowledge always acknowledges the contexts of its production and interpretation. Valuing the relationships that connect various knowledges, researchers in the complex domain ask how education experience is constructed and educational meaning is made (Cannella, & Kincheloe, 2002; Day, 1996; Denzin, & Lincoln, 2000). In such explorations they walk through a star gate into a more pragmatic dimension of empirical research. Understanding the contexts of knowledge production and the nature of its relation to practice, critical complex educational researchers study the half-life of their data in terms of its implementation.

How could it be used to improve education? How is educational improvement defined? Did it promote professional awareness? How does professional experience relate to practice? Within such analyses, reflections, and inquiries a new dawn breaks for the role of empirical knowledge in education.

## NORMATIVE KNOWLEDGE ABOUT EDUCATION

Normative knowledge concerns "what should be" in relation to moral and ethical issues about education. What constitutes moral and ethical behavior on the part of teacher educators and teachers? How do we develop a vision of practice that will empower educators to embrace these behaviors without fear of reprisals? Such questions began the theoretical work necessary to the development of a democratic, egalitarian sense of educational purpose. Such normative knowledge is central to the effort to establish just and rigorous colleges/schools/departments of education and schools of various kinds. Such knowledge is not produced arbitrarily but in relation to particular social visions, power relations, and cultural/historical contexts. With these concerns in mind we ask questions about the nature of education, the role of schools in a democratic society, and the philosophical issues raised in this process.

The "critical" in our critical complex teacher education is directly related to normative knowledge. Critical theorists such as Max Horkheimer, Theodor Adorno, and Herbert Marcuse directly addressed this normative dimension when they wrote about the concept of "eminent critique." Moral and ethical action, they argued, cannot take place until one can envision a more desirable state of affairs, alternatives to injustice. In this context, they argued, any domain of study is ethically required to examine not only "what is" but also "what could be"—the notion of eminence. In critical pedagogy—the educational articulation of critical theory buoyed by the work of feminist theorists and Brazilian educator, Paulo Freire—advocates have confronted the positivistic, decontextualized, and depoliticized education often found in mainstream teacher education and higher education in general, and elementary and secondary schools on normative grounds. These institutions, critical analysts maintain, have often failed to develop an ethical vision for the pedagogical process in a democratic society.

From the critical complex perspective developed in this essay, educational rigor and social justice cannot be ethically separated. Questions of oppression and empowerment are always implicated in visions of scholarship. When positivistic schools, for example are set up to serve the needs of individuals abstracted from their social, cultural, political, and economic context, the privileged will be rewarded and the marginalized punished. Thus, the critical perspective develops a language of critique to expose the way contemporary democratic societies maintain disparate social relations and in turn how these relationships shape pedagogy. The complex part of the critical complex equation insists that these dynamics are even more complicated than originally understood and that advocates of critical pedagogy must be consistently vigilant about their own oppressive tendencies. In this complex normative context they must always be reflective about modes of oppression growing up around their own relationship to issues of race, class, gender, sexuality, religion, geographic place, etc.

As critical professionals develop these modes of normative knowledge, they begin to understand how ethical concerns are often hidden in everyday life and professional practice. They observe such masking processes at work in many cultural sites, in many colleges of education, and in secondary and elementary schools. In this cloaking process educators are induced to accept the organizational structure and daily operations of schools as if they could be no other way. This hidden normative curriculum moves critical complex teacher educators to be concerned with positivist forms of educational knowledge production and the role it plays in this great denial of the moral and ethical dimensions of pedagogy. Moved by this concern criticalists argue that all of the other educational knowledges must be produced in close connection to normative knowledges.

Empirical knowledge produced outside of such normative concerns takes on the pseudo-neutrality of positivism that promotes an unexamined normative agenda even as it claims it does not. Moreover, as we clarify the distinctions between normative knowledge and empirical knowledge, we begin to realize that positivistic requests for empirical proof of what are normative questions are epistemologically naïve and misguided. One cannot "prove" a normative statement about educational purpose or professional ethics (Aronowitz, 1988; Fischer, 1998; Giroux, 1997; Goodlad, 1994; Hinchey, 1998). No study empirically proves the inadequacy of an educational purpose—this is a different form of knowledge. Teacher educators concerned with social justice and democracy have been confronted with such epistemological inconsistencies for decades. In my own work around issues of social justice in teacher education I have often been asked by colleagues to provide empirical evidence of the validity of such concerns. From the perspective of such educators, there was only one form of professional knowledge about education—empirical. If pedagogical insights could not be empirically proved or disproved, then they were relegated to the epistemological junk heap.

All educational programs and curricula are built on a foundation of normative knowledge—even if such knowledge is hidden or even not fully understood. This is what is so often not understood in teacher education and in schooling. Thus, a key dimension of the work of teacher education is to bring these norms, these ethical and moral assumptions, these visions to the light of day so they can be analyzed and discussed. Because many in teacher education have not conceptualized and talked about normative knowledge, those operating within a positivist culture of neutrality often view this analytical process with great discomfort. When we discuss concepts such as a political vision undergirding teaching, this often is heard as a "politicization of education." More attention to normative types of knowledge can sometimes clear up these misunderstandings.

When one claims neutrality and promotes a view of education that doesn't attend to effects of human suffering, exploitation, and oppression in relation to the teaching act, a serious contradiction arises. By failing to address such issues one has taken a distinct moral position. Such orientations in the analysis of normative knowledge are revealed and problematized. Indeed, critical complex educators consider it an ethical duty to disclose their normative perspectives, to admit their value structures, and to help students understand how such allegiances affect their teaching. Critical complex teacher education openly embraces democratic values, a vision of race, class, gender, and sexual equality, and the necessity of exposing the effects of power in shaping individual identity and educational purpose. This in not an act of politicization of education; education has always been politicized. Critical complex teacher educators are attempting to understand and act ethically in light of such politicization.

## CRITICAL KNOWLEDGE ABOUT EDUCATION

Critical knowledge is closely associated with normative knowledge, as it focuses on the political/power-related aspects of teacher education and teaching. In the context of critical knowledge the charges of politicization heard in the normative domain grow louder and often more strident. Critical complex teacher educators maintain that it is impossible to conceptualize curricula outside of a sociopolitical context. No matter what form they take all curricula bear the imprint of power. When teacher education students are induced to study the curriculum outside of such horizons, they are being deceived by a claim of neutrality concerning the production of knowledge. The culture of positivism defines the curriculum as a body of agreed-upon knowledges being systematically passed along to students as an ever evolving, but neutral, instructional process.

Critical complex teacher educators know too much to be seduced by the sirens of political neutrality. As a deliberate process, the curriculum is always a formal transmission of particular aspects of a culture's knowledge. Do we teach women's and African-American history in eleventh grade social studies? Do we read Toni Morrison and Alice Walker in twelfth grade literature? In colleges of education do we teach the history of Horace Mann's crusade for public education from a political economic perspective? These are all sociopolitical questions—this means they involve power and its influence. In this context critical complex teacher educators understand the need to build a teacher education that infuses this critical knowledge into all phases of professional education. As this takes place, teacher education students gain a far more rigorous and nuanced understanding of why education exists in its present form.

Teacher educators don't have to look very far to uncover critical knowledges in education, the exercise of power in shaping "the way things are." Colleges of education, themselves, are implicated in power relations shaped by interest-driven legislative intervention in academic life. Responding to the needs of business and corporate leaders, legislators often impose policies that presuppose a view of an educational profession that acts in the power interests of managerial elites. Appreciating such dynamics, critical complex teacher educators ground their curriculum on the notion that the socio-educational world has been constructed by dominant power and thus can be reconstructed by human action and savvy political organization. Thus, critical complex teacher educators inject a literacy of power into their professional education curriculum. Such an orientation studies critical knowledges such as hegemony, ideology, discursive power, regulatory power, disciplinary power, etc.

With these critical knowledges critical complex teacher educators gain greater familiarity with diverse cultural expressions and the ways teacher education and schooling brush against them. As researchers and knowledge workers they develop the analytical ability to expose the insidious ways dominant cultural inscriptions in educational contexts marginalize culturally diverse and lower socio-economic class groups. Thinking in terms of race, class, and gender differences, critical complex practitioners survey their classes for patterns developing along these lines. The critical respect for diversity allows such teachers the ability to conceptualize multiple perspectives on issues such as intelligence, student ability, evaluation, community needs, and educational justice. Such perspectives allow for the acceptance of a diversity of expressions that exposes the fingerprints of power, in the process bringing more parents and students to the negotiating table of educational purpose.

Appreciating that all knowledges about education, all disciplinary knowledges are produced in discourses of power, critical complex teacher education understands there is no neutral ground. Imbued with such critical knowledges, they see through positivistic technical rationality and its claim that objective researchers produce educational knowledge and theory which is then applied to neutral sites of practice. In the technical rational context the assumption of ideological innocence on the part of researchers and educational policymakers leads to unproblematized hierarchical assumptions between the educated and the uneducated. Wearing the badge of neutrality such hierarchies can quickly mutate into schooling as a neo-White Man's Burden where educational missionaries attempt to deliver the civilizing "gospel" of European high culture to the poor and/or "off-white" masses.

## ONTOLOGICAL KNOWLEDGE IN EDUCATION

There is nothing new in asserting that the ways one teaches, the pedagogical purposes one pursues is directly connected to the way teachers see themselves. At the same time, the ways teachers come to see themselves as learners, in particular the ways they conceptualize what they need to learn, where they need to learn it, and how the process should take place shape their teacher persona (CPRE, 1995). Such a persona cannot be separated from the various forms of knowledge delineated here and the larger notion of "professional awareness." Too infrequently are teachers in university, student teaching, or in-service professional education encouraged to confront why they think as they do about themselves as teachers—especially in relationship to the social, cultural, political, economic, and historical world around them. Teacher education provides little insight into the forces that shape identity and consciousness. Becoming educated, becoming a critical complex practitioner necessitates personal transformation.

With such dynamics in mind, critical complex teachers are asked to confront their relationship to some long-term historical trends rarely discussed in the contemporary public conversation. Critical complex teacher educators maintain these trends hold profound implications for the development of both professional awareness and a teacher persona. In my own case the understanding of my personal historicization in light of five centuries of European colonialism from the fifteenth to the twentieth century—and new forms of economic, geo-political, cultural, and educational colonialism picking up steam in the contemporary era—is essential knowledge. Indeed, everyone in the contemporary U.S. is shaped by this knowledge in some way whether or not they are conscious of it. We cannot contemplate our professional awareness without reference to these last five hundred and some years and their effects. I was born in 1950, in the middle of the post-colonial rebellion against this half millennium of colonial violence emerging in Africa, Asia, Latin America, and throughout the indigenous world.

While anti-colonial activity continues into the twenty-first century, such discontent reached its apex in the U.S. in the 1960s and early 1970s finding expression in the civil rights, women's, anti-Vietnam war, gay rights, and other liberation movements. By the mid-1970s a conservative counter-reaction was taking shape with the goals of "recovering" what was perceived to be lost in these movements. Thus, the politics, cultural wars, and educational debates, policies, and practices of the last three decades cannot be understood outside of these efforts to "recover" white supremacy, patriarchy, class privilege, heterosexual "normality," Christian dominance, and the European intellectual canon. I must decide where I stand in relation to such profound yet muffled historical processes. I cannot conceptualize my teacher persona outside of them. They are the defining macroconcerns of our time, as every topic is refracted through their lenses. Any view of education, any curriculum development, any professional education conceived outside of their framework ends up becoming a form of ideological mystification.

Once we turn our analysis to the examination of ontological knowledges vis-à-vis such historical processes, we set the teacher "self" in question. As self-images, inherited dogmas, and absolute beliefs are interrogated, teachers begin to see themselves in relation to the world around them. They perceive the school as a piece of a larger mosaic. With such a conceptual matrix, teachers start to see an inseparable relationship between thinking and acting, as the boundary between feeling and logic begins to fade from the map of teacher thinking—a map redrawn by the cartography of teacher education and its ontological knowledges. In such an ontological context, teachers derive the motivation to produce their own knowledge. If teachers hold power to produce their own knowledges, then they are empowered to reconstruct their own consciousness. The top-down tyranny of expert-produced interpretations of tradition and its oppressive power can be subverted and our futures can be reinvented along the lines of a critical complex system of meaning making.

If positivism prevails and successfully excludes ontological, normative, and critical knowledges from professional education, teaching will too often remain a technical act. These issues of self-production will be removed from the consciousness of prospective teachers, as they memorize the generic theories and the fragments of the "knowledge base." Relegated to a static state of being, teachers in the technicist paradigm are conceived as a unit of production of an assembly line—historically abstracted selves located outside of a wider social context. Standards reforms that decontextualize students in this manner are molded by the dynamics of history and social structure (Kincheloe, & Weil, 2001). Identity is never complete and always subject to modification in relation to prevailing ideologies, discourses, and knowledges. Critical complex teacher education encourages desocialization via ideological disembedding. Critical complex professional education coursework and practicum experiences focus on the ways in which the values of power-driven, information-saturated hyperreality of the twenty-first century shape the consciousness of both students and teachers (Apple, 1999; Britzman, 1991; Carson, 1997; Gordon, 2001; Macedo, 1994; Malewski, 2001; Soto, 2000). The rigorous study of cultural and historical context alerts prospective teachers to the ways dominant myths, behavior, and language shape their view of the teacher's role without conscious filtering.

## EXPERIENTIAL KNOWLEDGE ABOUT EDUCATION

Obviously, there are experiential knowledges of education. Educators need knowledges about practice; teacher educators need to take these knowledges seriously and place them neither above nor below other forms of knowledges about education. Knowledges about practice are inherently problematic, however, because the nature of what constitutes practice is profoundly complex. There are many different forms of educational practice:
– classroom teaching;
– teacher leadership involving areas of curriculum and instruction;
– educational administration;
– educational policy making;
– teacher education;
– knowledge production in education;
– political activism.

The point here is that there are many types of educational practice—these are just a few. Yet too often in teaching and teacher education the only type of practice signified by the term involves classroom teaching. We have to be very careful about this type of reductionism as we work to develop and put into practice a critical complex teacher education.

Thus, the model of teacher education advocated here recognizes that not only are there numerous forms of practice but that all of them are complex. Donald Schon (1995) has used the term, "indeterminate zones of practice" to signify the uncertainty, complexity, uniqueness, and contested nature of any practice. The positivistic epistemology of the contemporary university often is incapable of coping with the complexity of practice, as it applies scientific theories to practical situations. Instead, Schon promotes a practice grounded on reflection-in-action. Here practitioners engage in conscious thinking and analysis while "in practice." They have no choice, they have to do this Schon argues, because each situation a practitioner encounters is unique. This demands a rigor that falls outside the boundaries of positivistic technical rationality and its reductionistic rule following. As one technicist teacher educator put it: "Look to the overhead projector, class; here are the five steps to writing on the chalkboard:
- always keep chalk longer than two inches readily available in the chalk tray;
- before writing adjust shades to minimize glare on board;
- hold the chalk at a 45 degree angle relative to the board;
- write letters at least five inches tall;
- dust hands before leaving the board so not to wipe them inadvertently on clothing."

I actually endured this lesson in an undergraduate teacher education class in 1971. I am still trying to recover.

Thus, our meta-epistemological understanding reasserts itself here in the context of experiential knowledge. From such a perspective the knowledge derived from practice about education is shaped by an epistemology significantly different from the one shaping propositional empirical knowledge. Such a position undermines the technically rational notion that teacher education researchers should continue to produce positivist empirical knowledge about educational practice until they can tell teachers how to do it correctly (Hatton, & Smith, 1995; Munby, & Russell, 1996). Experiential knowledge in the critical complex paradigm is rooted in action and informed by a subtle interaction with the empirical, normative, critical, ontological, and reflective-synthetic knowledges. There is no way to specify these interactions and routinize practice accordingly. Professional practice is always marked by surprises. Such interruption forces the practitioner to restructure her understanding of the situation. Critical complex practitioners learn to improvise and develop new ways of dealing with the new circumstances, new modes of action. A new teaching situation, for example, may be created by a particular student's behavior or by a reprimand by the principal. How do I address the needs that are moving the student to be so violent? How do I work with the principal productively when she holds views of educational purpose so different from my own? Schon (1995) contends that such reflection-in-action brings the medium of words to the action orientation of practice. And this is the context in which experiential knowledge begins to come into its own as one of many knowledges related to education. Valuing this knowledge—not as the only important form of knowledge—brings practitioners to the negotiating table as respected participants in the professional conversation. With practitioners at the table no longer will education be subjected to mandated "expert-produced systems" with rules and scripts for teachers to follow (Capra, 1996; Goodson, 1999; Schon, 1983, 1987, 1995).

In this context it is important to note that a critical complex teacher education values experiential knowledge about teaching. Because of its value and because of teacher education students' concerns with obtaining such knowledge, it may be wise to begin teacher education in school settings. In this context teacher education students could be directed to take note of and analyze the experiential knowledges they encounter. A critical complex teacher education is dedicated to making sure that experiential knowledge is not deemed second class information about education. Given its importance and student concern with obtaining it, beginning teacher education with school experience with experiential knowledge may be desirable. Such a positioning would challenge the debasement of experiential knowledge, while helping students deconstruct the positivist view that we can only do after being told what to do. This epistemological assumption must be challenged before a critical complex teacher education can get students to analyze the diverse forms of knowledge involved in becoming a professional educator. In this context critical complex teacher educators listen carefully to the experiential knowledge of teachers and other types of educational practitioners. We must be sensitive to not only the value of such knowledge but the ways it is obtained, altered, and sophisticated in lived contexts. Understanding these features of experiential knowledge, we are better prepared to teach it and integrate it with the other forms of educational knowledge (Kincheloe, 2001; Munby, & Hutchinson, 1998; Munby, & Russell, 1996; Quinn, 2001).

## REFLECTIVE-SYNTHETIC KNOWLEDGE ABOUT EDUCATION

Acknowledging our debt to Schon's notion of the reflective practitioner, a critical complex teacher education includes a reflective-synthetic form of educational knowledge. Since our purpose is not to indoctrinate practitioners to operate in a particular manner but to think about practice in more sophisticated ways, a central dimension of teacher education involves reflecting on and examining all of these knowledges in relation to one another. A reflective-synthetic knowledge of education involves developing a way of thinking about the professional role in light of a body of knowledges, principles, purposes, and experiences. In this process educators work to devise ways of using these various knowledges to perform our jobs in more informed, practical, ethical, democratic, politically just, self-aware, and purposeful ways. At the same time they work to expose the assumptions about knowledge embedded in various conceptions of practice and in the officially approved educational information they encounter.

In the reflective-synthetic context the practitioners' purpose is not to commit various knowledges to memory or to learn the right answers. Instead, teachers and other practitioners work studiously to avoid generic forms of educational knowledge applicable in all situations. Neither does their reflection on and synthesis of all the knowledges we have described reduce the uncertainty of the profession. The recognition of such uncertainty and complexity elicits humility, an understanding that all teachers and teacher educators agonize over the confusing nature of everyday practice. To do otherwise would involve a reductionistic retreat to the dishonesty of positivism's veil of certainty. In the reflective-synthetic domain practitioners learn they cannot separate their knowledges from the context in which they are generated. Thus, they study their own usage of such knowledges and the schemas they develop in this process.

In the reflective-synthetic domain, teacher educators engage teacher education students and teachers in an examination of not only the contexts in which teaching has taken place but the various forces and cultural knowledges shaping everyone involved with the teaching act. How do cultural knowledges of educational purpose connected with racialized and class-inscribed definitions of what it means to be an "educated person" shape the pedagogical act? How do folk knowledges about the nature of children and the ways they must be treated insert themselves into pedagogy? How do craft knowledges of the proper role of the teacher shape practice? How does the larger depoliticization of American culture shape teachers', parents', and the public's view of the political role of schools in a democratic society? How does the public's view of the "ideal teacher" influence who chooses education as a career path? How do all of these dynamics intersect to shape education in the U.S. writ large, as well as the individual lives of teachers and students?

All teacher educators, educational leaders, and friends of democratic education must make sure that all teachers have the time and opportunity to cultivate such reflective-synthetic knowledges. Such knowledges help them come to terms with their early concerns with survival skills and move to a more sophisticated understanding of the diverse factors that shape teaching and the broad contexts that must be accounted for as pedagogy proceeds. When positivism reduces teacher education to training in methods of transferring knowledge in light of the demands of standards, a teacher possessing reflective-synthetic skills knows that such teacher education has already embraced many political assumptions about knowing. Synthesizing a variety of the educational knowledges we have studied, such teachers begin to put together the complex ways these political assumptions shape the purposes of schools, the image of the "good teacher," the validated knowledge about "best practices" they are provided, and the ways they are evaluated. In this synthetic context they know that the way particular knowledges are transmitted reflects a variety of value positions and hidden assumptions.

In this context, critical complex teachers use their insights to connect their students to these understandings. Such teachers get to know their students and help their students know them by producing a form of authentic dialogue. With their students, they analyze and reflect on classroom conversations (How do we talk to one another?), the nature of classroom learning (What do we call knowledge?), curriculum decisions (What do we need to know?), and assessment (Is what we are doing working?). In this conversation with students they ask how the macro-level decisions about larger educational, political, and moral issues shape these everyday classroom dynamics. When thinking advances and the dialogues grow in sophistication, students come to reflect on the socio-political, moral, and epistemological dimensions of their school experiences. When this happens, a new level of learning has been reached.

The concept of teachers as researchers becomes extremely important in critical complex practice (Kincheloe, 2003). If teachers and eventually students are to be able to engage in these types of exercises, they must become researchers of educational contexts. Bringing the various educational knowledges together with research skills, all parties are empowered to reveal the deep structures that shape school activities. In this process they develop a reflexive awareness that allows them to discern the ways that teacher and student perception is shaped by the socio-educational context with its accompanying linguistic codes, cultural signs, and tacit views of the world. This reflexive awareness, this stepping back from the world as we are accustomed to seeing it, requires that the prospective teachers construct their perceptions of the world anew. For teachers this reconstruction of perception is not conducted in a random way but in a manner that undermines the forms of teacher thinking that the culture makes appear natural. Reflexively aware teacher researchers ask where their own ways of seeing come from, in the process clarifying their own meaning systems as they reconstruct the role of the practitioner. The ultimate justification for such reflective research activity is practitioner and student empowerment. In this context teachers gain the skills to overcome the positivist tendency to discredit their integrity as capable, reflexively aware, self-directed professionals (Carson, & Sumara, 1997; Diamond, & Mullin, 1999; Hatton, & Smith, 1995; McLaren, 2000; Wesson, & Weaver, 2001). An awareness of these knowledges can elicit productive analyses, conversations, and actions that lead to new forms of pedagogical and intellectual rigor.

## REFERENCES

Apple, M. (1999). *Power, meaning, and identity: Essays in critical educational studies.* New York: Peter Lang.

Aronowitz, S. (1988). *Science as power: Discourse and ideology in modern society.* Minneapolis, MN: University of Minnesota Press.

Bereiter, C. (2002). *Education and the mind in the knowledge age.* Mahwah, NJ: Lawrence Erlbaum Associates.

Britzman, D. (1991). *Practice makes practice: A critical study of learning to teach.* Albany, NY: State University of New York Press.

Bruner, J. (1997). *The culture of education.* Cambridge, MA: Harvard University Press.

Cannella, G., & Kincheloe, J. L. (2002). *Kidworld: Childhood studies, global perspectives, and education.* New York: Peter Lang.

Capra, F. (1996). *The web of life: A new scientific understanding of living systems.* New York: Anchor Books.

Carson, T. (1997). Reflection and its resistances: Teacher education as living practice. In T. Carson & D. Sumara (Eds.), *Action research as a living practice.* NewYork: Peter Lang.

Carson, T., & Sumara, D. (1997). *Action research as a living practice.* NewYork: Peter Lang.

Center for Policy Research (CPRE). (1995). *Dimensions of capacity.* Retrieved from http://www.ed.gov/pubs/CPRE/rb18/rb18b.html

Day, R. (1996). LIS, method, and postmodern science. *Journal of Education for Library and Information Science, 37*(4), 317–325.

Denzin, N., & Lincoln, Y. (2000). Introduction: The discipline and practice of qualitative research. In N. Denzin & Y. Lincoln (Eds.), *Handbook of qualitative research* (2nd ed.). Thousand Oaks, CA: Sage.

Diamond, P. & Mullin, C. (Ed.), (1999). *The postmodern educator: Arts-Based inquiries and teacher development*. New York: Peter Lang.

Edwards, A. (2000). *Researching pedagogy: A sociocultural Agenda*. Inaugural Lecture: University of Birmingham.

Elmore, R. (1997). *Education policy and practice in the aftermath of TIMSS*. Retrieved from http://www.enc.org/TIMSS/addtools/pubs/symp/cd163/cd163.htm

Ferreira, M., & Alexandre, F. (2000). *Education for citizenship: The challenge of teacher education in postmodernity*. Retrieved from http://www.ioe.ac.uk./ccs/conference2000/papers/epsd/ferreiraandalexandre.html

Fischer, F. (1998). Beyond empiricism: Policy inquiry in postpositivist perspective. *Policy Studies Journal, 26*(1), 129–146.

Giroux, H. (1997). *Pedagogy and the politics of hope: Theory, culture, and schooling*. Boulder, CO: Westview.

Goodlad, J. (1994). *Educational renewal: Better teachers, better schools*. San Francisco: Jossey-Bass.

Goodson, I. (1999). The educational researcher as public intellectual. *British Educational Research Journal, 25*(3), 277–297.

Gordon, M. (2001). Philosophical analysis and standards—philosophical and analytical standards. In J. L. Kincheloe & D. Weil (Eds.), *Standards and schooling in the United States: An Encyclopedia* (3 Vols.). Santa Barbara, CA: ABC-CLIO.

Hatton, N., & Smith, D. (1995). *Reflection in education: Toward definition and implementation*. Retrieved from http://www2.edfac.usyd.edu.au/LocalResource/study1/hattonart.html

Hinchey, P. (1998). *Finding freedom in the classroom: A practical introduction to critical theory*. New York: Peter Lang.

Horn, R. (2000). *Teacher talk: A postformal inquiry into education change*. New York: Peter Lang.

Horn, R. & Kincheloe, J. L. (Eds.), (2001). *American standards: Quality education in a complex world*. New York: Peter Lang.

Kincheloe, J. L. (2001). *Getting beyond the facts: Teaching social studies/social science in the twenty-first century* (2nd ed.). New York: Peter Lang.

Kincheloe, J. L. (2003). *Teachers as researchers: Qualitative paths to empowerment*. New York: Falmer.

Kincheloe, J. L. & Weil, D. (Eds.), (2001). *Standards and schooling in the United States: An encyclopedia* (3 Vols.). Santa Barbara, CA: ABC-ClIO.

McLaren, P. (2000). *Che Guevara, Paulo Freire, and the pedagogy of revolution*. Lanham, MD: Rowan, & Littlefield.

Macedo, D. (1994). *Literacies of power: What Americans are not allowed to know*. Boulder, CO: Westview Press.

Malewski, E. (2001). Administration—Administrative leadership and public consciousness: discourse matters in the struggle for new standards. In J. L. Kincheloe & D. Weil (Eds.), *Standards and schooling in the United States: An encyclopedia* (3 Vols.). Santa Barbara, CA: ABC-CLIO.

McGuire, M. (1996). Teacher education: Some current challenges. *Social Education, 60*(2), 89–94.

McNeil, L. (2000). *Contradictions of school reform: Educational costs of standardized testing*. New York: Routledge.

Munby, H., & Hutchinson, N. (1998). Using experience to prepare teachers for inclusive classrooms: Teacher education and the epistemology of practice. *Teacher Education and Special Education, 21*(2), 75–82.

Munby, H., & Russell, T. (1996). *Theory follows practice in learning to teach and in research on teaching*. Paper presented to American Educational Research Association, New York.

Pozzuto, R., Angell, G., & Pierpont, J. (2000). *Power and knowledge in social work*. Retrieved from http://www.arcaf.net/social_work_proceedings/ftp_files5/pozzuto3.pdf

Quinn, M. (2001). *Going out, not knowing whither: Education, the upward journey, and the faith of reason.* New York: Peter Lang.
Report of the Undergraduate Teacher Education Program Design Team (University of Missouri-Columbia). (1997). Retrieved from http://www.cos.missouri.edu/syllabi/report.html
Schön, D. (1983). *The reflective practitioner: How professionals think in action.* New York: Basic Books.
Schön, D. (1987). *Educating the reflective practitioner.* San Francisco: Jossey-Bass.
Schön, D. (1995). The new scholarship requires a new epistemology. *Change, 27*(6), 9.
Schubert, W. (1998). *Toward constructivist teacher education for elementary schools in the twenty-first century: A framework for decision-making.* Retrieved from my.netian.com/~yhhknue/coned19.htm
Segall, A. (2002). *Disturbing practice: Reading teacher education as text.* New York: Peter Lang.
Smyth, J. (2001). *Critical politics of teachers' work.* New York: Peter Lang.
Soto, L. (Ed.). (2000). *The politics of early childhood education.* New York: Peter Lang.
Steinberg S. R. (Ed.). (2001). *Multi/Intercultural conversations.* New York: Peter Lang.
Strom, S. (2000). *Knowledge base for teaching.* Retrieved from http://www.ericsp.org/pages/digests/knowledge_base.html
U.S. Department of Education. (1998). *Improving teacher preparation.* Retrieved from http://www.ed.gov/pubs/prompractice/title.html
Wesson, L., & Weaver, J. (2001). Administration—Educational standards: Using the lens of postmodern thinking to examine the role of the school administrator. In J. L. Kincheloe & D. Weil (Eds.), *Standards and schooling in the United States: An Encyclopedia* (3 Vols.). Santa Barbara, CA: ABC-CLIO.

Reprinted with permission: Kincheloe, J. L. (2004). The knowledges of teacher education: developing a critical complex epistemology. *Teacher Education Quarterly, 31*(1), 49–66.

ELIZABETH P. QUINTERO

# THE KNOWLEDGES OF TEACHER EDUCATION IN ACTION

I first read about Joe Kincheloe's work in 1995 when I found *13 Questions: Reframing Education's Conversation*. Later, I met him and Shirley Steinberg, and knew immediately that they both were going to be mentors, friends, and inspirational kicks-in-the-soul by their example, intellectual rigor, generative energy, and sincere caring.

Joe Kincheloe was fearless. He was the ultimate questioner, and clearly, almost always, the most knowledgeable person in a room. He pushed boundaries of polite academic conversation to intellectual, philosophical dialogue connecting history to present, connecting policy and practice, and connecting future to potential for work that improves lives for human beings.

One work that shows aspects of his deep contribution and generative influence is "The Knowledges of Teacher Education: Developing a Critical Complex Epistemology." The questions that he addresses in his essay are "What is critical complex teacher education? What types of knowledges should professional educator possess?"

In this brief commentary, I will review his ideas and explore ways in which Joe Kincheloe's work represents a dialogic engagement with the historical and contemporary socio-political and cultural dynamics that have shaped the ways in which we produce, disseminate, and value knowledge. Throughout the commentary, I will comment on just a few of the ways in which Joe's work has served as a catalyst for the evolution of critical theory frameworks for me as a critical theorist in early childhood and family studies. The application of such frameworks has enhanced our understandings of knowledge work both in research and pedagogical practice. Of course, the beauty and strength of Kincheloe's work is that it crosses disciplinary lines in teacher education and pushes us all to look at *what is really going on* in learning contexts.

## A DIALOGIC ENGAGEMENT: HISTORICAL AND CONTEMPORARY SOCIO-POLITICAL AND CULTURAL DYNAMICS

We who are dedicated to and immersed in critical pedagogy have internalized that knowing and meaning making are pluralities. Yet, here we are in 2010, in a context in which power brokers create, proselytize, and use as threats standards based on a very narrow knowledge base that ignores much of the history, art, and information of human experience. Joe's tireless work putting the intellectually layered tenets of critical theory and critical pedagogy in to responsible and readable forms accessible to practicing teachers (Kincheloe, 2006) shows a dialogic engagement with the historical and contemporary socio-political and cultural dynamics that connects research knowledge with day-to-day work in classrooms. And we certainly need his work and his passion here at a time when political and economic "facts" are being manipulated by lobbyists and irresponsible news media to prevent health, financial, and environmental reform at the national level.

My career began years before I learned about Joe Kincheloe's work and even Paulo Freire's work. I am a teacher scholar passionate about multi-literacies and transformative action of children, families, and communities. I have spent many years working in classrooms with young children from a wide range of cultural, linguistic, and social class backgrounds from birth to third grade. As a beginning early childhood teacher with research frames that began with a range of foci from Vygotsky, Piaget, Bronfenbrenner, to Montessori, I grew to embrace critical theory as a frame for my research and practice in this complicated world of learners with multiple strengths, multiple histories, and multiple needs. By studying development from perspectives in addition to the Western "lens" which is still prevalent in many academic circles and development texts (Soto, 2000). I have worked at moving beyond more traditional approaches to child development by studying critical theory (Freire, 1984; Kincheloe, 2000).

It is through this personal journey about critical knowledges that Joe's work became a lifeline for me, and now for my teacher education students. I conduct research and support teachers and student teachers who work in programs for young children and their families. In addition, my work with immigrant and refugee families in the context of critical, multilingual literacy programs has illuminated the promise of the histories that young children (and their families) bring to our developing field of early care and education both in the United States and worldwide.

It is through the prism of working with this specific, yet varied, group of teacher education students, that I propose to concretize Kincheloe's wisdom from this important article, "The Knowledges of Teacher Education: Developing a Critical Complex Epistemology." The space here is limited, so I will highlight just a few examples of Joe's teachings that have guided my students and I as we work thinking about, designing and collaborating on what I hope Kincheloe might call critical complex teacher education.

My university classes specifically address integrated curriculum for learners aged birth to age 8. The class participants have been a combination of teacher education students in early childhood studies university classes. All participants are actively involved in working with children in either a student teaching or teaching situation. Some programs have been in urban schools, some in rural schools, and most (82%) programs served families in poverty. In almost every (96%) program children who were English Language Learners are represented. In the university classes, the participants study systems theory, critical theory, constructivist theories, and critical race theory in addition to other foundational theories relating to early care and education and family studies. The class participates in a variety of critical literacy activities in teacher education courses before they begin planning and implementing activities based on similar frameworks for the children they work with.

Kincheloe asked, "What is a critical complex teacher education? What types of knowledges should professional educators possess?" He proposed his vision of critical complex teachers as scholars and policy makers and insisted that critical complex teacher education must have a socially just and democratic notion of schooling. He reminded us that the cultural landscape of the twenty-first century must be connected to questions of educational purpose and practice (Bruner, 1997; Ferreira, & Alexandre, 2000; Horn, & Kincheloe, 2001). He delineated that teacher education students must delve into: 1) the context in which education takes place; 2) the historical forces that have shaped the purposes of schooling; 3) the ways dominant power uses schools for anti-democratic, transformative pedagogy; and 4) the specific ways all of these knowledges relate to transformative classroom teaching in general and to their particular curricular domain in particular. By looking briefly at his explanations of the types of knowledges that he believed were necessary to his vision of teacher education, we can see an overlay of how by addressing these knowledges, the four requirements above are addressed.

## A CATALYST FOR CRITICAL THEORY FRAMEWORKS: KNOWLEDGES EXPLORED

Joe Kincheloe had a way to get right to the point. He pointed out that in our current context and all future contexts, we must support educators to engage the public in responses, thoughtful and complex, to questions such as: What does it mean "to know" something? What is involved in the process of understanding? What are the moral responsibilities of understanding? What does it mean to act one's knowledge and understanding in the world? How do we assess when individuals have engaged these processes in a rigorous way?

In part, he believed that we must categorize the multiple forms of pedagogical knowledge. He believed that pedagogical knowledges include, but are not limited to, empirical, experiential, normative, critical, ontological, and reflective-synthetic domains.

Teaching practice is *epistemological*. It is not a set of skills. Kincheloe reminded us that,

> A critical complex empiricism understands that there may be many interpretations of the observations made and the data collected, that different researchers depending on their relative situatedness may see very different phenomena in a study of the same classroom. (Kincheloe, 2003).

My teacher education students working in multiple communities with children have assignments early in their coursework to observe children in the classrooms where they are working in terms of the children's strengths and interests. They are asked to document what the children know, what is the evidence, and how this knowledge relates to children's learning. One student wrote:

> It is the start of week three and I'm beginning to see cohesiveness among the children. This year we have 12 boys and 6 girls. Most of the children are used to the daily routine. They want to explore everything. They flutter from station

to station without hesitation. About 1/3$^{rd}$ of the children are Spanish speaking only and another 8 are English Language Learners, and 1 boy speaks Mandarin/English and 4 are English speakers only.

There are about four boys who really are into dinosaurs but most of the children really want to work with the play dough. To address some of the literacy and math skills and how I know they know these skills exist is not always clear-cut. For example, one of the boys today created a catapult out of two blocks (it looked like a teeter-totter) and he was bent on showing everyone his invention. I know he is manipulating geometric shapes, using symbolic representation, demonstrating memory and knowledge, cause and effect, measurement, timing and balance, being creative and showing competence. I know Reggio would have me elicit questions from the child and further explore. To address the literacy domain, many of the children are beginning to participate in our morning songs and chants. In the library the children are demonstrating an interest in literacy and concepts of print by holding a book the appropriate way and by wanting me to read over and over again. Right now we are encouraging color recognition in Chinese, Spanish and English. I am truly making a note of all of their special interests.

The student teacher's developing empirical knowledge about the children's knowledges was integral for her before she could even begin to think about curriculum.

*Normative knowledge about education* concerns "what should be" in relation to moral and ethical issues about education. This knowledge is not produced arbitrarily but in relation to particular social visions, power relations, and cultural/historical contexts. Moral and ethical action cannot take place until one can envision a more desirable state of affairs, alternatives to injustice.

In my world of using critical literacy a frame for approaching critical knowledges in curriculum development, my students and I define literacy in a way to build upon family and learner strengths. We define critical literacy as a **process of constructing and critically using language (oral and written) as a means of expression, interpretation and/or transformation of our lives and the lives of those around us.** We address the fact that most school programs promote "book culture" while in many homes families choose to share and transmit wisdom in different ways, such as through storytelling, music, or other ways. We see our responsibility as ensuring that the world of books and literacy is not presented as a wedge between parents and their children, but instead a connection that strengthens their interaction. One teacher education student remembered:

A memory I have of my mother with literacy is singing and dancing while doing chores. I remember her dancing around with broom and whistling. She taught me how to whistle and hum to music. My mother did not read or write but she would always sit down with us to do our homework. My mother would also buy the newspaper and read it, little did I know that all she did was look at pictures and cut the coupons. Now I understand a lot of things that happened when I was younger and appreciate my mother more.

*Critical knowledge about education* is closely associated with normative knowledge, as it focuses on the political/power-related aspects of teacher education and teaching.... critical complex teacher educators maintain that it is impossible to conceptualize curricula outside of a socio-political context. Much research documents that preschool education is beneficial to all children across all economic backgrounds, although children whose parents have the least formal education and lowest incomes appear to benefit most (Barnett, 1995, 2001; Schweinhart, Barnes, Weikart, Barnett, & Epstein, 1993). But this research seems to often be used to promote programs that try to push the schools' models of learning on families. This schoolwork rarely takes into account the knowledge and aspirations of the families.

One student teacher working in a state-funded preschool program for low-income families addressed these complexities:

... I have learned that *educacíon* is often explained in Spanish-speaking communities as a cultural concept that encompasses academic learning and nonacademic moral training such as learning the difference between right and wrong, respect for adults, and good manners.

If this is true then these families that I visited today have one heck of an education. I noticed in almost all of the homes we visited that the young children, of all ages present, were encouraged to shake our hand and they did without hesitation, regardless of their demeanor. The children were well behaved and greeted us with smiles. The adults were all involved in the conversations taking place about the child whether it was a parent, an uncle, or grandmother; they all had some input. It was apparent that they all had close bonds with each other as well as with the children.

*Ontological knowledge in education*, the ways one teaches and the pedagogical purposes one pursues, is directly connected to how teachers see themselves. Critical complex teachers are asked to confront their relationship to some long-term historical trends rarely discussed in the contemporary public conversation. For many early childhood professionals committed to critical pedagogy the intricacies of examining issues of family economic and social realities is both difficult and necessary. One student working in southern California wrote after some assigned readings:

Regarding how we perceive our Latino families and culture. We are obviously reading things wrong. This comment, "the harder their lives, the more coping and survival skills they develop," really hit home for me because I grew up in a family of 6 with a single mother. I believe that my experiences growing up, at times were both extremely difficult and also really taught me to strategize and be very resourceful.

One thing to keep in mind is that difficult socio-economic times can and most often do lead to questionable behaviors. My own brothers used to steal food when I was young ... then one day after seeing the behavior; I tried my hand at it. Fortunately for me, my sister marched me back up to the store manager and made me return the item. I cried all the way home! But my point is that when people struggle financially they may find it very difficult to remain honest and may even seek out ways to make life easier. First they are oppressed, then forced into inner city slums and fed the scraps, which only sends the message that that is all they are worth. They feel cheated and hunger for more, more of which they deserve so, they rebel against society by taking what they feel they have a right to and they do have that right to more. Essentially, they take the easiest road they know in order to survive.

*Experiential knowledge about education* is about practice; teacher educators need to take these knowledges seriously and place them neither above nor below other forms of knowledges about education. Through critical framework, teacher education students I work with look to the importance of literacy knowledges learned through family and community histories. One example is a journal assignment:

- Please reflect and write about a significant member of your family who influenced you when you were young. How did that person interact with you and what do you remember learning?

A student teacher examining her personal stories related to literacy history wrote in a journal entry:

My grandfather and I had very good relationship. When I was young, we used to live together as a big family. It was always the nighttime, when I was going to bed, he told me the folktales. He didn't have a book. It was a real folktale that he knew from a long time ago.... I imagined all the characters; and I imagined all the happenings that came out of my grandfather's mouth. While I was thinking about the story, I fell into sleep and dreamed about it.

On the other hand, my grandmother used to tell me her real life stories...She lived in a completely different society from mine. She talked about how her house, school, family, marriage, and the Korean war. It was about her. However, it was also a culture and history lesson for me. Every night, I begged for a story from them. Often times, they said, "I already told you about that story, didn't I?" I replied, "Yes, but that's okay, I can listen one more time..." I still remember every single story and moment that we shared. (Quintero, 2009, p. 83)

*Reflective-synthetic knowledge about education* involves developing a way of thinking about the professional role in light of a body of knowledges, principles, purposes, and experiences. Again, to use the example of the teacher education students working on integrated curriculum development, a part of the process is to engage in an onging system of self assessment. The students are taken through a series of activities using critical pedagogy that facilitates their connecting these personal beliefs and experiences with their current beliefs about teaching and learning. They are asked to refect and write about theories of education that they have studied and to identify the theories that resonate with them as professionals. Finally action is taken by group discussion and feedback assignments involving updating their knowledge base about particular relative theories, and documentation assignments from the field that support or contradict their theoretical beliefs.

One of the teachers in our participant group had planned her critical literacy integrated curriculum activities based upon critical theroy, with influences from theoretical knowledges of the Reggio Emilia model of child centered, community and family influenced, early education. She integrated the content areas of literacy, art, and science. She was working with multilingual three and four year olds. In her final self-assessment written response, she documented an anecdote that she felt illustrated the children's journey of learning by participating in the activities she had developed.

On the final day of curriculum activities I brought the children's stick (a version of a "talking stick" that they each had made) to group for them to share with their friends. Each child was holding/playing with their stick and I asked each of them to tell the others about their stick or to share a story again. The children were talking and sharing ideas, mostly unrelated to my request, until I got to the last child M. M said, "Someone chase me, they take my stick. And turn into monster. In my closet." I asked him, "Did you have a dream about someone chasing you, taking your stick, turning into a monster? He said, "Si, in my closet." I said, "There was a monster in your closet?" M said, "Si, but monsters no real." Just so you know, I followed up with the book, *There's a Nightmare in my Closet*. I really felt some gratification at the fact that at least this child could demonstrate understanding about the whole idea behind a story stick. Overall, my main goal was achieved by promoting oral language, vocabulary and self-expression.

*Kincheloe's Relevance Today: Knowledges in Times of Accountability*

Given the array of variation in histories, cultures, and languages represented by children in early childhood programs, there appears huge potential for multiple sources of knowledge and information. What is a responsible educator to do? How is it possible to incorporate all these important guidelines and activities into the few hours we have with children in our programs? And more important, how is the critical complex educator able to connect these standards and recommendations for learning to the children's learning contexts in their homes? Joe's work is an inspiration and a guide for ongoing scholarly research of teaching and learning. Joe Kincheloe's ideas about critical complex teaching are chilling in their relevance to the present.

## REFERENCES

Barnett, W. (1995). Long term effects of early education programs on cognitive and school outcomes. *The Future of Children*, 5, 25–50.

Barnett, W. S. (2001). Preschool education for economically disadvantaged children: Effects on reading achievement and related outcomes. In S. Neuman & D. Dickinson (Eds.), *Handbook of early literacy research* (pp. 421–443). New York: Guilford Press.

Bruner, J. (1997). *The culture of education*. Cambridge, MA: Harvard University Press.

Ferreira, M., & Alexandre, F. (2000). *Education for citizenship: The challenge of teacher education in postmodernity*. Retrieved from http://www.ioe.ac.uk/ccs/conference2000/papers/epsd/ferreiraandalexandre.html

Freire, P. (1984). *The politics of education: Culture, power, and liberation*. Granby, MA: Bergin, & Garvey.

Horn, R. & Kincheloe, J. L. (Eds.). (2001). *American standards: Quality education in a complex world*. New York: Peter Lang.

Kincheloe, J. L. (2000). Certifying the damage: Mainstream educational psychology and the oppression of children. In L. D. Soto (Ed.), *The politics of early childhood education* (pp. 75–84). New York: Peter Lang.

Moll, L. C., Gonzalez, N., & Amanti, C., (2005). *Funds of knowledge: Theorizing practices in households, communities, and classrooms*. New York: Lawrence Erlbaumm.

Schweinhart, L. J., Barnes, H. V., Weikart, D. P., Barnett, W. S., & Epstein, A. S. (1993). *Significant benefits: The High/Scope Perry preschool study through age 27*. Ypsilanti, MI: High/Scope Press.

*Joe regarded the bricolage as his most important work in the context of critical qualitative research. He refused to label it methodology; rather he saw it as a philosophical stance in which to create interpretation. Always the hermeneutic, he expected research to be rigorous, personal, transgressive, and to contain multiple, tentative interpretations. Like Hermes, he expected the message of research to be flexed, stretched, negated, and reinforced, and indeed, he saw the teacher/researcher/scholar to be a trickster of interpretation, a shapeshifter of scholarship. SS*

JOE L. KINCHELOE

# 11. ON TO THE NEXT LEVEL

*Continuing the Conceptualization of the Bricolage*

*The bricolage offers insight into new forms of rigor and complexity in social research. This article explores new forms of complex, multimethodological, multilogical forms of inquiry into the social, cultural, political, psychological, and educational domains. Picking up where his previous* Qualitative Inquiry *article on the bricolage left off, this article examines not only the epistemological but also the ontological dimensions of multimethodological/multitheoretical research. Focusing on webs of relationshipsinstead of simply things-in-themselves, the bricoleur constructs the object of study in amore complex framework. In this process, attention is directed toward processes, relationships, and interconnections among phenomena. Such analysis leads bricoleurs tomultiple dimensions of multilogicality. In this context, the article generates a variety of important categories in which multiple perspectives may be constructed: methodology, theory, interpretation, power relations, and narratology.*

For the past several years, with the help of Norm Denzin and Yvonna Lincoln, I have been working on the extension of their concept of bricolage—a multimethod mode of research referenced by a variety of researchers but not developed in detail. On one level, the bricolage can be described as the process of getting down to the nuts and bolts of multidisciplinary research. Ethnography, textual analysis, semiotics, hermeneutics, psychoanalysis, phenomenology, historiography, discourse analysis combined with philosophical analysis, literary analysis, aesthetic criticism, and theatrical and dramatic ways of observing and making meaning constitute the methodological bricolage. In this way, bricoleurs move beyond the blinds of particular disciplines and peer through a conceptual window to a new world of research and knowledge production. This article is the second half of "Describing the Bricolage: Conceptualizing a New Rigor in Qualitative Research" (Kincheloe, 2001), which

*k. hayes et al., (eds.), Key Work in Critical Pedagogy: Joe L. Kincheloe, 253–277.*
*© 2011 Sense Publishers. All rights reserved.*

appeared in *Qualitative Inquiry*. In that issue, Yvonna Lincoln (2001), William Pinar (2001), and Peter McLaren (2001) offered valuable responses/critiques of my thoughts on bricolage. I take their insights seriously in presenting the second part of my article.

In the first decade of the 21st century, bricolage is typically understood to involve the process of employing these methodological strategies as they are needed in the unfolding context of the research situation. Although this interdisciplinary feature is central to any notion of the bricolage, I propose that qualitative researchers go beyond this dynamic. Pushing to a new conceptual terrain, such an eclectic process raises numerous issues that researchers must deal with to maintain theoretical coherence and epistemological innovation. Such multidisciplinarity demands a new level of research self-consciousness and awareness of the numerous contexts in which any researcher is operating. As one labors to expose the various structures that covertly shape one's own and other scholars' research narratives, the bricolage highlights the relationship between a researcher's ways of seeing and the social location of his or her personal history. Appreciating research as a power-driven act, the researcher-as-bricoleur abandons the quest for some naïve concept of realism, focusing instead on the clarification of his or her position in the web of reality and the social locations of other researchers and the ways they shape the production and interpretation of knowledge.

In this context, bricoleurs move into the domain of complexity. The bricolage exists out of respect for the complexity of the lived world. Indeed, it is grounded on an epistemology of complexity. One dimension of this complexity can be illustrated by the relationship between research and the domain of social theory. All observations of the world are shaped either consciously or unconsciously by social theory—such theory provides the framework that highlights or erases what might be observed. Theory in a modernist empiricist mode is a way of understanding that operates without variation in every context. Because theory is a cultural and linguistic artifact, its interpretation of the object of its observation is inseparable from the historical dynamics that have shaped it. The task of the bricoleur is to attack this complexity, uncovering the invisible artifacts of power and culture and documenting the nature of their influence not only on their own scholarship but also scholarship in general. In this process, bricoleurs act on the concept that theory is not an explanation of nature—it is more an explanation of our relation to nature.

## AN ACTIVE VIEW OF RESEARCH METHODOLOGY

In its hard labors in the domain of complexity, the bricolage views research methods actively rather than passively, meaning that we actively construct our research methods from the tools at hand rather than passively receiving the "correct," universally applicable methodologies. Avoiding modes of reasoning that come from certified processes of logical analysis, bricoleurs also steer clear of preexisting guidelines and checklists developed outside the specific demands of the inquiry at hand. In its embrace of complexity, the bricolage constructs a far more active role for humans both in shaping reality and in creating the research processes and narratives that represent it. Such an active agency rejects deterministic views of social reality that assume the effects of particular social, political, economic, and educational processes. At the same time and in the same conceptual context, this belief in active human agency refuses standardized modes of knowledge production (Dahlbom, 1998; McLeod, 2000; Selfe, & Selfe, 1994; Young, & Yarbrough, 1993).

In many ways there is a form of instrumental reason, of rational irrationality, in the use of passive, external, and monological research methods. In the active bricolage, we bring our understanding of the research context together with our previous experience with research methods. Using these knowledges, we *tinker* in the Lévi-Straussian sense with our research methods in field-based and interpretive contexts. This tinkering is a high-level cognitive process involving construction and reconstruction, contextual diagnosis, negotiation, and readjustment. Researchers' interaction with the objects of their inquiries, bricoleurs understand, are always complicated, mercurial, unpredictable and of course, complex. Such conditions negate the practice of planning research strategies in advance. In lieu of such rationalization of the process, bricoleurs enter into the research act as methodological negotiators. Always respecting the demands of the task at hand, the bricolage, as conceptualized here, resists its placement in concrete as it promotes its elasticity. In light of Lincoln's (2001) delineation of two types of bricoleurs, those who (a) are committed to research eclecticism allowing circumstance to shape methods employed and those who (b) want to engage in the genealogy/archeology of the disciplines with some grander purpose in mind, my purpose entails both of Lincoln's articulations of the role of the bricoleur.

Research method in the bricolage is a concept that receives more respect than in more rationalistic articulations of the term. The rationalistic articulation of method subverts the deconstruction of wide varieties of unanalyzed assumptions embedded in passive methods. Bricoleurs, in their appreciation of the complexity of the research process, view research method as involving far more than procedure. In this mode of analysis, bricoleurs come to understand research method as also a technology of justification, meaning a way of defending what we assert we know and the process by which we know it. Thus, the education of researchers demands that everyone take a step back from the process of learning research methods. Such a step back allows us a conceptual distance that produces a critical consciousness. Such a consciousness refuses the passive acceptance of externally imposed research methods that tacitly certify modes justifying knowledges that are decontextualized and reductionistic (Denzin, & Lincoln, 2000; Foster, 1997; McLeod, 2000).

## CHASING COMPLEXITY: AVOIDING MONOLOGICAL KNOWLEDGE IN THE BRICOLAGE

Avoiding the reductionistic knowledge of externally imposed methods, the bricolage continues its pursuit of complexity by sidestepping monological forms of knowledge. Monological knowledge is produced in the rationalistic quest for order and certainty. In such a trek, a solitary individual, abstracted from the cultural, discursive, ideological, and epistemological contexts that have shaped him or her and the research methods and interpretive strategies he or she employs, seeks an objective knowledge of unconnected things-in-themselves. Monological knowledge not only reduces human life to its objectifiable dimensions, that is, what can be expressed numerically, but also is incapable of moving beyond one individual's unilateral experience of the world. At its core the bricolage struggles to find and develop numerous strategies for getting beyond this one-dimensionality. In this monological context, thick descriptions are lost to the forces of order and certainty that are satisfied with right and wrong answers that preclude the need for other perspectives. Thus, monological knowledge is a smug knowledge that is content with quick resolutions to the problems that confront researchers (Madison, 1988; Thomas, 1998).

Bricoleurs understand a basic flaw within the nature and production of monological knowledge: Unilateral perspectives on the world fail to account for the complex relationship between material reality and human perception. When this relationship is ignored, knowledge producers have hell to pay. Such an expenditure includes the costs of not taking into account that what we perceive is shaped by a panoply of factors. Mistaking perception for truth not only reduces our ability to make sense of the world around us but also harms those with the least power to pronounce what is true (Karunaratne, 1997). In his initial speculations on the nature of the bricolage, Lévi-Strauss (1966) emphasized this point. A knowledge producer, Lévi-Strauss argued, never carries on a simple dialogue with the world but instead, interacts "with a particular relationship between nature and culture definable in terms of his particular period and civilization and the material means at his disposal" (p. 19).

Lévi-Strauss (1966), of course, was delineating bricolage's concern with and understanding of the dialectical relationship between knowledge and reality. In the decades since his pronouncements, social analysts have argued that in the complexity of this relationship, knowledge and reality change both continuously and interdependently. In the recognition of this complexity, many researchers have come to the conclusion that the description of what really exists may be far more difficult than originally thought. In this context, bricoleurs seek multiple perspectives not to provide the *truth* about reality but to avoid the monological knowledge that emerges from unquestioned frames of reference and the dismissal of the numerous relationships and connections that link various forms of knowledge together.

Here rests a central epistemological and ontological assumption of the bricolage:

The domains of the physical, the social, the cultural, the psychological, and the educational consist of the interplay of a wide variety of entities— thus, the complexity and the need for multiple ways of seeing advocated by bricoleurs. As part of a larger process that is ever changing, the reality that bricoleurs engage is not a fixed entity. In its impermanence, the lived world presents special problems for researchers that demand attention to the nature of its changes and the processes of its movements. In this dynamic context, bricoleurs work to avoid pronouncements of final truth. Because of the changing and impermanent nature of the world, bricoleurs propose compelling insights into their engagement with reality and the unresolved contradictions that characterize such interactions (Karunaratne, 1997; Lomax, & Parker, 1996; Young, & Yarbrough, 1993).

## ON TO THE NEXT LEVEL

### COMPLEXITY DEMANDS THE RIGOR OF THE BRICOLAGE

As bricoleurs plan their escape from the limitations of monological knowledge, they envision forms of research that transcend reductionism. In this context, they understand that complexity sets the stage for the need for the bricolage, the necessity of new ways to understand the complications of social, cultural, psychological, and educational life. Once again, the complexity principle gets in our face: Knowledge production is a far more complex process than we originally thought; there are more obstacles to the act of making sense of the world than researchers had anticipated. It was with these understandings in mind that Denzin and Lincoln (2000) issued their rigorous conception of the bricoleur as intellectually informed, widely read, and cognizant of diverse paradigms of interpretation. Realizing that the world is too complex to be revealed as an objective reality, Denzin and Lincoln sought multiple methods to provide richness and depth to a study.

Lévi-Strauss (1966), in his delineation of the bricolage, maintained that the concept originated in an understanding of the complexity and unpredictability of the cultural domain. Complexity in the context of cultural inquiry demands that the researcher develop a thick description that avoids the reductionism of describing the "functional role" of an individual. Such a "literacy of complexity" understands the intersecting roles and social locations of all human beings and the multiple layers of interpretations of self, contexts, and social actors involved in rigorous research (Dicks, & Mason, 1998). Bricoleurs act on these understandings in the effort to address the complexity of everyday life. Such complexity is embedded in notions of:

- *Explicate and implicate orders of reality*—the explicate order consists of simple patterns and invariants in time. These characteristics of the world, as theorized by physicist David Bohm, seem to repeat themselves in similar ways and possess recognizable locations in time and space. The implicate order is a much deeper structure of the world. It is the level at which ostensible separateness disappears and all things seem to become a part of a larger unified process. Implicate orders are marked by the simultaneous presence of a sequence of many levels of enfoldment with similar dissimilarities existing among them (Bohm, & Peat, 1987). Bricoleurs who recognize complexity search for this implicate order as a process often hidden from social, cultural, psychological, and pedagogical researchers.
- *The questioning of universalism*—contextual specificities may interfere with a researcher's ability to generalize findings to a level of universal application. With the recognition of complexity, universal theories of intelligence, for example, might have to respect and, thus, account for the way individuals and groups in diverse social settings conceptualize the concept (Kincheloe, Steinberg, & Villaverde, 1999).
- *Polysemy*—interpretation is always a complex process and different words and phrases, depending on the context in which they are used, can mean different things to different individuals. Thus, the research process is always more complex than initially perceived.
- *The living process in which cultural entities are situated*—in the zone of complexity, processes may be more fundamental to understanding the sociocultural world than isolated entities. Knowledge in this process-oriented context

has a past and a future; researchers have traditionally viewed a phenomenon in a particular stage of its development. Bricoleurs operating on a terrain of complexity understand that they must transcend this tendency and struggle to comprehend the process of which an object of study is a part.
- *The ontology of relationships and connections*—in complexity theory, the concept of relatedness is deemed to possess properties and influences that are just beginning to be understood. For example, complexity theorists argue that the self is less stable and essentialized than was previously thought. In this context, the relationship between self and culture becomes a central focus in particular forms of social, cognitive, and psychological research. Culture is not merely the context in which the self operates but also "in the self"—an inseparable portion of what we call the self. Who we are as human beings is dependent on the nature of such relationships and connections.
- *Intersecting contexts*—bricoleurs operating in the complexity zone understand that knowledge can never stand alone or be complete in and of itself. When researchers abstract, they take something away from its context. Of course, we all abstract, but researchers as bricoleurs refuse to lose sight of the contextual field—indeed, the intersecting contextual fields—that provide separate entities diverse meanings. Contextualization is always a complex act, as it exposes connections between what were assumed to be separate entities. In this activity, researchers come to see dimensions of an object of study never before noticed. When researchers realize that there are always multiple contexts in which to view phenomena, they come to understand that some reductionistic notion of a definitive or final comprehension of an object of study is a reductionistic concept. There is always another context in which a phenomenon can be studied.
- *Multiple epistemologies*—depending on where observers stand in the multidimensional web of reality, they will come to see different phenomena in different ways. Bricoleurs understand that in this complex context, diverse epistemologies will develop in different historical and cultural locales. As opposed to European modes of knowledge production, diverse peoples of the planet have produced ways of knowing that often have come directly into conflict. In their appreciation of epistemological complexity, bricoleurs seek out diverse epistemologies for their unique insights and sophisticated modes of making meaning. In this search, they gain provocative insights into epistemological diversity on issues of the relationships between mind and body, Self and Other, spirit and matter, knower and known, things-in-themselves and relationships, logic and emotion, and so forth. These insights allow them to ask new questions of epistemology and the research act.
- *Intertextuality*—adding to the complexity of the bricoleur's understanding of the research act is the notion of intertextuality, defined simply as the complicated interrelationship connecting a text to other texts in the act of textual creation or interpretation. Central to the importance of intertextuality in the context of the bricolage and the effort to understand complexity involves the notion that all narratives obtain meaning not merely by their relationship to material reality but from their connection to other narratives. A research account in this context cannot

be understood without historically situating it in relation to other research narratives. With this understanding of intertextuality, bricoleurs are always aware that the researcher, the consumer/reader of the research, and exterior research narratives always occupy points on intersecting intertextual axes. In this way, they are always influencing one another and any effort to make meaning of any research act.

- *Discursive construction*—all knowledge production is shaped tacitly or consciously by discursive rules and practices. Bricoleurs exploring the complexity of the research act are always exploring the discursive construction of research narratives. They work to uncover the hidden rules that define what a researcher can and cannot say, who possesses the power to speak/write about particular topics and who must listen/read, and whose constructions of reality are valid and whose are unlearned and unimportant. Bricoleurs understand Michel Foucault's (1980) assertion that fields of knowledge take their forms as a result of the power relations of discursive practices.

- *The interpretive aspect of all knowledge*—as argued throughout this description of the bricolage, interpretation is always at work in the act of knowledge production—the "facts" never speak for themselves. As inhabitants of the world, researchers are oriented to it in a manner that prevents them from grounding their findings outside of it. Thus, whether we like it or not, all researchers are destined to be interpreters who analyze the cosmos from within its boundaries and blinders. To research, we must interpret; indeed, to live, we must interpret.

- *The fictive dimension of research findings*—because in the zone of complexity no fact is self-evident and no representation is "pure," any knowledge worker who believes research narratives are simple truths is operating in a naïve domain. Thus, bricoleurs assert that there are fictive elements to all representations and narratives. Such fictive dimensions may be influenced by a variety of forces, including linguistic factors, narrative emplotment strategies, and cultural prejudices.

- *The cultural assumptions within all research methods*—Western science as well as any form of knowledge production is constructed at a particular historical time and in a specific cultural place. These temporal and spatial dimensions always leave their mark on the nature of the research methods employed and the knowledges produced. As bricolage pursues complexity, it induces researchers to seek the specific ways these cultural assumptions shape knowledge production, their own research processes in particular. Researchers operating with a consciousness of these dynamics use the insights gleaned from it to seek more complex ways of producing knowledge that are conscious of the many tacit ways cultural assumptions wander unnoticed within the act of researching.

- *The relationship between power and knowledge*—power, like the research act itself, is more complex than we originally posited. Drawing on Foucault (1980), power can be a censor that excludes, blocks, and represses like a great superego. On the other hand, however, power is a great producer, creating knowledge and legitimate ways of seeing. As a censor in research, power serves to limit what constitutes a legitimate focus of research, excluding "dangerous" investigations. As a producer in the research context, power serves to reward particular ways of seeing and specific activities. For example, in higher education, researchers who desire success in their fields learn to follow particular research norms, allowing them the rewards of funded grants and promotions based on scholarly productivity. The way different research orientations draw boundaries between what is acceptable and what is not constitutes the ideological dimension of the act of inquiry. Here, bricoleurs understand, complexity abounds as power is at work promoting particular views of research rigor and validity and notions of "unscientific" or soft research unworthy of certification at any level. The ability to trace the footprints of power in the research domain is a central dimension in the bricoleur's efforts to understand complexity and knowledge production.

Bricoleurs acting on the complexity principle understand that the identification of social structures is always problematic, always open to questions of contextual contingency. This recognition does not mean that we dismiss the notion of structures but that we view them in a different way. For example, the structure of patriarchy is not some universal, fixed, unchanging reality. Patriarchy might better be described as an interpretive concept that varies in relation to time and place, and that is constantly mutating in relation to its connections to a plethora of historical, social, cultural, economic, political, psychological, and pedagogical forces. The effects of patriarchy on specific groups and individuals are real but always idiosyncratic and undetermined. Bricoleurs understand in this context that they cannot use a theory of patriarchy to tell them what has happened in a particular situation but must dig, scratch, and analyze from different angles and employ multiple research methods and interpretive strategies to examine different aspects of the situation. Structural analysis is too messy, contradictory, and complex to offer a universally valid and essentialized description of any social structure. As the complexity-sensitive bricolage theorizes structure as an untidy process, it views it like a model in a "fashion shoot"—from a variety of angles, in numerous contexts and backdrops, and in relation to different moods and affects. Chaos theory has provided bricoleurs with a compelling means of dealing with structures in its concept of fractals. Like social structures viewed through the lenses of the complexity principle, fractals are involved in the analysis of *loosely* structured entities. These irregular shapes, where their parts reflect the whole of the entity, are similar to social structures such as patriarchy that are non-linear, contextually specific, and irregular in their manifestation (Young, & Yarbrough, 1993). The similarities between fractals in physical reality and these social dynamics are compelling. These fractal dynamics deserve more study later in this article.

## CONSTRUCTING THE BRICOLAGE: DEVELOPING A SOCIAL, CULTURAL, PSYCHOLOGICAL, AND EDUCATIONAL SCIENCE OF COMPLEXITY

Some of the best work in the study of social complexity is now taking place in the qualitative inquiry of numerous fields from sociology, cultural studies, anthropology, literary studies, marketing, geography, media studies, informatics, library studies, women's studies, various ethnic studies, and education to nursing. Denzin and Lincoln (2000) are acutely aware of these dynamics and referred to them in the context of their delineation of the bricolage. Lincoln (2001), in her response to the first part of this expansion of the bricolage, maintained that the most important border work between disciplines is taking place in feminism and racial/ethnic studies. In his response, Pinar (2001) correctly pointed out that curriculum theory provides numerous examples of "radical forms of interdisciplinarity" similar to what I am describing as the bricolage. It is unfortunate that researchers in sociology, cultural studies, psychology, history, and other disciplines are not more familiar with curriculum theory.

In the move to transcend the objective certainty of positivism and the effort to avoid the nihilism of more radical modes of postmodernism, social and cultural analysis has migrated to a more undefined space where no particular paradigmatic view dominates. In this domain, an awareness of the complexity of knowledge production undermines efforts to fix the field of social research in a well-defined locale. The development of particular universal ways of operating as researchers is not so easy in a situation where more and more professional practitioners grasp the complexity of their task.

The bricolage does not enter into this paradigmatic situation as a knight on a white horse ready to "save" the field. Such bravado is not the point of constructing the bricolage. In light of the vicissitudes of the contemporary state of social, cultural, psychological, and educational research, the bricolage serves as a way of naming and organizing existing impulses. In this context, it serves to promote understanding and communication and create structures that allow for a better informed, more rigorous mode of knowledge production. Do not misread this humility: I strongly believe in the power of the bricolage to move the field in a positive direction; it is concurrently important, however, to understand its construction and limitations in the context of contemporary social research. The appreciation of the complexity of everyday life and the difficulty understanding it brings with it demands humility on the part of researchers.

Indeed, a complex social, cultural, and educational analysis is aware that a specific set of variables does not lead to the same outcomes in some linear cause-and-effect manner. Scholars in such an analysis transcend reductionistic assumptions such as only one entity can inhabit the same locale at the same time. In a complex ontology, patriarchy can coexist in the same time and space with religion, socioeconomic class, gender, sexuality, geographic place, and a plethora of other social dynamics. In such a context, the notion of causality and the nature of social interconnections become far more complex concepts and processes to research. With this complexity in mind, T. R. Young and James Yarbrough (1993) argued that the way researchers discursively define a social phenomenon produces the form the notion takes.

Using class as an example, Young and Yarbrough (1993) argued that it is possible to define it as a lifestyle, a function of formal education, a manifestation of one's father's occupation, or one's relationship to the means of production. Class as a social structure looks very different depending on what definition we choose. A sociology or a cultural studies of complexity understands that there is no final source of authority to which researchers can appeal for a validated definition. Such uncertainty, bricoleurs recognize, is a key aspect of the human condition of being-in-the-world—a complex ontology. Operating in this situation, bricoleurs employ "any means necessary," as many methods as possible to make their way through a world of diverse meanings—not to mention becoming researchers of such a world. These diverse meanings continuously circulate through language, common sense, worldviews, ideologies, and discourses, always operating to tacitly shape the act of meaning making.

Any social, cultural, psychological, or educational science of complexity takes these dynamics into account. No research act or interpretive task begins on virgin territory. Countless acts of meaning making have already shaped the terrain that researchers explore. In this context, bricoleurs need as much help as they can get to negotiate their way through such overwhelming complexity. This is why we develop the bricolage in the first place: Complexity demands a wider definition of *research* that would include modes of philosophical inquiry that account for these epistemological and ontological dynamics.

On the landscape of complexity, I am lost as a researcher if I do not possess an epistemological and ontological map to help me understand the nature of the territory I am exploring. To produce research that provides thick description and a glimpse of what could be, I need epistemological and ontological insights that alert me to the multidimensional, socially constructed, polyvocal, ever-changing, fractal-based nature of the social world. Such insights hold profound implications for research methods (Bridges, 1997; Lutz, Jones, & Kendall, 1997; McLeod, 2000). In this complex context, it becomes even more obvious that learning the bricolage is a lifelong process.

## AN ONTOLOGY OF COMPLEXITY: IMPLICATIONS FOR THE BRICOLAGE

I have alluded to a complex ontology in the description of the bricolage. Because of the importance of this concept, it is useful to specifically describe this notion before moving into new dimensions of the bricolage. As bricoleurs prepare to explore that which is not readily apparent to the ethnographic eye, that realm of complexity in knowledge production that insists on initiating a conversation about what it is that qualitative researchers are observing and interpreting in the world, this clarification of a complex ontology is needed. This conversation is especially important because it has not generally taken place. Bricoleurs maintain that this object of inquiry is ontologically complex in that it cannot be described as an encapsulated entity. In this more open view of the object of inquiry, it is always a part of many contexts and processes, it is culturally inscribed and historically situated. The complex view of the object of inquiry accounts for the historical efforts to interpret its meaning in the world and how such efforts continue to define its social, cultural, psychological, and educational effects.

In the domain of the qualitative research process, for example, this ontological complexity undermines traditional notions of triangulation. Because of its in-process (processual) nature, interresearcher reliability becomes far more difficult to achieve. Process-sensitive scholars watch the world flow by like a river, where the exact contents of the water are never the same. Because all observers view an object of inquiry from their own vantage points in the web of reality, no portrait of a social phenomenon is ever exactly the same as another. Because all physical, social, cultural, psychological, and educational dynamics are connected in a larger fabric, researchers will produce different descriptions of an object of inquiry depending on what part of the fabric they have focused—what part of the river they have seen. The more unaware observers are of this type of complexity, the more reductionistic the knowledge they produce about it. Bricoleurs attempt to understand this fabric and the processes that shape it in as thick a way possible (Blommaert, 1997).

The design and methods used to analyze this social fabric cannot be separated from the way reality is construed. Thus, ontology and epistemology are inextricably linked in ways that shape the task of the researcher. The bricoleur must understand these features in the pursuit of rigor. A deep interdisciplinarity is justified by an understanding of the complexity of the object of inquiry and the demands such complications place on the research act. As parts of complex systems and intricate processes, objects of inquiry are far too mercurial to be viewed by a single way of seeing or as a snapshot of a particular phenomenon at a specific moment in time.

In social research the relationship between individuals and their contexts is a central dynamic to be investigated. This relationship is a key ontological and epistemological concern of the bricolage; it is a connection that shapes the identities of human beings and the nature of the complex social fabric. Thus, bricoleurs use multiple methods to analyze the multidimensionality of this type of connection. The ways bricoleurs engage in this process of putting together the pieces of the relationship may provide a different interpretation of its meaning and effects. Recognizing the complex ontological importance of relationships alters the basic foundations of the research act and knowledge production process. Thin reductionistic descriptions of isolated things in themselves are no longer sufficient (Foster, 1997; Zammito, 1996).

What the bricolage is dealing with in this context is a double ontology of complexity: first, the complexity of objects of inquiry and their being-in-the-world; second, the nature of the social construction of human subjectivity, the production of human "being." Such understanding opens a new era of social research where the process of becoming human agents is appreciated with a new level of sophistication. The complex feedback loop between an unstable social structure and the individual can be charted in a way that grants human beings insight into the means by which power operates and the democratic process is subverted. In this complex ontological view, bricoleurs understand that social structures do not *determine* individual subjectivity but *constrain* it in remarkably intricate ways. The bricolage is acutely interested in developing and employing a variety of strategies to help specify these ways subjectivity is shaped.

The recognitions that emerge from such a multiperspectival process get analysts beyond the determinism of reductionistic notions of macro-social structures. The intent of a usable social or educational research is subverted in this reductionistic context as human agency is erased by the "laws" of society. Structures do not simply "exist" as objective entities whose influence can be predicted or "not exist" with no influences over the cosmos of human affairs. Once again, fractals enter the stage with their loosely structured characteristics of irregular shape—fractal structures. Although not *determining* human behavior, for example, fractal structures possess sufficient order to affect other systems and entities within their environment. Such structures are never stable or universally present in some uniform manifestation (Varenne, 1996; Young, & Yarbrough, 1993). The more we study such dynamics, the more diversity of expression we find.

Taking this ontological and epistemological diversity into account, bricoleurs understand there are numerous dimensions to the bricolage (Denzin, & Lincoln, 2000). As with all aspects of the bricolage, no description is fixed and final and all features of the bricolage come with an elastic clause. We can delineate, with the help of Denzin and Lincoln (2000), five dimensions of the bricolage: methodological bricolage, theoretical bricolage, interpretive bricolage, political bricolage, and narrative bricolage:

- *Methodological bricolage*: employs numerous data-gathering strategies from the interviewing techniques of ethnography, historical research methods, discursive and rhetorical analysis of language, semiotic analysis of signs, phenomenological analysis of consciousness and intersubjectivity, psychoanalytical methods, and Pinarian *currere* (Pinar, 1994) to textual analysis of documents.
- *Theoretical bricolage*: uses a wide knowledge of social theoretical positions from constructivism, critical constructivism, enactivism, feminism, Marxism, neo-Marxism, critical theory, postmodernism, poststructuralism, and cultural studies to queer theory to situate and determine the purposes, meanings, and uses of the research act.
- *Interpretive bricolage*: deploys a range of interpretive strategies that emerge from a detailed awareness of the field of hermeneutics and the ability to use the hermeneutic circle. In this context, bricoleurs work to discern their location in the web of reality in relation to intersecting axes of personal history, autobiography, race, socioeconomic class, gender, sexual orientation, ethnicity, religion, geographical place, and numerous other dynamics. These various perspectives are used to discern the role of self in the interpretive process. This process is combined with different perspectives offered by people located in diverse locations in the web to widen the hermeneutical circle and to appreciate the diversity of perspectives on a particular topic. These perspectives or interpretations are viewed in relation to one another and in relation to larger social, cultural, political, economic, psychological, and educational structures as well as the social theoretical positions previously referenced. In this way the complexity and multidimensionality of the interpretive process is comprehended by the bricoleur.
- *Political bricolage*: understands that all research processes hold political implications, are manifestations of power. No science, no mode of knowledge production is free from the inscriptions of power. In this context, bricoleurs study the information they collect and the knowledge they produce to discern the ways tacit forms of power have shaped them. In light of such awareness, bricoleurs attempt to document the effects of ideological power, hegemonic power, discursive power, disciplinary power, regulatory power, and coercive power. In this context, bricoleurs are informed by McLaren's (2001) response to my first delineation of the bricolage. In this political articulation of the concept, normative foundations are explored and questions of political economy, racism, sexism, and homophobia

are seen as central concerns of the criticality of the bricolage. A power literacy is sought that informs cultural workers of the ways oppressive power can be resisted.
- *Narrative bricolage*: appreciates the notion that all research knowledge is shaped by the types of stories inquirers tell about their topics. Such story types are not innocently constructed but reflect particular narratological traditions: comedy, tragedy, and irony. The bricoleur's knowledge of the frequently unconscious narrative formula at work in the representation of the research allows a greater degree of insight into the forces that shape the nature of knowledge production. Thus, more complex and sophisticated research emerges from the bricolage.

## SPECIFYING THE IMPORTANCE OF PHILOSOPHICAL RESEARCH IN THE BRICOLAGE

I have frequently alluded in this article to the importance of philosophical research to the bricolage. I use the phrase *philosophical research* to denote the use of various philosophical tools to help clarify the process of inquiry and provide insight into the assumptions on which it conceptually rests. In this section, I focus on this dimension and in the process, specify a few of the benefits such a form of inquiry might bring to this project. Informed by philosophical research, bricoleurs become smarter, more self-reflective about their own role and the role of researchers in general in the knowledge-and reality creating process. An appreciation of complexity, of course, demands such insights, as it insists on an understanding that conceptual categories are human constructions and posits that such categorization exerts a profound impact on modes of perception and human action itself. Little work has been undertaken on philosophy as research, not to mention its role in a research bricolage. The following offers a few ideas about how bricoleurs might begin to think through these dynamics in light of our previous contentions about the complexity of the bricolage.

The mode of philosophical consciousness advocated here helps bricoleurs bracket their own subjectivity as researchers in ways that force the intersection of notions such as researcher "invention" and researcher "discovery." The bricolage makes use of philosophical research into the boundary between the social world and the narrative representation of it. Such explorations provide profound and often unrecognized knowledge about what exactly is produced when researchers describe the social world. Rigor, I assert, is impossible without such knowledge and discernment. Exploring this complex, ever-shifting boundary between the social world and the narrative representation of it, philosophically informed bricoleurs begin to document the specific influences of life history, lived context, race, class, gender, and sexuality on researchers and the knowledge they produce (Denzin, & Lincoln, 2000; McLeod, 2000; Zammito, 1996).

These aspects of philosophical research help the bricoleur to highlight the ethical, epistemological, ontological, and political features of the research process and the knowledge it produces. Such tasks might be described as a form of research concerned with conceptual clarification. For example, what does it mean to exist in history? To live and operate as a social and historical subject? How do researchers begin the process of exploring such dynamics? How do the ways researchers conceptualize these features shape the research process and the knowledge it produces? How do social theoretical choices and assumptions affect these issues? All of these questions point to the role of science as first and foremost a cultural activity. Abstract and objective procedural and methodological protocols come to be viewed as the socially constructed entities that they are. Thus, bricoleurs are freed from reductionistic conventions in ways that facilitate their moves not to an anything-goes model of research but to a genuinely rigorous, informed multiperspectival way of exploring the lived world (Bridges, 1997; Foster, 1997; Morawski, 1997).

What bricoleurs are exploring in this philosophical mode of inquiry are the nature and effects of the social construction of knowledge, understanding, and human subjectivity. Realizing the dramatic limitations of so-called objectivist assumptions about the knowledge production process, bricoleurs struggle to specify the ways perspectives are shaped by social, cultural, political, ideological, discursive, and disciplinary forces. Understanding the specifics of this construction process helps multiperspectival researchers choose and develop the methodological, theoretical, and interpretive tools they need to address the depictions of the world that emerge from it. In the context of the philosophical inquiry as conceptual clarification, the bricolage understands that the objectivist view of knowledge assumes that meaning in the world exists separately from an individual's experience. In such an objectivist context, the research act simply involves identifying external objective reality and reflecting it in the research narrative. Such reductionism and its concurrent distortion is exactly what the bricolage seeks to avoid (Cronin, 1997; McLeod, 2000; Varenne, 1996).

## PHILOSOPHICAL INQUIRY IN THE BRICOLAGE: CONSTRUCTIVISM AND HISTORICITY

As bricoleurs gain insight into the social construction of knowledge, understanding, and human subjectivity, they gain a consciousness of their own and other's historicity. What many researchers have referred to as the crisis of historicity is really nothing more than the development of this consciousness, this understanding of historical, social, cultural, ideological, and discursive construction of science and the research it produces. In this context, bricoleurs understand that the effort to distinguish between different social realities and different interpretations of researchers is more difficult than originally assumed. With such an understanding in mind, bricoleurs always have to deal with levels of complexity ignored by less informed researchers. As bricoleurs negotiate their way between the constructed and discovered dimensions of knowledge work, they come to appreciate the blurred line between the historical and historiographical.

Naïveté is the result of dismissing these issues of constructivism and historicity. Philosophical inquiry in the bricolage moves us away from this lack of sophistication and rigor, as researchers gain insight into the existential grounds on which diverse approaches to research evolve. Such inquiry helps bricoleurs appreciate the principles and sources that fuel the production of knowledge by both self and others—a facility necessary for good research and good scholarship in general.

Indeed, bricoleurs employ philosophical inquiry to explore the logic and psychology of the development of research strategies and their use in the larger effort to produce knowledge. Such logics and psychologies can be appreciated only in historical context, in terms of their historicity. The historicization of research allows bricoleurs to ask questions of knowledge production that have previously gone unasked and, thus, to gain insight into previously invisible processes shaping the ways we come to describe and act in the world. In this way, the work of the bricolage becomes thicker, more insightful, savvier, and more rigorous (Bridges, 1997; McCarthy, 1997; Zammito, 1996).

The understanding of constructivism and historicity in relation to research cannot be separated from the interpretive dimension of the bricolage and its grounding in hermeneutics. In this context a notion of critical hermeneutics is employed by the bricoleur to understand the historical and social ways that power operates to shape meaning and its lived consequences. Critical hermeneutics alerts us to the ways power helps construct the social, cultural, and economic conditions under which meaning is made and research processes are constructed. Not all parties or all advocates of particular marginalized lived experiences are allowed to sit at the table of official meaning making. The bricoleur's awareness of constructivism and historicity helps her or him point out these omissions and their effects on the knowledge production processes.

In this context, critical hermeneutics facilitates bricoleurs' attempts to identify socially oppressive forms of meaning making and research processes. Bricoleurs understand that constructivism and historicity can be relatively unhelpful concepts without a recognition of this critical dimension of power and its effects. As McLaren (2001) pointed out in his response to the first part of this description of the bricolage, merely focusing on the production of meanings may not lead to "resisting and transforming the existing conditions of exploitation" (p. 702). I take his admonition seriously and assert that in the critical hermeneutical dimension of the bricolage, the act of understanding power and its effects is merely one part—albeit an inseparable part—of counterhegemonic *action*. Critical hermeneutics understands that meaning does not "just happen"—we do not see bumperstickers proclaiming "meaning happens." Instead, meaning is imposed on the world, and if researchers are not aware of such dynamics, they will unconsciously join in this imposition. Joining in the imposition is disguised by the assertion that meaning exists in the world independently and unconnected to the subjectivities of researchers and other "knowers." All objectivist researchers do, they innocently and reductionistically maintain, is discover this independent meaning and report it to their audience.

Power in this construction of knowledge, it is argued, plays no role in the process. Bricoleurs employing critical notions of historicity and constructivism know better. The objective knowledge and the validated research processes used by reductionists are always socially negotiated in a power-saturated context. Assertions that knowledge is permanent and universal are undermined and the stability of meaning is subverted. Forces of domination will often reject such historically conscious and power-literate insights, as such awareness undermines the unchallenged knowledge assertions of power wielders. Critical hermeneutics, bricoleurs come to understand, can be quite dangerous when deployed in the sacred temples of knowledge production. It is no surprise that this form of philosophical inquiry is typically excluded from the canon of official research (Cronin, 1997; Lutz et al., 1997). Again in reference to McLaren's (2001) concerns, the criticality of the bricolage is dedicated to engaging political action in a variety of social, political, economic, and academic venues.

## EPISTEMOLOGICAL ANALYSIS IN THE BRICOLAGE: EXTENDING PHILOSOPHICAL RESEARCH

If epistemology involves the exploration of how researchers come to know about the phenomena they study, how this knowledge is structured, and the grounds on which these knowledge claims are tendered, then epistemological understandings are central to the rigor of the bricolage. In multimethod/interdisciplinary research, these epistemological understandings become even more important, as different orientations assume different views of knowledge. In this context, researchers learn from comparative epistemological insights, developing a profound understanding of knowledge theory and production in the process. The development of such epistemological insight is yet another dimension of the philosophical inquiry of the bricolage.

Aided by these epistemological understandings, bricoleurs are better equipped to perform subtle forms of knowledge work. As philosophical inquirers working in the epistemological domain, bricoleurs ask informed questions, develop complex concepts, construct alternate modes of reasoning, and provide unprecedented interpretations of the data they generate. All these dimensions of research involve making sophisticated epistemological decisions and are inseparable from the larger task of producing high-quality research. With these epistemological insights in mind, bricoleurs are empowered to draw on their conceptual and methodological tool kits, depending on the nature of the research context and the phenomenon in question. They are emancipated from the tyranny of prespecified, intractable research procedures (Foster, 1997; Selfe, & Selfe, 1994; Willinsky, 2001).

Mainstream research traditions have been reluctant to admit philosophical inquiry and its associated epistemological analysis into the pantheon of acceptable research methods. Bricoleurs embrace philosophical research for a number of reasons, one of the most fundamental involving its notion that at its most basic articulation, research involves asking and answering an unanswered question. Obviously, philosophical inquiry meets this criterion, as it seeks out answers to the most compelling questions of human life and the purposes of research:
- What is the nature of being? In this ontological domain, bricoleurs examine not only the nature of human being (subjectivity) and its relation to knowledge production but also the nature of the object of study. In the case of the latter, bricoleurs ask: Do we study the object as a thing-in-itself or as a part of larger processes and relationships?
- What is the nature of living a good life? In this ethical domain, bricoleurs question the ways their research contribute to the social good. How does this work influence the lives of the researcher, the community, the world?

- What knowledge is of most worth? Epistemological questions are profoundly important to the bricoleur. This question demands modes of judgment that move bricoleurs to think about the value of their research projects. What researchers are producing knowledge of worth? What researchers are not producing knowledge of worth? How do we make such a distinction?
- What is knowledge? This epistemological question demands that researchers clearly understand the different ways that different paradigms define *knowledge* and its production. The awareness that comes from understanding these competing versions provides bricoleurs with a more profound understanding of the forces that tacitly shape all knowledge claims.
- What does it mean to know something? This question forces bricoleurs to seek out the insights of cognitive theory in relation to their epistemological questions. The cognitive insights gained from, for example, the Santiago School of enactivism and its notions of knowledge-in-action and the power of relationships informs epistemology in compelling ways. Such a synergy is yet another example of the benefits of the multiperspectivalism of the bricolage.
- How do we distinguish between worthy and unworthy knowledge? This question moves bricoleurs into the complex domain of validity. Here they can engage in the contemporary conversation about making judgments about research quality. Are the terms *external validity* and *internal validity* helpful in this context? What does knowledge produced about one context have to tell us about another context? Our philosophical grounding helps us formulate questions about the worth of research that might have never occurred to those without such insights. In this context, bricoleurs, with their philosophical grounding, seriously engage with the purposes of research. In this process, they invent concepts such as catalytic validity, ironic validity, paralogical validity, rhizomatic validity, voluptuous validity (Lather, 1991, 1993), hermeneutic validity, cognitive validity, and pragmatic validity (Kincheloe, 2003).
- What is rigor in the research process? Here bricoleurs take the opportunity to move beyond traditional definitions of *rigor* as the degree of fidelity to the unquestioned steps in the research process and the degree to which the research accurately reflects "true reality." In this context, they study the socially constructed nature of what passes as rigor in research. Doing so, they move a step closer to the complexity of the act of knowledge production. Such proximity helps them redefine rigor in a way that involves developing numerous ways of recognizing and working with this complexity.

If answering such questions is not an act of research, then bricoleurs are not sure what research involves.

In examining these issues, I have encountered several situations in schools of education where excellent scholars who perform philosophical inquiry have been told by administrators and tenure committees that their work does not constitute "real research." Such scholars have been punished and traumatized by these narrow and uninformed viewpoints. Exploring the dynamics at work in these academic assaults on philosophical researchers, the issue that emerges at the root of the attack is epistemological in nature. The guardians of "research purity" proclaim a clear distinction between empirical (scientific knowledge production) and philosophical inquiry (unscientific knowledge production). In this context, the epistemological and ontological analysis of philosophical inquiry questions this empirical and philosophical bifurcation.

The deep interdisciplinarity of the bricolage transgresses the boundary between the two domains, illustrating in the process their interaction and inseparability. Bricoleurs are not aware of where the empirical ends and the philosophical begins because such epistemological features are always embedded in one another. Avoiding reductionistic and uninformed notions of research that are monological and exclusive, the bricolage works to embrace and learn from various modes of knowledge production, including philosophical inquiry as well as historical and literary modes of scholarship. Employing the unconscious epistemological criteria of the elitist excluders, historical and literary inquiry would not meet the criteria of real research (Bridges, 1997). Such exclusion masquerades as a form of rigor, confusing narrow-mindedness with high standards.

## INTERPRETATION IN THE BRICOLAGE: THE CENTRALITY OF CRITICAL HERMENEUTICS

The research bricolage as articulated here is grounded in a critical notion of hermeneutics. Long concerned with the theory and practice of interpretation, hermeneutics is a form a philosophical inquiry that focuses on the cultural, social, political, and historical nature of research. In this context, hermeneutics maintains that meaning making cannot be quarantined from where one stands or is placed in the web of social reality. Thus, in a hermeneutic context, interpretation is denaturalized in the sense that certain events and/or phenomena do not imply a particular interpretation of their meaning. Interpretation is far more complex than assumed, far more a product of social forces than admitted.

Thus, bricoleurs focus great attention on the act of interpretation in research, appreciating the distinction between describing a phenomenon and understanding it. In this context, bricoleurs informed by hermeneutics understand that any act of rigorous research involves:
– connecting the object of inquiry to the many contexts in which it is embedded;
– appreciating the relationship between researcher and that being researched;
– connecting the making of meaning to human experience;
– making use of textual forms of analysis while not losing sight that living and breathing human beings are the entities around which and with which meaning is being made; and
– building a bridge between these forms of understanding and informed action.

Too often in mainstream forms of research, bricoleurs maintain, these interpretive understandings are deemed irrelevant.

The form of hermeneutics employed here is a critical hermeneutics—critical in the sense that it has engaged in a dialogue with the tradition of critical theory. Critical theory is always concerned with the ways power operates, the ways various institutions and interests deploy power in the effort to survive, shape behavior, gain dominance over others, or in a more productive vein, improve the human condition. Realizing that power is not simply one important force in the social process, critical theory understands that humans are the historical products of power. Men and women do not emerge outside the process of history. Human identities are shaped by entanglements in the webs that power weaves. Critical hermeneutics emerges in the dialogue between hermeneutics and critical theory's concern with power and social action (Jardine, 1998; Kincheloe, Steinberg, & Villaverde, 1999; McLaren, 2000; Smith, 1999).

In this hybrid context, critical hermeneutics pushes interpretation in research to new levels, moving beyond what is visible to the ethnographic eye to the exposure of concealed motives that move events and shape everyday life. As critical hermeneutics observes the intersection of power and omnipresent, prereflective cultural meanings, a sensitive and rigorous understanding of the social world begins to take shape. Critical hermeneutics takes the concept of historicity to a new conceptual level as it specifies the nature of the historicity that helps produce cultural meaning, the consciousness of the researcher, the construction of the research process, and the formation of human subjectivity and transformative action. In this interpretive context, critical theoretical concerns with praxis-based notions of social change are more easily addressed, as social action informed by thick description and rigorous understanding of a social and political circumstance is made possible (Lutz et al., 1997; Zammito, 1996).

## I WALK THE LINE: EMPOWERED SUBJECTS AND RIGOROUS ANALYSIS

In this critical hermeneutic context, bricoleurs are concerned with the empowerment of the subjects of research and the voice to the subjugated and the marginalized. Such efforts raise numerous questions about the research process. For example, do the acts of empowerment and giving voice involve simply highlighting the specific words of the research participants? Do they mean featuring the interactions of the participants and the researcher as the most important dimensions of the research narrative? Although in *no* way dismissing the importance of these dimensions of the empowerment process in the criticality of the bricolage, bricoleurs informed by critical hermeneutics worry that sometimes, in highlighting the specific words of participants and featuring research participant interaction, rigorous insights can be lost. In the specifics of the process, interpretation emerging from the interaction of the particular with macrosocial configurations can be set aside in the focus on the personal. Concurrently, psychologistic representations of abstract individuals can crowd out the contextual concerns of the hermeneutically informed bricolage. In such cases, the rigor of complexity is displaced not by scientific reductionism but by an excessive fascination with unsituated personal experience. As Johnny Cash once put it, one must "walk the line"; in this case, the line separates the decontextualization of the idiosyncrasy of the personal from the unreflective, authoritarian voice of truth of the reductionistic researcher.

Bricoleurs operating in a critical hermeneutical framework work to record the voice of the subjugated but to expand its meaning by engaging in the hermeneutic circle of interpretation. Even subjugated voices are better understood when studied in relation to numerous social, cultural, political, economic, philosophical, historical, psychological, and pedagogical dynamics (Dicks, & Mason, 1998). I attempted to walk this line in my recent book *The Sign of the Burger: McDonald's and the Culture of Power* (Kincheloe, 2002). As I highlight the voices of my ethnographic research participants, I always contextualize their perspectives within the frames of macrosocial, political, and economic concerns; the insights of social theory; and the discernment of critical hermeneutics. The rigorous demands of the bricolage insist that researchers engage in these deliberations and struggle with their implications for every project they undertake.

Researchers in this struggle draw strength from the multiple perspectives of the bricolage. Such multiperspectivalism is enhanced by critical hermeneutics and the interpretive collisions it promotes in the hermeneutic circle—hermeneuts often refer to this dynamic as the fusion of horizons. Here we return to the very basis of bricolage, learning from the juxtaposition of divergent ideas and ways of seeing. Metaphors abound in this context as the work of the bricoleur is compared to that of a jazz musician, quilt maker, and the producer of pictorial montage. In all of these processes, different dynamics are brought together in ways that produce a synergistic interaction—the whole is greater than the sum of the parts. The hermeneutic fusion of horizons helps bricoleurs consider numerous representations of reality simultaneously. In this context, the concept of simultaneity is important, as it takes precedence over more traditional research concerns with sequence and linearity. As hermeneutically grounded bricoleurs watch these conceptual collisions, they adeptly sidestep the danger of liberal eclecticism. Here in the hermeneutic circle, they chart the ways that the divergent representations both inform and transform one another (Denzin, & Lincoln, 2000; Kellner, 1995; Paulson, 1995; Pryse, 1998).

## MOVING TO THE MARGINS: ALTERNATIVE MODES OF MEANING MAKING IN THE BRICOLAGE

In its critical concern for just social change, the bricolage seeks insight from the margins of Western societies and the knowledge and ways of knowing of non-Western peoples. Such insight helps bricoleurs reshape and sophisticate social theory, research methods, and interpretive strategies as they discern new topics to be researched. This confrontation with difference, so basic to the concept of the bricolage, enables researchers to produce new forms of knowledge that inform policy decisions and political action in general. In gaining this insight from the margins, bricoleurs display once again the blurred boundary between the hermeneutical search for understanding and the critical concern with social change for social justice. Responding yet again to McLaren's (2001) important concern, not only are the two orientations not in conflict but they are also synergistic (DeVault, 1996; Lutz et al., 1997; McLaren, Hammer, Reilly, & Sholle, 1995; Soto, 2000; Steinberg, 2001).

To contribute to social transformation, bricoleurs seek to better understand both the forces of domination that affect the lives of individuals from race, class, gender, sexual, ethnic, and religious backgrounds outside of dominant culture(s) and the worldviews of such diverse peoples. In this context, bricoleurs attempt to remove knowledge production and its benefits from the control of elite groups. Such control consistently operates to reinforce elite privilege while pushing marginalized groups farther away from the center of dominant power. Rejecting this normalized state of affairs, bricoleurs commit their knowledge work to helping address the ideological and informational needs of marginalized groups and individuals. As detectives of subjugated insight, bricoleurs eagerly learn from labor struggles, women's marginalization, the "double consciousness" of the racially oppressed, and insurrections against colonialism (Kincheloe, & Steinberg, 1993; Kincheloe, Steinberg, & Hinchey, 1999; Young, & Yarbrough, 1993).

Thus, the bricolage is dedicated to a form of rigor that is conversant with numerous modes of meaning making and knowledge production—modes that originate in diverse social locations. These alternative modes of reasoning and researching always consider the relationships, the resonances, and the disjunctions between formal and rationalistic modes of Western epistemology and ontology and different cultural, philosophical, paradigmatic, and subjugated expressions. In these latter expressions, bricoleurs often uncover ways of accessing a concept without resorting to a conventional validated set of prespecified procedures that provide the distance of objectivity. This notion of distance fails to take into account the rigor of the hermeneutical understanding of the way meaning is preinscribed in the act of being-in-the world, the research process, and objects of research. This absence of hermeneutical awareness undermines the researcher's quest for a thick description and contributes to the production of reduced understandings of the complexity of social life (Paulson, 1995; Selfe, & Selfe, 1994).

Indeed, what bricoleurs are concerned with here is nothing less than the quality of the knowledge we produce about the world. In this context, they address both the reductionism of uninformed research methods and the quest for new ways of seeing. In the intersection of these concerns, they uncover new insights into research and knowledge production, new forms of reason that are directly connected to specific contexts, practical forms of analysis that are informed by social theory, and the concreteness of lived situations (Fischer, 1998). Understanding non-Western ways of knowing and the epistemologies of marginalized groups within Western societies, bricoleurs transcend regressive forms of reductionism. They see past reductionistic notions that researchers simply produce facts that correspond to external reality, information that is devoid of specific cultural values. With these understandings as valuable parts of their tool kits, bricoleurs expand the envelope of social research, of what we can understand about the world. They are empowered to produce knowledge that can change the world.

## SHE'S NOT THERE: RIGOR IN THE ABSENCE

In their move to the margins and transcendence of reductionism, bricoleurs seek to identify what is absent in particular situations—a task ignored by monological, objectivist modes of research. In this context, bricoleurs seek to cultivate a higher form of researcher creativity that leads them, like poets, to produce concepts and

insights about the social world that previously did not exist. This rigor in the absence can be expressed in numerous ways, including the bricoleur's ability:
- to imagine things that never were;
- to see the world as it could be;
- to develop alternatives to oppressive existing conditions;
- to discern what is lacking in a way that promotes the will to act; and
- to understand that there is far more to the world than what we can see.

As always, bricoleurs are struggling to transcend the traditional observational constraint on social researchers as they develop new ways and methods of exposing social, cultural, political, psychological, and educational forces not at first glance discernible. Pursuing rigor in the absence, bricoleurs document venues of meaning that transcend the words of interviewees or observations of particular behaviors (Dahlbom, 1998; Dicks, & Mason, 1998).

Of course, a central feature of this rigorous effort to identify what is absent involves excavating what has been lost in the naïveté of monological disciplinarity. As bricoleurs engaging in the boundary work of deep interdisciplinarity explore what has been dismissed, deleted, and covered up, they bring to the surface the ideological devices that have erased the lived worlds and perspectives of those living at the margins of power. In response to Lincoln's (2001) question about the use value of knowledge produced by the bricolage, I offer the following assertion: As researchers employ the methodological, theoretical, interpretive, political, and narrative dimensions of the bricolage, they make a variety of previously repressed features of the social world visible. Because they are describing dimensions of the sociocultural, political, economic, psychological, and pedagogical cosmos that have never previously existed, bricoleurs are engaging in what might be termed the fictive element of research.

The use of the term *fictive* as previously discussed should not be conflated with *unreal* in this context. Scientific inventors have engaged in a similar process when they have created design documents for the electric light, the rocket, the computer, or virtual reality. In these examples, individuals used a fictive imagination to produce something that did not yet exist. The bricoleur does the same thing in a different ontological and epistemological domain. Both the inventor and the bricoleur are future oriented as they explore the realm of possibility, a kinetic epistemology of the possible. In the process, the sophistication of knowledge work moves to a new cognitive level; the notion of rigor transmigrates to a new dimension. As in a 1950s sci-fi movie, bricoleurs enter the 4-D—the fourth dimension of research.

In this way, bricoleurs create a space for reassessing the nature of the knowledge that has been created about the social cosmos and the modes of research that have created it. In an era of information saturation and hegemony, this space for reassessing knowledge production and research methods becomes a necessity for democratic survival, the foundation of a pro democracy movement and as Pinar (2001) correctly maintained, the "labor of educational scholarship in general" (p. 698). Overwhelmed by corporate produced data and befuddled by the complex of the social issues that face us, individuals without access to the lenses of the bricolage often do not know how to deal with these debilitating conditions (Dahlbom, 1998;

Denzin, & Lincoln, 2000; DeVault, 1996). As the bricolage provides us new insights into the chaos of the contemporary, researchers become better equipped to imagine where we might go and what path we might take to get there through the jungle of information surrounding us. The bricolage is no panacea, but it does allow us new vantage points to survey the epistemological wilderness and the possibilities hidden in its underbrush.

## CONCLUSION: THE BRICOLAGE AND HUMAN POSSIBILITY

Obviously, my concern with the bricolage in social research involves not only improving the quality of research but also enhancing the possibility of being human or human being. Thus, the bricolage is not only a dynamic of research but operates in the connected domains of cognition and pedagogy as well. In the epistemological and ontological deliberations of the bricolage, we gain insight into new modes of thinking, teaching, and learning. In all of these domains, research included, bricoleurs move from convergent to divergent forms of meaning making, abandoning the short sightedness of prespecified, correct patterns of analysis in favor of more holistic, inclusive, and eclectic models. In this context, the "present awareness" of numerous cultural, historical, and philosophical traditions is explored for insights into new ways of thinking, seeing, being, and researching.

Laurel Richardson (2000) picked up on and expanded these ideas with her metaphor of the crystal. The bricolage, like a crystal, expands, mutates, and alters while at the same time reflecting and refracting the "light" of the social world. New patterns emerge and new shapes dance on the pages of the texts produced by the bricoleur—images unanticipated before the process took place. In this new textual domain, we trace the emergence of not only creative narratives but also new notions of humanness. In a humble context, bricoleurs maintain that there is a profound human drama playing out in this context. In their understanding of social complexity, they gain a larger perspective on post-Enlightenment Western history. Viewing the past 3½ centuries from a new multidimensional vantage point, bricoleurs understand that Westerners built not only a system of knowledge production but also a world that could have been very different than what came to be. The questions they now ask of that system and that world are dramatic in their implications for the future.

The system of knowledge production, with its epistemological blinders that developed and expanded across the centuries, shackled human agency to the gospel of so-called natural law and scientific procedures. In the name of an ethnocentric notion of scientific progress, it attempted to keep individuals ignorant of their potentials and confused cultural difference with deficiency. This procedure-bound science did not do a very good job of addressing questions involving what it means to be human, what it might mean to live in a good and just society, and the worthiness of those who live in cultures and locales different from the West. This is why bricoleurs ascribe such importance to the critical and hermeneutic traditions and their concern with such human questions. Drawing on these traditions, combining them with forms of paradigmatic and textual analyses, bricoleurs struggle to connect the research act to the emotion and heart of lived human experience (Lutz et al., 1997;

Pryse, 1998; Wexler, 2000). Understanding that research that fails to address the ontology of the human existential situation with all of its pain, suffering, joy, and desire is limited in its worth, bricoleurs search for better ways to connect with and illuminate this domain. In this context, much is possible.

## REFERENCES

Blommaert, J. (1997). *Workshopping: Notes on professional vision in discourse.* Retrieved from http://africana_rug.ac.be/texts/research-publications/publications_on-line/workshopping.htm

Bohm, D., & Peat, F. (1987). *Science, order, and creativity.* New York: Bantam.

Bridges, D. (1997). Philosophy and educational research: A reconsideration of epistemological boundaries. *Cambridge Journal of Education, 27*(2), 177–189.

Cronin, P. (1997). *Learning and assessment of instruction.* Retrieved from http://www.cogsci.ed.ac.uk/~paulus/work/vranded/litconsa.txt

Dahlbom, B. (1998). *Going to the future.* Retrieved from http://www.viktoria.infomatik.gu.se/~max/bo/papers.html

Denzin, N., & Lincoln, Y. (2000). *Handbook of qualitative research* (2nd ed.). Thousand Oaks, CA: Sage.

DeVault, M. (1996). Talking back to sociology: Distinctive contributions of feminist methodologies. *Annual Review of Sociology, 22,* 29–50.

Dicks, B., & Mason, B. (1998). Hypermedia and ethnography: Reflections on the construction of a research approach. *Sociological Research Online, 3*(3).

Fischer, F. (1998). Beyond empiricism: Policy inquiry in postpositivist perspective. *Policy Studies Journal, 26*(1), 129–146.

Foster, R. (1997). Addressing epistemologic and practical issues in multimethod research: A procedure for conceptual triangulation. *Advances in Nursing Education, 10*(1), 1–12.

Foucault, M. (1980). *Power/Knowledge: Selected interviews and other writings* (C. Gordon, Ed.). New York: Pantheon.

Jardine, D. (1998). *To dwell with a boundless heart: Essays in curriculum theory, hermeneutics, and the ecological imagination.* New York: Peter Lang.

Karunaratne, V. (1997). *Buddhism, science, and dialectics.* Retrieved from http://humanism.org/opinions/articles.html

Kellner, D. (1995). *Media culture: Cultural studies, identity and politics between the modern and postmodern.* New York: Routledge.

Kincheloe, J. L. (2001). Describing the bricolage: Conceptualizing a new rigor in qualitative research. *Qualitative Inquiry, 7*(6), 679–692.

Kincheloe, J. L. (2002). *The sign of the burger: McDonald's and the culture of power.* Philadelphia: Temple University Press.

Kincheloe, J. L. (2003). *Teachers as researchers: Qualitative inquiry as a path to empowerment* (2nd ed.). London: Falmer.

Kincheloe, J. L., & Steinberg S. R. (1993). A tentative description of postformal thinking: The critical confrontation with cognitive theory. *Harvard Educational Review, 63*(3), 296–320.

Kincheloe, J. L., Steinberg S. R., & Hinchey, P. (1999). *The postformal reader: Cognition and education.* New York: Falmer.

Kincheloe, J. L., Steinberg, S. R., & Villaverde, L. (1999). *Rethinking intelligence: Confronting psychological assumptions about teaching and learning.* New York: Routledge.

Lather, P. (1991). *Getting smart: Feminist research and pedagogy with/in the postmodern.* New York: Routledge.

Lather, P. (1993). Fertile obsession: Validity after poststructuralism. *Sociological Quarterly, 34,* 673–693.

Lévi-Strauss, C. (1966). *The savage mind.* Chicago: University of Chicago Press.

Lincoln, Y. (2001). An emerging new bricoleur: Promises and possibilities—a reaction to Joe Kincheloe's "Describing the bricolage. *Qualitative Inquiry, 7*(6), 693–696.

Lomax, P., & Parker, Z. (1996). *Representing a dialectical form of knowledge within a new epistemology for teaching and teacher education.* Paper presented at the American Educational Research Association, New York.

Lutz, K., Jones, K., & Kendall, J. (1997). Expanding the praxis debate: Contributions to clinical inquiry. *Advances in Nursing Science, 20*(2), 23–31.

Madison, G. (1988). *The hermeneutics of postmodernity: Figures and themes.* Bloomington, IN: Indiana University Press.

McCarthy, M. (1997). Pluralism, invariance, and conflict. *The Review of Metaphysics, 51*(1), 477–492.

McLaren, P. (2000). *Che Guevara, Paulo Freire, and the pedagogy of revolution.* Lanham, MD: Rowman and Littlefield.

McLaren, P. (2001). Bricklayers and bricoleurs: A Marxist addendum. *Qualitative Inquiry, 7*(6), 700–705.

McLaren, P., Hammer, R., Reilly, S., & Sholle, D. (1995). *Rethinking media literacy: A critical pedagogy of representation.* New York: Peter Lang.

McLeod, J. (2000). *Qualitative research as bricolage.* Paper presented at the Society for Psychotherapy Research annual conference, Chicago.

Morawski, J. (1997). The science behind feminist research methods. *Journal of Social Issues, 53*(4), 667–682.

Paulson, R. (1995). Mapping knowledge perspectives in studies of educational change. In P. Cookson Jr. & B. Schneider (Eds.), *Transforming schools* (pp. 137–180). NewYork: Garland.

Pinar, W. (1994). *Autobiography, politics, and sexuality: Essays in curriculum theory, 1972–1992.* New York: Peter Lang.

Pinar, W. (2001). The researcher as bricoleur: The teacher as public intellectual. *Qualitative Inquiry, 7*(6), 696–700.

Pryse, M. (1998). Critical interdisciplinarity, womens studies, and cross-cultural insight. *NWSA Journal, 10*(1), 1–11.

Richardson, L. (2000). Writing: Amethod of inquiry. In N. Denzin & Y. Lincoln (Eds.), *Handbook of qualitative research* (2nd ed., pp. 923–948). Thousand Oaks, CA: Sage.

Selfe, C., & Selfe, R. (1994). *The politics of the interface: Power and its exercise in electronic contact zones.* Retrieved from http://www.hu.mtu.edu/cyselfe/texts/politics.html

Smith, D. (1999). *Pedagon: Interdisciplinary essays in the human sciences, pedagogy, and culture.* New York: Peter Lang.

Soto, L. (Ed.). (2000). *The politics of early childhood education.* New York: Peter Lang.

Steinberg, S. R. (Ed.), (2001). *Multi/intercultural conversations.* New York: Peter Lang.

Thomas, G. (1998). The myth of rational research. *British Educational Research Journal, 24*(2), 141–161.

Varenne, H. (1996). The social facting of education: Durkheim's legacy. *Journal of Curriculum Studies, 27,* 373–389.

Wexler, P. (2000). *The mystical society: Revitalization in culture, theory, and education.* Boulder, CO: Westview.

Willinsky, J. (2001). Raising the standards for democratic education: Research and evaluation as public knowledge. In J. L. Kincheloe & D. Weil (Eds.), *Standards and schooling in the U. S.: An encyclopedia* (pp. 609–621). Santa Barbara, CA: ABC-CLIO.

Young, T., & Yarbrough, J. (1993). *Reinventing sociology: Mission and methods for postmodern sociologists* (Transforming Sociology Series, 154). Weidman, MI: Red Feather Institute.

Zammito, J. (1996). *Historicism, metahistory, and historical practice: The historicization of the historical subject.* Retrieved from http://home.cc.umanitoba.ca/sprague/zammito.htm

**Reprinted with permission: Kincheloe, J. L. (2005). On to the next level: continuing the conceptualization of the bricolage.** *Qualitative Inquiry, 11,* 323–350.

KATHLEEN S. BERRY

# EMBRACING RADICAL RESEARCH

*A Commentary on Joe L. Kincheloe's on to the Next Level:
Continuing the Conceptualization of the Bricolage*

TO SHIRLEY WITH RADICAL LOVE

Over the past century and into this century, research theories and methodologies have proliferated especially those constructed by quantitative discourses and designs. Although, more recently, qualitative theories and methodologies, such as anthropological, phenomenological, narrative or grounded theory research have gained some credibility, the studies produced still tend to be monological; that is singular in design and reductionistic in knowledge. Questions raised by socio-historical worlds as racialized, gendered, sexualized, classed and so forth have problematized monological research even further. Other theoretical and methodological discourses such as postmodernism, postcolonialism and poststructuralism continue to challenge and expand traditional fields of modern research. The interdisciplinary mingling and collapsing of epistemological borders in the natural sciences, humanities, arts and social sciences are rearranging what counts as research and knowledge. Chaos and complexity theories from physics and the influence of major theorists in social history, the arts and literature such as, to name a few, Michael Foucault, Jacques Derrida, and Judith Butler present multiple possibilities for conducting research. Knowledge restored and reclaimed from non-Eurocentric histories and people such as Indigenous nations is changing the face of research. Globalization, transnationalism, and needless to say, the plethora of media and digital age technologies increase not only the volume of research possibilities but the speed at which knowledge is generated. This list is far from complete but acts as a brief indication that radical changes are occurring in many different modern disciplinary and professional fields including educational research.

With the availability of these endless possibilities, there is no question that all fields of knowledge production must embrace radical research theories and methodologies. Why, what, how and when to do so is the task Joe L. Kincheloe undertakes in his many books and articles employing the notion of the bricolage; specifically for this commentary, *On to the Next Level: Continuing the Conceptualization of the Bricolage* (2005). His many writings on the bricolage problematize, address and articulate a rationality for radical research immediately and in the future. He courageously and rigorously continued to explore the notion of the bricolage as first introduced by Levi-Strauss in *The Savage Mind* (1966); discussed briefly in the introduction of Denzin and Lincoln's voluminous text *Handbook of Qualitative*

*Research* (2000); expanded on in *Rigour and Complexity in Educational Research: Conceptualizing the Bricolage* (Kincheloe and Berry, 2004) and put into practice in *The Sign of the Burger: MacDonald's and A Culture of Power* (Kincheloe, 2002).

First and foremost, however, every reader of Joe's writings on the bricolage must never lose sight of his dedication to all research informed by Critical Theories and his positioning in the works as a Critical Pedagogue (yes all with a capital letter!). With this key point in mind, we recognize that Joe's renderings of the bricolage are not simply a mosaic, accumulation, combination and permutation, or unintentional, convenient selections of available research theories and methodologies. To Joe, unless the complexity of the bricolage considers critical theory frameworks as the overriding rationality for employing multiple areas, such as those listed in the beginning paragraph of this commentary, research is nothing more than a fallback to reductionist, monological, linear research hierarchies. In other words, releasing the bricoleur to choose from the multitude of research theories and methodologies without embracing critical theory frameworks is a misuse of the bricolage and still permits one or two theories and methodologies to dominate the fields of research. Thus power to produce and disseminate knowledge is assigned to one or two research designs. And the power becomes produced as the singular, knowledge, truth and value; circulated through graduate programs and dissertation requirements, research committees and funding agencies; and finally hegemonically maintained by institutional and societal discourses and policies. Peter McLaren (2001) admires Joe's description of the bricolage but very adamantly cautions all bricoleurs that abandoning the Critical theories, especially the foundations provided by Marxism, is dangerous. Several of my Critical Study colleagues agree. When we collaborate on engaging the bricolage in research studies, graduate courses, dissertations, research committees and so forth, if there is an absence or weak inclusion of Critical theories, methodologies or even the lack of critical theory questioning, to us the knowledge produced is valueless and non-transformative. In spite of Joe's extensive and detailed descriptions in *On to the Next Level* and other works on the bricolage, his emphasis on the CRITICAL bricolage needs, to me and others, to be more heavily weighted and clarified; a task that both novice and seasoned bricoleurs should consider emphatically. Henceforth, I attach Critical to the bricolage - thus The Critical Bricolage always. I hope Joe concurs.

Reading his sequence of writings on the (critical) bricolage is very helpful for understanding the evolution of Joe's concern for the construction of knowledge through research In *Describing the Bricolage* (2001), the prelude article to *On to the Next Level* (2005), Joe very clearly warns us of the possibilities, limitations, struggles and politics inherent in engaging the bricolage as research. Without hesitation in the prelude article, he opens research fields to the possibility of breaking disciplinary boundaries. Inspirationally, in *On to the Next Level*, he delineates in more detail and with broad conceptual descriptions, how the complexity of the bricolage is embedded with notions of: explicate and implicate orders of reality; the questioning of universalism; polysemy; the living process in which cultural entities are situated; the ontology of relationships and connections; intersecting contexts; multiple epistemologies; intertextuality; discursive constructions; the interpretative aspect of all knowledge; the fictive dimension of research findings; the cultural assumptions within all research methods (I would also add the socio-historical assumptions the researcher brings to the research—thus a critical autobiographical positioning of the bricoleur in the research); and finally—and most importantly to maintaining the critical theory frameworks of the bricolage—the relationship of power and knowledge.

As an important first step in embarking on a research process and/or introducing novice and seasoned researchers to the bricolage, Joe, whether in a book, address, or journal article, always contextualizes and problematizes the history of research and knowledge production under headings such as *Bricolage in the Cosmos* and *Rigour in the Ruins* (in Describing the Bricolage, 2001) and *An Active View of Research Methodology* and *Chasing Complexity: Avoiding Monological Knowledge in the Bricolage* (On to the Next Level, 2005). I find that without these contextualizing and problematizing discussions, novice and seasoned researchers, graduate students and professors (myself included) tend to *chase* the bricolage as a potpourri of facts and methodologies. Thus the research and researchers are merely resorting to a superficial or redundant construction of knowledge. In my own work with graduate students, whether a research or content oriented course, they are introduced to the history of knowledge production mainly through Joe's writings. It seems once they grasp the notion of contextualizing and problematizing knowledge production, the plethora of possibilities (such as summarized in the first paragraph of this commentary and in the many works of Joe's and others) made available to them, are understood in a manner diligent about avoiding reductionism and cogent about the choices they select to construct new knowledge. Needless to say, however, the *chase* is always informed by critical theories, practices and pedagogy; a constant concern of Joe's.

Another strong feature of Joe's writings is his delineated summary of various dimensions of the bricolage borrowed from Denzin and Lincoln (2002). In a further attempt to cover all the possibilities for organizing and legitimizing the bricolage as research, in *On to the Next Level*, Joe expands their five dimensions: the methodological bricolage, the theoretical bricolage, the interpretative bricolage, the narrative bricolage and the political bricolage. These areas, however, tend to be inclusive of what I consider to meet the established academic requirements for graduate dissertations and research funding proposals. The dimensions seem to follow the traditional five empirical chapters usually organized as: Introduction, Literature Review, Methodology, Data Analysis and Conclusions. The similarity between the two organizational structures potentially slips the bricolage into the very abyss of scientific rationale, monological, objective construction of knowledge that Joe constantly writes against. In the seductive rush to embrace the bricolage, novice and seasoned researchers, graduate students and professors under pressure to consent to the hegemonic practices of doing research within institutional and academic settings often resort to the familiarity and convenience of traditional empirical research. In addition, with a lack of historical, creative, and innovative precedents on how to organize and disseminate the knowledge produced by the bricolage, even Joe's dimensions can fall prey to the traditional empirical ways and means of constructing knowledge through research. The names may have changed but the knowledge remains the same. Which in turn means institutional and societal power, discourses, structures, practices, and ethics continue social injustices, exclusions and inequities unfettered by what the bricolage might challenge and dismantle.

As mentioned previously, it is the dimension of the political bricolage that should be threaded throughout all research dimensions and works no matter the source, field or purpose. And as was once mandatory for all academics and researchers to be able to access knowledge/understand more than one language, the application of the political bricolage should be compulsory for all research works and knowledge workers. I know Joe would wish this for the future of knowledge production, value and dissemination. In other words, requiring the political bricolage as the overriding discourse and application to all research is the turn to embracing radical research!

In the article, *On To The Next Level*, and in many of his other writings, Joe frames research utilizing the bricolage as a process of rigour and complexity. In fact, in our co-authored book (2004), Joe invited me to write my chapters based on graduate courses in which I regularly taught the bricolage as a process of complexity. In so doing, he and I noted the emphasis on the theories, discourse and practices borrowed from those of Chaos and Complexity. To us, framing the bricolage as such seems the best metaphor that makes the entry into, doing of and completing (if this is possible?) the process of constructing knowledge/research possible, accessible, and innovative. Might it also be that as politically visionary as Joe and I are, we see the discourse of complexity as cultural capital in the emerging postmodern, already-here digital world? A mere employment, however, of the concepts associated with complexity is not enough. Bricoleurs need to understand the concepts that drive the bricolage as rigour and complexity. How is a process that builds complexity different from a process that is reductionistic? In his steady problematizing of the current dominance of scientific rationality as monological, linear, hierarchical, and logical positivism Joe answers why a bricoleur needs to understand and accept the bricolage as a process of complexity. To me, in addition to the importance of attaching Critical theories, questions and practices to the concept of the bricolage, understanding and accepting the principles and practices of complexity are necessary to embracing the radical aspects of the bricolage.

Joe's explorations of the Critical and Complexity of the bricolage represent both a dialectic (as intended by the Critical and previously noted in this commentary) and a dialogic engagement (as premised by complexity) with the historical and contemporary socio-poltical and cultural dynamics that have shaped the ways in which we produce, disseminate and value knowledge. In hand with the Critical dimensions of the bricolage that challenge any constructions of knowledge in all realms of temporal and spatial worlds, complexity only builds if the dialogic is present. Conditions of complexity include: self-organization, far-from-equilibrium conditions, feedback looping, randomness, spontaneity, and bifurcations. Coupled with the dialectic of the Critical bricolage, complexity increases the dialogic of the process. The interaction between the possible fields of the bricolage and the presence of conditions of complexity call forth the dialectic and the dialogic. Joe continuously reminds us of the conversations, whether oral, printed, visual, auditory and so forth that speak with the tongues of the Critical Bricolage and Complexity: conversations that point out sites of hegemony, conflicts, contradictions, inequities, social injustices and exclusions in the ways and products that produce, disseminate and value knowledge. Both the tension of Critical questions and the features of building complexity such as feedback looping, self-organization, and far-from-equilibrium create and maintain the dialectic and dialogic dynamics of the bricolage. Just as a hint of reductionism or the fear of complexity enters into the research process, it becomes the responsibility of all those involved in embracing the 'radical', to critically question, challenge, feedback loop, borrow, collect, dig and connect (archeological genealogy), track, dismantle and so forth all the 'tools' available in the theories and practices of the bricolage. In this way, there is limited to nil escape from Joe's belief in the significance of the bricolage. To read Joe's works otherwise, I assume, is epistemologically and ontologically inexcusable.

Perhaps some examples borrowed in part from actual research and/or dissertations works might help to clarify what Joe means about the significance of the dialectic and the dialogic. In one example, the PhD researcher investigated nurse's daily work conditions by gathering 'data' through interviews and the application of grounded theory. No other aspects of the bricolage were considered. Yet all the nurses interviewed, except one, were women. Some of the interviewees were from different racialized/classed backgrounds than that of the dominance of white middle classed nurses in the area. The 'findings' were interpreted, thematized and generalized. When asked why not the application of feminist theories and/or theories from the field of race studies, or even a brief discussion borrowed from the political bricolage, the supervisor baulked at the questions. So the conversation ended—the dialogic closed. So Joe, how would a Critical Bricoleur respond?

In another example, a student teacher/researcher worked with ten secondary school students to produce a film that related their personal experiences of being categorized as drop-outs, failures, druggies, and so forth. The student researcher is an excellent teacher. What he got from these marginalized students was, as all ten students echoed; "awesome, changed my life, never forget."

At the individual, personal level, yes it was life altering in many respects for the secondary students. But as they walked away from the experience, and in the long run, what had really been transformative at the personal, societal and institutional levels? How could the researcher draw from different areas of the bricolage to make the personal political? What discourse and questions could be threaded through his analysis/interpretation to shed light on what policies and practices were hegemonically discursive in the society, history, and institutions that placed these students in the margins initially? What transformative knowledge could he have extracted and/or created from the bricolage that would challenge and resist the marginalization of these students and Others positioned as such in the dominant power? For help in exploring these questions and applying the Critical bricolage and building complexity—read Joe's work.

While the near-ending possibilities of knowledge constructions of the bricolage are infinite, an end must be reached at some point. As a colleague responded to one student's thesis using the bricolage, "So What?" In the spirit of both critical theories and the bricolage, the end point of the knowledge production is transformative action.

In what ways does Joe's work remain relevant and need to be leveraged anew within our contemporary social and academic contexts? Although Joe ends the article with a conclusion, the discourse of scientific rationality, those of us who worked with him as a friend, colleague, and ally of critical pedagogy know full well that he did not intend to slip into closure. My use of the slippery slopes of past, present and future tenses (grammatically inconsistent) throughout this commentary is a further indication that Joe's works need to be continued "On to the Next Level" from this article (2005). I know firsthand the importance of doing so. After working for years with Linda Eyre and others to establish a program at the university level through Critical Studies in Education with Joe and Shirley's help, then having to fight constantly against the political, faculty and administrative backlash to the program; developing courses and dissertations with limited to nil support from the bureaucratic structures that deploy graduate students to more acceptable fields (such as curriculum and instruction or special education); while university faculties of education align themselves with conservative, neo-liberal, Christian right ideologies of State Departments of Education and a host of other factors that continue the marginalization and oppression of the production, circulation and maintenance of different ways of knowing and being, how can democracy thrive? Witness the recent power of corporations to squash unions or of capitalism to provide a quality life for all—the very foundational promises of democracy. Joe's works help to light the torch of social justice. It's for many to keep it burning.

## REFERENCES

Denzin, N, & Lincoln, Y. (2002). *Handbook of qualitative research* (2nd ed.). Thousand Oaks, CA: Sage.

Kincheloe, J. L. (2005). On to the next level: Continuing the conceptualizing of the bricolage. *Qualitative Inquiry, 11*(3), 323–350.

Kincheloe, J. L., & Berry, K. S. (2004). *Rigour and complexity in educational research: Conceptualizing the bricolage.* England: Open University Press.

Kincheloe, J. L. (2002). *The sign of the burger: Macdonald's and the culture of power.* Philadelphia: Temple University Press.

Kincheloe, J. L. (2001). Describing the bricolage: Conceptualizing a new rigour in qualitative research. *Qualitative Inquiry, 7*(6), 679–692.

Levi-Strauss, C. (1966). *The savage mind.* Chicago: University of Chicago Press.

McLaren, P. (2001). Bricklayers and bricoleurs: A Marxist addendum. *Qualitative Inquiry, 7*, 700–705.

*1993, Atlanta, Georgia. It was the first year that Joe realized his work was actually being read. We lived in South Carolina, so put our weimaraner, Amber, in the van and drove to Atlanta. We were excited to meet up with Peter and Jenny McLaren, and to meet Yvonna Lincoln. Peter had arranged a meeting with Joe and Yvonna to discuss a project. Joe was pretty overwhelmed at the idea of meeting and lunching with Yvonna, his work was grounded in Lincoln and Guba, and he had no idea what Peter had in mind. Earlier that morning, Jenny and I were off somewhere (it was our first meeting and we were instantly friends) and Joe and Peter were at the hotel on the terrace eating breakfast with Amber sitting at Joe's feet. They were crazed laughing, as was their habit, creating their own language much like twins do. It was at that conference that Joe and Peter determined they had to be twins from different mothers, that they were obviously zygotes who were separated at birth. At any rate, they turned to look at the man eating next to them and realized with glee that it was Red Skelton. They both jumped on the opportunity to meet Red and to listen to him tell stories. However, their notion of being star-struck took new meaning as Skelton continually spewed scrambled eggs in their faces. But the time Yvonna got there, Joe and Peter were hardly the controlled scholars they intended to be.*

*The reason for the meeting was clarified almost instantly. After Joe and Yvonna did their redneck southern roots bonding, and an instant rapport emerged with the three, Yvonna invited Joe to join Peter in writing a piece for Norm Denzin's and her new Handbook of Qualitative Research. As she named the scholars who would be included in the book, Joe couldn't contain his shock and pleasure at being invited to work with Peter on this project. Indeed, Peter insisted Joe be the lead author on the chapter, which has become known throughout the research world as a seminal piece on critical theory and research, first published in 1994, 2000, and this piece in 2005 and 2010. Neither Joe nor I could read this piece without thinking of the weimaraner, Red Skelton, the zygote twins, and Yvonna Lincoln. This little sidebar is a note of love and friendship to Peter McLaren and Jenny McLaren, and to Yvonna and Norm for inviting "the boys" to contribute this piece. SS*

JOE L. KINCHELOE AND PETER MCLAREN

# 12. RETHINKING CRITICAL THEORY AND QUALITATIVE RESEARCH

THE ROOTS OF CRITICAL RESEARCH

Some 70 years after its development in Frankfurt, Germany, critical theory retains its ability to disrupt and challenge the status quo. In the process, it elicits highly charged emotions of all types—fierce loyalty from its proponents, vehement hostility from its detractors. Such vibrantly polar reactions indicate at the very least that critical theory still matters. We can be against critical theory or for it, but, especially at the present historical juncture, we cannot be without it. Indeed, qualitative research that frames its purpose in the context of critical theoretical concerns still produces, in our view, undeniably dangerous knowledge, the kind of information and insight that upsets institutions and threatens to overturn sovereign regimes of truth.

*Critical theory* is a term that is often evoked and frequently misunderstood. It usually refers to the theoretical tradition developed by the Frankfurt school, a group of writers connected to the Institute of Social Research at the University of Frankfurt. However, none of the Frankfurt school theorists ever claimed to have developed a unified approach to cultural criticism. In its beginnings, Max Horkheimer, Theodor Adorno, and Herbert Marcuse initiated a conversation with the German tradition of philosophical and social thought, especially that of Marx, Kant, Hegel, and Weber. From the vantage point of these critical theorists, whose political sensibilities were influenced by the devastations of World War I, postwar Germany with its economic depression marked by inflation and unemployment, and the failed strikes and protests in Germany and Central Europe in this same period. The world was in urgent need of reinterpretation. From this perspective, they defied Marxist orthodoxy while deepening their belief that injustice and subjugation shape the lived world (Bottomore, 1984; Gibson, 1986; Held, 1980; Jay, 1973). Focusing their attention on the changing nature of capitalism, the early critical theorists analyzed the mutating forms of domination that accompanied this change (Agger, 1998; Gall, Gall, & Borg, 1999; Giroux, 1983, 1997; Kellner, 1989; Kincheloe, & Pinar, 1991; McLaren, 1997).

Only a decade after the Frankfurt school was established, the Nazis controlled Germany. The danger posed by the exclusive Jewish membership of the Frankfurt school, and its association with Marxism, convinced Horkheimer, Adorno, and Marcuse to leave Germany. Eventually locating themselves in California, these critical theorists were shocked by American culture. Offended by the taken-for-granted empirical practices of American social science researchers, Horkheimer, Adorno, and Marcuse were challenged to respond to the social science establishment's belief that their research could describe and accurately measure any dimension of human behavior. Piqued by the contradictions between progressive American rhetoric of egalitarianism and the reality of racial and class discrimination, these theorists produced their major work while residing in the United States. In 1953, Horkheimer and Adorno returned to Germany and reestablished the Institute of Social Research. Significantly, Herbert Marcuse stayed in the United States, where he would find a new audience for his work in social theory. Much to his own surprise, Marcuse skyrocketed to fame as the philosopher of the student movements of the 1960s. Critical theory, especially the emotionally and sexually liberating work of Marcuse, provided the philosophical voice of the New Left. Concerned with the politics of psychological and cultural revolution, the New Left preached a Marcusian sermon of political emancipation (Gibson, 1986; Hinchey, 1998; Kincheloe, & Steinberg, 1997; Surber, 1998; Wexler, 1991, 1996b).

Many academicians who had come of age in the politically charged atmosphere of the 1960s focused their scholarly attention on critical theory. Frustrated by forms of domination emerging from a post-Enlightenment culture nurtured by capitalism, these scholars saw in critical theory a method of temporarily freeing academic work from these forms of power. Impressed by critical theory's dialectical concern with the social construction of experience, they came to view their disciplines as manifestations of the discourses and power relations of the social and historical contexts that produced them. The "discourse of possibility" implicit within the constructed nature of social experience suggested to these scholars that a reconstruction of the social sciences could eventually lead to a more egalitarian and democratic social order. New poststructuralist conceptualizations of human agency and their promise that men and women can at least partly determine their own existence offered new hope for emancipatory forms of social research when compared with orthodox Marxism's assertion of the iron laws of history, the irrevocable evil of capitalism, and the proletariat as the privileged subject and anticipated agent of social transformation. For example, when Henry Giroux and other critical educators criticized the argument made by Marxist scholars Samuel Bowles and Herbert Gintis—that schools are capitalist agencies of social, economic, cultural, and bureaucratic reproduction—they contrasted the deterministic perspectives of Bowles and Gintis with the idea that schools, as venues of hope, could become sites of resistance and democratic possibility through concerted efforts among teachers and students to work within a liberatory pedagogical framework. Giroux (1988), in particular, maintained that schools can become institutions where forms of knowledge, values, and social relations are taught for the purpose of educating young people for critical empowerment rather than subjugation.

## CRITICAL HUMILITY: OUR IDIOSYNCRATIC INTERPRETATION OF CRITICAL THEORY AND CRITICAL RESEARCH

Over the past 20 years of our involvement in critical theory and critical research, we have been asked by hundreds of people to explain more precisely what critical theory is. We find that question difficult to answer because (a) there are many critical theories, not just one; (b) the critical tradition is always changing and evolving; and (c) critical theory attempts to avoid too much specificity, as there is room for disagreement among critical theorists. To lay out a set of fixed characteristics of the position is contrary to the desire of such theorists to avoid the production of blueprints of sociopolitical and epistemological beliefs. Given these disclaimers, we will now attempt to provide one idiosyncratic "take" on the nature of critical theory and critical research at the beginning of the millennium. Please note that this is merely our subjective analysis and there are many brilliant critical theorists who will find many problems with our pronouncements.

In this humble spirit we tender a description of a reconceptualized, end-of-century critical theory that has been critiqued and overhauled by the "post-discourses" of the 20th century (Bauman, 1995; Carlson, & Apple, 1998; Collins, 1995; Giroux, 1997; Kellner, 1995; Roman, & Eyre, 1997; Steinberg, & Kincheloe, 1998) In this context a reconceptualized critical theory questions the assumption that societies such as the United States, Canada, Australia, New Zealand, and the nations in the European Union, for example, are unproblematically democratic and free. Over the 20th century, especially since the early 1960s, individuals in these societies have been acculturated to feel comfortable in relations of domination and subordination rather than equality and independence. Given the social and technological changes of the last half of the century that led to new forms of information production and access, critical theorists argued that questions of self-direction and democratic egalitarianism should be reassessed. In this context critical researchers informed by the "post-discourses" (e.g., postmodern, critical feminism, poststructuralism) understand that individuals' views of themselves and the worlds even more influenced by social and historical forces than previously believed. Given the changing social and informational conditions of late-20th-century media-saturated Western culture, critical theorists needed new ways of researching and analyzing the construction of individuals (Agger, 1992; Flossner, & Otto, 1998; Hinchey, 1998; Leistyna, Woodrum, & Sherblom, 1996; Quail, Razzano, & Skalli, 2000; Smith, & Wexler, 1995; Sünker, 1998). The following points briefly delineate our interpretation of a critical theory for the new millennium.

## A RECONCEPTUALIZED CRITICAL THEORY

In this context it is important to note that we understand a social theory as a map or a guide to the social sphere. In a research context it does not determine how we see the world but helps us devise questions and strategies for exploring it. A critical social theory is concerned in particular with issues of power and justice and the ways that the economy, matters of race, class, and gender, ideologies, discourses, education, religion, and other social institutions, and cultural dynamics interact to construct a social system.

*Critical enlightenment.* In this context critical theory analyzes competing power interests between groups and individuals within a society—identifying who gains and who loses in specific situations. Privileged groups, criticalists argue, often have an interest in supporting the status quo to protect their advantages; the dynamics of such efforts often become a central focus of critical research. Such studies of privilege often revolve around issues of race, class, gender, and sexuality (Carter, 1998; Howell, 1998; Kincheloe, & Steinberg, 1997; Kincheloe, Steinberg, Rodriguez, & Chennault, 1998; McLaren, 1997; Rodriguez, & Villaverde, 1999; Sleeter, & McLaren, 1995). In this context to seek critical enlightenment is to uncover the winners and losers in particular social arrangements and the processes by which such power plays operate (Cary, 1996; Fehr, 1993; King, 1996; Pruyn, 1994; Wexler, 1996a).

*Critical emancipation.* Those who seek emancipation attempt to gain the power to control their own lives in solidarity with a justice-oriented community. Here critical research attempts to expose the forces that prevent individuals and groups from shaping the decisions that crucially affect their lives. In this way greater degrees of autonomy and human agency can be achieved. At the beginning of the new millennium we are cautious in our use of the term *emancipation* because, as many critics have pointed out, no one is ever completely emancipated from the socio-political context that has produced him or her. Also, many have questioned the arrogance that may accompany efforts to emancipate "others." These are important criticisms and must be carefully taken into account by critical researchers. Thus, as critical inquirers who search for those forces that insidiously shape who we are, we respect those who reach different conclusions in their personal journeys (Butler, 1998; Cannella, 1997; Kellogg, 1998; Knobel, 1999; Steinberg, & Kincheloe, 1998; Weil, 1998).

*The rejection of economic determinism.* A caveat of a reconceptualized critical theory involves the insistence that the tradition does not accept the orthodox Marxist notion that "base" determines "superstructure"—meaning that economic factors dictate the nature of all other aspects of human existence. Critical theorists understand at the beginning of the 21st century that there are multiple forms of power, including the aforementioned racial, gender, sexual axes of domination. In issuing this caveat, however, a reconceptualized critical theory in no way attempts to argue that economic factors are unimportant in the shaping of everyday life. Economic factors can never be separated from other axes of oppression (Aronowitz, & DiFazio, 1994; Carlson, 1997; Gabbard, 1995; Gee, Hull, & Lankshear, 1996; Gibson, 1986; Haymes, 1995; Kincheloe, 1995, 1999; Kincheloe, & Steinberg, 1999; Martin, & Schumann, 1996; Rifkin, 1995).

*The critique of instrumental or technical rationality.* A reconceptualized critical theory sees instrumental/technological rationality as one of the most oppressive features of contemporary society. Such a form of "hyperreason" involves an obsession with means in preference to ends. Critical theorists claim that instrumental/technical rationality is more interested in method and efficiency than in purpose. It delimits its questions to "how to" instead of "why should." In a research context, critical theorists claim that many rationalistic scholars become so obsessed with issues of technique, procedure, and correct method that they forget the humanistic purpose of the research act. Instrumental/technical rationality often separates fact from value in its obsession with "proper" method, losing in the process an understanding of the value choices always involved in the production of so-called facts (Alfino, Caputo, & Wynyard, 1998; Giroux, 1997; Hinchey, 1998; Kincheloe, 1993; McLaren, 1998; Ritzer, 1993; Stallabrass, 1996; Weinstein, 1998).

*The impact of desire.* A reconceptualized critical theory appreciates poststructuralist psycho analysis as an important resource in pursuing an emancipatory research project. In this context critical researchers are empowered to dig more deeply into the complexity of the construction of the human psyche. Such a psychoanalysis helps critical researchers discern the unconscious processes that create resistance to progressive change and induce self-destructive behavior. A poststructural psychoanalysis, in its rejection of traditional psychoanalysis's tendency to view individuals as rational and autonomous beings, allows critical researchers new tools to rethink the interplay among the various axes of power, identity, libido, rationality, and emotion. In this configuration the psychic is no longer separated from the sociopolitical realm; indeed desire can be socially constructed and used by power wielders for destructive and oppressive outcomes. On the other hand, critical theorists can help mobilize desire for progressive and emancipatory projects. Taking their lead from feminist theory, critical researchers are aware of the patriarchal inscriptions within traditional psychoanalysis and work to avoid its bourgeois, ethnocentric, and misogynist practices freed from these blinders, poststructuralist psychoanalysis helps researchers gain a new sensitivity to the role of fantasy and imagination and the structures of sociocultural and psychological meaning they reference (Alford, 1993; Atwell-Vasey, 1998; Barrows, 1995; Block, 1995; Britzman, & Pitt, 1996; Elliot, 1994; Gresson, 2000; Kincheloe, Steinberg, & Villaverde, 1999; Pinar, 1998; Pinar, Reynolds, Slattery, & Taubman, 1995; Samuels, 1993).

*A reconceptualized critical theory of power: hegemony.* Our conception of a reconceptualized critical theory is intensely concerned with the need to understand the various and complex that power operates to dominate and shape consciousness. Power, critical theorists have learned, is an extremely ambiguous topic that demands detailed study and analysis. A consensus seems to be emerging among criticalists that power is a basic constituent of human existence that works to shape the oppressive and productive nature of the human tradition. Indeed, we are all empowered and we are all unempowered, in that we all possess abilities and we are all limited in the attempt to use out abilities. Because of limited space, we will focus here on critical theory's traditional concern with the oppressive aspects of power, although we understand that an important aspect of critical research focuses on the productive aspects of power- its ability to empower, to establish a critical democracy, to engage marginalized people in the rethinking of their sociopolitical role (Apple, 1996b; Fiske, 1993; Freire, 2000; Giroux, 1997; Macedo, 1994; Nicholson, & Seidman, 1995).

In the context of oppressive power and its ability to produce inequalities and human suffering, Antonio Gramsci's notion of hegemony is central to critical research. Gramsci understood that dominant power in the 20th century is not always exercised simply by physical force but also through social psychological attempts to win people's consent to domination through cultural institutions such as the media, the schools, the family, and the church. Gramscian hegemony recognizes that the winning of popular consent is a very complex process and must be researched carefully on a case-by-case basis. Students and researchers of power, educators, sociologists, all of us are hegemonized as our field of knowledge and understanding is structured by a limited exposure to competing definitions of the sociopolitical world. The hegemonic field, with its bounded sociopsychological horizons, garners consent to an inequitable power matrix- a set of social relations that are legitimized by their depiction as natural and inevitable. In this context critical researchers note that hegemonic consent is never completely established, as it is always contested by various groups with different agendas (Grossberg, 1997; Lull, 1995; McLaren, 1995a, 1995b; McLaren, Hammer, Reilly, & Sholle, 1995; West, 1993).

*A reconceptualized critical theory of power: ideology.* Critical theorists understand that the formulation of hegemony cannot be separated from the production of ideology. If hegemony is the larger effort of the powerful to win the consent of their "subordinates" then ideological hegemony involves the cultural forms, the meanings, the rituals, and the representations that produce consent to the status quo and individuals' particular place within it. Ideology vis-à-vis hegemony moves critical inquirers beyond simplistic explanations of domination that have used terms such as *propaganda* to describe the way media, political, educational, and other sociocultural productions coercively manipulate citizens to adopt oppressive meanings. A reconceptualized critical research endorses a much more subtle, ambiguous, and situationally specific form of domination that refuses the propaganda model's assumption that people are passive, easily manipulated victims. Researchers operating with an awareness of this hegemonic ideology understand that dominant ideological practices and discourses shape our vision of reality (Lemke, 1995, 1998). Thus our notion of hegemonic ideology is a critical form of epistemological constructivism buoyed by a nuanced understanding of power's complicity in the constructions people make of the world and their role in it (Kincheloe, 1998). Such an awareness corrects earlier delineations of ideology as a monolithic unidirectional entity that was imposed on individuals by a secret cohort of ruling-class czars. Understanding domination in the context of concurrent struggles among different classes, racial and gender groups, and sectors of capital, critical researchers of ideology explore the ways such competition engages different visions, interests, and agendas in a variety of social locales- venues previously thought to be outside the domain of ideological struggle (Brosio, 1994; Steinberg, 2000).

*A reconceptualized critical theory of power: linguistic/discursive power.* Critical researchers have come to understand that language is not a mirror of society. It is an unstable social practice whose meaning shifts, depending upon the context in which it is used. Contrary to previous understandings, critical researchers appreciate the fact that language is not a neutral and objective conduit of description of the "real world." Rather, from a critical perspective, linguistic descriptions are not simply about the world but serve to construct it. With these linguistic notions in mind, criticalists begin to study the way language in the form of discourses serves as a form of regulation and domination. Discursive practices are defined as a set of tacit rules that regulate what can and cannot be said, who can speak with the blessings of authority and who must listen, whose social constructions are valid and whose are erroneous and unimportant. In an educational context, for example, legitimated discourses of power insidiously tell educators what books may be read by students, what instructional methods may be utilized, and what belief systems and views of success may be taught. In all forms of research discursive power validates particular research strategies, narrative formats, and modes of representation. In this context power discourses undermine the multiple meanings of language, establishing one correct reading that implants a particular hegemonic/ideological message into the consciousness of the reader. This is a process often referred to as the attempt to impose discursive closure. Critical researchers interested in the construction of consciousness are very attentive to these power dynamics (Blades, 1997; Gee, 1996; Lemke, 1993; Morgan, 1996; McWilliam, & Taylor, 1996; Steinberg, 1998).

*Focusing on the relationships among culture, power, and domination.* In the last decades of the 20th century, culture has taken on a new importance in the effort to understand power and domination. Critical researchers have argued that culture has to be viewed as a domain of struggle where the production and transmission of knowledge is always a contested process (Giroux, 1997; Kincheloe, & Steinberg, 1997; McLaren, 1997; Steinberg, & Kincheloe, 1997; Steinberg, 1998). Dominant and subordinate cultures deploy differing systems of meaning based on the forms of knowledge produced in their cultural domain. Popular culture, with its TV, movies, video games, computers, music, dance, and other productions, plays an increasingly important role in critical research on power and domination. Cultural studies, of course, occupies an ever-expanding role in this context, as it examines not only popular culture but the tacit rules that guide cultural production. Arguing that the development of mass media has changed the way the culture operates, cultural studies researchers maintain that cultural epistemologies at the beginning of the new millennium are different from those of only a few decades ago. New forms of culture and cultural domination are produced as the distinction between the real and the simulated is blurred. This blurring effect of hyperreality constructs a social vertigo characterized by a loss of touch with traditional notions of time, community, self, and history. New structures of cultural space and time generated by bombarding electronic images from local, national, and international spaces shake our personal sense of place. This proliferation of signs and images functions as a mechanism of control in contemporary Western societies. The key to successful counterhegemonic cultural research involves a) the ability to link the production of representations, images, and signs of hyperreality to power in the political economy; and b) the capacity, once this linkage is exposed and described, to delineate the highly complex effects of the reception of these images and signs on individuals located at various race, class, gender, and sexual coordinates in the web of reality (Ferguson, & Golding, 1997; Garnham, 1997; Grossberg, 1995; Joyrich, 1996; Thomas, 1997).

*The role of cultural pedagogy in critical theory.* Cultural production can often be thought of as a form of education, as it generates knowledge, shapes values, and constructs identity. From our perspective, such a framing can help critical researchers make sense of the world of domination and oppression as they work to bring about a more just, democratic, and egalitarian society. In recent years this educational dynamic has been referred to as cultural pedagogy (Berry, 1998; Giroux, 1997; Kincheloe, 1995; McLaren, 1997; Pailliotet, 1998; Semali, 1998; Soto, 1998). *Pedagogy* is a useful term that has traditionally been used to refer only to teaching and schooling. By using the term *cultural pedagogy*, we are specifically referring to the ways particular cultural agents produce particular hegemonic ways of seeing. In our critical interpretive context, our notion of cultural pedagogy asserts that the new "educators" in the electronically wired contemporary era are those who possess the financial resources to use mass media. This corporate-dominated pedagogical process has worked so well that few complain about it at the beginning of the new millennium—such informational politics doesn't make the evening news. Can we imagine another institution in contemporary society gaining the pedagogical power that corporations now assert over information and signification systems? What if the Church of Christ was sufficiently powerful to run pedagogical "commercials" every few minutes on TV and radio touting the necessity for everyone to accept that denomination's faith? Replayed scenes of Jews, Muslims, Hindus, Catholics, and Methodists being condemned to hell if they rejected the official pedagogy (the true doctrine) would greet North Americans and their children 7 days a week. There is little doubt that many people would be outraged and would organize for political action. Western societies have to some degree capitulated to this corporate pedagogical threat to democracy, passively watching an elite gain greater control over the political system and political consciousness via a sophisticated cultural pedagogy. Critical researchers are intent on exposing the specifics of this process (Deetz, 1993; Drummond, 1996; Molnar, 1996; Pfeil, 1995; Steinberg, & Kincheloe, 1997).

## CRITICAL RESEARCH AND THE CENTRALITY OF INTERPRETATION: CRITICAL HERMENEUTICS

One of the most important aspects of a critical theory-informed qualitative research involves the often-neglected domain of the interpretation of information. As we have taught and written about critical research in the 1990s, this interpretive or hermeneutical aspect has become increasingly important. Many students of qualitative research approach us in classes and presentations with little theoretical background involving the complex and multidimensional nature of data interpretation in their work. Although there are many moments within the process of researching when the *critical* dynamic of critical theory-informed research appears, there is none more important than the moment(s) of interpretation. In this context we begin our discussion of critical qualitative research, linking it as we go to questions of the relationship between critical hermeneutics and knowledge production (Madison, 1988; Slattery, 1995).

The critical hermeneutic tradition (Grondin, 1994; Gross, & Keith, 1997; Rosen, 1987; Vattimo, 1994) holds that in qualitative research there is only interpretation, no matter how vociferously many researchers may argue that the facts speak for themselves. The hermeneutic act of interpretation involves in its most elemental articulation making sense of what has been observed in a way that communicates understanding. Not only is all research merely an act of interpretation, but, hermeneutics contends, perception itself is an act of interpretation. Thus the quest for understanding is a fundamental feature of human existence, as encounter with the unfamiliar always demands the attempt to make meaning, to make sense. The same, however, is also the case with the familiar. Indeed, as in the study of commonly known texts, we come to find that sometimes the familiar may be seen as the most strange. Thus it should not be surprising that even the so-called objective writings of qualitative research are interpretations, not value-free descriptions (Denzin, 1994; Gallagher, 1992; Jardine, 1998; Smith, 1999).

Learning from the hermeneutic tradition and the postmodern critique, critical researchers have begun to reexamine textual claims to authority. No pristine interpretation exists— indeed, no methodology, social or educational theory, or discursive form can claim a privileged position that enables the production of authoritative knowledge. Researchers must always speak/write about the world in terms of something else in the world, "in relation to..." As creatures of the world, we are oriented to it in a way that prevents us from grounding our theories amid perspectives outside of it. Thus, whether we like it or not, we are all destined as interpreters to analyze from within its boundaries amid blinders. Within these limitations, however, the interpretations emerging from the hermeneutic process can still move us to new levels of understanding, appreciations that allow us to "live our way" into an experience described to us. Despite the impediments of context, hermeneutical researchers can transcend the inadequacies of thin descriptions of decontextualized facts and produce thick descriptions of social texts characterized by the contexts of their production, the intentions of their producers, and the meanings mobilized in the processes of their construction. The production of such thick descriptions/ interpretations follows no step-by-step blueprint or mechanical formula. As with any art form, hermeneutical analysis can be learned only in the Deweyan sense— by doing it. Researchers in the context practice the art by grappling with the text to be understood, telling its story in relation to its contextual dynamics and other texts first to themselves and then to a public audience (Carson, & Sumara, 1997; Denzin, 1994; Gallagher, 1992; Jardine, 1998; Madison, 1988).

## CRITICAL HERMENEUTICAL METHODS OF INTERPRETATION

These concerns with the nature of hermeneutical interpretation come under the category of philosophical hermeneutics. Working this domain, hermeneutical scholars attempt to think through and clarify the conditions under which interpretation and understanding take place. The critical hermeneutics that grounds critical qualitative research moves more in the direction of normative hermeneutics in that it raises questions about the purposes and procedures of interpretation. In its critical theory-driven context, the purpose of hermeneutical analysis is to develop a form of cultural criticism revealing power dynamics within social and cultural texts. Qualitative researchers familiar with critical hermeneutics build bridges between reader and text, text and its producer, historical context and present, and one particular social circumstance and another. Accomplishing such interpretive tasks is difficult, and researchers situated in normative hermeneutics push ethnographers, historians, semioticians, literary critics, and content analysts to trace the bridge-building processes employed by successful interpretations of knowledge production and culture (Gallagher, 1992; Kellner, 1995; Kogler, 1996; Rapko, 1998).

Grounded by the hermeneutical bridge building, critical researchers in a hermeneutical circle (a process of analysis in which interpreters seek the historical and social dynamics that shape textual interpretation) engage in the back-and-forth of studying parts in relations to the whole and the whole in relation to parts. No final interpretation is sought in this context, as the activity of the circle proceeds with no need for closure (Gallagher, 1992; Peters, & Lankshear, 1994; Pinar et al., 1995). This movement of whole to parts is combined with an analytic flow between abstract and concrete. Such dynamics often tie interpretation to the interplay of larger social forces (the general) to the everyday lives of individuals (the particular). A critical hermeneutics beings the concrete, the parts, the particular into focus, but in a manner that grounds them contextually in a larger understanding of the social forces, the whole, the abstract (the general). Focus on the parts is dynamic that brings the particular into focus, sharpening our understanding of the individual in light of the social and psychological forces that shape him or her. The parts and the unique places they occupy ground hermeneutical ways of seeing by providing the contextualization of the particular- a perspective often erased in traditional inquiry's search for abstract generalizations (Gallagher, 1992; Kellner, 1995; Miller, & Hodge, 1998; Peters, & Lankshear, 1994).

The give-and-take of the hermeneutical circle provokes analysts to review existing conceptual matrices in light of new understandings. Here the analysts reconsider and reconceptualize preconceptions so as to provide a new way of exploring a particular text. Making use of an author's insights hermeneutically does not mean replicating his or her response to his or her original question. In the hermeneutical process the author's answer is valuable only if it catalyzes the production of a new question for our consideration in the effort to make sense of a particular textual phenomenon (Gallagher, 1992). In this context participants in the hermeneutical circle must be wary of techniques of textual defamiliarization that have become clichéd. For example, feminist criticisms of Barbie's figure and its construction of the image of ideal woman became such conventions in popular cultural analysis that other readings of Barbie were suppressed (Steinberg, 1997). Critical hermeneutical analysts in this and many other cases have to introduce new forms of analysis to the hermeneutical circle— to defamiliarjze conventional defamiliarizations—in order to achieve deeper levels of understanding (Berger, 1995; Steinberg, 1998).

Within the hermeneutical circle we may develop new metaphors to shape our analysis in ways that break us out of familiar modes. For example, thinking of movies as mass-mediated dreams may help critical researchers of popular culture to re-conceptualize the interpretive act as a psychoanalytic form of dream study. In this way, critical researchers could examine psychoanalytic work in the analysis of dream symbolization for insights into their cultural studies of the popular culture and the meanings it helps individuals make through its visual images and narratives. As researchers apply these new metaphors in the hermeneutical circle, they must be aware of the implicit metaphors researchers continuously bring to the interpretive process (Berger, 1995; Clough, 1998). Such metaphors are shaped by the socio-historical era, the culture, and the linguistic context in which the interpreter operates. Such awarenesses are important features that must be introduced into the give-and-take of the critical hermeneutical circle. As John Dewey (1916) observed decades ago, individuals adopt the values and perspectives of their social groups in a manner that such factors come to shape their views of the world. Indeed, the values and perspectives of the group help determine what is deemed important and what is not, what is granted attention and what is ignored. Hermeneutical analysts are aware of such interpretational dynamics and make sure they are included in the search for understanding (Madison, 1988; Mullen, 1999).

Critical researchers with a hermeneutical insight take Dewey's insight to heart as they pursue their inquiry. They are aware that the consciousness, and the interpretive frames, they bring to their research are historically situated, ever changing, ever evolving in relationship to the cultural and ideological climate (Hinchey, 1998; Kincheloe, Steinberg, & Hinchey, 1999). Thus there is nothing simple about the social construction of interpretive lenses—consciousness construction is contradictory and the result of the collision of a variety of ideologically oppositional forces. Critical qualitative researchers who understand the relationship between identity formation and interpretive lenses are better equipped to understand the etymology of their own assertions—especially the way power operates to shape them. Linguistic, discursive, and many other factors typically hidden from awareness insidiously shape the meanings researchers garner from their work (Goodson, 1997). It was this dynamic that Antonio Gramsci had in mind when he argued that a critical philosophy should be viewed as a form of self-criticism. The starting point, he concluded, for any higher understanding of self involves consciousness of oneself as a product of power-driven sociohistorical forces. A critical perspective, he once wrote, involves the ability of its adherents to criticize the ideological frames that they use to make sense of the world (see Coben, 1998). Analyzing Dewey's and Gramsci's notions of self-production in light of the aims of critical hermeneutics vis-à-vis critical qualitative research, we begin to gain insight into how the ambiguous and closeted interpretive process operates. This moves us in a critical direction, as we understand that the "facts" do not simply demand particular interpretations.

## HERMENEUTICAL HORIZONS: SITUATING CRITICAL RESEARCH

Researchers who fail to take these points into account operate at the mercy of unexamined assumptions. Because all interpretation is historically and culturally situated, it is the lot of critical researchers to study the ways both interpreters (often the analysts themselves) and the objects of interpretation are constructed by their time and place. In this context the importance of social theory emerges. Operating in this manner, researchers inject critical social theory into the hermeneutical circle to facilitate an understanding of the hidden structures and tacit cultural dynamics that insidiously inscribe social meanings and values (Cary, 1996; Gallagher, 1992; Kellner, 1995). This social and historical situating of interpreter and text is an extremely complex enterprise that demands a nuanced analysis of the impact of hegemonic and ideological forces that connect the micro-dynamics of everyday life with the macro-dynamics of structures such as white supremacy, patriarchy, and class elitism. The central hermeneutic of many critical qualitative works involves the interactions among research, subject(s), and these situating sociohistorical structures.

When these aspects of the interpretation process are taken into account, analysts begin to understand Hans-Georg Gadamer's (1989) contention that social frames of reference influence researchers' questions, which, in turn, shape the nature of interpretation itself. In light of this situating process, the modernist notion that a social text has one valid interpretation evaporates into thin air. Researchers, whether they admit it or not, always have points of view, disciplinary orientations, social or political groups with which they identify (Kincheloe, 1991; Lugg, 1996). Thus the point, critical hermeneuts argue, is not that researchers should shed all worldly affiliations but that they should identify those affiliations and understand their impacts on the ways the researchers approach social and educational phenomena. Gadamer labels these world affiliations of researchers their "horizons" and deems the hermeneutic act of interpretation the "fusion of horizons." When critical researchers participate in the fusion of horizons, they enter into the tradition of the text. Here they study the conditions of its production and the circle of previous interpretations. In this manner they begin to uncover the ways the text has attempted to over determine meaning (Berger, 1995; Ellis, 1998; Jardine, 1998; Miller, & Hodge, 1998; Slattery, 1995).

The hermeneutical tradition puts the politics of interpretation at center stage. Like ordinary human beings, critical researchers make history and live their lives within structures of meaning they have not necessarily chosen for themselves. Understanding this, critical hermeneuts realize that a central aspect of their sociocultural analysis involves dissecting the ways people connect their everyday experiences to the cultural representations of such experiences. Such work involves the unraveling of the ideological codings embedded in these cultural representations. This unraveling is complicated by the taken-for-grantedness of the meanings promoted in these representations and the typically undetected ways these meanings are circulated into everyday life (Denzin, 1992; Kogler, 1996). The better the analyst, the better he or she can expose these meanings in the domain of the "what-goes-without-saying," that activity previously deemed noise unworthy of comment.

At this historical juncture, electronic modes of communication become extremely important to the production of meanings and representations that culturally situate human beings in general and textual interpretations in particular (Goldman, & Papson, 1994; Hall, 1997). In many ways it can be argued that the postmodern condition produces a secondhand culture, filtered and performed in the marketplace and constantly communicated via popular and mass media. Critical analysts understand that the pedagogical effects of such a mediated culture can range from the political/ideological to the cognitive/epistemological. For example, the situating effects of print media tend to promote a form of rationality, continuity, and uniformity; on the other hand, electronic media promote a nonlinear immediacy that may encourage more emotional responses that lead individuals in very different directions (duGay, Hall, Janes, MacKay, & Negus, 1997; Shelton, & Kincheloe, 1999). Thus the situating influence and pedagogical impact of electronic media of the postmodern condition must be assessed by those who study cultural and political processes and, most important at the turn of the millennium, the research processes itself (Bell, & Valentine, 1997; Berger, 1995; Bertman, 1998; Denzin, 1992; Kellner, 1995).

## CRITICAL HERMENEUTICS: LAYING THE GROUNDWORK OF CRITICAL RESEARCH

Critical hermeneutics is suspicious of any model of interpretation that claims to reveal the final truth, the essence of a text or any form of experience (Goodson, &

Mangan, 1996). Critical hermeneutics is more comfortable with interpretive approaches that assume that the meaning of human experience can never be fully disclosed—neither to the researcher nor even to the human who experienced it. Because language is always slippery, with its meanings ever "in process," critical hermeneutics understands that interpretations will never be linguistically unproblematic, will never be direct representations. Critical hermeneutics seeks to understand how textual practices such as scientific research and classical theory work to maintain existing power relations and to support extant power structures (Denzin, 1992). As critical researchers we draw, of course, on the latter model of interpretation, with its treatment of the personal as political. Critical hermeneutics grounds a critical research that attempts to connect the everyday troubles individuals face to public issues of power, justice, and democracy. Typically, within the realm of cultural studies and cultural analysis in general critical hermeneutics has deconstructed sociocultural texts that promote demeaning stereotypes of the disempowered (Denzin, 1992; Gross, & Keith, 1997; Rapko, 1998). In this context critical hermeneutics is also being deployed in relation to cultural texts that reinforce an ideology of privilege and entitlement for empowered members of the society (Allison, 1998; Fine, Weis, Powell, & Wong, 1997; Frankenberg, 1993; Kincheloe et al., 1998; Rains, 1998; Rodriguez, & Villaverde, 1999).

In its ability to render the personal political, critical hermeneutics provides a methodology for arousing a critical consciousness through the analysis of the generative themes of the present era. Such generative themes can often be used to examine the meaning-making power of the contemporary cultural realm (Peters, & Lankshear, 1994). Within the qualitative research community there is still resistance to the idea that movies, television, and popular music are intricately involved in the most important political, economic, and cultural battles of the contemporary epoch. Critical hermeneutics recognizes this centrality of popular culture in the postmodern condition and seeks to uncover the ways it impedes and advances the struggle for a democratic society (Kellner, 1995). Appreciating the material effects of media culture, critical hermeneutics traces the ways cultural dynamics position audiences politically in ways that not only shape their political beliefs but formulate their identities (Steinberg, & Kincheloe, 1997). In this context, Paulo Freire's (1985) contribution to the development of a critical hermeneutics is especially valuable. Understanding that the generative themes of a culture are central features in a critical social analysis, Freire assumes that the interpretive process is both an ontological (pertaining to being) and an epistemological (pertaining to knowledge) act. It is ontological on the level that our vocation as humans, the foundation of our being, is grounded on the hermeneutical task of interpreting the world so we can become more fully human. It is epistemological in the sense that critical hermeneutics offers us a method for investigating rile conditions of our existence and the generative themes that shape it. In this context we gain the prowess to both live with a purpose and operate with the ability to perform evaluative acts in naming the culture around us. This ability takes on an even greater importance in the contemporary electronic society, where the sociopolitical effects of the cultural domain have often been left unnamed, allowing our exploration of the shaping of our own humanness to go unexplored in this strange new social context. Critical hermeneutics addresses this vacuum (Kincheloe, & Steinberg, 1997; McLaren, 1997; Peters, & Lankshear, 1994).

Critical hermeneutics names the world as a part of a larger effort to evaluate it and make it better. Knowing this, it is easy to understand why critical hermeneutics focuses on domination and its negation, emancipation. Domination limits self-direction and democratic community building, whereas emancipation enables them. Domination, legitimated as it is by ideology, is decoded by critical hermeneuts who help critical researchers discover the ways they and their subjects have been entangled in the ideological process. The exposé and critique of ideology is one of the main objectives of critical hermeneutics in its effort to make the world better. As long as our vision is obstructed by the various purveyors of ideology, our effort to live in democratic communities will be thwarted (Gallagher, 1992). Power wielders with race, class, and gender privilege (Kincheloe, & Steinberg, 1997) have access to the resources that allow them to promote ideologies amid representations in ways individuals without such privilege cannot (Bartolomé, 1998; Carlson, & Apple, 1998; Denzin, 1992; Gresson, 1995; Hinchey, 1998; Jipson, & Paley, 1997; Leistyna et al., 1996; Peters, & Lankshear, 1994; Pinar, 1998).

## PARTISAN RESEARCH IN A "NEUTRAL" ACADEMIC CULTURE

In the space available here it is impossible to do justice to all of the critical traditions that have drawn inspiration from Marx, Kant, Hegel, Weber, the Frankfurt school theorists, Continental social theorists such as Foucault, Habermas, and Derrida, Latin American thinkers such as Paulo Freire, French feminists such as Irigaray, Kristeva, and Cixous, or Russian sociolinguists such as Bakhtin and Vygotsky—most of whom regularly find their way into the reference lists of contemporary critical researchers. Today there are criticalist schools in many fields, and even a superficial discussion of the most prominent of these schools would demand much more space than we have available.

The fact that numerous books have been written about the often-virulent disagreements among members of the Frankfurt school only heightens our concern with the "packaging" of the different criticalist schools. Critical theory should not be treated as a universal grammar of revolutionary thought objectified and reduced to discrete formulaic pronouncements or strategies. Obviously, in presenting our idiosyncratic version of a reconceptualized critical theory, we have defined the critical tradition very broadly for the purpose of generating understanding; as we asserted earlier, this will trouble many critical researchers. In this move we decided to focus on the underlying commonality among critical schools of thought, at the cost of focusing on differences. This, of course, is always risky business in terms of suggesting a false unity or consensus where none exists, but such concerns are unavoidable in a survey chapter such as this. We are defining a criticalist as a researcher or theorist who attempts to use her or his work as a form of social or cultural criticism and who accepts basic assumptions: that all thought is fundamentally mediated by power relations that are social and historically constituted; that facts can never be isolated from the domain of values or removed from some form of ideological inscription;

that the relationship between concept and object and between signifier and signified is never stable or fixed and is often mediated by the social relations of capitalist production and consumption; that language is central to the formation of subjectivity (conscious and unconscious awareness); that certain groups in any society are privileged over others and, although the reasons for this privileging may vary widely, the oppression that characterizes contemporary societies is most forcefully reproduced when subordinates accept their social status as natural, necessary, or inevitable; that oppression has many faces and that focusing on only one at the expense of others (e.g., class oppression versus racism) often elides the interconnections among them; and, finally, that mainstream research practices are generally, although most often unwittingly, implicated in the reproduction of systems of class, race, and gender oppression (Kincheloe, & Steinberg, 1997).

In today's climate of blurred disciplinary genres, it is not uncommon to find literary theorists doing anthropology and anthropologists writing about literary theory, or political scientists trying their hand at ethnomethodological analysis, or philosophers doing Lacanian film criticism. We offer this observation not as an excuse to be wantonly eclectic in our treatment of the critical tradition but to make the point that any attempts to delineate critical theory as discrete schools of analysis will fail to capture the hybridity endemic to contemporary critical analysis.

Readers familiar with the criticalist traditions will recognize essentially four different "emergent" schools of social inquiry in this chapter: the neo-Marxist tradition of critical theory associated with the work of Horkheimer, Adorno, and Marcuse; the genealogical writings of Michel Foucault; the practices of post-structuralist deconstruction associated with Derrida; and postmodernist currents associated with Derrida, Foucault, Lyotard, Ebert, and others. In our view, critical ethnography has been influenced by all of these perspectives in different ways and to different degrees. From critical theory, researchers inherit a forceful criticism of the positivist conception of science and instrumental rationality, especially in Adorno's idea of negative dialectics, which posits an unstable relationship of contradiction between concepts and objects; from Derrida, researchers are given a means for deconstructing objective truth, or what is referred to as "the metaphysics of presence." For Derrida, the meaning of a word is constantly deferred because the word can have meaning only in relation to its difference from other words within a given system of language; Foucault invites researchers to explore the ways in which discourses are implicated in relations of power and how power and knowledge serve as dialectically reinitiating practices that regulate what is considered reasonable and true. We have characterized much of the work influenced by these writers as the "ludic" and "resistance" postmodernist theoretical perspectives.

Critical research can be best understood in the context of the empowerment of individuals. Inquiry that aspired to the name *critical* must be connected to an attempt to confront the injustice of a particular society or public sphere within the society. Research thus becomes a transformative endeavor unembarrassed by the label *political* and unafraid to consummate a relationship with emancipatory consciousness. Whereas traditional researchers cling to the guard rail of neutrality, critical researchers frequently announce their partisanship in the struggle for a better world.

Traditional researchers see their task as the description, interpretation, or reanimation of a slice of reality, whereas critical researchers often regard their work as a first step toward forms of political action that can redress the injustices found in the field site or constructed in the very act of research itself. Horkheimer (1972) puts it succinctly when he argues that critical theory and research are never satisfied with merely increasing knowledge (see also Agger 1998; Andersen, 1989; Britzman, 1991; Giroux, 1983, 1988, 1997; Kincheloe, 1991; Kincheloe, & Steinberg, 1993; Quantz, 1992; Shor, 1996; Villaverde, & Kincheloe, 1998).

Research in the critical tradition takes the form of self-conscious criticism—self-conscious in the sense that researchers try to become aware of the ideological imperatives and epistemological presuppositions that inform their research as well as their own subjective, inter-subjective, and normative reference claims. Thus critical researchers enter into an investigation with their assumptions on the table, so no one is confused concerning the epistemological and political baggage they bring with them to the research site. Upon detailed analysis, these assumptions may change. Stimulus for change may come from the critical researchers' recognition that such assumptions are not leading to emancipatory actions. The source of this emancipatory action involves the researchers' ability to expose the contradictions of the world of appearances accepted by the dominant culture as natural and inviolable (Giroux, 1983, 1988, 1997; McLaren, 1992a, 1997; San Juan, 1992; Zizek, 1990). Such appearances may, critical researchers contend, conceal social relationships of inequality, injustice, and exploitation. For instance, if we view the violence we find in classrooms not as random or isolated incidents created by aberrant individuals willfully stepping out of line in accordance with a particular form of social pathology, but as narratives of transgression and resistance, then this could indicate that the "political unconscious" lurking beneath the surface of everyday classroom life is not unrelated to practices of race, class, and gender oppression but rather intimately connected to them.

## BABES IN TOYLAND: CRITICAL THEORY IN HYPERREALITY

*Postmodern Culture*

Over the last quarter of the 20$^{th}$ century, traditional notions of critical theory have had to come to terms with the rise of postmodernism. Our reconceptualized notion of critical theory is our way of denoting the conversation between traditional criticalism amid postmodernism (Kincheloe, Steinberg, & Tippins, 1999). We will first analyze postmodernism and then address the relationship between it and our notion of critical theory.

In a contemporary era marked by the delegitimation of the grand narratives of Western civilization, a loss of faith in the power of reason, and a shattering of traditional religious orthodoxies, scholars continue to debate what the term *postmodernism* means, generally positing it as a periodizing concept following modernism. Indeed, scholars have not agreed if this epochal break with the "modern" era even constitutes a discrete period. In the midst of such confusion it seems somehow appropriate that scholars are fighting over the application of the term *postmodernism* to the contemporary condition. Accepting postmodernism as an apt moniker for the end of the 20$^{th}$ century, a major feature of critical academic work has involved the exploration of what happens when critical theory encounters the postmodern condition, or hyperreality. *Hyperreality* is a term used to describe an information society socially saturated with ever-increasing forms of representation: filmic, photographic, electronic, and so on. These have had profound effects on the construction of the cultural narratives that shape our identities. The drama of living has been portrayed so often on television that individuals, for the most part, are increasingly able to predict the outcomes and consider such outcomes to be the "natural" and "normal" course of social life (Fraser, 1995; Gergen, 1991; Heshusius, & Ballard, 1996; Kellner, 1994; Morley, & Chen, 1996; Nicholson, & Seidman, 1995).

As many postmodern analysts have put it, we become pastiches, imitative conglomerations of one another. In such a condition we approach life with low affect, with a sense of postmodern ennui and irremissible anxiety. Our emotional bonds are diffused as television, computers, VCRs, and stereo headphones assault us with representations that have shaped our cognitive and affective facilities in ways that still remain insufficiently understood. In the political arena, traditionalists circle their cultural wagons and fight off imagined bogeymen such as secular humanists, "extreme liberals," and utopianists, not realizing the impact that postmodern hyperreality exerts on their hallowed institutions. The nuclear family, for example, has declined in importance not because of the assault of radical feminists but because the home has been redefined through the familiar presence of electronic communication systems. Particular modes of information put individual family members in constant contact with specific subcultures. While they are physically in the home, they exist emotionally outside of it through the mediating effects of various forms of communication (Gergen, 1991; McGuigan, 1996; McLaren, 1997; Poster, 1989; Steinberg, & Kincheloe, 1997). We increasingly make sense of the social world and judge other cultures through conventional and culture-bound television genres. Hyperreality has presented us with new forms of literacy that do not simply refer to discrete skills but rather constitute social skills and relations of symbolic power. These new technologies cannot be seen apart from the social and institutional contexts in which they are used and the roles they play in the family the community, and the workplace They also need to be seen in terms of how "viewing competencies" are socially distributed and the diverse social and discursive practices in which these new media literacies are produced (Buckingham, 1989; Hall, 1997; Taylor, & Saarinen, 1994).

Electronic transmissions generate new formations of cultural space and restructure experiences of time. We often are motivated to trade community membership for a sense of pseudo belonging to the mediascape. Residents of hyperreality are temporarily comforted by proclamations of community offered by "media personalities" on the 6 o'clock *Eyewitness News*. "Bringing news of your neighbors in the Tri-State community home to you," media marketers attempt to soften the edges of hyperreality, to soften the emotional effects of the social vertigo. The world is not brought into our homes by television as much as television brings its viewers to a quasi-fictional place—hyperreality (Luke, 1991).

## Postmodern Social Theory

We believe that it is misleading to identify postmodernism with poststructuralism. Although there are certainly similarities involved, they cannot be considered discrete homologies. We also believe that it is a mistake to equate postmodernism with postmodernity or to assert that these terms can be contrasted *in* some simple equivalent way with modernism amid modernity. As Michael Peters (1993) notes, "To do so is to frame up the debate in strictly (and naïvely) modernist terminology' which employs exhaustive binary oppositions privileging one set of terms against the other" (p. 14). We are using the term *postmodernity* to refer to the postmodern combination that we have described as *hyperreality* and the term *postmodern theory* as an umbrella term that includes antifoundationalist writing in philosophy and the social sciences. Again, we are using this term in a very general sense that includes poststructuralist currents.

Postmodern theoretical trajectories take as their entry point a rejection of the deeply ingrained assumptions of Enlightenment rationality, traditional Western epistemology, or any supposedly "secure" representation of reality that exists outside of discourse itself. Doubt is cast on the myth of the autonomous, transcendental subject, and the concept of praxis is marginalized in favor of rhetorical undecidability amid textual analysis of social practices. As a species of criticism, intended, in part, as a central requestioning of the humanism amid anthropologism of the early 1970s, postmodernist social theory rejects Hegel's ahistorical state of absolute knowledge and resigns itself to the impossibility of an ahistorical, transcendental, or self-authenticating version of truth. The reigning conviction that knowledge is knowledge only if it reflects the world as it "really" exists has been annihilated in favor of a view in which reality is socially constructed or semiotically posited. Furthermore, normative agreement on what should constitute and guide scientific practice amid argumentative consistency has become an intellectual target for epistemological uncertainty (Pinar et al., 1995; Shelton, 1996).

Postmodern criticism takes as its starting point the notion that meaning is constituted by the continual, playfulness of the signifier, and the thrust of its critique is aimed at deconstructing Western metanarratives of truth and the ethnocentrism implicit in the European view of history as the unilinear progress of universal reason. Postmodern theory is a site of both hope and fear, where there exists a strange convergence between critical theorists and political conservatives, a cynical complicity with status quo social and institutional relations and a fierce criticism of ideological manipulation and the reigning practices of subjectivity in which knowledge takes place.

## Ludic and Resistance Postmodernism

Postmodernist criticism is not monolithic, and for the purposes of this essay we would like to distinguish between two theoretical strands. The first has been astutely described by Teresa Ebert (1991) as "ludic postmodernism" (p. 115)—an approach to social theory that is decidedly limited in its ability to transform oppressive social and political regimes of power. Ludic postmodernism generally occupies itself with a reality that is constituted by the continual playfulness of the signifier and the heterogeneity of differences. As such, ludic postmodernism (see, e.g., Lyotard, Derrida, Baudrillard) constitutes a moment of self-reflexivity in the deconstruction of Western metanarratives, assenting that "meaning itself is self-divided and undecidable."

We want to argue that critical researchers should assume a cautionary stance toward ludic postmodernism critique because, as Ebert (1991) notes, it tends to reinscribe the status quo and reduce history to the supplementarity of signification on the free-floating trace of textuality. As a mode of critique, it rests its case on interrogating specific and local enunciations of oppression, hut often fails to analyze such enunciations in relation to larger dominating structures of oppression (Aronowitz, & Giroux, 1991; McLaren, 1995a; Sünker, 1998).

The kind of postmodern social theory we want to pose as a counterweight to skeptical and spectral postmodernism has been referred to as "oppositional postmodernism" (Foster, 1983), "radical critique-al theory" (Zavarzadeh, & Morton, 1991), "postmodern education" (Aronowitz, & Giroux, 1991), "resistance postmodernism" (Ebert, 1991), "affirmative post-modernism" (Slattery, 1995), "critical postmodernism" (Giroux, 1992; McLaren, 1992b, 1997; McLaren, & Hammer, 1989), amid "post-formalism" (Kincheloe, 1993, 1995; Kincheloe, & Steinberg, 1993; Kincheloe, Steinberg, & Hinchey, 1999; Kincheloe, Steinberg, & Villaverde, 1999). These forms of critique are not alternatives to ludic postmodernism but appropriations and extensions of this critique. Resistance postmodernism brings to ludic critique a form of materialist intervention because it is not based solely on a textual theory of difference but rather on one that is also social and historical. In this way, postmodern critique can serve as an interventionist and transformative critique of Western culture. Following Ebert (1991), resistance postmodernism attempts to show that "textualities (significations) are material practices, forms of conflicting social relations" (p. 115). The sign is always an arena of material conflict and competing social relations as well as ideas. From this perspective we can rethink a signifier as an ideological dynamic ever related to a contextually possible set of signifieds. In other words, difference is politicized by being situated in real social and historical conflicts.

The synergism of the conversation between resistance postmodernism and critical theory involves an interplay between the praxis of the critical and the radical uncertainty of the postmodern. As it invokes its strategies for the emancipation of meaning, critical theory provides the postmodern critique with a normative foundation (i.e., a basis for distinguishing between oppressive amid liberatory social relations). Without such a foundation the post-modern critique is ever vulnerable to nihilism and inaction. Indeed, the normatively ungrounded postmodern critique is incapable of providing an ethically challenging and politically transformative program of action. Aronowitz, Giroux, Kincheloe, and McLaren argue that if the postmodern critique is to make a valuable contribution to the notion of schooling as an emancipatory form of cultural politics, it must make connections to those egalitarian impulses of modernism that contribute to an emancipatory democracy. In doing this, the postmodern critique can extend the project of an emancipatory democracy and the schooling that supports it by promoting new understandings of how power operates and by incorporating groups who had been excluded because of race, gender, or class (Aronowitz, & Giroux, 1991; Codd, 1984; Godzich, 1992; Kincheloe, 1995, 1999; Lash, 1990; McLaren, 1997, 1999; Morrow, 1991; Pinar, 1994, 1998; Rosenau, 1992; Steinberg, & Kincheloe, 1998; Surber, 1998; Welch, 1991; Wexler, 1996a, 1997; Yates, 1990).

*Cultural Research and Cultural Studies*

Cultural studies is an interdisciplinary, transdisciplinary, and sometimes counter-disciplinary field that functions within the dynamics of competing definitions of culture. Unlike traditional humanistic studies, cultural studies questions the equation of culture with high culture; instead, cultural studies asserts that myriad expressions of cultural production should be analyzed in relations to other cultural dynamics and social and historical structures. Such a position commits cultural studies to a potpourri of artistic, religious, political, economic, and communicative activities. In this context, it is important to note that although cultural studies is associated with the study of popular culture, it is not primarily about popular culture. The interests of cultural studies are much broader and generally tend to involve the production and nature of the rules of inclusivity and exclusivity that guide academic evaluation—in particular the way these rules shape and are shaped by relations of power. The rules that guide academic evaluation are inseparable from the rules of knowledge production and research. Thus cultural studies provides a disciplinary critique that holds many implications (Abercrombie, 1994; Ferguson, & Golding, 1997; Grossberg, 1995; Hall, & du Gay, 1996; McLaren, 1995a; Woodward, 1997).

One of the most important sites of theoretical production in the history of critical research has been the Centre for Contemporary Cultural Studies (CCCS) at the University of Birmingham. Attempting to connect critical theory with the particularity of everyday experience, the CCCS researchers have argued that all experience is vulnerable to ideological inscription. At the same time, they have maintained that theorizing outside of everyday experience results in formal amid deterministic theory. An excellent representative of the CCCS's perspectives is Paul Willis, whose *Learning to Labour: How Working Class Kids Get Working Class Jobs* was published in 1977, seven years after Colin Lacey's *Hightown Grammar* (1970). Redefining the nature of ethnographic research in a critical manner, *Learning to Labour* inspired a spate of critical studies: David Robins and Philip Cohen's *Knuckle Sandwich Growing Up in the Working Class City* in 1978, Paul Corrigan's *Schooling the Smash Street Kids* in 1979, and Dick Hebdige's *Subculture: The Meaning of Style* in 1979.

Also following Willis's work were critical feminist studies, including an anthology titled *Women Take Issue* (Women's Studies Group, 1978). In 1985, Christine Griffin published *Typical Girls?*, the first extended feminist study produced by the CCCS. Conceived as a response to Willis's *Learning to Labour, Typical Girls?* analyzes adolescent female consciousness as it is constructed in a world of patriarchy. Through their recognition of patriarchy as a major disciplinary technology in the production of subjectivity, Griffin and the members of the CCCS gender study' group move critical research in a multicultural direction. In addition to the examination of class, gender and racial analyses are beginning to gain importance (Quantz, 1992). Poststructuralism frames power not simply as one aspect of a society, but as the basis of society. Thus patriarchy is not simply one isolated force among many with which women must contend; patriarchy informs all aspects of the social and effectively shapes women's lives (see also Douglas, 1994; Finders, 1997; Fine et al., 1997; Frankenberg, 1993; Franz, & Stewart, 1994; Shohat, & Stam, 1994).

Cornel West (1993) pushes critical research even further into the multicultural domain as he focuses critical attention on women, the Third World, and race. Adopting theoretical advances in neo-Marxist postcolonialist criticism and cultural studies, he is able to shed greater light on the workings of power in everyday life. In this context, Ladislaus Semali and Joe Kincheloe, in *What Is Indigenous Knowledge? Voices from the Academy* (1999), explore the power of indigenous knowledge as a resource for critical attempts to bring about social change. Critical researchers, they argue, should analyze such knowledges in order to understand emotions, sensitivities, and epistemologies that move in ways unimagined by many Western knowledge producers. In this postcolonially informed context, Semali and Kincheloe employ concerns raised by indigenous knowledge to challenge the academy, its "normal science," and its accepted notions of certified information. Moving the conversation about critical research in new directions, these authors understand the conceptual inseparability of valuing indigenous knowledge, developing postcolonial forms of resistance, academic reform, the reconceptualization of research and interpretation, and the struggle for social justice.

In *Schooling as a Ritual Performance*, Peter McLaren (1999) integrates poststructuralist, postcolonialist, and Marxist theory with the projects of cultural studies, critical pedagogy, and critical ethnography. He grounds his theoretical analysis in the poststructuralist claim that the connection of signifier and signified is arbitrary yet shaped by historical, cultural, and economic forces. The primary cultural narrative that defines school life is the resistance by students to the school's attempts to marginalize their street culture and street knowledge. McLaren analyzes the school as a cultural site where symbolic capital is smuggled over in the form of ritual dramas. *Schooling as a Ritual Performance* adopts the position that researchers are unable to grasp themselves or others introspectively without social mediation through their positionalities with respect to race, class, gender, and other configurations. The visceral, bodily forms of knowledge, and the rhythms and gestures of the street culture of the students, are distinguished from the formal abstract knowledge of classroom instruction. The teachers regard knowledge as it is constructed informally outside of the culture of school instruction as threatening to the universalist and decidedly Eurocentric ideal of high culture that forms the basis of the school curriculum.

As critical researchers pursue the reconceptualization of critical theory pushed by its synergistic relationship with cultural studies, postmodernism, and poststructuralism, they are confronted with the post-discourses' redefinition of critical notions of democracy in terms of multiplicity and difference. Traditional notions of community often privilege unity over diversity in the name of Enlightenment values. Poststructuralists in general and poststructuralist feminists in particular see this communitarian dream as politically disabling because of the suppression of race, class, and gender differences and the exclusion of subaltern voices and marginalized groups whom community members are loath to engage. What begins to emerge in this instance is the movement of feminist theoretical concerns to the center of critical theory. Indeed, after the feminist critique, critical theory can never return to a paradigm of inquiry in which the concept of social class is antiseptically privileged and exalted as the master concept in the Holy Trinity of race, class, and gender. A critical theory reconceptualized by poststructuralism and feminism promotes a politics of difference that refuses to pathologize or exoticize the Other. In this context, communities are more prone to revitalization amid revivification (Wexler, 1996b, 1997); peripheralized groups in the thrall of a condescending Euro-centric gaze are able to edge closer to the borders of respect, and "classified" objects of research potentially acquire the characteristics of subjecthood. Kathleen Weiler's *Women Teaching for Change: Gender, Class, and Power* (1988) serves as a good example of critical research framed by feminist theory. Weiler shows not only how feminist theory can extend critical research, but how the concept of emancipation can be reconceptualized in light of a feminist epistemology (Aronowitz, & Giroux, 1991; Behar, & Gordon, 1995; Bersani, 1995; Brents, & Monson, 1998; Britzman, 1995; Christian-Smith, & Keelor, 1999; Clatterbaugh, 1997; Clough, 1994; Cooper, 1994; Hammer, 1999; Hedley, 1994; Johnson, 1996; Kelly, 1996; King, & Mitchell, 1995; Lugones, 1987; Maher, & Tetreault, 1994; Morrow, 1991; Rand, 1995; Scott, 1992; Sedgwick, 1995; Steinberg, 1997; Young, 1990).

*Focusing on Critical Ethnography*

As critical researchers attempt to get behind the curtain, to move beyond assimilated experience, to expose the way ideology constrains the desire for self-direction, and to confront the way power reproduces itself in the construction of human consciousness, they employ a plethora of research methodologies. In this context, Patti Lather (1991, 1993) extends our position with her notion of catalytic validity. Catalytic validity points to the degree to which research moves those it studies to understand the world and the way it is shaped in order for them to transform it. Noncritical researchers who operate within an empiricist framework will perhaps find catalytic validity to be a strange concept. Research that possesses catalytic validity will not only display the reality-altering impact of the inquiry process, it will direct this impact so that those under study will gain self-understanding and self-direction.

Theory that falls under the rubric of *post-colonialism* (see McLaren, 1999; Semali, & Kincheloe, 1999) involves important debates over the knowing subject and object of analysis. Such works have initiated important new modes of analysis, especially in relation to questions of imperialism, colonialism, and neocolonialism. Recent attempts by critical researchers to move beyond the objectifying and imperialist gaze associated with the Western anthropological tradition (which fixes the image of the so-called informant from the colonizing perspective of the knowing subject), although laudatory and well-intentioned, are not without their shortcomings (Bourdieu, & Wacquaat, 1992). As Fuchs (1993) has so presciently observed, serious limitations plague recent efforts to develop a more reflective approach to ethnographic writing. The challenge here can be summarized in the following questions: How does the knowing subject come to know the Other? How can researchers respect the perspective of the Other and invite the Other to speak (Abdullah, & Stringer, 1999; Ashcroft, Griffiths, & Tiffin, 1995; Brock-Utne, 1996; Goldie, 1995; Macedo, 1994; Myrsiades, & Myrsiades, 1998; Pieterse, & Parekh, 1995; Prakash, & Esteva, 1998; Rains, 1998; Scheurich, & Young, 1997; Semali, & Kincheloe, 1999; Viergever, 1999)?

Although recent confessional modes of ethnographic writing attempt to treat so-called informants as "participants" in an attempt to avoid the objectification of the Other (usually referring to the relationship between Western anthropologists and non-Western culture), there is a risk that uncovering colonial and postcolonial structures of domination by, in fact, unintentionally validating and consolidating such structures as well as reasserting liberal values through a type of covert ethnocentrism. Fuchs (1993) warns that the attempt to subject researchers to the same approach to which other societies are subjected could lead to an "'othering' of one's own world" (p. 108). Such an attempt often fails to question existing ethnographic methodologies and therefore unwittingly extends their validity and applicability while further objectifying the world of the researcher.

Michel Foucault's approach to this dilemma is to "detach" social theory from the epistemology of his own culture by criticizing the traditional philosophy of reflection. However, Foucault falls into the trap of ontologizing his own methodological argumentation and erasing the notion of prior understanding that is linked to the idea of an "inside" view (Fuchs, 1993). Louis Dumont fares somewhat better by arguing that cultural texts need to be viewed simultaneously from the inside amid from the outside. However, in trying to affirm a "reciprocal interpretation of various societies among themselves" (Fuchs, 1993, p. 113) through identifying both transindividual structures of consciousness and transubjective social structures, Dumont aspires to a universal framework for the comparative analysis of societies. Whereas Foucault and Dumont attempt to "transcend the categorical foundations of their own world" (Fuchs, 1993, p. 118) by refusing to include themselves in the process of objectification, Pierre Bourdieu integrates himself as a social actor into the social field under analysis. Bourdieu achieves such integration by "epistemologizing the ethnological content of his own presuppositions" (Fuchs, 1993, p. 121). But the self-objectification of the observer (anthropologist) is not unproblematic. Fuchs (1993) notes, after Bourdieu, that the chief difficulty is "forgetting the difference between the theoretical and the practical relationship with the world and of imposing on the object the theoretical relationship one maintains with it" (p. 120). Bourdieu's approach to research does not fully escape becoming, to a certain extent, a "confirmation of objectivism," but at least there is an earnest attempt by the researcher to reflect on the preconditions of his own self-understanding—an attempt to engage in an "ethnography of ethnographers" (p. 122).

Postmodern ethnography often intersects—to varying degrees—with the concerns of postcolonialist researchers, but the degree to which it fully addresses issues of exploitation and the social relations of capitalist exploitation remains questionable. Postmodern ethnography—and we are thinking here of works such as Paul Rabinow's *Reflections on Fieldwork in Morocco* (1977), James Boon's *Other Tribes, Other Scribes* (1982), and Michael Taussig's *Shamanism, Colonialism, and the Wild Man* (1987)—shares the conviction articulated by Marc Manganaro (1990) that "no anthropology is apolitical, removed from ideology and hence from the capacity to be affected by or, as crucially, to effect social formations. The question ought not to be if an anthropological text is political, but rather, what kind of sociopolitical affiliations are tied *to* particular anthropological texts" (p. 35).

Judith Newton and Judith Stacey (1992–1993) note that the current post-modern textual experimentation of ethnography credits the "post-colonial predicament of culture as the opportunity for anthropology to reinvent itself" (p. 56). Modernist ethnography, according to these authors, "constructed authoritative cultural accounts that served, however inadvertently, not only to establish the authority of the Western ethnographer over native others but also to sustain Western authority over colonial cultures" (p. 56). They argue (following James Clifford) that ethnographers can and should try to escape the recurrent allegorical genre of colonial ethnography—the pastoral, a nostalgic, redemptive text that preserves a primitive culture on the brink of extinction for the historical record of its Western conquerors. The narrative structure of this "savage text" portrays the native culture as a coherent, authentic, and lamentably "evading past," whereas its complex, inauthentic, Western successors represent the future (p. 56).

Postmodern ethnographic writing faces the challenge of moving beyond simply the reanimation of local experience, an uncritical celebration of cultural difference (including figural differentiations within the ethnographer's own culture), and the employment of a framework that espouses universal values and a global role for interpretivist anthropology (Silverman, 1990). What we have described as resistance postmodernism can help qualitative researchers challenge dominant Western research practices that are underwritten by a foundational epistemology and a claim to universally valid knowledge at the expense of local, subjugated knowledges (Peters, 1993). The choice is not one between modernism and postmodernism, but one of whether or not to challenge the presuppositions that inform the normalizing judgments one makes as a researcher. Vincent Crapanzano (1990) warns that "the anthropologist can assume neither the Orphic lyre nor the crown of thorns, although I confess to hear salvationist echoes in his desire to protect his people" (p. 301).

Connor (1992) describes the work of James Clifford, which shares an affinity with ethnographic work associated with Georges Bataille, Michel Lerris, and the College de Sociologic, as not simply the "writing of culture" but rather "the interior disruption of categories of art and culture correspond (ing) to a radically dialogic form of ethnographic writing, which takes place across and between cultures" (p. 251). Clifford (1992) describes his own work as an attempt "to multiply the hands amid discourses involved in 'writing culture' not to assert a naïve democracy of plural authorship, but to loosen at least somewhat the monological control of the executive writer/anthropologist and to open for discussion ethnography's hierarchy amid negotiation of discourses in power changed, unequal situations" (p. 100).

Citing the work of Marcus and Fischer (1986), Clifford warns against modernist ethnographic practices of "representational essentializing" and "metonymic freezing" in which one aspect of a group's life is taken to represent the group as a whole; instead, Clifford urges forms of multilocale ethnography to reflect the "transnational, political, economic and cultural forces that traverse and constitute local or regional worlds" (p. 102). Rather than fixing culture into reified textual portraits, culture needs to be better understood as displacement, transplantation, disruption, positionality, and difference.

Although critical ethnography allows, in a way conventional ethnography does not, for the relationship of liberation and history, and although its hermeneutical task is to call into question the social and cultural conditioning of human activity and the prevailing sociopolitical structures we do not claim that this is enough to restructure the social system. But it is certainly, in our view, a necessary beginning. We follow Patricia Ticineto Clough (1992) in arguing that "realist narrativity has allowed empirical social science to be the platform and horizon of social criticism" (p. 135). Ethnography needs to be analyzed critically not only in terms of its field methods but also as reading and writing practices. Data collection must give way to "rereadings of representations in every form" (Clough, 1992, p. 137). In the narrative construction of its authority as empirical science, ethnography needs to face the unconscious processes upon which it justifies its canonical formulations, processes that often involve the disavowal of oedipal or authorial desire and the reduction of differences to binary oppositions. Within these processes of binary reduction, the male ethnographer is most often privileged as the guardian of "the factual representation of empirical positivities" (Clough, 1992, p. 9).

*New Questions Concerning Validity in Critical Ethnography*

Critical research traditions have arrived at the point where they recognize that claims to truth are always discursively situated and implicated in relations of power. Yet, unlike some claims made within "ludic" strands of postmodernist research, we do not suggest that because we cannot know truth absolutely that truth can simply be equated with an effect of power. We say this because truth involves regulative rules that must be met for some statements to be more meaningful than others Otherwise truth becomes meaningless and, if that is the case, liberatory praxis has no purpose other than to win for the sake of winning. As Phil Carspecken (1993, 1999) remarks, every time we act, in every instance of our behavior, we presuppose some normative on universal relation to truth. Truth is internally related to meaning in a pragmatic way through normative referenced claims, intersubjective referenced claims, subjective referenced claims, and the way we deictically ground or anchor meaning in our daily lives. Carspecken explains that researchers are able to articulate the normative evaluative claims of others when they begin to see them in the same way as their participants by living inside the cultural and discursive positionalities that inform such claims.

Claims to universality must be recognized in each particular normative claim, and questions must be raised about whether such norms represent the entire group.

When the limited claim of universality is seen to be contradictory to the practices under observation, power relations become visible. What is crucial here, according to Carspecken, is that researchers recognize where they are ideologically located in the normative amid identity claims of others and at the same time be honest about their own subjective referenced claims and not let normative evaluative claims interfere with what they observe. Critical research continues to problematize normative and universal claims in a way that does not permit them to be analyzed outside of a politics of representation, divorced from the material conditions in which they are produced, or outside of a concern with the constitution of the subject in the very acts of reading and writing.

In his book, *Critical Ethnography Educational Research* (1996), Carspecken addresses the issue of critical epistemology, an understanding of the relationship between power and thought, and power and truth claims. In a short exposition of what is "critical" to critical epistemology, he debunks facile forms of social constructivism and offers a deft criticism of mainstream epistemologies by way of Continental phenomenology, poststructuralism, and postmodernist social theory, mainly the work of Edmund Husserl and Jacques Derrida. Carspecken makes short work of facile forms of constructivist thought purporting that what we see is strongly influenced by what we already value and that criticalist research simply indulges itself in the "correct" political values. For instance, some constructivists argue that all that criticalists need to do is to "bias" their work in the direction of social justice. This form of constructivist thought is not viable, according to Carspecken, because it is plainly ocular-centric; that is, it depends upon visual perceptions to form the basis of its theory. Rather than rely on perceptual metaphors found in mainstream ethnographic accounts, critical ethnography, in contrast, should emphasize communicative experiences amid structures as well as cultural typifications. Carspecken argues that critical ethnography needs to differentiate among ontological categories (i.e., subjective, objective, normative-evaluative) rather than adopt the position of "multiple realities" defended by many constructivists. He adopts a principled position that research value orientations should not determine research findings, as much as this is possible. Rather critical ethnographers should employ a critical epistemology; that is, they should uphold epistemological principles that apply to all researchers. In fecundating this claim, Carspecken rehabilitates critical ethnography from many of the misperceptions of its critics who believe that it ignores questions of validity.

To construct a socially critical epistemology, critical ethnographers need to understand holistic modes of human experience and their relationships to communicative structures. Preliminary stages of this process that Carspecken articulates include examining researcher bias and discovering researcher value orientations. Following stages include compiling the primary record through the collection of monological data, preliminary reconstructive analysis, dialogical data generation, discovering social systems relations, and using systems relations to explain findings. Anthony Giddens's work forms the basis of Carspecken's approach to systems analysis. Accompanying discussions of each of the complex stages Carspecken develops are brilliantly articulated approaches to horizontal and vertical validity reconstructions and pragmatic horizons of analysis. In order to help link theory to practice, Carspecken uses data from his study of an inner-city Houston elementary school program that is charged with helping students learn conflict management skills.

Another impressive feature is Carspecken's exposition and analysis of communicative acts, especially his discussion of meaning as embodiment and understanding as intersubjective, not objective or subjective. Carspecken works from a view of intersubjectivity that combines Hegel, Mead, Habermas, and Taylor. He recommends that critical ethnographers record body language carefully because the meaning of an action is not in the language, it is rather in the action and the author's bodily states. In Carspecken's view subjectivity is derivative from intersubjectivity (as is objectivity), and intersubjectivity involves the dialogical constitution of the "feeling body." Finally, Carspecken stresses the importance of macro-level social theories, environmental conditions, socially structured ways of meeting needs and desires, effects of cultural commodities on students, economic exploitation, and political and cultural conditions of action.

Much of Carspecken's inspiration for his approach to validity claims is taken from Habermas's theory of communicative action. Carspecken reads Habermas as grasping the prelinguistic foundations of language and intersubjectivity, making language secondary to the concept of intersubjectivity. Yet Carspecken departs from a strict Habermasian view of action by bringing in an expressive/praxis model roughly consistent with Charles Taylor's work. Although Habermas and Taylor frequently argue against each other's positions, Carspecken puts them together in a convincing manner. Taylor's emphasis on holistic modes of understanding and time act constitution that Carspecken employs make it possible to link the theory of communicative nationality to work on embodied meaning and time metaphoric basis of meaningful action. It also provides a means for synthesizing Giddens's ideas on part/whole relations, virtual structure, and act constitution with communicative rationality. This is another way in which Carspecken's work differs from Habermas and yet remains consistent with his theory and the internal link between meaning and validity.

*Recent Innovations in Critical Ethnography*

In addition to Carspecken's brilliant insights into critically grounded ethnography, the late 1990s have witnessed a proliferation of deconstructive approaches as well as reflexive approaches (this discussion is based on Trueba, & McLaren, in press). In her important book *Fictions of Feminist Ethnography* (1994), Kamala Visweswaran maintains that reflexive ethnography, like normative ethnography, rests on the "declarative mode" of imparting knowledge to a reader whose identity is anchored in a shared discourse. Deconstructive ethnography, in contrast, enacts the "interrogative mode" through a constant deferral or a refusal to explain or interpret. Within deconstructive ethnography, the identity of the reader with a unified subject of enunciation is discouraged. Whereas reflexive ethnography maintains that the ethnographer is not separate from the object of investigation, the ethnographer is still viewed as a unified subject of knowledge that can make hermeneutic efforts to establish identification between the observer and the observed (as in modernist interpretive traditions).

Deconstructive ethnography, in contrast, often disrupts such identification in favor of articulating a fractured, destabilized, multiply positioned subjectivity (as in postmodernist interpretive traditions). Whereas reflexive ethnography questions its own authority, deconstructive ethnography forfeits its authority. Both approaches to critical ethnography can be used to uncover the clinging Eurocentric authority employed by ethnographers in the study of Latino/a populations. The goal of both of these approaches is criticalist in nature: that is, to free the object of analysis from the tyranny of fixed, unassailable categories and to rethink subjectivity itself as a permanently unclosed, always partial, narrative engagement with text and context. Such an approach can help the ethnographer to caution against the damaging depictions propagated by Anglo observers about Mexican immigrants. As Ruth Behar (1993) notes, in classical sociological and ethnographic accounts of the Mexican and Mexican American family,

> Stereotypes similar to those surrounding the Black family perpetuated images of the authoritarian, oversexed, and macho husband and the meek and submissive wife surrounded by children who adore their good and suffering mother. These stereotypes have come under strong critique in the last few years, particularly by Chicana critics, who have sought to go beyond the various "deficiency theories" that continue to mark the discussion of African-American and Latina/Latino family life. (p. 276)

The conception of culture advanced by critical ethnographers generally unpacks culture as a complex circuit of production that includes myriad dialectically reinitiating and mutually informing sets of activities such as routines, rituals, action conditions, systems of intelligibility and meaning making, conventions of interretation, systems relations, and conditions both external and internal to the social actor (Carspecken, 1996). In her recent ethnographic study *A Space on the Side of the Road* (1996), Kathleen Stewart cogently illustrates the ambivalent character of culture, as well as its fluidity and ungraspable multilayeredness, when she remarks:

> Culture, as it is seen through its productive forms and means of mediation, is not, then, reducible to a fixed body of social value and belief or a direct precipitant of lived experience in the world but grows into a space on the side of the road where stories weighted with sociality take on a life of their own. We "see" it ... only by building up multilayered narratives of the poetic in the everyday life of things. We represent it only by roaming from one texted genre to another—romantic, realist, historical, fantastic, sociological, surreal. There is no final textual solution, no way of resolving the dialogic of the interpreter/interpreted or subject/object through efforts to "place" ourselves in the text, or to represent "the fieldwork experience," or to gather up the voices of the other as if they could speak for themselves. (p. 210)

According to E. San Juan (1996), a renewed understanding of culture—as both discursive and material—becomes the linchpin for any emancipatory politics. San Juan writes that the idea of culture as social processes and practices that are thoroughly grounded in material social relations—in the systems of maintenance (economics), decision (politics), learning and communication (culture), and generation and nurture (the domain of social reproduction) must be the grounding principle, or paradigm if you like, of any progressive and emancipatory approach (p. 177; Gresson, 1995).

Rejecting the characterization of anthropologists as either "adaptationalists" (e.g., Marvin Harris) or "ideationalists" (e.g., cognitivists, Lévi-Straussian structuralists, Schneiderian symbolists, Geertzian interpretivists), E. Valentine Daniel remarks in his recent ethnography *Charred Lullabies: Chapters in an Anthropology of Violence* (1996) that culture is "no longer something out there to be discovered, described, and explained, but rather something into which the ethnographer, as interpreter, enter[s]" (p. 198). Culture, in other words, is cocreated by the anthropologist and informant through conversation. Yet even this semeiosic conceptualization of culture is not without its problems. As Daniel himself notes, even if one considers oneself to be a "culture-comaking processualist," in contrast to a "culture-finding essentialist," one still has to recognize that one is working within a logocentric tradition that, to a greater or lesser extent privileges words over actions.

Critical ethnography has benefited from this new understanding of culture and from the new hybridic possibilities for cultural critique that have been opened up by the current blurring and mixing of disciplinary genres—those that emphasize experience, subjectivity, reflexivity, and dialogical understanding. The advantage that follows such perspectives is that social life is not viewed as preontologically available for the researchers to study. It also follows that there is no perspective unspoiled by ideology from which to study social life in an antiseptically objective way. What is important to note here is the stress placed on the ideological situatedness of any descriptive or socioanalytic account of social life. Critical ethnographers such as John and Jean Comaroff (1992) have made significant contributions to our understanding of the ways in which power is entailed in culture, leading to practices of domination and exploitation that have become naturalized in everyday social life. According to Comaroff and Comaroff, hegemony refers to "that order of signs and practices, relations and distinctions, images and epistemologies- drawn from a historically situated cultural field- that come to be taken-for-granted as the natural and received shape of the world and everything that inhabits it" (p. 23). These axiomatic and yet ineffable discourses and practices that are presumptively shared become "ideological" precisely when their internal contradictions are revealed, uncovered, and viewed as arbitrary and negotiable. Ideology, then, refers to a highly articulated worldview, master narrative, discursive regime, or organizing scheme for collective symbolic production. The dominant ideology is the expression of the dominant social group.

Following this line of argument, hegemony "is nonnegotiable and therefore beyond direct argument," whereas ideology "is more susceptible to being perceived as a matter of inimical opinion and interest and therefore is open to contestation" (Comaroff, & Comaroff, 1992, p. 24) Ideologies become the expressions of specific groups, whereas hegemony refers to conventions and constructs that are shared and naturalized throughout a political community. Hegemony works both through silences and repetition in naturalizing the dominant world-view. There also may exist oppositional ideologies among subordinate or subaltern groups- whether well formed or loosely articulated- that break free of hegemony. In this way hegemony is never total or complete; it is always porous.

## CONCLUSION: CRITICAL RESEARCH IN A GLOBALIZED, PRIVATIZEED WORLD

A critical postmodern research requires researchers to construct their perception of the world anew, not just in random ways but in a manner that undermines what appears natural, that opens to question what appears obvious (Slaughter, 1989). Oppositional and insurgent researchers as maieutic agents must not confuse their research efforts with the textual suavities of an avant-garde academic posturing in which they are awarded the sinecure of representation for the oppressed without actually having to return to those working-class communities where their studies took place. Rather, they need to locate their work in a transformative praxis that leads to the alleviation of suffering and the overcoming of oppression. Rejecting the arrogant reading of metropolitan critics and their imperial mandates governing research, insurgent researchers ask questions about how what is has come to be, whose interests are served by particular institutional arrangements, and where our own frames of reference come from. Facts are no longer simply "what is"; the truth of beliefs is not simply testable by their correspondence to these facts. To engage in critical postmodern research is to take part in a process of critical world making, guided by the shadowed outline of a dream of a world less conditioned by misery, suffering, and the politics of deceit. It is, in short, a pragmatics of hope in an age of cynical reason. The obstacles that critical postmodern research has yet to overcome in terms of a frontal assault against the ravages of global capitalism and its devastation of the global working class has led McLaren to a more sustained and sympathetic engagement with Marx and the Marxist tradition.

The educational left in the United States has not been able to provide a counter-force to resist the ferocious orbit of capital and what we believe is the creation of a transnational global society in which the nation-state as the principal form of social organization has been superseded. We see as already under way an integration of all national markets into a single international market and division of labor and the erosion of national affiliations of capital (Robinson, 1998). The transnationalism of labor and capital has brought about material shifts in cultural practices and the proliferation of new contradictions between capitalism and labor. The deepening instability following in the wake of global capitalism has been driven by over-accumulation, overinvestment, overcapacity, overproduction, and new developments in the theater of global finance. The bottom line is the production of goods must return a profit by selling at market prices. Despite efforts of working classes throughout the globe to resist capital's drive to exploit their labor, capitalism is able dynamically and continuously to reorganize and reengineer itself such that its drive to accumulate is unhampered. Efforts at regulating markets are not effective at overcoming capital's reign of global terror. What is called for is the overturning of the basic laws of capitalism and the defeat of the dominion of capital itself. Capitalism's concentration, centralization, and transnationalism have reterritorialized the laws of motion of capital. We need to view the phenomena of globalized capitalism not merely in terms of market competition but rather from the perspective of production. Given that the logic of privatization and free trade—where social labor is the means and measure of value, and surplus social labor lies at the heart of profit—now odiously shapes archetypes of citizenship, manages our perceptions of what should constitute the "good society," and creates ideological formations that produce necessary functions for capital in relation to labor, it stands to reason that new ethnographic research approaches must take global capitalism not as an end point of analysis, but as a starting point. As schools are financed more by corporations that function as service industries for transnational capitalism, and as neoliberalism continues to guide educational policy and practice, the U.S. population faces a challenging educational reality (Kincheloe, 1999). It is a reality that is witnessing the progressive merging of cultural pedagogy and the productive processes within advanced capitalism (Giroux, & Searles, 1996; McLaren, 1997). Although, as researchers, we may not be interested in global capitalism, we can be sure that it is interested in us.

Critical ethnography faces a daunting challenge in the years to come, especially because capitalism has been naturalized as commonsense reality—even as a part of nature itself—and the term *social class* has been replaced by the less antagonistic term *socioeconomic status*. The focus of much recent postmodern ethnography is on asymmetrical gender and ethnic relations, and although this focus is important, class struggle has become an outdated issue (Kincheloe, & Steinberg, 1999). When social class is discussed, it is usually viewed as relational, not as oppositional. In the context of discussions of "social status" rather than "class struggle," postmodern ethnography has secured a privileged position that is functionally advantageous to the socially reproductive logic of entrepreneurial capitalism, private ownership, and the personal appropriation of social production (McLaren, 1995b) More than ever before research needs to address the objective, material conditions of the workplace and labor relations in order to prevent the further resecuring of the ideological hegemony of the neoliberal corporatist state.

In many ways the globalization process, and the strengthening of the free market capitalism that accompanies it, takes us back to the roots of critical research. As we have gained profound insights into the impact of the inscriptions of patriarchy, white supremacy, and class elitism on the consciousness of researchers operating under the banner of humanistic values, we also appreciate—mainly because it has profound implications for defeating the exploitation of human labor and the consolidation of a global ruling elite—critical insights into the domination of capital. In this context we envision important new developments of Marxist ethnographic -practices that both complement and extend many of the exciting new approaches that we are witnessing within the precincts of post-modern and postcolonial ethnography. Future practitioners of critical research must take all of these crucial dynamics into account if their work is to help create a more just, democratic, and egalitarian world. The realm of the critical has yet to reach the potential it envisions. We hope that this essay challenges its readers to engage in the hard work and research necessary to move critical praxis closer to its realization.

## REFERENCES

Abdullah, J., & Stringer, E. (1999). Indigenous knowledge, indigenous learning, indigenous research. In L. Semali & J. L. Kincheloe (Eds.), *What is indigenous knowledge? Voices from the academy*. Bristol, PA: Falmer.
Abercrombie, N. (1994). Authority and consumer society. In R. Keat, N. Whiteley, & N. Abercrombie (Eds.), *The authority of the consumer*. New York: Routledge.
Agger, B. (1992). *The discourse of domination; From the Frankfurt school to postmodernism*. Evanston, IL: Northwestern University Press.
Agger, B. (1998). *Critical social theories: An introduction*. Boulder, CO: Westview.
Alfino, M., Caputo, J., & Wynyard, R. (Eds.). (1998). *McDonaldization revisited: Critical essays on consumer and culture*. Westport, CT: Praeger.
Alford, C. (1993). Introduction to the special issue on political psychology and political theory. *Political Psychology, 14*, 199–208.
Allison, C. (1998). Okie narratives: Agency and whiteness. In J. L. Kincheloe, S. R. Steinberg, N. M. Rodriguez, & R. E. Chennault (Eds.), *White reign: Deploying whiteness in America*. New York: St. Martin's Press.
Anderson, G. (1989). Critical ethnography in education: Origins, current status, and new directions. *Review of educational research, 59*, 249–270.
Apple, M. (1996a). Dominance and dependency: Situating the bell curve within the conservative restoration. In J. L. Kincheloe, S. R. Steinberg, & A. D. Gresson III (Eds.), *Measured lies: the Bell curve examined*. New York: St. Martin's Press.
Apple, M. (1966). *Cultural politics and education*. New York: Teacher's College Press.
Aronowitz, S., & Di Fazio W, (1994). *The jobless future*. Minneapolis, MN: University of Minnesota Press.
Aronowitz, S., & Giroux, H. *Postmodern education: Politics, culture, and social criticism*. Minneapolis, MN: University of Minnesota Press.
Ashcroft, B., Griffiths, G., & Tiffin, H. (Eds.). (1995). *The post-colonial studies reader*. New York: Routledge.
Atwell-Vasey, W. (1998). Psychoanalytic feminism and the powerful teacher. In W. F. Pinar (Ed.), *Curriculum: Toward new identities*. New York: Garland.
Barrows, A. (1995). The ecopsychology of child development. In T. Roszak, M. Gomes, & A, Kanner (Eds.), *Ecopsychology: Restoring the earth, healing the mind*. San Francisco: Sierra Club Books.
Bartolomé, L. I. (1998). *The misteaching of academic discourses: The politics of language in the classroom*. Boulder, CO: Westview.
Bauman, Z. (1995). *Life in fragments: Essay's in postmodern morality*. Cambridge, MA: Blackwell.
Behar, R. (1993). *Translated woman: Crossing the border with Esperanza's story*. Boston: Beacon.
Behar, R., & Gordon, D. A. (Eds.), (1995). *Women writing culture*. Berkeley, CA: University of California Press.
Bell, D., & Valentine, G. (1997). *Consuming geographies: We are where we eat*. New York: Routledge.
Berger, A. A. (1995). *Cultural criticism: A primer of key concepts*. Thousand Oaks, CA: Sage.
Berry, K. (1998). Nurturing the imagination of resistance: Young adults as creators of knowledge. In J. L. Kincheloe & S. R. Steinberg (Eds.), *Unauthorized methods: Strategies for critical teaching*. New York: Routledge.
Bersani, L. (1995). Loving men. In M. Berger, B. Wallis, & S. Watson (Eds.), *Constructing masculinity*. New York: Routledge.
Bertman, S. (1998). *Hyperculture: The human cost of speed*. Westport, CT: Praeger.
Blades, D. (1997). *Procedures of power and curriculum change: Foucault and the quest for possibilities in science education*. New York: Peter Lang.
Block, A. (1995). *Occupied reading: Critical foundations for an ecological theory*. New York: Garland.
Boon, J. A. (1982). *Other tribes, other scribes: Symbolic anthropology in the comparative study of cultures, histories, religions, arid texts*. Cambridge: Cambridge University Press.
Bottomore, T. (1984). *The Frankfurt school*. London: Tavistock.

Bourdieu, P., & Wacquaat, L. (1992). *An invitation to reflexive sociology.* Chicago: University of Chicago Press.
Brents, B., & Monson, M. (1998). Whitewashing the strip: The construction of whiteness in Las Vegas. In J. L. Kincheloe, S. R. Steinberg, N. M. Rodriguez, & R. E. Chennault (Eds.), *White reign: Deploying whiteness in America.* New York: St. Martin's.
Britzman, D. (1991). *Practice makes practice: A critical study of learning to teach.* Albany, NY: State University of New York Press.
Britzman, D. (1995). What is this thing called love? *Taboo: The Journal of Culture and Education, 1,* 65–93.
Britzman, D., & Pitt, A. (1996). On refusing one's place: The ditchdigger's dream. In J. L. Kincheloe, S. R. Steinberg, & A. D. Gresson III (Eds.), *Measured lies: The bell curve examined.* New York: St. Martin's.
Brock-Utne, B. (1996). Reliability and validity in qualitative research within Africa. *International Review of Education, 42,* 605–621.
Brosio, R. (1994). *The radical democratic critique of capitalist education.* New York: Peter Lang.
Buckingham, D. (1989). Television literacy: A critique. *Radical Philosophy, 51,* 12–25.
Butler, M. (1998). Negotiating place: The importance of children's realities. In S. R. Steinberg & J. L. Kincheloe (Eds.), *Students as researchers: Creating classrooms that matter* (pp. 94–112). London: Taylor, & Francis.
Cannella, G. (1997). *Deconstructing early childhood education: Social justice and revolution.* New York: Peter Lang.
Carlson, D. (1997). *Teachers in crisis.* New York: Routledge.
Carlson, D. & Apple, M. (Eds.). (1998). *Power/knowledge/pedagogy: The meaning of democratic education in unsettling times.* Boulder, CO: Westview.
Carson, T. R. & Sumara, D. (Eds.). (1997). *Action research as a living practice.* New York: Peter Lang.
Carspecken, P. F. (1993). *Power, truth, and method: Outline for a critical methodology.* Unpublished manuscript.
Carspecken, P. F. (1996). *Critical ethnography in educational research: A theoretical and practical guide.* New York: Routledge.
Carspecken, P. F. (1999). *Four scenes for posing the question of meaning and other essays in critical philosophy and critical methodology.* New York: Peter Lang.
Carter, V. (1998). Computer-assisted racism: Toward an understanding of cyber-whiteness. In J. L. Kincheloe, S. R. Steinberg, N. M. Rodriguez, & R. E. Chennault (Eds.), *White reign: Deploying whiteness in America.* New York: St. Martin's.
Cary, R. (1996). IQ as commodity: The "new" economics of intelligence. In J. L. Kincheloe, S. R. Steinberg, & A. D. Gresson III (Eds.), *Measured lies: The bell curve examined.* New York: St. Martin's.
Christian-Smith, L., & Keelor, K. S. (1999). *Everyday knowledge and women of the academy: Uncommon truths.* Boulder, CO: Westview.
Clatterbaugh, K. (1997). *Contemporary perspectives on masculinity: Men, women, and politics in modern society.* Boulder, CO: Westview.
Clifford, J. (1992). Traveling cultures. In L. Grossberg, C. Nelson, & P. A. Treichler (Eds.), *Cultural studies* (pp. 96–116). New York: Routledge.
Clough, P. T. (1994). *Feminist thought: Desire, power and academic discourse.* Cambridge, MA: Blackwell.
Clough, P. T. (1992). *The end(s) of ethnography: From realism to social criticism.* Newbury Park, CA: Sage.
Clough, P. T. (1998). *The end(s) of ethnography: From realism to social criticism* (2nd ed.). New York: Peter Lang.
Coben, D. (1998). *Radical heroes: Gramsci, Freire and the politics of adult education.* New York: Garland.
Codd, J. (1984). Introduction. In J. Codd (Ed.), *Philosophy, common sense, and action in educational administration* (pp. 8–28). Geelong, Victoria, Australia: Deakin University Press.
Collins, J. (1995). *Architectures of excess: Cultural life in the information age.* New York: Routledge.

Comaroff, J., & Comaroff, J. (1992). *Ethnography and the historical imagination*. Boulder, CO: Westview.
Connor, S. (1992). *Theory and cultural value*. Cambridge, MA: Blackwell.
Cooper, D. (1994). Productive, relational, and everywhere? Conceptualizing power and resistance within Foucauldian feminism. *Sociology, 28*, 435–454.
Corrigan, P. (1979). *Schooling the Smash Street kids*. London: Macmillan.
Crapanzano, V. (1990). Afterword. In M. Manganaro (Ed.), *Modernist anthropology: From fieldwork to text* (pp. 300–308). Princeton, NJ: Princeton University Press.
Daniel, E. V. (1996). *Charred lullabies: Chapters in an anthropology of violence*. Princeton, NJ: Princeton University Press.
Deetz, S. A. (1993, May). *Corporations, the media, industry, and society: Ethical imperatives and responsibilities*. Paper presented at the annual meeting of the International Communication Association, Washington, DC.
Denzin, N. K. (1992). *Symbolic interactionism and cultural studies*. Newbury Park, CA: Sage.
Denzin, N. K. (1994). The art and politics of interpretation. In N. K. Denzin & Y. S. Lincoln (Eds.), *Handbook of qualitative research* (pp. 500–515). Thousand Oaks, CA: Sage.
Dewey, J. (1916). *Democracy and education*. New York: Free Press.
Douglas, S. (1994). *Where the girls are: Growing up female in the mass media*. New York: Times Books.
Drummond, L. (1996). *American dreamtime: A cultural analysis of popular movies, and their implications for a science of humanity*. Lantham, MD: Littlefield Adams.
du Gay, P., Hall, S., Janes, L., MacKay, H., & Negus, K. (1997). *Doing cultural studies: The story of the Sony Walkman*. London: Sage.
Ebert, T. (1991). Political semiosis in/or American cultural studies. *American Journal of Semiotics, 8*, 113–135.
Elliot, A. (1994). *Psychoanalytic theory: An introduction*. Cambridge, MA: Blackwell.
Ellis, J. (1998). Interpretive inquiry as student research. In S. R. Steinberg, & J. L. Kincheloe (Eds.), *Students as researchers: Creating classrooms that matter* (pp. 49–63). London: Taylor, & Francis.
Fehr, D. (1993). *Dogs playing cards: Powerbrokers of prejudice in education, art, and culture*. New York: Peter Lang.
Ferguson, M. & Golding, P. (Eds.). (1997). *Cultural studies in question*. London: Sage.
Finders, M. (1997). *Just girls: Hidden literacies and life in junior high*. New York: Teachers College Press.
Fine, M., Powell, L. C., Weis, L., & Wong, L. M. (Eds.). (1997). *Off white: Readings on race, power and society*. New York: Routledge.
Fiske, J. (1993). *Power works, power plays*. New York: Verso.
Flossner, G. & Otto, H. (Eds.). (1998). *Towards more democracy in social services: Models of culture and welfare*. New York: de Gruyter.
Foster, H. (Ed.). (1983). *The anti-aesthetic: Essays on postmodern culture*. Port Townsend, WA: Bay.
Frankenbeng, R. (1993). *White women, race matters: The social construction of whiteness*. Minneapolis, MN: University of Minnesota Press.
Franz, C. & Stewart, A. (Eds.). (1994). *Women creating lives*. Boulder, CO: Westview.
Fraser, N. (1995). Politics, culture, and the public sphere: Toward a postmodern conception. In L. J. Nicholson & S. Seidman (Eds.), *Social postmodernism: Beyond identity politics*. New York: Cambridge University Press.
Freire, A. M. A. (2000). Foreword by Ana Maria Araujo Freire. In P. McLaren, *Che Guevara, Paulo Freire, and the pedagogy of revolution*. Boulder, CO: Rowman and Littlefield.
Freire, P. (1985). *The politics of education: Culture, power, and liberation*. South Hadley, MA: Bergin, & Garvey.
Fuchs, M. (1993). The reversal of the ethnological perspective: Attempts at objectifying one's own cultural horizon. Dumont, Foucault, Bourdieu? *Thesis Eleven, 34*, 104–125.
Gabbard, D. (1995). NAFTA, GATT, and Goals 2000: Reading the political culture of post-industrial America. *Taboo: The Journal of Culture and Education, 2*, 184–199.
Gadamer, H. G. (1989). *Truth and method* (2nd Rev. ed., J. Weinsheimer & D. G. Marshall, Eds. & Trans.). New York: Crossroad.

Gall, J., Gall, M., & Borg, W. (1999). *Applying educational research: A practical guide*. New York: Longman.
Gallagher, S. (1992). *Hermeneutics and education*. Albany, NY: State University of New York Press.
Garnham, N. (1997). Political economy and the practice of cultural studies. In M. Ferguson & P. Golding (Eds.), *Cultural studies in question*. London: Sage.
Gee, J. (1996). *Social linguistics and literacies: Ideology in discourses* (2nd ed.). London: Taylor, & Francis.
Gee, J., Hull, G., & Lankshear, C. (1996). *The new work order: Behind the language of the new capitalism*. Boulder, CO: Westview.
Gergen, K. J. (1991). *The saturated self: Dilemmas of identity in contemporary life*. New York: Basic Books.
Gibson, R. (1986). *Critical theory and education*. London: Hodder, & Stroughton.
Giroux, H. (1983). *Theory and resistance in education: A pedagogy for the opposition*. South Hadley, MA: Bergin, & Garvey.
Giroux, H. (1988). Critical theory amid the politics of culture and voice: Rethinking the discourse of educational research. In R. Sherman & R. Webb (Eds.), *Qualitative research in education: Focus and methods* (pp. 190–210). New York: Palmer.
Giroux, H. (1992). *Border crossings: Cultural workers and the politics of education*. New York: Routledge.
Giroux, H. (1997). *Pedagogy and the politics of hope: Theory, culture, and schooling*. Boulder, CO: Westview.
Giroux, H., & Searles, S. (1996). The bell curve debate and the crisis of public intellectuals. In J. L. Kincheloe, S. R. Steinberg, & A. D. Gresson III (Eds.), *Measured lies: The bell curve examined*. New York: St. Martin's.
Godzich, W. (1992). Afterword: Reading against literacy. In J. F. Lyotard (Ed.), *The postmodern explained*. Minneapolis, MN: University of Minnesota Press.
Goldie, T. (1995). The representation of the indigene. In B. Ashcroft, C. Griffiths, & H. Tiffin (Eds.), *The post-colonial studies reader*. New York: Routledge.
Goldman, R., & Papson, S. (1994). The post-modernism that failed. In D. Dickens & A. Fontana (Eds.), *Postmodernism and social inquiry*. New York: Guilford Press.
Goodson, I. (1997). *The changing curriculum: Studies in social construction*. New York: Peter Lang.
Goodson, I., & Mangan, J. (1996). Exploring alternative perspectives in educational research. *Interchange*, 27(1), 41–59.
Gresson, A. (1995). *The recovery of race in America*. Minneapolis, MN: University of Minnesota Press.
Gresson, A. (2000). *America's atonement: Racial pain, recovery discourse and the psychology of healing*. New York: Peter Lang.
Griffin, C. (1985). *Typical girls? Young women from school to the job market*. London: Routledge, & Kegan Paul.
Grondin, J. (1994). *Introduction to philosophical hermeneutics* (J. Weinsheimer, Trans.). New Haven, CT: Yale University Press.
Gross, A., & Keith, W. (Eds.). (1997). *Rhetorical hermeneutics: Invention and Interpretation in the age of science*. Albany, NY: State University of New York Press.
Grossberg, L. (1995). What's in a name (one more time)? *Taboo: The Journal of Culture and Education, 1*, 1–37.
Grossberg, L. (1997). *Bringing it all back home: Essays on cultural studies*. Durham, NC: Duke University Press.
Hall, S. (Ed.), (1997). *Representation: Cultural representations and signifying practices*. London: Sage.
Hall, S. & du Gay, P. (Eds.). (1996). *Questions of cultural identity*. London: Sage.
Hebdige, D. (1979). *Subculture: The meaning of style*. London: Methuen.
Hedley, M. (1994). The presentation of gendered conflict in popular movies: Affective stereotypes, cultural sentiments, and men's motivation. *Sex Roles, 31*, 721–740.
Held, D. (1980). *Introduction to critical theory: Horkheimer to Habermas*. Berkeley, CA: University of California Press.

Heshusius, L. & Ballard, K. (Eds.). (1996). *From positivism to interpretivism and beyond: Tales of transformation in educational and social research.* New York: Teachers College Press.

Hicks, D. E. (1999). *Ninety-five languages and seven forms of intelligence.* New York: Peter Lang.

Hinchey, P. (1998). *Finding freedom in the classroom: A practical introduction to critical theory.* New York: Peter Lang.

Horkheimer, M. (1972). *Critical theory.* New York: Seabury.

Howell, S. (1998). The learning organization: Reproduction of whiteness. In J. L. Kincheloe, S. R. Steinberg, N. M. Rodriguez, & R. E. Chennault (Eds.), *White reign: Deploying whiteness in America.* New York: St. Martin's.

Jardine, D. (1998). *To dwell with a boundless heart: Essays in curriculum theory, hermeneutics, and the ecological imagination.* New York: Peter Lang.

Jay, M. (1973). *The dialectical imagination: A history of the Frankfurt school and the Institute of Social Research 1923–1950.* Boston: Little Brown.

Jipson, J., & Paley, N. (1997). *Daredevil research: Recreating analytic practice.* New York: Peter Lang.

Johnson, C. (1996). Does capitalism really need patriarchy? Some old issues reconsidered. *Women's Studies International Forum, 19,* 193–202.

Joyrich, L. (1996). *Reviewing reception: Television, gender, and postmodern culture.* Bloomington, IN: Indiana University Press.

Kellner, D. (1989). *Critical theory, Marxism, and modernity.* Baltimore: Johns Hopkins University Press.

Kellner, D. (Ed.). (1994). *Baudrillard: A critical reader.* Cambridge, MA: Blackwell.

Kellner, D. (1995). *Media culture: Cultural studies, identity and politics between the modern and the postmodern.* New York: Routledge.

Kellogg, D. (1998). Exploring critical distance in science education: Students researching the implications of technological embeddedness. In S. R. Steinberg & J. L. Kincheloe (Eds.), *Students as researchers: Creating classrooms that matter* (pp. 212–227). London: Falmer.

Kelly, L. (1996). When does the speaking profit us? Reflection on the challenges of developing feminist perspectives on abuse and violence by women. In M. Hester, L. Kelly, & J. Radford (Eds.), *Women, violence, and male power.* Bristol, PA: Open University Press.

Kincheloe, J. L. (1991). *Teachers as researchers: Qualitative paths to empowerment.* London: Falmer.

Kincheloe, J. L. (1993). *Toward a critical politics of teacher thinking: Mapping the postmodern.* Granby, MA: Bergin, & Garvey.

Kincheloe, J. L. (1995). *Toil and trouble: Good work, smart workers, and the integration of academic and vocational education.* New York: Peter Lang.

Kincheloe, J. L. (1998). Critical research in science education. In B. Fraser & K. Tobin (Eds.), *International handbook of science education* (Pt. 2). Boston: Kluwer.

Kincheloe, J. L. (1999). *How do we tell the workers? The socioeconomic foundations of work and vocational education.* Boulder, CO: Westview.

Kincheloe, J. L., & Pinar, W. F. (1991). Introduction. In J. L. Kincheloe & W. F. Pinar (Eds.), *Curriculum as social psychoanalysis: Essays on the significance of place* (pp. 1–23). Albany, NY: State University of New York Press.

Kincheloe, J. L., & Steinberg, S. R. (1993). A tentative description of postformal thinking: The critical confrontation with cognitive theory. *Harvard Educational Review, 63,* 296–320.

Kincheloe, J. L., & Steinberg, S. R. (1997). *Changing multiculturalism: New times, new curriculum.* London: Open University Press.

Kincheloe, J. L., Steinberg, S. R., & Hinchey, P. (Eds.), (1999). *The postformal reader: Cognition and education.* New York: Palmer.

Kincheloe, J. L., Steinberg, S. R., Rodriguez, N. M., & Chennault, R. E. (Eds.). (1998). *White reign: Deploying whiteness in America.* New York: St. Martin's.

Kincheloe, J. L., Steinberg, S. R., & Tippins, D. J. (1999). *The stigma of genius: Einstein, consciousness and Education.* New York: Peter Lang.

Kincheloe, J. L., Steinberg, S. R., & Villaverde, L. (Eds.). (1999). *Rethinking intelligence: Confronting psychological assumptions about teaching and learning.* New York: Routledge.

King, J. (1996). Bad luck, bad blood, bad faith: Ideological hegemony and the oppressive language of hoodoo social science. In J. L. Kincheloe, S. R. Steinberg, & A. D. Gresson III (Eds.), *Measured lies: The bell curve examined*. New York: St. Martin's.

King, J., & Mitchell, C. (1995). *Black mothers to sons*. New York: Peter Lang.

Knobel, M. *Everyday literacies: Students, discourse, and social practice*. New York: Peter Lang.

Kogler, H. (1996). *The power of dialogue: Critical hermeneutics after Gadamer and Foucault*. Cambridge, MA: MIT Press.

Lacey, C. (1970). *Hightown Grammar: The school as a social system*. London: Routledge & Kegan Paul.

Lash, S. (1990). Learning from Leipzig . . . or politics in the semiotic society. *Theory, Culture, & Society*, 7(4), 145–158.

Lather, P. (1991). *Getting smart: Feminist research and pedagogy with/in the postmodern*. New York: Routledge.

Lather, P. (1993). Fertile obsession: Validity after poststructuralism. *Sociological Quarterly*, 34, 673–693.

Leistyna, P., Woodrum, A., & Sherblom, S. (1996). *Breaking free: The transformative power of critical pedagogy*. Cambridge, MA: Harvard Educational Review.

Lemke, J. (1993). Discourse, dynamics, and social change. *Cultural Dynamics*, 6, 243–275.

Lemke, J. (1995). *Textual politics: Discourse and social dynamics*. London: Taylor, & Francis.

Lemke, J. (1998). Analyzing verbal data: Principles, methods, and problems. In B. Fraser & K. Tobin (Eds.), *International handbook of science education* (Pt. 2). Boston: Kluwer.

Lugg, C. (1996). Attacking affirmative action: Social Darwinism as public policy. In J. L. Kincheloe, S. R. Steinberg, & A. D. Gresson III (Eds.), *Measured lies: The bell curve examined*. New York: St. Martin's.

Lugones, M. (1987). Playfulness, "world"-traveling, and loving perception. *Hypatia*, 2(2), 3–19.

Luke, T. (1991). Touring hyperreality: Critical theory confronts informational society. In P. Wexler (Ed.), *Critical theory now* (pp. 1–26). New York: Falmer.

Lull, J. (1995). *Media, communication, culture: A global approach*. New York: Columbia University Press.

Macedo, D. (1994). *Literacies of power: What Americans are not allowed to know*. Boulder, CO: Westview

Madison, G. B. (1988). *The hermeneutics of postmodernity: Figures and themes*. Bloomington, IN: Indiana University Press.

Maher, F., & Tetreault, M. (1994). *The feminist classroom: An inside look at how professors and students are transforming higher education for a diverse society*. New York: Basic Books.

Manganaro, M. (1990). Textual play, power, and cultural critique: An orientation to modernist anthropology. In M. Manganaro (Ed.), *Modernist anthropology: From fieldwork to text* (pp. 3–47). Princeton, NJ: Princeton University Press.

Marcus, G. E., & Fischer, M. M. J. (1986). *Anthropology as cultural critique: An experimental moment in the human sciences*. Chicago: University of Chicago Press.

Martin, H., & Schuman, H. (1996). *The global trap: Globalization and the assault on democracy and prosperity*. New York: Zed Books.

McGuigan, J. (1996). *Culture and the public sphere*. New York: Routledge.

McLaren, P. (1992a). Collisions with otherness: "Traveling" theory, post-colonial criticism, and the politics of ethnographic practice—the mission of the wounded ethnographer. *International Journal of Qualitative Studies in Education*, 5, 77–92.

McLaren, P. (1992b). Literacy research and time postmodern turn: Cautions from the margins. In R. Beach, J. Green, M. Kamil, & T. Shanahan (Eds.), *Multidisciplinary perspectives on research*. Urbana, IL: National Council of Teachers of English.

McLaren, P. (1995a). *Critical pedagogy and predatory culture: Oppositional politics in a postmodern era*. New York: Routledge.

McLaren, P. (1995b). *Life in schools* (3rd ed.). New York: Longman.

McLaren, P. (1997). *Revolutionary multiculturalism: Pedagogies of dissent for the new millennium*. New York: Routledge.

McLaren, P. (1998). Revolutionary pedagogy in Post-revolutionary times: Rethinking the political economy of critical education. *Educational Theory*, 48, 431–462.

McLaren, P. (1999). *Schooling as a ritual performance: Toward a political economy of educational symbols and gestures* (3rd ed.). Boulder, CO: Rowman & Littlefield.

McLaren, P. (2000). *Che Guevara, Paulo Freire, and the pedagogy of revolution.* Boulder, CO: Rowman & Littlefield.

McLaren, P., & Hammer, R. (1989). Critical pedagogy and the post-modern challenge. *Educational Foundations, 3*(3), 29–69.

McLaren, P., Hammer, R., Reilly, S., & Sholle, D. (1995). *Rethinking media literacy: A critical pedagogy of representation.* New York: Peter Lang.

McWilliam, E. & Taylor, P. (Eds.). (1996). *Pedagogy, technology, and the body.* New York: Peter Lang.

Miller, S., & Hodge, J. (1998). *Phenomenology, hermeneutics, and narrative analysis: Some finished methodological business.* Unpublished manuscript.

Molnar, A. (1996). *Giving kids the business: The commercialization of America's schools.* Boulder, CO: Westview.

Morgan, W. (1996). Personal training: Discourses of (self) fashioning. In E. McWilliam & P. Taylor (Eds.), *Pedagogy, technology, and the body.* New York: Peter Lang.

Morley, D. & Chen, K. H. (Eds.), (1996). *Stuart Hall: Critical dialogues in cultural studies.* New York: Routledge.

Morrow, R. (1991). Critical theory, Gramsci and cultural studies: From structuralism to post-structuralism. In P. Wexler (Ed.), *Critical theory now* (pp. 27–69). New York: Falmer.

Mullen, C. (1999). Whiteness, cracks, and ink stains: Making cultural identity with Euro-american preservice teachers. In P. Diamond & C. Mullen (Eds.), *The postmodern educator: Arts-based inquiries and teacher development.* New York: Peter Lang.

Myrsiades, K. & Myrsiades, L. (Eds.). (1998). *Race-ing representation: Voice, history, and sexuality.* Lanham, MD: Rowman & Littlefield.

Newton, J., & Stacey, J. (1992–1993). Learning not to curse, or, feminist predicaments in cultural criticism by men: Our movie date with James Clifford and Stephen Greenbatt. *Cultural Critique, 23,* 51–82.

Nicholson, L. J. & Seidman, S. (Eds.). (1995). *Social postmodernist critics: Beyond identity politics.* New York: Cambridge University Press

Pailliotet, A. (1998). Deep Viewing: A critical look at visual texts. In J. L. Kincheloe & S. R. Steinberg (Eds.), *Unauthorized methods: Strategies for critical teaching.* New York: Routledge.

Peters, M. (1993). *Against Finkielkraut's la defaite de la pensee: Culture, postmodernism and education.* Unpublished manuscript.

Peters, M., & Lankshear, C. (1994). Education and hermeneutics: A Freirean interpretation. In P. McLaren & C. Lankshear (Eds.), *Politics of liberation: Paths from Freire.* New York: Routledge.

Pfeil, F. (1995). *White guys: Studies in post-modern domination and difference.* New York: Verso.

Pieterse, J., & Parekh, B. (1995). Shifting imaginaries: Decolonization, internal decolonization, and post-coloniality. In J. Pieterse & B. Parekh (Eds.), *The decolonialization of imagination: Culture, knowledge, and power.* Atlantic Highlands, NJ: Zed.

Pinar, W. F. (1994). *Autobiography, politics, and sexuality: Essays in curriculum theory, 1972–1992.* New York: Peter Lang.

Pinar, W. F. (Ed.). (1998). *Curriculum: Toward new identities.* New York: Garland.

Pinar, W. F., Reynolds, W., Slattery, P., & Taubman, P. (1995). *Understanding curriculum.* New York: Peter Lang.

Poster, M. (1989). *Critical theory and poststructuralism: In search of a context.* Ithaca, NY: Cornell University Press.

Prakash, M., & Esteva, C. (1998). *Escaping education: Living as learning within grassroots cultures.* New York: Peter Lang.

Pruyn, M. (1994). Becoming subjects through critical practice: How students in an elementary classroom critically read and wrote their world. *International Journal of Educational Reform, 3*(1), 37–50.

Pruyn, M. (1999). *Discourse wars in Gotham-West: A Latino immigrant urban tale of resistance and agency.* Boulder, CO: Westview.

Quantz, R. A. (1992). On critical ethnography (with some postmodern considerations). In M. D. LeCompte, W. L. Millroy, & J. Preissle (Eds.), *The handbook of qualitative research in education* (pp. 447–505). New York: Academic Press.

Quail, C. B., Razzano, K. A., & Skalli, L. H. (2000). *Tell me more: Rethinking daytime talk shows*. New York: Peter Lang.

Rabinow, P. (1977). *Reflections on fieldwork in Morocco*. Berkeley, CA: University of California Press.

Rains, F. (1998). Is the benign really harmless? Deconstructing some "benign" manifestations of operationalized white privilege. In J. L. Kincheloe, S. R. Steinberg, N. M. Rodriguez, & R. E. Chennault (Eds.), *White reign: Deploying whiteness in America*. New York: St. Martin's.

Rand, E. (1995). *Barbie's queer accessories*. Durham, NC: Duke University Press.

Rapko, J. (1998). Review of The power of dialogue: Critical hermeneutics after Gadamer and Foucault. *Criticism, 40*(1), 133–138.

Ritzer, C. (1993). *The McDonaldization of society*. Thousand Oaks, CA: Pine Forge.

Robins, D., & Cohen, P. (1978). *Knuckle sandwich: Growing up in the working—class city*. Harmondsworth: Penguin.

Robinson, W. (1998). Beyond nation-state paradigms: Globalization, sociology, and the challenge of transnational studies. *Sociological Forum, 13*, 561–594.

Rodriguez, N. M., & Villaverde, L. (2000). *Dismantling whiteness*. New York: Peter Lang.

Roman, L. & Eyre, L. (Eds.). (1997). *Dangerous territories: Struggles for difference and equality in education*. New York: Routledge.

Rosen, S. (1987). *Hermeneutics as politics*. New York: Oxford University Press.

Rosenau, P. M. (1992). *Post-modernism and the social sciences: Insights, inroads, and intrusion*. Princeton, NJ: Princeton University Press.

Samuels, A. (1993). *The political psyche*. New York: Routledge.

San Juan, E., Jr. (1992). *Articulations of power in ethnic and racial studies in the United States*. Atlantic Highlands, NJ: Humanities Press.

San Juan, E., Jr. (1996). *Mediations: From a Filipino perspective*. Pasig City, Philippines: Anvil.

Scheurich, J. J., & Young, M. (1997). Coloring epistemologies: Are our research epistemologies racially biased? *Educational Researcher, 26*(4), 4–16.

Scott, J. W (1992). Experience. In J. Butler & J. W Scott (Eds.), *Feminists theorize the political* (pp. 22–40). New York: Routledge.

Sedgwick, E. (1995). Gosh, Boy George, you must be awfully secure in your masculinity? In M. Bergen, B. Wallis, & S. Watson (Eds.), *Constructing masculinity*. New York: Routledge.

Semali, L. (1998). Still crazy after all these years: Teaching critical media literacy. In J. L. Kincheloe & S. R. Steinberg (Eds.), *Unauthorized methods: Strategies for critical teaching*. New York: Routledge.

Semali, L., & Kincheloe, J. L. (1999). *What is indigenous knowledge? Voices from the academy*. New York: Falmer.

Shelton, A. (1996). The ape's IQ. In J. L. Kincheloe, S. R. Steinberg, & A. D. Gresson III (Eds.), *Measured lies: The bell curve examined*. New York: St. Martin's.

Shohat, E., & Stam, R. (1994). *Unthinking Eurocentrism: Multiculturalism and the media*. New York: Routledge.

Shor, I. (1996). *When students have power: Negotiating authority in a critical pedagogy*. Chicago: University of Chicago Press.

Silverman, E. K. (1990). Clifford Geertz: Towards a more "thick" understanding? In C. Tilley (Ed.), *Reading material culture* (pp. 121–159). Cambridge, MA: Blackwell.

Slattery, P. (1995). *Curriculum development in the postmodern era*. New York: Garland.

Slaughter, R. (1989). Cultural reconstruction in the post-modern world. *Journal of Curriculum Studies, 3*, 255–270.

Sleeter, C. & McLaren, P. (Eds.), (1995). *Multicultural education, critical pedagogy, and the politics of difference*. Albany, NY: State University of New York Press.

Smith, D. G. (1999). *Interdisciplinary essays in the Pedagon: Human sciences, pedagogy and culture*. New York: Peter Lang.

Smith, R. & Wexler, P. (Eds.). (1995). *After Post-modernism: Education, politics, amid identity.* London: Falmer.

Smyth, J. (1989). A critical pedagogy of classroom practice. *Journal of Curriculum Studies, 21*(6), 483–401.

Soto, L. (1998). Bilingual education in America: In search of equity and just-ice. In J. L. Kincheloe & S. R. Steinberg (Eds.), *Unauthorized methods: Strategies for critical teaching.* New York: Routledge.

Stallabrass, J. (1996). *Gargantua: Manufactured mass culture.* London: Verso.

Steinberg, S. R. (1997). Kinderculture: The cultural studies of childhood. In N. Denzin (Ed.), *Cultural studies: A research volume* (Vol. 2, pp. 17–44). Greenwich, CT: JAI.

Steinberg, S. R. (Ed.). (2000). *Multi/intercultural conversations.* New York: Peter Lang.

Steinberg, S. R. (1997). The bitch who has everything. In S. R. Steinberg & J. L. Kincheloe (Eds.), *Kinderculture: The corporate construction of childhood.* Boulder, CO: Westview.

Steinberg, S. R. & Kincheloe, J. L. (Eds.), (1997). *Kinderculture: Corporate constructions of childhood.* Boulder, CO: Westview.

Steinberg, S. R. & Kincheloe, J. L. (Eds.), (1998). *Students as researchers: Creating classrooms that matter.* London: Taylor, & Francis.

Stewart, K. (1996). *A space on the side of the road: Cultural poetics in an "other"America.* Princeton, NJ: Princeton University Press.

Sünker, H. (1998). Welfare, democracy, and social work. In G. Flosser & H. Otto (Eds.), *Towards more democracy in social services: Models of culture and welfare.* New York: deGruyter.

Surber, J. (1998). *Culture and critique: An introduction to the critical discourses of cultural studies.* Boulder, CO: Westview.

Taussig, M. (1987). *Shamanism, colonialism, and the wild man: A study in terror and healing.* Chicago: University of Chicago Press.

Taylor, M., & Saarinen, E. (1994). *Imagologies: Media philosophy.* New York: Routledge.

Thomas, S. (1997). Dominance and ideology in cultural studies. In M. Ferguson & P. Golding (Eds.), *Cultural studies in question.* London: Sage.

Trueba, E. T., & McLaren, P. (in press). Critical ethnography for the study of immigrants. In E. T. Trueba & L. I. Bartolomé (Eds.), *Immigrant voices: In search of educational equity.* Boulder, CO: Rowman, & Littlefield.

Vattimo, G. (1994). *Beyond interpretation: The meaning of hermeneutics for philosophy.* Stanford, CA: Stanford University Press.

Viergever, M. (1999). Indigenous knowledge: An interpretation of views from indigenous peoples. In L. Semali & J. L. Kincheloe (Eds.), *What is indigenous knowledge? Voices from the academy.* Bristol, PA: Falmer.

Villaverde, L., & Kincheloe, J. L. (1998). Engaging students as researchers: Researching and teaching Thanksgiving in the elementary classroom. In S. R. Steinberg & J. L. Kincheloe (Eds.), *Students as researchers: Creating classrooms that matter* (pp. 149–166). London: Falmer.

Visweswaran, K. (1994). *Fictions of feminist ethnography.* Minneapolis, MN: University of Minnesota Press.

Weil, D. (1998). *Towards a critical multi-cultural literacy: Theory and practice for education for liberation.* New York: Peter Lang.

Weiler, K. (1988). *Women teaching for change: Gender, class, and power.* South Hadley, MA: Bergin, & Garvey.

Weinstein, M. (1998). *Robot world: Education, popular culture, and science.* New York: Peter Lang.

Welch, S. (1991). An ethic of solidarity and difference. In H. Giroux (Ed.), *Postmodernism, feminism, and cultural politics: Redrawing educational boundaries* (pp. 83–99). Albany, NY: State University of New York Press.

West, C. (1993). *Race matters.* Boston: Beacon.

Wexler, P. (1991). Preface. In P. Wexler (Ed.), *Critical theory now.* New York: Falmer.

Wexler, P. (1996a). *Critical social psychology.* New York: Peter Lang.

Wexler, P. (1996b). *Holy sparks: Social theory, education, and religion.* New York: St. Martin's.

Wexler, P. (1997). *Social research in education: Ethnography of being*. Paper presented at the international conference on the Culture of Schooling, Halle, Germany.
Willis, P. E. (1977). *Learning to labour: How working class kids get working class jobs*. Farnborough, UK: Saxon House.
Women's Studies Group, Centre for Contemporary Cultural Studies. (1978). *Women take issue: Aspects of women's subordination*. London: Hutchinson, with Centre for Contemporary Cultural Studies, University of Birmingham.
Woodward, K. (Ed.). (1997). *Identity and difference*. London: Sage.
Yates, T. (1990). Jacques Derrida: "There is nothing outside of the text". In C. Tilley (Ed.), *Reading material culture* (pp. 206–280). Cambridge, MA: Blackwell.
Young, I. (1990). The ideal of community and the politics of difference. In L. J. Nicholson (Ed.), *Feminism/postmodernism* (pp. 300–323). New York: Routledge.
Zavarzadeh, M., & Morton, D. (1991). *Theory, (post)modernity, opposition*. Washington, DC: Maisonnieuve.
Zizek, S. (1990). *The sublime object of ideology*. London: Verso.

Reprinted with permission: Kincheloe, J. L., & McLaren, P. (2005). Rethinking critical theory and qualitative research. In N. Denzin and Y. Lincoln (Eds.), *The handbook of qualitative research* (pp. 279–313). Thousand Oaks, CA: Sage Publications.

KECIA HAYES

# REFLECTING ON CRITICAL THEORY AND QUALITATIVE RESEARCH

In *Rethinking Critical Theory and Qualitative Research*, Kincheloe and McLaren detail how critical social theory and qualitative research methodology can be intentionally leveraged to decolonize knowledge production by destabilizing the dominance of Western epistemologies and by creating sacred space for indigenous epistemologies. They explain how the work of a criticalist researcher is principally shaped by the understanding "...that all thought is fundamentally mediated by power relations that are social and historically constituted; that facts can never be isolated from the domain of values or removed from some form of ideological inscription; that the relationship between concept and object and between signifier and signified is never stable or fixed and is often mediated by the social relations of capitalist production and consumption; that language is central to the formation of subjectivity (conscious and unconscious awareness); that certain groups in any society are privileged over others and, although reasons for this privileging may vary widely, the oppression that characterizes contemporary societies is most forcefully reproduced when subordinates accept their social status as natural, necessary, or inevitable; that oppression has many faces and that focusing on only one at the expense of other (e.g., class oppression versus racism) often elides the interconnections among them; and finally, that mainstream research practices are generally, although most often unwittingly, implicated in the reproduction of systems of class, race, and gender oppression" (Kincheloe & McLaren, p. 291).

Within their conceptual framework, there is a recognition of Madison's belief that "[s]cientific knowledge is, therefore, no passive copying of reality but is, rather, an active construction or constitution of it... science is but one way in which we creatively interpret reality, and no more than in any other mode of interpretation do we have access here to absolute reality and truth" (Madison, p. 17). Furthermore, a fervent and exclusive adherence to scientific knowledge and its modernist epistemologies further institutionalizes the hegemonic logic and oppressive power dynamics of our society through an assertion of "...who is allowed to proclaim truth and to establish the procedures by which truth is to be established..." (Semali & Kincheloe, p. 31). Kincheloe understood that the modernist epistemologies of research and pedagogy decontextualize knowledge and its production from all aspects of its sociocultural context thereby generating fragmentations and distortions; establish absolutisms through claims of scientific neutrality; obscure inherent dynamics of hegemonic power that mute the voices of individuals who occupy subjugated social spaces; and alienate the knowledge worker or student from the knowledge or learning produced. Throughout his extensive body of scholarship as well as the text of his life, Kincheloe demonstrated how an epistemology of criticality enables us to restore or achieve dynamics of justice and humanity for the oppressed and for the privileged by unmasking the hidden agendas, dynamics of power, repressive assumptions, false neutrality, and certainty that cloaks modernist epistemologies; and by recognizing frameworks of knowing that are more relevant to and reflective of the complex lived experiences of all individuals within our society. In doing so, he mapped a path to authentic enlightenment, empowerment, and transformation.

As an educator who primarily is concerned with the ways in which poor urban youth and families of color experience education and schooling within our society, I think our contemporary urban education discourses, policies, and practices are devoid of a substantive understanding of how urban youth are impacted by the power dynamics of schooling and education as they attempt to navigate the complex and multi-layered social spheres of their lives. Our failure to achieve a critical perspective of their educational engagements has hindered our ability to create meaningfully relevant reforms of urban schooling. For me, Joe's scholarship on the intersections of critical social theory and qualitative research methodology is invaluable because it provides a viable analytical framework to move us beyond the aggregated statistical data of urban youth's educational outcomes to a nuanced understanding of the complex phenomena that circumscribe how and why urban youth engage and resist schooling as they do. If we are genuinely interested in the construction of urban education discourses, policies, and practices that effectively attend to the needs of our urban young people, then we must commit ourselves to the work of critical research wherein the phenomena of their experiences with education and schooling are examined and understood through an interpretative analysis that acknowledges the formidable dynamics of power that impact their efforts to obtain an education in our public schools including the ways in which sociohistorical inequities persistently shape their contemporary experiences, and their disempowered social positionality.

In consideration of Kincheloe's framework of critical research as well as the need to substantively reform the ways in which we structure the work of urban education and schooling, I want to intentionally conduct research that is a decidedly "… phenomenological and hermeneutical study of human existence: phenomenology because it is the descriptive study of lived experience (phenomena) in the attempt to enrich lived experience by mining its meaning; hermeneutics because it is the interpretive study of the expressions and objectifications (texts) of lived experience in the attempt to determine the meaning embodied in them" (van Manen, p. 38). What follows is a brief discussion of one such study wherein I examined the emergent ideological narratives and acts of agency around school engagement for a small group of urban high school youth of color through the use of focus group and semi-structured individual interviews. Hopefully, this account will help to illuminate the value of the critical research framework for which Kincheloe advocated.

Of the intersection of critical social theory and qualitative research methodology, Kincheloe and McLaren note, "[i]n a research context it does not determine how we see the world but helps us to devise the questions and strategies for exploring it" (Kincheloe & McLaren, p. 281). Consequently, I initiated the focus group discussion with the following question: Most people would argue that education empowers people. Since schools are the primary place where we educate young people in our society, it would seem that schools should be a place where you are having experiences that help you to gain a sense of empowerment. Have your experiences to get an education in your various schools been empowering? To this question, all of the students expressed an initial agreement with the idea that education should empower people; and then began to recount specific experiences in their schools to illustrate their thoughts about whether schools helped them to develop a sense of empowerment.

One student, who attended five different high schools in a four-year period and was at that time working towards his General Equivalency Diploma (GED), explained that his school experiences were not positive or empowering. He contended that the major reason for this circumstance was his encounters with teachers who displayed uncaring attitudes, who were unresponsive to students' needs, and who appeared unconcerned with whether students were actually learning. He said, "They don't really care because they know they can't make a difference." Other students in the group echoed this sentiment. They reported that they believed that some teachers believed that their generation wasn't really interested in obtaining an education so it didn't make sense to try to provide it to them. As evidence of this idea, the research participants noted that they observed that some teachers, who didn't want particular students in their classes, immediately would call security for the slightest misbehaviors in order to have the students removed. The teachers wouldn't make any attempts to handle or de-escalate the situation. Another student commented that, "Teachers just try to rip you down and say it is to prepare you for the real world but it is just about ripping you." In discussing their learning experiences, the students felt that they needed better teachers "who know the curriculum, who know the plan to make it [the school] a better place, who know what they are doing, who understand youth better, who know how to communicate it [the curriculum] to students in different ways, and who are able to make a connection with the students." There also was concern about the culturally monolithic curricula of their schools, especially in terms of classes on U.S. history, "They should teach more about Black history, and dealing with U.S. history, they should teach more on Black culture than American culture because a lot of it is not true."

As the students continued to discuss their specific experiences and the culture of learning that permeated their schools, notions of power dynamics began to emerge, which helped to illuminate the extent to which the students' experiences in school reflected education as empowerment. The students had a keen sense of the fact that the structure of schools has a very distinct power differential wherein students are the most subordinate. Interestingly, the students problematized the abuse of power by teachers rather than the existence of the power differential. They felt that there wasn't a need to equalize power because hierarchies exist in society and it's unrealistic to level power in such a way that teachers and students have the same degrees of power. They did, however, express an expectation that "the teachers should [consider], knowing that there is someone telling you what to do and you know how you feel about that person, how do you think the student is gonna feel about the teacher when she's doing the same thing that is done to her." The students agreed with one participant who summarized with the idea that "the hierarchy should not be oppressive." The students recognized that one manifestation of the oppressive hierarchy was the strengthening of school security and implementation of 'high stakes discipline policies'. They felt that there was no space within the hierarchy of oppression for the consideration that young people are experiencing higher levels of frustration and pressure inside and outside of the schoolhouse.

I then asked the students to discuss the ways in which they and their classmates reacted to the cultures of learning and power hierarchies that they believed existed within their schools. For the most part, the young people recounted acts of agency that were strategic rather than oppositional in resisting the problematic school policies and practices. Two of the young men had especially poignant examples of deliberate acts of strategic agency. The first involved a student who decided to transfer to another school; and the second involved a student working on his GED after attending four different high schools in a four-year period. Both of the students revealed that the goal of educational attainment, as symbolized by a diploma, was a priority despite the obstacles and frustrations that they experienced within the school system. They said that dropping out was not an option. For them, persistence in the wake of the oppressive and obstructed environment represented strength that would serve them well in other endeavors throughout life. A third student interjects with the thought, "You take the good with the bad. Like, the criticism that a teacher will give you, instead of them acting out towards it, they will just use it against them, against the teacher because all it is doing is making them a better person. A teacher says that you will never make it because you are a bad student. Instead of being a bad student and fighting everyday, he'll graduate with his high school diploma, go to college, and then go back to the school and let her know how far he came in life so how could she say he was a bad student. Even though he didn't get good grades, he wasn't a bad student." The students seemed to embody, albeit to different degrees, an understanding that is reflected in the educational experiences of Villanueva, "School becomes his obsession. There is the education. But the obsession is as much, if not more, in getting a degree, not with a job in mind, just the degree, just because he thinks he can, despite all that has said he could not" (Villanueva, p. 71).

The young people who participated in the research demonstrated that they are so much more than the socially prevalent representations of who they are—representations that primarily are defined by modernist epistemological conclusions based upon decontextualized examinations of their educational outcomes. Their discussions reflected a propensity to critically read the rhetorical text of society's policies and practices for urban education and schooling juxtaposed against their lived experiences. They did not allow their recognition of the rhetorical text to linger as a hegemonic logic that displaces their hermeneutic sense-making of their educational experiences within schools. In this respect, they are knowledge workers excavating their own lived experiences and attempting to achieve what Kincheloe and McLaren have described as critical enlightenment "...to uncover the winners and losers in particular social arrangements and the processes by which such power plays operate" (Kincheloe & McLaren, p. 281).

In their discussion, Kincheloe and McLaren argue that there is a need for critical researchers to "...construct their perception of the world anew, not just in random ways but in a manner that undermines what appears natural, that opens to question what appears obvious" (Kincheloe & McLaren, p. 303). They recognize ever-evolving manifestations of entrenched and emergent power dynamics within our hegemonic society and consequently, critical researchers must be vigilant in their questioning of the hegemonic logic that attempts to normalize the oppression. Power is never stagnant and always finds novel formations that expand the dynamics of oppression and marginalization. In addition to these concerns that Kincheloe and McLaren delineate for the field of critical research, it also is important for workers within this tradition to determine how to use the research to move people from a place of critical enlightenment to enactivism wherein we transform our own perceptions, cognitions, and actions based upon the knowledges that we produce through the excavation of the embedded meanings of our lived experiences within an evolving hegemonic society. This work is fundamentally about building people's capacity for increasingly strategic and intentional responses of resistance to the oppressive power dynamics that insidiously structure their lives. The two young men who sought alternative educational options (i.e., transfer to another school and enrollment in a GED program) represent movement in this direction but there is a need to help them and other urban youth of color, especially those who do not readily see viable alternatives, to achieve deeper levels of enactivism as a result of their expanding critical enlightenment. This idea is consistent with Kincheloe and McLaren's belief that the work to "...name the *critical* must be connected to an attempt to confront the injustice of a particular society or public sphere within the society. Research thus becomes a transformative endeavor unembarrassed by the label *political* and unafraid to consummate a relationship with emancipatory consciousness" (Kincheloe & McLaren, p. 291).

Simultaneously, critical researchers must work to ensure that the knowledges produced are amplified within the policymaking arena. The themes embedded in the hermeneutic narratives of the subjugated need to be authentically considered and integrated into the construction of the social policies and practices that overwhelmingly structure their lives. In order to realize the full transformative potential of critical research, critical researchers need to publicly leverage the knowledges produced as a means to disrupt the oppressive master narratives that permeate the sociopolitical discourses within public domain. In doing so, critical researchers can effectively subvert the hegemonic logic that overwhelmingly structures our contemporary policymaking endeavors and begin to embed new understandings that seek to achieve social justice for the marginalized. Consider the extent to which No Child Left Behind would be different if the policy discourse reflected a deeper understanding of young people's hermeneutic narratives of the phenomenon of being left behind; or the extent to which our discourse on school safety would be upended by a recognition of all of the ways in which young people articulate their experiences of school as an unsafe environment. We need to end the overreliance of our policymaking on modernist epistemologies because they covertly are value-laden and politicized as well as privilege those who possess different forms of social power over the disempowered. Furthermore, they constrict our abilities to create a more equalized power dynamic in the policymaking process by achieving a more comprehensive and nuanced understanding of the phenomenon being addressed. In essence, we need to ask ourselves "[m]ay we presume to hope that the work of these and other socially engaged researchers somehow goes beyond the documentation of existing evils to effect real change in the world outside the texts?" (Barone, p. 593). An affirmative response is required to manifest the potential of critical research as a tool for transformative social justice.

## REFERENCES

Barone, T. (2009). Narrative researchers as witnesses of injustice and agents of social change? *Educational Researcher, 38*(8), 591–597.

Kincheloe, J. L., & McLaren, P. (2000). Rethinking critical theory and qualitative research. In N. Denzin & Y. Lincoln (Eds.), *Handbook of Qualitative Research* (pp. 279–314). Thousand Oaks, CA: Sage Publications, Inc.

Madison, G. B. (1988). *The hermeneutics of postmodernity*. Bloomington, IN: Indiana University Press.

Semali, L., & Kincheloe, J. L. (1999). Indigenous knowledge and schooling: A continuum between conflict and dialogue. In L. Semali & J. L. Kincheloe (Eds.), *What is indigenous knowledge?: Voices from the academy* (pp. 3–57). New York: Falmer Press.

van Manen, M. (1990). *Researching lived experience*. Ontario, Canada: The Althouse Press, Faculty of Education, The University of Western Ontario.

Villanueva, V., Jr. (1993). *Bootstraps: From an American academic of color*. Illinois, IL: National Council of Teachers of English.

*In 1980, Joe finished his dissertation and found it impossible to get a job. He applied everywhere, but no luck. He got to the point that he was certain he would go back to construction (a field in which he had proven to really fail in). A last ditch effort was to apply for Department Chair in Education at Sinte Gleska College, on the Rosebud Sioux Reservation in South Dakota. A kid from Tennessee, Joe's notions of non-dominant cultural people were framed by the Appalachian poor–both Black and White. His knowledge of colonialism and oppression had been enhanced through university research, but living in South Dakota contextualized a consciousness which had only just begun. Along with teaching at the College and chairing the department, Joe joined the small community, living in a trailer home out on the wind swept prairies of the frozen land. He learned to walk the balance between understanding and naming oppression, and how to not be a savior, nor anticipate that anyone on the res needed saving. His work on the Rosebud brought him to a living palate of Paulo Freire's work—he saw power work, power corrupt, and indigenous peoples negotiate their lives in the conditions of imperialism and American greed. His work in South Dakota informed every day of his life, along with Sioux spiritualism and wisdom, he began to create a conversation about the complexities of writing with indigenous peoples. SS*

JOE L. KINCHELOE

# 13. CRITICAL ONTOLOGY AND INDIGENOUS WAYS OF BEING

*Forging a Postcolonial Curriculum*

Mainstream teacher education provides little insight into the forces that shape teacher identity and consciousness. Becoming educated, becoming a postcolonial teacher-scholar-researcher necessitates personal transformation based on an understanding and critique of these forces. In this context this chapter develops a notion of critical ontology (ontology is the branch of philosophy that studies what it means to be in the world, to be human) and its relationship to *being* a teacher in light of indigenous knowledges and ontologies. As teachers from the dominant culture explore issues of indigeneity, they highlight both their differences with cultural others and the social construction of their own subjectivities. In this context they come to understand themselves, the ways they develop curriculum, and their pedagogy in a postcolonial world. Such issues become even more important at a time where new forms of economic, political, and military colonialism are reshaping both colonizing and colonized societies. This chapter makes three basic points:

Critical ontology is grounded on the epistemological and ontological power of difference.

The study of indigeneity and indigenous ways of being highlights tacit Western assumptions about the nature and construction of selfhood.

A notion of critical ontology emerges in these conceptual contexts that helps us push the boundaries of Western selfhood in the twenty-first century as we concurrently gain new respect for the genius of indigenous epistemologies and ontologies.

## WHAT IS CRITICAL ONTOLOGY?

In this context we engage in the excitement of attaining new levels of consciousness and "ways of being." Individuals who gain such a critical ontological awareness understand how and why their political opinions, religious beliefs, gender role, racial positions, and sexual orientation have been shaped by dominant cultural perspectives. A critical ontological vision helps us in the effort to gain new understandings and insights as to who we can become. Such a vision helps us move beyond our present state of being–our ontological selves–as we discern the forces that have made us that way. The line between knowledge production and being is blurred, as the epistemological and the ontological converge around questions of identity. As we employ the ontological vision we ask questions about ethics, morality, politics, emotion, and gut feelings, seeking not precise steps to reshape our subjectivity but a framework of principles with which we can negotiate. Thus, we join the quest for new, expanded, more just and interconnected ways of being human.

An important dimension of a critical ontology involves freeing ourselves from the machine metaphors of Cartesianism. Such an ontological stance recognizes the reductionism of viewing the universe as a well-oiled machine and the human mind as a computer. Such colonial ways of being subvert an appreciation of the amazing life force that inhabits both the universe and human beings. This machine cosmology has positioned human beings as living in a dead world, a lifeless universe. Ontologically, this Western Cartesianism has separated individuals from their inanimate surroundings, undermining any organic interconnection of the person to the cosmos. The life-giving complexity of the inseparability of human and world has been lost and social/cultural/pedagogical/psychological studies of people abstracted–removed from context. Such a removal has exerted disastrous ontological effects. Human beings, in a sense, lost their belongingness to both the world and to other people around them.

The importance of indigenous (Semali and Kincheloe, 1999; Steinberg, 2001) and other subjugated knowledges emerges in this ontological context. With the birth of modernity, the scientific revolution and the colonial policies they spawned, many pre-modern, indigenous ontologies were lost. Ridiculed by Europeans as primitive, the indigenous ways of being were often destroyed by the colonial conquerors of not only the military but the political, religious, and educational variety as well. While there is great diversity among pre-modern worldviews and ways of being, there do seem to be some discernible patterns that distinguish them from modernist perspectives. In addition to developing systems of meaning and being that were connected to cosmological perspectives on the nature of creation, most premodern viewpoints saw nature and the world at large as living systems. Western, often Christian, observers condescendingly labeled such perspectives as pantheism or nature worship and positioned them as an enemy of monotheism. Not understanding the subtlety and nuance of such indigenous views of the world, Europeans subverted the sense of belonging that accompanied these enchanted understandings of nature. European Christomodernism transformed the individual from a connected participant in the drama of nature to a detached, objective, depersonalized observer.

The Western modernist individual emerged from the process alienated and disenchanted. As Edmund O'Sullivan (1999) puts it, Cartesianism tore apart "the relationship between the microcosmos and the macrocosmos" (p. 18). Such a fragmentation resulted in the loss of cosmological significance and the beginning of a snowballing pattern of ontological imbalance. A critical ontology involves the process of reconnecting human beings on a variety of levels and in numerous ways to a living social and physical web of reality, to a living cosmos. Of course, in this process Westerners have much to learn from indigenous educators. Teachers with a critical ontological vision help students connect to the civic web of the political domain, the biotic web of the natural world, the social web of human life, and the epistemological web of knowledge production. In this manner, we all move to the realm of critical ontology where new ways of being and new ways of being *connected* reshape all people.

## THE POWER OF DIFFERENCE

The concept of difference is central to a critical ontology. Gregory Bateson uses the example of binoculars to illustrate this point. The image of the binocular—a singular and undivided picture—is a complex synthesis between images in both the left and right side of the brain. In this context a synergy is created where the sum of the images is greater than the separate parts. As a result of bringing the two different views together, resolution and contrast are enhanced. Even more important, new insight into depth is created. Thus, the relationship between the different parts constructs new dimensions of seeing (Bateson in Newland, 1997). Employing such examples of synergies, critical ontologists maintain that juxtapositions of difference create a bonus of insight. This concept becomes extremely important in any cognitive, epistemological, social, pedagogical, or self-production activity.

## DEPLOYING DIFFERENCE: USING SUBJUGATED/INDIGENOUS KNOWLEDGES IN CRITICAL ONTOLOGY

Cartesian rationalism has consistently excluded subjugated/indigenous knowledges from validated databases in diverse disciplines. These local, unauthorized knowledges are central to the work of the bricolage. Too often in Western colonial and neo-colonial history Europeans have viewed the knowledges and ways of seeing of the poor, the marginalized, and the conquered in a condescending and dismissive manner. Many of these perspectives, of course, were brimming with cosmological, epistemological, and ontological insight missing from Western perspectives. Western scholars were often simply too ethnocentric and arrogant to recognize the genius of such subjugated/indigenous information. Critical ontologists unabashedly take a hard look at these perspectives—not in some naïve romantic manner but in a rigorous and critical orientation. They are aware that Western scientific thinking often promotes contempt for indigenous individuals who have learned about a topic such as farming from the wisdom of their ancestors and a lifetime of cultivating the land. Many of the subjugated knowledges critical ontologists employ come from postcolonial backgrounds. Such ways of seeing force such scholars and teachers to account for the ways colonial power has shaped their approaches to knowledge production while inscribing the process of self-production.

Starting research and pedagogy with a valuing of non-Western knowledges, critical ontologists can spiral through a variety of such discourses to weave a multilogical theoretical and empirical tapestry. They can even juxtapose them with Western ways of seeing. For example, using a Hindu-influenced ontology that delineates the existence of a non-objective, purposely constructed reality, a critical theory that traces the role of power in producing this construction, a Santiago cognitive theory that maintains we bring forth this constructed world via our action within and upon it, and a poststructuralist feminist theory that alerts us to the ways patriarchal and other structures shape our knowledge about this reality, we gain a more profound understanding of what is happening when human beings encounter the world. The insights we gain and the knowledges we produce with these concepts in mind move us to new levels of both epistemological and ontological awareness. Such an awareness may be similar to what the Vajrayana tradition of Buddhism calls "crazy wisdom." Critical ontologists seek the multilogical orientation of crazy wisdom in their efforts to push the envelope of knowledge production and selfhood (Thomas, 1998; Parmar, 2003; Progler, 2001; Berry, 2001; Capra, 1996; Varela, 1999).

With these insights in mind scholar-teachers can operate in a wide diversity of disciplines and use an infinite number of subjugated and indigenous forms of knowledge. Ethnomathematical knowledges can be used to extend understanding of and knowledge production about math and math pedagogy (Appelbaum, 2003). Organic African American knowledges of grandmothers, beauticians, and preachers can provide profound insight into the nature of higher order cognition (Dumas, 2003). Hip hop musicians can help educators working to develop thicker and more insightful understandings of youth cultures and their implications for pedagogy (Parmar, 2003). Ancient African epistemologies and ontologies can help shape the theoretical lenses one uses to study and teach about contemporary racism and class bias.

Feminist understandings are important as they open doors to previously excluded knowledges. Such knowledges often point out the problems with the universal pronouncements of Cartesianism. The presence of gender diversity in this context reveals the patriarchal inscriptions on what was presented as universal, always true, validated knowledge about some aspect of the world. Indeed, this psychological pronouncement about the highest form of moral reasoning may apply more to men than it does to women—and even then it may apply more to upper-middle class men than to lower socio-economic class men or more to Anglo men than to Asian and African men. With these feminist insights in mind, critical ontologists find it easier to view the ways the knowledges they produce reflect the cultural, historical, and gendered contexts they occupy. In this context universality is problematized. Indeed, the more we are aware of those different from us on a variety of levels, the harder it is to produce naive universal knowledges. In our heightened awareness, in our crazy wisdom, we produce more sensitive, more aware modes of information (Burbules and Beck, 1999). Once the subjugated/indigenous door is open the possibilities are infinite.

## THE BRICOLAGE, DIFFERENCE, AND SELF-AWARENESS IN RESEARCH

When researchers, for example, encounter difference in the nature of the other, they enter into symbiotic relationships where their identity is changed. Such researchers are no longer merely obtaining information but are entering a space of transformation where previously excluded perspectives operate to change consciousness of both self and the world. Thus, research in a critical ontological context changes not only what one knows but who one actually is. In this process the epistemological and ontological domains enter into a new relationship that produces dramatic changes. Lev Vygotsky was on the right track as he documented the importance of the context in which learning takes place—the zone of proximal development (zpd). Difference in the sense we are using it here expands the notion of the zpd into the domain of research, drawing upon the power of our interactions in helping shape the ways we make meaning. In the new synergized position ontologically sensitive researchers construct new realities where they take on new and expanded roles.

Aware of the power of difference, these researchers develop a new consciousness of the self: 1) the manner in which it has been constructed; 2) its limitations; and 3) a sense of immanence concerning what it can become. Self-awareness is a metacognitive skill that has historically been more valued in Eastern traditions such as Buddhism, Taoism, and Yoga than in the West. Time and again we see the value of pluralism manifest itself in this discussion of difference and the bricolage. A pluralistic epistemology helps us understand the way we are situated in the web of reality and how this situatedness shapes what we see as researchers. Such an awareness reveals the limited nature of our observations of the world. Instead of researchers making final pronouncements on the way things are, they begin to see themselves in a larger interdisciplinary and intercultural conversation. Critical ontologists attuned to this dynamic, focus their attention on better modes of listening and respecting diverse viewpoints. Such higher order listening moves them to new levels of self-consciousness (Williams, 1999; Newland, 1997; Lepani, 1998; Thayer-Bacon, 2000).

Of course, difference does not work as an invisible hand that magically shapes new insights into self and world. Humans must exercise their complex hermeneutic abilities to forge these connections and interpret their meanings. In this context critical ontologists confront difference and then decide where they stand in relation to it. They must discern what to make of what it has presented them. With this in mind these critical scholar-educators work hard to develop relationships with those different from themselves that operate to create new meanings in the interactions of identity and difference. In this interaction knowledge producers grow smarter as they reject modernist Cartesian notions that cultural conflicts can be solved only by developing monological universal principles of epistemology and universal steps to the process of research. Too often, these scholars/cultural workers understand that these "universal" principles simply reflect colonial Western ways of viewing the world hiding in the disguise of universalism. Rigorous examination of the construction of self and society are closed off in such faux-universalism. Indeed, it undermines the development of a critical self-consciousness.

In the face of a wide variety of different knowledges and ways of seeing the world, the cosmos human beings think they know collapses. In a counter-colonial move critical ontologists raise questions about any knowledges and ways of knowing that claim universal status. In this context they make use of this suspicion of universalism in combination with global, subjugated, and indigenous knowledges to understand how they have been positioned in the world. Almost all of us from Western backgrounds or non-Western colonized backgrounds have been implicated in some way in the web of universalism. The inevitable conflicts that arise from this implication do not have to be resolved immediately. At the base of these conflicts rest the future of global culture as well as the future of research and pedagogy. Recognizing that these are generative issues that engage us in a productive process of analyzing self and world is in itself a powerful recognition. The value of both this recognition and the process of working through the complicated conceptual problems are treasured by critical ontologists. Indeed, they avoid any notion of finality in the resolution of such dilemmas (Richardson and Woolfolk, 1994; Degenaar, 1995; Howley, Pendarvis, and Howley, 1993; O'Sullivan, 1999; Fenwick, 2000).

## INDIGENEITY AND THE CONSTRUCTION OF SELFHOOD

Always looking for multiple perspectives, insight in diverse places, the power of difference, critical ontologists examine human interconnectedness via the lens of indigenous knowledges. Many systems of indigenous knowledge illustrate the *enaction* of interconnectedness and raise profound questions about the ways Western scholars have constructed knowledge, scientific methods, and the scholarly disciplines. While there is great diversity in these indigenous knowledges, most assume that humans are part of the world of nature. Extending this holism many indigenous scholars maintain that the production and acquisition of knowledge involves a process of interactions among the human body, the mind, and the spirit (Dei, 1995). R. Sambuli Mosha (2000) writes that among the East African Chagga peoples knowledge that is passed along to others must further the development of morality, goodness, harmony, and spirituality. Indeed, he continues, in the Chagga worldview it is impossible to separate these domains. Such fragmentation simply does not make sense to the Chagga. Embedded in every Chagga child is a part of the divine dimension of reality, illustrating the interconnectedness of all aspects of reality. Thus, knowledge production and the construction of selfhood cannot take place outside this intricate web of relationships.

In Cartesian-Newtonian modes of colonial science the interrelationships cherished by the Chagga are not as *real* as their individual parts. For example, in Cartesian psychology consciousness is often reduced to neural and chemical dynamics. Researchers in this context often study nothing outside the narrow confines of brain chemistry from graduate school to retirement. The notion that the understanding of human consciousness might be enhanced by anthropological, theological, or philosophical investigations rarely, if ever, occurs to such researchers over the decades of their research.

Making use of indigenous knowledges and the theological insights of Buddhism in this domain, cognitive theorist Francisco Varela develops a dramatically different concept of consciousness. Understanding the indigenous notion that the individual cannot be understood outside the community of which she is a part, Varela posits that human consciousness *emerges* from the social and biological interactions of its various parts. This understanding may over the next couple of decades revolutionize the fields of cognitive science, psychology, and even pedagogy. When scholars grasp the multilogical, interrelated nature of the possibilities for dramatic changes in the ways scholars and educators operate begin to take place. Using the indigenous metaphor, knowledge *lives* in the cultures of indigenous peoples. As opposed to the disciplinary knowledges of Cartesian-Newtonianism, which are often stored in archives or laboratories, indigenous knowledges live in everyday cultural practices (Woodhouse, 1996; Dei, 1995; Maurial, 1999).

Critical ontologists ask hard questions of indigenous knowledges. They know that folk knowledges–like Western scientific knowledges–often help construct exploitation and oppression for diverse groups and individuals. With this caution and resistance to essentialism in mind, ontological scholars study the ways many indigenous peoples in Africa construct the interrelationships of their inner selves to the outer world. This indigenous tendency to avoid dualism that when unacknowledged undermines the balance of various relationships is profoundly important. For example, the dualism between humans and nature can wreak havoc in an indigenous social system. In many indigenous African conceptions of humanness are viewed as a part of nature, not separate from it. Unlike scholars in the Cartesian-Newtonian disciplines, the world was too sacred for humans to study and dominate or conquer. Once humanness and the environment were viewed as separate entities, forces were unleashed that could destroy the delicate eco- and social systems that sustained the indigenous culture. Thus, to accept the dualism between humanness and nature in the minds of many African peoples was tantamount to committing mass suicide.

Another example of indigenous culture whose knowledges critical ontologists deem valuable is the Andean peoples of South America. Everyone and everything in traditional Andean culture is sentient, as, for example, the rivers and mountains have ears and eyes. Acting in the world in this cultural context is a dimension of being in relationship to the world. In one's actions within the physical environment, an Andean individual is in conversation with the mountains, rivers, trees, lakes, etc. This language of conversation replaces in Andean culture a Western traditional scientific language of knowing. A profound epistemological shift has taken place in this replacement. In Andean culture the concept of knower and known is irrelevant. Instead humans and physical entities engage in reciprocal relationships, carrying on conversations in the interests of both.

These conversations have been described as mutually nurturing events, acts that enhance the ontological evolution of all parties involved via their tenderness and empathy for the living needs of the other. Thus, the epistemology at work here involves more than simply knowing about something. It involves tuning oneself in to the other's mode of being–its ontological presence—and entering into a life generating relationship with it (Apffel-Marglin, 1995). Critical ontologists take from this an understanding of a new dimension of the inseparable relationship between knowing and being. Those working in the academic disciplines of Western societies must enter into ontological relationships with that which they are studying. Such relationships should be enumerated and analyzed. How am I changed by this relationship? How is the object of my study changed or potentially changed by the relationship?

Great change occurs as a result of the Andean people's conversation with nature. Nature's voice is heard through the position and brilliance of planets and stars; the speed, frequency, color, and smell of the wind; and the size and number of particular wild flowers to mention only a few. Such talk tells Andeans about the coming weather and various dimensions of cultivation and they act in response to such messages. Because of the overwhelming diversity of ecosystems and climates in the Andes mountains and valleys, these conversations are complex. Interpretations of meanings– like any hermeneutic acts–are anything but self-evident. Such conversations and the actions they catalyze allow the Andean peoples to produce an enormous variety of cultivated plant species that amaze plant geneticists from around the world. As Frederique Apffel-Marglin (1995) describes this diversity:

> The peasants grow and know some 1,500 varieties of quinoa, 330 of kaniwa, 228 of tarwi, 250 of potatoes, 610 of oca (another tuber) and so forth... The varieties differ according to regions, altitude, soils, and other factors. Such incredible diversity cannot only be due to ecological diversity. The manner in which peasants converse with plants and all the other inhabitants of the world, be they animate or inanimate, with not only an infinite attention to detail but with a receptive, open, and direct or embodied attitude is at the heart of such diversity (p. 11).

The Andeans actually have a word for those places where the conversation between humans and the natural world take place. *Chacras* include the land where the Andeans cultivate their crops, the places where utensils are crafted, and the places where herds and flocks live and graze. According to the Andeans these are all places where all entities come together to discuss the regeneration of life. The concept of interrelationship is so important in the Andean culture that the people use the word, *ayllu*, to signify a kinship group that includes not only other human beings but animals, mountains, streams, rocks, and the spirits of a particular geographical place. Critical ontological scholars adapt these indigenous Andean concepts to the rethinking of the ways they study, as they identify the methodologies, epistemologies, ontologies, cultural systems, social theories, ad infinitum that they employ in their multilogical understanding of the research act. Those who research the social, psychological, and educational worlds hold a special responsibility to those concepts and the people they research to select critical and life affirming logics of inquiry. A critical hermeneutics demands that relationships at all levels be respected and engaged in ways that produce justice and new levels of understanding—in ways that regenerate life and, central to our ontological concerns, new ways of being.

Thus, critical ontologists are able to make use of the power of difference in the context of subjugated/indigenous knowledges. The power of difference or "ontological mutualism" transcends Cartesianism's emphasis on the thing-in-itself. The tendency in Cartesian-Newtonian thinking is to erase mutualism's bonus of insight in the abstraction of the object of inquiry from the processes and contexts of which it is a part. In this activity it subverts difference. The power of these synergies exists not only in the cognitive, social, pedagogical, and epistemological domains but in the physical world as well. Natural phenomena, as Albert Einstein illustrated in physics and Humberto Maturana and Francisco Varela laid out in biology and cognition, operate in states of interdependence. These ways of seeing have produced perspectives on the workings of the planet that profoundly differ from the views produced by Western science.

What has been fascinating to many is that these post-Einsteinian perspectives have in so many ways reflected the epistemologies and ontologies of ancient non-Western peoples in India, China, and Africa and indigenous peoples around the world. Thus, critical ontology's use of indigenous knowledge is not offered as some new form of postcolonial exploitation—as in pharmaceutical companies' rush into indigenous locales to harvest plants that indigenous peoples have known for millennia possess medicinal qualities. In this context such products are then marketed as culturally sensitive postcolonial forms of exotica. The hipness of such entrepreneurial diversity provides little benefits for the indigenous people watching the process—they are not the beneficiaries of the big profits. Instead, a critical ontology *uses* indigenous peoples as teachers, as providers of wisdom. In their respect for such indigenous knowledges and indigenous peoples critical ontologists use such indigenous teachings to create a world more respectful and hospitable to indigenous peoples' needs and ways of being.

## CONSTRUCTING A CRITICAL ONTOLOGY

Making use of our concept of difference and the insights provided by indigenous knowledges and ways of being, we are ready to construct our critical ontological postcolonial curriculum. In a critical ontology the teaching, learning, and curriculum development processes emerge as profoundly exciting enterprises because they are always conceptualized in terms of what we can become—both in an individual and a collective context. In our socio-ontological imagination we can transcend the

Enlightenment category of abstract individualism and move toward a more textured concept of the relational individual. While abstract individualism and a self-sufficient ontology seem almost *natural* in the Western modernist world, of course, such is not the case in many indigenous cultures and has not been the case even in Western societies in previous historical eras. In ancient Greece, for example, it is hard to find language that identified "the self" or "I"—such descriptions were not commonly used because the individual was viewed as a part of a collective who could not function independently of the larger social group (Allen, 2000). In the "common sense" of contemporary Western society and its unexamined ontological assumptions this way of seeing self is hard to fathom.

Enlightenment ontology discerns the natural state of the individual as solitary. The social order in this modernist Eurocentric context is grounded on a set of contractual transactions between isolated individual atoms. In other works I (Kincheloe, 1993) have referred to Clint Eastwood's "man with no name" cinematic character who didn't need a "damn thing from nobody" as the ideal Western male way of being–the ontological norm. Operating in this context, we clearly discern, for example, cognitive psychology's tradition of focusing on the autonomous development of the individual monad. In our critical complex ontology a human being simply can't exist outside the inscription of community with its processes of relationship, differentiation, interaction, and subjectivity. Indeed, in this critical (and complex) ontology the relational embeddedness of self is so context dependent that psychologists, sociologists, and educators can never isolate a finalized completed "true self." Since the self is always in context and in process, no final delineation of a notion such as ability can be determined. Thus, we are released from the rugged cross of and such hurtful and primitive colonial conceptions of "intelligence." In this context it is interesting to note that famed psychometricians Richard Herrnstein and Charles Murray (1994) in *The Bell Curve* noted without any data that the average IQ of African is probably around 75–epistemological/ontological neo-colonialism in a transparent form.

One can quickly discern the political consequences of a Cartesian ontology. Human beings in Western liberal political thought become abstract bearers of particular civic rights. If individuals are relational, context-embedded beings, however, these abstract rights may be of little consequence. A critical ontology insists that individuals live in specific places with particular types of relationships. They operate or are placed in the web of reality at various points of race, class, gender, sexual, religious, physical ability, geographical place, and other continua. Where individuals find themselves in this complex web holds dramatic power consequences. Their location shapes their relationship to both dominant culture and Western colonialism and the psychological and curricular assumptions that accompany them. In other words the intelligence mainstream psychology deems these individuals to possess profoundly depends on this contextual, power-inscribed placement. A prime manifestation of ontological alienation involves a lack of recognition of the dramatic effect of these dynamics on everything that takes place in the psycho-educational cosmos.

In the context of our critical ontology the autonomous self with a fixed intellectual ability becomes an anachronism. As an effort to appreciate the power of human beings to affect their own destinies, to exercise human agency, and to change social conditions, critical ontologists study selfhood in light of the sociological, cultural studies, cultural psychological, and critical analytical work of the last few decades. Much of what dominant psychology and education consider free will and expressions of innate intelligence are simply manifestations of the effects of particular social, cultural, political, and economic forces. While we can make decisions on how we operate as human beings, they are never completely independent of these structuring forces. This is true whether we are Diane Ravitch or Michel Foucault–neither person can operate outside of society or free from cultural, linguistic, ideological influences.

It is important to note here that neo-positivist educational policy makers contend that their work takes place outside of the influence of these dynamics. They claim that their work avoids cultural values and morally inscribed issues and because of such diligence, they have presented us the truth about how students learn and how teachers should teach. In the critical ontological context developed here, such researchers must take a closer look at who they are and the structuring forces that have shaped their views of the world, mind, and self. Their inability to discern the effects of these forces reflects ontological alienation. Such alienation undermines their ability to imagine new and better ways of being human both for themselves and for the teachers and students their knowledges and policies oppress.

A postcolonial curriculum informed by a complex ontology asks the question: how do we move beyond simply uncovering the sources of consciousness construction in our larger attempt to reconstruct the self in a critical manner? Critical teachers must search in as many locations as possible for alternate discourses, ways of thinking and being that expand the envelopes of possibility. In this context teachers explore literature, history, popular culture, and ways of forging community in subjugated/indigenous knowledges. In this context teachers develop their own and their students' social and aesthetic imaginations. Here we imagine what we might become by recovering and reinterpreting what we once were. The excitement of curriculum as ontological quest is powerful.

## THE INFRASTRUCTURE OF A CRITICAL ONTOLOGY

Employing an understanding of complexity theory, Maturana and Varela's Santiago enactivism as the process of life, a postcolonial appreciation of indigeneity, critical theoretical foundations, the critique of Cartesianism, and poststructuralist feminist analysis, we can lay the conceptual foundations for a new mode of selfhood. Such a configuration cannot be comprehensively delineated here, but we can begin to build theoretical pathways to get around the Cartesian limitations on the ontological imagination. With Humberto Maturana and Francisco Valera's concept that living things constantly remake themselves in interaction with their environments, our notion of a new self or a critical ontology is grounded on the human ability to use new social contexts and experiences, exposure to new knowledges and ways of being to reformulate subjectivity. In this context the concept of personal ability becomes a de-essentialized cognition of possibility. No essentialized bounded self can access the cognitive potential offered by epiphanies of difference or triggered by an "insignificant" insight.

As we begin to identify previously unperceived patterns in which the self is implicated, the possibility of cognitive change and personal growth is enhanced. As the barriers between mind and multiple contexts are erased, the chance that more expanded forms of "cognitive autopoiesis"—self-constructed modes of higher-order thinking—will emerge is increased. A more textured, a thicker sense of self-production and the nature of self and other is constructed in this process. As we examine the self and its relationship to others in cosmological, epistemological, linguistic, social, cultural, and political contexts, we gain a clearer sense of our purpose in the world especially in relation to justice, the indigenous-informed notion of interconnectedness, and even love. In these activities we move closer to the macro-processes of life and their micro-expressions in everyday life.

A key aspect of the life processes is the understanding of difference that comes from recognition of patterns of interconnectedness. Knowing that an individual from an upper-middle class European background living in a Virginia suburb will be considered culturally bizarre by a group of tribespeople from the Amazon rainforest is a potentially profound learning experience in the domain of the personal. How is the suburbanite viewed as bizarre? What cultural practices are seen as so unusual? What mannerisms are humorous to the tribespeople? What worldviews are baffling to them? The answers to such questions may shock the suburbanite into reorienting her view of her own "normality." The interaction may induce her to ask questions of the way she is perceived by and the way she perceives others. Such a bracketing of the personal may be quite liberating. This interaction with the power of difference is another example of Maturana and Valera's structural coupling that creates a new relationship with other and with self. In Maturana and Varela's conceptualization a new inner world is created as a result of such coupling (Maturana and Varela, 1987; Varela, 1999; Sumara and Davis, 1997).

Such explorations on the ontological frontier hold profound curricular implications. As students pursue rigorous study of diverse global knowledges, they come to understand that the identities of their peer groups and families constitute only a few of countless historical and cultural ways to be human. As they study their self-production in wider biological, sociological, cultural studies, historical, theological, psychological and counter-canonical contexts, they gain insights into their ways of being. As they engage the conflicts that induce diverse knowledge producers to operate in conflicting ways, students become more attuned to the ideological, discursive, and regulatory forces operating in all knowledges. This is not nihilism, as many defenders of the Eurocanon argue; this is the exciting process of exploring the world and the self and their relationship in all of the complexity such study requires.

The processual and relational notions of self structurally couple with the sociocultural context and can only be understood by studying them with these dynamics in mind. These characteristics of self hold profound implications politically, psychologically, and pedagogically. If our notion of the self emerges in its counter-colonial relationship with multiple dimensions of the world, it is by its nature a participatory entity. Such an interactive dynamic is always in process and thus demands a reconceptualization of the concept of individualism and self-interest (Pickering, 1999). The needs of self and others in this context begin to merge, as the concept of self-reliance takes on new meanings. Notions of educational purpose, evaluation, and curriculum development are transformed when these new conceptions of the personal domain come into the picture. In the first decade of the twenty-first century we stand merely on the threshold of the possibilities this notion of selfhood harbors.

ENACTIVISM AS A WAY OUT: EXPLORING THE ONTOLOGICAL POSSIBILITIES

A critical ontology understands that the effort to explain complex cognitive, biological, social, or pedagogical events by the reductionistic study of their components outside of the larger processes of which they are a part will not work. It will not move us to new levels of understanding or set the stage for new, unexplored modes of being human. The social, biological, cognitive, or the curricular domain is not an assortment of discrete objects that can be understood in isolation from one another (Pickering, 1999). The fragmented pieces put forth in such studies do not constitute reality–even if commonsense tells Westerners they do. The deeper structures, the tacit forces, the processes that shape the physical world and the social world will be lost to such observers. As I argue in the introduction to *The Stigma of Genius: Einstein, Consciousness, and Education* (1999), Einstein's General Theory of Relativity could not have been produced without this ontological understanding of connectedness, process, and the limitations of studying only things-in-themselves.

For 250 years physicists had been searching for the basic building block of gravity–some contended it was a particle (a graviton), others argued it was a gravity wave. Einstein pointed out that it was neither, that it was not a *thing* at all. Gravity, he maintained, was a part of the structure of the universe that existed as a relationship connecting mass, space, and time. This insight, of course, changed the very nature of how we conceptualize the universe. It should have changed how we conceptualize epistemology, cognition, pedagogy, and ontology. Of course, it didn't–and that's what we are still working on. The emphasis on studying and teaching about the world as a compilation of fragmented things-in-themselves has returned with a vengeance, of course, in recent educational reforms and mandates for use of only positivistic forms of educational research.

In this context the work of Humberto Maturana is instructive. Maturana and Varela's Santiago enactivism employ the same ontological concept of interconnectedness that Einstein's used in the General Theory of Relativity to explain life as a process, a system of interconnections. Indeed, they argue, that the process of cognition is the process of life. In enactivism mind is not a thing-in-itself but a process–an activity where the interactions of a living organism with its environment constitute cognition. In this relationship life itself and cognition are indelibly connected and reveal this interrelationship at diverse levels of living and what are still considered non-living domains. Where mind ends and matter begins is difficult to discern, a situation that operates to overturn the long-standing and problematic Cartesian separation of the two entities. In Maturana's and Varela's conception mind and matter are merely parts of the same process–one cannot exist without the other. A critical ontology seeks to repair this rupture between mind and matter, self and world. In this re-connection we enter into a new phase of human history, new modes of cognition, and dramatic changes in pedagogy and curriculum.

According to the enactivists perception and cognition also operate in contradiction to Cartesianism, as they construct a reality as opposed to reflecting an external one already in existence. The interactive or circular organization of the nervous system described by Maturana is similar to the hermeneutic circle as it employs a conversation between diverse parts of a system to construct meaning. Autopoiesis as the process of self-production is the way living things operate. Self-construction emerges out of a set of relationships between simple parts. In the hermeneutic circle the relationships between parts "self-construct" previously unimagined meanings. Thus, in an ontological context meaning emerges not from the thing-in-itself but from its relationships to an infinite number of other things. In this complexity we understand from another angle that there is no final meaning of anything; meanings are always evolving in light of new relationships, new horizons. Thus, in a critical ontology our power as meaning makers and producers of new selfhoods is enhanced. Cognition is the process in which living systems organize the world around them into meaning. With this in mind critical ontology creates a new era of immanence— "what could be" has never implied so much.

Specifically, Maturana and Varela argue that our identities do not come with us into the world in some neatly packaged unitary self. Since they "rise and subside" in a series of shifting relationships and patterns, the self can be described using the Buddhist notion that the "self is empty of self-nature." Understanding this, Francisco Varela (1999) maintains, self-understanding and self-change become more possible than ever before. The self, therefore, is not a material entity but takes on more a virtual quality. Human beings have the experience of self, but no self–no central controlling mechanism–is to be found. Much is to be gained by an understanding of the virtual nature of the self. Such knowledge is an important dimension of a critical ontology. According to the enactivists this knowledge helps us develop intelligent awareness–a profound understanding of the construction and the functioning of selfhood. Intelligent awareness is filled with wisdom but devoid of the egocentrism that undermines various notions of critical knowing. In such a context intelligent awareness cannot be separated from ethical insight. Without this ontological understanding many of pedagogies designed to empower will fan the flames of the egocentrism they attempt to overcome. If nothing else a critical ontology cultivates humility without which wisdom is not possible.

## MATURANA AND VARELA'S ENACTIVISM AND THE DEVELOPMENT OF THE RELATIONAL SELF

From Maturana and Varela's perspective learning takes place when a self-maintaining system develops a more effective relationship with the external features of the system. In this context enactivism is highlighting the profound importance of *relationship* writ large as well as the centrality of the nature and quality of the relationships an organism makes with its environment. In a cognitive context this is an extension of Vygotsky's notion of the zone of proximal development to the ontological realm–it is our assertion here that indigeneity should become a part of Westerners' zpd. In the development of a critical ontology we learn from these ideas that political empowerment vis-à-vis the cultivation of the intellect demand an understanding of the system of relationships that construct our selfhood. In the case of a critical form of curriculum development these relationships always involve students' connections to cultural systems, language, economic concerns, religious belief, social status, and the power dynamics that constitute them. With the benefit of understanding the self-in-relationship teachers gain a new insight into what is happening in any learning situation. Living on the borderline between self and external system and self and other, learning never takes place outside of these relationships (Pickering, 1999). Such knowledge changes our orientation to curriculum development and pedagogy.

Thus, a critical ontology is intimately connected to a relational self (Noddings, 1990; Thayer-Bacon, 2000). Humans are ultimately the constructs of relationships, not fragmented monads or abstract individuals. From Varela's perspective this notion of humans as constructs of relationships corresponds precisely to what he is labeling the virtual self. A larger pattern–in the case of humans, consciousness–arises from the interaction of local elements. This larger pattern seems to be driven by a central controlling mechanism that can never be located. Thus, we discern the origin of traditional psychology's dismissal of consciousness as irrelevant. This not only constituted throwing out the baby with the bath water but discarding the tub, the bathroom fixtures, and the plumbing as well. In this positivistic articulation the process of life and the basis of the cognitive act were deemed unimportant. A critical ontology is always interested in these processes because they open us to a previously occluded insight into the nature of selfhood, of human being. The autopoiesis, the self-making allows humans to perpetually reshape themselves in their new relationships and resulting new patterns of perception and behavior.

There is no way to predict the relationships individuals will make and the nature of the self-(re)construction that will ensue. Such uncertainty adds yet another element of complexity to the study of sociology, psychology, and pedagogy, as it simultaneously catalyzes the possibilities of human agency. It causes those enamored with critical ontology yet another reason to study the inadequacies of Cartesian science to account for the intricacies of the human domain. Physical objects *don't necessarily* change their structures via their interaction with other objects. A critical ontology understands that human beings do change their structures as a result of their interactions. As a result the human mind moves light years beyond the lifeless cognitivist computer model of mind—a psychological way of seeing that reduced mental activity to information processing (Lapani, 1998).

The human self-organization process—while profoundly more complex than the World Wide Web—is analogous to the way the Web arranges itself by random and not-so-random connections. The Web is an autopoietic organism that constructs itself in a hypertextual mode of operation. Unanticipated links create new concepts, ways of perceiving, and even ways of being among those that enter into this domain of epistemological emergence. Such experience reminds one that a new cultural logic has developed that transcends the mechanical dimensions of the machine epistemologies and ontologies of the modernist industrial era. Consider the stunning implications that when numerous simple entities possessing simple characteristics are thrown together—whether it be websites on the Internet or individuals' relationships with aspects of their environments—amazing things occur. From such interactions emerge a larger whole that is not guided by a central controlling mechanism. Self-awareness of this process of creation may lead to unanticipated modes of learning and new concepts of human being.

Students of critical curriculum have no choice; they must deal with these ontological issues. When they are considered within the context of our understanding of the power of difference and the specific benefits of indigeneity, a postcolonial curriculum begins to take shape that is truly global in its scope, its concerns and its influences. Such a curriculum is transformative in ways that other "transformative" curricula have not been in its connection to a plethora of knowledges and ways of being. Employing interconnectedness with difference to push the boundaries of the Western alienated self, this postcolonial curriculum sets off an autopoietic process energized by the interplay of multiple forms of difference—cultural, political, epistemological, cognitive, and, of course, ontological. It will be fascinating to watch where a critical ontology can take us in the coming years.

## REFERENCES

Allen, M. (2000). *Voice of reason*. Retrieved from http://www.curtin.edu.au/learn/unit/10846/arrow/vorall.htm

Apffel-Marglin, F. (1995). Development or decolonization in the Andes? *Interculture: International Journal of Intercultural and Transdisciplinary Research, 28*(1), 3–17.

Appelbaum, P. (2003). Mathematics education. In D. Weil & J. L. Kincheloe (Eds.), *Critical thinking and learning: An encyclopedia*. New York: Greenwood.

Berry, K. (2001). Standards of complexity in a postmodern democracy. In J. L. Kincheloe & D. Weil (Eds.), *Standards and schooling in the United States: An encyclopedia*. Santa Barbara, CA: ABC-Clio.

Burbules, N., & R. Beck (1999). Critical thinking and critical pedagogy: Relations, differences, and limits. In T. Popkewitz & L. Fendler (Eds.), *Critical theories in education*. New York: Routledge.

Capra, F. (1996). *The web of life: A new scientific understanding of living systems*. New York: Anchor Books.

Degenaar, J. (1995). Myth and the collision of cultures. *Myth and Symbol, 2*.

Dei, G. (1995). Indigenous knowledge as an empowerment tool. In N. Singh & V. Titi (Eds.), *Empowerment: Toward sustainable development*. Toronto: Fernwood Press.

Dumas, M. (2003). Critical thinking as black existence. In D. Weil & J. L. Kincheloe (Eds.), *Critical thinking and learning: An encyclopedia*. New York: Greenwood.

Fenwick, T. (2000). *Experiential learning in adult education: A comparative framework*. Retrieved from http://www.ualberta.ca/~tfenwick/ext/aeq.htm

Howley, A., Pendarvis, E., & Howley, C. (1993). Anti-intellectualism in U.S. schools. *Education Policy Analysis Archives, 1*, 6.

Kincheloe, J. L. (1993). *Toward a critical politics of teacher thinking: Mapping the postmodern*. Westport, CT: Bergin and Garvey.

Kincheloe, J. L., Steinberg, S. R., & Tippins, D. J. (1999). *The stigma of genius: Einstein, consciousness, and education*. New York: Peter Lang.

Lepani, B. (1998). *Information literacy: The challenge of the digital age*. Retrieved from http://www.acal.edu.au/lepani.htm

Maturana, H., & Varela, F. (1987). *The tree of knowledge*. Boston: Shambhala.

Maurial, M. (1999). Indigenous knowledge and schooling: A continuum between conflict and dialogue. In L. Semali & J. L. Kincheloe (Eds.), *What is indigenous knowledge? Voices from the academy*. New York: Falmer.

Mosha, R. (2000). *The heartbeat of indigenous Africa: A study of the Chagga educational system*. New York: Garland.

Newland, P. (1997). *Logical types of learning*. Retrieved from http://www.envf.port.ac.uk/newmedia/lecturenotes/EMMA/at2n.htm

Noddings, N. (1990). Review symposium: A response. *Hypatia, 5*(1), 120–126.

O'Sullivan, E. (1999). *Transformative learning: Educational vision for the 21st century*. London: Zed.

Parmar, P. (2003). The pedagogy of KRS-One. In D. Weil & J. L. Kincheloe (Eds.), *Critical thinking and learning: An encyclopedia*. New York: Greenwood.

Pickering, J. (1999). The self is a semiotic process. *Journal of Consciousness Studies, 6*(4), 31–47.

Progler, Y. (2001). Social Studies—Social Studies standards: Diversity, conformity, complexity. In J. L. Kincheloe & D. Weil (Eds.), *Standards and schooling in the United States: An Encyclopedia* (3 Vols.). Santa Barbara, CA: ABC-CLIO.

Richardson, F., & Woolfolk, R. (1994). Social theory and values: A hermeneutic perspective. *Theory and Psychology, 4*(2), 199–226.

Semali, L., & Kincheloe, J. L. (1999). *What is indigenous knowledge? Voices from the academy*. New York: Falmer.

Steinberg, S. R. (2001). *Multi/intercultural conversations: A reader*. New York: Peter Lang.

Sumara, D., & B. Davis (1997). Cognition, complexity, and teacher education. *Harvard Educational Review, 67*(1), 75–104.

Thayer-Bacon, B. (2000). *Transforming critical thinking: Thinking constructively*. New York: Teachers College Press.

Thomas, G. (1998). The myth of rational research. *British Educational Research Journal, 24*(2).

Varela, F. (1999). *Ethical know-how: Action, wisdom, and cognition*. Stanford, CA: Stanford University Press.

Williams, S. (1999). Truth, speech, and ethics: A feminist revision of free speech theory. *Genders, 30*. Retrieved from http://www.genders.org

Woodhouse, M. (1996). *Paradigm wars: Worldviews for a new age*. Berkeley, CA: Frog.

**Reprinted with permission: Kincheloe, J. L. (2006). Critical ontology and indigenous ways of being: forging a postcolonial curriculum. In Y. Kanu (Ed.), *Curriculum as cultural practice: postcolonial imaginations* (pp. 181–202). Toronto: University of Toronto Press.**

CHRISTOPHER EMDIN

# ON CRITICAL ONTOLOGY AND INDIGENEOUS WAYS OF BEING

*Framing a Kincheloean Agenda for Education*

### INTRODUCTION

As an urban educator, deeply committed to providing opportunities for marginalized youth to be successful in the sciences, Kincheloe's work stands as a portal through which my work and others that focus on expanding deficit perspectives of youth from non-dominant backgrounds must travel. His work uncovers the hidden truth that the work of any teacher, school administrator or researcher that aims to be transformative in regards to the lives of marginalized populations must first begin with a questioning of the paradigms within which the work operates. Kincheloe argues that this questioning is the key to a critical ontological vision that provides insight into who we are and how the contexts we are embedded in shape the decisions we make. Not considering questions about the educators' stances, the students' lifeworlds, the paths that bring the teacher and the student to the classroom, the history of the institutions in which teaching must take place, and the political and historical baggage that the educator inherits, means that these questions go unanswered and that the information that would otherwise have been uncovered through this questioning lies dormant within an untapped realm of consciousness that lies beneath the present one. It also means that the existent paradigm inevitably shapes the work that is done within it, and limits opportunities to move beyond established conceptions. It does this in a way that is piercing, yet subtle, ignorant, and yet cunning. I use the words piercing and subtle in order to convey the idea that Kincheloe describes existent structures penetrate through well-intentioned goals of practitioners and researchers—shifting their core mission, while leaving them with the idea that their goals have been unchanged. By ignorant, yet cunning, I describe the fact that existent thought in regards to school and schooling is ignorant of the ways of knowing and being outside of existent norms yet able to convince the population at large that it is inclusive and considerate of all. For example, "science for all" or the U.S. department of education's ethos of "Promoting Educational Excellence for all Americans" leads one to believe that working within the established structures of schools or education in the United States means doing good for all; including populations that have been traditionally marginalized. In reality, these structures within schools function to inhibit the localized knowledge's of certain populations in the attainment of educational excellence. Therefore, traditional ways of knowing and the structures that support them do not truly promote "all." In fact, they actually function to promote excellence for only a specific population that ascribes to an established way of knowing and being that it validates. For a more easy-to-grasp example of how this occurs, we can consider Kincheloe's work in regards to the experiences of the contemporary educator and the structures of schooling that combat students' abilities to gain positive experiences in schools. Consider standardized exams that supposedly mark intelligence or knowledge by multiple choice and one-word answers. These exams can be, and have been described as being good for all students because they provide opportunities for students to show what they know. They have also been described as a means to ensure that students are taught all the information that they need. In these widely accepted descriptions of the purpose of these exams, they are framed as having a true benefit for all students. However, if one focuses on the ways that these exams may alienate students who express their knowledge about a subject or topic by describing it, talking about it, or acting it out, or who have knowledge that extends beyond what is required for the exam, it becomes obvious that the exam categorically renders the expansive knowledge and skills that certain students possess as extraneous to the ultimate goals of school. Therefore, while these exams are presented as a means to, "do good by students," they actually serve ulterior purposes that are counter to students' best interests. I make these points to echo a key theme of Kincheloe's work, which is that, to do good work without defining goodness for those whom the work is being done, sets the stage for well-intentioned oppression. In other words, working to transform the schooling experiences of indigenous populations by simply working within the existing order, and without some effort to change the larger structures that deny them the opportunity to be successful within schools is merely a feel good exercise with no long-term traction. This process is analogous to massaging a wound area without treating the wound. Kincheloe (2006) works to both massage and treat by describing both the need for critical ontology and an understanding of indigenous ways of being. In so doing, he troubles our comfort with the hegemony of colonialism and arms educators with tools that allow them to fight the deleterious effects of a western approach to schooling that has proven to be counter-indigenous.

## CRITICAL ONTOLOGY

For educators enveloped in a world where teaching and learning have evolved to become prescribed sciences rooted in the colonial tradition of teaching to fill an empty or "uncivil" indigenous mind, critical ontology plants the seed that no one enters the classroom as a blank state. It then blossoms into the idea that everyone has complex understandings developed through their ties to the worlds in which they are embedded. It is at this point; where individuals who are considered not to have knowledge become valued because of the knowledge they have developed within the contexts in which they are embedded, that critical ontology invokes a set of necessary quandaries for the traditional educator. For the most part, these quandaries are internal in the sense that they may involve the educators' confrontation with the fact that who they are as educators and the instruction they deliver in classrooms does not promote other cultures. They may have to make a decision about whether or not they are willing to confront who they are, the way they teach, and how these facts mediate instruction. These quandaries may also involve the educators' unspoken acceptance that the belief that the classroom is a "lifeless space" devoid of any true application to the real world. For example, in contemporary urban science education, the quandary may be what to do after realizing the divergent lines of thought that exist between traditional science and the urban youth experience. For example, when teachers begins to see that the heroes of school science and their backgrounds are different from that of Black and brown urban students, they are placed in a space where a decision must be made about continuing to teach in ways that they always have, or in ways that consider their students' backgrounds.

As Kincheloe alludes to in the previous chapter, the tools for addressing these quandaries or dilemmas are found through a particular focus on indigenous and subjugated knowledges and a viewing of the environments where culture is produced as a part of the lives of those who are birthed from them. For example, when participants in hip hop are rapping to each other on a street corner, the acknowledgement that they are expressing contemporary forms of indigenous ontologies through their gestures and rituals opens up new realities. These forms of knowledge, rife with themes that suggest ways of looking at the world that vary from the silencing force of western Cartesian structures, must be accepted as a key component of teaching and learning youth from non-western backgrounds.

At its core, Kincheloe's argument is for an identification of, and value for difference. This approach has tentacles that extend to both the work of practitioners and researchers. For practitioners, opportunities for new more inclusive pedagogical approaches are formed, curriculum gets re-interpreted, and changes in practice are implemented. For researchers, new theoretical frameworks that are either rooted in, or that inform non-traditional ways of thinking and being are embraced. Through Kincheloe's naming of the bricolage as a worthwhile approach to combining frameworks that may have been previously perceived as unrelated to each other and to the construction of a framework for study, traditional approaches to research are challenged, and indigenous ways of being are not only valued in practice but in research. Furthermore, this approach supports the notion that a construction of self as educator, researcher, and thinker need not be a set of separate exercises that exist at different times in specific locales at specific times. The pluralist stance that the bricolage is rooted in blurs the boundaries between pre-existent categories and sets the stage for multiple permutations within the traditional educator, researcher, and scholar paradigms. These categories get fused together in ways that allow for more complex hyphenated identities to develop. For example, a teacher that transforms into a teacher-researcher-scholar becomes a better teacher, researcher than any one who had previously been categorized into just one of these roles.

## THE PROVISIONS OF CRITICAL ONTOLOGY

Not only does Kincheloe's work suggest that teachers and researchers commit themselves to viable alternatives to the normative and objectivist traditions of schools and schooling, it also presents opportunities for an alternate reality where goodness, love, and a responsibility for each other are as significant as the delivery of content or the theorizing of what guides what is happening in classrooms. The beauty in this approach to sharing the work is not just in the descriptions of a new way to doing things, but a modelling of how to incorporate alternate frameworks into academic work. This is evident in Kincheloe's use of indigenous metaphors, his call for revolutionary practices in his work, and his referencing and analysing the work of scholars who have pushed traditional boundaries in their work. Bringing in Varela's (1999) exploration of ethics through social and biological constructs and Apfel-Marglin's (1995) descriptions of the advanced knowledge of the indigenous displays the folly of scholars in the Cartesian-Newtonian tradition and positions the previously subjugated as the expert.

Without an appreciation for the ways of thinking, knowing, and being of subjugated populations, teachers fail to recognize the brilliance of their communal practices and the complex and layered modes of communication within their culture. Because these parts of subjugated and indigenous knowledges are necessary for the advancement of teaching and learning, critical ontology, through its focus on difference is particularly focused on the advancement of education for youth from non-dominant backgrounds whose needs have traditionally not been met within schools. This process requires a postcolonial pedagogy that is informed by the indigenous and considers their perspectives on everything from the way students sit in the class to the subject matter delivery methods and the ways students are assessed. Kincheloe argues that through the posing of questions to self and to the world within which one is embedded, alternative discourses and pedagogical approaches that reflect the needs of indigenous populations emerge. I argue that this approach breeds dialogue with youth and supports discussions with students about the purpose of school and schooling from their perspective.

## CONCLUSIONS

The work described in this chapter is merely an additional lens through which Kincheloe's work can be viewed. It is one of many possible insights that can be taken on the impact or goals of the work. As I respond to, and reflect on Kincheloe's work, I am guided by my position as a man of color from the hip hop generation who is focused on transforming urban science education in the midst of the historical, socio-political and cultural dynamics that dictate that I do not have a place in the world of the science or a say in the way that the subject matter is taught. Through the work that Kincheloe produced, and its call for an examination of who I am in the world and its implication on teaching and learning, I have come to see strength in difference, the need for addressing the internal conflicts related to being a part of the structures of the existing system, and have come to grips with how my withholding of the knowledges that I hold as a result of my urbanness and Blackness has been a paining experience that forces me to create an in-school self that is completely different from whom I am outside of schools.

I see Kincheloe's work, his shaping of critical theory frameworks, and his commitment to filling us with the passion to fight for the subjugated, as being in the tradition of musicians like Fela Kuti who lived and died for the cause of anti-oppression, anti-establishment, pro-freedom movements. This is because of how my multiple selves are constructed. I draw from my Nigerian roots, my New York hip-hop roots and my deep connection to Fela's words on freedom for the oppressed. Kincheloe's critique of established norms and nesting of self outside of cultural and political norms for the sake of providing inroads into alternative realities invokes the same timeless emotions as Fela's work. These emotions constantly move us to expand our knowledge and serve as a catalyst for hope when the constant force of hegemony has beaten it down.

For a new generation of scholars who have not had the pleasure to meet and talk with Joe Kincheloe or engage with his work, both the preceding chapter and this one, serve as points from which deeper interrogations of his work can begin, and his mission to transform schools, schooling, teaching, and learning can continue to grow.

## REFERENCES

Kincheloe, J. L. (2006). Critical ontology and indigenous ways of being: Forging a postcolonial curriculum. In Y. Kanu (Ed.), *Curriculum as cultural practice: Postcolonial imaginations* (pp. 181–202). Toronto: University of Toronto Press.

Varela, F. (1999). *Ethical know-how: Action, wisdom, and cognition*. Stanford, CA: Stanford University Press.

*Certainly, an invitation to write a piece for Manning Marable's journal: Souls: A Critical Journal of Black Politics, Culture and Society was met with great enthusiasm. Joe was anxious to integrate his work on whiteness with his original work looking at the South and place. Placing his piece in this journal was a way to meet a new audience, outside of education. Anyone who has ever worked with or learned with Joe knows that positionality is an essential element in cognition and empowerment. Joe has often discussed his notion that ideology must always trump positionality...that what one knew and felt was more significant than how one appeared. Taking this idea to heart, every moment of Joe's life was spent with recognition that he was privileged, that he was white, middle class, educated, and identified with the dominant culture. Taking note of Aaron Gresson's theory of recovery, Joe blended his work on the Old South, the Modern South, and the contemporary South with the articulation of whiteness. This piece, in my opinion, is one of Joe's finest articles. In a sort of second degree of separation motif, our son, Ian, was the managing editor of Souls at the time. To say Joe was incredibly proud of Ian would be, indeed, an understatement. SS*

JOE L. KINCHELOE

# 14. THE SOUTHERN PLACE AND RACIAL POLITICS

*Southernification, Romanticization, and the Recovery of White Supremacy*

The political changes that have rocked the United States over the last few decades are profound. In other work I have argued that a central dimension of a right-wing movement in American political life has revolved around the perception among many white people that because of the Civil Rights Movement and social policies such as affirmative action, the real victims of racism in America in the late twentieth and early twenty-first centuries are white people, white men in particular. In this essay I would like to employ what my colleague, Aaron Gresson first labeled as the recovery-of-white-supremacy thesis (subsequently referenced as the recovery movement) in relation to some important issues in African American studies as they relate to views of the South—especially the romanticization of the region—and the larger process of the Southernification of the United States. Using a critical theoretical/ pedagogical base, such analysis opens new perspectives on Black politics in the last half of the first decade of the twenty-first century.[1]

THE SOUTH, RACIAL POLITICS, AND THE WHITE RECOVERY MOVEMENT

In the tradition of Black Studies' radical eye, my work as a white Southerner engages a critical interracialism that avoids essentialism as it works for racial, class, and gender justice. In this context I've used the conceptual lenses of a critical multiculturalism to explore the evolving nature of racism and racial identity in the contemporary era. In my work in whiteness studies I have operated on the assumption that whiteness studies conducted by white people must always be undertaken as an interracial act. A study of whiteness suffers when it is not directly connected to African American studies, Latino/Chicano studies, indigenous studies, ethnic studies, and postcolonialism and the way white power and the historical white construction of "reason" have attempted to position non-white peoples. Obviously, the histories of the world's various peoples in general as well as non-European peoples in Western societies in particular have often been told from a white historiographical perspective. Such accounts have erased the values, epistemologies, ontologies, and belief systems that grounded the cultural practices of these diverse peoples. In this essay these concerns and modes of analysis will be brought to bear on the South, the growing Southernification of the United States, and the racial politics surrounding this larger manifestation of whiteness.

A critical understanding of whiteness/white power and its effect on racial politics is possible only if we understand in great specificity the multiple meanings of whiteness and their effects on the way white consciousness is historically structured and socially inscribed. Without such appreciations and the meta-consciousness they ground, an awareness of the privilege and dominance of white Northern European vantage points is buried in the cemetery of power evasion. The mutations in white consciousness over the last few decades join other occluded insights into whiteness in this conceptual graveyard. Students of African American studies need to exhume such concepts in the pursuit of a contemporary understanding of Black life in the twenty-first century.

One way to mitigate the repressive effects of this hegemonic white power is bring the multilogicality of postcolonialism to the conceptual mix. Central to the critical study of whiteness and its effects on people of color is an appreciation of the historical origins of the twentieth century anti-colonial rebellion movements that emerged in Africa, Latin America, and parts of Asia. All of these movements, including indigenous peoples' movements around the world, can be connected to a more inclusive anti/postcolonialism whose origins can be traced to these movements. Familiarity with the multiple perspectives emerging from such an anti/postcolonialism moves disciplines of knowledge to new conceptual domains. In the ruins of traditional disciplinarity the multilogicality of these new perspectives and their relationships to other ways of seeing are invaluable to critical scholars.

Inject the South and Southern studies into this critical theoretical mix. Many white Southerners in the contemporary socio-cultural landscape prefer to focus on the wounds inflicted on them rather than on the injustices they have imposed on others. Here rests a central force driving contemporary American socio-political life. As working class and numerous middle level jobs have been outsourced to parts unknown, many white males have been introduced to a situation African Americans and other people of color have suffered with for a long time—a declining domain for individual development and progression. In this new context fewer white men are going to college. In this twenty-first century context some of these southern

THE SOUTHERN PLACE AND RACIAL POLITICS

(and of course American in general) men are sensing a decline in the traditional privileges accorded them. At the same time they feel this loss, they are watching media images and representations of them as the subjugators of African Americans, Latinos, Native Americans, women, and others. For a majority of these men, history and its influence on the present is not a topic understood or deemed important.

In this dehistoricized context the representation of white male as victim can be promoted in a way that resonates with the larger society to such a degree that it alters the political landscape. With the image of white male as racial victim firmly entrenched, any discussion of racism in the national political discourse or even in classrooms can be characterized as a personal attack on white people and their "traditional values." When this is the case a new form of racial politics dominates the cultural landscape. On such a terrain the idea of multilogicality and its postcolonial multiple perspectives become threats to the existing social order that must be squelched. Without such perspectives monological forms of knowledge, unilateral perceptions begin to emerge. Uncontested [concepts] such a racialized reductionism comes to dominate educational and other socio-political institutions. A radical re-education of the public is the result. While there are many sources of redress and many individuals who challenge such a racial politics, these cultural dynamics are certainly at work in contemporary America. To attempt to understand the South and its relation to racial politics outside these conceptual boundaries is to fall into the trap of a one-dimensional region-done-wrong story, a socio-cultural country song.[2]

Manning Marable[3] contends that the creation of a living history for African Americans is not possible without understanding it in the context of the larger society and grander social movements. Marable's thesis applies directly to the purpose of this essay—the effort to understand the role of the South in the complex racial politics of the twenty-first century. Willie Morris[4], the famous Mississippi chronicler, argued that somewhere buried in the experience of the South exists something of great value for America. What happens in small town Mississippi, he concluded, will be of enduring importance to America's quest for its soul. In this context I believe that an understanding of the racial politics of that Southern place can, in Marable's words, "reshape contemporary civic outcomes…and transform the objective material and cultural conditions and subordinate status of marginalized groups."[5] Indeed, without an understanding the South, its relation to the recovery movement, and the impact of these dynamics on contemporary racial politics in particular and American politics in general, interracial struggles against racial oppression and ideologies of racism will find it difficult to prosper.

Without such understandings it will be difficult for white people to transform racial identities being forged around new articulations of white supremacy. The critical analysis of racial politics pursued here seeks, of course, to engage readers of all racial backgrounds; it is, however, particularly interested in challenging and pushing the boundaries of whiteness. Such confrontation attempts to move white people to examine the privilege of white identity in a manner that induces them to change the way they live their lives, the way they relate to the people with whom they come into contact. In other words such work attempts to promote a "Freedom Summer of racial consciousness"—a form of critical ontological labor that understands the construction of self so that we can become more than we presently are. Here white people—as well as individuals from other races and ethnicities—come to understand how their political opinions and racial identities have been shaped by dominant power.

## FROM THE ANTI-COLONIAL MOVEMENT TO THE RECOVERY MOVEMENT

A critical understanding of racial politics is acutely focused on the larger historical context in which the issues we are dealing with in this essay are situated. The last 500 years of Euro-American colonialism exerts a dramatic everyday effect on socio-political, economic, cultural, philosophical, psychological, and pedagogical structures and, in turn, everyday life. After several centuries of exploitation, the early twentieth century began to witness a growing impatience of colonized peoples with their status. A half millennium of colonial violence had convinced many Africans, Asians, Latin Americans, and indigenous peoples around the world that enough was enough. Picking up steam after World War Two, colonized peoples around the world threw off colonial governmental strictures and set out on a troubled journey toward independence. The European colonial powers, however, were not about to give up such lucrative socio-economic relationships so easily. With the United States leading the way Western societies developed a wide-array of neo-colonial strategies for maintaining the benefits of colonialism. This neo-colonial effort continues unabated and in many ways with a new intensity in an era of transnational corporations and the "war on terror" in the twenty-first century.

As students of African American studies know these anti-colonial rebellions constructed the theoretical foundation for the Civil Rights Movement and other liberation struggles in the 1950s, 1960s, and 1970s. For example, Martin Luther King wrote his dissertation on the anti-colonial rebellion against the British led by Mohandas Gandhi in India. King focused his scholarly attention on Gandhi's non-violent colonial resistance tactics, later drawing upon such strategies in the Civil Rights Movement. The generation of Black intellectuals emerging at the time such as Martin Luther King, Malcolm X, and Frantz Fanon were profoundly affected by these anti-colonial movements. Central to the issues of recovery, the Southern place, and Southernification is that in the United States by the mid-1970s a conservative counterreaction to these liberation movements was taking shape. Its goal was make sure that white people would recover what they perceived to have lost in the liberation process.[6]

While, of course, there are many other factors that play a profound role in shaping the racial politics of the last three decades, the effort to recover white supremacy is a very important and often overlooked aspect of the process. The "culture wars," the educational and psychological debates about intelligence and school policy, and the political discourse and policies of the era all reflect the influence of the recovery movement. In my field of education one does not have to look hard to see the finger-prints of recovery on educational policy in recent American educational history. Efforts to diversify the American elementary, secondary, and university curricula, for example, to reflect the knowledge produced by various cultural traditions has been meet by fierce resistance. Understanding that progressive educators were attempting to extend the goals of the liberation movements, right-wing strategists sought to subvert the public and civic dimensions of schooling. Instead of helping to prepare society for a socially mobile and egalitarian democracy, education in the formulation of the right-wing recovery movement redefined schooling as a private concern.

In this context the recovery movement's cognitive theorists, Richard Herrnstein and Charles Murray,[7] provided bogus "proof" that efforts to use education to provide social mobility to students of color could not work because of their intellectual inferiority. Recovery, thus, was necessary in such a construction to save the nation from the racially inferior incompetents moving into positions of authority. Deploying a rhetoric of loss, the promoters of recovery made reference to a loss of standards, personal discipline, civility, and proper English. America was in decline directly because of the pursuit of racial justice and cultural diversity. In the discourse of recovery the notion of loss and falling standards was always accompanied by strategically placed critiques of affirmative action, racial preferences, and multiculturalism. Though the connection was obvious, plausible deniability was maintained—"we are not racists, we only want to protect our country from the destruction of its most treasured values."

Not surprisingly, another rhetorical device of the recovery is the accusation of "reverse racism." In the recovery discursive cosmos anti-racist activity and work for racial justice can always be represented as a form of Black racism toward white people. We have reached "end of racism" toward people of color, as recovery poster boy Dinesh D'Souza[8] proclaimed in 1995. Given this new non-racist social reality, many white citizens, politicians, students, and activists express great anger when Black, Latino and indigenous peoples keep bringing up historical and contemporary racism. We are victims of "political correctness," advocates of recovery contend. Before the liberation movements, the recovery narrative tells us, we lived in a safe country where you could leave your doors unlocked, schools maintained strong discipline and high standards, and there were no language police to take away our freedom to express ourselves freely.

The advocates of recovery possess a disconcerting similarity to the advocates of retrenchment in the South of the late nineteenth century. After the attempts of Reconstruction to bring about more racial power sharing in the South, advocates of the "recovery" of white domination regained political power in the region. In control of southern statehouses by the 1890s the "Redeemers" established Jim Crow legislation that worked to disenfranchise and segregate African Americans while denying them legal protection from lynching and other forms of violence. Northern journalists and authors of the period shifted their representations of the South from rebellious foe to noble partner. By the end of the nineteenth century the South in the national consciousness had become a land of dignity, a place whose (white) people were characterized by chivalry and honor.[9] The image of the Southerners as genteel plantation owners had been "recovered" from the representation of Southerner as rebellious and violent slave owner.

This late nineteenth century recovery of southern nobility helped set the tone of racial politics throughout the next fifty years. It was much more difficult, for example, to pass anti-lynching legislation in an era where white Southerners were represented in the public mind as chivalrous and honorable. Thus, this laudatory image of the Southerner interacted with the politics of whiteness during the era. The white privilege of universalizing its characteristics as the "proper way to be" has continuously undermined the efforts of African Americans to improve their condition in numerous twentieth and now twenty-first century contexts. At times such universalizing has produced self-loathing among individual members of oppressed groups, as they internalize the "truths" about themselves. A critical racial politics that studies whiteness reveals such power-related processes to whites and people of color alike, exposing how individuals from both of these groups are stripped of self-knowledge—an understanding of socio-historical construction.

Without the help of such a critical racial politics white people in the twenty-first century were unconsciously shaped by the tacit epistemology and ontology of the recovery movement. Robert Bork, for example, in *Slouching Towards Gomorrah: Modern Liberalism and American Decline* argues that "American culture is Eurocentric and it must remain Eurocentric or collapse into meaningless."[10] In this book the famous jurist maintains that white people must relearn their [supremacy]. If there are any questions Charles Murray, co-author of *The Bell Curve*, assures whites that their racial supremacy is validated by hard science.

This re-validation of white supremacy and Western ways of seeing the world and producing knowledge is a key dimension of the recovery movement. In this context the politics of knowledge, the control of information has emerged as a central aspect of white recovery. By the last half of the first decade of the twenty-first century it is growing more difficult to find anti-colonial, anti-racist perspectives in the mainstream print and visual media. The representations of whiteness that are typically found in the contemporary media follow a Forrest Gump model: they portray an innocent whiteness. In this context 9–11 can be represented in the white-as-victim and innocent-whiteness modality. America did nothing to the Muslim world to elicit such an attack—we (white Americans) are as chaste as the virgin lamb.[11]

In this recovery mode no place in the United States has presented itself as more "purely American" than the South. In many ways racial recovery begins in the South, as Southern history has been marked by events and Southern whites' reaction to them that anticipate a more general white recovery movement. As with the late nineteenth century "redemption" of the South and its recovery of its genteel image, the contemporary recovery movement is intimately connected to a neo-romanticization of the South reflected over the last couple of decades in movies such as "Forrest Gump," "Driving Miss Daisy," and "Fried Green Tomatoes." In the hands of these filmmakers Southern racism is transformed into a warm and fuzzy interaction between races and "good" Black characters unconcerned with racial injustice populate the landscape. An interesting dimension of the new and improved image of the South emerging in the few decades is that some African Americans have joined this southern rehabilitation project.

We can see this dynamic in Black migration statistics indicating that by the end of the 1960s more Black migration *into* rather than *out of* the South. The failure of the Northern urban dream is obviously an important factor in this return migration, but nevertheless there are many other manifestations of changing African American perspectives toward the South during this era. Even in the work of Toni Morrison and Alice Walker we witness dimensions of this trend as the South becomes a venue of racial redemption and the discovery of one's identity. As the place where Africa is most alive, Morrison's and Walker's South offers possibility and hope to African Americans. Even rap groups such as Arrested Development pick up on the need for African Americans to return to the South for racial redemption.[12] These portrayals of the South are extremely important to the issues raised in this essay. At the intersection of the concepts of the rehabilitation vis-à-vis the romanticization of the South rests the complex issues of racial politics that I want to focus on in the remainder of this essay.

## SOUTHERNIFICATION

There is much evidence to suggest that over the last four decades the nation as a whole has become more like the South. This is not to make the argument that while the North, Midwest, and West have experienced Southernification, no more regional differences exist. Regional distinctions, while not as great as they once were, still matter between the South and the rest of the nation. Black and progressive white Southerners grew up in the first seven decades of the twentieth century believing that the North was a place where racism was hard to find and erudition reigned supreme. I was sure as a politically **precocious** child in the mountains of Tennessee that the North would help us Southerners overcome our racial problems by example or even by force.

Of course, such images came crashing down by the late 1960s and 1970s with overt Northern racism exhibiting itself time and again in various non-Southern venues in a variety of ways. As an education professor, I have said and written on numerous occasions that the most overt racism I've ever faced from white students was not in my teaching in Tennessee, Virginia, Louisiana, South Carolina, or Florida but in Brooklyn. In no way is this assertion meant to romanticize the South—Southern white students were uncomfortable expressing their racism in racially mixed groups. The point is that the white students in Brooklyn conveyed it so unabashedly.

In the "moral rebirth" of America, the "spiritual awakening" found especially in the evangelized, now majority Republican Party, one witnesses in all regions of the United States Southern-style fundamentalist Christian concerns with abortion and homosexuality but deafening silence on the issue of racism. In such circles one dare not raise the issue of racism lest they be accused of playing the race card or being oppressively politically correct. In this context the question emerges: how did the rest of the country become more South-like? Political concerns raised initially by Southerners involving "reverse racism," the (selected) intrusions of big government, the role of religion in political domain, and social issues such as muliticulturalism and prayer in schools reverberate in the North and West in ways unimagined only a few years ago. Another question that comes up in this context is: why has the rest of the country been so receptive to these long-time white Southern anxieties?

One dimension of a possible answer to that question may involve the effects of military defeat and the dishonor that accompanies it. Humiliating defeat—as in Germany after World War I—often elicits a right-wing reaction replete with absolutist belief structures, hyper-nationalism, cultural chauvinism, vilification of "others," and an exaggerated fidelity to racial, ethnic, and group identity. Both the South's defeat in the Civil War and Reconstruction and America's defeat in Vietnam almost exactly one century later elicited these right-wing reactions. Southerners in the nineteenth and early twentieth centuries and many white Americans in the twentieth and early twenty-first centuries sensed threats to white supremacy and, thus, the need to recover it.

When the Civil Rights Movement and the other liberation movements were added to the defeat in Vietnam the perceived need for many whites to recover their racial supremacy was exacerbated. Indeed, Vietnam's struggle for independence from French colonial rule and later American intervention was itself a part of the same anti-colonialism-based liberation framework. In the decades following the 1960s one can discern recovery constructs, discourses, and images permeating the media. One of the first interruptions to this recovery-based ideology has been the television representation of unattended African American victims of Hurricane Katrina in New Orleans. In light of such desperation and neglect it is difficult to maintain the recovery assertion that whites are the *real* victims of racism in America.

One can see the mounting white reaction to the anti-colonialist movement and its African American expression by the late 1950s and early 1960s. The capture of the Republican Party by anti-Civil-Rights-Act Goldwater conservatives in 1964 and his victory in numerous Southern states in the presidential election point to the early manifestations of recovery. A few years later Nixon's so-called southern strategy was grounded on the construction of an alliance with former Dixiecrat Strom Thurmond and George Wallace's segregationist Democrats. Wallace's overwhelming [victory] in the 1972 Michigan Democratic primary provides fascinating insight into the political expressions of the Southernification process. Ronald Reagan, however, was the figure who consummated the political dimension of white recovery.

Reagan's first campaign stop after winning the 1980 Republican presidential nomination was in Philadelphia, Mississippi—the small southern town where the Ku Klux Klan and the local sheriff's department had conspired to murder the northern civil rights workers, Michael Schwerner, Andrew Goodman, and James Chaney. Reagan vowed on this "recovery pilgrimage" to almost all white audiences to protect "states' rights"—a code word for anyone who grew up or lived during the Civil Rights Movement to denote the maintenance of white supremacy and Jim Crow. If someone had failed to get the message, Reagan told his white audiences stories about welfare queens in designer jeans—a folk myth told by white Southerners since the New Deal.[13] The northern son was coming to the South to assure his white political base that they had been right all along—America is a white Eurocentric nation and all of this multicultural, racial justice nonsense had to go. With Reagan's victories in both the South and the North and West in the 1980 and 1984 elections, Southernification and the political recovery had become dominant themes of American life. The South had made good on its promise to "rise again"—not in a military sense but in a socio-political and cultural formulation.

In this Southernification context a metaphoric gag rule reminiscent of the one imposed in the antebellum period prohibiting any Congressional discussion about the abolition of slavery began to take shape. In the national political discourse and increasingly with the standardization of elementary and secondary curricula in contemporary right-wing school reforms[14] white consciousness of historical and contemporary racism directed toward people of color is being erased. Aaron Gresson[15] writes of the "disconnect white people now exhibit with respect to racism" and the socio-political and cultural consequences of this scrubbing of white consciousness. The refusal of many contemporary white people in the North and West to confront the reality of racism in America is disturbing as it reflects the response to racial progress of many white Southerners of a generation ago. The politics of knowledge is a central issue in Southernification and contemporary racial politics.

Indeed, in contemporary American colleges and universities many white student organizations maintain that curricula that deal with white racism constitute a violation of white students' rights. Such teaching is often deemed to be in violation of Principle 5 of the Students For Academic Freedom's "Academic Bill of Rights"—freedom from "political indoctrination."[16] Such Southernification dynamics were unthinkable during and immediately after the Civil Rights Movement. Many of the racial arguments—deemed by most Americans at the time as extreme and frightening—that Strom Thurmond made in his 1948 presidential campaign and George Wallace championed in his tenure as Alabama governor and presidential candidate in the 1960s and early 1970s are now mainstream white American perspectives. With the ever-increasing erasure of the nation's consciousness of historical and contemporary racism, many young whites are developing forms of racial/racist identity that would make South Carolina's race baiting Retrenchment Governor and U.S. Senator Pitchfork Ben Tillman proud.

Another answer to our earlier question about the rest of the country's receptiveness to Southern perspectives and anxieties about race and many other matters may involve what is often labeled the breakdown of community in Northern, Midwestern, and Western urban locales. The alienation that many Americans of all racial and ethnic backgrounds experience in these domains is real and increasing. There is little doubt that such Americans are searching for places where community exists and the bonds of friendship and belongingness are real. In this context the South has presented itself as a region where such things are possible. When the search for community is combined with the post-military defeat right-wing search for certainty and comfort in absolutist belief structures, hyper-nationalism, cultural chauvinism, vilification of "others," and an exaggerated fidelity to racial, ethnic, and group identity, one can begin to discern the attractiveness of a region where many white people had experienced these needs for generations.

In this context it is less surprising that the overwhelmingly white Southern Baptist Convention (SBC)—the largest Protestant denomination in the United States—has witnessed much growth in the North, Midwest, and West in the decades following its ouster of "moderates" from its leadership in the early 1980s. A central dimension of the fundamentalist Baptists' objection to the moderates' *modus operandi* was their scholarly employment of historical-critical methods of scriptural hermeneutics. The anti-intellectualism of the fundamentalists appealed to a majority of the Southern Baptist laity and to the Northern, Midwestern, and Western believers who have joined not only the SBC but other even more fundamentalist churches in increasing numbers.[17] This rise of fundamentalism around the nation has brought the racial politics and conservative values of the white rural South to a mainstream America searching for an antidote to a gnawing sense of alienation.

These and many other factors have operated to "southernify" American ideology, to move the United States toward the status of "greater Alabama." In this rearranged context individuals who once considered themselves liberal in matters of race—even former "freedom riders" of the 1960s—now support privatization efforts in areas such as social services and education that undermine Black access to opportunity and socio-economic mobility. Indeed, the same liberals that fought against racial segregation in the 1960s fail to see issues of economic democracy as inherently racial in the twenty-first century. Jacob Levinson[18] maintains that the South in the twenty-first century is a reflection of what America has become—at least, I might add what a "recovered" America has become. This reflection is one that includes:
- NASCAR as the nation's most popular spectator sport
- the explosive growth of fundamentalist Christianity in the North, Midwest, and West
- the national dominance of right-wing politics
- a growing assertion of white supremacy
- the nationalization of the confederate flag as a symbol of white power
- white militias that often use the Ku Klux Klan as their model
- pervasive anti-unionism complete with an obsession with producing "good business climates" with their excessive profits and dismissal of health and safety concerns for workers
- growing anti-intellectualism that undermines local school and state university budgets
- Top 40 country music with its right-wing politics of knowledge
- and with global warming, tornados.

## UNDERSTANDING THE RETURN MIGRATION OF AFRICAN AMERICANS TO THE SOUTH: ROMANTICIZATION AND MULTIPLE PERSPECTIVES

Returning to our earlier discussion of Black migration, in the late 1960s and early 1970s the migration dynamics of the last five decades began to change. African Americans began returning to the South in increasingly greater numbers in search of better economic and vocational prospects than they had found in Northern, Midwestern, and Western locations as well as more affective and community-based dimensions of everyday life. Approximately two-thirds of the African Americans who moved back to the South in this period were returning to the land where they were born. Most of those migrants who had not been born in the South were northern people going to a place where they possessed deep-seated and enduring familial connections. This return migration was no statistical aberration, as more and more Black people returned to the South in succeeding decades. The 1990s witnessed a dramatic increase in the movement, and the numbers have continued to increase throughout the first decade of the twenty-first century. From a contemporary perspective it is apparent that the Black migration to the South over the last four decades constitutes one of the greatest migrations in American history.

THE SOUTHERN PLACE AND RACIAL POLITICS

Profound insights into the conceptual connections and meanings of the main concerns of this essay—the Southern place, racial politics, Southernification, and the recovery of white supremacy—dwell within the motivations and lived dimensions of this return migration. As referenced in the introduction to this essay, the multilogicality post/anti-colonial perspectives are very important in this context. Without the criticality of such ways of seeing it is easy for observers to lapse into a regressive romanticism of all things Southern that simply catalyzes the recovery movement. A survey of the return migration reveals that along with a more general American romanticization of the South, scholars can find a similar tendency among African Americans. Maya Angelou[19], herself a return migrant to the South—writes about the migration:

> The answer to the question why are so many young Black people moving South today? is that the American South sings a siren song to all Black Americans. The melody may be ignored, despised or ridiculed, but we all hear it ... They return and find or make their places in the land of their foreparents. They find and make friends under the shade of trees their ancestors left decades earlier. Many find themselves happy, without being able to explain the emotion. I think it is simply that they feel generally important.

While Angelou alludes to the complexities of the move—"the melody may be ignored, despised or ridiculed"—there is still a depoliticized celebration of Southern elation in her words. Non-southern observers reading Angelou and scores of other African American writers and/or interviewing numerous Black Southerners may begin to realize that Black people are Southerners too. And like many white Southerners, many Black Southerners like to attend church on Sundays and Wednesday nights, watch high school and college football, go to barbecues, arrange family reunions, garden, fish, and hunt. For a people historically in need of "safe spaces," the South evoked by Angelou, Toni Morrison, and Alice Walker can provide them in both a literal and figurative manner. One sees this theme safe space in a clearly romanticized manner in Julia Dash's 1992 film, "Daughters of the Dust." Here the migration north is portrayed as a mistake for African Americans. Through the use of imagery and various cinemagraphic techniques, Dash creates a bucolic view of Georgia's Sea Islands vis-à-vis the overcrowded, violence-ridden despair of the urban North.[20]

This same Southern romanticization is depicted in 2005 in a set of promotions developed by the Turner South television network. In these "My South" commercials for an all Southern television station, Black poets and rappers are featured reciting their compositions about the virtues of Southerness. All of the compositions emphasize cornbread, grits and other Southern cuisine, the strict discipline of children, memories of happy and innocent childhoods, family values, and Jesus. My point in referencing these romantic portrayals is not to ridicule them in some condescending hip, cynical, urbane manner but to explore their meaning in relation to the themes of the essay. Celebrating community, shared experiences, family, and religion does not have to serve as a romantic reification of the status quo. With critical input, postcolonial multilogicality, and the addition of dangerous memory such images can be deployed for resistance, for more emancipatory outcomes. These contradictory dynamics reflect the dialectic of place that is central to the themes developed here.

For example, in Toni Morrison's *Song of Solomon*, Milkman's return to a bucolic South is a journey of self-discovery and transformation, an effort to gain a historical consciousness that leads to racial redemption. Such a narrative is no simple ritual of romanticization—it is far more complex. Yet, the portrait of the South presented is not one of racial violence and oppression. Arrested Development, as previously referenced, is after all going home to Tennessee. Such reconstructions of the South in the African American collective consciousness could not have developed, of course, without the profound failure of the North as the Promised Land. From the vantage point of the Northern urban ghettos the more recognizable and intimate interpersonal associations of the South looked good to many African Americans. To many such interactions seemed superior to the insidious racism, the invisible structural oppression of the North, Midwest, and West. Gladys Knight and the Pips expressed the concept unambiguously in their 1973 hit, "Midnight Train to Georgia"—the first post-Civil Rights Movement song to address the return migration and the failure of the non-Southern Black urban experience. Gladys sings of following her man home to Georgia. Although Georgia is a "different place in time," it is still superior to the California dream that morphed into a Watts and South Central nightmare.

There is no doubt that a romantic impulse permeates many Black—and, of course, white (a perusal of country music quickly illustrates the pervasiveness of white romanticization)—artistic representations of the South in the last four decades. A central problem in such narratives is the erasure of the South's continuing racial oppression. In this context it is important to emphasize that the "Southern affirmations," the valued dimensions of Southern life, celebrated by Black and white observers are real. I agree that they can be found in unlikely places among people of all races and ethnicities, socio-economic classes, and genders. For those interested in racial justice, however, such celebrations cannot be one-dimensional and de-historicized. The affirmations may exist, but they live within a complex dialectic of pain and psychic malformation.

Without a critical multilogical grounding the Southern affirmations of both Black and white people lapse into an apologia for the racism, class-bias, sexism, and homophobia of the region. Without an understanding of the affirmations and the empowerment they portend—an insight not found among many Northern white progressives—the South recedes into a region without redeeming value or hope. In my own autobiographical case as a white Southerner, I can act on these understandings by becoming (or continuing to be) an existential outsider. Such a status allows me the critical distance necessary to escape the Southern ghosts of racism, sexism, class bias, homophobia, fundamentalism, provincialism, anti-intellectualism, etc. William Faulkner understood this dynamic of distance, appreciating the fact that Oxford, Mississippi could be his "expertise" but not his home. Alternatively in love with it and offended by it, Faulkner had to pull back. He lived his life in the South as a double agent—an insider and an outsider.[21]

One doesn't have to look too far into popular culture to see the manifestations of the unchallenged, romanticized Southern affirmations deployed for the ideology of

THE SOUTHERN PLACE AND RACIAL POLITICS

recovery. As previously referenced, over the last couple of decades Hollywood has paid romantic homage to Southerness in movies such as "Fried Green Tomatoes," and "Driving Miss Daisy." Such movies are recovery efforts to recapture a Southern past that exists only in the white imagination. Indeed, such a past can exist in the contemporary consciousness only if racial history is erased. Such a construction protects white people from the negativity that comes from confronting the mutating phenomenon of racism in American life.

If racism in the South never existed in a violent and virulent form, then it is easy to proclaim in contemporary artistic works that a separate-but-equal "Driving Miss Daisy" variety of racial politics no longer exists. It is then just a short step to one of the recovery project's central tenets: racism is dead. Without multiple perspectives from diverse participants and a critical historiographical orientation, the neo-romanticization of the South operates like D. W. Griffith's "Birth of a Nation" in the first recovery movement to further the causes of a new, albeit mutated, form of twenty-first century white supremacy. Recovery history and popular cultural historical representations constitute a view of the past devoid of dangerous memory.[22]

Such histories are adept in crafting an innocent representation of whiteness. As a historical figure Forrest Gump is the archetypal innocent white male who was present at all the great events of the last one-third of the twentieth century. Aaron Gresson[23] captures the power of "Forrest Gump," pointing out that Forrest has no conception of evil, cannot conceive of hurting others, and is present but not responsible for events surrounding him. The innocent but slow Alabama boy becomes a symbol for an era plagued with a case of social amnesia. Forrest calls to Americans to forget the postcolonial lessons of Vietnam, the realities that motivated the Civil Rights Movement, the genocide of Manifest Destiny, the role of women in a pre-feminist America, etc.... **Forrest** offers atonement to country that some believe has strayed from its white supremacist, colonialist, and patriarchal origins. Here the recovery's path of redemption runs through Alabama.

Trent Lott's wish that Strom Thurmond had won the presidency as a white supremacist Dixiecrat in 1948 travels this same road to recovery taking it into Mississippi. When Lott proclaimed that the country would not have had all of "these problems" if Thurmond had become president at the beginning of the Civil Rights Movement, his audience knew he was referencing the liberationist effort to empower African Americans and in turn destroy the "Mississippi way of life." Indeed, if America had followed Missisipi's lead and voted for Thurmond, Lott maintained, we'd all be a lot better off today. As with the movie, Forrest Gump, Lott's comments emerged from a recovery-informed discursive universe. Socio-historical amnesia is a pre-condition necessary to consenting to such constructs: the filmmakers and Lott assume that there was no problem in need of fixing in the 1950s South—or America in general. Life was good as it was—disenfranchisement, lynching, poverty, legal rights, and the **lack of** protection of law enforcement aside.

In the recovery discourse we can clearly see the need for multiple perspectives, for multilogical knowledges. Scholars in diverse disciplines who explore contemporary racial politics are obligated to get beyond monological, neo-colonialist perspectives and engage in new ways of understanding. In this exploration I have employed power theories that help uncover the hidden artifacts of power and the ways they construct ways of seeing and the knowledges a society produces in relation to racial politics. Multilogical frameworks have never been more important, as we examine the monological ways of perceiving advanced by the recovery movement. In the next section of the essay I will examine the complexity of Southerness in light of our larger concerns with racial politics and this multilogicality.

## GHOSTS AND AFFIRMATIONS: THE DIALECTIC OF THE SOUTHERN PLACE

An examination of African American consciousness over the last century[24] reveals a complex Black view of the South. This dialectic of Southern place frames the South concurrently as a locus of violence and a setting for ancestorial wisdom. These two dynamics exist in dialectical tension, one always shaping and influencing the other. Black enslavement, pain, and blood provide the down payment for not only African American moral entitlement to the land but also for the evolution of racial identity and redemption. Negotiating this dialectic of place, African Americans understand the underside of the South as Black home, yet they elect to go back there. This dialectic of Southern place is discernible in the Black literary tradition. In the middle decades of the twentieth century Ralph Ellison and Albert Murray refused to view their own Southern pasts as unmitigated disasters despite the prevailing consensus in the 1950s and 1960s that they should do so. By the 1980s and 1990s Morrison, Walker, Angelou, and Ernest Gaines were making the same observation.

With his college political awakening in the 1950s, white Southern essayist Willie Morris felt shame for his Mississippi origins. While in New York City in the 1960s, Morris came to appreciate the need to transcend such a sentiment. Shame, he wrote, was a simplistic and debilitating emotion—like bitterness it was too reductionistic, too predictable. Moving to the dialectical zone, Morris was challenged to understand the Southern experience and to appreciate its meaning in light of human experience emanating from other places. In the spirit of Albert Murray's understanding of the blues idiom, the dialectic of Southern place is a blues construction. We mourn the pain of the place but we concurrently celebrate its possibility, its redemptive challenge for us to carry on despite the blood that fertilized the strange fruit.[25] It is hard to think of Billie Holliday singing "Strange Fruit" without conjuring images of the dialectic of the sweet and bitter Southern place. The juxtaposition of the sweet scent of magnolia trees with the smell of burning flesh leaves no doubt about the duality.

In recent Black literature numerous writers have drawn upon this dialectical Southern theme to offer hope and possibility for the Black future. Toni Morrison's *Song of Solomon* well represents this motif, as Milkman interprets the family history he recovers in the South as a larger racial history. In this context African Americans—and hopefully progressive whites—can use the ghosts of Southern history as a historical source of wisdom and insight. The tree once used for lynching innocent Black people now cradles Morrison's Milkman like the loving hands of a grandfather.[26] Such literary dynamics evoke great hope and are powerful sociopolitical forces in contemporary American life. Nevertheless, the Southern ghosts are not about to give up their haunting of the Southern place. The rural South of the twenty-first century, for example, is a place of waning agricultural opportunities and contracting numbers of land owners. Education is limited for Black residents, poverty persists, and little is being done to change these harsh realities. So while the South as safe space of healing is a fashionable literary construct, political economic realities on the sacred Southern land are not as encouraging as we would hope. The dialectic of place with its competing affirmations and bloody ghosts persists.

Indeed, I don't sense safety and redemption in the recent actions of Mississippi Senators Trent Lott and Thad Cochran in relation to their refusal to join their Senate colleagues in apologizing for the institution's inaction on Southern lynching. Cochran's vote against the apology was even more revealing in light of his earlier co-sponsorship of resolutions of contrition in relation to the treatment of Native Americans and the interment of Japanese-Americans during World War Two. Of course, such actions are symbolic and don't increase educational and economic opportunities for Black children. Nevertheless, they do illustrate the continuation and evolution of a white mindset that holds dramatic consequence for contemporary racial politics and the recovery movement. While the South offers many things to elicit hope for a more just racial order, the point being made here is that we must be careful not to romanticize Southern racial politics in light of our disappointment with Northern, Midwestern, and Western racism. Indeed, what are referred to here as the Southern affirmations of community, interracialism, closeness to the land, redemptive refuge, **breeding ground of the artistic imagination**, etc. can easily be bastardized and transformed into family values, parochialism, complacency, political apathy, religious tyranny, and conformity.[27]

## THE SOUTHERN GHOSTS

First, I will examine what I am calling the Southern ghosts—those regressive dimensions of Southern history and contemporary life that oppress individuals from all racial backgrounds, albeit in diverse ways.

1) *Virulent racism—a sense of white supremacy that permeated all dimensions of Southern society.* Both Black and white consciousness was shaped by this relentless racism. Facing such a threat and the exclusions it carried with it, Southern Blacks sought shelter in their own culture and institutions. Whites, of course, were scarred by the delusion of superiority and the dehumanizing influences that accompanied it. Every aspect of the Southern experience has been haunted by this often unacknowledged elephant in the parlor. Willie Morris[28] captured the Southern white discourse of white supremacy in his autobiography, *North Toward Home*. Black people, he wrote, were always ours to do with as we wished with their degenerate lifestyles and distasteful habits.

Dirty whites were said to keep house like niggers. A nigger car was dilapidated and didn't run well. Staying out all night and being seen with a variety of male companions made a white female guilty of acting like a nigger woman. Conversation filled with lies and superstition was described by whites as nigger talk. Over the last few years I have studied young whites who perpetuate this racist discourse, albeit more self-consciously and oppositionally than their ancestors. In the contemporary South an entire right wing, white supremacist counterculture has arisen that with its racist discourse and symbology holds much appeal for young whites outside of the South.

2) *Religious tyranny—the white Protestant fundamentalism of the South that imposes its beliefs by fear and rote.* This white religious fundamentalism that has gained so much power and influence in all areas of the country over the last three decades. For the most part this fundamentalism is a right-wing reactionary movement that often excludes non-whites, as it promotes an ethnocentric ideological agenda.[29] Willie Morris wrote about the power of this fundamentalism in his Mississippi home. As a fourth grader, Morris found himself entrusted to public school teacher Miss Abbott and her white-bearded, king of clubs, American sympathizing anthropomorphic God.

Miss Abbott passed along God's pronouncements on the niggers and the Japs while the white children of Yazoo City, Mississippi spent a good portion of their mornings memorizing and reciting Bible verses. The lessons, buoyed by the omnipresent threat of hell, were not lost on the Yazoo youth. "Our fundamentalism was so much a part of us that its very sources, even its most outrageous gyrations and circumlocutions went unquestioned."[30] In the twenty-first century these same historical impulses continue on with a new sense of urgency. As Southern fundamentalists have come to believe that they are the victims of racial and religious persecution in late twentieth and early twenty-first century America, they have worked to "recover" their dominance with a vengeance.

3) *A history of violence—a blood and darkness that has caused and still causes great trauma.* Power in Southern history has not been subtle—Antonio Gramsci's notion of hegemony has been somewhat irrelevant for few white Southerners were trying to win the consent of African Americans. Power over Black people was won by force—rape, castration, beating, and lynching. Violence against the Black body is one of the central themes of Southern history and literature. As the crime scene for such violence, the world often lost sight of the diverse and more subtle ways racism took place in other areas of the country. The ghost of violence still haunts the twenty-first century South, albeit in new forms and circumstances.

4) *Patriarchy—a history of male dominance characterized by a paternalistic chivalry, male bonding rituals, and good ol' boyism.* James Baldwin in *Go Tell It on the Mountain* captured the historical horror of this patriarchy in his description of the South as the white man's great whorehouse—a brothel filled with Black women over whom he held complete power. In Southern patriarchy sexism and racism are intermeshed, as white privilege becomes intertwined with male privilege. As a child of the South, I watched young white males attempt to claim their "birthright" with Black women. When their sexual demands were resisted, such young men became excessively abusive and sometimes violent. Such rituals were male power plays designed to illustrate their social power and privilege to all onlookers. In this regressive world of gender a Southern boy's most important friends, those among whom he felt comfortable being himself, were to be found in the male peer group. Even in upper middle class settings association with popular and attractive white girls was not pursued merely for its intrinsic worth—such

associations brought with them increased good ol' boy status in the male group. Such patriarchy and the good ol' boyism that accompanies it continue to oppress southern women and repress the ontological possibility of Southern men.

5) *An anti-intellectualism that undermines the support of educational institutions that would benefit all dimensions of Southern life.* For years after Reconstruction most white Southerners opposed any form of public education on the grounds that they did not want to pay for the education of African Americans or support racially integrated schools. Thus, in the mind of the South education was associated with interracialism and African American mobility—a kiss of death in the milieu. In a patriarchal domain education was viewed as an effeminate **pursuit** unworthy of manly attention.

6) *A parochialism that undermines efforts to become more than one already is.* Familiarity with place—especially for individuals in privileged groups—and comfort with "what is" crushes the desire to go beyond it. Again, Willie Morris[31] provides insight into this parochial complacency, as he describes his comfort in Yazoo City, Mississippi, his majorette girlfriend, and his family's land. What more could there possibly be? he only occasionally wondered. After a Saturday night of high school partying at the house of some Yazoo parents who had traveled to Oxford for the Ole Miss football game, Morris was satisfied. I was with the little plantation girl I loved, and old friends who had been friends for as long as I could remember in a town as familiar and settled to me as anything I would ever know, I would never wander very far away.[32]

## THE SOUTHERN AFFIRMATIONS

The Southern affirmations that many white and Black progeny of the region understand and appreciate are qualities that have helped catalyze the Southernification process. In this study of contemporary racial politics in light of these Southern dynamics, it is profoundly important to interrogate such affirmations in their dialectical relationship with the ghosts—a process that protects us from both romanticization and the use of these virtues in the larger recovery efforts of the contemporary era.

1) *Even as the racist ghosts haunt, the South is a Black and white place—an interracial location where cultural hybridity exists in spite of historical forces that would subvert it.* Southern schools, politic institutions, and suburbs—to the shock of many non-Southerners—are the most racially integrated in America.[33] Southern consciousness certainly cuts across racial and class lines, connecting in remarkable ways professors, journalists, Black preachers, members of the NAACP, and NASCAR enthusiasts with Confederate flags on their rear bumpers. I have stood in Tennessee and Louisiana among racially mixed groups and hear Black ministers and Klansmen agree that they would rather raise their children in the South than in any other part of the country. Even Southern music is interracial, as the blues and jazz are more of a hybrid of African, African American, and white musical forms **than** previously understood. Of course, rock n' roll is the paragon of interracial music.

2) *Community exists in the South in many localities—the perception of the existence of community is so strong that the South-as-home theme emerges time and again in both Black and white literary/cultural expression.* Cornel West[34] captures this dynamic, maintaining that African Americans possess a long history of pain, toil, and struggle for endurance that has been soothed by registers of meaning and emotion that constructed and maintained communities. Within these communities committed members labored and sacrificed in service to others. Willie Morris[35] echoes West's sentiments in a white context, contending that Southern people shared certain things: a love of mutually known geographic places, a consciousness of particular beloved landmarks that were central to individual and group identity, and a reverence toward the concept of friendship. All of these dynamics led to a unique and obdurate sense of community.

3) *The South is a site of redemption forged by trauma and pain.* The trauma and darkness of the South's racial history obviously has crushed hope and emancipatory impulses. Yet, in the midst of pain derived from such realities, resting at the core of the dialectic of place, emerges the possibility of grace of character gained via anguish and bereavement. The question quickly emerges from such an assertion: does historical liberation require trauma? The tyrannies of the South are all too real: the region's shattered dreams, the tragedy of its history, the enlightenment that could be gained by living with a great sin, and an "un-American" poverty. Toni Morrison has been acutely aware of such dynamics in her oeuvre. As the place haunted by trauma, where Africa is most present, where home exists in reality and in the imagination, Morrison's South is a place of redemption.

4) *The South is a place where Black and white people both maintain a closeness to the land and a feel for the rhythms of nature.* Richard Wright in *Inheritors of Slavery: Twelve Million Black Voices—a Folk History of the Negro in the United States* (1941) wrote about the Southern land with its

red and black and brown clay, with fresh and hungry smells, with pine trees and palm trees, with rolling hills and swampy delta—an unbelievably fertile land....

Our southern springs are filled with quiet noises and scenes of growth. Apple buds laugh into blossom. Honeysuckles creep up the sides of houses. Sunflowers nod in the hot fields. From mossy tree to mossy tree—oak, elm, willow, aspen, sycamore, dogwood, cedar, walnut, ash, and hickory–bright green leaves jut from a million branches to form an awning that tries to shield and shade the earth.[36]

Obviously, as much as Wright hated the injustices that scarred the South, he loved the land. Willie Morris writes in the same key, insisting that the powerful delta land with all of its mysteries and strengths was always tugging at the Southern soul. We were never far away from the land, the growing plants, and nature's wilder moods. One's closeness to the textures of the land with its sensual if not erotic rhythms staved off **at least** one form of alienation, as it constantly confronted one with births and deaths, the long forgotten victories and tragedies, and the sadnesses and joys of human existence in this unique Southern place.

5) *The South is a place where people love storytelling and believe that this tradition builds community by linking us to our past, by creating common memories.* Eudora Welty argued that we must become our own storytellers. Nothing ever happens once and is finished, the past lives on. As Southerners tell their stories, enhance their reputations as raconteurs; they construct their individual versions of the past. Welty, like William Faulkner, saw history as a dialectical process— an interchange between the "out there" and the "in here." Each time a story is told there is a reweaving of facts—some details are omitted, some reemphasized. Tradition is challenged, the presentation of past as myth is overcome.

Morris joins this conversation, maintaining that a story worth telling is worth telling again. The storyteller assigns his or her listeners the responsibility to pass the tale along to a different audience, hopefully in a distant future. In this way family and cultural continuity is assured. The stories are the proper province of one's oldest living relative. They are most effective, Morris posits, when they are told in the dark of a summer evening, the whole family gathered on a screened porch, quiet in their listening so that the thumping of the night-flying beetles against the screens and the whine of locusts and cicadas merge with the storyteller's voice to become part of the tale. Such a setting reaching past into the fiber of childhood, endures as vividly in the memory as the tale itself.[37] Many African Americans have returned to the South in search of these stories lost to them via their migrations. The significance of the work of Morrison, Walker, Gaines, Angelou and other African American "storytellers" cannot be **properly appreciated** outside this dynamic. At its best Southern storytelling operates as a catalyst for personal and social transformation, as it helps forge the bonds of community.

6) *The South is a place where people revere the impulses of the imagination that shape speech, music, literature, love of place, and potential.* The atmosphere of small Southern towns and rural areas, Willie Morris argues, did amazing things to the imagination of children. When clocks moved slowly the southern sense of fancy had time to develop—people had to focus their imagination on something. Many have asserted that the Southern imagination is the region's greatest asset; it saved Willie Morris from the philistine concerns of the small town bourgeoisie and it saved Louis Armstrong from the ravages of Louisiana racism that so easily could have consumed him. It is no accident that all uniquely American music (i.e., African American music) has its origins in the South.

7) *The South possesses a sense of place unlike no other American region.* This fidelity to place in the South, of course, has too often taken on regressive, racist, sexist, and right-wing forms. Yet, many Black and white Southerners believe that it can be employed as an affirmation, serving interracial and liberatory purposes in the twenty-first century. The Southern sense of place in this progressive sense transcends the ghost of provincialism with its exclusivity, as it serves to connect the world of daily affairs with history and the memory of people across generations. Such a notion not only builds a literature that elevates cultural renewal to a central concern but fashions a politics (a pedagogy) of possibility.

A notion of racial and cultural politics emerges with this liberatory sense of place that is acutely concerned with the death of history and social amnesia. This liberatory sense of place dominates the consciousness of many Black and progressive white Southern expatriates. Willie Morris wrote that during his exile in New York he shared far more cultural sensibilities with Black Southerners than with many of the Yankee Wasps he encountered on a daily basis. A central feature of *North Toward Home* involves the sense of Southern place Morris, Ralph Ellison, and Albert Murray shared and their mutual enjoyment of New Year's dinners consisting of collard greens, black-eyed peas, ham hocks, cornbread, and bourbon.[38]

## CONCLUSION: THE PROMISE OF THE SOUTHERN AFFIRMATIONS, THE HORROR OF THE SOUTHERN GHOSTS

Both the Southern ghosts and the affirmations call out to contemporary America, both strike affective chords. Such a reality reaffirms Willie Morris's belief that what happens in the South is not only important **to Southerners but potentially holds great consequence for the nation.** In this time of regressive politics and new mutated forms of racism and class bias, the Southern ghosts have moved north and west. The siren call of the affirmations in their regressive articulation as family values and communities (often gated) that are exclusive, ethnocentric, homophobic, and parochial continue to influence twenty-first century American cultural politics. Of course, the South is in a struggle for its own survival as corporatism and the alienation of global market economics continues to homogenize the Southern place with their good business climates, cheap labor, Wal-marts, and McDonald's. If such trends continue, the South and its particularities of place may simply fade into regional oblivion, reemerging as the Sunbelt.

Thus, it is the burden of proponents of progressive cultural and racial politics to understand the complexities of the South, its deployment in contemporary American life, and the possibilities its affirmations offer for racial healing and liberation. Like Howard Dean—but with more sensitivity to the emotional register of references to the Confederate Flag—I do not want to "write off" the South as a regressive racial/ cultural domain. If we are to be Southernified, the process should involve the development of a lived interracialism, an inclusive sense of community and its importance in everyday life, a collective racial consciousness based on a shared historical memory of the nation's blood and darkness, a racial redemption in which we all participate, an appreciation of the land and our collective cultivation of it, a recognition of the interracial contributions to the nation's most imaginative and innovative artistic production, and an understanding that one of the dominant socio-political impulses of our time, the recovery movement, is leading us down a path of inevitable ethical and political devastation.

## NOTES

[1] Gresson's work on these topics includes Aaron Gresson, *The Recovery of Race in America* (Minneapolis: University of Minnesota Press, 1995 and *America's Atonement: Racial Pain, Recovery Rhetoric, and the Pedagogy of Healing* (New York: Peter Lang, 2004); my work includes Joe L. Kincheloe, & Shirley Steinberg, *Changing Multiculturalism* (London: Open University Press, 1997); Joe L. Kincheloe, Shirley Steinberg, Nelson Rodriguez, & Ronnald Chennault, *White Reign: Deploying*

*Whiteness in America* (NewYork: St. Martin's Press, 1998); Joe L. Kincheloe, *Getting Beyond the Facts: Teaching Social Studies/Social Science in the Twenty-First Century* (New York: Peter Lang, 2001).

[2] James Cobb, "Vienna Sausage, Faulkner, and Elvis." *Georgia Magazine*, 2003. http://cobblog.blogspot.com/2005_03_01_cobblog_archive.html; Aaron Gresson, *America's Atonement*.

[3] Manning Marable, "Living Black History: Resurrecting the African American Intellectual Tradition," *Souls: A Critical Journal of Black Politics, Culture, and Society*, **6**, 3/4 (2004): 5–16.

[4] Willie Morris, *North Toward Home* (Oxford, Mississippi: Yoknapatawpha Press, 1967).

[5] Marable, "Living Black History," 13–14.

[6] Aaron Gresson, *The Recovery of Race in America*; Nelson Rodriguez, & Leila Villaverde (Eds.), *Dismantling White Privilege* (New York: Peter Lang, 2000); Gresson, *America's Atonement*; Joe L. Kincheloe, & Shirley Steinberg (Eds.), *What You Don't Know about School* (New York: Palgrave, 2006).

[7] Richard Herrnstein, & Charles Murray, *The Bell Curve: Intelligence and Class Structure in American Life* (New York: Basic Books, 1994); Joe L. Kincheloe, Shirley Steinberg, & Aaron Gresson, *Measured Lies: The Bell Curve Examined* (New York: St. Martin's Press, 1996).

[8] Dinesh D'Souza, *The End of Racism* (New York: The Free Press, 1995).

[9] Joe L. Kincheloe, & William Pinar (Eds.), *Curriculum as Social Psychoanalysis: Essays on the Significance of Place* (Albany, New York: State University of New York Press, 1991); John Beck, Wendy Frandsen, & Aaron Randall, "Will Southern Culture Survive? Three Views," 2005. http://oit.vgcc.cc.nc.us/hum122/concl.htm

[10] Robert H. Bork, *Slouching Towards Gomorrah: Modern Liberalism and American Decline* (New York: Regan Books, 1996).

[11] Gresson, *America's Atonement*; Joe L. Kincheloe, & Shirley Steinberg, *The Miseducation of the West: How Schools and the Media Distort Our Understanding of the Islamic World* (Westport, CT: Praeger, 2004).

[12] Farah Jasmine Griffin, *Who Set You Flowin'? The African American Migration Narrative* (New York: Oxford University Press, 1995); Valerie Grim, & Anne B. W. Effland, "Sustaining a Rural Black Farming Community in the South." *Rural Development Perspectives*, 1997, **12**, 3: 47–55.
Jacob Levinson, "Divining Dixie," *Columbia Journalism Review*, **2**, 2004.

[13] Jacob Levinson, "Divining Dixie," *Columbia Journalism Review*, **2**, 2004. http://www.cjr.org/issues/2004/2/levenson-dixie.asp

[14] Kincheloe, & Steinberg, *What You Don't Know about School*.

[15] Gresson, *America's Atonement*, 113.

[16] Students for Academic Freedom, "Academic Bill of Rights," 2004. http://www.studentsforacademicfreedom.org/abor.html

[17] Betty A. DeBerg, "Response to Sam Hill, 'Fundamentalism in Recent Southern Culture,'" *Journal of Southern Religion*, 1998. http://www.as.wvu.edu/coll03/relst/jsr/deberg.htm

[18] Kincheloe, & Pinar, *Curriculum as Social Psychoanalysis*; African American Migration Experience (AAME), "Return Migration to the South," 2005. http://www.inmotionaame.org

[19] Angelou quoted in AAME, "Return Migration to the South."

[20] Griffin, *Who Set You Flowin'?*; Beck, Frandsen, & Randall, "Will the South Survive?"; AAME, "Return Migration to the South."

[21] Richard Gray, *Writing the South: Ideas of an American Region* (New York: Cambridge University Press, 1986); Griffin, *Who Set You Flowin'?*; AAME, "Return Migration to the South."

[22] Griffin, *Who Set You Flowin'?*; Gresson, *America's Atonement*.

[23] Gresson, *America's Atonement*.

[24] Lawrence W. Levine, *Black Culture and Black Consciousness* (New York: Oxford University Press, 1977); Griffin, *Who Set You Flowin'?*

[25] Morris, *North Toward Home*; Frances Jones-Sneed, "Memories of the Civil Rights Movent. A Review Essay of *The Children* by David Halberstam," 1999. http://www.mcla.mass.edu/publications/faculty_publications/the_minds_eye_spring_99/sneed.htm; Albert Murray, *The Blue Devils of Nada: A Contemporary American Approach to Aesthetic Statement* (New York: Vintage, 1996).

[26] Toni Morrison, *Song of Solomon* (New York: Random House, 1977); Griffin, *Who Set You Flowin'?*
[27] Grim and Effland, "Sustaining a Rural Black Farming Community in the South"; James Cobb, "So Another Racist Finds Himself Behind Bars...So?" 2005. http://cobblog.blogspot.com2005/05/my-latest-rant.html
[28] DeBerg, "Response to Sam Hill."
[29] Beck, Frandsen, & Randall, "Will the South Survive?"
[30] Morris, *North Toward Home.*
[31] Ibid.
[32] Ibid, 139–40.
[33] Cobb, "So Another Racist Finds Himself Behind Bars."
[34] Cornel West, *Race Matters* (Boston: Beacon Press, 1993).
[35] Morris, *North Toward Home.*
[36] Wright quoted in Griffith, *Who Set You Flowin'?*, p. 33.
[37] Morris, *North Toward Home*; Eudora Welty, "Place in Fiction." In Eudora Welty, *The Eye of the Story* (New York: Random House, 1977).
[38] Morris, *North Toward Home.*

**Reprinted with permission: Kincheloe, J. L. (2006). The southern place and racial politics: Southernification, romanticization, and the recovery of white supremacy. *Souls: A Critical Journal of Black Politics, Culture, and Society, 8*(1), *27–46*.**

AARON DAVID GRESSON III

# KINCHELOE AND INTERRACIAL RECOVERY

*A Child of the South on Dialogic Engagement*

In the mid 1990s I published *The Recovery of Race in America* (Gresson, 1995). There I argued that much of the social, political, and cultural struggle between 1970 and 1990 could be read as an effort to address losses—real and perceived—spawned by the social activism of the 1960s. I called this cultural struggle "recovery work." Joe Kincheloe was among the most insightful and persistent scholars engaging this recovery discourse. In his 2006 essay on the South and African American Studies, he is especially brilliant in arguing that a process of "southernification" characterized this recovery work. Specifically, he uses the recovery paradigm to explore ways in which southern traditions, visions, and values seemed to influence the nation at large. In this essay, Kincheloe's imaginative energies illumine the enduring significance of his advocacy for vigilance and critique/ activism. Most important, perhaps, Joe employs his own remembrance/ engagement with the South to call for an enlarged interracial recovery, one that replaces an emergent white racial recovery. Through this initiative we are able to see critical aspects of Joe's theory and praxis, and gain some sense of the depth, scope, and enduring significance of his scholarship.

## KNOWLEDGE PRODUCTION, DISSEMINATION AND VALUE

Joe Kincheloe's scholarship has probably always been a *dialogical engagement*—a challenging conversation with those who sought to shape ideas. In his reflections on the New Right, for instance, one could see both recognition of the emergent reactionary conservative impulse and a commitment to challenge it. Focusing on social studies and the critical education of America's youth, he recognized in the conservative teaching about Vietnam a struggle for the high school and postsecondary students' critical understanding of the nation (Kincheloe and Staley, 1983). Over the next two decades, Kincheloe deepened and enlarged the scope of cultural, social, and political phenomena touched by this dialogic engagement. In the 2006 essay, notably, Joe returned to an early interest in the South—his birthplace—with a new rhetorical twist: its significance for African American and related area studies. In this essay Joe names/situates himself as white male southerner and thereby embarks on a refreshing take on dialogic engagement.

The essay is exciting on multiple levels; but on each Kincheloe pleas for dialogic engagement—to speak as a white southerner to an emergent yet currently expanding equally dialogic other: the Africana studies scholar. His goal is to invite, nay, impel, recognition of intertwining forces: the inevitable arrival of minority-guided production and dissemination of knowledge about race and racism in the national and global contexts, set against a backdrop of counter-forces, namely *white recovery work*. Critical to Kincheloe's effort in this essay is a review of the role of emergent area studies in critiquing both white and colored identities. Pertinent to this effort, we might recall the nature of the *dispersal* and its implications for knowledge production and dissemination. Sally Tomlinson (2003, p. 213) offers one understanding of this dispersal:

> The second half of the twentieth century saw unprecedented mass movement of peoples around the world. This movement included forced migrations as attempts were made to separate ethnic and cultural groups; voluntary migrations as groups embraced political and religious freedoms; economic migrations from "old" to "new" worlds and from former colonial countries in Africa, the Caribbean, and Asia to fill Europe's labour markets; and increasing numbers of political refugees and asylum seekers from war and conflicts.

As people move around, they bring ideas and information with them. They also send ideas and information back home. The information or knowledge that occurs as a result of being people in motion has been called *diaspora knowledge* (Yang, 2002). Thus, there are millions of people living in the United States and elsewhere who not only learn what we choose to teach; they also participate in constructing knowledge. Today there are many *disaporic* intellectual traditions—Asian, African, Caribbean, and Latin. These produce alternative knowledge about what has been and are their achievements, interests, and priorities.

The combined impact of globalization and disasporic knowledge on race and identity is both exciting and challenging. The question/quest posed by Joe Kincheloe is how to make sense of the stubborn resistance of whiteness to join the diasporic discourse where identities are enlarged via vulnerable engagement. This is perhaps one of Joe's greatest gifts to us: to see that recovery persists, and plays out in the vast global identity politics of today.

## RECOVERY AND CRITICAL THEORY: EVOLUTIONARY SYNERGY

Shortly after I met Joe and Shirley, Hernnstein and Murray's *The Bell Shaped Curve* (1994) was published amid much fanfare. Joe and Shirley, realizing the implications of failure to respond in kind to this vanguard illustration of white racial recovery, assumed a now-familiar leadership role in proffering a critical praxis to this kind of reactionary scholarship. We teamed up to edit *Measured Lies: The Bell Curve Reexamined* (1996). This volume used critical perspectives to ask and answer why a return to scientific racism made sense in the 1990s. It also set forth a critical positionality sensitive to the symbolic and substantive importance of recovery dynamics in knowledge production and dissemination. Joe understood, in a profound way, that criticality itself must be formulated in ways sensitive to the subjective experiences of and response to interracialism. By challenging assertions that race and ethnic-linked intelligence accounted for differential academic and social achievement, *Measured Lies* was a strategic opportunity to relate critical theoretical frameworks to race and education.

Joe's 2006 essay on southernification, revisits the theme of racial recovery, with a difference: he traces the regional recovery of a "redeemed" South as it expands to engulf a larger segment of the American racial imagination. In his words:

> In the tradition of Black Studies' radical eye, my work as a white Southerner engages a critical interracialism that avoids essentialism as it works for racial, class, and gender justice. In this context I've used the conceptual lenses of a critical multiculturalism to explore the evolving nature of racism and racial identity in the contemporary era. In my work in whiteness studies I have operated on the assumption that whiteness studies conducted by white people must always be undertaken as an interracial act.

For Joe and so many other critical educators, multiculturalism often failed because it lacked *criticality*. That is, the emphasis on many cultural traditions gaining their individual recognition on the cultural or social stage was insufficient to deal with the challenges posed by *power* in its various guises and positions. Through a critical multiculturalism Joe and his colleagues hoped to explode those falsehoods perpetrated in so many books and curricula on cultural diversity. In this regard, he notes:

I have operated on the assumption that whiteness studies conducted by white people must always be undertaken as an interracial act. A study of whiteness suffers when it is not directly connected to African American studies, Latino/Chicano studies, indigenous studies, ethnic studies, and postcolonialism and the way white power and the historical white construction of "reason" have attempted to position non-white peoples.

Kincheloe lays out the terms of engagement between a developing area of studies agenda such as represented by Africana Studies and the growth of recovery work among diverse segments of white social, cultural, and politico-economic America. If by *critical*, we understand, in part, the capacity for reflexivity—looking at oneself in the equation—then Kincheloe lives and illumines criticalness through his effort to clarify the dynamic scope of white recovery efforts in contemporary time. In the essay, he is at pains to make clear this point:

> A critical understanding of whiteness/white power and its effect on racial politics is possible only if we understand in great specificity the multiple meanings of whiteness and their effects on the way white consciousness is historically structured and socially inscribed. Without such appreciations and the meta-consciousness they ground, an awareness of the privilege and dominance of white Northern European vantage points is buried in the cemetery of power evasion. The mutations in white consciousness over the last few decades join other occluded insights into whiteness in this conceptual graveyard. Students of African American studies need to exhume such concepts in the pursuit of a contemporary understanding of Black life in the twenty-first century.

Whether or not Africana scholars will agree with the extent to which whiteness/ white power are the central concerns of emergent diaspora studies, most will most likely appreciate the way that Kincheloe inserts himself as critical scholar *and* son of the South in the dual discourse of a reconstituted South and a Redeemed American Nation. Few critical theorists could or have provided, for instance, the kind of conclusions enumerated in the final section of this essay: Kincheloe cogently and concisely captures the range of emotion, belief, and behavior that constitutes the "Southernification" of the Nation. These very premises become a critical research agenda for further cultural workers and scholars as they portray a reality that feels real but requires further exploration. This leads us to consider a final matter— Kincheloe's continuing importance in the discourse of critical theory and praxis.

By situating Africana Studies also as critical agenda, Kincheloe furthers a project he has been singularly concerned with: how to help whites under the influence of whiteness recover a broader humanity through overcoming the negativities of racial exceptionalism. He joins and enjoins the Africana/Diaspora Studies initiative to consider the implications of whiteness studies for an enlarged interracial discourse. For the past few decades the global disaporic trend has intensified interest in multiple identities among people of color. Highly visible persons like Tiger Woods and Barack Obama celebrate their diverse racial/ethnic identities; thereby reminding us that race is a social construction that must be continually defined and renegotiated. In a 1999 essay on whiteness and shifting identities, Joe anticipated the emergent challenge facing whites who would join this broader global diasporic trend. This 2006 essay extends Kincheloe's hope that an interracially motivated critical perspective might both explore and liberate whites from the narrow, limiting and dehumanizing outcomes of whiteness. By taking his ongoing critique of whiteness to the threshold of Africana Studies, he was both returning home to the South of his youth and re-imaging its possible role as an influence on the national recovery motive.

## THE CONTINUING IMPORTANCE OF KINCHELOE

In 2009, former President Jimmy Carter opined on a possible reason for some of the opposition to the nation's first African American president:

> I think an overwhelming portion of the intensely demonstrated animosity toward President Barack Obama is based on the fact that he is a Black man, that he's African American," Carter said. "I live in the South, and I've seen the South come a long way and I've seen the rest of the country that shared the South's attitude toward minority groups at that time ... and I think it's bubbled up to the surface, because of a belief among many white people, not just in the South but around the country, that African-Americans are not qualified to lead this great country. (CNN, 2009, p. 1)

Carter, a son of the South, found a shared "geographical unconscious" in the racially-tinged opposition to President Barack Obama. While decried by many as misguided in his words, he is nonetheless reminiscent of Joe Kincheloe's argument in the 2006 essay. Joe saw that recovery bore cyclical and geographic (pedagogy of place) properties. In particular, racial recovery impulses threaten, like Anti-Semitism, to resurface whenever a perceived danger gives rise to the group's "lesser angel" and a convenient scapegoat can be found. Throughout Kincheloe's scholarship we see this vision; and we continue to draw inspiration and insight from it. In the essay, in particular, Joe recognizes, as Carter in his own remembrance, that "the Southern ghosts have moved north and west." But Kincheloe also knows that the challenge cannot stop at merely naming the danger. Rather, in his words, "it is the burden of proponents of progressive cultural and racial politics to understand the complexities of the South, ... if we are to be Southernified, the process should involve the development of a lived interracialism, an inclusive sense of community and its importance in everyday life, a collective racial consciousness based on a shared historical memory of the nation's blood and darkness..."

By situating Africana Studies as a progressive political agenda, Kincheloe furthers a critical project that he has long advocated. In this, he joins the Africana/Diaspora Studies initiative that has been emerging for the past few decades; as diverse peoples of color respond to their multiple identities. In a 1999 essay, Kincheloe anticipated how what I call "white pain" (Gresson, 2004) figures in this larger global construction of identity. The current essay is a hopeful step in this identity shifting process; one in which Kincheloe seems to recognize himself as both creator and created. Through his own engagement of this duality, he stands as a model of a continuing dialectic: He is no stranger to "white pain"; yet he emerges as the "wounded healer" for remembering he is a son of the South. In him, as in President Carter, we meet men of remembrance who invite an enlarged racial—hence interracial—discourse.

The arguments put forth in this essay remain relevant not only for the remembrance factor. Currently, a malaise born of both economic and political shifts within the Academy has threatened Africana Studies and other area studies. Interestingly, Kincheloe's essay posits a less often articulated position in the face of real threats to Africana Studies by University politics: consider an interracial recovery. When whites join others in partnership in the dialogic enlargement of democracy and social justice, the multivocal and multifocal move to a more exciting, potentiated place begins. *Authority* assumes a different meaning and role in the dialogic discourse of social justice and democratic enlargement. In his career, Kincheloe saw the role of communicative approaches and values that aided both the learning of the given and inherited knowledge/truths, but also their revision, reconstruction, and reliving. As diverse "authors" introduce new or alternative ideas, perspectives, and lived experiences, these can be commented upon, in both validational and counter-authoritative ways. Kincheloe saw himself, and others, *bricoleurs*, engaging in teaching and learning using a variety of available and emergent materials: prescriptive discursive norms, situated, contingent, and collaborative projects were an ongoing part of who he had become at the height of his intellectual and critical presence.

## REFERENCES

CNN. (2009, September 17). *Carter again cites racism as factor in Obama's treatment*. Retrieved January 11, 2009, from http://www.cnn.com/2009/POLITICS/09/15/carter.obama/index.html

Gresson, A. D. (2004). *America's atonement: Racial pain, recovery rhetoric and the pedagogy of healing*. New York: Peter Lang Press.

Gresson, A. D. (1995). *The recovery of race in America*. Minneapolis, MN: University of Minnesota Press.

Herrnstein, R. J., & Murray, C. (1995). *The bell curve: Intelligence and class structure American life*. New York: Free Press.

Kincheloe, J. L. (1999). The struggle to define and reinvent whiteness: A pedagogical analysis. *College Literature*, 6(3), 162–195.

Kincheloe, J. L., Steinberg, S. R., Rodriguez, N. M., & Chennault, R. E. (Eds.). (1998). *White reign: Deploying whiteness in America*. New York: St. Martin's Press.

Kincheloe, J. L., Steinberg S. R., & Gresson, A. D. (Eds.). (1996). *Measured lies: The bell curve examined*. New York: St. Martin's Press.

Kincheloe, J. L., & Staley, G. (1983, July). Vietnam to Central America: A case of educational failure. *USA Today*, 122(2483), 30–32.

Tomlinson, S. (2003). Globalization, race, and education: continuity and change. *Journal of Education*, 4, 213–230.

Yang, L. (2002). Theorizing Asian America: On Asian American and postcolonial Asian diasporic women. *Intellectuals Journal of Asian American Studies*, 5, 139–178.

*The sci-fi movie Joe refers to in this article is still playing, and we are all in the cast. It was incredible to him that institutions of higher learning could blatantly insist that criticality was dangerous, subversive, and lacking in rigor. Moving from institution to institution, Joe was always re-surprised when his academic honeymoon would end (usually within a semester) and became a tenured marriage from hell. Aliens would rise their ugly heads out of the bodies of the formerly rayon-clad colleagues who had wined and dined him during his hiring process. The very peers who fought to bring him into Clemson, Florida International University, Penn State, Brooklyn College, and McGill University, were peeling their human skins off to reveal the positivistic school marms of faculties of education. Joe moved a lot, usually because he believed his good work, and that of his students, was being overshadowed by the negative notions harbored by many peers. Joe never played the victim, rather he understood that critical work is accompanied by unsettled, nervous reactions. Certainly, Henry learned that early in his career at Boston, and many who read this book are learning it even now. Originally expecting knowledge wars to stem from the Right, Joe found that even the most "liberal" appearing institution was usually a shill for the status quo. Yes, we are all in that sci-fi movie, the one that demonizes those who ask for social justice, equity, and democracy, and forces them to move on, trying to find a place just to do their thing. SS*

JOE L. KINCHELOE

# 15. CRITICAL PEDAGOGY AND THE KNOWLEDGE WARS OF THE TWENTY-FIRST CENTURY

We live in nasty and perilous times. Those of us in critical pedagogy cannot help but despair as we watch the U.S. and its Western collaborators instigate imperial wars for geopolitical positioning and natural resources, and mega-corporations develop and spend billions of dollars to justify economic strategies that simply take money from the weakest and poorest peoples of the world and transfer them to the richest people in North American and Europe. In this context, the politics of knowledge become a central issue in the educational and social domains of every nation in the world. The politics of knowledge firmly entrenched around the planet are characterized by a few rich individuals and transnational corporations controlling most of the "validated" data we can access. Thankfully, there is a rich source of counter-data on the Internet and several book publishers and journals—but students and other people are warned about the politicized nature of this information. Thus, many individuals are exposed over and over again to phony rationalizations for

k. hayes et al., (eds.), Key Work in Critical Pedagogy: Joe L. Kincheloe, 385–405.
© 2011 Sense Publishers. All rights reserved.

indefensible governmental, military, financial, and social actions of power wielders in the U.S. and its Western allies. The Iraqi War, as merely one example, is not simply a story about a brutal and unnecessary policy, but a chronicle of the way the knowledge war operates in the twenty-first century. Those who wage the war employ the authority of science and media to spread a plethora of great untruths about Iraq's danger to the world and the necessity of continuing military action against the "nation." As I write this, they deploy the same type of knowledge tactics against Iran. The power of such knowledge work is at times overwhelming as millions of individuals in the U.S. and around the world have been profoundly influenced by such misleading information. Those of us in critical pedagogy find it hard to believe that such lies and misrepresentations could still have credibility years after they had been exposed, but, just as an example, nearly one-third of the people in the contemporary U.S. still believe that Saddam Hussein's regime possessed WMDs, was responsible for 9–11, and had prepared to leave American cities under a mushroom cloud. Such a crazy politics of knowledge tells us that something is deeply wrong with not only the ethical behavior and sanity of power wielders, but that one of the most powerful weapons in their multidimensional and frightening arsenal is their ownership of much of the world's knowledge. In this context, contemporary standardized educational systems contribute to the imperial task as they pass along the official verities of the regime and promote its sociopolitical and economic interests. The focus of this essay involves analyzing the ways critical pedagogy might conceptualize and enact a response to the knowledge wars being waged against peoples in North America, Australia, New Zealand and Europe; marginalized peoples living in these regions; and the most destitute peoples living around the world.

## THE WEST WORKS TO GAIN MULTI-LEVEL SUPREMACY OVER THE REST OF THE WORLD

The politics of knowledge and the contemporary knowledge wars cannot be separated from the relationship between the epistemological, ontological, the political economic, and the ideological. All four of these domains constantly interact in a synergistic manner to shape the nature of the knowledge produced by Western power wielders in the contemporary era. Utilizing a crypto-positivistic, evidence-based science that excludes complexity; context; power; multiple modes of research design; the ever-changing, in-process nature of the phenomena of the social world; subjugated and indigenous knowledges from diverse social and geographical locales; and the multiple realities perceived and constructed by different peoples at divergent historical times and cultural places, dominant power brokers attempt with a great deal of success to regulate what people view as legitimate knowledge. There is no way around it; the task of the critical pedagogue as teacher, researcher, and knowledge worker is profoundly complex and demanding in our proto-fascist era. I hate to use the word *fascist* because of the accusations of overstatement that it will evoke, but at this historical point I sense that we can no longer avoid it.

The neo-liberal, market-driven, and crypto-fascist logic of the contemporary Western empire with its "recovered" forms of white supremacy, patriarchy, class politics, homophobia, and fundamentalist Christian intolerance represents a new "fall of Western civilization." We are all affected by the fact that as a culture "we have fallen and we can't get up," and in this context our critiques of hegemonic knowledges constitute just one aspect of a larger effort to "get well," to mend our psyches that have been broken in this social descent (Sardar, 1999; Nelson, 2000). As I visit North American schools and study the curricula taught in most of them, I am reminded yet again of the preparation of young pioneers for the empire.

The superiority of the European heritage, Christianity, and Western knowledges are now firmly re-entrenched. The notion that we might study the knowledges or entertain the perspectives of peoples from other cultures, religions, or ideological perspectives is quickly fading like the Morning Star as the sun rises over Fallujah. Along with geo-political, military, political economic and other forms of power, the power of knowledge (episto-power) plays its role in reinforcing these other forms of power by placing the various peoples of North American, Europe, and the rest of the world into hierarchical categories. Poor people, individuals from Diasporas from the most economically depressed parts of the world, and residents of the "developing countries" are positioned on these hierarchies as less intelligent, less civilized, and more barbaric than upper-middle class, white, Christian, and often male Westerners. The superiority of those who fall under the parasol of dominant positionality is made so obvious by educational and other social institutions that everyone knows where they fit on the status ladder. This knowing where one fits on the ladder does great harm—obviously to those who at the bottom rungs feel inferior—but also to those at the top rungs who develop a sense of privilege and superiority (Weiler, 2004). It is the charge of critical pedagogy to throw a monkey wrench into a system of knowledge—an episteme as Foucault labeled his regime of truth—that perpetuates such perspectives and the human suffering that accompanies them.

## DIVERSALITY: THE DIRE NEED FOR DIFFERENT PERSPECTIVES, FOR MULTIPLE FORMS OF KNOWLEDGE IN THE EFFORT TO EXPOSE AND RESIST THE NEW EMPIRE

A key task of critical pedagogy involves helping people understand the ideological and epistemological inscriptions on the ways of seeing promoted by the dominant power blocs of the West. In such work, criticalists uncover both old and new knowledges that stimulate our ethical, ideological, and pedagogical imagination to change our relationship with the world and other people. Concurrently, such critical labor facilitates the construction of a new mode of emancipation derived from our understandings of the successes and failures of the past and the present. Such an undertaking is essential to the planet's survival at this moment in history. In the last years of the first decade of the twenty-first century, the hegemonic politics of knowledge and the crypto-positivistic epistemology that is its conjoined twin are destroying the world.

As I write these words, I feel as if I've been magically positioned in a 1950s sci-fi movie in which the people of the earth mobilize to fight off their destruction. Of course, it is not the lizard people from the planet Enyon that threaten us; it is the power wielders of the West with their free market economic policies, geo-political military actions, and the episto-rays of consciousness constructing information that we must confront. Dominant crypto-positivist modes of these episto-rays are the most difficult of the tools of hegemonic power to recognize. They travel under the cover of phrases such as "scientific proof" and other high status monikers. Flying under the public radar of perception, they justify murder in the name of national security and ecological devastation in the name of economic growth.

Such "knowledge weapons" help deaden our ethical senses and compassion for those harmed by transnational economic scams, and Eurocentric and Americocentric ways of seeing that subvert the development of a critical consciousness. Indeed, the episto-rays move us to support—under the flag of high standards—schools that obscure more than enlighten.

Our critical pedagogical effort to thwart these power plays, I believe, involves engaging in a transformative multilogicality. By this, I refer to gaining the capability and the resolve to explore the world not from the Western imperial vantage point but from diverse perspectives—often standpoints forged by pain, suffering, and degradation. The imperial, neo-liberal rationalization for the construction of a planetary empire ruled by the U.S. and its collaborators is grotesquely disturbing to hundreds of millions of people around the world. Given the flagrance of the imperial abuses and the perversity of the Iraqi War, more and more Westerners are beginning to understand the brutality of the military violence, the material disparity, and the ecological harm that such policies and knowledges create. The empire's neo-liberal adulation of market-driven modes of sociopolitical and educational organization shapes its efforts to adjust children and youth to their imperial roles as human capital and cannon fodder for the wars of geo-political advantage and resources demanded by the needs of the imperial machine. Key to the multilogical critical pedagogy advocated here is the notion that while theoretical and knowledge frameworks help elucidate phenomena, they also work to mystify our understanding of them. This is one of the reasons that I have worked so hard to develop the concept of the bricolage delineated by Norman Denzin and Yvonna Lincoln (2000) in a critical context (Kincheloe, 2001a; Kincheloe, & Berry, 2004; Kincheloe, 2005a). Bricolage involves the process of rigorously rethinking and reconceptualizing multidisciplinary research. Ethnography, textual analysis, semiotics, hermeneutics, psychoanalysis, phenomenology, historiography, discourse analysis combined with philosophical analysis, literary analysis, aesthetic criticism, and theatrical and dramatic ways of observing and making meaning typically constitute the methodological bricolage. Employing these multi-perspectival (Kellner, 1995) dynamics, bricoleurs transcend the parochial blinders of mono-disciplinary approaches and open new windows onto the world of research and knowledge production.

In the contemporary domain, bricolage is usually understood to involve the process of employing these methodological strategies when the need arises in fluid research situations. In the critical articulation of the bricolage, I contend that qualitative researchers move beyond mere interdisciplinarity as it refers to research designs and methodologies, and move to a new conceptual domain. Bricoleurs employing a variety of research methodologies must also employ a variety of theoretical insights coming obviously from a deep understanding of critical theory as well as feminist theory, social theory from diverse geographical places, anti-racist theories, class theories, post-structuralism, complexity and chaos theories, queer theory, and post/anti-colonial theories. This, of course, is a lot to ask of critical scholars/activists, but perilous times demand great commitment. Such multidisciplinary insight and theoretical dexterity helps researchers not only gain a more rigorous (not in the positivistic sense) view of the world but also a new mode of researcher self-awareness.

Critical bricoleurs understand the diverse contexts in which any knowledge producer operates. Transformative researchers struggle to uncover the insidious ways that dominant power blocs work to shape the knowledge they produce, they begin to better understand the relationship between any researcher's ways of seeing and the social location of her personal history. As the bricoleur appreciates the ways that research is a power-inscribed activity, she abandons the quixotic quest for some naïve mode of realism. At this point, the bricoleur concentrates on the expose of the multiple ways power harms individuals and groups and the way a knowledge producer's location in the web of reality helps shape the production, interpretation, and consumption of data. At every space, the critical bricoleur discerns new ways that a hegemonic epistemology in league with a dominant power-soaked politics of knowledge operates to privilege the privileged and further marginalize the marginalized.

In the context of the critical bricolage, the power of difference, of diverse perspectives, and of insights coming from different locales in the web of reality reveal their significance. All of these worldviews—especially when they are juxtaposed in dialogue with one another—contribute to our understanding of the world in general and the oppression that leads to human suffering in particular. Such diversal knowledges enhance our socio-political and educational imagination and our ability to imagine new ways of seeing and being and interacting with other people and the physical world. I believe that a multilogical critical pedagogy can lead the way to these new social, ideological, epistemological, ontological, and cognitive domains. So-called "primitive peoples" were much more influenced by the unconscious dimension of the human mind than modern Western peoples. In many ways such Western distancing from the subconscious may lead to forms of disconnection with the world and its people that undermine the psychological and cognitive well being of contemporary, highly educated people from dominant cultural backgrounds.

In the engagement with diverse knowledges promoted by the critical bricolage, critical pedagogues attempt to reengage with these ancient indigenous knowledges in the process integrating them with political economic, socio-cultural, and pedagogical insights. The outcomes can be profoundly transformative on both an individual and a social scale. Indeed, the thanocentric impulses of contemporary Western ideological orientations and actions demand a form of social psychoanalysis (Kincheloe and Pinar, 1991) that can repair the social unconsciousness of the West. Diversal knowledges—ancient indigenous and other types—can help in this therapeutic process. As contemporary Westerners stare into what Mr. Lahey from the Canadian TV series "Trailer Park Boys" would call the "shit abyss," there is a great need for alternative ontologies, epistemologies, cosmologies, and ideologies to which they can compare their present views of self and world. In the interaction with the diverse ways of thinking, Westerners and Western educators can begin to develop an eros to counter the dead end thanatos of the empire.

## DIVERSALITY WITH A CRITICAL FOUNDATION

In an era of imperial wars and concomitant information control to elicit support for such "preemptive strikes," critical pedagogues need to develop knotholes in the center field fence through which teachers, students, and other individuals can view unregulated pictures of socio-cultural reality. The public's consciousness is shaped just as much by what is not perceived as it is by what is. This is why diversal knowledges are so important in this time and place. Critical pedagogues explore data from Asia, Africa. Latin America, the Islamic World, the oppressed in North America, Australia, New Zealand, and Europe, and indigenous communities around the world. In this context, we attempt to construct a political economic ecology of knowledges that lead to new ways of seeing and being. Simply in the act of attending to and learning from the insights of marginalized peoples, we operate as allies in their struggle against the oppression of Western power blocs. Such support cannot be separated from the necessity of white, upper middle class, male Westerners to step back and examine the effects of their own immersion in such a politics of knowledge.

As we understand the compelling perceptions of indigenous peoples, we can gain new vantage points on the sentient and mysterious life force that inhabits both our being and the cosmos surrounding us. The insights peoples from diverse cultural and historical locales in the web of reality have accessed about this life force in unconscious and other states of consciousness should be a source of fascination and study by scholars from a wide variety of academic domains, critical pedagogy being merely one of many. Yet, this often does not happen because of the crypto-positivistic stigma attached to the exploration of such yet to be understood domains. The intelligence of the earth—which may simply be a pale reflection of the intelligence of the universe—is not something that mainstream scholars are ready to discuss. The insights we may gain from connecting to such a larger cognitive force—insights often appreciated by indigenous peoples more than Western scholars—can become one of the most important dimensions of emancipatory knowledge work of the future. This is one of the dimensions of the value of the work of Humberto Maturana and Francisco Varela (1987) in their work on life as a cognitive process (see Kincheloe, 2004a for an expansion of the relation of this work to criticality).

Thus, again and again we confront the power of difference, alterity, and diversality by pushing critical theory and critical pedagogy to a more intellectually rigorous and in turn praxiologically powerful position. A critically complex and diversal critical pedagogy is simply better equipped to confront those waging a knowledge war against the world in the twenty-first century. The power of diverse perspectives is, thankfully, recognized by more and more scholars who appreciate the notion that forms of cultural renewal can come from places long viewed as irrelevant and peripheral to Western power wielders. In this diversal domain, we become more capable of critically scrutinizing the process of imperial political economic, geopolitical, and epistemological globalization. In this process, criticalists also monitor the role that all levels of education play in this imperial process in order to develop more pragmatic strategies for transformative intervention. Elementary and secondary schools as well as colleges and universities must become "trading zones" of intercultural exchange and global meeting places. This, of course, is a central goal of the Paulo and Nita Freire International Project for Critical Pedagogy at McGill University. As cultural and epistemological crossroads, the purpose of schools in a global world would forever be transformed. The politics of knowledge would become a central dimension of any curriculum, and the contrast and comparison of different cultural perspectives on a wide array of issues would emerge as a familiar aspect of the study of any topic. In such a transformed diversal education, critical pedagogues would establish working relationships with scholars and schools around the world. Such educators would seek the help of scholars from educational institutions in developing nations who have already begun to challenge hegemonic systems of Western knowledge. The curricula these innovative scholars have developed by incorporating subjugated knowledges of their own and other cultures can profoundly help critical educators from all parts of the world rethink, diversalize, and revitalize existing pedagogies (Nandy, 2000; Weiler, 2004; Orelus, 2007).

## THE CRITICAL BRICOLAGE VIS-À-VIS DIVERSALITY: ENHANCING AGENCY IN A SOCIALLY CONSTRUCTED WORLD

Such proposals represent a sea change in the everyday teaching, learning, and knowledge production of all educational institutions. The moribund status quo is no longer acceptable—not that it ever was. The bricolage in this context becomes a central research/epistemological/theoretical motif for incorporating the diversal intersections of knowledges that would be welcomed into schools of all types. The hidden positivism that insidiously shapes so much of Western curriculum, instruction, and research is remarkably uninterested in the contexts and processes of which a phenomenon is a part—dynamics that I and many other researchers find essential to the study and understanding of any topic imaginable. It should not be surprising that insight into the contexts and processes of which phenomena are a part often help explain the role that dominant power blocs play in shaping them. Thus, the dismissal of context and process is often an insidious and effective way of hiding the influence of dominant power and maintaining the status quo. A critical form of hermeneutics and textual analysis counters such cryptopositivist tactics, using context and process to undermine the easy production of *universal* knowledge of the reductionist tradition of research. When phenomena are viewed within the contexts and processes that have shaped both them and the consciousness of the individual observing them, a far more complex picture begins to emerge. An awareness of the contexts and processes in which a phenomenon takes place and the contexts and processes in which an observer of the phenomenon is located provides us profoundly divergent understandings and perspectives on the entity. In the knowledge wars of the contemporary era, such epistemological insights are "dangerous," as they expose the way episto-power operates to exclude diversality from curricula and public knowledge (Clark, 2001; Marcel, 2001).

Employing the bricolage vis-à-vis diversality will inevitably promote paradox where there is certainty, open-endedness where there is finality, multiple perspectives where there is one correct answer, insight into ideological and cultural inscription where there is objectivity, and defamiliarization where there is comfort and security. In a sense the type of knowledge work produced by the bricolage vis-à-vis diversality creates research narratives without endings. Closure simply can't take place when we know that phenomena are always in process, and that as times and locales change the ways we understand them also changes. Thus, our critical knowledge work offers insights from this point in time and from this particular ideological/cultural perspective. Such a positioning of our work does not weaken it—to the contrary, it makes it stronger, more in touch with the ways the world, the mind, epistemology, and ontology operate.

When we view a Western social organization for the first time, for example, from the perspective of a marginalized individual who has experienced a form of existential death at the hands of the institution, we have crawled through a new conceptual wormhole in our effort to make sense of the phenomenon in question. Such an insight destroys any notion of closure we might have had. In these situations we have been touched by Walter Benjamin's Angel of History in a way that forever changes us, the knowledge we generate, and the reasons we produce it in the first place. This is how the bricolage vis-à-vis diversality works—it refuses to allow us to be content with monological and monocultural perspectives. It places abrasive grains of epistemological sand in our pants and makes us uncomfortable with reductionism and its consequences.

A key anti-hegemonic dimension of the bricolage vis-à-vis diversality is that it alerts us to the ways contexts, processes, and relationships shape both the phenomena of the world and consciousness itself. This is a powerful and life-changing insight that must always be coupled with the appreciation that humans have agency—they do not have to be pawns that passively submit to the demands of dominant power. As many critical social theorists have maintained, this agency doesn't mean that people can just simply do what they want. These contexts, processes, and relationships—always inscribed by dominant forms of power—construct a playing field on which human agents operate. Thus, human activity is influenced by such dynamics but not determined. As individuals begin to understand this power-related and socially constructed dimension of the world, they sometimes feel like refugees in relation to the hegemonic cosmos to which they can never return. Critical pedagogy, of course, maintains that we don't have to live like refugees, as we re-construct the world and create new, shared spaces with individuals from diverse places around the world.

In any critical orientation, researchers, educators, and activists always have to be careful of inadvertently endorsing structural modes of determinism. The failure to recognize human agency in the struggle for justice and in the knowledge wars of the contemporary era is to create nihilistic forms of pedagogy and cultural work. The critical bricolage viewed in this context is literally the toolbox from which critical teachers and cultural workers draw to better understand the hegemonic mystifications of dominant power blocs in the contemporary world. While existing tools can be and are used for valuable effect, an evolving notion of criticality (see Kincheloe, 2008) attempts to create the most rigorous and useful forms of knowledge work and social activism possible. All critical teachers and cultural workers must become adept hermeneuts who hone their ability to make sense of the diverse and complex forces at work in divergent situations. Concurrently, they gain the ability to identify and discern the effects of where they are situated in diverse social and political frameworks. In this same interpretive context, critical bricoleurs acting on their understanding of diversality deploy their interpretive skills in the effort to make sense of the way members of dominant power blocs from race, class, gender, sexual, colonial, and religious perspectives see the world and rationalize their often oppressive actions. In previous work on race, class, and gender (Kincheloe and Steinberg, 1997) on whiteness and racism (Kincheloe, Steinberg, Rodriguez, and Chennault, 1998), patriarchy (Kincheloe, 2001b), and dominant economic constructs (Kincheloe and Steinberg, 2007), my colleagues and I have attempted to understand not only the nature of oppression and its effects on the oppressed, but also the knowledge frameworks and cognitive/affective matrixes that shape both the consciousness and actions of members of dominant groups whose deeds often perpetuate subjugation. In this complex context, critical bricoleurs always examine such sociopolitical and pedagogical dynamics within the interaction of relationship and individuality (Steinberg, 2006).

There is no universal formula for such interaction—indeed, each encounter is idiosyncratic and erratic. Although we may recognize tendencies, we cannot count on regularity or consistency in such complex encounters. We must study each situation as a unique occurrence with diverse players, divergent contexts and processes, and distinct outcomes. The critical bricolage vis-à-vis diversality presents a transformative, anti-hegemonic view zealous in its effort to address and end oppression but concurrently nuanced in its understanding of the slippery relationship between agency and structure. Human beings do not fade away into the ice fog of power structures. The process of social construction is always a coconstructive process as individual and structure create one another. As agential beings who make our way through the ice fog, individuals who grasp the critical complex insights to power, agency, knowledge, and action delineated here, criticalists understand that they have to rethink what they are going to do the rest of their lives. Previously operating in only limited dimensions of reality, they had not been faced with the ethical and ideological decisions now placed before them in the multilogical domains they have entered. At this moment they realize that there is nothing easy about living in a critical manner, about living critical pedagogy (Faulconer and Williams, 1985; Livezey, 1988; Marcel, 2001).

## THE POLITICS OF KNOWLEDGE IN THE EMPIRE: THE CONTINUING CRISIS OF KNOWLEDGE

Since the time of Rene Descartes in the seventeenth century, many Western knowledge producers have held up their notion of reason and research as the one pathway to enlightenment and emancipation from ignorance. In the contemporary era, the dominant imperial politics of knowledge want to recover this one universal pathway to truth via the reassertion of positivist logic. Evidence-based research has become a code word for a kind of crypto-positivism that, like a CIA operative, always maintains "plausible deniability" that it is not really positivism. As referenced earlier, the decontextualizing dimensions of this crypto-positivism often works effectively to uphold the status quo, a Bush-Harper-Howard reality. These politics of knowledge become even more important in an era where privatization and corporatization of education becomes a key dimension of the public conversation about schooling and more and more of an actual reality.

In higher education, the self-direction and independence of colleges and universities have already been compromised by corporate influences. Every day that passes witnesses new forms of dependency on corporate support and funding as governments back away from fiscal support of higher education. The fact that a pharmaceutical company pays for research on the effectiveness of particular drugs is part of the context that often shapes the nature of the knowledge that is produced. If researchers know that their multi-million dollar corporately-funded center may be closed down if they produce data at odds with the fiscal interests of the funding agency, they may find it hard not to be influenced by such pressure. Knowledge is never free and unconnected to diverse power blocs because it is always produced as part of a web of power relationships. In corporate hyperreality, these power matrices become even more complex and interwoven into every dimension of the social order with the development of diverse knowledge technologies that disperse corporatized data everyday around the clock. Thus, the ghosts of the new and improved Western empire constantly haunt us with both cognitively directed information and affectively aimed images and representations designed to win our consent to the needs of capital and dominant power. The hobgoblins of the imperial mind are omnipresent and they have become so adept at producing hegemonic data that most individuals are unable to recognize ideologically charged information when they consume it. The twenty-first century imperial politics of knowledge flies under the radar like a B-2 Spirit stealth bomber dropping epistemological "payloads" on domestic and foreign targets.

In the everyday life of universities, these critical insights into the politics of knowledge are still not a typical aspect of the conversation about the institutional research mission. The idea that the production and mediation of information in higher education is a highly politicized process demanding careful monitoring of the ideological interests involved is still unwelcome in academic circles. Most researchers, politicians, and educators still live in a state of denial about the political dimension to knowledge production and the relationship between validated information and the international purveyors of economic power. One is inseparable from the other. The sooner the politics of knowledge become a central aspect of all dimensions of research, politics, and education, the sooner we may be able to leave the global Gitmo of ideological mystification in which we are all held captive (Livesey, 1988; Weiler, 2004; Smith, 2006).

Academics, from Jean-Francois Lyotard's (1979/1984) *The postmodern condition: A report on knowledge* to diverse contemporary analyses of the nature of knowledge production, have been talking about the crisis of knowledge for decades. Lyotard linked the flood of knowledge produced in academic institutions of the 1970s to the breakdown of the Western "modernist" grand narratives. In a diverse world such narratives, Lyotard argued, had outlived their usefulness and were incapable of producing data that was not inscribed by Western epistemological traditions. While Lyotard was quite correct in his understanding of the limitations of Western knowledge work, he might not have anticipated how dramatically the crisis would intensify in the twenty-first century. With the expansion of the power and concentration of capital over the last couple of decades, scholarship and social movements have not kept up with the ways that power frameworks insidiously inscribe knowledge coming from diverse social locations (Weiler, 2004; Kincheloe, 2005b). Neither have those who serve as the guardians of the quality and rigor of research developed satisfactory ways of monitoring the production of knowledge under these ideological conditions.

In my own experience, many editors of prestigious journals in a variety of disciplines have no idea what my critical colleagues and I are talking about when we make reference to the ideological conditions under which particular knowledge is produced. Such guardians of the epistemological status quo often do not understand the episto-political factors at work in their own journals. Their ideological naiveté grants insight into the ways that critical analyses of the insidious impact of dominant power on the research act are not commonly taught in research courses in the physical sciences, the social sciences, and the humanities.

When such issues of power and knowledge fall outside the purview of the professional awareness of scholars sufficiently prominent to edit prestigious journals, we know that a regressive, hegemonic politics of knowledge is accomplishing its goals. Those corporate advocates of privatization and empire may not be winning in Iraq, but they are certainly finding success in their preemptive strikes in the knowledge wars.

The politics of imperial knowledge will continue to exacerbate the twenty first century crisis of knowledge until Western scholars, politicos, and educators begin to understand the intimacy between dominant power blocs and information as well as the cultural hegemony of monological Western epistemologies and the data they validate. Our call for diversal knowledges reemerges in this context. Until we understand the ways that power not only validates but rank orders the knowledges produced by individuals with differing amounts of academic and cultural capital, an epistemological hegemony legitimizing a political economic hegemony will only grow more acute and inhumane. Indeed, it will perpetuate and legitimate unacceptable forms of human suffering. The alienation contemporary people experience from the physical, historical, ethical, political, ecological, cosmological, ontological, and epistemological contexts of which they are intimately embedded will also continue to deepen in this episteme. The crisis of imperial knowledge leads to harder stuff, more intense problems for more and more of the planet's inhabitants.

## THE FAILURE OF SOCIAL SCIENCE: THE POSSIBILITIES OF NEW WAYS OF SEEING

After all the paradigmatic debate and discord surrounding the production of knowledge, the nature of epistemology and ontology, and nature of research design in the social, psychological, and educational domains, many of the issues addressed here about power, justice, empire, and the socio-cultural location of knowledge are simply not addressed in the twenty-first century. Much of the analysis involving paradigmatic typologies—e.g., positivism, post-positivism, constructivism, interpretivism, criticality, feminism, poststructuralism, etc.—have failed to adequately deal with these concerns. The effort to bring a form of crypto-positivism back to the socio-educational sciences is currently successful with the support of many Western governments and corporate interests. It will ultimately fail, however, for many reasons. One of the most surprising of these reasons is that such a recovery of positivism on many levels dismisses what future historians may see as the most important advances in twentieth-century science: the advent of complexity from Einstein's relativity (see Kincheloe, Steinberg, and Tippins, 1999), quantum physics, Heisenberg's uncertainty principle, and complexity and chaos theory and the related science of emergent properties coming from the biological and psychological work of Humberto Maturana and Francisco Varela.

Instead of focusing on the power of this complexity and multilogicality of scientific pursuit, contemporary crypto-positivists have re-adjusted their lens in a reductionist manner. Rather than taking a cue from the insight into complexity to be drawn from the aforementioned and much other scientific work, the crypto-positivists have concentrated on the isolation of what they believe to be fixed and intractable social, psychological, and educational phenomena. The idea that things-in-the-world are in flux, always changing, in the process of becoming that is drawn from the move to complexity has been swept under the epistemological and ontological rug. Thus, a neo-mechanism has emerged that fears the recognition of epistemological, ontological, and even cosmological changes demanded by complexity and diversity. If the physical, biological, social, psychological, and education cosmos is more like an indivisible, at-first-glance imperceptible matrix of experiences in process and ever evolving relationships then a reductionist science simply doesn't work. Indeed, such a neo-positivist view of knowledge provides tobacco companies, pesticide manufacturers, pharmaceutical producers, standardized test makers, and all their political beneficiaries with a way of getting the answers they want from a "validated" (but corrupted) science.

For reductionist researchers, such words sting. The possibility of rethinking the nature of how we approach social, psychological, and educational science is a disturbing consideration for neo-positivist researchers. Obviously there are researchers who fall into the reductionist camp who are simply naïve and do not understand the epistemological, ontological, ideological, and political economic dynamics of their work. Concurrently, there are those who make conscious decisions to sell their souls to tainted money, in the process doing the bidding of their benefactors and dancing to the devil's fiddle. As I write these words, I know I will not win the Miss Congeniality award in the world of research. I want to make clear I am not lumping all researchers who disagree with me about the complex and complicated domain of knowledge production into the categories of naïve scholars or playmates of the corporate devils. Obviously, there are brilliant, socially conscious researchers who profoundly disagree with me and go about doing first-rate research in ways very different than mine. Still, the epistemological and ideological bastardization of research practices in a variety of domains is a reality that cannot be ignored.

In addition to the complexity-based scientific traditions I have previously referenced, numerous other researchers over the last century have laid a foundation for many of the arguments presented here about the failures of social, psychological, and educational inquiry. John Dewey's (1916) challenge to positivism in the first decades of the twentieth century with his epistemological and ontological questions about the reality of intractable and timeless truths has influenced so many researchers and educators, me included. Obviously, in a critical theoretical essay the work of Max Horkheimer (1974), Theodor Adorno (1973), Herbert Marcuse (1955), and Walter Benjamin (1968) from the Frankfurt School from the 1920s to the 1960s is central in understanding the oppressive uses to which positivist modes of inquiry have been put. Antonio Gramsci's (1988) work in Mussolini's fascist prisons in the 1920s and 1930s against hegemony and his insights into the transformative role of the organic intellectual are key aspects of the critical research tradition.

Of course, the anti-colonial revolutionary ideas articulated so profoundly by Franz Fanon (1963) and Albert Memmi (1965) that so powerfully influenced the emergence of the Civil Rights Movement, the women's movement, the queer rights movement and the challenges to reductionist scholarly knowledge these collectives inspired constitute a central thread in development of critical knowledge work in the twenty-first century. Indeed, the work of those involved with the post-discourses and postcolonialism are central dimensions of the body of insights on which contemporary criticalists draw. Running this work through the filter of feminist scholars such as bell hooks (1981), Gayatri Spivak (1987), Patricia Hill Collins (1991), Vandana Shiva (1993), and Sandra Harding (1986) to name only a few, a powerful multidimensional canon of critique begins to emerge.

This canon—including the previously mentioned scholars and many, many other critical knowledge workers around the world—have generally argued that Western reductionist sciences have rarely produced knowledge that was in the best interests of the casualties of Western colonialism and numerous other forms of racial, class-based, gender, sexual, religious, and physical ability-related oppression. These aforementioned scholars all understood from diverse cultural, theoretical, and epistemological perspectives that something was egregiously wrong with the reductionist knowledges produced by Western and Western-influenced scholars. Providing only narrow strips of decontextualized information on a topic, such knowledges often missed the larger epistemological and ideological forest for the cultural trees in front of them. In such a knowledge cosmos, great damage was and continues to be done to those in the most vulnerable situations. The consistency of such scientific damage over the decades is disconcerting, as too many scholars/researchers have failed to learn the lessons the previously mentioned knowledge producers taught. The knowledge wars never seem to end.

As the knowledge wars continue, the U.S./Western empire continues to fall deeper and deeper into the epistemological, ideological, ethical, cultural, sociopolitical, psychological, and pedagogical abyss. The machine metaphors of Western Cartesian-Newtonian-Baconian epistemology and ontology persist in the work of the crypto-positivists and the dead universe they promote. Individuals reared in an educational domain grounded on a thanocentric cosmology struggle to existentially survive, reaching out to fundamentalist Christianity, Judaism, Islam, New Age mysticism, or the contents of an ever-growing pharmacopoeia to "enliven," to bring something transcendent into their daily lives. While many of these individuals are shielded from educational experiences that would help them articulate their alienation, they intuitively sense that there is something crucial missing from the world machine metaphor permeating the socio-cultural, psychological, and political dimensions of their lived worlds. Thus, understandably, they are put off by political discourse, rigorous theological inquiry, and education as it generally exists in the contemporary era. They are searching for meaning and engaging affective experiences. Such dynamics are generally not to be found in these domains. At least fundamentalist religion provides affective stimulation in a world where the "experts" too often promote deadening, thanocentric "expertise." Yet at the same time this neo-Marcusean thano-virus morphs into its twenty-first century configuration, we know that there is an alternative to such ways of seeing and being in the world. While by no means does criticality offer an "answer" to ultimate human questions or "salvation" in any sense of the term, it does provide us a different and *less mad path* than the one being followed and promoted by many Westerners and their dominant social institutions. Make no mistake, human beings are existentially condemned to a life without final answers and ultimate revelations of meaning—that is just part of life on earth. We have to simply get used to the uncertainty and ambiguity of the human condition.

As we accept the inevitability of uncertainty and ambiguity in light of epistemological, ontological, and cosmological complexity, we can also begin to explore with the help of the critical bricolage vis-à-vis diversality an alternative view of the nature of the cosmos and our role in it. Grounded on a critical theoretical commitment to social justice, anti-oppressive ways of being, and new forms of connectedness and radical love, we can help set in motion an analysis of the universe not as a lifeless machine but as a living cognitive process that is changeable and ever connected to human consciousness. Most great theological traditions have at some point in their history pondered this notion of cosmological intelligence, but now it is becoming a more important dimension of complexity-grounded physical sciences—physics and the life sciences in particular. Here life is connected to the cognitive ingenuity embedded in the cosmos. Here creativity and historically significant work become important in an ontology of becoming. In this living universe, the inner world of consciousness is never unconnected to physical cosmos we see around us (Prigogine and Stengers, 1984; Prigogine, 1996). Developing a variety of sociopolitical, economic, ethical, aesthetic, cognitive, and educational ways to put these ideas into action is the challenge of the twenty-first century—a charge central to our survival.

Thus, the more we know about positivism and its contemporary hidden strain, the better able we are to get beyond a static existence and more into a dynamic and erotic becoming. In addition, such knowledge empowers us to understand that positivism is not misguided simply because it presents a deceptive picture of the physical and social worlds. As if that wasn't enough, positivism and the culture it constructs around it are grounded on an indefensible epistemology, ontology, and cosmology—of course, I could add axiology, teleology, and ethics to this list as well. Indeed, positivism's view of the nature of humanness and life itself is highly problematic. Mechanistic, positivistic ways of viewing the world and ourselves has led and is leading us down a primrose path to great human suffering and planetary destruction. In the twenty-first century Imperial Court of Corporate Greed and Knowledge Control, criticalists must be the ones who expose the corruption and deception.

As critical pedagogues we must gain the ability to look at the world anew and ask completely different questions about it—questions that expose what's going on at diverse levels of reality and the way these events influence the lived world. It is only at this juncture that we can produce knowledges that alert the world to the understanding that "reality" is not exactly what it appears to be. Crypto-positivists are trapped in a never-ending game of three hand monty with its delusions of "normal" ways of seeing that use the name of neutrality to conceal the machinations of power. Using our multiperspectival methodologies, we begin to reframe our windows on the world in a way that allows us not only to view diverse dimensions of reality in different ways but that also permits to resituate the problems that confront us. As I look at the way, for example, the U.S. and many of its Western allies have dealt with Iran over the last several decades, I appreciate multiple ways of seeing the web of colonial and political economic relationships that has shaped mainstream knowledge production and policies toward the nation. It is absurd to ignore this web of interactions that have led us to this particular point in diplomatic history. The ever-worsening relations between the U.S. and Iran represent a failure of imperial ambitions, economic greed, and ways of producing knowledge that help us understand the larger dynamics at work in this situation (see Kincheloe, 2004 for an expansion of these ideas). Thus, we fall back into our crypto-positivist trap of limited ways of seeing. Critical pedagogy with its critical bricolage vis-à-vis diversality in its concern with multiple perspectives and divergent forms of power identifies the normalizing voices that "naturalize" dominant perspectives and invalidate the views of the "other," the marginalized. The ability of positivism to exclude a wide variety of information and experiences from consideration is one of the keys to its success as an invaluable partner to the dominant power blocs over the past couple of centuries. Crypto-positivism continues this tradition undercover and more effectively in the twenty-first century wars. Critical pedagogy in this unfortunate state of affairs delivers a jolt to dominant epistemologies and the empire's politics of knowledge (Falconer and Williams, 1987; Livezey, 1988; Pickering, 1999; Nelson, 2000).

## LOST: LOSING CONNECTION EVEN IN THE AGE OF THE WORLD WIDE WEB – OUR MISPLACED SENSE OF PURPOSE

No matter how much traditional modes of science have learned about the physical world, humans are still children in the effort to understand the workings of the cosmos. In the world of physics and biology—just to mention a couple of physical scientific disciplines—there are so many things about the structure and workings of the universe as well as the nature of the life process that elude experts. The same could be said of any scientific domain, where the notion of interconnection and purpose gives way to positivism's ontological delusion of separateness—of things-in-themselves, not things-in-connection or things-in-relationship. It takes ideological and intellectual fortitude to challenge the knowledge warriors of crypto-positivism. We know they will hit back every time with challenges to the legitimacy of one's scholarly or cultural work.

Young criticalists must prepare themselves for attacks from those who would deny them tenure, question the purpose of their pedagogy, use their work in criticality as exhibits of their potential criminality in trials and legal proceedings, and publicize their efforts in public media as dangerous challenges to community values and Western civilization itself (all of these are actual examples). Indeed, critical pedagogy is not for the faint of heart. I can't help but find nasty humor in mainstream scholars telling criticalists to quit using provocative language (such as the kind I'm using right now), while they destroy the lives of critical scholars or stand silently by while some of the previously referenced assaults take place. But to be provocative, this is often the modus operandi of the academic bourgeoisie who many times have no problem with people destroying other people's lives and careers as long as the demolition is carried out with a low affect, a quiet voice, and a faint smile on one's face.

I fervently believe in the importance of education and the research mission of the university. Such pedagogy and knowledge work help shape the consciousness of people both directly and indirectly connected to educational institutions. If such work were not important, there wouldn't be so many efforts to counter the work of criticalists. Thus, in an era of knowledge wars, the contested space of critical pedagogy and the knowledge it produces takes on a consequence greater than before. In the purposeless world of crypto-positivism, the effort to address human suffering and the power asymmetries that continue to expand or the consideration of critical notions of affective investment and radical love are quite out of place. Such commitments can be held in private, but they have no place in the objective and covert world of crypto-positivism. Critical research takes place outside the matrix of global domination and, in this locale, works to expose and respond to the dominant power wielders' brutal operations justified under the flag of verified truth (Pickering, 1999; Smith, 2006; Monchinski, 2007). In the positivist universe, the notion of critical transformation of unacceptable social conditions is not relevant to those researchers who operate around such horror.

Critical researchers have a passion for social justice in research that transcends reductionistic modes of distancing and disinterestedness. This means that we must challenge forms of knowledge that are presented to us as value-free. Concurrently, we must also challenge the removal of humanness from objectivist knowledges that are deployed in the world. I have long been fascinated by the use of the passive voice in positivistic research, e.g., the Lwiindi ceremony of the people (Tonga tribe of Zambia) was observed with the natives dancing and giving thanks to the gods that provided a good harvest. In such a construction the human observer, the researcher, is erased in the same way a physical scientist would write in her protocols that 88 mls of sulfuric acid was added to 1.3g of mixed nitroesters of nitrobenzyl alcohols. In both examples no human dimension of the research activity was present to contaminate the objective description of the Lwiindi ceremony or the chemical process. No matter how oblivious the Western researchers may have been to the Tonga people's ways of seeing and being, they were providing an objectively true account of the harvest ritual.

What many critical, postcolonial, and indigenous researchers have of course often found in ethnographic research of this variety from every conceivable part of the world is that the original investigators had completely missed the point of the cultural practice in question. The information they provided was sometimes humorous and always offensive to the peoples under scrutiny. As Dakota Sioux singer/ songwriter Floyd "Red Crow" Westerman wrote in his song, "Here Come the Anthros," the anthropologists flock to the reservation to study "their feathered freaks with funded money in their [the anthropologists'] hands." None of the money, however, Westerman writes later in the song, ever goes to the Native peoples. The purpose of such culturally oblivious, positivist-inscribed research was not to help indigenous peoples throw off the shackles of colonial or neo-colonial bondage but to provide an objective report about them.

Even in epistemological domains such as generalizability of data, the positivistic lack of purpose and the removal of humanness exhibit themselves in harmful ways. The generalizability of research involves taking that which is learned from inquiry and utilizing it in another situation. Thus, what researchers ascertain in one situation is applied to the larger population. The point in the generalization process is that which is ascertained from one population and applied to another in social, psychological, and educational science always implicates human beings in at least two different settings. The researcher simply can't remove human beings from this process. In order for generalizability to be achievable, the human agents in the new situation must be just like those in the first inquiry. Given the specific contextual construction of all human actors, it appears profoundly difficult to exchange a person in the original study with a person in the larger populace. Research that takes humanness seriously cannot take on faith the interchangeability of people coming from the two sets of subjects. Thus in this case, the removal of humanness in the name of objectivity and rigor ends up undermining the quality of the data produced (Livesey, 1988; Geeland, 1996; Tobin, forthcoming).

Such a positivist science may be incapable of adequately dealing with even the most uncomplicated dimensions of lived experience in a way that provides not only unprecedented insights into social, psychological, or educational phenomena but also useful knowledges that can improve human life. Positivism is far more comfortable exploring fragments of lived experience rather than wholes, interconnections, and meanings. The all-important scholarly act of making sense of data is more a poetic activity than a positivistic scientific one. Deriving the living meaning out of human science is a profoundly difficult task that demands exploring the micro-experiences experiences through diverse theoretical frameworks to figure out how they might be interpreted (van Manen, 1991; Lloyd and Smith, 2006; Pinar, 2006). This process is never simple and will never yield some facile mode of certainty. Any physical or human science that is grounded on the quest for certainty must remove phenomena of the world and human beings from its design because such things-in-the-world are always in process and cannot by definition be described with final certainty. In the next moment, in the next interaction they engage, they are by definition something different. The metaphysics of positivism will always lead it astray.

This complex, in process, poetic dimension of all research will not be discussed in the Parliament of Positivism—the gag rule has been invoked. The poetic power of the critical researcher's imagination is a crucial dimension of difference-making research. Such creativity always stands in awe of the autopoetic dimension of the physical, biological, and social domains—the phenomenon of emergence that could be called the intelligence of the universe. Indeed, compelling critical research possesses an aesthetic dimension where researchers make use of a hermeneutic muse to help them make sense of particular situations. Artists construct their own interpretations of the world in diverse media. Such constructions can by no means be explained in any exactitude by positivist psychology or science of any kind, arising as they do from the interaction of the unconscious, a socially constructed consciousness, and a variety of other factors.

Psychoanalysis can certainly grant us some insights into the process—but by no means can it produce what positivists would label validated knowledge. Thus, some of our most compelling, life-altering, and world-changing knowledges come from parts unknown. It would seem in this context that researchers and people in general who developed a critical consciousness of the world connected to an appreciation of many of the unconscious dimensions of their psyche would be best equipped to produce brilliant knowledge and accomplish great things in the world. In the warped neighborhood of positivism, however, the idea of cultivating the poetic imagination and integrated, transformative consciousness of the researcher as a key dimension of a rigorous education is viewed as idiocy. In this and scores of other ways—a few of which are referenced here—crypto-positivism crushes the sociological, psychological, and pedagogical imagination. In this context, one front of the knowledge wars involves the crusade against the scientific imagination.

## WHAT TO DO ABOUT THE WARS: DEALING WITH VIOLENT KNOWLEDGE WHEN ONE ESCHEWS VIOLENCE

The imperial political economic knowledge wars of the contemporary era help pave the way for criminal acts by corporations and their government allies against the poorest people around the world. In this context, I'm reminded of a public debate I had with a very personable and caring economist while I was a professor in Louisiana. Because he came from a very positivistic econometric perspective, he took issue with a statement I had made about the ethical dimensions of economics and economic policy. There is no ethical dimension to economics, he argued, maintaining that one simply had no choice but to follow universal laws of the market. But what about the purpose of our studies of economics? I asked him. Is it simply to maximize profits of particular corporations or specific sectors of one nation's economy or is it to make sure that wealth is produced and then distributed in a way where everyone would benefit? My friend was perplexed at my question and answered that my query was not an economics question but a moral or a theological question. The two domains were separate in his consciousness and had nothing to do with one another.

Later, my friend told me that he had been very troubled by my questions because in receiving a B.A., M.S., and Ph.D. in economics he had never been confronted with or thought about such issues—and that really disturbed him. He had compartmentalized his life; he was an economist in one dimension of his life, and in another he was a compassionate man who sincerely cared about the welfare of his fellow human beings. How could it be, he asked me, that the twain never met? How could he be "indoctrinated" (his word) in a way that convinced him that there were no ethical dimensions of the "dismal science"? One doesn't have to be a genius to anticipate what I said to him. I hope I didn't overdo it, but I gave him a treatise on the politics of knowledge and epistemology. It's in the interests of corporate power wielders, I told him, to keep economists from thinking of these dynamics. And it's more than coincidental, I speculated, that positivist modes of economics keeps "facts" and "values" so neatly separate. How, we both wondered, could one obtain three academic degrees in economics and not deal with these issues?

In this interaction with my friend rests a micro-manifestation of some of the macro-issues dealt with in this essay. The economist was a good man but had been academically "reared" in a culture where positivist assumptions were the only game in town. Economics was defined without challenge in his experience as the study of markets and profit making and he had never imagined another way of viewing the field. The idea of who was hurt by such ways of seeing was simply never raised in such a positivistic culture. How do we deal with similar circumstances in other fields such as psychology and education? Do we continue to educate scholars devoid of soul and civic courage? Do we continue to ignore the violent inscriptions on much of the knowledge that's produced in the social, political, economic, psychological, and pedagogical domains? How do we "fight" in these knowledge wars when we hate the notion of fighting? These are some of the challenges that face proponents of critical pedagogy in the last years of the first decade of the twenty-first century.

The logic and power of capital and its willingness to hurt whoever gets in the way of quarterly profit margins never ceases to amaze me. I am even more amazed that the educational cronies of dominant power blocs are willing to destroy lives of teachers and students while subverting critique of practices that lead to injustice and human suffering to the name of objectivity and neutrality—or, even worse, doing so with their institutional mission statements saturated with the language of democracy and social justice. To all of those courageous critical pedagogues who expose these travesties without allies or supporters in diverse educational and social institutions, I hope you know how much many of us appreciate your unrewarded work. Many of us have felt that sense of being alone, of questioning our own sanity, as superiors in the hierarchy deem the critical work we do as a form of social pathology and an insult to the academy. This is the sociopsychological and phenomenological dimension of the knowledge wars. I hope in this dark hour that critical pedagogy has the intellectual and political facility to change the course of history.

## REFERENCES

Adorno, T. (1973). *Negative dialectics*. New York: The Seabury Press.
Benjamin, W. (1968). *Illuminations: essays and reflections*. New York: Pantheon.
Clark, C. (2001). *Surely teaching hypertext in the composition classroom qualifies as a feminist pedagogy?* Retrieved from http://english.ttu.edu/kairos/6.2/coverweb/gender/clark/index.htm
Collins, P. (1991). *Black feminist thought: Knowledge, consciousness, and the politics of empowerment*. New York: Routledge.
Denzin, N., & Lincoln, Y. (2000). *Handbook of qualitative research* (2nd ed.). Thousand Oakes, CA: Sage.
Dewey, J. (1916). *Democracy and education*. New York: The Free Press.
Fanon, F. (1963). *The wretched of the Earth*. New York: Grove Press.
Faulconer, J., & Williams, R. (1985). Temporality in human action: An alternative to positivism and historicism. *American Psychologist, 40*(11), 1179–1188.
Geeland, D. (1996). *Learning to communicate: Developing as a science teacher*. Retrieved from http://bravus.port5.com/learn.htm
Gramsci, A. (1988). *An Antonio Gramsci reader* (D. Forgacs, Ed.). New York: Schocken Books.
Harding, S. (1986). *The science question in feminism*. Ithaca, NY: Cornell University Press.
hooks, b. (1981). *Ain't I a woman: Black women and feminism*. Boston: South End Press.
Horkheimer, M. (1974). *Critique of instrumental reason*. New York: Seabury Press.
Kellner, D. (1995). *Media culture: Cultural studies, identity and politics between the modern and postmodern*. New York: Routledge.
Kincheloe, J. L. (2001a). Describing the bricolage: Conceptualizing a new rigor in qualitative research. *Qualitative Inquiry, 7*(6), 679–692.
Kincheloe, J. L. (2001b). *Getting beyond the facts: Teaching social studies/social sciences in the twenty-first century*. New York: Peter Lang.
Kincheloe, J. L. (2004a). Into the great wide open: Introducing critical thinking. In D. Weil & J. L. Kincheloe (Eds.), *Critical thinking and learning: An encyclopedia for parents and teachers*. Westport, CT: Greenwood Press.
Kincheloe, J. L. (2004b). Iran and American miseducation: Cover-ups, distortions, and omissions. In J. L. Kincheloe & S. R. Steinberg (Eds.), *The miseducation of the West: Constructing Islam*. New York: Greenwood.
Kincheloe, J. L. (2005a). On to the next level: Continuing the conceptualization of the bricolage. *Qualitative Inquiry, 11*(3), 323–350.
Kincheloe, J. L. (2005b). *Critical constructivism*. New York: Peter Lang.
Kincheloe, J. L. (2008). *Critical pedagogy* (2nd ed.). New York: Peter Lang.
Kincheloe J. L., & Berry, K. (2004). *Rigor and complexity in educational research: Conceptualizing the bricolage*. London: Open University Press.
Kincheloe, J. L., & Pinar, W. (1991). *Curriculum as social psychoanalysis: Essays on the significance of place*. Albany, NY: State University of New York Press.
Kincheloe, J. L., & Steinberg, S. R. (1997). *Changing multiculturalism*. London: Open University Press.
Kincheloe, J. L., & Steinberg, S. R. (2007). *Cutting class: Socio-economic status and education*. Boulder, CO: Rowman and Littlefield.
Kincheloe, J. L., Steinberg S. R., Rodriguez, N., & Chennault, R. (1998). *White reign: Deploying whiteness in America*. New York: St. Martin's Press.
Livezey, L. (1988). Women, power, and politics: Feminist theology in process perspective. *Process Studies, 17*(2), 67–77.

Lloyd, R., & Smith, S. (2006). Motion-sensitive phenomenology. In K. Tobin & J. L. Kincheloe (Eds.), *Doing educational research: A handbook*. Rotterdam: Sense Publishing.
Lyotard, J. (1979/1984). *The postmodern condition: A report on knowledge* (G. Bennington & B. Massumi, Trans.). Minneapolis, MN: University of Minnesota Press.
Marcuse, H. (1955). *Eros and civilization*. Boston: Beacon Press.
Marcel, V. (2001). *The constructivist debate: Bringing hermeneutics (properly) in*. Retrieved from http://www.isanet.org/archive/isa01.pdf
Maturana, H., & Varela, F. (1987). *The tree of knowledge*. Boston: Shambhala.
Memmi, A. (1965). *The colonizer and the colonized*. New York: The Orion Press.
Monchinski, T. (2007). *The politics of education: An introduction*. Rotterdam: Sense Publishers.
Nandy, A. (2000). Recovery of indigenous knowledge and dissenting futures of the university. In S. Inayatullah & J. Gidley (Eds.), *The university in transformation: Global perspectives on the future of the university*. Westport, CT: Bergin and Garvey.
Nelson, L. (2000). Feminist epistemology as and in practice. *Newsletter on Feminism and Philosophy, 99*, 2. Retrieved from http://www.apa.udel.edu/apa/publications/newsletter//v99n2
Orelus, P. (2007). *Education under occupation: The heavy price of living in a neocolonized and globalized world*. Rotterdam: Sense Publishers.
Pickering, J. (1999). The self is a semiotic process. *Journal of Consciousness Studies, 6*(4), 31–47.
Pinar, W. (2006). Literary study as educational research: "More than a pungent and corrosive school story". In K. Tobin & J. Kincheloe (Eds.), *Doing educational research: A handbook*. Rotterdam: Sense Publishing.
Prigogine, I. (1996). *The end of certainty: Time, chaos, and the new laws of nature*. New York: The Free Press.
Prigogine, I., & I. Stengers (1984). *Order out of chaos*. New York: Basic Books.
Shiva, V. (1993). *Monocultures of the mind*. London: Zed.
Smith, D. (2006). *Trying to teach in a season of great untruth: Globalization, empire, and the crises of pedagogy*. Rotterdam: Sense Publishers.
Spivak, G. (1987). *In other worlds: Essays on cultural politics*. New York: Methuen.
Steinberg S. R. (2006). Critical cultural studies research: Bricolage in action. In K. Tobin & J. L. Kincheloe (Eds.), *Doing educational research: A handbook*. Rotterdam: Sense Publishers.
van Manen, M. (1991). *Researching lived experience: Human science for an action sensitive pedagogy*. Albany, NY: State University of New York Press.
Weiler, H. (2004). *Challenging the orthodoxies of knowledge: Epistemological, structural, and political implications for higher education*. Retrieved from http://www.stanford.edu/~weiler/unesco_paper_24.pdf

**Reprinted with permission: Kincheloe, J. L. (2008). Critical pedagogy and the knowledge wars of the twenty-first century.** *International Journal of Critical Pedagogy, 1*(1), 1–22.

CURRY STEPHENSON MALOTT

# THE ANTI-IMPERIALIST PEDAGOGY OF JOE L. KINCHELOE

In "Critical Pedagogy and the Knowledge Wars of the Twenty-First Century" (2008) Joe L. Kincheloe highlights the role of critical pedagogy as a tool to resist the unjust ways empires use knowledge to deceive and perpetuate a system of oppression and exploitation. Obvious examples, of course, are ways schools in the U.S. teach a social studies of white supremacist manifest destiny that situates Western civilization and industrial capitalism as evidence of progress and Euro-supremacy and, simultaneously, positions Indigenous peoples in America, Africa, and elsewhere, as backwards, primitive, and lucky to be under the protective care of their natural superiors, even if these bosses do have an occasional genocidal mean streak. Unlike many critical pedagogues, however, Kincheloe has consistently positioned his approach as dialectically opposed to not only political and economic indoctrination in the interest of colonization and domination, but to the dominant mechanistic form of educational psychology, which, ultimately, serves the same hegemonic functions.

For this, Kincheloe's unique perspective is invaluable. That is, because education is founded upon psychology, a real, viable, critical challenge must address its underlying assumptions. What we find is that the behaviorist form of educational psychology is in fact not based on the objective science it claims to be, but is part of the empire's knowledge wars. In this case, the goal is to control people through classroom management and curriculum, and to convince the population that the world is naturally organized hierarchically or that certain cultures produce smarter, more intelligent people—these are verifiable lies the empire deceptively presupposes are objective and thus neutral facts.

Mainstream educational psychology, to be sure, is founded upon the presupposition that the mind and consciousness are knowable and measurable properties, and therefore controllable. Since around the beginning of the twentieth century neo-mechanicalists, such as Frederick Taylor, have argued that intelligence is not only measurable, but is naturally hierarchical, rendering the elite few natural leaders. The mechanical worldview is based on the assumption that there are no non-material entities in the world rendering all that is real is measurable. Because the mechanical philosophy behind this paradigm was disproved by Newton in the seventeenth century with his *action at a distance* discovery, which acknowledges that the force or cause of life is a non-material, immeasurable property, which is commonly referred to as free will/spirit/soul/consciousness, and therefore largely unknowable and mysterious, education, as a field of study or discipline, is grounded on antiquated ideas the scientific community long ago abandoned.

From the perspective of empire, however, there are no alternatives—in other words, the *bosses*, as it were, cannot admit to the true nature of reality. That is, a universe governed *not* by order and predictability, but one with an unchangeable and untamable spirit is not acceptable, even if science suggests it to be so. Consequently, the empire must ignore science and work in the less than admirable domain of indoctrination and propaganda and pretend people are robots and the earth is a bottomless shopping mall, and the world will live happily ever after as long as we do not challenge or question the man behind the curtain. In this context Joe's critical pedagogy is absolutely transformative because it is firmly grounded in knowledge regarding the immeasurable free will that makes possible the human agency and consciousness that has created and recreated critical pedagogy.

"Knowledge Wars," therefore, transgresses the dominant paradigm because it refuses to accept the existence of a lifeless world that can be manipulated by naturally superior individuals (or *races*) with unwavering certainty. That robotic world *does not* and *has not* ever existed. However, capitalist schooling, as Kincheloe demonstrates, assumes students are empty vessels waiting to be filled with content, the truthfulness dependent upon the particular needs of business and the perpetuation of the basic structures of power. Rejecting the passivity of the mechanical paradigm, educators and students are free to unmask the biases built into what the ruling elite validate as legitimate data, again, a process based not on facts or the truth, but on political and economic interests. Kincheloe names the theory underlying contemporary education as "crypto-positivistic" because it is an unstated bias presented as a non-perspective or *just the way it is.*

Why, we may ask, would educational policy makers, many of whom are glorified workers themselves, serve the interests of empire and engage their practice from outdated theories? The answer is simple enough. Most policy makers, it is safe to assume, have internalized the dominant paradigm so extensively, they believe the natural order of the world is hierarchical and the role of education is to save the ignorant masses from their own inferiority through a process of social control, that is, behaviorism. Consequently, policy makers, and the rest of us socialized within the same system, tend not to be aware, without rigorous self-reflection, that we see and act upon the world through an internalized, unconscious philosophy.

Because capitalist education is based more on indoctrination and control than on the legitimate quest for factual knowledge and the alleviation of human suffering, the terrain of education has historically represented a contested field, or knowledge wars. That is, Joe's critical pedagogy, or form of education designed to fight oppression and strengthen the democratic imperative, like critical pedagogy in general, is interested in increasing student critical consciousness through the development of analytical tools for reading the world and challenging unjust relationships such as white supremacist race relations and the capitalist relations of economic and social reproduction for something similar to what we might call, for lack of a term more pregnant with descriptive imagery, a *socialist* future.

Again, however, unlike many critical pedagogues, Joe Kincheloe's place of departure or primary target is not *fighting the dictators of capital outright*, but challenging the architects of capital's system of education—both foci, we should note, are equally important in these troubling times. Meeting these complex challenges, which requires highlighting the interconnectedness of the social and physical with the mental and non-material, requires mounting an effective critique of mainstream educational psychology and offering a viable alternative to capitalist hegemony. In his essay and throughout much, if not all, of his work, Kincheloe, in his own beautiful way, is able to achieve both goals.

Kincheloe has often attributed his relevance as a critical pedagogue, although stated in much humbler terms, to the tendency among Frankfurt School scholars operating in Germany and the U.S. during WWII to acknowledge the changing nature of capitalism, and therefore the changing nature of oppression. From this perspective, an effective critical pedagogy must too continuously adapt to a perpetually changing world. Rejecting the modern Western belief in one true reality or paradigm, Kincheloe's post-modernism presupposes a highly complex social reality that produces many equally valid perspectives, not just between marginalized communities, but within them as well. This passion for complexity and different perspectives is the heart or the venom of Kincheloe's anti-imperialist pedagogy.

Why, one may query, would we point to the seemingly mild acknowledgement of the obvious existence of multiple perspectives as so potentially transformative? Precisely because it is a necessary safeguard against the paternalistic tendency of imperialism where the assumed natural leaders or responsible men, speak *for* rather than *with*. In other words, Kincheloe suggests that if our critical pedagogy is to be anti-imperialist, it must not attempt to speak for those most oppressed by the ravages of imperialist war and capital, but should rather seek to form alliances and work in solidarity with one another for a more democratic future. Kincheloe then reminds us that in practice researchers must be aware of the power-inscribed nature of producing knowledge. To highlight this idea that multiple perspectives are indispensable in combating modern imperialism we will turn our attention to an example of the many ways social class and poverty are experienced, which demonstrates the democratic value of always striving for greater complexity and depth of understanding. While the following descriptions are useful for us here, they are still *my* interpretations of what was shared with me through discussion and experience.

***

In the highly techno-industrially developed United States the working class has a long history of struggle centered around collective bargaining as a method of holding onto more of the value produced through the exertion of one's labor power. Recently, the working class has been enraged over cut backs and downsizing in many industries, most notably the automobile industry and manufacturing in general. However, those relegated to the status of worker in the United States have also historically been unwilling to fully break with the system, regardless of their many legitimate grievances. These *first world* workers experience capitalism and class oppression vastly differently, from those in the so-called *third world*. The perspectives of third world peoples therefore becomes central to Kincheloe's democratic project because imperialism has always legitimated itself by excluding the voices and points of view of those most oppressed and abused. To demonstrate we will turn to a few recent examples from Jamaica.

Some Jamaican townships and communities suffer as high as sixty to seventy percent unemployment rates, especially in areas far removed from the hubs of tourism. People in these parishes often gaze to the U.S. dreaming they too had the opportunity to more directly participate in the labor-capital relationship. For these folks the significance of the American working class is not that they suffer and are exploited for their labor power, as they often view themselves, but are privileged and ungrateful for what they have. However, we are not here to judge the accuracy of these sentiments—that happens through dialogue. We are simply affirming that it is a perspective that is held by real people in the Jamaican countryside.

At the same time, many economically excluded people in these rural areas remain strong supporters of Jamaica's former social democratic Prime Minister, Michael Manley, who the U.S. covertly worked to remove from power during the 1970s because he sought to ensure that the wealth generated in Jamaica should benefit Jamaicans (Malott and Malott, 2008). Many of these folks are also unapologetic supporters of Fidel Castro and more recent socialist leaders such as Hugo Chavez of Venezuela—when you have little to no political power, which, in this world, is buying power, you are not as likely to say no to something or some power, especially *socialist* power. In my travels and engagements I found this socialist spirit of sharing and working together alive and well in rural Jamaica. For example, around the rocky points that speckle much of Jamaica's coastline congregate locale fisherman skillfully landing everything from barracudas to sharks with makeshift line and hook devices, who, at the end of the day, tend to share the catch so everyone leaves with either nothing or something.

At the same time however there exists differences between those who came of age during Manley's era of socialist promises and possibility for real justice, and today's generation coming of age in the computerized and cellularized twenty-first century. Many of Jamaica's youth appear to be intoxicated by the romantic dream of *America's* consumer culture and consequently less interested in the Indigenous knowledge of community building and of plants and farming and the sea and fishing. Reports of similar media-induced Westernization phenomena are emerging from all corners of the planet, from socialist Cuba to the American Indian Reservations in the United States and Canada. The information age, marked by the World Wide Web, has not only been used counter-hegemonically, but it too serves hegemonic, imperialist interests, as it was created *by* that system *for* that system.

In rural corners of the Island the youth crowd around computer screens view the romantic images of the good life in America embedded within its movies and music videos, and other highly fictitious cultural texts. As a result of this opulence in the face of their own poverty, an overwhelming vast majority of Jamaicans would leave the island if they could, according to recent polls. With neoliberal global capitalisms' flooding of the first world with inexpensive commodities made possible by nearly eliminating the cost of labor, barrels of these products are flooding the Jamaican countryside as overseas relatives, endowed with their sense of community and sharing, are providing the physical material to support the youths' romantic images. That is, a pair of paints might be *fly* or *nice*, but they can tell the consumer nothing of the suffering that fueled their manifestation. But even if the pants could talk, and sometimes they do, the mantra of the twenty-first century has been: *all for self, nothing for anyone else; fuck em; if you're not with us, you're against us.* In short, American corporate-military gangsterism has set the tone on the global stage.

These short examples highlight Kincheloe's emphasis on the need to know context, worldview, and their relationship. It also demonstrates the arrogance of Americans who think they know what is best for oppressed people in countries they know little to nothing about. White American critical educators, crippled by their own romantic images of third world revolution, have argued that Jamaicans who so desperately want to leave their country need to be told that it is not that easy in the U.S. and that they should stay and try and make it better there fighting the socialist fight against global capitalism. I find this sentiment highly troubling as it assumes Westerners are better equipped to make decisions for those in impoverished and excluded countries than those who live that life everyday. It is problematic because it keeps intact the paternalistic relationship of colonialism, although from a supposedly critical or revolutionary perspective.

Again, Joe's critical pedagogy cautions against this paternalism that refuses to listen because it assumes that poor people do not know what is best for them because of their assumed ignorance. If there is any truth to this, then it is equally true of Westerners. That is, we are all equally ignorant of some things and knowledgeable of some things. This is our democratic place of departure and part of the strength of Kincheloe's radically democratic project of unity.

\*\*\*

Risking unnecessary repetition it is worth restating that Kincheloe situates his critical pedagogical approach to knowledge production in the context of challenging the oppressive nature of the current hegemony—global, neo-liberal capitalism that controls officially sanctioned information and ideas, and, as a result, manipulates what we might call *the public ontology*. Subverting what Kincheloe and others identify as the undemocratic and unjust nature of empire requires confronting the view of the world advanced by the institutions, such as schools and the mass media, that serve the interests of the elite, whose wealth comes not from their own toil, but from the unpaid labor hours of the vast majority. Joe here is sensitive to the ways the exploitative relationship between capitalists and labor are perpetuated by hegemonizing the ways people understand the world and themselves in it. Consequently, establishing a new, more democratic future requires the democratization of the knowledge production process.

Kincheloe's critical pedagogy here clearly draws on the postmodern rejection of the idea that the world *consists of an objective reality that can be comprehended by the logical and predictable mind* because language and discourse shape the ways in which knowledge is constructed about the nature of existence and, ultimately, how relationships are understood and responded to. Marxists might therefore accuse such a focus as perpetuating a form of neo-idealism for over-emphasizing language and discourse at the expense of *real* class struggle against the process of value production—in a word, capitalism.

However, without confronting the philosophies and worldviews embedded within all language usage and discourse, such as questions of the nature of human existence that inform notions of intelligence, which inform the construction and practice of education, for example, Marxists run the risk of advancing a sort of critical banking pedagogy as they argue for curriculum reform that engages students in developing their sociological imagination by imaging a world without capitalism, for example. Kincheloe's radical epistemological and ontological inclusiveness appreciates such Marxist-informed insights, but also values perspectives coming from different experiences, such as the third world views from Jamaica outlined above. His work is therefore of extreme relevance here because it *hangs out in and learns from the epistemological bizarre*, paraphrasing Kincheloe's other writings. What is of most importance here, in Kincheloe's critical contribution, is not *just* the critical pedagogy of the educator or teacher, but the experiential knowledge of oppression and how to survive and fight it. This, of course, demands of the educator not only the courage to speak, but the humility to listen and learn from those whose life experiences and worldviews are vastly divergent from your own.

*Joe would laugh at the irony that the last chapter he wrote for a book was on critiquing fundamentalist Christians and capitalistic religion. He would be sure that "they" got the last laugh by his death a month before the book came out. As a little boy, Joe was apprenticed to his Uncle Marvin, a fundamentalist Methodist circuit preacher in the mountains of East Tennessee. Every week little Jodie would be tied tight in a Sunday suit and accompany Marvin to witness souls being saved. And every week, little Jodie would become more and more convinced he would not, or could not be saved. The son of older parents, Jodie was the only hope of his father, Joe Sr., and the other Kincheloe Brothers. Joe Sr.'s male siblings had not sired children, and certainly, the children adopted by his brothers were not considered to carry on Uncle Marvin's sacred mission. These church visits were the foundation of Joe's ability to speak in public, and as a little kid, he learned to imitate then improve upon the preachers of the South. By the time he was twelve, he admitted that, one, He knew how to preach, and two, that he would never be saved. Uncle Marvin and Joe Sr. were devastated, and little Jodie lost his position as apprentice minister.*

*The church greatly influenced Joe's life, however, and he wrote his dissertation on the fundamentalist camp meetings in Tennessee during the 1800s. He was obsessed by fundamentalism, in every way, and along with emulating preachers in his own lectures and public speaking style, he continued to research and follow religious extremists. The new millennium was ripe for Joe's rhetorical pickings, and after the installation of a right wing born again in the Whitehouse in the moronic body of W., Joe was convinced that capitalism had a new best friend. Our notion of Christotainment was clear when we started to do political economic readings of American Christian fundamentalism. SS*

JOE L. KINCHELOE

## 16. SELLING A NEW AND IMPROVED JESUS – CHRISTOTAINMENT AND THE POWER OF POLITICAL FUNDAMENTALISM

Christotainment could have only materialized in this particular historical moment with its particular social and political characteristics. How long this moment will last, I don't know—I'm afraid it's not going away very soon. Popular culture has been a site of great consternation for evangelical fundamentalists. Understanding possibly on a subconscious level that they couldn't beat it, conservative Christians decided to counter it—and in the end appropriate it. This book is a story of that appropriation and its expanding effects. Indeed, this appropriation has marked a new era in theological and as we will see social and political history. In this Christotainment saturated context, what I am calling political fundamentalism is growing. Very importantly, its social and political influence is strengthening. Near the end of the first decade of the twenty-first century

- over 70 million Americans call themselves evangelicals, millions of others share beliefs with this group
- four out of ten view the Bible as the literal word of God
- 84% believe that Jesus is the son of God
- eight out of ten believe they will stand before God on Judgment Day and will face consequences based on the Creator's decision
- one-half believe that angels exist
- over 66% openly say they have made an allegiance to Jesus
- over one-third believe in the literal truth of the Book of Revelations description of the Rapture (Prothero, 2003; Hedges, 2006; Sheler, 2006).

When these statistics are compared to Europeans, for example, stark differences emerge. Christianity in general is not as important to Europeans as it is to Americans. But where the real difference emerges is around fundamentalism, especially in its Americanized politicized phase that now exerts more influence than ever before on U.S. theology, society, and politics. While political fundamentalists can be found in Europe for the most part they remain far out on the fringe of everyday sociopolitical and theological life. The U.S. case is unique, although with fundamentalist missionary efforts growth is occurring in diverse corners of the planet.

## DEFINING EVANGELICALISM AND FUNDAMENTALISM

It would be remiss to deal with these issues without attempting to define the terms evangelicalism and fundamentalism. When I first wrote about these topics 35 years ago, this was a relatively easy exercise. Over the last three and one half decades, however, there have been numerous challenges to traditional definitions, coming both from the scholarly community and fundamentalists and evangelicals themselves. Fundamentalists often feel that those who are establishing the definitions are individuals who despise their beliefs. There is some truth to this, as fundamentalists correctly argue that the "definers" use the term in a consistently negative way. Nevertheless, for those of us who are not fundamentalists what we observe about fundamentalist beliefs and actions may, by necessity, strike us harmful and threatening. With these concerns in mind and in an effort to be as fair as possible, the following is as generic a definition for evangelicalism and fundamentalism as I deem possible.

Evangelicalism is characterized by a belief in the infallibility of Scriptures, the sovereignty of God, the depravity of human beings, and the centrality of the conversion experience. Evangelicals have long accepted that salvation can be achieved only through the grace of God, the value of preaching, the death of Jesus for the sins of human beings, the supremacy of faith in the attainment of salvation, and the ethical content of Christian living presented in the New Testament. Never a separate denomination, evangelicalism does not have a single moment when it was born as it represents a convergence of numerous theological and sectarian movements that slowly came together in America in the eighteenth and nineteenth centuries. Within evangelicalism there is great diversity, theologically, socially, and ideologically. Any effort to generalize about the history of evangelicalism and its present status is virtually impossible.

Many evangelicals in the late nineteenth century embraced the social gospel movement; many contemporary evangelicals act bravely against prevailing beliefs about the poor and the racially and sexually marginalized. Obviously, the evangelical African American church would be a prime example of this diversity. While over 78% of them describe themselves as politically conservative, there is evidence that this is changing. In 2004, for example, over seven million voted for John Kerry and over nineteen million did not vote. In the contemporary era wedge issues such as abortion and homosexual marriage keep many evangelicals voting Republican even though they disagree with many of the party's domestic and foreign policies. Thus, it would be unfair to evangelicals to lump them all together as a monolithic right wing group with the same view of Jesus, the demands of faith, and other doctrinal issues (Moore, 1994; Sheler, 2006, Goldberg, 2007). In *Christotainment* the editors and authors will make every effort to avoid such distortion.

Now, carefully turning to fundamentalism, we can historically trace from the early nineteenth century a persistent radical strain of the evangelical movement. While maintaining the basic doctrinal tenets of evangelicalism, this radical contingent has often embraced an even more emotion-based, revival-oriented theology suspicious of clergy-mandated rituals. A key dimension of this dissenting tradition has been its consistent anti-intellectualism and distrust of rationality. Again, while there is diversity among fundamentalists—from Missouri Synod Lutherans and Pentacostals, for example—there is a *degree* of consistency among contemporary fundamentalists in their exclusionary perspectives toward God's truth and those who they consider non-believers. I won't go into detail about fundamentalist history here—that has been covered elsewhere on numerous occasions—but in the second and third decades of the twentieth century, the group that would come to be known as fundamentalists laid down the gauntlet against evangelicals and other Christians seen to be "modernizing" the faith with theological scholarship. In 1909, they produced a twelve-volume set of books entitled *The Fundamentals* to proclaim doctrinal truth to the world.

It took a decade, but by around 1919 conservative Christian panic over liberal influences in Christendom and the moral decay of American culture induced evangelical radicals to build new networks of like-minded believers. The soon-to-be-labeled fundamentalists came together to discuss what they could do to bring Christians back from their encounter with modernity, especially what to do with anti-Christian Darwinism. In their meetings they expressed their dire concern with evolution and the changing role of women. The independence of the women of the twenties, they believed, was undermining the social fabric and the God-ordained dominance of men. From the fundamentalist perspective scientific Darwinism and the ostensible breakdown of patriarchy and the social chaos surrounding it were evidence of the coming of the end of days. Believing tribulation and the Rapture were eminent, the word of Jesus had to be spread as quickly as possible. Thus, fundamentalists embraced radio with a proselytical vengeance (Thomas, 2005; Frykholm, 2005; Sheler, 2006). This fervor to engage the world through popular media has never abated. Twentieth century Christotainment had taken a great leap forward.

## AN AMERICAN JESUS: SELLING THE SAVIOR ACROSS THE DECADES

In the evangelicalism of the nineteenth century we see the emergence of another theological phenomenon that would reach its zenith in the last half of the twentieth and the first decade of the twenty-first centuries: the Americanization of Jesus, especially in forms of Christotainment. Especially by the time of the flowering of post-World War II anti-Communism and nationalism, Jesus virtually had to be an American so not to disrupt the conflation of Christianity with Americanism. By the post-1960s conservative effort to "recover" what had been perceived to have been "lost" by white Americans, men, and heterosexuals to the various liberation movements of the era, Jesus had to be *sold* as a true-blue American who was disgusted by the decadence and anti-Western undercurrents of the anti-Vietnam War, civil rights, sexual, feminist, Native American liberation, Latino pride, and gay rights movements. Indeed, Jesus had emigrated from Palestine and had secured his new American persona.

With the Son of Man's identity secure, the evangelicals could use their American marketing skills to plug him. Numerous examinations of "public opinion about Jesus" indicate that Jesus marketing has been a great success. Americans of all religious persuasions look at Jesus in a positive manner now that He is omnipresent in the domain of American pop culture. At the end of the first decade of the twenty-first century, you can't turn on the radio or TV, go to the movie theater, listen to contemporary music, or attend on and off Broadway musicals without encountering Jesus. This book wants to understand this merging of popular culture and Christian fundamentalism. In this context, we use a bricolage of methods to understand religious marketing, what such theotainment looks like, and its theological, cultural, social, and political effects. Our assertion is that such dynamics are changing the world in a dangerous and frightening manner (Neiwart, 2003; Prothero, 2003; Mahan, 2005).

Of course, there's nothing new about evangelicalism, marketing, and entertainment in the U.S. From the time of eighteenth century revivalist George Whitefield, the dramatic was fused with the religious in such an entertaining way that tens of thousands of people would come to his services. So finely tuned was Whitefield's voice to the nuance of the theatrical, contemporary observers reported that he could bring thousands to tears by him merely uttering the word, Mesopotamia. The sermons of the great evangelists of the First Great Awakening (1730s and 1740s) and Second Great Awakening (first three decades of the nineteenth centuries) including Jonathan Edwards, Charles Finney, Lorenzo Dow successfully merged drama and theology. The post-Civil War revivals of former shoe salesman Dwight Moody and his song leader, Ira B. Sankey brought thousands all around the nation to be entertained.

Paul Rader, Aimee Semple McPherson, and many other early radio preachers of the 1920s exhibited great showmanship and maintained thousands and thousands of listeners around the country.

One of the most uniquely American dimensions of Christotainment—and one of the earliest and most successful—was the camp meetings of the Second Great Awakening. One of the most famous contemporary descriptions of these meetings was that more souls were begot than saved. The meetings were like nineteenth century Woodstocks replete with outrageous preaching, wild displays of religious enthusiasm, prostitutes, moonshiners, gamblers, and other characters. I have long been fascinated by these "wild displays of religious enthusiasm." Once the Holy Spirit had descended on the assemblages, men and women filled with the spirit would engage in what were called the "exercises." These included such activities as barking, running in a straight line (there were always reports of broken noses from runners hitting trees), laughing (the holy laugh), jerking, marrying (a woman would be directed by the Lord to marry a particular man in the congregation), whirling, and many more. Some of these meetings held throughout the nation but predominantly on the Tennessee and Kentucky frontier would attract over 200,000 people.

Over a century and one half later Jim and Tammy Faye Bakker of Praise the Lord (PTL) Club fame and infamy would carry the tradition of the camp meeting into the late 1970s and 1980s hyperreality. As we'll discuss later, hyperreality is a term used to describe the contemporary cultural landscape marked by the saturating presence of electronic information and high-tech communication. In such a landscape individuals begin to lose touch with the traditional notions of time, community, self, and history. In this circumstance those phenomena displayed on electronic media assume a "realness" greater than when directly observed. Thus, in their heyday Jim and Tammy—or many other media personalities, seem to be more a presence in the life of their viewers than everyday real life relationships. Thus, in this new cultural atmosphere the Bakkers merged Disneyland with the orgasmic delights of the camp meeting. With the sexual and financial scandals that beset the couple, their version of Heritage USA fell apart. Evangelicals knew they had a good marketing idea and numerous efforts to reconstitute the fundamentalist theme park continue into the twenty-first century. Suffice it to say that the Jesus marketed at Heritage USA was an American patriot (Moore, 1994; Romanowski, 2005).

## THE IMPACT OF CHRISTOTAINMENT

In any cultural study it is always difficult to assess the effects of the phenomenon in question. After visiting Christotainment centers, the Holy Land Experience in Orlando for example, it is easy to see that many of those in attendance were visibly moved and took the entire experience very seriously. Others, it seemed, were curious cultural voyeurs who were astounded and clearly not emotionally and ideologically engaged by the events taking place in front of them. Individuals are active readers of Christotainment and other cultural forms, that is, they don't passively sit back and let the producers of popular culture impose particular belief structures on them. In the same context, the popularity of Christotainment in its diverse forms and the ideological movement of the American to more and more conservative politics seem to indicate that something is happening. Such forms of interaction at the most engage people in particular theological and ideological ways of seeing while at the least reaffirm the predispositions individuals bring to the rendezvous. We are particularly interested in the producers of Christotainment in this book, for we have reached the conclusion that there are dangerous agendas transcending merely the profit motive circulating among many creators of these phenomena.

## DOMINIONISM AND THE RADICAL POLITICIZATION OF FAITH

The central group we are pondering in this context is the fundamentalist Christian group who are sometimes referred to as dominionists. Most Americans are not as yet familiar with this term that refers to the biblical interpretation that God gave *man* dominion over all things earthly. In the contemporary use of the term, this notion of dominion has been expanded to include control over the U.S. and in turn a fundamentalist Christian dominion over the world. These are not abstract ideas, as dominionists now operate in all aspects of American life. In fact, during the second Bush Administration dominionists were brought into most executive departments and to the courts. This special brand of fundamentalists has been successful in tapping into the fear, loneliness, and lack of connection Americans harbor in the twenty-first century. Many times, they gain support from fundamentalist Christians who don't know about or fully understand their ideological and geo-political ambitions. Numerous Christians have been attracted to the dominionists by their promise of a better day, a righteous, fundamentalist America that subdues all enemies and runs the world American style.

Employing the American Jesus and Christotainment, dominionists do not numerically dominate fundamentalism—but, historically, smaller radical groups can guide larger movements. This has already happened to some degree with this group. Dominionists have carefully engaged in their surreptitious political activities—sometimes successfully, sometimes not so—in the process putting together mass communications complexes. Indeed, at the end of this decade they own six TV networks, 2000 Christian radio stations, and control the leadership of the Southern Baptist Convention—the largest Protestant denomination in the U.S. This gives them access to most people in the country with their new language of democracy and freedom. Even long-standing definitions, not to mention progressive updates of the concepts, of such terms fade away in the fundamentalist "newspeak" of the Dominionists. Using the language of Christian love, empathy, and equality, Dominionists act on an entirely different set of values. In this way they have set out to reshape the nation and the world.

The more malignant aspirations of the Dominionists have already and will continue to evoke backlash from diverse groups, even many who fall within the evangelical orbit. When a group openly speaks of the suppression of non-believers— "America is a Christian nation," the increased use of the death penalty, the end to all abortion no matter what the circumstances, the closing of "government schools" (read, public education), some people are going to react negatively. In an age of de-politicization and cynicism far too many Americans are ignorant of the Dominionists' goals, don't believe "it could ever happen here," agree with many of their points, or are too cynical to think they can do anything about the damage such groups are exacting on the cultural fabric in general and social and political institutions in particular.

In addition, Dominionists strategically use a stealth language to push forward some of their ideological issues. In the domain of same-sex marriage, for example, Glenn Stanton, a senior official of Dominionist-oriented Focus on the Family, confides that with this and other issues you want to make God's case in secular language. This is the best way to win a Dominionist argument, for those who are political fundamentalists will already support the "correct" position. Stanton maintains that he and his fellow fundamentalists appeal to universal norms—by this he is referring to Western standards. Thus, using these tactics, Stanton maintains that he can speak about politics to his own community without alienating people who don't really know the relationship between his theological and political positions. These careful maneuverings have worked better than almost anyone expected, as Dominionists and their fundamentalist brothers and sisters in Jesus make a new path for America.

A central, if not *the* central figure, in Dominionist Christotainment is Tim LaHaye. I have been writing about LaHaye—who was recently named the most influential evangelical of our time—for almost thirty years. In the late 1970s and early 1980s LaHaye and his wife Beverly were writing about the successful historical effort of the "secular humanists" to take over America and destroy all of the traditions Christian Americans held dear. Arguing that institutions such as the public schools were secular humanist plots to wipe out Christianity, LaHaye ended up in Ronald Reagan's White House telling the president about the Dominionist interpretation of American history. In recent years—as Doug Kellner and Rhonda Hammer explore in their chapter in this book—LaHaye has become the most successful writer of a series of books in publishing history.

LaHaye's *Left Behind* series co-authored with Jerry Jenkins has sold over seventy million copies. In book, children's book, movie, and video game formats, *Left Behind* has become a blueprint for the Dominionist future. In this context Dominionist Christotainment works its magic. Take LaHaye on the War in Iraq. Using his many outlets for disseminating data, the world's most important evangelical promotes the view that the Book of Revelations foretold of the war. Following the logic that made LaHaye famous, his audiences learn that before the Rapture comes, that Babylon (Iraq) must be rebuilt as the home of Satan (Saddam Hussein). This, LaHaye contends, is what Hussein was doing before George W. Bush decided to invade in 2003. Continuing, LaHaye warns that Hussein was not a Muslim but a Satanist and had plans to build a temple to Satan in Iraq.

Thus, for the millions of true believers who read LaHaye's non-fiction and his fiction and watch his movies—he and Jenkins write about the world government of the Anti-Christ in one of their *Left Behind* novels, *New Babylon*—the Iraqi War had an extra theological justification. Whether President Bush exploited these beliefs is a subject of debate. From a discursive perspective Bush peppered his speeches about the war with Biblical phrases and language that reflected portions of the

Book of Revelations. The nation is riddled by debates over whether or not Bush purposefully employed this Revelations discourse to garner support for his policies. Honestly, I see no evidence to conclude whether he did or did not. It is safe to say, however, that the president benefited from the connections made by many of the fundamentalist faithful (Mahan, 2005; Thomas, 2005; Hedges, 2006; Pfohl, 2006; Klemp, 2007).

As previously mentioned, it is very difficult to determine the effects of any body of information including popular culture, propaganda, advertising, or Christotainment on the belief structures of groups and individuals. We do know, however, that producers of Christotainment such as LaHaye continue to turn out their products believing they have a religious and ideological effect, and that America, clearly for a plethora of reasons, has become more fundamentalist theologically and more right-wing politically. Just because someone reads a few of the *Left Behind* books or plays the *Left Behind: Eternal Forces* video game, they don't necessarily buy into a Dominionist theo-political model.

Some readers and players view these books and games as they would any artifact from a science fiction or horror genre. Indeed, *Left Behind* has been reviewed and talked about on sci-fi and horror websites by fans who also love *Star Wars* and *Star Trek*. Like such popular culture icons, *Left Behind* also markets CDs, coffee cups, T-shirts, fan fiction, mousepads, screen savers, ad infinitum. The Apocalypse and the Rapture now reside at the center of Christotainment—the end of the world is just so damned exciting. Books, publishing houses such as Warner and Bertelsmann, movies, videos, radio, interactive games, and local and national fun events push a Rapture politics and theology embedded in everyday concerns of evangelical Christians.

Such commonplace concerns involve everything from tax preparation, child-rearing, missionary activity, weight loss to marriage problems. The purveyors of Dominionism know that everytime one speaks or writes to someone about their physical fitness, an opportunity will present itself to further their theological and ideological agenda. Fundamentalist leaders have found that the appropriation of popular culture via Christotainment works far better than simply denouncing it—the failed strategy of the past. Dominionists and other fundamentalists/evangelicals are busily working to produce a Christianized multidimensional popular culture to create an alternate universe of amusement and leisure activities. What has emerged is Christotainment, a religiously and politically inscribed consumer's earthly paradise where boredom can be quashed, practical advice can be given, and hearts, minds, and souls can be won for a new and improved Jesus and the baggage He has been burdened with in the twenty-first century (McAlister, 2003).

## DOMINIONIST POWER

I would not be honest if I didn't admit that the Dominionist success in promoting a shadowy view of an exclusionary, theocratic, anti-rational U.S. still amazes me after growing up in a Tennessee Mountain culture saturated by Protestant fundamentalism. I am amazed but not surprised. Understanding the power and the potential theo-political influence of fundamentalism, I knew I had to understand everything about it.

With this in mind, I wrote a master's thesis in history on the effect of evangelicalism on American political institutions and a doctoral dissertation on the tradition's capacity to shape educational organizations. Some of the first articles I published in the late 1970s and first years of the 1980s involved the emerging power of fundamentalism in American political life and social institutions. From my Tennessee vantage point I could clearly see the storm that was brewing around the role of religion in U.S. political life. Writing and editing this book at the end of the first decade of the twenty-first century, my worst nightmares have materialized as this minority, albeit millions of people, gains more and more control over governmental, social, and religious institutions.

One of the central strategies of the Dominionists involves their readiness to take advantage of the fear engendered by a military, social, cultural, or ideological emergency to promote seemingly simple solutions to the confusion that ensues—for example, "turn your lives over to Jesus," "trust in the Lord," "make America follow the dictates of the Bible," or "let us establish dominion over those who don't accept the word of God." September 11, 2001 was one of these moments of crisis. With a President and a Congress *sensitive* to their support, the Dominionists became the vanguard for demonizing the Muslim enemy (Kincheloe and Steinberg, 2004), for suspending Constitutional guarantees to those under suspicion of terrorism, for preemptive wars in the Middle East to conquer the enemy and hasten the Rapture and the Apocalypse. Already strong in some political positions, the Dominionists gained power after 9–11 that allowed them to officially move from the margins of the political order to the legislative, judicial, and executive branches of government.

Now a dominant force in the Republican Party, Dominionists often control or maintain a powerful presence in state GOP operations. Fronted by numerous organizations such as the Family Resource Council, Dominionist senators and representatives promote Creationism in public schools, capital punishment for doctors who perform abortions, stricter sodomy laws, more preemptive wars, bans on single mothers teaching in "government schools," a Bible-based legal system, and many more right wing issues. While there are many dedicated organizations devoted to publicizing—there's no need to expose, they are mainly in open public view—these Dominionist activities, the American public still seems unmindful of the implications of such political fundamentalist pursuits. In part this is a manifestation of the American public's political naiveté and the politics of knowledge that dominates American media in general and news coverage and education in particular.

One of the important ways that such radical political fundamentalist ideas move from the fringe to the mainstream involves the Dominionists' media empire that broadcasts fundamentalist preachers who take positions emanating from extremist circles and legitimizing them on TV and radio. Such ideas find their way into various dimensions of Christotainment that work to reinforce the ideas promoted by the ministers in a more palatable "politics of pleasure." Political positions that only a few years ago were thought to be the viewpoint of irrational zealots continue to move into the Republican Party and mainstream American socio-political life.

The idea of installing a "Christian" government whose legal system is grounded on a particular and highly problematic interpretation of Scriptures, not the Constitution, has now moved into the mainstream of American political life. Numerous conservative officeholders as well as organizations such as the prominent Council for National Policy now endorse such a position. My, how the American political landscape has changed; less than a decade ago the label, Conservative, described an individual who argued that the Constitution was the legal foundation of American government and should be followed in a strict and literal manner. Although, this position is problematic in its dismissal of changing conditions and contextual data, it is a reasonable, moderate perspective in light of the Dominionists' Bible-based political and legal standpoint.

Consider for a moment the implications of such a Scriptural political and legal framework. Those who would object to such a system are dismissed as heathen, atheists, outsiders, or secular humanists. Liberal concepts such as universal human rights crumble as the focus of the system involves the security of the "saved" who are the keepers of the truth. Here, entire sectors of the U.S. population are deleted from legal protection and political participation. The fact that a particular and highly problematic interpretation of the Bible is used as the grounding for a Scriptural-based system is profoundly significant in this context. Not only would non-Christians be excluded from the legal protections and civil rights of the Dominionist system but so also would many devote Christians whose interpretations of the Bible were deemed "incorrect." Depending on one's theological hermeneutics (the way she makes sense of Scriptures), a Bible-based schema could and has been used to justify everything from slavery, gender violence, to acts of cruelty against "outsiders" in general (Neiwert, 2003; Blumenthal, 2005; Hedges, 2006).

## CHRISTOTAINMENT, LIBIDINAL INVESTMENT, AND NAVY SEALS FOR JESUS

In the Christotainment domain we see various groups working to spread these militant, aggressive, and threatening perspectives into diverse groups—young people in particular. In recent years an array of entertainment- and proselytical-based groups and organizations have emerged to immerse youth in macho, patriarchal, and militaristic modes of political fundamentalist belief systems, lifestyle, and activities. Take, for example, the work of Ryan Dobson, son of the powerful founder of the Dominionist Focus on the Family and media personality. Dobson the younger in three recent books, *Be intolerant: Because some things are just stupid*, *2Die4*, and *2Live4*, has grounded his brassy work with young people around the notion that kids need to get ready to die in the pursuit of a Dominionist revolution in America. In a manner not too different from Mujahideen suicide bombers, Ryan with the apparent blessing of his father and other fundamentalist leaders shepherds his flock toward martyrdom for Dominionism (Hedges, 2006).

Ron Luce's BattleCry, a fundamentalist Christian youth movement proclaims to his followers that we are in a war against the secular forces in the nation. As he and his staff put together Christian rock concerts that have drawn 25,000 attendees in numerous cities across the country, Luce tells his wildly enthusiastic and cheering fans that only the violent will gain hold of "the Kingdom." To accentuate the point he combines his rock concerts with elaborate light shows that spotlight military equipment, posters with young people modeling military weapons, Navy Seals giving testimony to their fundamentalist beliefs and battle plans for the coming Dominionist revolution, endorsements of the War in Iraq, and letters from President George W. Bush validating the patriotic activities taking place at the events (Hubert, 2006; Hedges, 2006). Here is a description of the BattleCry spectacle from a reporter who attended a concert in Philadelphia in 2006:

> After Franklin "Islam is a Wicked Religion" Graham [Dominionist evangelist son of Billy Graham] came out to thunder against the evils of homosexuality and the Iraqi people (whom he considers to be exactly the same people as the ancient Babylonians who enslaved the tribes of Israel and deserving, one would assume, the exact same fate) we heard an explosion. Flames shot out on stage and a team of Navy Seals was shown on the big TV monitors in full camouflage creeping forward down the hallway from the locker room with their M16s. They were hunting us, the future Christian leaders of America. Two teenage girls next to me burst into tears and even I, a jaded middle-aged male, almost jumped out of my skin. I imagined for that moment what it must have felt like to have been a teacher at Columbine high school. 10 seconds later they rushed out onstage and pointed their guns in our direction firing blanks spitting flames. About 1000 shots and bang, we were all dead (WorldCantWait, 2006).

Delirious is a Christian rock band that sometimes plays at BattleCry events singing words such as: "We're an army of God and we're ready to die... Let's paint this big ol' town red ... We see nothing but the blood of Jesus" (Hedges, 2006, p. 30). As the band blasted out their heavy Christian metal at the concert in Philadelphia, their lyrics were simultaneously projected on giant rock concert screens to make sure the young crowd didn't miss the Dominionist message being delivered. They didn't, as 17,000 young believers chanted in response to the band, "We are warriors." This, of course, is only one dimension of the Christian music scene as Philip Anderson and Curry Mallot will illustrate in their chapters in this book. There are growing numbers of Christian bands performing in a wide variety of musical genres and within the theological and ideological diversity of evangelicalism/fundamentalism. There are Christian music festivals such as Creation that takes place every summer in the hills of south central Pennsylvania drawing almost 100,000 young people.

These bands and concert promoters are keenly aware of the registers of affect such music and such events traverse. Dominionist Focus on the Family understands the absurdities of the old fundamentalists' idea that if a listener plays a record backwards Satanic messages can be heard or that rock is a form of "jungle music"—read African American-inspired and not to be tolerated. Focus music promoters know that pop music is a key theater in the "war" for youth libidinal investment, desire. In the spirit of what Philip Anderson writes in his chapter, rock and other forms of beat-based music no matter what the lyrics engage a bodily relationship with the listener. Secular observers of Christian music concerts regularly observe discern a libidinal frenzy among stimulated concert crowds that points to the visceral power of the beat. Similar to the transcendent ecstasy produced by the camp meetings in the early nineteenth century—many husbands did not want their wives attending such meetings—many contemporary fundamentalists fear that if not authoritatively directed such energy will be used in ways not conducive to the fundamentalist cause. Among the Dominionists, such ecstasy is central to manipulating young people to serve their militaristic, 2die4, ambitions (Hendershot, 1995; Hedges, 2006; Sheler, 2006).

### SETTLING THE SCORE WITH NON-BELIEVERS: DOMINIONISM AS A CHRISTOFASCIST MOVEMENT

The new and improved Jesus referenced in the subtitle of this chapter refers, as previously mentioned, to an Americanized Jesus as well as a macho, kick-the-heathens'- ass Savior. One of the great American evangelical/fundamentalist theological innovations has been to re-make Jesus as an epic *personality* whose "eye is on the sparrow" and with whom we develop a personal relationship. This notion seems so commonplace, so natural among contemporary evangelicalism/fundamentalism that it is hard to believe that in Christian history it is a relatively recent invention of nineteenth century American theologians. This epic personality has continued to evolve in recent years as fundamentalist groups—Dominionists in particular—have produced the badass Savior, only employing in limited contexts the Prince-of-Peace persona. No wimpy, girly Jesus for me, Jerry Falwell wrote in the early 1980s, setting a trend of fundamentalist calls to represent Jesus to the world (in Falwell's words) as a "he-man."

Dominionist leaders and the producers of Christotainment heard these calls loud and clear. In the last volume of the *Left Behind* series, for example, *The Glorious Appearing*, the Jesus who returns to earth would never be confused with the loving Lord who promoted selfless love and forgiveness. That guy is long departed for calmer climes. The new Jesus has undergone an extreme makeover and is now the judge executioner for the Jews, Muslims, Hindus, Buddhists, atheists, agonistics, and even members of the United Church of Christ. This killer Jesus, as described by LaHaye and Jenkins, releases a metaphorical sword from his mouth that invisibly spins through the air exacting God's judgment on the unbelieving swine. We Christians, the story goes, gave the unbelievers chance after chance to accept Jesus as their personal Savior. The time finally came when we did what we had to do to establish our rule, His rule on Earth (Little, 2006; Pfohl, 2006).

Like George W. Bush and his good-versus-evil rhetoric in the War on Terror, the political fundamentalists allow no ambiguity in their war against the sinners and non-believers. Those who don't fit into the narrow definitions of Christianity offered are undoubtedly headed for the divine tortures that media commentators such as Pat Robertson or Russ Limbaugh seem to wish on those who would pursue social justice. In *Left Behind* many of those who are slaughtered at the Battle of Armageddon are the leftists that describe good Christians as "right-wing, fanatic, fundamentalist faction" zealots. They are the American Jews descended from the barbarians who were responsible for the brutal whipping and crucifixion of Jesus in the gospel according to Mel Gibson in the *Passion of the Christ*. Gibson's portrayal of the violence of the crucifixion is so exaggerated that Jesus would have been dead many times before getting to Calvary. In the film Jesus moves from macho he-man to dark graphic novel superhero. He even bursts out of the tomb looking gallant and fearless—and very marketable—rising from the dead to the soundtrack of military drums. Batman, Superman, Spiderman, and Gibson's Jesus are all consumable products who are ready for sequels (McAlister, 2003; Smiga, 2006; Little, 2006; Marquez, 2006).

Historical analyses consistently make the argument that fascism always takes years and years to emerge into its mature form—in the case of Hitler's Germany with its brownshirts, mass political gatherings, violence, tactical harassment, and genocide. Even in Nazi Germany, fascism emerged slowly as a dispersed rural phenomenon and slowly moved to Munich and the other cities around the country. Emerging in the U.S. as previously referenced in a society marked by a loss of a sense of belongingness, community disintegration, and socio-political amnesia, rural grounded hyper-patriotic/nationalist groups have come closer together with a rural-based political fundamentalism. In this emerging coalition aided and abetted by Christotainment's fundamentalist talk shows and right-wing radio a revolutionary movement is taking shape. A blueprint for a theocratic utopian society is being constructed that creates a political fundamentalist tyranny, a catalyst for a theo-fascist state.

Americans do not presently live in a fascist state. I want to make that perfectly clear. What I am grappling with here involves analyzing Dominionism and the Christotainment that accompanies it in relation to questions about an emerging fascism or fascist tendencies. These questions are asked with an open mind and no final pronouncement on the answers. Indeed, I may eventually find that examining Dominionism and other forms of political fundamentalism through this lens may not contribute to our understanding of the theo-political phenomena in question. It is important to note that historically fascism has been comprised of dynamics that are culturally familiar and in and of themselves seem rather harmless even noble. Moreover, such dynamics have to be viewed in this comfortable way for the fascistic process to successfully emerge. Thus, when social conditions reach a crisis status the emerging movement is ready to take advantage of a new receptivity to its message.

In the cyber-world of the blogosphere one of the great postulates that has surfaced in the collective wisdom of the cyber-community is that she who first mentions fascism in a thread of debate loses the argument. According to this axiom, I just lost any argument I was making. In this political fundamentalist context I am willing to take the chance, because there do seem to be fascistic tendencies dancing around in the cultural ether. This articulated, I bristle at the inappropriate usage, the hyperbole of the way the term, fascism has been employed in the public conversation by the Right and the Left. Unfitting usage of the term so egregiously dishonors those millions of individuals who have lost their lives to real-life fascist movements around the world. Suffice it to say, I am careful with the term.

My point within the critical ideological context from which I emerge (see Kincheloe, 2008a and 2008b) is that American and other Western societies need to be intimately acquainted with political fundamentalism and the Christotainment it produces to win adherents via a politics/theology of pleasure. Not only is it the civic duty of all Americans to understand political fundamentalism and its fascist tendencies, but, in particular, I believe it is the ethical obligation of all individuals who call themselves Christian to know what is being done in the name of their faith. Many Christians who come from different theological and political orientations often ask me: "I am shocked by the new Jesus being sold by the Dominionists. What happened to the Jesus who counseled us to love our enemies?" As an educator, I would argue that not knowing the Bible and the religious texts of many other religions severely handicaps one in the effort to become a good citizen of the world, an educated person, a human being who understands history, philosophy, politics, literature, art, ad infinitum. This lack of knowledge pushes one into a precarious naiveté, a truncated outlook as restricted who proclaim with no rigorous investigation that any holy scripture is the literal, unfiltered word of the Creator. Such modes of ignorance undermine the civic and theological conversation and contribute to the destruction of democratic and positive theological spheres of human activity (Neiwert, 2003; Leupp, 2005; Hedges, 2006).

In this uninformed state, individuals become highly vulnerable to the colonizing effects of this emerging Christo-fascism. Here the political fundamentalists steal peoples' individual stories only to replace them with narratives in which the uninformed are relegated to low rungs of the crypto-fascist status hierarchy. In these low level roles they become characters in constructions that serve the needs of those in leadership positions. In this fascist cosmos leaders place great emphasis on the iconographic and aesthetic dimensions of the meetings they plan, always focusing on the romantic and mystical dimensions of the belief structure. Such dynamics work to enhance the seductive aspects of the group, placing even more affective pressure on the uninformed to grant their consent. Christotainment picks up on these romantic and mystical elements of fascist aesthetics and takes them to new levels of sophistication.

BattleCry's rock concerts are excellent examples of the fascist spectacle that operates to manipulate and guide the affective investments of young people. BattleCry and countless other types of similar Christotainment elicit jouissance, love, desire, hate, and feelings of belonging. In numerous ways participants feel empowered, endowed with a new sense of purpose in life. When religious news broadcasts from the Christian Broadcasting Network (CBN) and the public affairs programming are added to the libidinal experience of the gatherings, a new theological and political consciousness emerges. Such knowledge producers operate much like those data producers at Walt Disney World who provide narratives on American history to the park's visitors. These faux-historians have provided narratives to connect a plethora of facts and pseudo-facts in the process turning American history into a fairy tale of virtuous heroes who wanted only to do good in the world. Of course in hyperreality these stories become more real than any other national narratives.

Political fundamentalist history books used by home schoolers and Christian schools tell a similar story of the founding and early decades of American history. As the story progresses we begin to see a litany of Satanic enemies from the founders of public schooling to government leaders who established social policies for the poor. Novelist and social theorist Umberto Eco (Neiwert, 2003) contends that contemporary Dominionist and political fundamentalist discourse and knowledge politics are grounded on a fascist marinated Orwellian Newspeak that unites the believers and degrades those who are in someway "different." Multiple sources, forms of knowledge employing a wide variety of media create a discursive universe of

Newspeak that manipulates meanings for the larger good of the cause. In the process Christotained political fundamentalism with its fascist tendencies induces millions to become God's soldiers against the multiple enemies of Jesus.

Mel Gibson's establishment of "validity" in *The Passion of the Christ* illustrates well the validation of such knowledge processes. Careful to produce tiny details of supposed historical accuracy including the use of the Aramaic language, Gibson and his production team induced viewers to believe that if this depiction of the crucifixion is true then the contemporary fundamentalist proclamation of Jesus's message must be literally true. He is simply more believable when he is portrayed on the dominant media of the day. Numerous individuals asserted after seeing the film, "Jesus is so human in the film ... Jesus is really one of us" (Smiga, 2006). This is Newspeak in hyperreality, as the "realer real" of Christotainment productions such as *The Passion* bring innumerable converts. When these factors are added to the vile and often gratuitous dimensions of the anti-Semitism of the film, the Christo-fascistic imprint is indelibly darkened.

The theological bigoted and naïve Gibson and his political fundamentalist fellow-travelers seem to be totally unaware that the blaming of the Jews for the death of Jesus only emerged as a political strategy as the early Christians sought favor as they operated in the Roman Empire. It was much easier and most definitely politically expedient to exonerate the Romans and scapegoat the Jews in such a matrix of power. Gibson completely ignores these well-established historical (see Gertrud Schiller's book *The iconography of Christian art* for a seminal expansion of these themes) dimensions of the early Christians' cynical blaming of the Jews in a fascistic effort to demonize and otherize the non-believers. A close reading of the Aramaic screenplay reveals almost unbelievable anti-Semitic background dialogue that places the Jews at the time of the crucifixion in a most unfavorable light. We don't even need to bring in Gibson's and his father's diatribes against Judaism to clearly see the hatred of Jews embedded in the film (Mazur, & Koda, 2001; Miles, 2006).

In the next chapter, we continue to examine these themes, especially the way Christotainment and political fundamentalism fit into larger sociopolitical movements. In this context, we examine the way Christotainment has helped "recover" forms of dominant power believed to have been severely subverted by anti-Christian elements in American society. In this context, Christotainment becomes a central force in contemporary American culture and politics.

## REFERENCES

Blumenthal, M. (2005). Air Jesus. *Media transparency*. Retrieved August 29, 2008, from http://media transparency.org

Frykholm, A. (2005). The gender dynamics of the left behind series. In B. Forbes & J. Mahan (Eds.), *Religion and popular culture in America* (2nd ed.). Berkeley, CA: University of California Press.

Goldberg, M. (2007). The rise of Christian nationalism. *The Humanist, 67*(5), 29–33.

Hedges, C. (2006). *American fascists: The Christian right and the war on America*. New York: Free Press.

Hendershot, H. (1995). *Shaking the world for Jesus: Media and conservative evangelical culture*. Chicago: University of Chicago Press.

Hubert, D. (2006). G. I. Jesus? Denouncement of right-wing Christian battleCry. BuzzFlash.net. Retrieved August 29, 2008, from www.buzzflash.com/contributors/06/05/con06203.html

Hutson, J. (2007). Pentagon adopts missionary position on homoerotic art. *Talk2Action*. Retrieved from http://www.talk2action.org/story/2007/8/8/182310/3445

Kincheloe, J. L. (2008a). *Critical pedagogy primer* (2nd ed.). New York: Peter Lang Publishing.

Kincheloe, J. L. (2008b). Critical pedagogy and the knowledge wars of the twenty-first century. *International Journal of Critical Pedagogy*, 1(1), 1–22.

Kincheloe, J. L., & Steinberg, S. R. (2004). *The miseducation of the West: How schools and the media distort our understanding of the Islamic world*. Westport, CT: Praeger.

Klemp, N. (2007). Beyone God-talk: Understanding the Christian right from the ground up. *Polity, 39*, 522–544.

Leupp, G. (2005). Fighting for the work of the Lord: Everybody's talking about Christian fascism. *Counterpunch*. Retrieved August 29, 2008, from www.counterpunch.org/leupp01131005.htm

Little, W. (2006). Jesus's extreme makeover. In T. Beal & T. Linafelt (Ed.), *Mel Gibson's bible: Religion, popular culture, and The Passion of the Christ*. Chicago: University of Chicago Press.

Mahan, J. (2005). Conclusion: Establishing a dialogue about religion and popular culture. In B. Forbes & J. Mahan (Eds.), *Religion and popular culture in America* (2nd ed.). Berkeley, CA: University of California Press.

Marquez, J. (2006). Lights! Camera! Action! In E. Mazur & K. McCarthy (Eds.), *God in the details: American religion in popular culture*. New York: Routledge.

Mazur, E., & T. Koda. (2001). Happiest place on Earth: Disney's America and the commodification of religion. In E. Mazur & K. McCarthy (Eds.), *God in the details: American religion in popular culture*. New York: Routledge.

McAlister, M. (2003, September 4). An empire of their own. *Nation*. Retrieved August 29, 2008, from www.thenation.com/doc/20030922/mcalister

Miles, J. (2006). The art of The Passion. In T. Beal & T. Linafelt (Eds.), *Mel Gibson's Bible: Religion, popular culture, and The Passion of the Christ*. Chicago: University of Chicago Press.

Moore, R. (1994). *Selling God: American religion in the marketplace of culture*. New York: Oxford University Press.

Neiwwert, D. (2003). Rush, newspeak, and fascism: An exegesis. *Orcinus*. Retrieved July 15, 2008, from http://dneiwert.blogspot.com/rush%20newspeak%20%20fascism.pdf

Pfohl, S. (2006). *Left behind: Religion, technology, and the flight from the flesh*. ctheory.net. Retrieved August 29, 2008, from www.ctheory.net/articles.aspx?id=557

Prothero, S. (2003). *American Jesus: How the son of God became a national icon*. New York: Farrar, Straus, and Giroux.

Romanowski, W. (2005). Evangelicals and popular music: The contemporary Christian music industry. In B. Forbes & J. Mahan (Eds.), *Religion and popular culture in America* (2nd ed.). Berkeley, CA: University of California Press.

Sheler, J. (2006). *Believers: A journey into evangelical America*. New York: Penguin.

Smiga, G. (2006). The good news of Mel Gibson's Passion. In T. Beal & T. Linafelt (Eds.), *Mel Gibson's Bible: Religion, popular culture, and The Passion of the Christ*. Chicago: University of Chicago Press.

Thomas, P. (2005). Christian fundamentalism and the media. *Media Development*. Retrieved July 18, 2008, from www.wacc.org.uk/wacc/publications/media_development/2005_2christian_fundamentalism_and_themedia

WorldCantWait. (2006). A carnival of theocrats. *Daily Kos*.Retrieved from http://www.dailykos.com.story/2006/5/15/04817/0699

**Reprinted with permission: Kincheloe, J. L. (2009). Selling a new and improved Jesus – Christotainment and the power of political fundamentalism. In S. R. Steinberg and J. L. Kincheloe (Eds.), *Christotainment: selling Jesus through popular culture* (pp. 1–21). Boulder, CO: Westview Press.**

DOUGLAS J. SIMPSON

# JOE KINCHELOE

*A Proponent of Democracy and Christianity?*

Joe Kincheloe: A Proponent of Democracy and Christianity? may be considered an extremely odd title by some, including both Joe's supporters and detractors. Many friends of Joe may consider the title preposterous or outrageous, especially considering the possible implication that he was a proponent of Christianity. I do not necessarily disagree with their sentiments when I think about how Joe could be and was stereotyped at times. But when I think of Joe's love of life and others and his openness and reflection, I am less hesitant to concur with the idea that the title reflects inanity. I believe his wide-awakeness (Greene, 1978) and passion for life influenced him to enjoy ironies, comparisons, and critiques. Similarly, his wide reading and understanding led him to think eclectically. This is not to say, that Joe would agree with my approach to or conclusions regarding this subject. Conversely, it is to say that Joe shared the radical love that stimulated Freire (2002, p. 10) to claim that the radical "is convinced he [or she] is right, but respects another man's [or woman's] prerogative to judge him [her]self correct. He [or she] tries to convince and convert, not to crush his opponent." Given his radical love, Joe would at worse probably seek to convince me I was mistaken as I pursued this topic.

In addition to some of Joe's friends who may find the title off putting, there may be detractors who consider the title irreverent. I do not completely disagree with their sentiments, especially if the title is misinterpreted to somehow be an insult to Jesus. But when I think of Jesus rather than certain ideologies, I am less hesitant to see eye to eye with the idea that the title is by implication sacrilegious. I think Jesus' love of people, his passion for life, his regard for the well being of others, and his wish for a kingdom of the heart rather than the heartland reveals a person that is frequently distorted by if not absent from many of the cathedrals of Christendom. I consider his radical love, a love that stimulated him to assert, "Love your enemies, do good to those who hate you, bless those who curse you, pray for those who mistreat you" (Luke 6, 27–28), to be substantively different from that which is promulgated in some quarters. This is not to say, that Jesus would agree with my opinions or my approach to this topic, either. Conversely, it is to maintain that significant portions of the teachings of Jesus seem foreign to many who call themselves Christians. This departure from the teachings of Jesus is partially understandable because his affirmations are so frequently both idealistic and countercultural. But a consistent, habitual, and unending dichotomy between belief and practice seems to have been a key target of Jesus' own critiques. Everything considered, however,

Jesus too might seek to convince me that my propensity to see the weird and the wonderful is at least on this occasion mistaken.

This said, then, it remains to be seen if the ideals of Joe included both democracy and Christianity. I conduct this inquiry via discussing three themes that I find in the first chapter of *Christotainment: Selling Jesus through Popular Culture*. The themes are explicated under the following headings: Fairness in the Midst of Disagreement, Critique in the Achievement of Fairness, and Democratic Values in the Pursuit of Liberation. Of course, a full and rich treatment of my topic would require a much deeper journey into many if not most of Joe's works.

## FAIRNESS IN THE MIDST OF DISAGREEMENT

Anyone who knew Joe realizes that he was an artist with words, written and spoken, and sought to communicate clearly and fairly with and about others and their ideas and ideals. This fairness is easily noted in his nuanced treatment of fundamentalists and evangelicals even though he strongly disagreed with them about a variety of the basic issues of life and thought. For example, he noted that many fundamentalists are chagrined with the way the term *fundamentalist* is used. He clarified their mortification by stating, "Fundamentalists often feel that those who are establishing the definitions are individuals who despise their beliefs" (Kincheloe, 2009, p. 2). His personal distaste for many aspects of fundamentalism and evangelicalism, however, did not lead him to reject this claim outright. Instead, he acknowledged that the accusation was partially accurate. He knew well that the definers of experience and belief have great power, even when the definitions are directed toward a powerful religious ideology (Freire, 2005). So, he understood the difficulties of describing without demonizing and added:

> Nevertheless, for those of us who are not fundamentalists, our observations of fundamentalist beliefs and actions may, by necessity, strike us as harmful and threatening. With these concerns in mind and in an effort to be as fair as possible, the following is as generic a definition of ... fundamentalism as I deem possible. (Kincheloe, 2009, p. 2)

Joe did not subscribe to the idea that we can be perfectly objective or neutral in our descriptions of beliefs and believers, whether rightwing neo-Nazis or leftwing neo-Stalinists, much less Christians. Yet, he did argue that fair-mindedness is an essential quality for social, political, religious, and educational critics. To a substantial degree, then, he attempted to be and was "as fair as possible." Thus, he wrote in an anti-stereotypical fashion of the "great diversity" found in evangelicalism in the areas of theology, political commitments, and social backgrounds (Kincheloe, 2009, p. 3) and the unfairness of lumping them together as "a monolithic right-wing group" (Kincheloe, 2009, p. 3). Moreover, he stressed that there are "many contemporary evangelicals [who] act bravely against prevailing beliefs about the poor and the racially and sexually marginalized" (Kincheloe, 2009, p. 3). He achieved his desire to be fair but also pursued the objective of scrutinizing the foibles and fears of fundamentalists and evangelicals, including an extremist sub-group labeled

Dominionists, noting that they were sometimes "radicals" who wanted to "build new networks of [control and] like-minded believers" (Kincheloe, 2009, p. 4). But even as he sought to understand, evaluate, and counteract the anti-democratic tendencies of some fundamentalists and evangelicals, he confessed that he needed to pursue his study of them and their religious, social, and political beliefs and practices with an "open mind and not final pronouncement" (Kincheloe, 2009, p. 17). In view of his ideals and practices, then, it seems appropriate to conclude that Joe practiced a key teaching of at least one strand of thought about democracy and Christianity: being open- and fair-minded in the pursuit of understanding and human relationships is essential.

## CRITIQUE IN THE ACHIEVEMENT OF FAIRNESS

Being fair-minded in the midst of disagreement, of course, did not mean to Joe that he was supposed to ignore, compromise, or mute the reasons for his disagreement. Thus, the fact that he believed that he should fairly describe the diversity within fundamentalism and evangelicalism did not silence his voice as a critical pedagogue. Nor did his recognition of the accuracy of some fundamentalist and evangelical beliefs and arguments cause him to overlook the inaccuracies and weaknesses he saw. Indeed, for Joe, being fair-minded involved examining the pros and cons, the strengths and weaknesses, and the contributions and liabilities of any position, regardless of its ideological roots. For instance, Kincheloe (2005) critiqued his own roots when he concluded that critical pedagogy sometimes failed to live up to its ideals and opportunities.

In *Christotainment: Selling Jesus through popular culture*, Joe continued to demonstrate his penchant for critique as well as his inclination for fairness. Evenhandedly, he admitted that, "there's nothing new about evangelicalism, marketing, and entertainment in the United States" (Kincheloe, 2009, p. 5). Simultaneously, he averred that, "there are dangerous agendas transcending merely the profit motive circulating among many creators of these [Christotainment] phenomena" (Kincheloe, 2009, p. 7). At the heart of his criticism was his objection to what he identified as "the Americanization of Jesus" (Kincheloe, 2009, p. 4). Although he was raised in the midst of and rejected a protestant fundamentalist form of American Christianity, the contemporary American Christianity and Jesus that he saw he deemed more dangerous, in part because he thought that even fundamentalism is in danger of being commandeered by a rather small militant and extremist group called Dominionists. In brief, Dominionists are interested in solidifying their "control over the United States and ... over the world" (Kincheloe, 2009, p. 7). The techniques that they use to promote their Dominionist causes, including using "their new language of democracy and freedom" (Kincheloe, 2009, p. 8) and using popular culture's entertainment industry—was antithetical to his view of an open and reflective democracy that valued all individuals and population groups. Like Paz (1985, p. 45), he recoiled from any ideology that nullifies, cancels out, and turns another person into "nothingness." Turning people who disagree with you into meaningless Nobodies is precisely what he thought the Dominionists are about, if not intentionally and directly, at least operationally and indirectly.

A question emerges in this context: What happened to Jesus as he was Americanized by the Dominionists and their witting and unwitting allies? With candor, Joe said that Jesus as the Americanized leader of the Dominionists has become "a true-blue American," (Kincheloe, 2009, p. 4) "a macho, kick-the-heathens'-ass savior," "the badass savior," "he-man" (Kincheloe, 2009, p. 15), and a "gallant and fearless" superhero (Kincheloe, 2009, p. 16). In short, "The new Jesus has undergone an extreme makeover and is now the judge executioner of Jews, Muslims, Hindus, Buddhists, atheists, agnostics" (Kincheloe, 2009, p. 15). The new "killer Jesus" (Kincheloe, 2009, p. 16) has replaced "the loving Lord who promoted selfless love and forgiveness" (Kincheloe, 2009, p. 15). Joe repeated with approval a question he had sometimes been asked by shocked Christians who do not share the political and doctrinaire agendas of Dominionists, "What happened to the Jesus who counseled us to love our enemies" (Kincheloe, 2009, p. 17)?

At this juncture, Joe paused in his writing and, in what may seem like an unusual move, spoke to everyone who calls her or himself a Christian. Echoing Camus's (1985, p. 71) call for Christians in Europe to speak out clearly and forcefully against Nazi and fascist ideologies and atrocities so that their condemnation of such beliefs and behaviors would leave no doubt about where they stood even to "the simplest man [or woman]," Joe asserted, "I believe it is the ethical obligation of all individuals who call themselves Christian to know what is being done in the name of their faith" (Kincheloe, 2009, p. 17). But tying his ideas to his praxis, it appears that Joe wanted Christians to move beyond merely knowing about Dominionists to saying and to acting on behalf of democratic and Christian values and all peoples. To do less, in his opinion, was neither democratic nor Christian.

## DEMOCRATIC VALUES IN THE PURSUIT OF LIBERATION

Although Joe was keenly interested in democratic values, his references to them in "Selling a New and Improved Jesus: Christotainment and the Power of Political Fundamentalism" are largely but not exclusively implicit and, consequently, are frequently attached to or embedded in his other ideas. Raising a question, however, helps us uncover and understand his commitment to a democratic set of values. The question—Why did he co-edit *Christotainment* and write the introductory chapter "Selling a new and improved Jesus"?—moves us toward seeing his democratic rationale. Of course, he no doubt had many reasons for editing and writing, but a major reason seems to be that he believed that the ideas he introduced were designed to counter what he deemed "harmful and threatening" (Kincheloe, 2009, p. 2). But what, in his mind, do some forms of fundamentalism, evangelicalism, and, in particular, Dominionism teach and do that strike him as being detrimental and menacing? The answer is more complicated and complex than my conclusion. Nevertheless, for the sake of efficiency, I conclude that Joe believed that these three isms— or, better, at least some people who subscribe to them—are teaching and practicing ideas and ideals that are antithetical to and subversive of democratic values.

But where, you may wonder, does Joe suggest that he is concerned about democracy? Several of his arguments help us answer this question. First, his answer is implied when he discusses the idea that Dominionists are interested in controlling not just the United States but the world (Kincheloe, 2009, p. 7). Certainly, the desire to control nations and the world has been a longstanding ambition of many ideological, economic, and political groups. Colonizers of minds and actions are in every country. Even so, this is no reason to ignore them. And Joe did not, for he believed that minds and people need to be liberated rather than dominated. Second, we find another hint of Joe's belief that democratic values are important in the pursuit of liberation. Notice his warning that Dominionists use their "new language of democracy and freedom" and as well as "the language of Christian love, empathy, and equality" as they "act on an entirely different set of values" (Kincheloe, 2009, p. 8). Was Joe implying that many Dominionists and their partners are opposed to democracy, freedom, love, empathy, and equality? Was he, perhaps, unconsciously implying an answer to the question in our title: Joe Kincheloe: A proponent of democracy and Christianity? Regardless of how we answer this question, it does seem obvious that Joe was concerned about a set of values that were in his mind contrary to democracy, Christianity, freedom, love, empathy, and equality.

There are at least three other reasons for thinking that Joe was greatly concerned about democratic values and they are important both as means and as ends. To begin, notice his reference to "constitutional guarantees" being suspended in the name of protecting our democracy after the Twin Towers in New York City were destroyed along with the lives of thousands of people (Kincheloe, 2009, p. 11). His implications? At a minimum he appears to have implied that a democratic country should not set aside its democratic values of respecting Muslims and prisoners and their rights in the name of defending democracy. But there are many other constitutional guarantees that undoubtedly troubled Joe as he examined Dominionists' ideas. So, secondly, he wrote, "my worst nightmares have materialized as this [Dominionist] minority ...gains more and more control over governmental, social, and religious institutions" (Kincheloe, 2009, p. 11). In many of his works, Joe demonstrated his apprehension that any diverse liberal democracy might become controlled by a group of ideologues that reshapes society in its own dogma-dominated image. Obviously, societies are dominated to varying degrees by the socially, economically, and politically powerful in them, but this is not a grounds for being indifferent to the power in society. The degree of control and domination can become greater and will if Joe's interpretation of the Dominionist plan materializes. Third, democracy was in the forefront of his thinking when Joe argued that developing a Dominionist government would be contrary to the current constitutional government (Kincheloe, 2009, p. 12). Joe recognized multiple and deep contradictions exist in our present quasi-democratic governmental form, but he also recognized that a government based on a dogmatic religious orientation has much, much less to offer. Unless we favor dehumanizing and marginalizing those defined as "heathens, atheists, outsiders" (Kincheloe, 2009, p. 12) and want to "demonize and otherize" (Kincheloe, 2009, p. 19) opponents, we should be more critically conscious of the values and political philosophy being promoted by Dominionists.

One final point—both a fourth and a sixth thought, depending on the way one counts—needs to be mentioned about Joe's democratic commitments. In his discussion of religious and theological ignorance and misunderstanding, he observed that such undermines "the civic and theological conversation and contribute[s] to the destruction of democratic and positive theological spheres of human activity" (Kincheloe, 2009, p. 18). Once again Camus (1995) comes to mind. He was so convinced that dialogue is essential to the preservation of society that he suggested that our options are to choose between "the forces of terror" and "the forces of dialogue" (Kincheloe, 2009, p. 73). Even more radical, Camus insisted that the dialogue should be based on the premise that "the only possible dialogue is the kind between people who remain what they are and speak their minds" (Kincheloe, 2009, p. 70). In context, this would mean that Dominionists would remain Dominionists, and critical pedagogues would remain critical pedagogues as they dialogued. Would Joe be a comrade with Camus on this thought? If his love and respect for others is as radical as it appears, the answer may appear to be yes. But Joe—and likely Camus—would probably say that few if any people remain exactly "what they are" when they seek to learn what others think. Therein rests the hope of dialogue, whatever the parameters that are set. Of course, there is always the possibility that someone of any viewpoint may prefer the ignorance of silence and separation over the enlightenment of speaking and meeting. But that is a conversation that we must leave for another occasion.

## CONCLUSION

We close with a return to our question regarding whether or not Joe was a proponent of democracy and Christianity? In addition to the snippets that have been mentioned above regarding Joe's commitment to a set of democratic values, it is interesting to note that his life as a scholar assumed such values. That is to say, his belief in and practice of fairness in the midst of disagreement assumes that there is the freedom to disagree about important ideas, to share grounds of disagreement, and to follow arguments and evidence wherever they led. Moreover, open critique lives and flourishes in the freedom of a vibrant democracy. Likewise, love, empathy, equality, fairness, and human rights seem, in Joe's case, to be contextualized in the freedoms of expression, inquiry, and dialogue. His belief in a rich and strong mutual respect of persons—even of those who may be or are guilty of human atrocities—is likely ruinous to any inhumane, closed, and undemocratic society.

If we agree that Joe was a proponent of democracy, we need not agree that he was a proponent of Christianity. Indeed, it is manifest that he was opposed to at least some of the religious beliefs (Kincheloe, 2009, p. 1), political understandings (Kincheloe, 2009, pp. 7–9, 12–13), and every-day practices (Kincheloe, 2009, p. 4) of many Christians. He detested the Americanization of Jesus (Kincheloe, 2009, p. 4), the Christotainment of popular culture (Kincheloe, 2009, pp. 1–20), and the sociopolitical trappings of Dominionists (pp. 10–13). Given these transparent beliefs, how could anyone even raise much less entertain the question of Joe's being a proponent of Christianity? Well, perhaps—but perhaps not—we can agree that Joe promoted the Christian values of "love, empathy, equality," loving "our enemies," and "selfless love and forgiveness." Maybe we would agree that he sympathized with the values of those Christians who were "shocked" to discover what some

Dominionists teach in the name of the Christian faith. If not, why would he conclude that it is their ethical responsibility to understand and confront those who distort their faith?

In view of the aforementioned information, it may be tempting to conclude that Joe was an advocate of little more than the ethics of Jesus and that this support is hardly grounds for concluding that he promoted Christianity. Admittedly, the answer to the question—was Joe a proponent of democracy and Christianity?—appears yes to democracy and no to Christianity, at least largely. On the other hand, when Joe turned his mind—as he so often did—to the so-called democracies of the west, he identified serious flaws in belief and practice. He was not a proponent of a capitalistic or bourgeois democracy any more than he was for an Americanized Christianity. In fact, he saw that the two ideologies—bourgeois democracy and Americanized Christianity—were so close as to be indistinguishable at times. In a more comprehensive study of the answer to the question, therefore, the conclusion might be, for the most part, no to both democracy and Christianity. But this tentative conclusion needs to be qualified in that it applies to the distorted and popularized views of both democracy and Christianity that Joe interrogated. If Joe's overall critique of these two domains is as briefly described, his critical analyses demonstrate one of his most admirable qualities: he was disposed to appreciate the nuggets of accuracy in the ideas and practices of those with whom he usually disagreed and surface the boulders of inconsistency in the ideas and practices of those with whom he often agreed. His approach, if the above scenario is reasonably accurate, might stimulate proponents of both democracy and Christianity to reexamine their beliefs and practices to determine which elements are valid expressions of their respective faiths. Certainly, Joe would claim that the unexamined faith, whether democratic or Christian, is not worth keeping.

## REFERENCES

Book of Luke. (1978). *New international version.* Grand rapids, MI: Zondervan.
Camus, A. (1985). The unbeliever and Christians. In A. Camus (Ed.), J. O'Brien (Trans.), *Resistance, rebellion, and death* (pp. 67–74). New York: Vintage International.
Freire, P. (2002). Education as the practice of freedom. In P. Freire (Ed.), *Education for critical consciousness.* New York: Continuum.
Freire, P. (2005). *Teachers as cultural workers.* Boulder, CO: Westview Press.
Greene, M. (1978). *Landscapes of learning.* New York: Teachers College Press.
Kincheloe, J. L. (2009). Selling a new and improved Jesus: Christotainment and the power of political fundamentalism. In S. R. Steinberg & J. L. Kincheloe (Eds.), *Christotainment: Selling Jesus through popular culture* (pp. 1–21). Boulder, CO: Westview Press.
Kincheloe, J. L. (2005). *Critical constructivism primer.* New York: Peter Lang.
Paz, O. (1985). *The labyrinth of solitude.* New York: Grove Press.

JOHN WILLINSKY

# THE MUSIC[1]

*Afterword*

The music in Joe L. Kincheloe's life forms its own afterword and then some. That music was both commentary and reflection, and it came before and after, at every turn in his life. Music was there in the beginning, when he taught himself the piano as an only child growing up in East Tennessee. Music and word were there, in the notebooks he filled with song lists and lyrics for the songs he was writing from his early high school days in a band that he played in around the town of Kingsport. Music was in the grand piano and Fender Rhodes, the B-3 organ and Moog synthesizer, that Joe and Shirley had about the home that they made home for so many, wherever the two of them were living.

The music came first, too, the first time Joe and I spoke at a publishers' dinner many years ago, and would return, like sleeping dog awakened at his master's voice, in almost every conversation that followed. As one not given to dawdling, musically, Joe was ready to put together a band, by the end of our first conversation, a band devoted to relieving conference monotony and rocking out the day-long string of presentations. *Afterword.* That might have been a good name for the band, except that the music proved to be rich enough in words, stories, satires, and polemics, with the best of them in Joe's hand. Thus, it seems worth attending, in this afterword, to a few of the songs that he wrote, sang, and played, over the course of a decade of raising the conference-exhausted to their feet, and having them shake their minds free of the day-long flow of compressed research pitches and PowerPoint(less) slides.

Music represented a long unbreakable thread running through Joe's life. It held him true to growing up rebellious and Southern. It formed the narrative center to so many of the stories he would tell about the treacherous small-town band circuit of his youth. To lend your keyboard to another musician was to learn that it had been hocked at the end of the evening for a couple of cases of beer, and to drop a poor performer from the band was to have to face up to the boy's whole family and fire him outright in his own living room. But then the music was to form the core of many stories to come playing the academic conference circuit, as we stood trapped for a good part of the evening in a hotel freight elevator with our equipment, or as we found ourselves running desperately after a departing cab in Chicago as it drove off with the band's instruments in its trunk.

Although Joe brought a great depth of musical experience and knowledge to the band, what he managed to teach us above all – and he taught us much through his patience as much as his pedagogy ("now listen carefully this time") – was that what really stood behind the musical integrity and tightness of the band, was this

## AFTERWORD

thing he referred to as *band etiquette*. It was a phrase that I found remarkable, coming out of the very era of ego-strutting, drug-fueled rock-star indulgences that otherwise marked 1960s band life. Joe didn't even mention band etiquette until long after he had so thoroughly demonstrated it, beginning with our early performances. But then that, too, I came to realize, was band etiquette.

Let me explain. When we first came together as a group in 1998, Joe did not even suggest that he might sing, because he saw that the bass player I brought in had been singing in the group with me, and thus had, by this grace known as band etiquette, a prior claim to the vocals, at least initially. Nor did Joe even refer to his own compositions for some time, although he had notebooks full of them, running back to his high school days, and extending to five-act rock operas. Only after he had felt that he had paid his dues, serving us all so very well on keyboards, did he bring forward a song or two, always apologizing profusely, with understated, half-self-mocking graciousness. "Let me play this for you," he would say, "although I don't know if you'll like it or not, and that is entirely okay with me, either way." After the first go around with one of his songs, we would then smile at this routine, as if there would be any doubt about whether we'd go for the song or not.

Joe wrote songs that honored, in musical structure and his Tennessee baritone, the rhythm and blues traditions that he grew up in. Yet they were not imitations or simple variations on old themes. They were meditations on that history, as in "Soul," which never failed to work on the audience's sense of the musical history that he brought to bear:

> I wanna tell you bout the history of soul
> From out of the delta it rocked and it rolled
> Moved to the city where it really took hold
> All that followed was cast in its mold.

It was a history that he could render vivid, with the words painting their own grainy historical picture against the slow rocking back and forth of this song's determined beat, that might have kept time for those marching in that earlier era, whether behind death's hearse or in hope's protest:

> It smoldered deeply like a fire in the night
> It laid the soundtrack for the civil rights fight
> Warmongers quivered in the light of its might
> We all were inspired by its power to incite

"Soul" let us rock out, by all means. It did so in ways, from its opening chord, that allowed us to approach the illusive perfection of a sound we only had imagined reaching but a few years before. But "Soul" only did so while asking questions, echoed by those of us singing backup, that kept going round in your head, long after the last chorus was over:

> But I wanna know, I wanna know, I wanna know
> What happened to soul?
> Where did it go?
> What happened to soul?

It was a refrain that had in its final version, at the song's end a reminder that what was but a musical genre was also something more, and more precious for that:

> Bring back the soul, bring back the soul
> It's more precious than gold
> We gotta bring back the soul

Yet Joe did not always look back in his songs. They were as often about the present moment, as much as we were a twenty-first century band during this new century's false, tragic start with the Bush years. In "The World's Gone Mad," Joe set out in a series of vivid images across a rock beat just how bad things had become. It was a siren song of warning, a prophetic caution, at once too late, much in the spirit of Critical Theory, with the hope that in not letting the issue go by unaddressed and unannounced, it would be affected by explication:

> I see it on TV
> I see it on the sidewalks
> And the penitentiaries
> It's bad, the world's gone mad.

The song is unrelenting in this blunt depiction, marked by a resigned sense of a world *already* gone mad. Musically, its driving structure moves minor to major chords, with a bit of reprise on the comma in – "It's bad, the world's gone mad" – as the singular line of the chorus:

> I see it in the rivers
> I see it in the air
> I see it in the melting snow
> And in my worst nightmares
> It's bad, the world's gone mad.

Yet the air was thick at the time with impending Bush-affected disasters, and we also introduced P. F. Sloan's sardonic "Eve of Destruction" from 1965 into our set ("You're old enough to kill, but not for votin'").

Yet the litany of nightmares in "World Gone Mad" was broken by the song's "bridge." It's not so much a *bridge* to some other, less mad world, but a *break*, a break in the storm clouds of that song. The music changed up for the song's bridge (which is what bridges do), from driving rock beat to a more reflective and complex sequence (oh, so complex a musical sequence, that when we all got it right, Joe would give us in the band that most-treasured gift – a quick wink and an approving smile). The bridge signaled that there was more to this world gone mad after all:

> But there's gonna come a new day
> When the world cries out no more, no more
> When people say were not going back to the killin' floor
> We're gonna take back our souls
> We're gonna break all the molds
> We're going to set them free, set them free.

## AFTERWORD

That *new day* would come when this world-gone-mad would be returned to its proper bearings. It called for nothing less than our own actions of taking back, breaking out, and setting free. Yet it was hard to play, as I said, this intricate upbeat bridge across the abyss of this song And with the bridge's final "set them free," the song clouded over again, to the return of the relentless beat, the tight sharp rhyme, only with the terms of endangerment turned up:

> I see it in oxycotin
> I see it in crystal meth
> I see it in Ritalin
> I smell it on his breath
> It's bad, the world's gone mad.

The drug-fouled breath brings home the medicated, zoned-out response, the science-noir quality of how bad things were becoming, with only that bridge of hope to what we can still do.

There was also a satirical side to Joe's writing, in the academic tradition of Tom Lehrer ("Once the rockets are up, who cares where they come down? / That's not my department, says Wernher von Braun") from the 1950s. Yet in his own inimical way, Joe preferred to turn the foibles of our times unto himself, as if to absorb our sins – most often, the great conference sin of vanity – and do so in the Methodist revivalist manner of his circuit-preaching uncle Marvin, with whom he made the prayer-tent rounds so often as a child. So Joe had learned this way of reminding us of how far we have come, how much we have in hand, and how far we have strayed:

> I got lost in cyberspace.
> When Facebook rejected me, the chatroom knew I was thoroughly disgraced;
> I knew that a change was coming when Apple stock soared,
> But worshippin' Steven Jobs made me lose faith in a brick and mortar Lord.

In a thoroughly topical song such as, "Lost in Cyberspace," he could offer the redemption of satire, with a beat to it to which you could certainly dance (amen). And the song's constant refrain had a way of reminding us all of how swept up we were in the shallow swill of digital life (suffer the little children) again using his own sorry state as the prime instance:

> I got lost in cyberspace.
> Since my website crashed, I can't even show my face.
> Worst of all, I got no friends on MySpace;
> Calling all computer geeks, get me back in the race.

The website misery of which he sang, it should be noted, belies all that Joe and Shirley were to do with The Paulo and Nita Freire International Project for Critical Pedagogy. They managed, in a very short time, to craft a masterful social networking community centered on the website set up at McGill University as part of Joe's Canada Research Chair. Here an extremely adept Joe demonstrated unsung Dick Cavett-like talents in drawing out critical pedagogues in splendid web-streaming conversation.

Still, it was not that such technical finesse came readily to Joe, in cyberspace or right here on earth, as his hands were trained, after all, solely (soulfully) in four-four time rhythm and blues. It was at the 1999 American Educational Research Association annual conference held in Montreal that we played our first gig together. A few hours before we were to go on at the University of British Columbia reception, we found ourselves with drummer and bass player standing on the Hilton Hotel loading bay platform at the rear of the hotel. A truck had just unloaded all of the rented band equipment, and we started to unpack it right there, as the idea of a quick practice seemed to make some sense, given that we had never played together, and that some of us did not have a lot of band experience to fall back on.

As hotel workers carried huge cuts of beef from the back of trucks into the kitchen, we all ended up standing silently around the sound board with cables and jacks in our hands. We did not have a clue among us as to what went where. A sound board presents a majestic honeycomb of knobs, buttons, and variously shaped receptacles for plugging instruments and speakers into. Such a device, Joe explained as we turned to the most experienced musician among us, was far more than his Kingsport band of the 1960s had been able to swing, if there even were such things *then*, he added with a degree of finality. For what seemed like the longest time, we tried combination after combination of inputs and outputs, buttons and knobs, only to raise increasingly embarrassing prospects for this first fateful performance together.

Finally and inevitably, inputs and outputs matched. To our surprise and delight, we were able to rock that loading bay, finding the first traces of a groove that was to run for a decade across academic conference locations in the United States and Canada, from hotel ballrooms to jazz bars, deserted theatres to dock-bound paddle-wheel boats (complete with pole-dancing academics), from outdoor patios to stuffy faculty clubs. And after that first gig, we added a sound technician to our equipment list, although we relied as much on Shirley for our ongoing performance sound check, as well as for the better part of the crowd that would begin the dancing, among those heavy-footed academics. Yet if technical finesse was not Joe's strength, he was at least able to turn that to lyrical and humorous advantage in "Lost in Cyberspace":

> Nothing comes up, when you Google me
> I'm a natural born loser with technology
> As my wife walked out, she called a cyber rube
> And told me she placed my bedroom failure, you guessed it, on YouTube

Finally, it has to be said that Joe could be straightforwardly political in the fearless spirit of his near-namesake Country Joe and the Fish ("And it's one, two, three / What are we fighting for?/ Don't ask me, I don't give a damn, / Next stop is Vietnam"). Joe L. Kincheloe was not one to stand idly by, playing elevator music on our ride to the bottom of those trying Bush years:

> I've had enough of George Bush, enough of Dick Cheney too
> Do unto them as they've done unto you
> I know the devil will get their souls
> But until then, boys.... I'll see you at Gitmo

In "I've Had Enough of George Bush," Joe managed not only to pin Bush's disregard for human rights to the wall, but he proved himself one of rock 'n roll's

AFTERWORD

few song writers to utilize the five-syllable accusative ("prevaricator"), without missing (or adding) a beat:

> What about Alberto, Alberto Gonzo
> He didn't even know what he didn't know
> He fancied himself a smooth operator
> But in the end, he was just a *prevaricator*.

He certainly didn't pull his punches when it came to naming what we have still to come to grips with, in terms of the legal consequences of the Bush years. Bush also brought another side of Joe's irrepressible musical and poetic talents, as well. In the midst of a song like "Cocaine" by J. J. Cale, once the night had worn on, and people were bopping on the dance floor, Joe would let the verses go, and start to preach against the political hypocrisy of George W. Bush. He'd tell the story of Bush's cocaine days, drawing the crowd in, bringing the band down low, until finally the whole room would be moving up and down, shouting out with him, over and over, in the revealed truth of it all, "George Bush did the cocaine."

One time and once only, in the midst of "Jumpin Jack Flash" ("I was schooled with a strap right across my back"), as we riffed on and on, Joe told the story of his grade four teacher who had warned the class about the dangers of this new music known as rock 'n roll. He described sitting at his desk, looking up at this earnest teacher exhorting each of them to steer clear of what was Negro music, to avoid the temptations of such evils, even if your older brothers and sisters have fallen prey to its devil beat. And he told the story of that segregated Tennessee classroom to the beat of the Rolling Stones, as if to serve notice to Mrs. Hennessey, I think it was, that the music held sway and that he was part of that transformation of that classroom.

Then, too, Joe did not only do stories. He dared to go with ideas and theory where other lyricists feared to tread. He managed to move beyond, for example, the educational theorizing of Frank Zappa ("Brown shoes don't make it / Quit school, why fake it?") in what was the final forging of another sort of bridge, larding rock 'n roll with scholarly themes in "Critical Pedagogy" the song:

> Emancipated and historicized,
> Seeing thru subjugated eyes.
> Part to whole and whole to part,
> Posing problems is where we start.

Afterword? With Joe, the afterword is to be found in the word and melody, in the voice and rhythm of his music and his writing. It is found throughout the chapters of this book, among his colleagues. It is found among his friends, children, and students, and it is found, as Joe reminds us so poignantly now in the "Critical Pedagogy" song, in how "nothing is static, nothing is fixed, / radical love is always worth the risk."

NOTES

[1] Song lyrics in this chapter by Joe Kincheloe © 1998–2008, used with permission.

# ABOUT THE CONTRIBUTORS

**Kathy Berry** was a professor of Critical Studies in Education until mandatory retirement required she retire at 65. Her main interest is literacy and critical pedagogy. She has written several chapters and a couple of books for Joe and Shirley over the past 20 years. She continues to write and hopefully find a world where discrimination based on age and physical being is illegal. Success in her university career was, in large part, thanks to Shirley and Joe. Kathy can be reached at kberry@unb.ca.

**Robert Duggan, Jr.** is currently a student in the Master's Plus Teaching Certification program at Villanova University. He plans to use both that degree and his Master's in English Literature to teach high school English literature starting in the fall of 2010. Bob's main academic areas of interest include 19th century British and American literature, the novels of Herman Melville, the poetry of the British Romantic movement, and modern poetry. Since 2007 he has written a blog on art history that has appeared on several "best of" lists of blogs dealing with the visual arts.

**Christopher Emdin** is an assistant professor in science education at Teachers College, Columbia University. He has taught middle school science and mathematics, high school physics and chemistry, and was chair of science departments in New York City public schools. Dr. Emdin was recently awarded the 2008 Best paper for Innovation in Teaching Science Teachers from The Association for Science Teacher Education and the 2008 Phi Delta Kappa Outstanding Dissertation Award. His research focuses on issues of race, class, and diversity in urban science classrooms, the use of new theoretical frameworks to transform science education, and urban science education reform.

**Gene Fellner** returned to academia in 2005 after spending over twenty years as an artist and a political organizer because he felt the need to acquire new epistemologies and methodologies to shape and be shaped by his practice. Gene now is in his third year as a doctoral student at the City University of New York where he has acquired much of what he sought. He also is part of the literacy faculty at New Jersey City University and a mentor to middle-school language arts teachers in Newark, NJ. Doctoral studies tend to lack the lyrical that is so integral to art, organizing, and a full life, but it was alive and well in Joe's thinking and practice.

**Lee Gabay** is a doctoral candidate in the Urban Education Program at the Graduate Center of the City University of New York. He teaches incarcerated students in New York City. His published works can be found in Teaching City Kids: Understanding and Appreciating Them (2006), The Praeger Handbook of Education and Psychology (2007) and KICKS Magazine (2009).

**Aaron David Gresson III** is a community mental health consultant and advocate in Maryland. He is the author of several books, notably, *Race and Education: A Primer,*

ABOUT THE CONTRIBUTORS

and *The Recovery of Race in America.* Holding a PhD in psychology and another in education, Gresson is retired from Penn State University.

**kecia hayes** received her PhD in Urban Education from the Graduate Center of the City University of New York. Currently, she is an assistant professor in the College of Education and Human Services at Montclair State University. Her research interests include the education of court-involved youth, the impact of social policies and practices on the educational experiences of urban youth and families, and educational leadership in urban schools.

**Ray Horn**, associate professor of education at Saint Joseph's University, is a retired public school educator, the Director of the Interdisciplinary Doctor of Education Program for Educational Leaders, and the Department of Educational Leadership Chairperson. His books include *Standards Primer, Understanding Educational Reform: A Reference Handbook,* and *Teacher Talk: A Postformal Inquiry into Educational Change.* Joe Kincheloe and he co-edited *The Praeger Handbook of Education and Psychology,* and *American Standards: Quality Education in a Complex World—The Texas Case.* In addition, he is the co-editor of the scholarly journal, *Scholar-Practitioner Quarterly.*

**Bal Chandra Luitel** has completed doctoral study at the Science and Mathematics Education Centre, Curtin University of Technology. He has been working in Nepal as a teacher educator for about a decade. Guided by multiple paradigms of integralism, postmodernism, interpretivism and criticalism, Bal's research aims at developing a transformative philosophy of mathematics education in Nepal, a country that hosts more than 92 language groups and different cultural traditions arising from Vedic, Buddhist and Animist belief systems. Subscribing to multiple epistemic metaphors of knowing as imagining, reconceptualising self, deconstructing, reconstructing and poeisis, Bal engages with dialectical, metaphorical, poetic and narrative logics as a means for developing a vision of an inclusive and transformative mathematics education in Nepal.

**Curry Stephenson Malott** currently lives in New York City as a writer and teacher. Formerly an assistant professor at D'Youville College in Buffalo, NY, he has worked as an educational consultant for Menominee Tribal School and Menominee High School on the Menominee Indian Reservation in Wisconsin. His most recent books include *A Call to Action: An Introduction to Education, Philosophy, and Native North America* (2008, Peter Lang); *The Destructive Path of Neoliberalism: An International Examination of Urban Education* (2008, Sense) co-edited with Bradley Porfilio; *Teaching Native America Across the Curriculum: A Critical Inquiry* (2009, Peter Lang) with Chairwoman Lisa Waukau and Lauren Waukau-Villagomez; *Critical Pedagogy in the 21$^{st}$ Century: A New Generation of Scholars* (Information Age, 2010) co-edited with Bradley Porfilio; *Policy and Research in Education: A Critical Pedagogy for Educational Leadership* (Peter Lang, 2010); and *Critical Pedagogy and Cognition: An Introduction to Postformal Psychology* (Springer, forthcoming).

# ABOUT THE CONTRIBUTORS

**Elizabeth J. Meyer** is an assistant professor in the Department of Education at Concordia University in Montreal, Quebec, Canada. Her work has been published in journals such as *Gender and Education* and *The Journal of LGBT Youth*. She is the author of Gender, bullying, and harassment: Strategies to end sexism and homophobia in schools (2009) and *Gender and Sexual Diversity in Schools* (2010). She also has chapters in several books including: *Media Literacy: A Reader* (Macedo, & Steinberg, 2007), *Queering Straight Teachers* (Rodriguez, & Pinar, 2007), *Rocking your World* (Churchill, 2009) and *Diversity and Multiculturalism: A Reader* (Steinberg, 2009).

**Elizabeth Quintero**, is a professor of education at California State University Channel Islands and has worked in the U.S. as well as several countries as teacher and research scholar with programs that serve families in multilingual communities representing a variety of cultural and historical backgrounds. Recent publications include: Quintero, E. P. (2009). *Critical Literacy in Early Childhood Education: Artful Story and the Integrated Curriculum*, NY: Peter Lang Publishing; Quintero, E. P. (2009) Children Using Story to Connect with Others, in Naidich, Fernando (Editor) *Educação*, Rio de Janero, Brazil; Quintero, E. P. (2009). In a World of Migration: Rethinking Literacy, Language, & Learning Texts in *Context, The Journal of Educational Media, Memory, and Society,* Georg Eckert Institute for International Textbook Research, Braunschweig, Germany.

**Douglas J. Simpson** is a professor and holder of the Helen DeVitt Jones Chair in Teacher Education at Texas Tech University. His research explores the normative grounds of educational and curriculum theory by examining questions of ethical, epistemological, and theoretical adequacy. His articles in British, Canadian, and American journals and his dozen books and monographs—e.g., *John Dewey: Primer* (Lang), *John Dewey and the Art of Teaching* (Sage), *Educational Reform: A Deweyan Perspective* (Garland), *Re-creating Schools* (Corwin), *The Teacher as Philosopher* (Methuen)—have earned him an international reputation for his scholarship.

**John Smyth** is Research Professor of Education, and Research Theme Leader Addressing Disadvantage and Inequality in Education and Health, University of Ballarat, Australia. He is author/editor of 20 books including: 'Hanging In with Kids' in Tough Times (Peter Lang, 2010); Critically Engaged Learning; Connecting to Young Lives (Peter Lang, 2008); Activist and Socially Critical School and Community Renewal: Social Justice in Exploitative Times (Sense Publishers, 2009); Teachers in the Middle: Reclaiming the Wasteland of the Adolescent Years of Schooling (Peter Lang, 2007); and, 'Dropping Out', Drifting Off, Being Excluded: Becoming Somebody Without School (Peter Lang, 2004).

**Chaim M. Steinberg** is a secondary school teacher. After leaving the South, he lived through losing his house in Hurricane Andrew in Miami, then moved to Central Pennsylvania to complete school. A graduate of the Master's of Education program at the University of Pittsburgh, his first teaching position was at Bialik High School in

Montreal. He is now living in Hamilton, Ontario and teaching at an alternative school in Toronto. His sports consciousness was molded by Joe Kincheloe, and he carries on the legacy of loyalty to the Atlanta Braves, the Tennessee Volunteers, and Peyton Manning.

**Shirley R. Steinberg** is the Director of the Paulo and Nita Freire International Project for Critical Pedagogy. Recently a Research Professor at the University of Barcelona, she currently is at McGill University, where she teaches critical media literacy, cultural studies, and critical pedagogy. Her recent books include: *Diversity and Multiculturalism: A Reader; 19 Urban Questions: Teaching in the City,* and many books with Joe L. Kincheloe, including: *Christotainment: Selling Jesus through Popular Culture*; *Changing Multiculturalism: New Times, New Curriculum; Kinderculture: The Corporate Construction of Childhood;* and *Measure Lies: The Bell Curve Examined.* An internationally known speaker, she is a frequent contributor to CBC TV and Radio, CTV, *The Toronto Globe and Mail,* and Canadian Press International. Joe Kincheloe's partner for twenty years, she worked with him in developing Postformalism, Kinderculture, Critical Multiculturalism, and to create a Critical Pedagogy Global Network at freireproject.org.

**Peter Charles Taylor** is associate professor of transformative education at the Science and Mathematics Education Centre, Curtin University of Technology, Western Australia. His research focuses on the contextualisation of science and mathematics education with/in postcolonial societies, especially culture-sensitive ways of harnessing global forces of modernisation. This research involves excavating personal educational histories and alternative knowledge systems, examining critically the legacy of (neo)colonial educational policies and practices, and envisioning transformative curricular possibilities for creating *third space* classrooms. Of particular interest are auto/ethnography, literary genres of narrative, fictive and impressionistic writing, nondual logics such as dialectics and poetics, and agentic standards of critical reflexivity and pedagogical thoughtfulness.

**Connie Titone** is professor in the Department of Education and Human Services at Villanova University. She received her doctorate in the Philosophy of Education from Harvard University. Connie has published two books: *Women's Philosophies of Education: Thinking through our Mothers* (1999) with co-author Karen Maloney and *Gender Equality in the Philosophy of Education: Catharine Macaulay's Forgotten Contribution* (2004). In addition, she has published numerous articles on the topic of women in the philosophy of education and topics related to diversity and teacher education.

**Kenneth Tobin** is Presidential Professor of Urban Education at the Graduate Center of CUNY. In 2004 Tobin was recognized by the National Science Foundation as a *Distinguished Teaching Scholar* and by the Association for the Education of Teachers of Science as *Outstanding Science Teacher Educator of the Year.* Prior to commencing a career as a teacher educator, Tobin taught high school science and mathematics in Australia and was involved in curriculum design. His research interests are focused on the teaching and learning of science in urban schools, which involve mainly African American students living in conditions of poverty. A parallel program of research focuses on coteaching as a way of learning to teach in urban high schools.

**John Willinsky** is Khosla Family Professor of Education at Stanford University and director of the Public Knowledge Project at Stanford, the University of British Columbia, and Simon Fraser University. Much of his work, including his book, *The access principle: The case for open access to research and scholarship* (MIT Press, 2006), as well as PKP's open source software for journals and conferences, is free to download through the project's website (http://pkp.sfu.ca).

CPSIA information can be obtained at www.ICGtesting.com
259897BV00004B/47/P